IN SPANISH TRENCHES

# IN SPANISH TRENCHES

## THE MINDS AND DEEDS OF THE IRISH WHO FOUGHT FOR THE REPUBLIC IN THE SPANISH CIVIL WAR

Barry McLoughlin & Emmet O'Connor

UNIVERSITY COLLEGE DUBLIN PRESS
PREAS CHOLÁISTE OLLSCOILE BHAILE ÁTHA CLIATH
2020

First published 2020
by University College Dublin Press
UCD Humanities Institute,
Belfield,
Dublin 4
Ireland
www.ucdpress.ie

Text and notes © Barry McLoughlin & Emmet O'Connor 2020

ISBN 978-1-910820-58-2 *pb*

All rights reserved. No part of this publication may be
reproduced, stored in a retrieval system, or transmitted in
any form or by any means, electronic, photocopying, recording
or otherwise without the prior permission of the publisher.

CIP data available from the British Library

*The right of Barry McLoughlin & Emmet O'Connor to be identified as the
author of this work has been asserted by them*

Typeset in Scotland in Adobe Caslon
and Bodoni Oldstyle by Ryan Shiels
Text design by Lyn Davis
Printed in Scotland on acid-free paper by
Bell & Bain Ltd, Glasgow, G46 7UQ, UK

# Contents

Dedication
viii

Acknowledgements
ix

Abbreviations
xiii

List of Maps and Images
xv

INTRODUCTION
xvii

ONE
IRELAND AND THE SPANISH CIVIL WAR
1

TWO
THE WAR AT HOME
28

THREE
THE WAR IN THE NORTH
60

FOUR
THE INTERNATIONAL BRIGADES AND
THEIR IRISH CONTINGENT
85

### FIVE
### THE ROAD TO THE LINCOLNS
108

### SIX
### BLOOD AND BOREDOM ON THE JARAMA, FEBRUARY–JUNE 1937
138

### SEVEN
### FIRST OFFENSIVE: BRUNETE
169

### EIGHT
### FAILED OFFENSIVES: ARAGON AND TERUEL
202

### NINE
### RETREAT AND CAPTURE
228

### TEN
### ENDGAME ON THE EBRO
249

### ELEVEN
### DISCIPLINE, DESERTION AND PUNISHMENT
272

### TWELVE
### THE TRIAL AND IMPRISONMENT OF FRANK RYAN, JUNE 1938–JUNE 1939
296

### THIRTEEN
### FRANK RYAN: RELEASE ATTEMPTS, JUNE 1939–JULY 1940
330

Epilogue: Withdrawal, Homecoming, and the Politics of Commemoration
355

Appendix: List of the Irish in the International Brigades
380

Bibliography
389

Index
405

*In memory of our fathers:*
*Captain James Joseph McLoughlin, Cavalry Corps, Irish Army*
*Sergeant Peter O'Connor, Abraham Lincoln Battalion, 15th International Brigade*

# *Acknowledgements*

This book has a long pre-history. Emmet's father, Peter, fought in Spain under Frank Ryan, while Barry knew Frank Ryan's biographer Seán Cronin, and International Brigade (IB) veterans in Britain and Austria from the 1980s.

Visits to Moscow during the chaotic rule of Yeltsin in the mid-1990s sparked the idea for a joint study on the Irish in the IB. Our main port of call there was the former Institute for Marxism–Leninism of the Central Committee of the Communist Party of the Soviet Union, a modernist stone building in the Bolshaya Dimitrovka street, known to Muscovites as 'The Three Blind Men' because of the granite busts of Marx, Engels and Lenin glowering through empty sockets at the passers-by. The Institute for Marxism–Leninism, now called the Russian State Archive for Political and Social History (RGASPI), housed innumerable archival stocks (fondy) – the files of the Comintern, the papers of Soviet leaders and 3,365 thick dossiers generated within the IB and shipped from France to Leningrad in 1939. The only photographic portraits of the Irish or British in the brigadas mixtas of the Spanish Republic that we unearthed in Moscow are from the summer of 1938: young men tanned almost black, smiling figures in sweat-soaked shirts and usually unshaven. They look extremely thin and vulnerable, and they were: most of them were killed shortly afterwards.

University teaching and other historical projects meant that our 'Spanish' book was deferred again and again, but a quarter of a century later we located important material on Frank Ryan and other foreign captives of Franco deposited in Spanish archives (Alcalá de Henares, Guadalajara, El Ferrol, Madrid), and hitherto unseen correspondence on the Frank Ryan 'release' case in the archive of the German Foreign Office in Berlin (Politisches Amt des Auswärtigen Amtes, PAAA). Also in Ireland many primary sources had become available in the intervening years – files in the Irish National Archives, primarily documents on Irish–Hispanic relations and partially published by the Royal Irish Academy (www.difp.ie). As always, the National Library in Kildare Street was an obligatory address, especially the Manuscripts Collection containing the diaries of Rosamond Jacob, Frank Ryan's close friend.

In Britain we found important deposits (mainly memoirs, interview transcripts and communist party correspondence) in Marx Memorial Library

(London), Modern Records Centre (University of Warwick), National Museum of Labour History (Manchester), South Wales Miners' Library (Swansea), Working Class Movement Library (Salford) and Southampton City Archives. Among documentation made accessible in recent years in the British National Archives in Kew (TNA) we garnered reports from the archives of the Foreign Office and MI5. We have profited from individuals or institutions who interviewed brigade veterans (Imperial War Museum, London). Last but not least, Ciaran Crossey's online collection on the Spanish Civil War and Ireland (www.irelandscw.com) was a source we frequently consulted.

Six visits to the main battle sites in Spain, usually in sweltering weather, with our friends Christian Lendl, Richard Baxell and John Halstead, made us familiar with the topography of the areas so fiercely fought over (Jarama, Brunete, Teruel, Belchite, Calaceite, Corbera and Gandesa), the training bases (Albacete, Villanueva de la Jara, Madrigueras, Tarazona and Marçà), Franco's headquarters at Burgos and the former concentration camps of San Pedro de Cardeña and Miranda de Ebro near the city. The trips also deepened our knowledge of the country and its language and brought home to us why the Spanish Civil War is still a highly contested topic in the country.

Richard Baxell, chronicler of the British in the IB, shared his encyclopaedic knowledge of the British battalion and answered our countless enquiries about individual Irish brigadistas with estimable patience and good humour. He also pointed out errors in the original manuscript and challenged some of our conclusions. Christina O'Shaughnessy, an old friend and professional editor, read our proofs with great diligence and found countless formal mistakes. We also thank others who provided information, photos or documents on Irish volunteers and aspects of the war and its aftermath: Werner Abel, Andrew Boyd (RIP), Jim Carmody (RIP), Guillem Casañ, Frank Clissmann, Maeve Clissmann, Nicholas Cummins, Diarmuid Duggan (maps), Fred Firsov, Nóirín Greene, Erich Hackl, Carmel Hanna, Wladislaw Hedeler, Ray Hoff, Douglas McIldoon, Mike McLoughlin, Myron Momryk, Joe Mooney, André Novak (maps), Mark O'Sullivan, Harry Owens, Amina Parkes, Danny Payne, Georg Pichler, Sean Quinn, Aideen Ryan, Des Ryan, Juan Carlos Salavera Pardos (Belchite Tourism Office), Eleanor Updale and David Yorke. Will Burton and Jason McGeoghan were the best of postgraduate students of Spain. Barry Whelan of Dublin City University, and Michael Kennedy and his colleague Kate O'Malley of the Royal Irish Academy, helped us to assess the role of Irish and British diplomats in Spain, while Isaac Rilova Pérez was our host in Burgos: he showed us Franco's office in the city's La Isla mansion and directed us to places where Internationals had been interned. Anna Martí and Enric Comas were our guides around the Ebro and Belchite battle sites. In our efforts to access Spanish archives, Barry's Spanish teacher

Joaquin de Otaola Zamora was a masterful drafter of letters in Castilian bureaucratic prose that proved successful on every occasion. Michael Ó hAodha kindly allowed us to use his translation of the Irish language memoir of brigadista Eugene Downing, while the late Gerald O'Reilly of New York made the generous gift of copies of his correspondence with Frank Ryan between 1935 and 1939.

A vote of thanks is also due to archival and library staff in five countries: Ireland: Michael Kennedy, Ken Robinson (National Archives of Ireland); James Harte, Gerry Kavanagh, Glenn Dunne (National Library of Ireland); Jayne Dunlop (Ulster University); Britain: Meirian Jump (Marx Memorial Library); Germany: Annegret Wilke (PAAA, Berlin); Russia: Svetlana Rosental (RGASPI, Moscow); Spain: Daniel Gozalbo Gimeno and Evelia Vega González (Archivo General de Administración, Alcalá de Henares); Miguel Saiz Martínez (Archivo General Militar, Guadalajara); José Benito and Dolores Vázquez Rodríguez (Archivo Intermedio Militar Noroeste, El Ferrol).

Finally, we are obliged to Professor Ian Thatcher, Research Director of History, Ulster University for subventing research visits to Spain and the maps and the indexing of the book.

*Barry O'Loughlin & Emmet O'Connor*
*October 2020*

# Abbreviations

### ORGANISATIONS, NAMES, PLACES, AND TITLES

| | |
|---|---|
| ATGWU | Amalgamated Transport and General Workers' Union |
| AWOL | Absent Without Official Leave |
| BBC | British Broadcasting Corporation |
| CNT | Confederación Nacional del Trabajo |
| CP | Communist Party |
| CPGB | Communist Party of Great Britain |
| CPI | Communist Party of Ireland |
| CPUSA | Communist Party of the United States of America |
| ECCI | Executive Committee of the Communist International |
| ERP | Ejército Republicano Popular |
| FARE | Fuerzas Aéreas de la República Española (Republican Air Force) |
| GRU | Soviet Military Intelligence |
| HQ | Headquarters |
| IB | International Brigades |
| IBA | International Brigade Association (UK) |
| ILP | Independent Labour Party |
| IRA | Irish Republican Army |
| KPD | Kommunistische Partei Deutschlands |
| NILP | Northern Ireland Labour Party |
| NKVD | Narodnyi Komissariat Vnutrennikh Del (Soviet Ministry of the Interior) |
| OKW | Oberkommando der Wehrmacht |
| PCE | Partido Comunista de España |
| PCF | Parti Communiste Français |
| POUM | Partido Obrero de Unificación Marxista |
| POW | Prisoner of War |
| PSOE | Partido Socialista Obrero Español |
| PSUC | Partit Socialista Unificat de Catalunya, the Catalan CP |
| RUC | Royal Ulster Constabulary |
| RWG | Revolutionary Workers' Groups |
| SAP | Sozialistische Arbeiterpartei Deutschlands (Germany) |

| | |
|---|---|
| SIM | Servicio Investigación Militar |
| SPNI | Socialist Party (Northern Ireland) |
| TD | Teachta Dála |
| UCD | University College Dublin |
| UK | United Kingdom |
| UME | Unión Militar Española |
| UMRA | Unión Militar Antifascista |
| US | United States |
| USSR | Union of Soviet Socialist Republics |

## ARCHIVES AND SOURCES

| | |
|---|---|
| AGA | Archivo General de la Administración |
| AIMNOR | Archivo Intermedio Militar Noroeste |
| AMGu | Archivo General Militar Guadalajara |
| COFLA | Cardinal Tomás Ó Fiaich Memorial Library and Archive |
| DFA | Department of Foreign Affairs |
| DIFP | Documents on Irish Foreign Policy |
| IWM | Imperial War Museum |
| MML | Marx Memorial Library |
| NA | National Archives |
| NLI | National Library of Ireland |
| PAAA | Politisches Archiv des Auswärtigen Amtes |
| PRONI | Public Record Office of Northern Ireland |
| RGASPI | Rossiiskii Gosudarstvennyi Arkhiv Sotsialno-Politischeskoi Istorii (Russian State Archive for Social and Political History). Files are cited by fond (f.), opis' (o.), delo (d.), and list (l.) |
| ROR | Correpondence between Frank Ryan and Gerald O'Reilly, donated to Barry McLoughlin |
| TNA | The National Archives of the UK |
| UCDA | University College Dublin Archives |
| WCML | Working Class Movement Library |

# List of Maps and Images

*Maps*

1. Battles and Training Bases of the 15th IB 1936–38 (courtesy of André Novak)
2. Jarama Front (from *The Book of the XV Brigade*)
3. Jarama Front, British attack, 12 February 1937 (courtesy of Diarmuid Duggan)
4. Brunete battle area, July 1937 (courtesy of André Novak)
5. Battle of Brunete, July 1937: Positions of 13th and 15th IB (courtesy of André Novak)
6. Battle of Brunete, July 1937: Limits of Republican advance (from *The Book of the XV Brigade*)
7. Aragon Offensive, August–October 1937 (from *The Book of the XV Brigade*)
8. Belchite attack, August–September 1937 (from *The Book of the XV Brigade*)
9. Teruel battle area, 1938 (courtesy of André Novak)
10. The retreat from Aragon 9th March–3rd April 1938 (courtesy of André Novak and Diarmuid Duggan)
11. Battle of the Ebro, July–September 1938 (courtesy of André Novak)

*Plates*

1. Frank Ryan in the kitchen of R. M. Fox and Patricia Lynch, no date (courtesy of National Library of Ireland)
2. Showers at Jarama, March 1937. Facilities like these were rare and Brigadistas complained regularly about living conditions at the front (courtesy of Peter O'Connor)
3. The CPGB's suspicion of the IRA was set aside for the war and the *Daily Worker* lionised the Irish Brigadistas (courtesy of Emmet O'Connor)
4–7. Clockwise from the top left: Paddy O'Daire (Donegal); John O'Shea (Waterford); Richard McAleenan (Down); Bob Clark (Liverpool).

The Brigadistas saw themselves as a citizen army, but in public perception abroad, the motley dress of Republican troops contrasted unfavourably with the uniform appearance of the Fascists (courtesy of RGASPI)

8. Jim Woulfe (courtesy of Amina Parkes)
9. San Agustín Church, Belchite, after the battle. Jim Woulfe was mortally wounded in the cloisters on the right (courtesy of Belchite Tourist Office)
10. Zaragoza, 4 April 1938. Fascist officers and propagandists talk to the captured members of the International Brigades (courtesy of Archivo Capúa)
11. Zaragoza, 4 April 1938. A foreign journalist (possibly Kim Philby) talks to the captured members of the International Brigades (courtesy of Archivo Capúa)
12. San Pedro de Cardeña monastery near Burgos today (courtesy of Barry McLoughlin)
13. 8 July 2004. Unveiling the Waterford IB memorial: Mayor Cllr Seamus Ryan, Michael O'Riordan and Jack Jones (British Batt.), and Moe Fishman (Lincoln Batt.) (courtesy of John Power Photography)
14. Zaragoza, 5 April 1938. Frank Ryan, photographed on the orders of the Francoist High Command (courtesy of Archivo Capúa)
15. Spain created the first rallying point for liberals in independent Ireland, and women were prominent in organising support for the Republic in Dublin (courtesy of East Wall History Group)
16. Madrid, 10 April 1939. Minister Kerney refusing the fascist salute when handing over his credentials to Franco (courtesy of Kerney family)

# *Introduction*

Very few Irish people still alive have participated in a major international war. The veterans of Flanders and France we knew as old men when we were boys are long since dead, as are almost all those Irish who fought for the Allies in the Second World War. As regards the Irish veterans of the International Brigades (IB) who fought for the Spanish Republic (1936–1938), the last survivor was Vincent 'Paddy' Cochrane who died in 2011, at the age of 98.

Many of the earlier works on the history of the IB were motivated by political party adherence and ideologically driven; others downplayed controversial subjects such as atrocities committed by the Left in the Spanish War, the ramifications of communist control within the IB or the strategical and tactical errors of the Republican high command. All these negative factors, when one reflects, actually enhance the sacrifice of some 240–250 Irishmen who arrived in Spain from five different countries (Ireland, Britain, Australia, Canada and the United States) to fight in a struggle they saw as just: to halt the spread of fascism in Europe. Compared to their countrymen who fought in both world wars, the Irish brigadistas were certainly treated worst of all, being in no way the 'soldiers of fortune' their enemies implied, but rather 'soldiers of misfortune'. The food was often inedible and inadequate, the uniforms were shoddy, the arms they received were often antiquated and prone to malfunction, the pay was derisory and more or less worthless in the 'shortages economy' of Republican Spain, operations to treat wounds were frequently carried out without anaesthetics and, finally, there would be no pension should the volunteers fall in combat or be severely disabled.

Seeing that the Irish contingent was less than one per cent of the total number who joined the IB (32,000–35,000), any description of the Irish participation has to take into account the officers and infantrymen from other countries in any unit they were posted to; likewise the increasing importance of communist cadre policy in running the battalions and judging the men's performance. Although Frank Ryan was the accepted leader of the Irish in Spain from December 1936 to March 1938, many of the Irish volunteers knew about him only from hearsay or not at all. That applies especially to those Irish radicalised by the poverty of interwar Britain or, for that matter, those who undertook the long journey to Spain from the US, Canada, and Australia. In the main, these men were communists and easily integrated into the British, American, and Canadian battalions.

Our book, probably more than most on this subject, looks at each battle in some detail, its strategic goal and the tactical measures adopted to attain it. We were also exercised by the desire to do justice to all, not forgetting the deserters or others who dissented or were disaffected, persons often written out of history by 'true believer' narrators. Another criterion was to place the Irish contingent *within* the history of the Brigades as a whole, i.e. to outline the political as well as the military context at any one point in the war. The English-speaking units, especially before the People's Army was organised on conventional lines in autumn 1937, were a collection of men usually in their late twenties, from all walks of life, predominantly from the working classes and with links to the labour movement. However, from about mid-1937 the Brigades began to repatriate older soldiers, those badly wounded or teenagers who had lied about their age on joining. An unknown number of English-speakers were rejected outright either in Paris or in Figueras (the reception centre in Spain) on grounds of age, physical disability, or bad behaviour. Among the Irish volunteers, card-carrying communists were in a minority, others had experience in the Irish Republican Army (IRA), while a few (hitherto underestimated) had served in the British armed forces or the Irish Free State Army in the inter-war era. A still smaller group had seen military action during World War One or during the Irish War of Independence and the Irish Civil War.

Besides describing the military and political situation in our accounts of the main battles, we devote much space to describing aspects of the volunteers' experience on a day-to-day basis: their living conditions, relations with other nationalities and the internal tensions with the respective battalion leaderships (British and American). Comintern politics and the dissent it created, from the top brass in Albacete or Madrid to infantry company level, is also addressed, a strand in our book that other colleagues have dealt with cursorily, if at all.

Back in Ireland, the Spanish war greatly exercised emotions because of atrocities against religion in the early months of the war. Interest waned when Irish right-wing politicians' campaigns against the elected Spanish Republican Government was increasingly perceived as an anti-Fianna Fáil ramp. Franco's ferocious methods of warfare, not least the bombing of the Catholic Basque capital of Guernica in April 1937, made many realise that the Spanish conflict was more complex than a black-and-white struggle between atheism and Christianity.

During 1936–1939, several factors motivated Éamon de Valera to maintain the diplomatic relations with the Spanish Republic initiated in 1935. He did not want the Irish Free State/Éire to be the only democratic state in Europe to recognise the Spanish dictator early in the war, which would have placed Ireland in the same camp as Mussolini and Hitler; he wished Ireland to continue its membership of the Non-Intervention Committee (which favoured Franco) and, as always, he was mindful of the Vatican's foreign policy: the Papacy sent a chargé d'affaires to Burgos in October 1937, but full diplomatic recognition followed only in May 1938 when a Nuncio was accredited to Burgos.[1] Moreover, de Valera was hesitant in according Franco full diplomatic honours ahead of Neville Chamberlain's National Government, although he was entitled to do so by virtue of the External Relations Act of 1936.[2] Finally, the Irish Premier was anxious not to be seen as surrendering to Irish right-wing pressure groups, the main opposition party Fine Gael, and his clerical critics.

By staying his hand, de Valera was in essence pursuing a 'wait and see' attitude, a course advocated by Michael Rynne of the Department of External Affairs as early as November 1936: 'compromising (and, perhaps temporizing) between the alternatives (de facto status for the Franco regime or continuing de jure accreditation to the Republican Government)'.[3] Rynne foresaw, one year in advance, Britain's de facto recognition of the insurgents' administration by the appointment of Sir Richard Hodgson as British agent to Burgos.[4] While Dublin felt it had to follow the British Government's intention to enforce the Foreign Enlistment Act of 1870, the subsequent legislation passed by the Dáil [Parliament] in February 1937 forbade the recruitment and transportation of volunteers to the Spanish battlefield, but actual participation was not prohibited. While the Gardaí [Police force] were instructed to inform the Department of External Affairs of the departure of suspected men to Spain, nothing could be done if the volunteers did not apply for a passport.

In the end, neither the British nor the Irish Government thought it politic to prosecute their national participants on either side.[5] Following Franco's victory in 1939, Irish interest in the Spanish war decreased further: the defeated limped home to indifference, and their contribution to democracy was forgotten, not least because of political prejudice and the immeasurable horror that ensued – the Second World War.

Chapter 1 sets out the international context. Two reasons why so many Irishmen went to Spain to fight, on both sides, are Spanish anti-clericalism and the fact that Ireland was one of the most globalised countries in the world in the 1930s. Neither are popular explanations, and both need affirmation. The former was problematic, even unfathomable, in Ireland. And the latter has been obscured by the myth of Irish isolation before joining the European Economic Community. Given that post-war globalisation has come to mean Americanisation, Ireland was in some respects more European in the 1930s than it is today.

Chapters 2 and 3 discuss the response at home, chiefly in Dublin and Belfast, to events in Spain. Ireland was obsessed with Spain between the summers of 1936 and 1937. While public opinion was overwhelmingly pro-Franco, the war also led to a revival of communist and radical republican elements and generated an imaginative response from the small liberal middle class, which anticipated the emergence of secular Ireland in the 1970s. Of note too is the writing of women authors with first-hand knowledge of Spain, such as Kate O'Brien, Máirín Mitchell, and Maura Laverty. The descending fist of clericalism in the Free State made the North the more liberal part of Ireland for the first time since partition and inaugurated a purple patch for the Belfast left. The six-county Catholic and Protestant communities had their own take on events in Spain, their perspectives refracted through their experience of living in a divided society, each seeing themselves as a beleaguered people.

Chapter 4 addresses the role of the Soviet Union in the IB. We delineate the outlines of Soviet foreign policy and Stalin's other preoccupations during the war, demonstrate that Soviet military aid was considerable, even if irregularly delivered, and try to come to a balanced judgement on the role of the Comintern's leading figures in running the brigades: André Marty and Palmiro Togliatti (Ercoli). The Irish contingent is then analysed on the basis of county of birth, political affiliation, and military experience. It was a gathering of the Irish diaspora: the majority travelled to Spain from Britain; others from Ireland, the US and Australia. Noteworthy, at over ten per cent, is the number of Irish-born among enforcements sent from Canada who formed their own battalion (MacKenzie–Papineau) and fought in all major battles after Brunete.

Chapter 5 examines why recruits were mobilised for service in Spain. Direct engagement with the war was not inevitable, and many on the left were sceptical about its worth to begin with. For decades, the critical decision of some Irishmen to forsake the British for the Lincoln Battalion remained shrouded in obfuscation and was treated with embarrassment. Even Ryan's explanation of events was discounted.

Chapter 6 deals with the traumatic frontal assaults and dogged rearguard actions with very high casualty rates in the valley of the Jarama (February–June 1937). This section ends with an excursion to the Irish, British and Americans fighting in the hills of western Andalusia.

Chapter 7 is a lengthy and detailed account of the Battle of Brunete (July 1937), fought over three weeks in intense heat. Brunete is arguably the key battle of the whole war, as its outcome presaged further offensives of the Republic: minimal gains in territory and enormous losses in men and equipment, due in part to lack of resources, hesitant leadership, rivalry between communist commanders and professional officers, and bad logistics. The superiority of the fascists in artillery and airpower proved decisive. For the Internationals involved, the battle was a horrible blur of killings, hunger, and thirst, but we try to depict the advance and retreat of the 15th (Anglo-American) and the 13th (German-Austrian-French-Spanish) IB in a taut chronology.

Chapter 8 deals with how Togliatti and other Comintern luminaries oversaw a thorough re-organisation of the brigades. The next offensive, into Aragon, in August 1937, failed for more or less the same reasons that the initial gains won in the Brunete salient could not be held: bad coordination between armour and infantry and the egotistical behaviour of self-important communist commanders. The first copybook success was the capture of Quinto by the 15th, 11th and 13th brigades, and later of Belchite. The focus on them moves to the wintry landscape of Teruel in the mountains, an operation launched for political motives and where the 15th Brigade, called in late to stem fascist counter-attacks, proved effective but was later deployed in a costly diversionary attack at Segura de los Baños.

Chapter 9 describes how Republican forces, severely attenuated after Teruel, were in no condition to stop Franco's Army of Manoeuvre that poured into Aragon in two major drives in early March 1938. The retreat was chaotic, many Internationals were taken prisoner, killed or went 'missing believed dead'; others were drowned trying to swim the swollen Ebro, but one group of the British battalion pushed through the mountains near Gandesa and reached the eastern bank of the Ebro in boats. The British Battalion ran into the spearhead of the renewed Francoist offensive – Italian tanks and infantry. Among the prisoners was Frank Ryan, who had sent the manuscript of *The Book of the XV Brigade* to the printers, and was now an unarmed soldier, but conspicuous because of his officer's uniform.

The narrative then shifts to London and the egregious attempts of Captain Clifford Wattis, a deserter from Aragon, to denigrate his former comrades (and denounce Frank Ryan to Franco's agent in London) in speeches to the House of Commons and upholders of Britain's imperial role in the world. The following sub-chapters recount the first efforts of Leopold H. Kerney, Irish Minister to the Spanish Republic, to have Frank Ryan released, and the leading part Ryan played in boosting morale among the prisoners in the disused monastery of San Pedro de Cardeña outside Burgos.

Chapter 10 begins with the longest period of rest and training that the 15th International Brigade enjoyed during the war, in villages between the Mediterranean and the Ebro. The growing influence of the 'politicos' was accompanied by fervent propaganda: adhering to the communist belief that shortcomings should be attributed to a 'lack of political will' among the riflemen. The brigades crossed the Ebro on 25 July 1938 in high spirits, driving the enemy back, but the initial success broke on the granite hills south of the main objective, Gandesa. The British and Irish were bled white during attacks on Hill 481, and the attrition continued on higher ground and ended in virtual annihilation on the road between Gandesa and Les Camposines on 23 September. The chapter ends with the long journey home.

Chapter 11 examines the controversial subject of discipline, desertion and punishment within the brigades. Executions after due procedure (military tribunals) were very rare in the English-speaking units. 'Unofficial' ones, when some officer shot a notorious delinquent out of hand, were more frequent but hardly widespread, especially in the last months.

Chapters 12 and 13 concern the detention, trial, and extradition to Germany of Frank Ryan. As Ryan was the undisputed leader of the Irish in the brigades, the attention given to him in these pages is justifiable. The interrogation of Ryan by Franco's military had parallels with Stalinist persecution: the foreign prisoner was primarily accused of 'crimes' committed in the past in the home country (in Russia 'deviation from the Party line', 'Trotskyism'). So, it was also in Ryan's case: his prosecutors had little knowledge of his career in the brigades, and they therefore built their arguments on half-truths and down-right lies about his colourful past, furnished willingly by his hostile compatriots.

Chapter 13 opens with the gathering pace of public meetings in Britain and Ireland to agitate for Ryan's release in the summer of 1939 and describes conditions in Burgos prison. The chapter ends with an estimation of Kerney's acquiescence to the release of the prisoner to the Germans and why Frank Ryan accepted it.

The epilogue looks at how brigadistas made their way home and what awaited them on arrival. It is doubtful if more than a minority stayed in Ireland. Aside from the unsympathetic political environment, prospects for employment in Éire were not good. Nor was there an understanding of what would now be called post-traumatic stress disorder. Few survived to see the resurgence of interest in the Spanish Civil War in the 1980s. The values driving the revival offer an additional perspective on the wider, topical debate on remembrance and the politics of commemoration during the 'decade of centenaries'.

NOTES

1. Dermot Keogh, *Ireland and the Vatican: The Politics and Diplomacy of Church-State Relations, 1922–1960* (Cork, 1995), pp 127–32; Paul Preston, *Franco: A Biography* (London, 1995), p. 273.

2. Fearghal McGarry, *Irish Politics and the Spanish Civil War* (Cork, 1999), p. 302.
3. Michael Kennedy et al. (eds), *Documents on Irish Foreign Policy, vol. 4, 1932–1936*, (Dublin, 2004), hereafter DIFP, pp 504–6, memorandum by Rynne to Walshe, 11 November 1936.
4. *Daily Telegraph*, 5 November 1937 (House of Commons debate).
5. McGarry, *Irish Politics and the Spanish Civil War*, pp 213–15.

ONE

# IRELAND AND THE SPANISH CIVIL WAR

## THE SETTING

The Spanish Civil War began on Friday, 17 July 1936 with a revolt led by the Army of Africa and the veteran General José Sanjurjo.[1] The target was Spain's Popular Front government. Politics in Spain was both fragmented and polarised. The Frente Popular was an electoral coalition of Republicans, the Partido Comunista de España (PCE) and socialists, initiated in January 1936 in hopes of defeating the centre-right government in the forthcoming elections to the Cortes. The anarchists gave it conditional support. Its chief opponent was the equally makeshift Spanish Confederation of Right-wing Autonomous Groups (CEDA), comprising a fractious assortment of conservatives, monarchists, falangists and centrists.

The Front won the elections on 16 February with a narrow lead in votes over the right and a bigger lead in seats in the Cortes. Just 16 of the Front's 278 deputies were communists.[2] The Front promised to extend workers' rights, reform landholding, curb the role of the Catholic Church in education and trim the bloated army.

The military conspiracy began. With 690 generals and one commissioned man for every six privates, the officer corps had much to lose.[3] The plan to trigger a series of simultaneous seizures of power in regional centres and install a military government did not go as expected. In the Basque Country, Catalonia, Madrid and most areas to the south, popular militias and armed forces who remained loyal to the Republic retained control. As early as 19 July it became clear that geographically as well as politically, Spain was split, more or less down the middle. Sanjurjo was killed in a plane crash near Lisbon on 20 July as he returned from exile. To hold the rebellion together he was promptly replaced by General Emilio Mola. In a desperate gesture, the prime minister offered him a seat in the cabinet. 'With a little patience', according to Brenan, 'the Right would have gained much of what it sought without a war, for the

Popular Front was breaking up rapidly through its inner discord'.[4] Events, said Mola, were now beyond their control, and in the hands of implacables. One of the implacables was General Francisco Franco.

From 22 July it became increasingly evident that he was the coming man on the insurgent side. Franco had made his name as a ruthless, brave and effective soldier in Spain's Moroccan pocket-colony, the heel-tap of a once vast empire where the inept Spanish army struggled to beat the Rifs in a long and savage war. He was hungry to forge the soul of Spain anew and regarded the falling away of his rivals as providential. Franco would ensure that there would be no compromise with the Republic, that the war was less about winning Spain than about eradicating the enemy, and that its goal was not to complete a military coup but to establish *Franquismo*, an authoritarian ideology of his own composition, based on medieval Catholicism, nationalism, anti-modernism and fascism. On 30 September he was formally appointed 'head of state' and supreme commander of Nationalist forces.[5]

Spain had suffered chronic political instability and violent changes of regime for over a century. Twenty-seven military coups had been attempted between 1846 and 1932. Six succeeded.[6] The revolt of 1936 was modelled on a military coup by General Miguel Primo de Rivera in 1923. Primo de Rivera's dictatorship was overthrown in 1930. The king, Alfonso XIII, was deposed in 1931 and the Second Republic declared. Sanjurjo led a failed rebellion in 1932 and the left attempted a revolution in 1934. For some Spaniards, the events of July 1936 were more of the same. But for foreigners, they were different because of the way they intersected with European politics.

Immediately, Spain became a divisive issue between left and right internationally. As the left saw it, the end of the World War, the war to end all wars, was supposed to have been followed by a new age of democracy. President Woodrow Wilson himself had promised it with his 14-point plan for peace. Democracy in turn would ensure that there would be no return to the pre-War regimes that had blundered into the holocaust of 1914–1918. Instead, fascism emerged to destroy the democracies of Europe one by one.

The Spanish people were the first to rise up against a fascist takeover. They had drawn a line in the sand, and anti-fascists believed that after the defeats in Italy (1922), Germany (1933) and Austria (1934), now was the time to stand with them. As the right saw it, increasingly polarised Spain was drifting towards communism or anarchy. After the February 1936 elections the country was shaken by church-burnings, bombings, strikes and assassinations, and the Government seemed helpless to impose order. It was but a matter of time before parliamentary democracy collapsed, and just as well that the army moved first.[7]

Fascism was better than communism. That would be the attitude of most radio broadcasts, newsreels and newspapers in Britain and the US over the following three years. One of the two most popular newsreel companies, Movietone, was owned by Fox News and controlled in Britain by Lord Rothermere, a cheerleader for the British Union of Fascists in his *Daily Mail*.[8]

Another reason why events in Spain took on such international importance was that by 1936 many people felt that Europe was moving towards another world war, and that what happened in Spain might determine if that war took place or else might undermine the balance of forces in the war. In 1935, Benito Mussolini had invaded Abyssinia. Adolf Hitler had torn up the Treaty of Versailles and begun the re-armament of Germany. On 7 March 1936 German troops re-occupied the Rhineland.

The left believed that war was intrinsic to fascism and the ambition of fascist leaders for war was limited only by the material at their disposal. Mussolini could make small wars. Hitler could make a big one. The right, apart from the fascists themselves, saw fascism as just the latest incarnation of dictatorship. Hitler had a fair case against the punitive Versailles settlement: Germany was as entitled to an army as Britain or France, and the Rhineland was German, after all. War could be avoided through compromise, and with memories of the carnage of the World War so fresh, serious compromises were well worth making.

Almost from the outset, the Spanish war intersected with these international anxieties. On 19 July Franco asked Mussolini for bombers. A Nationalist victory would suit the *Duce*'s ambitions to turn the Mediterranean into '*mare nostrum*', and he could not resist the lure of military glory. Unlike Hitler, he would pour material into Spain with no regard for the consequences for Europe's balance of power. Intervention brought Rome closer to Berlin and further from its old wartime allies who still hoped to keep Italy onside.

Hitler was pleased, and grasped the advantage of the war for combat training and for reinforcing his anti-Bolshevik credentials with the British and French middle class. On 22 July he promptly acceded to Franco's request for transports to lift his Legionnaires from Spanish Morocco over the patrol ships of the loyal Spanish navy and across the Straits of Gibraltar. It was the first such airlift in history, and without it the revolt might have faltered.[9] Portugal's fascist regime was sympathetic and assisted with troops, logistics and diplomacy, using its ancient alliance with England to persuade London that Franco would be a force for stability rather than a second Mussolini.

Britain and France, on whom the survival of European democracy depended, wrung their hands. Britain's Conservative governments remained enthusiastic for appeasement until Hitler broke the Munich Agreement in

1939. France, like Spain, had elected a Popular Front Government, in 1936. Comprising radicals and socialists, and supported in parliament by the communists, it was deeply divided over how it should respond. The French Prime Minister, Léon Blum, favoured the dispatch of France's woeful war planes initially, and the Minister of Aviation exploited the dithering to rush 60 machines across the Pyrenees in July and early August. Small amounts of more covert aid followed intermittently, in a few brief interludes. Blum had recoiled from a backlash in the press. Intervention, he told his colleagues, would lead to a fascist France, not a democratic Spain. Crucially, he was warned by the British Foreign Secretary to 'be prudent'.[10]

Like deer in the headlights of Nazi belligerence, French politicians saw the oncoming danger better than London but were terrified of provoking another Great War. The Maginot Line was supposed to allow France to be firm with Germany, irrespective of Britain. Now that was trumped by the Führer, and France's foreign policy fell back on the conviction that it had to have British support in a war with Germany.

The British were circumspect about the French. Opposing the leading continental power was ingrained in Foreign Office thinking since the days of Louis XIV. Aside from its belief in appeasement, the British Government was suspicious of French imperial designs and there were rumours of concessions in Spanish Morocco in return for aid.

As a fig leaf for inaction, and to prevent the conflict escalating into a European conflagration, Blum promoted a Non-Intervention Pact in August. The British warmed to the idea and would apply it more thoroughly. The London-based Non-Intervention Committee aimed to discourage all external involvement in Spain, and it was eventually endorsed by 27 countries, including Ireland, Soviet Russia, Italy, Germany, Portugal and, privately, the United States. Pandit Nehru described the Non-Intervention Agreement as 'the supreme farce of our time'.[11] It served as an alibi for the democracies to ignore the Republic's pleas for help and restrained the Spanish Government in its quest for the sinews of defence. The dictatorships made their own excuses. Josef Stalin said Russia would comply with the pact if Italy, Germany and Portugal did the same, which, of course, they didn't.

Spain was a headache for Stalin. He had been sanguine about Hitler's accession to power, in keeping with 'third period' thinking. The Moscow-based Communist International, or Comintern, the controlling body of all Communist parties, had adopted its 'third period' thesis in 1928. According to this doctrine, the Bolshevik revolution was followed by a period of working-class advance, followed by one of stabilisation and stalemate between left and right. Now the world was entering a third period of economic depression, a profits squeeze, and heightened ideological conflict, leading to a final showdown of communists and fascists. As, ultimately, one was either a communist or a fascist, the social democrats should be denounced as 'social fascists' to discredit their leaders and win their rank and file to the communist parties.

After Hitler became chancellor on 30 January 1933, the *Irish Workers' Voice*, organ of the Revolutionary Workers' Groups (RWG) declared, 'the Social Democratic Party has actually been the main prop of German capitalism, holding back masses of the workers and preventing them from coming into the struggle against Fascist terror'.[12] It was still expected that the Nazis would get rid of the social democrats and the workers would get rid of the Nazis. In fairness to this much derided scenario, there were many in contemporary Germany who despaired of the social democrats as ever ready to roll over and who reckoned the communists alone would stand up to Hitler.[13]

To rectify a catastrophic error, the Comintern endorsed the popular front idea in 1935. Where fascism was a threat, communists should now about-turn and ally with all democratic elements. Stalin began courting Britain and France for an alliance against Hitler. A Franco–Soviet Treaty of Mutual Assistance became effective in March 1936. What it really meant was unclear. Paris was nervous about giving it military application, leaving Stalin apprehensive about scaring the French with interference in Spain. On the other hand, the Comintern would lose credibility if Soviet Russia did nothing on Spain, and by the 1930s the Comintern had become subordinated to Soviet foreign policy and was Stalin's first line of defence. Reluctantly, the Soviet Union became the Republic's chief source of munitions. There is no evidence for George Orwell's canard that Stalin did not want a Republican victory and that he cunningly contrived to keep the war going; but he did want an outcome that would not alarm the financiers and middle classes of Britain or France. The Spanish government's most whole-hearted ally was Mexico, which was of great moral but less material support. Other countries, notably Poland and Czechoslovakia, sold arms to the Republic – for commercial reasons.

## THE IMPACT ON IRELAND

There was no escaping the Spanish question in Ireland between July 1936 and the summer of 1937. For decades the level of Irish engagement with Spain was a puzzle for Irish historians also. The conventional wisdom, and one happily endorsed by liberal elites, was that nationalism had condemned Ireland to centuries of isolation before the arrival of the European (Economic Community) enlightenment in 1973. Interest in the war was regarded as a relic of the ideological clash over the Anglo-Irish treaty, the only thing that seemed to explain the politics of independent Ireland. In 1971 Lyons wrote of Blueshirts and republicans reprising the Irish Civil War in 'the will-o'-the wisp of the Spanish Civil War... that had nothing to do with any of them'.[14] Eighteen years later, the most acclaimed study of twentieth-century Ireland made not a single mention of the Spanish situation.[15]

In reality, the opening up of North America in the eighteenth century shifted contemporary Ireland from being a cul-de-sac on the edge of Europe to being on one of the great global highways of trade and ideas. The English language, chronic emigration, the British empire and the Catholic Church then made it one of the most globalised countries in the world. Since the Volunteers of 1778, every political movement of any significance has been an echo of things happening elsewhere, and all major wars – from the American War of Independence to the US invasion of Iraq – have impinged on Irish politics. Recent researchers have been impressed with how European Irish mentalities were in 1936.[16] The contemporary Irish were more European than succeeding generations. Certainly, they were less American.

Globalisation explains the impact of Spain; Catholicism accounts for its intensity. Continental Catholicism was familiar to the Irish through icons, devotions to saints, and places of pilgrimage. Spain was the land of St John of the Cross and St Teresa of Avila. Few understood the politics of the Spanish Church. Fewer still understood the counterculture of anticlericalism, and even the communists in Ireland found it unpalatable.

The Church was by far the most powerful institution in Spain. In addition to its role in society and grip on education, it held considerable amounts of property. Though not a big landowner, it had sizable investments in industry, and may have owned as much as one third of Spain's wealth in the early twentieth century.[17] Reminders of its prestige and reach were everywhere – in its sumptuous vast cathedrals and awesome public rituals.

Since the Reconquista – the reconquest of Spain from the Moors – Catholicism had defined the state, and its status was not challenged constitutionally until the Second Republic. But after the Napoleonic occupation had cruelly exposed its weakness, there were many who blamed the Church for Spain's increasingly evident backwardness. Anticlericalism took root among bourgeois liberals and anarchists especially and, by European standards, anarchism and anarcho-syndicalism were relatively strong in Spain. Moreover, the Spanish were not so taken with the Bolshevik turn: like the Irish for a few years, they preferred their own varieties of syndicalism.

The Spanish hierarchy's discovery of the social question in response to Pope Leo XIII's encyclical *Rerum Novarum* merely compounded the problem.

Outside the Basque country, the Catholic trade unions and social clubs that it sponsored came to be regarded as 'yellow' for their cosy connections with employers. In Barcelona they were used as bureaux for blacklegs.

After the trauma of humiliating defeat and loss of empire in the Spanish–American war, 'el desastre' as the Spaniards called it, anticlericalism allied with organised labour in campaigns to clip the power of the priests, who were seen as emblematic of all that was wrong with official Spain. The violence that was endemic in Spanish industrial relations bled into anticlericalism, and hostility to the Church acquired a virulence that may have been instigated by the bishops but was ready to be thrown at the nearest cassock.

Barcelona's 'semana tragica' in July 1909, when a general strike against a call-up of reservists for the Second Rif War led to assaults on dozens of churches and convents, was a portent. For the most part, the priests counter-punched, condemned modernists of the left or the centre, and closed ranks with the rich, the landowners, the monarchy and the army.

With enthusiasts for the Second Republic pushing for secular education, subordination of religious orders to civil law, imposition of regular taxation on the Church and restrictions on clerical ownership of property, attitudes to religion became shibboleths separating the masses on the right and left and shaping a widening cultural divide.

The Vatican declined to recognise the Republic and condemned its liberal government in 1933. When the Civil War erupted, religion was part of the conflict, but with contrasting outcomes. Catholicism served the Nationalists well, ennobling the cause and providing a point of unity. Anticlericalism proved to be more problematic for the Republic. The desecration of altars, smashing of icons and execution of 6,832 clerics made a terrible impression internationally, overshadowing the greater number and more systematic character of atrocities on the Nationalist side.[18] Some 150,000 were shot in Nationalist 'limpieza' or cleansing operations.[19]

Awakening to the propaganda disaster, the Comintern advised the PCE to make overtures to Catholic workers, and the party duly condemned 'the provocative burning down of churches and monasteries, since such acts only go to help counter-revolution'.[20] It cut little ice in Spain, where communists were much fewer than anarchists. On the outbreak of the war the PCE had about 100,000 members, whereas the Confederación Nacional del Trabajo (CNT), the main anarchist trade union, had well over one million. It cut no ice at all in Ireland, where hostility to 'the Reds' made no distinction between them.

Ireland had been conditioned to 'red scares' since February 1930. The Church had said little on communism in the 1920s. Pope Benedict XV regarded the disestablishment of the Russian Orthodox Church as an opportunity for western Catholicism. Expecting that economics would soon take care of the Bolsheviks, he and his successor, Pius XI, sought a concordat with the Kremlin to permit the Roman clergy to proselytise in Russia. It remained a prized mission territory. Generations of Irish children were taught to pray, not for Russia's misfortunate Christians, but for its conversion.

Vatican policy changed after 1929, when Stalin condemned religion and included Catholics in his routine persecution of believers. Pius retaliated with calls for expiatory masses to atone for the crimes of communism to be said throughout the Catholic world.[21] It had been a difficult decade for Irish communists too. Their efforts to establish a party, often in cahoots with the Irish Republican Army (IRA), met with repeated frustration at the hands of Jim Larkin. Larkin's break with Moscow encouraged a new initiative from the Executive Committee of the Communist International (ECCI), leading to the formation of the Revolutionary Workers' Groups (RWG). Unfortunately for the communists, it coincided with the shift in Vatican policy.

The Cumann na nGaedheal government had earlier failed to secure a condemnation of republicanism from the hierarchy. Joseph MacRory, who had become Archbishop of Armagh in 1928 and a cardinal in 1929, was an outspoken anti-partitionist. In 1931, Eoin O'Duffy, then Garda Commissioner, urged the government to crush the emergent republican-communist nexus in the campaign against land annuities.[22] Playing the red card, President W. T. Cosgrave tried again, sending MacRory a report on Saor Éire. 'We are confronted with a completely new situation,' he wrote. 'Doctrines are being taught and practiced which were never before countenanced amongst us and I feel that the influence of the Church alone will be able to prevail in the struggle against them'.[23]

In reality, the RWG regarded Saor Éire as a rival, telling the ECCI: 'The organisation of Saor Éire is an attempt on the part of the petty bourgeois leaders [in the IRA] to steer the rising tide of unrest among the masses into channels where they can control it, and prevent the formation of a Communist Party'.[24] O'Duffy's security report acknowledged that Saor Éire was a 'National Communist Party, free from all foreign control' and that 'Russian Communism, as an organised force. . ., is not a menace to the country'.[25] Both Cosgrave and MacRory had their own agendas. The Church was already confronting International Lenin School agitators, who had surfaced in Dublin in 1929–1930 with an inexplicable supply of funds and pro-Soviet propaganda.

Dáil Éireann enacted the Public Safety Bill on 17 October 1931, proscribing 14 organisations. Next day, a pastoral letter read at Sunday masses described Saor Éire as aiming 'to set up a Communist State upon the Catholic soil of

Ireland, with its fanatical hatred of God, as now dominates Russia and threatens to dominate Spain'. The pastoral went on to stress that one 'cannot be a Catholic and a Communist. One stands for Christ, the other for Anti-Christ'.[26]

This level of censure was unprecedented. The Irish were used to episcopal denunciations in politics, and many were inured to them. But usually the censures applied to republicans, or occasionally to socialists, in particular contexts, for specific actions, or were made by a bishop or groups of bishops. Here was the entire hierarchy, patently backed by the Pope, anathematising an ideology in the most extreme terms, even to the point of urging priests to 'diligently instruct [the laity] on the satanic tendencies of Communism'.[27]

And what gave the tiny forces of communism in Ireland credibility, for communists as much as anti-communists, was their status as part of a world movement, completing the revolution in the remaining five sixths of the earth. Communists looked to Soviet Russia; their enemies bracketed Spain with Russia and Mexico. Cumann na nGaedheal sustained the red scare in the 1932 General Election with the suggestion that the IRA would play Lenin to Éamon de Valera's Kerensky.

The election of a Fianna Fáil Government ushered in a regime more sceptical of the bishops and anti-communism. Yet the people, and their Government, were no less Catholic, as became clear in the mass mobilisation for the Eucharistic Congress in June 1932 and public interest in less well-known propaganda initiatives such as the World-Wide Anti-God Campaign of Militant Atheism Exhibition that toured Ireland in 1935.[28] Anti-communism was given an intellectual appeal by Pope Pius XI's promotion of Catholic action in politics and society to build an alternative to fascism or communism. Implicitly the Pope was suggesting that liberal democracy was on the way out. A call to Catholic action was set out in one of the most influential papal encyclicals, *Quadragesimo Anno*, in 1931. One of its key concepts was vocationalism. Article 15 of the 1937 constitution allowed the Oireachtas to recognise vocational representation in economic and social life; articles 18 and 19 made vocationalism the electoral basis of Seanad Éireann, and in 1939 the Government appointed a Commission on Vocational Organisation to consider its application to Ireland generally.[29]

In the front row of politics, the three pillars of Francoism in Ireland were Fine Gael, the *Irish Independent* and the Irish Christian Front. The change of government in 1932 was the most important in independent Ireland: Cumann na nGaedheal *was* the Free State. Rattled by the threat to the regime it had created, Cumann na nGaedheal merged in 1933 with the National Centre Party and the National Guard to form Fine Gael under the leadership of O'Duffy.

The National Guard, commonly known as the Blueshirts, was the most obvious link between Ireland and continental fascism. The Blueshirts enjoyed a mushroom growth – to some 48,000 members in mid-1933 – in reaction to the muscular presence of IRA men at political rallies, fears that Fianna Fáil was crypto-communist and the devastating impact of the Economic War on cattle graziers.

When O'Duffy's promises of big electoral gains failed to materialise, he was quickly side-lined by Fine Gael. He left the party in 1935 to form the tiny National Corporate Party and its minuscule paramilitary wing, the Greenshirts.[30]

Aside from the Roman salutes, the parades, the street fights with the IRA, the anti-communism, the anti-Semitism and the attempt to develop a leadership cult around O'Duffy, a forthright fan of Mussolini, the Blueshirts had a programme based on Italian corporatism. The reluctance of historians to describe them as fascist echoes academic disbelief in a globalised Ireland before entry into the European Economic Community. 'Fascism was far too intellectually demanding for the bulk of the Blueshirts,' concluded Lee, with a condescension exceptional only in its swaggering hubris.[31] The same could be said of Blackshirts and Brownshirts.

Another blinkered argument is that the Blueshirts weren't fascist as they were the product of events in Ireland rather than the continent.[32] More credible is the protest that they were authoritarian conservatives, without the anti-capitalism and ambition to sweep away old elites found in early theorists of fascism and in the Brownshirts especially. Yet that objection ignores, as historians have been wont to do, the fact that O'Duffy tried to give the Blueshirts a radical dynamic by demanding action to end partition.[33] There were varieties of fascism. Hitler was disgusted by Mussolini's deference to the king and nobility in Italy. Franco's fascism might more precisely be called falangism and was selective, self-serving and contingent on Axis success in Second World War. He discarded it for traditional authoritarianism after 1945.

Reports of the trouble in Spain started to appear in Irish newspapers from 20 July 1936. One indication of public interest is that all three Dublin dailies sent correspondents to Spain at a time when it was highly unusual for Irish papers to maintain reporters abroad.[34] The *Irish Times* dispatched Lionel Fleming with £50 from editor R. M. 'Bertie' Smyllie. With a readership identified with the Protestant community and liberals of all persuasions, the *Times* had a relatively small circulation, and daily sales of 25,500. Its starting point was that 'At the last general election a Government was returned to power in a perfectly democratic way,' and that subsequent events were rooted in the complexities of Spanish history.[35] It also made plain its aversion to communism or fascism and its opinion that there was no good reason for the

Irish to bother about benighted Spain. While the *Times* is invariably credited with the most objective reportage, Fleming later admitted that he saw the Republic as fighting a 'legitimate struggle, both against the evils of Nazism and Fascism and the claim of the Catholic Church, that it should be allowed to control almost every aspect of Spanish life'.[36] His reports were published in a ten-part series in August and September 1936, and outraged the Catholic clergy. John Charles McQuaid, then president of Blackrock College, instigated a threat to withdraw advertising by Catholic schools from the paper. Smyllie recalled Fleming from Spain.[37]

The *Irish Press* was the most partisan of the three Dublin dailies. Arguably the partisanship was both a strength and a weakness, explaining why its daily sales of 95,000 were high, but not commensurate with Fianna Fáil's standing as the most popular party in the country. On Spain, as on everything else, the *Press* followed the Fianna Fáil government's line, endorsing its accession to the Non-Interventionist Pact.

Before Éire's unilateral neutrality in September 1939, de Valera's foreign policy favoured collective security. Because the most ardent Francoists were Fine Gaelers, Fianna Fáil adopted a more impartial position on Spain, and the *Irish Press* was happy to ridicule the Blueshirts and challenge the 'hysteria' of the more popular *Independent*. The stance met criticism from within the paper, and its managing editor, Chris O'Sullivan, an Irish-Australian, was sacked by de Valera in early 1937 for sending an undercover reporter to Spain with O'Duffy's brigade.[38]

For 30 years, the *Independent* was regarded as the voice of Catholic Ireland and had long boasted the biggest circulation of any Irish newspaper, with daily sales of 123,000 in 1935. Together with the provincial press in the Free State, the *Independent* represented what it called 'the Patriot army' as saviours and the war as one to protect the Catholic Church from the 'Red atrocities' of the atheist government. Franco was depicted as an exemplary Christian soldier, doing his duty to save Spain from Red anarchy. Between July and September 1936, the *Independent* devoted 22 editorials to Spain, compared with 16 by the *Irish Times* and 3 by the *Irish Press*.[39] Its line on Spain was reinforced by British newspapers, those with the greatest circulation in Ireland tending to be the more conservative ones, and Tories were overwhelmingly pro-Franco.[40]

Most cross-channel titles took an editorial stance on Spain. The *Daily Mail*, *Observer*, *Morning Post* and *Daily Sketch* endorsed Franco. The *News Chronicle*, *Daily Herald* and *Daily Worker* were for the Republic. The papers with the biggest circulations, the *Manchester Guardian*, *Daily Mirror* and *Daily Express* favoured appeasement and non-intervention. Only *The Times* and the *Daily Telegraph* attempted impartiality.[41] British newsreels, which monopolised news reportage in the cinema, were largely pro-Franco. Pro-Franco propaganda was available too in the Catholic media, which included two weeklies, 10 monthlies, a quarterly, 4 annuals, 11 periodicals devoted to the missions, 17 organs of religious orders and 3 youth magazines. The most militant and influential, the *Standard*, claimed a circulation of 28,000 per week.[42] The equally pro-Franco English Catholic papers, the *Tablet*, the *Universe* and the *Catholic Herald* also circulated in Ireland. Even the Scottish edition of the *Irish Weekly* warned British Labour against supporting 'the Communists' in Spain.[43]

The fate of the one home-grown liberal periodical available at the time seemed to confirm the futility of challenging the Church. *Ireland To-day* aimed to be a forum for 'constructive and critical thought, whether orthodox or not'. The first issue appeared in June 1936. The editor, James L. O'Donovan, was an old IRA man and contributors included numerous republicans. *Ireland To-Day* was the only mainstream periodical open to writers who were anti-Franco, and while it protested its neutrality there were limits to Catholic tolerance.

Spain dominated the September 1936 issue, which included a symposium on the war, with articles by Ambrose V. Martin, Máirín Mitchell and Peadar O'Donnell. Martin was a Fianna Fáil activist and businessman, trading with Republican Spain. Mitchell was a travel writer and London-based correspondent for the *Irish Press*. O'Donovan apologised for his inability to attract a more balanced line-up.

Months later, the cold shoulder gave way to the elbow. Owen Sheehy Skeffington's satires on inconsistencies in the Church's positions on Spain led to letters of protest and then to boycotts in the shops. Most of the journal's editorial committee wished to make a point of resisting the pressure, but O'Donovan had 'Skeff' replaced as foreign affairs correspondent and reined in the magazine's anti-Franco content. The clerical opposition persisted. *Ireland To-day* folded in March 1938.[44]

Another indication of the temper of the times was the breach of the notional distinction between religion and politics by the Irish Christian Front, formed in Dublin's Mansion House on 31 August 1936 by Fine Gael TD Patrick Belton with the encouragement of the Church and the *Irish Independent*. Few would defy its chief aims to defend Franco and 'unmask communism in Ireland'.[45] More controversially, it strayed into criticism of Fianna Fáil, demanded that the Government implement the Papal encyclicals, and advocated corporatism. Suspicions of fascism were not allayed by the Front adopting its own salute: arms crossed above the head. Shocked by anti-clerical atrocities – one gruesome photo reproduced in Irish papers from

*L'Écho de Paris* showed Spanish women looking aghast at 12 semi-decomposed cadavers of Carmelite nuns exhibited in open coffins outside a church in Barcelona – crowds of up to 40,000 thronged rallies of the Front.[46] Both the Christian Front and the Catholic hierarchy donated funds to the Nationalists. The Comintern was amazed that £32,000 had been collected 'from the poverty-stricken people [of Ireland] to help the Spanish fascists'. In fact the hierarchy had raised over £43,000, ostensibly for Spanish Catholics. The Christian Front collected £30,000 more.[47] The first of a proposed eight ambulances, built in Dublin, left for Spain in January 1937, blessed by the Rev. F. Wall, auxiliary Bishop of Dublin and titular Bishop of Thasos.[48]

The Church's most memorable contribution was to help the creation of O'Duffy's 'Irish Brigade'. The idea was put to Cardinal MacRory in August 1936 by the London-based Carlist Count Ramírez de Arellano, who thought it would help to project the insurgents as crusaders if volunteers could be raised in a country so identified with the Catholic Church. MacRory recommended O'Duffy, who had previously offered to fight with the Italians in Abyssinia.[49] With the aid of the extensive infrastructure of Catholic organisations like the Catholic Young Men's Society, O'Duffy claimed to have 7,000 volunteers by the end of August.[50] As Ramirez expected, the Brigade acquired a significant propaganda value as a unique phenomenon and because it was assumed that it was of Brigade strength. The Comintern thought it numbered 2,000, and even the *Irish Democrat* of 24 April 1937 was astounded to learn from the London *Times* that it was actually a battalion of some 640 men, including a pipe band.[51]

## WHAT'S LEFT IN THE FREE STATE?

The electoral strength of the left in the Free State reached a nadir in 1932–1933 as Fianna Fáil ate into the popular vote. The Labour Party, which near monopolised the left-wing vote during these years, saw its tally fall to 5.7 per cent in the 1933 general election. Fortuitously, the party's immediate requirement in the seventh Dáil was a replacement for its unseated leader. The succession fell to William Norton, general secretary of the Post Office Workers' Union. Professional and pragmatic, Norton was the party's first real leader. Tom Johnson had put the constitution first. T. J. O'Connell put the unions first. Norton put the party first.

That Labour survived at all owed much to Norton's shrewd tactical judgment. He soon ditched Labour's ambiguity on nationalism for a straightforward acceptance of consensus republicanism, and pledged backbench support for minority Fianna Fáil governments up to 1938. In return, Labour secured the introduction of unemployment assistance, widows and orphans' pensions, reform of public transport, protection for the flour-milling industry, control of food prices, economic development and the construction of 40,000 houses. In 1936 Labour adopted a new constitution, committing it to a 'Workers' Republic'. Norton's aim was not so much to take the party to the left as to distinguish it from Fianna Fáil. He was also responding to pressure from far-left accretions to the party. By 1937 the Labour vote had climbed to 10.3 per cent.[52]

Norton took a firm line against the Blueshirts, denouncing them as 'Hitlerite' and speaking at anti-fascist rallies around the country. He also accused Fine Gael politicians of sympathy with continental fascism:

> It is the Blueshirt movement to-day; it may be the Brownshirt, or any other kind of movement, another day... Do they want to see established here the system of Parliamentary parties that has been established in Germany, in Italy and in Austria; and [do] they want to see these Parliamentary parties end, as they must inevitably end, with the same tyranny that has disgraced Germany, disgraced Italy and disgraced Austria in later years?[53]

Arguably, Norton's primary aim was to win adherents from the fragmenting republican and Communist movements. He rejected appeals from the far left for a united front against fascism, and Labour's annual conference in 1934 affirmed its opposition to the introduction of 'anti-Christian communist doctrines into the movement'.[54] Norton's bottom line was to avoid confrontation with the Catholic Church. How much of this was due to his legendary expediency is debatable. As Labour leader he invoked *Rerum Novarum* on the right to a life of 'frugal comfort' and was a member of the lay sodality, the Knights of St Columbanus, which was widely seen as a Catholic version of the Freemasons. On the other hand, John Charles McQuaid, Archbishop of Dublin from 1940, believed his abiding concern was with 'votes from anywhere and how to get them'.[55] Nonetheless, he felt free in 1934 to include Austria in an international arraignment of fascist regimes, despite the claims of the Austrian dictatorship to be a Catholic-corporate state.

Spain posed a more severe challenge to Norton. Something had to be said to give direction to the party and discourage internal dissention. Michael Keyes, TD, had stood on a Christian Front platform at a rally in Limerick. There were others like Keyes who regarded communism as the supreme menace, and others yet, including Norton, who found the Christian Front obnoxious. Voices of the left came from the Dublin and university branches, including former Republican Congress members.[56]

At the same time, no offence could be given to Catholic groups in Ireland. After doing his best to avoid the issue, Norton published an evasive pamphlet, *Cemeteries of Liberty: Communist and Fascist Dictatorships*. The text was drawn from a speech he gave to Labour's annual conference during a heated debate on fascism in February 1937. It was introduced by William O'Brien, general secretary of the Irish Transport and General Workers' Union and the most powerful man in the trade union movement. Unlike in 1934, Norton made no reference to the Blueshirts and just one vague allusion to 'curbing Fascist tendencies in this country'. Giving credibility to fascism in Ireland would have strengthened demands on the left for action against it. Skirting both Spanish and Irish politics, Norton treated fascism as Nazism, and equated Nazism with Stalinism.[57] Labour, as Norton would have it, was anti-fascist but not anti-Franco; not pro-Franco, but definitely anti-communist. However slithering the strategy, it was successful in minimising accusations of communism against the party, and in waterproofing it from those that were made. It was an achievement for Norton to impose discipline and astuteness on a parliamentary party not known for either quality before his election as leader.

Trade unions in the Free State had something of a tradition of isolation, sharing with the Catholic Church a suspicion of internationalism as ideological. The Irish Trade Union Congress had severed connections with the international labour movement in 1920. A motion to affiliate to the International Federation of Trade Unions in 1934 was heavily defeated.[58] Unions in the Free State were less circumspect than the left and more inclined to be openly pro-Franco.

On 10 October 1936 over 10,000 people, with four bands and banners inscribed 'Long live Franco, Long live our faith', assembled in Waterford to form a branch of the Christian Front. Speaking from the platform, the president of the trades council said the workers of Waterford had 'sent him there to show that they were with the movement heart and soul'.[59] Even Larkin banned officials of his union from speaking in public on Spain, though it must have been an acute embarrassment to his eldest and favourite son, Young Jim, and his old pal, Jack Carney. Carney, who had served Big Jim for 25 years, took the boat to London and a new career in journalism. Young Jim ceased to attend meetings of the Communist Party of Ireland (CPI).[60] The loss of his name was a blow to the CPI.

'The amalgamateds', as British-based unions were called euphemistically – so many of them had been styled 'Amalgamated Society of...' on first entering the Irish market – became an obvious target in consequence of British Labour's sympathy for Republican Spain. The Catholic press and clerics urged Irish members not to let themselves be 'led by the noses', and there were protests, resignations, and a few defections en masse from branches of the Amalgamated

Transport and General Workers' Union (ATGWU). In Athenry the entire branch defected when the union gave £1,000 to the British Trades Union Congress Solidarity Fund for 'victims' of the war. While an Irish delegate conference of the union endorsed the gift, the ATGWU general secretary Ernest Bevin insisted that the money was for humanitarian aid only and spent on medical supplies in England. Other unions affected included the National Union of Railwaymen, the National Union of Boot and Shoe Operatives and the Amalgamated Society of Woodworkers.

It was a time of acute tension between Irish and British unions, and of calls for an exclusively Irish-based movement. The Spanish Civil War near coincided with the deliberations of an Irish Trade Union Congress commission on union restructuring. Against this contentious backdrop, and with the very future of the amalgamateds in Ireland hanging in the balance, the Congress retreated into neutrality, ignoring appeals for action on Spain from the International Federation of Trade Unions and the British National Joint Committee for Spanish Relief.[61] Very much an exception was John Swift, national organiser of the Bakers', Confectioners' and Allied Workers' Union, who took an openly pro-Republic line.[62]

Irish support for the Spanish Republic was orchestrated primarily by the CPI and the Republican Congress. The CPI had been founded by the RWG in June 1933. It was not a propitious time for the initiative. The anti-communist campaign underway since 1930 had climaxed between 27 and 30 March 1933. Inflamed by Lenten pastorals and sermons at missions and led by St Patrick's Anti-Communism League and the Catholic Young Men's Society, crowds in Dublin made nightly attacks on premises associated with the RWG or Larkin's Workers' Union of Ireland. The bulk of communists went to ground for the next few weeks. Seán Murray, the RWG's general secretary, took to carrying a gun after 'several strangers' made enquiries at his lodgings.[63] On one occasion he was chased from the CPI's usual Friday night rally in Abbey Street and jumped onto the nearest bus in O'Connell Street. The conductor helpfully pulled down the 'Bus Full' sign.[64]

In practice the CPI would suffer a semi-legal status in the Free State until the Spanish Civil War, and blamed its lack of progress on a pervasive 'spirit of illegality' among comrades.[65] Even so, there was a genuine reluctance to criticise religion, which had always been a source of contention between the RWG and the ECCI. Underestimating its grip on the masses, Moscow's Irish experts made little allowance for the anticipated hostility from the Catholic Church when preparing their renewed intervention in Ireland in 1929. A resolution drafted by the Anglo-American secretariat, which handled ECCI business in English-speaking countries, concluded: 'the confused ideologies prevailing among the radical republican and labour groups, make it essential to combat all inclinations to capitulate to religious and other prejudices.'[66] The *Workers' Voice* qualified this line somewhat by combining criticism of clerical attitudes in Ireland with frequent articles on religious freedom in Russia. For some fellow travellers, the *Voice* was still too blunt. Helena Molony expressed her reservations to Moscow, saying that Friends of Soviet Russia was more effective in addressing clerical hostility as it was led by 'people familiar and sympathetic with the National and religious psychology of the Irish people'. The approach of the *Workers' Voice*, she thought, 'leaves much to be desired'.[67]

Under Murray's editorial direction the *Voice* tried to be less dogmatic on religion, and he evidently broached the question in Moscow in 1932. He was informed by the ECCI's political commission:

> The RWG in the fight against the influence of the clergy who keep the masses divided on religious grounds in order to secure their subjection to capitalist and imperialist domination must base themselves on the basis of furthering class interests of the workers and small farmers... Every case of the clergy openly aiding the capitalists and imperialists against the workers and small farmers must be utilised to expose the class basis and role of religion and the church... No religious barriers should be allowed to interfere with the development of the united workers' struggle.
>
> As regards accepting members into the RWG who are imbued with religious prejudices no barriers should be raised, but it should be made clear that loyalty to the Communist Party, and Party discipline, comes first... and that they cannot as Communists use the Party platform to propagate religious beliefs. The Party must carry on a systematic educational campaign to overcome religious prejudices.[68]

Weeks after the anti-communist riots of 1933, the RWG managed to issue a stopgap *Workers' Bulletin* in place of the *Workers' Voice*. In the circumstances, it said relatively little on the riots or the Church and blamed 'rascally capitalist propagandists' for 'the use of religious feelings for political purposes against the militant workers'.[69] Misuse of religion would become a regular trope in Irish communist propaganda on the subject. Reports on the riots by T. A. Jackson in the *Daily Worker*, organ of the Communist Party of Great Britain (CPGB), were not appreciated. According to the Comintern agent in Dublin: 'The Anti-Religious touch is inevitable with him and the comrades here don't think it the best way to tackle the question.'[70]

In truth, the coverage was fairly restrained. Just a year earlier, the ECCI had directed the CPGB to be more sensitive towards the Irish and to produce a special edition of the *Daily Worker* without birth control advertisements. But Jackson, one of the CPGB's Irish experts, had recently published on the necessity of atheism and was secretary of the Soviet-based League of Militant Atheists.[71] As the ECCI dismissed the disasters in Dublin and continued to push for the transformation of the RWG into a proper party, Murray begged Moscow to avoid putting 'communist' in the title. The word had now acquired an extraordinary taboo, which would persist into the 1960s. The ECCI replied that Irish comrades had avoided the label for long enough – it had demanded a party by 1932 – and the time to advertise the brand was overdue.

According to British intelligence, Murray then suggested that 'the Communist Movement in Ireland should, like the IRA, obtain support by using the Bible. It is easy to interpret the teaching of Christ in a communist fashion, and this policy would gain many adherents as well as weakening opposition'. He was advised to apply the Comintern programme in 'easy stages'.[72] Even as it reported the Dublin riots, the *Daily Worker* was urging the RWG to press on with the party. Bizarrely, the founding congress of the second CPI convened at 5 Leinster Street, Dublin in a room rented from the Franciscans by the 'Dublin Total Abstinence Association', with a card outside the door saying 'Temperance meeting'.[73] Showing a saintly innocence, the good friars entertained no suspicions.

At the conference, Murray set out the line on religion:

> There is no mention of religion in the document [the founding manifesto] and this is not done for tactical reasons but as a question of principle. Religion is not a fundamental question and it is on the economic issues that we must lead the fight. The capitalists are pressing into the fight the powerful weapon of religion. They are over-reaching themselves and our party stands and will insist on our members giving first allegiance to the class, their party and the cause of the Irish people. The clergy are making it clear, as Marx once said, that 'they are the spiritual policy of the master class'. In the Soviet Union the solution of the religious issues was reached by breaking the secular power of the church. This is the solution to the questions here. While is it not a fundamental question we must make our position clear.[74]

No one challenged the policy.

Externally, the mischief-making continued. The *Daily Express* claimed that 20 per cent of those who attended the CPI congress were in the IRA, prompting the army council to send a blunt message to all within and without, affirming a standing order preventing members from belonging to the CPI. Having braved red scares since 1930, the IRA had first started to wobble over the Gralton affair. Jimmy Gralton was deported to New York in February 1933 at the instigation of the local clergy for socialist republican activism in Leitrim. Some Republicans were to the fore in defending Gralton. Others were conspicuously silent or quietly hostile. Wagering an each-way bet, the Leitrim battalion agreed that he deserved a fair trial – as his supporters were demanding – and suggested the IRA 'distance itself from all anti-God doctrines'.[75] After the March riots, the army council first dissociated the IRA from the communists, while deploring the attacks as comparable with Hitlerism.[76] The *Daily Express* pushed it into capitulating to the zeitgeist. On 17 June *An Phoblacht* decided that:

> The movement which is known as Communism throughout the world today has become definitely associated with atheism and irreligion. Hence any good or bad in the Communist economic theory is submerged. While a movement towards Communism makes a denial of God and activity hostility to religion and Christianity a dogma, it will fail.

Army order no. 4 forbade volunteers from being members of communist organisations. For Murray, an old IRA man himself from the glens of Antrim, it was a cruel blow to the CPI and a gratuitous gift to the most mindless of its enemies. The army council, however, did not see the break with the CPI as a shift to the right. It simply decided that the communists were more trouble than they were worth, and switched tack to strengthening links with mainstream Labour. But it was too much for the fellow travellers in the IRA, and O'Donnell was the quintessential fellow traveller. Hogan singled him out in Could Ireland Become Communist? as an Irish version of Willi Muenzenberg, the Comintern's propaganda wunderkind. Here was no 'useful idiot', warned Hogan, but a willing accomplice with an astute understanding of the Irish mind and Comintern tactics.[77]

Fifteen years later Orwell included O'Donnell in a list of 38 writers, journalists and actors whom he considered 'crypto-communists, fellow travellers or inclined that way' and which he showed to a secret section of Britain's Foreign Office.[78] O'Donnell had tabled a motion at the 1933 IRA general army convention for an alliance with other radical groups. When the proposal was defeated again in 1934, he and his supporters decamped unilaterally to call for a Republican Congress. It was not a split between left and right, but one over tactics.

Within months, a sprouting network of social agitation blossomed into a 'united front' of some 8,000 republicans and trade unionists. To the CPI the Republican Congress was another Saor Éire. To the CPGB, which handled Irish communications with Moscow through encrypted radio signals, it was a 'most dangerous situation'.[79] Like the Comintern, the British feared that

Murray was too close to O'Donnell, and that the communists would end up joining the republicans, rather than vice versa. It was, perhaps, one aspect of communist thinking that O'Donnell didn't quite grasp.

On 26–27 March 1922 Murray had attended the convention in Dublin at which the IRA withdrew its allegiance from the pro-Treaty Provisional Government. It was here that he met O'Donnell, who became his closest friend and confidante. 'We found each other somehow,' O'Donnell recalled, in a curiously intimate phrase. 'There are not many people at whose feet I would willingly sit but I would sit at Sean Murray's feet.'[80]

The CPI meanwhile struggled to reconcile its third period strategy of supporting 'united fronts from below' with the united front strategy of the Republican Congress. To begin with, the CPI offered joint action with the Congress only on specifics, such as anti-fascism. Fortuitously, the Comintern was allowing national sections to drift from third period thinking in response to the left's failure to stop the Nazis. On 1 September the CPI was able to endorse a united front with the Congress on the central issue of anti-imperialism.

The first convention of the Republican Congress in Rathmines Town Hall on Saturday 29 and Sunday 30 September marked the high-point of the far left in 1930s Ireland and illustrates the types of organisation it was given to produce. There were 186 accredited delegates representing local Congress groups, the revived Citizen Army, 16 trade union sections and trades councils, tenant leagues, the Kerry-based Republican Labour Party and the Socialist Party, formerly the Belfast branch of the British Independent Labour Party; the sizable communist contingent included representatives of the CPI, the Labour League Against Fascism, the Labour Defence League, the Irish National Unemployed Movement and fraternal delegates of the New York Irish Workers' Clubs, the League Against Imperialism, the British Anti-War League and the Indian Defence League.

Some 36 people carrying Eucharistic Congress flags picketed the Town Hall. At local level, clerical efforts to depict the Congress as communist were already under way. The most famous casualty was a future International Brigader, Frank Edwards, who lost his job as a teacher in Waterford.[81] The clerical censure was not without opposition. Gardaí were posted within and without Waterford cathedral when Bishop Kinane declared it a mortal sin to belong to the Republican Congress.[82]

The big issue in Rathmines was whether to continue as a united front or form a political party. There was no dispute over policy. But the controversy is usually remembered as abstruse debate over the slogan or a clash exposing the contradictions between left republicanism and true socialism.[83] O'Donnell and a minority on the Congress organising bureau wanted to continue as a united front that would appeal to everyone from the CPI to Fianna Fáil. Michael Price and a majority on the bureau wanted to create a political party. The minority proposed 'a republic'. The majority demanded 'a workers' republic'. At this point, the CPI should have called for 'a workers' and farmers' republic'.

The Comintern did not want a new party, but neither did it want the Irish comrades backing an ostensibly moderate slogan over a more left-wing slogan. For communists, the slogan was always very important. The instructions were radioed late in the day to CPGB secretary Harry Pollitt but never passed on to Dublin. So the communists voted with O'Donnell and the united front option was adopted by 99 to 84 votes. Price and the minority withdrew, and the stricken Congress never recovered. The Price faction blamed 'Moscow'.[84] Conversely, the remnant of the Republican Congress moved closer to the CPI. They had few other friends. The Comintern remained contemptuous of the Republican Congress and 'the evil results ensuing from submitting to petty-bourgeois nationalism'.[85]

At the seventh world congress of the Comintern in July and August 1935, which formally endorsed the popular front idea, Murray welcomed what he saw as a ratification of the united front strategy, and the terms 'united front' or 'people's front' were usually employed by the CPI. Admitting that the CPI 'has to bear a very heavy responsibility' for the split at Rathmines, and had made 'a very serious error of principle' in endorsing O'Donnell's slogan, Murray pleaded for a return to the anti-imperialist formula agreed with the RWG in 1932, on the ground that republicans were indispensable allies:

> the [Republican] Congress movement has enabled us to have a very valuable ally in the struggle against the fascists and against the church, and for the development of a mass movement in Dublin, and its future lies in the development of Congress groups in the countryside and in the rural areas. . . a broad united front of the working class [i.e. industrial workers] has, in my opinion, no possibility, and would be just an ideal.[86]

In August the Irish delegates submitted 'Proposals for the application of the united front in Ireland', intended to end 'the confusion around the fundamental slogan' and take a 'definite' stand for 'complete unity and independence of the country and [a] Workers' and Farmers' Republic'. Unity was the theme. The Republican Congress was to be encouraged to seek readmission to the IRA, and united fronts were to be offered to the Labour Party, the IRA and farmers' associations.[87]

The new policy was implemented in September by the Labour League Against Fascism and War as it campaigned on the Italian aggression against Abyssinia.[88] The internal response to the popular front was uniformly enthusiastic. Comrades felt the more moderate line gave them a better chance of winning support.[89] Organisational unity had become popular on the far left as it recoiled – not necessarily in the one direction – from the shambolic legacy of Rathmines.

In June the Michael Price faction of the Citizen Army had voted to join the Labour Party or the Northern Ireland Labour Party (NILP). The Abyssinian crisis was seen as a major step towards a new European war into which the Free State would be dragged unless the people united in opposition. At the same time, there were severe limits to the application of the popular front strategy. With whom were the fronts to be formed? Even the bizarre stratagem of a front without communists made little headway. In the People's Anti-Imperialist Front, created with members of Fianna Fáil, Conradh na Gaeilge, the Labour Party and trade unions, the CPI let the Republican Congress act as its proxy. But *Republican Congress* hit terminal problems in December 1935, as its eponymous publishers continued to atrophy.[90]

Beyond the far left, the preconditions for a popular front did not exist. Not only was the political climate not moving left in fear of fascism, it was in some respects moving right, and made more paranoid by popular frontism. Apprehensions about what the twentieth anniversary of the Easter Rising might encourage, and Labour's 'workers' republic' constitution, provided timely copy for Lenten pastorals denouncing socialism and radical republicanism. Catholic actionists were on the march again. The Catholic Young Men's Society attempted to disrupt a meeting addressed by Pollitt in January. On Easter Sunday it harried the Republican Congress and CPI sections on a parade to Glasnevin. An IRA cycling corps pedalling along behind declined to intervene.

Next evening some 5,000 gathered at College Green to prevent a CPI rally, at which the CPGB's Willie Gallacher was to speak. After the platform lorry failed to show up, O'Donnell famously shinned up a lamp post in a foolhardy bid to harangue the throng. The crowd responded with stones, wrecked the premises of the Republican Congress and tried to do the same to the CPI offices.[91] The suppression of the IRA followed in June, after outrage at two assassinations gave de Valera his chance to act with impunity. *An Phoblacht* closed in July, the third revolutionary paper to fold in six months. Special branch infiltration of the CPI had resumed, and it too would soon be considered for proscription.

In any case the 'spirit of illegality' had again taken a grip. The party had been on the defensive since January and suspended public meetings after

Easter. Murray and Jim Larkin Jr withdrew from the Dublin municipal elections in June. Frank Ryan and George Gilmore stood for the Republican Congress with mixed results, Gilmore gleaning a respectable, if inadequate, tally.[92] The closure of Republican Congress's Co-op Press, which had printed the *Workers' Voice* since August 1935, completed another frustrating chapter in the history of the young CPI. The last issue of the *Voice* appeared on 13 June 1936. Pollitt regarded Murray's inertia in the face of a foreseeable disaster as characteristic. Since January he had told the Comintern repeatedly that the state of the party was due entirely to poor leadership and had discussed the issue openly with comrades in Dublin.[93]

Days before Sanjurjo's revolt in Spain, Max Raylock, who had represented the British Anti-War League at the Rathmines conference, sent a grave report to the ECCI in which he combined Pollitt's damning assessment of Murray with the iron optimism of a true Bolshevik:

> There is a crisis facing our Irish party. On the most important questions of the day, the struggle for peace, and the building of the anti-imperialist people's front, it has no line. . . Ireland is one of the most important strategical countries in Europe. There are tremendous possibilities for us – a rising anti-imperialist movement, a big strike movement, and a tremendous desire for unity in the Labour movement against British imperialism. It is clear that the situation in the Party is holding this back and cannot be altered by the Central Committee of the British Party alone, it requires the attention of the Communist International.[94]

As Murray faced a summons to Moscow and a bleak future, there was little to indicate that the CPI and the Republican Congress would soon find their most imperishable cause.

NOTES

1. There is a vast literature, exceeding 40,000 volumes, on the Spanish Civil War. Recent major studies include Antony Beevor, *The Battle for Spain: The Spanish Civil War 1936–1939* (London, 2007); and Paul Preston, *The Spanish Civil War: Reaction, Revolution and Revenge* (London, 2006).
2. E. H. Carr, *The Comintern and the Spanish Civil War* (London, 1984), p. 3.
3. Gerald Brenan, *The Spanish Labyrinth: The Social and Political Background of the Spanish Civil War* (Cambridge, 1960), p. 60; Lawrence Dundas, *Behind the Spanish Mask* (London, 1943), p. 32.
4. Brenan, *The Spanish Labyrinth*, p. viii.

5. Enrique Moradiellos, *Franco: Anatomy of a Dictator* (London, 2018), pp 112–19.
6. Carlos Barciela López, Xavier Tafunell and Albert Carreras, *Estadísticas Históricas de España Siglos XIX–XX, Vol. I* (Bilbao, 2005), p. 152.
7. Patrick Turnbull and Jeffrey Burn, *The Spanish Civil War, 1936–39* (Oxford, 1978), pp 3–4.
8. Len Deighton, *Blood, Tears and Folly: In the Darkest Hour of the Second World War* (London, 1993), pp 330–1; Richard Baxell, *Unlikely Warriors, The British in the Spanish Civil War and the Struggle Against Fascism* (London, 2012), pp 28, 45.
9. For details on the value of foreign aid to both sides in Spain see Hugh Thomas, *The Spanish Civil War* (Harmondsworth, 1965), appendix 3.
10. Paul Preston, *The Spanish Civil War, 1936–39* (London, 1986), p.63; 'Britain and the Basque campaign of 1937: the government, the Royal Navy, the Labour Party and the press', in *European History Quarterly*, 48:3 (2018), pp 490–515.
11. Preston, *The Spanish Civil War, 1936–39*, p. 84.
12. *Irish Workers' Voice*, 11 February 1933.
13. Sebastian Haffner, *Defying Hitler: A Memoir* (London, 2003), pp 75, 90, 98–9.
14. F. S. L. Lyons, *Ireland Since the Famine* (London, 1971), p. 533.
15. J. J. Lee, *Ireland 1912–1985: Politics and Society* (Cambridge, 1989).
16. Fearghal McGarry, *Irish Politics and the Spanish Civil War* (Cork, 1999), p. 234; Robert A. Stradling, *The Irish in the Spanish Civil War, 1936–1939: Crusades in Conflict* (Manchester, 1999). Aside from these two general academic studies, more specific monographs have been appearing steadily.
17. Brenan, *The Spanish Labyrinth*, pp 47–8.
18. See Maria Thomas, *Faith and Fury: Popular Anti-Clerical Violence and Iconoclasm in Spain, 1931–1936* (Brighton, 2013); Paul Preston, *The Spanish Holocaust: Inquisition and Extermination in Twentieth-Century Spain* (New York, 2013).
19. Barry McLoughlin, *Fighting for Republican Spain, 1936–38: Frank Ryan and the Volunteers from Limerick in the International Brigades* (Lulu Books, 2014), p. 20.
20. Carr, *The Comintern and the Spanish Civil War*, pp 5–7.
21. Anthony Rhodes, *The Vatican in the Age of Dictators, 1922–45* (London, 1973), pp 131–40.
22. Jonathon Hamill, 'Saor Éire and the IRA: an exercise in deception?', in *Saothar*, 20 (1995), p. 63.
23. National Archives, Dublin (NA), Dept of the Taoiseach, DT/S 5864B.
24. Russian State Archive for Social and Political History, Moscow (RGASPI), 'The situation in Ireland: material for Anglo-American Secretariat meeting, 6 November 1931', f. 495, o. 89, d. 64, l. 22.
25. Cardinal Tomás Ó Fiaich Memorial Library and Archive, Armagh (COFLA), Cardinal MacRory Papers, Box 2, Folder 2, Report re The Spread of Communism in Ireland [Late] 1931.
26. COFLA, Cardinal MacRory Papers, Box 2, Folder 1, Joint Pastoral of the Archbishops and Bishops of Ireland, 18 October 1931.
27. Ibid.
28. Emmet O'Connor, *A Labour History of Waterford* (Waterford, 1989), p. 241.

29. See Don O'Leary, *Vocationalism and Social Catholicism in Twentieth-Century Ireland: The Search for a Christian Social Order* (Dublin, 2000).
30. Mike Cronin, 'The Blueshirt movement, 1932–5: Ireland's fascists?', in *Journal of Contemporary History*, 30 (1995), pp 311–32.
31. Lee, *Ireland, 1912–1985*, p. 181. See also Maurice Manning, *The Blueshirts* (Dublin, 2006); Mike Cronin, *The Blueshirts and Irish Politics* (Dublin, 1997).
32. R. M. Douglas, *Architects of the Resurrection: Ailtirí na hAiséirghe and the Fascist 'New Order' in Ireland* (Manchester, 2009), p. 9.
33. Fearghal McGarry, *Eoin O'Duffy: A Self-Made Hero* (Oxford, 2005), p. 209.
34. See Mark O'Brien, '"In war-torn Spain": the politics of Irish press coverage of the Spanish Civil War', in *Media, War, and Conflict*, 10:1 (2017), pp 1–14.
35. *Irish Times*, 5 August 1936.
36. Lionel Fleming, *Head or Harp* (London, 1965), p. 169.
37. John Cooney, *John Charles McQuaid: Ruler of Catholic Ireland* (Dublin, 1999), pp 90–2.
38. O'Brien, '"In war-torn Spain"', pp 9–12.
39. Fearghal McGarry, 'Irish newspapers and the Spanish Civil War', in *Irish Historical Studies*, 22:129 (May 2002), p. 69.
40. Richard Griffiths, *Fellow Travellers of the Right: British Enthusiasm for Nazi Germany* (Oxford, 1983), pp 261–4.
41. Deacon David, *British News Media and the Spanish Civil War: Tomorrow May Be Too Late* (Edinburgh, 2008); L. B. Shelmerdine, 'Britons in an "unBritish" war: domestic newspapers and the participation of UK nationals in the Spanish Civil War', in *North West Labour History*, 22 (n.d.), pp 20–47.
42. Stephen Brown, S.J., *The Press in Ireland: A Survey and A Guide* (Dublin, 1937), pp 242–56. The *Standard* was currently in trouble. See *Nationalist and Leinster Times*, 10 December 1938; *Irish Times*, 8 August 1977.
43. Ben Edwards, *With God on Our Side: British Christian Responses to the Spanish Civil War* (Newcastle upon Tyne, 2013), p. 227.
44. Andrée Sheehy Skeffington, *Skeff: A Life of Owen Sheehy Skeffington, 1909–1970* (Dublin, 1991), pp 80–3; Frank Shovlin, *The Irish Literary Periodical, 1923–1958* (Oxford, 2003), pp 69–94.
45. Niamh Puirséil, *The Irish Labour Party, 1922–73* (Dublin, 2007), p. 58.
46. *Irish News*, 1 August 1936, among others, printed it to illustrate 'the ferocious anti-clericalism which rules the mobs of fanatics armed by the Government'.
47. McGarry, *Irish Politics and the Spanish Civil War*, p. 161; *Standard*, 19 March 1937.
48. *Belfast News-Letter*, 14 January 1937.
49. Cian McMahon, 'Eoin O'Duffy's Blueshirts and the Abyssinian crisis', in *History Ireland*, 2:10 (summer 2002), pp 36–9.
50. McGarry, *Irish Politics and the Spanish Civil War*, p. 25.
51. RGASPI, Proposals in connection with the Communist Party of Ireland, 8 May 1937, f. 495, o. 89, d. 102, ll. 1-9.
52. Emmet O'Connor, *A Labour History of Ireland, 1824–2000* (Dublin, 2011), pp 142–6; Puirséil, *The Irish Labour Party*, p. 55.

53. William Norton, Dáil Debates, 2 March 1934.
54. Cited in Michael Gallagher, *The Irish Labour Party in Transition, 1957–82* (Manchester, 1982), pp 12–14.
55. Niamh Puirséil, 'Catholic Stakhanovites? Religion and the Irish Labour Party, 1922–73', in Francis Devine, Fintan Lane and Niamh Puirséil (eds), *Essays in Irish Labour History: A Festschrift for Elizabeth and John W. Boyle* (Dublin, 2008), pp 183–6.
56. *Limerick Leader*, 21 November 1936; Gallagher, *The Irish Labour Party in Transition, 1957–82*, pp 12–14; Vincent Geoghegan, 'Cemeteries of liberty: William Norton on communism and fascism', in *Saothar*, 18 (1993), pp 106–9.
57. Geoghegan, 'Cemeteries of liberty', pp 106–9.
58. Francis Devine, *Organising History: A Centenary of SIPTU, 1909–2009* (Dublin, 2009), p. 257.
59. *Munster Express*, 16 October 1936.
60. O'Connor, *James Larkin*, p. 100.
61. Emmet O'Connor, *Big Jim Larkin: Hero or Wrecker?* (Dublin, 2015), p. 296; O'Connor, *A Labour History of Ireland*, pp 148–50; McGarry, *Irish Politics and the Spanish Civil War*, pp 156–7, 182–90; *Derry Journal*, 11, 21 September 1936.
62. John P. Swift, *John Swift: An Irish Dissident* (Dublin, 1991), pp 101–3.
63. National Archives of the United Kingdom, London (TNA), KV2/1185, Sean Murray (PF 399.199).
64. Communist Party of Ireland, *Outline History* (n.d. [1975]), pp 21, 29.
65. RGASPI, CPI, resolution, central committee meeting, 10–11 March 1934, f. 495, o. 89, d. 99, ll. 5-12.
66. RGASPI, Draft resolution on Ireland for meeting of Anglo-American secretariat, 20 April 1930, f. 495, o. 89, d. 61, ll 2-9.
67. RGASPI, letter from Helena Molony, August 1930, f. 534, o. 7, d. 286, ll. 98-99.
68. RGASPI, Letter to Ireland, 23 September 1932, f. 495, o. 20, d. 251, ll. 89-98.
69. RGASPI, *Workers' Bulletin*, 23 April 1933, f. 495, o. 89, d. 91, l. 41.
70. RGASPI, Report from Dublin, undated [April 1933?], f. 495, o. 89, d. 91, ll. 59-61.
71. RGASPI, Letter to the CPGB on the Irish question, adopted by the Pol-Commission, 9 August 1932, f. 495, o. 4, d. 205, l. 6; *Daily Worker*, 29, 30 March, 1, 3–4 April 1933.
72. TNA, KV2/1185, Sean Murray (PF 399.199).
73. Emmet O'Connor, *Reds and the Green: Ireland, Russia, and the Communist Internationals, 1919–43* (Dublin, 2004), pp 187–8.
74. RGASPI, Report on the CPI, June 1933, f. 495, o. 89, d. 88, l. 18.
75. Adrian Grant, *Irish Socialist Republicanism, 1909–36* (Dublin, 2012), p. 187.
76. *An Phoblacht*, 1–8 April 1933.
77. James Hogan, *Could Ireland Become Communist? The Facts of the Case* (Dublin, 1935), vi–ix.
78. *Irish Times*, 28 June 2003.
79. RGASPI, To the secretariat, CPI, 19 September 1934, f. 495, o. 14, d. 334, ll. 24-27; memo to the CPI, 16 September 1934, f. 495, o. 89, d. 96, ll 46-47; TNA, Government Code and Cypher School decrypts of Comintern messages, 1930–45, HW 17/17.
80. Michael McInerney, *Peadar O'Donnell, Irish Social Rebel* (Dublin, 1974), pp 97, 99.

81. *Republican Congress*, 6 October 1934; University College, Dublin Archives (UCDA), Seán MacEntee papers, Notes on the Republican Congress movement, P67/527, p. 12.
82. *Belfast News-Letter*, 7 January 1935.
83. Richard English, 'Socialism and republican schism in Ireland: the emergence of the Republican Congress in 1934', in *Irish Historical Studies*, xxvii, 195 (May, 1990), pp 48–65, was influential in arguing for the incompatibility of socialism and republicanism.
84. Nora Connolly O'Brien, *We Shall Rise Again* (London, 1981), p. 72.
85. RGASPI, 'The Communist Party of Ireland and the Irish Republican Congress', f. 495, o. 18, d. 1059.
86. RGASPI, Seán Murray before the Anglo-American secretariat, 19 July 1935, f. 495, o. 14, d. 20, ll. 1-27.
87. RGASPI, Proposals for the application of the united front in Ireland (by Irish delegation), 26 August 1935, f. 495, o. 14, d. 335, ll. 84-86.
88. RGASPI, [CPI] against war and fascism since the 7th congress, 2 June 1936, f. 495, o. 14, d. 341, ll. 56-71.
89. UCDA, Seán MacEntee papers, Notes on communism in Saorstát Éireann, P67/523(5), pp 39–42; RGASPI, Report of the conference of the CPI, 5–6 October 1935, f. 495, o. 14, d. 337, ll. 9-27.
90. RGASPI, The national question and the policy of the CPI since the 7th congress CI, 26 May 1936, f. 495, o. 14, d. 337, ll. 168-171.
91. RGASPI, [CPI] against war and fascism since the 7th congress, 2 June 1936, f. 495, o. 14, d. 341, ll. 56-71; UCDA, Seán MacEntee papers, Special Branch report, 13 April 1936, P67/526(10); *Irish Press*, 14 April 1936.
92. RGASPI, [CPI] against war and fascism since the 7th congress, 2 June 1936, f. 495, o. 14, d. 341, ll. 56-71; UCDA, MacEntee papers, Notes on communism in Saorstát Éireann, P67/523(5), pp 3–5, 20; Seán Cronin, *Frank Ryan: The Search for the Republic* (Dublin, 1980), p. 68.
93. TNA, Government Code and Cypher School decrypts of Comintern messages, 1930–45, HW 17/22, London to Moscow, 26 June 1936; RGASPI, Report on situation in Ireland, July 1936, f. 495, o.14, d. 337, ll. 1-8; UCDA, Seán MacEntee papers, *Trade Union Information Bulletin*, no.1, November 1936, P67/526(1).
94. RGASPI, M. Raylock, Concerning the CPI, 29 July 1936, f. 495, o. 14, d. 341, ll. 98-101; J. Shields, 'Struggle in Ireland entering a new stage', in *Inprecorr*, 54, 12 October 1934.

TWO

# THE WAR AT HOME

Why did people and parties in Ireland support the Republic in the Civil War? What was their understanding of events in Spain? How did they make their case and deal with the arguments of their more numerous and powerful opponents? How did they relate to each other? And what informed the politics of the Connolly Column, the name that has become a blanket term for all Irish who fought in defence of the Spanish Republic? The term is misleading in suggesting that the Irish fought in one unit, inspired by the writings of James Connolly. It was coined in the 1970s by Peter O'Connor when Michael O'Riordan was seeking a title for his *Connolly Column: The Story of the Irishmen Who Fought in the Ranks of the International Brigades in the National Revolutionary War of the Spanish People, 1936–1939*, and a mercy perhaps that the subtitle was prefixed.

As used here, the term is broadened to include all Irish men and women who reported in Spain for medical or military service for the Republic. By Irish is meant Irish-born, with the exception of three volunteers, born in London and Glasgow but raised in Ireland. Variations on 'Connolly Column' were used during the war. On joining the Lincoln battalion, the Irish called themselves the James Connolly Centuria or James Connolly Unit. Máirín Mitchell in her *Storm Over Spain* referred to 'the Connolly Brigade, led by Frank Ryan', and Seán O'Casey to 'Frank Ryan, who leads the Communist Irish in Spain'. The *Worker*, the *Irish Democrat* and *The Book of the XV Brigade* wrote of 'the international column', 'the Irish column', 'the Irish unit', or 'Irish sections' in the British and Lincoln battalions.[1]

There was a core political unity that justifies 'Connolly Column' and it existed in Dublin as well as in Spain, though in more diverse formats. For pro-Republic elements, the politics on the home front has been read backwards from the politics, or the perceived politics, of the Connolly Column. Those who supported the Republic are seen in the light of the heroes in 'the good fight', and treated blandly as defenders of democracy and victims of reaction. While that was true, they also had their own agenda, and their interests and values were reflected in their two newspapers, the CPI's the *Worker* and its successor the *Irish Democrat*, a joint enterprise of the CPI, the Republican Congress and the Socialist Party (Northern Ireland) (SPNI). The cross-border *Democrat* reflected the unique way in which Spain could draw different factions together. The opposite too was true, and the *Democrat* would fall victim to Irish echoes of the infighting on the left in Spain. Inevitably, the Connolly Column reflected Irish political divisions, and the relative strengths of republicanism and communism at home, so that by international standards, the Irish contribution to the International Brigades was unusual in its ideological complexion, something that would lead to problems in Spain and an infamous incident in 1937.

The communists were first out of the traps, with blanket solidarity for the Spanish Republic. The Republican Congress hesitated, and then tried to fillet the cause by selecting the Basques as allies, before finally committing to a united front with the CPI. As public opinion divided over Spain, a popular front atmosphere, of sorts, emerged. Although the popular front was primarily a Comintern directive to the communists to build alliances with other groups against fascism, Spain broadened the concept as it drew artists and progressives towards various aid-to-Spain projects and generated some imaginative initiatives. Other countries had previous experience of similar developments and the late 1930s saw an appreciable inflow of intellectuals into the communist parties.

Ireland had a tenuous history of middle-class engagement with the left, confined to exceptional people or exceptional events like the 1913 lockout, when the force and flair of Big Jim Larkin compelled an awakening of intellectual curiosity. Otherwise, the Labour movement seemed too mundane and timid to excite the passions, and, for its part, Labour held middle-class people in some suspicion. It was no accident that O'Casey chose to improve his credentials as the hard-bitten lad from the slums by personifying the prejudice. The fringe left was more exciting but too fringe, ephemeral and authoritarian when under ECCI control. Spain on the other hand was a central concern and a great liberal cause of global significance, and the response in Ireland was unprecedented in its social and intellectual range. The upsurge of Catholic social power, the misrepresentation of events in Spain, and the intolerance of debate or comment on exaggerations of anti-clerical atrocities and the legitimacy of the generals' revolt in particular was seen to require a response. For the Free State's small liberal bourgeoise, it was a call to arms. Even if its reach remained much more restricted than its range, and scarcely bore comparison with other countries, Spain spawned a tradition that survived, guttering through the Cold War, until it flourished in the 1960s.

### THE WORKER, THE CPI AND THE REPUBLICAN CONGRESS

On 11 July 1936 Seán Murray replaced the *Workers' Voice* with the *Worker*, a cyclostyled four-page weekly, edited and largely written by himself. Published from 32 Lower Ormond Quay, Dublin, it sold for one penny.[2] Plans to have it printed were frustrated when the printer reneged on the contract and another could not be found at less than exorbitant prices.[3] In line with the resolutions of the seventh world congress of the ECCI, the CPI was still persevering with the People's Anti-Imperialist Front, seeking to unite 'all Labour forces (Party, Trade Unions, etc.) with all national-Republican forces (IRA, Fianna Fáil, etc.)' against Fine Gael and the Northern premier, Craigavon.[4]

The obvious anomaly here is that in the Free State it was seeking to ally with the government against the opposition. Spain removed that incongruity by creating a cause great enough to justify it. And for the next 12 months Spain became the alpha and omega of the CPI. Quite simply, it reaffirmed the Comintern line. The line was not known publicly until announced in the ECCI's gazette, *International Press Correspondence*, or *Inprecorr*, in August. But after the victory of the Frente Popular in the elections to the Cortes in February, the Comintern commended the PCE to forestall reaction by maximising unity against fascism and prioritising democracy before social revolution, a strategy that would be opposed by the anarchists and the Partido Obrero de Unificación Marxista (POUM). On 22 May the ECCI endorsed PCE efforts to back the Spanish government and reach out to anarchist-syndicalist and Catholic workers.[5]

Evidently the CPI and CPGB were not reliant on *Inprecorr* for directions. From 25 July the *Worker* would concentrate on the war as it was fought at home and abroad, and become the only anti-Franco paper in Ireland. On 26 July Harry Pollitt told a rally in Trafalgar Square to 'render every assistance to the Spanish people's front government'.[6] While the *Worker* made occasional references to the class basis of the Spanish antagonists, it followed the PCE and other communist parties in depicting the war as one of democracy against fascism, the defence of bourgeois liberalism being seen as a logical extension of the popular front.

As Spain became the measure of all things, the paper judged people by their stand on the war, and even by the terminology they used to describe the forces in conflict. Within the context of the Comintern position, the line was tweaked to address the peculiarities of the Irish situation. Thus, the People's Anti-Imperialist Front charm offensive was modified to excoriate the 'cowardly' Labour Party and trade union leaders for their silence and, in some cases, open collusion with Francoists.[7] Conversely, any anti-Franco comment, whatever its provenance, was sure of a welcome. While communists everywhere lionised Catholic critics of Franco, Ireland required considerable emphasis on rebutting the Catholic view of the war as a crusade for religion. The *Worker* featured articles entitled 'They would have condemned St Ambrose', 'Archbishop doubts atrocity stories' and 'Spanish priest attacks rebels.'[8] Peadar O'Donnell took a related line in *Ireland To-Day* in September 1936, noting that he and the communists were defending bourgeois democracy and 'Catholic Spain against the Moors and Legionnaires'.

Franco's use of Muslim troops to save Christianity was too obvious a contradiction to ignore. The *Worker* referred to 'heathen Moors', headlining the Badajoz massacre with 'Franco's Moors Massacre Christian Workers.'[9] Socialists frequently labelled the Moors as 'black', 'colonial' or 'Mahommedan'. 'You are asked in this country,' said Frank Ryan, 'to believe that the whole people are anti-religious and that the adventurers, the Mohommedan Moors, and the godless scum of the Foreign Legion are crusaders for Christianity.'[10] He also told of how women in captured towns were handed over to the Moors for rape.[11]

Ireland's oldest student magazine, *TCD Miscellany*, remarked on how the 'pinks' were horrified 'if one called the Abyssinians 'blacks' and had much to say about Ethiopian civilisations, etc., but they did not hesitate to call the Moors 'blacks' when they were fighting on the Anti-Red side in Spain'.[12] The left also ridiculed the paradox of self-styled 'Nationalists' importing auxiliaries from Italy, Germany and Portugal to fight the people of Spain. Again and again, the *Worker* used Irish history to explain events. The land question in Spain was compared to the Land War and parallels were drawn with the misuse of religion by Franco and by Edward Carson in his claim that Home Rule would mean 'Rome Rule'.

Republicans placed an even greater emphasis on Irish history and politics as they gradually attuned to the popular obsession with Spain. They had the additional provocation of Eoin O'Duffy. The Carlist Count de Ramírez de Arellano had written to Joseph Cardinal MacRory in August 1936, requesting Irish aid for Spain. Soldiers from a country so identified with Catholicism could be of significant symbolic value to the Nationalists' claim to be fighting for the defence of the Church. The cardinal referred him to O'Duffy, who offered to enlist an 'Irish brigade' with the help of his latest political group, the

National Corporate Party and its paramilitary wing, the Greenshirts. As a hate-figure for republicans, O'Duffy was a convenient excuse and motivation.

At a Republican Congress street meeting in Dublin on 17 August the only mention of Spain came from hecklers who suggested O'Donnell return there. One week later, George Gilmore and Frank Ryan, as Congress secretaries, congratulated the NILP on its decision to send a medical unit to Spain and urged southern workers to make common cause with the North. On 15 September, the Dublin Republican Congress agreed unanimously to cable a message of solidarity with the 'Spanish, Catalan and Basque people in their fight against Fascism' to Spanish Premier Francisco Largo Caballero. Much of the telegram was taken up with denunciation of the Christian Front, O'Duffy and the *Irish Independent* and their 'shameless' use of religion to 'obstruct national advance and hinder the movement of the working class'.[13]

More than any other, Ryan embodied the mind of the Connolly Column. Born in Limerick in 1902, the son of relatively well-off national school teachers, Ryan joined the East Limerick Brigade of the IRA during the Truce of July 1921 and graduated in Celtic Studies in UCD in 1925. Over the next 12 years he lived in Dublin, working as an Irish language teacher and a journalist, editing *Irish Travel* for the Tourist Board and *An tÓglach* for the IRA, and serving as adjutant of the Dublin Brigade of the IRA. He acquired a formidable reputation as an orator, organiser and fearless street fighter, whether confronting the Blueshirts or the Guards. In 1930 he spent a few weeks in the US, speaking to Clan na Gael branches.

Up to the 1980s Ryan was an iconic figure in the rockpool of socialist republicanism. Since then, he has become better known as the leader of the Connolly Column. His early life in the republican movement is presented as a backdrop to his more illustrious career in Spain. Many see it as being in contradiction to his role as a brigadista and juxtapose the two. The first biography of Ryan, by Seán Cronin in 1980, was published by Sinn Féin/The Workers' Party and sub-titled *The Search for the Republic*. It was followed in 2004 by Adrian Hoar's *In Green and Red*, the title emphasising the distinction between socialism and republicanism.

A similar approach was taken in McGarry's 2010 biography and Bell's 2012 documentary *The Enigma of Frank Ryan*. Bell emphasised the Ryan who went to Nazi Germany after Spain and has Ryan tell his story in a series of flashbacks from his flat in wartime Berlin. Publicity for the film included a lot of swastikas. It's a favourite criticism of anti-republicans. Republicanism's claim to be internationalist and socialist was a fraud, and Ryan exposed that in his decision to go with the Nazis. A popular twist on the theme is found in the novel and film *The Eagle Has Landed*, which features broth of a boy 'Liam

Devlin', an IRA veteran captured by Spanish Falangists, who agrees to join a Nazi plot to kidnap Winston Churchill. The swastika will always stick to Ryan for the same reason that Adolf Hitler is rarely off our television screens and the Wehrmacht marches through our living rooms every evening. But Spain was a logical conclusion to the evolution of left republicanism, and the Connolly Column saw it as an extension of battles in Ireland rather than a new departure.

Ryan and O'Donnell had led the development of socialist republicanism since the mid-1920s. If O'Donnell saw himself as Murray's disciple, Ryan was O'Donnell's protégé.[14] Modestly, O'Donnell attributed the biggest influence on Ryan's transition to socialism to the League Against Imperialism, a Comintern front, founded at a meeting of the Congress of Oppressed Nationalities in Brussels in 1927. Ryan was present as an IRA delegate. That same year the IRA pledged support for Russia in the event of an Anglo-Soviet war. Ryan was shocked by the poverty he witnessed in America after the Wall Street crash, and believed Russia to be a land of full employment and rapid industrialisation. Like many republicans he admired the Bolsheviks as the experts in revolution. A movement had credibility if it had succeeded in one sixth of the globe and was completing the job in the other five sixths. What he didn't like was the command structure or the blanket acceptance of Leninism that went with communism. He and O'Donnell were convinced that only an Irish rebel spirit could mobilise the people, as Michael Davitt or Charles Stewart Parnell had done, or as Sinn Féin had done in 1918. What they wanted was mass, radical Fenian unity, not communism but the discipline and vision of communism tempering the character and focus of republicanism.

Ryan's famous open letter to Cardinal MacRory captured the key themes of pro-Republic propaganda in Ireland. Distinguishing between religion and politics, and assuring MacRory that he took his religion 'from Rome', Ryan compared episcopal denunciation of Republicans in Spain and of Irish republicans during the Civil War, highlighted the anomaly of Franco's use of Moorish troops and questioned the veracity, extent and origin of atrocities, noting parallels with stories of German atrocities in Belgium in 1914. The exposure of exaggeration in tales of German outrages cast doubt on all similar propaganda in the post-war years. Ryan and Gilmore expanded on Ryan's points in a lengthy press release and followed up with a foolhardy meeting in College Green that only served to provide another outlet for the venom of pro-Franco elements. The Congress would learn to follow the CPI into semi-secrecy. And then there were the Basques. Ryan's letter cited them in support and referred to the telegram of sympathy with the Spanish, Catalan and Basques 'peoples', taking care to use the plural.[15]

'We utilised the Basque issue fairly fully and with considerable effect,' Murray assured the ECCI.[16] The Spanish government granted autonomy to the Basques on 1 October and an autonomous government was established in Bilbao. Whether Basque separatism triggered thoughts of freedom or partition and bore comparison with the Ireland in the United Kingdom or Ulster Unionism in Ireland was a point of debate in the letters pages of the press. Some Unionist newspapers drew parallels between Ulster Protestants and the Basques.[17] But on the question of religion, the Catholic Basque people fighting Franco with the blessing of their clergy were undoubtedly an asset for the Republican cause in Ireland. Initially the Republican Congress hoped the Basques might be their Schwerpunkt and despatched Gilmore to find Father Ramón Laborda. Laborda had attended the Eucharistic Congress in Dublin in 1932 and presented a Basque flag to Eithne Coyle, president of Cumann na mBan.

Cumann na mBan had inspired the foundation of Emakume Abertzale Batza, the Basque nationalist women's organisation in 1922 and Coyle later received an inscribed book from Basque women.[18] Language was another link. Like many activists in Conradh na Gaeilge Coyle admired the Basques as a people who valued their language and culture and Laborda enjoyed some renown in Ireland for his broadcasts of Basque songs. After a narrow escape when his flight from Paris got lost in fog and ditched on a beach, Gilmore arrived in Bilbao as a guest of the Lehendakari, José Antonio Aguirre.[19] On 5 November 1936 Ernie O'Malley chaired a meeting in the Engineers' Hall in Dawson Street, convened by Owen Sheehy Skeffington and Gilmore. Mindful of the College Green debacle, entry was by invitation only. Its stated aim was to counter the anti-Spanish Government ramp of the *Independent* and the Christian Front. O'Malley dwelt on the parallels between Ireland and Catalonia, which he had visited in 1925 to offer his services as a distinguished guerrilla cadre to the Catalan underground. But attention soon shifted to the Basques.

Ambrose Martin, an Irish-Argentinian whom O'Malley mistook for a Basque, said he represented the Basque government and read a telegram from Aguirre: 'Basque Nationalist Party in struggle in these bloody moments for God and liberty, fatherland and democracy, thank your intentions and work to make known the truth in Ireland. Euzkadi remembers once more with emotion the Irish patriots.'[20] Martin was managing director of the Irish Iberian Trading Company, founded in 1933 to create alternative commercial outlets for Ireland during the Economic War. Leopold Kerney, now Irish minister to the Spanish Republic, had been involved in its establishment, and Fianna Fáil TD Seán Hayes was a director. Despite the war, it continued to export cattle, pork, potatoes and eggs to Bilbao, Gibraltar and ports in the south of Spain. The meeting agreed to form committees for propaganda and medical aid for Spain, and saluted MP Harry Midgley for his work in Belfast.

Laborda arrived in Dublin in January, hosted by Martin and billeted with May and Seán Keating in Rathfarnham.[21] May worked as secretary to Hanna Sheehy Skeffington. On 17 January, billed as a 'Patriot Basque Priest' Laborda spoke to a packed Gaiety Theatre in Dublin and argued that the war was political rather than religious. Opening with the sign of the cross, he said he came 'to defend the attitude of the Catholic Basque patriots' and affirm that 'we have resisted Communism both on the platform and in the press, not with violence but with argument through public meetings and writing.'[22] Providing another stick to beat the Francoites, he said some of the insurgent generals were Freemasons.

Martin read Laborda's paper – his English being limited – from a translation by May Keating, who had been educated at a convent school in Seville. Laborda would later tell the *Irish Press*, 'Basque Nationalists readily admit their opposition to the unity of Spain, which is to us as the unity of the British Empire is to Irish Republicans', and opened an exhibition on Basque life in Egan's Art Galleries in Dublin.[23]

His presence was a serious embarrassment to the Catholic authorities. He was forbidden to say mass in public by the Dublin archdiocese, and the Jesuit fathers Stephen J. Brown and P. J. Gannon directed a ramp against him.[24] Brown had just completed *The Press in Ireland*, which revealed an obsession with communism and stated that 'Alone [the *Irish Independent*] gave the Irish public the full facts about the persecution of the Church and the atrocities committed against priests and nuns' in Spain. With the paternalism and sense of entitlement so typical of the Irish clergy at the time, it was subtitled *A Survey and a Guide*.[25]

After Laborda visited Ireland a second time, in February, the Government came to regard him as an alien partisan, in breach of the spirit of non-intervention. Ryan claimed he was 'virtually deported'. The meeting in the Gaiety was chaired by another priest, the veteran Sinn Féiner Michael O'Flanagan, whose ancient quarrels with Irish bishops may have sharpened his scepticism of the Spanish hierarchy. Anglophobia was a factor too. He had endorsed the Italian invasion of Abyssinia as an embarrassment for British foreign policy.[26] O'Flanagan was the only prominent Catholic cleric in Ireland to champion the Spanish Republic and, warmly embraced by the left, his stance on Abyssinia quietly forgotten. O'Flanagan also deputised for Ryan on speaking tours of America. The collar allowed him to go further than any CPI comrade would have dared at the time. In Madison Square Garden he praised the practical Christianity of the Soviet Russians and 'their great big-hearted Stalin who reminds me of our own James Connolly'. Equally, his clerical status infuriated Irish-American and Catholic groups.[27]

Ireland's Francoists were no less incensed by the 'Basque issue'. Patrick Belton accused the Irish Iberian Trading Company of 'feeding the Red soldiers of anti-Christ'. Ludicrously, he denounced Martin as 'one of the most pronounced and prominent Communists in this country'.[28] The January 1937 issue of the *National Student*, edited by Thomas Hughes and published by the Student Representative Council of University College, Dublin (UCD), ran into fierce opposition for featuring an article by Father Laborda. Commissioning the article was a brave and unusual move. University students at the time were socially select and self-important. Trinity student publications were freer in comment on Spain, but given to detachment and whimsy. The February issue of the *National Student* generated more trouble by reprinting 'An Appeal from Spanish Catholics to Catholics of the Entire World' by José Maria de Semprún. Semprún's *A Catholic Looks at Spain* was subsequently published by the Spanish embassy in London. Being a distinguished writer and diplomat, his 'Appeal' against the fascist bombardment of Madrid drew the attention of the mainstream press. The next meeting of UCD's Literary and Historical Society condemned the *National Student* by a 'substantial majority'.[29] In March, Father Francis Shaw, Professor of Irish at UCD, attacked Laborda's representation of the Basque people and clergy. The Student Representative Council then dissociated itself from the *National Student* and called for Hughes's resignation.[30] Shaw returned to Hughes and his 'anti-"fascist" and rationalist' propaganda in 1938, clearly regarding him as an unfortunate aberration. 'Why', he wondered, in weasel words, 'the article by Father Laborda should ever have appeared in the *National Student* it is not easy to see'.[31]

Another embarrassment was the bombing of Guernica on 26 April 1937 when the German Condor Legion killed some 250 civilians in a quiet market town of no military importance. At a time of mounting apprehension over the use of aerial bombing to cause mass terror in the next war, the first carpet bombing in history made a shocking impression. The *Irish Independent* initially reported the destruction of the town by 'fleets of Patriot planes' and later printed denials of responsibility by Franco and the Luftwaffe. Confusion persisted. The Catholic press shifted uncomfortably between silence, excuses, or articles blaming 'the Reds' for the bombing in a cynical propaganda stunt.[32] Irish Friends of the Spanish Republic addressed the Guernica atrocity at an eve of May Day rally in Hatch Street Hall, presided over by Hanna Sheehy Skeffington. Hanna was much in demand as a spokeswoman for worthy causes and had worked with Ryan on *An Phoblacht* up to 1932.[33] Speakers included three members of the Connolly Column: Ryan, Willoughby 'Bill' Scott and Domhnall O'Reilly, and a motion of solidarity was passed with the Basque, Catalan and Spanish 'peoples' in their fight for 'democracy and Republicanism'.[34]

Before Guernica the Basque government had discussed an exodus of Biblical proportions with a plan to evacuate 30,000 children in the event of

Euskadi being overrun. The bombing compelled the British government to admit some children on condition their maintenance and welfare would be the responsibility of the Basque Children's Committee. The Catholic Church in England assisted reluctantly, resenting the implicit aspersions on Franco and fearing the children might be tainted with communism.[35] The Committee's appeals for aid included letters to Irish newspapers.[36]

On 23 May 3,840 children, 80 teachers, 120 helpers, 15 priests and two doctors arrived at Southampton on the severely overcrowded SS *Habana*. Other children went to France, Czechoslovakia, Switzerland, the Netherlands, Denmark and Russia. In Ireland the pro-Franco press and Catholic periodicals variously evaluated the evacuation as a public relations trick or worried about the implications for proselytism in Protestant or socialist homes with studied detachment.

Gertrude Gaffney, formerly the special correspondent of the *Irish Independent* in Spain, thought it 'passing strange that in this country so full of Convents and other Catholic institutions not a single Basque child of the thousands brought to England has been offered hospitality'.[37] After Hanna Sheehy Skeffington and the Women's Aid Section of Irish Friends of the Spanish Republic opened a fund for victims of Guernica, Mitchell suggested that Irish families adopt some of the children.[38] Memories of Dora Montefiore's ill-fated 'Save the kiddies' scheme in 1913 would not have been an encouragement. A rare exception was a family who moved to live with Martin and his people in the newly founded Gaeltacht at Gibbstown.[39]

## THE IRISH DEMOCRAT

The final issue of the *Worker* appeared on 13 March 1937. Murray's promise that it would continue as a monthly, to maintain a distinct communist voice, was not realised. At this stage, the CPI consisted of two branches, with 75 members in Dublin and 40 in Belfast. Quality was as much a problem as quantity. In Dublin, Murray *was* the secretariat. A Women's Aid Committee had been created to support the International Brigaders and had raised over £50 and sent two consignments of comforts to Spain. Younger comrades had put up 1,300 posters and distributed 800 leaflets. But there were no reports of a CPI public meeting and it was admitted that the sale of literature and propaganda work was 'far from satisfactory'. The failure of its latest campaign to penetrate the trade unions, together with difficulties in organising the unemployed, was minuted.[40] Compared with Belfast, where the CPI was gaining ground in the unions and the SPNI was beavering away, the record was sluggish. The CPI's most precious contribution was the Connolly Column, but, as we shall see, it could not claim to be overburdened in this respect.

Fortunately for the CPI, a new departure was at hand. Its origins went back to the formation of the Left Book Club in May 1936 by John Strachey, Stafford Cripps, and Victor Gollancz. Broadly pro-communist, the Club aimed to educate British workers about the danger of fascism especially. Each month Gollancz, Strachey and Harold Laski would select a bright orange paperback marked 'Not for sale to the public', which members could buy for the bargain price of 2s6d. Over 45,000 joined in the first year, far exceeding expectations, and the Club had 730 local discussion groups.

In December 1936 members of the Left Book Club in Belfast established the Progressive Publications Society to foster anti-fascist unity. The Society in turn launched the weekly *Irish Democrat* on 27 March 1937 at a meeting chaired by Owen Sheehy Skeffington. The main backers behind the *Democrat* were the Republican Congress, the CPI and the SPNI. The project also won support from some old antagonists within the Republican Congress like Michael Price and Nora and Roddy Connolly.[41]

The SPNI was more or less the Protestant republican wing of the NILP, unusual in blending the routine Anglo-centrism of Belfast with the aspiration to Irish unity, and in combining support for Spain with suspicion of communists and the International Brigades. Formerly the Belfast branch of the (British) Independent Labour Party (ILP), it performed the same role in the NILP as the ILP within the British Labour Party.

When the ILP disaffiliated from the British Labour Party in June 1932, the Belfast branch went independent in order to continue as a ginger group within the NILP rather than follow the ILP's leftward drift to isolation. Cash-rich, thanks to compensation for the burning of the ILP hall in Belfast by loyalists in 1921, the SPNI contributed one third of the seed capital. Other financial contributions are unknown, apart from a grant of £280 secured on a visit to the CPGB's head office in 16 King Street, Covent Garden, by Murray and Frank Ryan.[42]

The eight-page *Democrat* was a big improvement on the *Worker*, better produced with a much wider range of writers and features. Opposition, too, improved and the *Democrat* regularly featured appeals to 'break the boycott' by newsagents. Formally, its aims were to promote working class unity, protect democratic liberties, demand intellectual freedom and 'equal rights for women with men' and oppose imperialist wars. In practice, it maintained the *Worker*'s weather-eye on Spain, its interpretation of the war and its tactics to offset pro-Franco propaganda. Murray implied it would be 'out and out Republican'.[43] Ryan served as editor and printed the paper on the machinery of the

Republican Congress's old Co-op Press, which was renamed the Ralahine Press after the socialist commune in County Clare in the 1830s. Taking a bullet on the Jarama front, Ryan was hospitalised in Alicante, travelled to London for treatment and paid several visits to O'Casey, one with Jack Carney. Despite Ryan's role in disrupting *The Plough and the Stars* at the Abbey in 1926, the peppery playwright thought him 'a splendid fellow' and begged him to stay out of the war. Ryan then returned to Ireland.[44]

Ryan and O'Donnell were still sanguine about building a united front of socialists and republicans in the spring of 1937. Rosamond Jacob, Ryan's Waterford-born lover and a selfless activist herself, offers a glimpse of the socialist republican mindset in her diary of the Hatch Street Hall meeting on Guernica. The entry never mentioned Guernica, and noted that Ryan's 'most interesting' speech 'dwelt mainly on the likenesses of events & parties here & in Spain'.[45] She went on to log a familiar litany for republicans: the bishops' denunciation of Saor Éire at the behest of the Cosgrave Government, the Church's support for O'Duffy, the alleged attempt of Ernest Blythe and Richard Mulcahy to incite an army mutiny after the 1932 elections, the role of the bankers and landlords and the success of working class unity in fighting fascism. It was a two-way process. Ryan was making sense of Spain through Irish history and citing Spain as an example for Ireland.

As the war progressed, the CPI took an increasingly republican line, even to the point of jeopardising the effort for Spain. The CPI's relations with the IRA improved when Tom Barry became chief of staff in June 1936. Barry favoured broadening the movement to draw in everyone from the CPI to Fianna Fáil. While he banned volunteers from going to Spain, he ended the IRA's proscription on CPI membership and the party found him 'very sympathetic and helpful'.[46]

During his convalescence back in Ireland Ryan resumed collaboration with the IRA for the first time since the split in 1934 and printed six issues of *An Phoblacht* as well as contributing a few anonymous articles. At Easter, foregoing the indignity of a sling and letting his wounded arm hang limp, he marched at the head of the IRA's commemoration to Glasnevin. The Republican Congress, Murray, and the CPI brought up the rear. In May, Ryan and Barry were batoned side by side at a banned protest against the coronation of George VI, who was constitutionally their king. Both received a rousing reception at a second meeting a few days later.[47]

Disputes on the editorial board of the *Irish Democrat* were usual, and not confined to Irish politics. The SPNI shared the ILP's suspicion of communists and preference for the POUM rather than the International Brigades, while the CPI swallowed the Comintern line on Trotskyists as troublemakers. In its only reference to events in Moscow – Spain making Russia impolitic – the *Worker* had applauded the trial of 'Trotsky terrorists' and denounced Leon Trotsky by name.[48] The POUM was tiny and could not accurately be described as Trotskyist, but was seen as such in Dublin and Moscow, and the CPGB believed the SPNI to have a nucleus of 30 Trotskyists. Certainly, Victor Halley, who, with Jack Macgougan, represented the SPNI on the *Irish Democrat* editorial board, disliked the communist parties, and as a Shankill Road republican he was not shy of controversy.[49]

The *Democrat* of 1 May covered the re-organisation of the Spanish Republican army sympathetically, reprinting the 'ten-point plan for victory' of the Catalan government. It followed several months of anti-government agitation by the POUM. Point seven demanded 'the concentration of all arms in the hands of the government'. The POUM, anarchists and anarcho-syndicalists resisted the plan, and fighting erupted in Barcelona on 3–7 May between their militias on one side and the Catalan government and communists on the other. On 8 May the *Democrat* featured an article entitled 'Trotskyites sabotage in Barcelona', denouncing the POUM as 'a Fascist force in the rear', and repeated the points on 22 May. Probably written by Ryan and echoing the Comintern view, they provoked objections from the SPNI.[50] The Moscow line persisted. In July the *Democrat* applauded the execution of Marshal Tukhachevsky and eight Red Army generals in 'the Case of Trotskyist anti-Soviet Military Organisation' as it was labelled. The *Democrat* decided they were guilty because generals had revolted in Spain, and Ireland knew all about treachery.

The *Irish Democrat* survived tensions over Spain. It did not survive the Irish question. On 28 March, one day after the launch, the various parties met in O'Donnell's house. Tommy Watters of the CPI's Belfast branch joined the SPNI representatives in objecting to the amount of space devoted to republicanism. It was agreed to concentrate on anti-fascism and class struggle, but on 27 May the Belfast CPI repeated its concerns.[51] Murray grumbled about having to exclude IRA-targeted material and Ryan complained: 'Half of my energy goes in avoiding Republicanism in it – because of the North, Halley... and others think it too Republican.'[52] Ryan went so far as to suggest separate editions for Dublin and Belfast, defending the partitionist proposal with the plea that fear of suppression in the six counties was preventing them from 'dealing with the IRA'.[53]

In June the *Democrat*'s tolerance was tested by Owen Sheehy Skeffington. Freshly evicted from *Ireland To-Day*, he agreed to contribute a fortnightly column 'And Yet It Moves' to the *Democrat*. The title echoed Galileo's supposed response to Pope Urban VIII's insistence that the earth was the centre of creation and did not orbit the sun. 'Skeff's' first column was on Spain. The second was on the new constitution for Éire. The third questioned the legitimacy of a private army like the IRA in a democracy. It signed off humorously: 'perhaps I am only swayed by a hope that *Ireland To-Day* will take an Open Letter from me when I am banned in the *Democrat* for Republican heresy.' Halley wrote in, rejecting the description of the paper as 'republican' or representative of the IRA, as socialists could not base their politics on terrorism, assassination or conspiracy. But 'Skeff' was closer to the truth. It was the column's last appearance in the *Democrat*. Ryan's return to Spain did not end the tug-of-war between Dublin and Belfast. Rose Jacob noted of an editorial meeting on 30 July:

> One blighter wanted all trace of nationality left out of it – it seems it can't be as Republican as it sh[oul]d [and not] be banned in the six Cos. & they are also trying to please the Protestant working people in Belfast. All [sic] makes it impossible for it to be a really good paper.[54]

Another challenge to republicanism came at the NILP's annual conference in November, when Midgley's supporters defeated an amendment calling for all-Ireland labour unity in favour of a motion proposing cooperation with Labour 'throughout the British Commonwealth'.[55] 'Amazing Decision', headlined the *Democrat*, hitting back with a major riposte by Connolly biographer Desmond Ryan, among others, which compared the episode with the 'Connolly-Walker' controversy in 1911. The editor, Johnny Nolan, a young Dublin printer in the CPI, told Ryan he had modified two paragraphs, explaining: 'We can't be over sharp on Midgeley [sic], bearing in mind his attitude on Spain, when the rest of the Labour people just funked it.'[56]

That Midgley was criticised at all contrasted with the admiration for him among republicans in November 1936 and said much about the priorities of the *Irish Democrat*: the unity of Ireland was more important than victory in Spain. The *Democrat*'s narrow base, and a slackening of popular interest in Spain after the July general election, saw the paper shipping water. Murray blamed its collapse on mounting debts and 'the growing estrangement' of the SPNI: linked factors, as the party was relatively rich with a war chest of almost £1,500. In Murray's estimation the SPNI's 'main objection is that the paper leans too much to Republicanism and they want it to cater for the Protestant workers exclusively', a pejorative view somewhat corroborated by Macgougan, who subsequently 'drifted out' of the party because it had 'become hopelessly sectarian'.[57] The final issue appeared on 18 December.

## A POPULAR FRONT?

The escalating trouble in Europe generated a heightening of interest in international affairs and culture. Nineteen thirty-six saw the foundation of the Irish Film Society, which specialised in continental films, the Irish Society for the Study of International Affairs and the All-Ireland Anti-War Crusade, later the Irish Pacifist Movement. More specifically, the Civil War in Spain produced divers organisations inspired by the popular front idea. All failed to break into the mainstream and were sustained by a small and overlapping cohort of socialists and middle-class liberals.

Irish Friends of the Spanish Republic was formed to bring together trade unionists, socialists, communists, republicans and what were called 'cultural representatives'. Its address was Davy McClean's Progressive Bookshop in Union Street, Belfast. Halley was chairman, Sam Haslett, SPNI, was secretary, and other founding members included Midgley, Denis Johnston, R. N. Tweedy, Nora McCormick, Nora Connolly O'Brien, Sheila Bowen Dowling, Hanna and Owen Sheehy Skeffington and Dorothy Macardle. In Dublin a Spanish Aid Committee was formed, with Hanna as chair, John Swift as vice-chairman and an office in the Quaker-related Court Laundry in Harcourt Street. In addition to fundraising, it hosted lectures on Spain.[58] There was also a New York based Irish Committee to Aid Spanish Democracy, affiliated to the North American Committee to Aid Spanish Democracy.[59]

In October 1936 an Irish Left Book Club was founded at a meeting in Wynn's Hotel, Dublin, convened by Owen Sheehy Skeffington. The membership of about 100 included a few Labour Party luminaries like Tom Johnson and Archie Heron, TD.[60] Operating de facto as a branch of its British counterpart, the Dublin group produced a monthly bulletin, *Left News*, and subdivided into smaller discussion groups of ten or so readers each. Its headquarters in 14 Sackville Place would also serve as a base for kindred projects like the New Theatre Group and a debating circle called the Unity Club. Owen's wife Andrée recalled wistfully:

> We were very earnest about it on the whole. We anticipated big changes in society, hoping the Popular Front style of government would spread further, and wanted to be prepared to help. Preserving liberal values against fascism or other dictatorships and injecting more social justice into democracy seemed goals nearly within our grasp. We were full of optimism, or tried to be; some might say we were rather naïve. A dose of naivety and optimism is needed for progress.[61]

Leading lights in the club were instrumental in launching the New Theatre Group in early 1937. It was another reflex of the popular front idea. In

1936 the Unity Theatre in London had emerged from the Workers' Theatre Movement. Gollancz established the Left Book Club Theatre Guild in April 1937. Within a year it had led to the formation of 200 theatre groups in the UK, including the Theatre Guild in Belfast. The New Theatre Group conducted a regular correspondence with the Gollancz's Theatre Guild, and its aims were broadly similar: to present 'plays with a purpose', ideally about workers, by workers, and for workers. Its first production was two one-act plays, Clifford Odets's *Waiting for Lefty* and *Strike*, in the Engineers' Hall in Dawson Street. According to Tom O'Brien, who was prominent in the Group before and after his time in the Connolly Column: 'On that first night the audience roared its approval. They were delighted. They had a theatre group and a play which was their very own.' Accustomed to reaction, several patrons were panicked by 'interrupters' dispersed throughout the hall, before realising they were part of the drama! O'Brien had no doubt that he was playing to a select, beleaguered demographic that was 'buffeted, bludgeoned, sat-upon and, generally speaking, all-in-wrestled with'.[62]

The Secular Society of Ireland, for example, founded in 1933 with some 40 members, met in semi-secrecy with attendance by invitation only. The disclosure of its venue in the *Irish Press* in 1934 led to meetings being held in members' homes or in the Dublin mountains. It was dissolved in 1936 and its bank balance – usually healthy thanks to some well-heeled sympathisers – was donated to the Spanish government.[63] The Secular Society had been formed out of the Contemporary Club, which offered a neutral venue for topical debate. At one meeting in October 1936, Thomas Gunning, O'Duffy's personal secretary, championed fascism while Murray defended Soviet Russia, 'in two or three monstrous propositions of the strong having the right to be a despot' according to Jacob. The club collapsed in the 1940s under the weight of religious disapproval.[64]

The New Theatre Group's second production opened in February 1938. Thereafter new plays were staged every two or three months, with week-long runs. When the company tired of plays by foreign authors, Tom O'Brien was 'instructed' to write one on the Spanish Civil War. He duly wrote *The Last Hill*. Its message was unvarnished.[65]

> Let me take the trigger when they come;
> A hundred rounds a minute suits my mood.
> I was in Barcelona when we rushed the machine guns with bare hands.[66]

The Group defined its politics simply as 'anti-fascist'. 'In the beginning', wrote O'Brien, 'the Group had a very definite political bias. It was in line with the Popular Front movement in Europe. . .'.[67] The most common affiliation of activists was the Republican Congress, and the great majority of activists were republicans rather than communists. Significantly, the Group was scarcely harmed by the Molotov-Ribbentrop pact, which adversely affected the Left Book Club in Britain and contributed to the collapse of its Theatre Guild, but was damaged by internal debate on the world war, which led to its departure from the Unity Club and terminal decline. By 1943 it had lost all political motivation.[68]

A fine example of the uniquely Irish combination of republicanism and the popular front spirit is *Good-Bye, Twilight: Songs of Struggle in Ireland*, compiled by Leslie Daiken in 1936 and illustrated with woodcuts by Harry Kernoff, a fellow Dublin Jew and member of Friends of Soviet Russia. It was dedicated to Tom Mooney, one of America's most famous political prisoners, and published by the new CPGB and popular front associated imprint, Lawrence and Wishart. Daiken, or 'Yod' to his friends, was born Yodaiken in Dublin's 'Little Jerusalem' in 1912, and joined the CPI in 1934. In 'Shamrocks for Mayakovsky' he remembered:

> On the Liffey Quay, beside the greasy water
> I was selling *Workers' Voices*
> To dockers who preferred their pints of porter.
> Blowing up the Basin, like teeth of a curry comb,
> The East wind cut through threadbare flannels. . .

The flannels reflected his student days in Trinity College. When Daiken moved to London to work in journalism and public relations, he took Ireland with him. In a basement flat in Kilburn, he and Charlie Donnelly edited 23 issues of *Irish Front*, a monthly voice of the London Republican Congress, Gestetnered in the office of the League Against Imperialism.[69] Contributors included O'Casey and Seán Ó Faoláin.

*Good-Bye, Twilight* was a collection of 75 poems and ballads by 40 Irish writers and workers, all 'showing unmistakeably out of the experience of the proletariat, that revolutionary poets, playwrights, and novelists are developing an art which reveals more forces in the world than the love of the lecher and the pride of the Narcissist'.[70] Daiken recalled life in London as 'one long continuum of 'agit-prop'', but sourced *Twilight* not in agit-prop but in James Connolly's recognition of Fenian ballads as weapons of revolution, highlighting the parallel with the clerical 'clap-trap' confronting the Fenian poets.[71]

Revolutionary art was emerging from the bourgeois self-indulgence of the Celtic twilight and the Yeatsian cynicism that followed. Daiken's introduction defied the trajectory of the intellectuals he had known at Trinity and UCD, and anticipated the caricature of the 1930s by future liberals.[72] Attributing 'almost every anomaly in recent Irish social events. . . *to the betrayal of the national aspirations by the Treaty of 1921* [his emphasis]', he delineated two main tendencies in Irish poetry: 'modernist' and 'traditionalist'. The greatest of Irish writers had retreated into modernism:

> Futility, or more often an inconsequential groping in the dark for a new bourgeois aesthetic, drove the more sensitive poets away from 'politics' (i.e. Ireland: and all its problems) to Paris, where the soul of Joyce ever presides as a source of inspiration to all thorough-going isolationists. Thither, with Thomas MacGreevy as a vanguard, trekked younger men like Samuel Beckett, Denis Devlin, and Brian Coffey; driven by the psychology of escape, then become a cult, across the wastelands of interiorisation, and technical experiment, they eventually found a mecca in a sort of essentially-celtic surrealism – as far from Ireland as they could get, in art.
> 
> 'For I prefer a grand-piano to a harp'.[73]

Daiken saw himself and his fellow republicans as 'authenticists'. In other words, he was rejecting the idea that Irish culture was backward and needed cosmopolitanism, and arguing that the key to revolution in Ireland was to be found in its republican heritage.[74]

*Good-Bye Twilight* varied in quality. The *Irish Democrat* conceded as much, and Ó Faoláin gave it a blistering review in *Ireland To-Day*. Ó Faoláin would have been very much a 'modernist' rather than a 'traditionalist'. 'What', he asked, 'is the use in singing about bold rapparees, spears, bivouacs and so on in 1936?' In addition, he was one of the few leading writers not to support the Spanish Republic. In a *Left Review* poll of authors, Ó Faoláin was listed as one of 16 'neutrals'. Just five favoured Franco and 100 backed the Republic.[75] In Britain, it was impossible to separate the literature from the politics. In Ireland, as the *Democrat* suggested, the remarkable thing about *Good-Bye Twilight* is not that it was done badly, but that it was done at all. Daiken was sanguine: 'Things were beginning to hum with optimism [in] heroic days of dream and struggle.'[76] Daiken supplies another snapshot of the communist republican mentality in a photo of himself and others of the Republican Congress in Trafalgar Square in 1938. Their banner put an Irish spin on Spain with the legend 'Irish Republicans greet Spanish Republicans. Smash All Imperialisms.'

Whereas Daiken has been neglected, Donnelly, the best known of Ireland's Spanish Civil War poets, has been misrepresented. A near contemporary of Denis Devlin et al. at UCD, Donnelly, with Frank Ryan and Owen Sheehy

Skeffington, had brought Trinity and UCD students together in Student Vanguard in May 1934. The first anti-fascist action on an Irish campus, Vanguard aimed to oppose both 'Blueshirt Fascism in the south and Craigavon Fascism in north'. It was also a response to control of the Student Representative Council by the Student Christian Movement and Pro Fide.[77] Donnelly went on to edit its organ *Student Vanguard*. He was a rare intellectual accretion to the left and, with Ryan, the only UCD man in the Connolly Column. Donnelly's literary tastes may have been more international than Daiken's, but he was an Irish republican who had written in UCD's *Comhthrom Féinne*: 'The modern Irish artist cannot throw over modern thought. Neither can he [. . .] throw over Ireland. In his consciousness, the two must fuse.'[78] Neither did Donnelly take world communism too seriously. Eugene Downing recalled one instance when he and Donnelly were printing leaflets in Connolly House. Murray was horrified to see they carried the slogan 'For a workers' republic!'. That should be 'For a workers' and small farmers' republic', said Murray, giving the latest ECCI line. As the leaflets were for distribution among Dublin workers, Downing and Donnelly nearly burst out laughing.[79]

Donnelly was also critical of Josef Stalin's purges. In Dublin he joined the Republican Congress rather than the CPI, and in England he chose to found the London Republican Congress with ex-IRA man Seán Mulgrew and Mick Kelly, fellow tenants of Daiken's flat, rather than join the CPGB. Donnelly and Daiken got on well and worked together for the League Against Imperialism in addition to editing *Irish Front*. Some issues were written entirely by Donnelly. Through the League, Donnelly was connecting with other nationalities, but he remained focused primarily on his own. *Irish Front* targeted the Irish community. And while it echoed *Republican Congress* in content, it carried Irish language articles, unlike the Dublin paper. Donnelly's name appeared in Irish on occasion. He also wrote a 30-page pamphlet *The Irish Republic at the Crossroads* and contributed a poem to *Good-Bye Twilight*. Yet *Even the Olives Are Bleeding* and the elegiac *Heroic Heart* remembered him as a 'modernist' and a victim of 'traditionalism' in a manner symptomatic of the lazy equation of nationalism with xenophobia and of the Connolly Column with the cosmopolitanism excoriated by Daiken.[80]

Socialist republican sensibilities found an earthy expression in the satirical ballads of 'Somhairle MacAlastair', pseudonym of ex-IRA man Diarmuid MacGoille Phádraig, which appeared in the *Worker*, the *Irish Democrat* and *Good-Bye Twilight*.[81] The ballads lampooned the republicans' rogues gallery: O'Duffy, the Christian Front, William Lombard Murphy and his *Irish Independent*, Italian and German fascism, British Tories and the *Daily Mail*. On religion, he was more indignant about Moslems than priests. 'Oh, blessed

God! The heathen Moor is lord of Malaga', ran 'The sack of Malaga' after Thomas Davis's 'The sack of Baltimore'. Málaga had fallen to the fascists in February 1937.[82] Most of the ballads are hilarious. 'Ballyseedy befriends Badajoz', the title linking sites of massacres of Irish and Spanish republicans, is venomous:

> O'Duffy's dupes are killing as their Fascist masters bid.
> Gas bombs are falling on the Mothers of Madrid.
> (The birds at Ballyseedy picked flesh from off the stones
> And the Spanish suns at Badajoz are bleaching baby bones.)
> *GOD*, they claim, is *FASCIST-THE VOICE* that Pilate feared
> Is spitting streams of hellish hate from a Moorish soldier's beard!
> They use the Cross of Calvary to veil their foul designs.
> 'Vivat Hispania' the voice of Hitler whines.
> Vivat Hispania, but not as they would ask-
> 'Defend the Young Republic' cries out the sturdy Basque.
> 'Tis the Crescent not the Sickle is looming over Spain,
> But the servants of Mohammed will sate their lust in vain.
> The hireling hordes of Italy that come with ev'ry tide
> Will conquer proud Iberia when all her sons have died.
> O'Duffy calls his 'godly band' and leads them to the fray.
> (They murdered Liam Mellows upon *Our Lady's Day*.)
> God help you! Spanish 'Connollys' if Lombard Murphy's crew
> Should blood their drunken hellhounds and send them after you![83]

Daiken's misgivings on anti-clericalism were teased out tortuously by O'Donnell in one of three books on Spain published by Irish writers in 1937. The self-confessed 'bigoted Tir Conaillian' had grown anxious about finding peace and quiet to finish his novel *The Big Windows* and, with no thought of politics, hesitated between the warmth of kindred Scotland and the heat of exotic Spain.[84] Concluding that fishing folk were the same the world over, he set off with his wife, Lile, to the seaside village of Sitges, near Barcelona. It was July 1936. Instead of the novel he would write *Salud!*, an account of his time in Spain at the start of the war. *Salud!*, commissioned by Methuen, is almost obsessive in finding parallels with Ireland. He opened with flashbacks to an episode in which he was caught up in a dispute over a sub-post office on Achill Island.

> I can imagine few things more exciting than to watch the days unfold against home conditions under a foreign sky; your own village is most exciting when you

meet it between strange mountains... I walked into a Civil War in Achill just as I walked into one in Spain, and it was the same Civil War... A picture of Achill is a map of Spain.[85]

O'Donnell, being O'Donnell, had a singular take on aspects of the war in Spain, and *Salud!* is unusual for its candour on the flaws and contradictions in Spanish Republican politics and O'Donnell's own conflicted feelings. Whereas others were given to deny anti-clerical excesses, O'Donnell admitted it in Ireland and condemned it in Spain, which would not have been easy listening for comrades in either country. '[T]he story of this sorry business of church burning', he insisted, 'needs frank telling within working-class movements'.[86]

He was more typically Irish in rationalising anti-clericalism as an understandable response to the Church's identification with fascism or its collusion with the scandalous extremes of wealth and poverty in Spain. Basque fidelity to the faith appeared to confirm his analysis. Yet he knew that in some respects he was rationalising the irrational to make it more palatable to Irish audiences.

Though frequently a victim of clerical power himself, he struggled to fathom the motivation for desecration even as he chewed over case after case in Ireland when the boot was on the other foot. The sight of looted churches and children in chasubles swinging chalices for the amusement of their parents depressed him profoundly. He knew too it was a propaganda disaster. *Salud!* included a detailed interrogation of the excuses behind the sacking of a church in Barcelona and dismissed them all with derision. Lile could not bear to watch the sacrilege: 'The fools, can't they even see they will smash the Movement, bewilder people. Look at the crowd,' she appealed to Peadar.[87] Her husband decided they amounted to a lumpen minority from the slums, just like the anti-communist 'animal gangs' in Dublin, directed by cadres with personal grudges against the clergy. Daiken too deplored 'a reactionary self-consciousness in a certain type of Catholic intellectual who frequently repaid a Higher Education with flamboyant heresies...'. One English militiaman, 'strutting around' in an altar cloth, earned O'Donnell's contempt as 'a robust little bigot, typical of Protestant opinion as I encountered it in Spain: and there is a touch of the same militant Protestantism in the Communist Movement in Britain'.[88] Mistaking anti-clericalism for anti-Catholicism was a very Irish prejudice.

Historians have given more attention to O'Donnell's sympathy with the anarchists. He was exhilarated by the Catalan people's spontaneous defence of the Republic, fascinated by the Anarchist Farmers' Congress where peasants discussed how land should be collectivised, and found the 'free' atmosphere of 'anarchist' Barcelona more congenial than that of 'communist' Madrid, a perspective he kept under wraps in Ireland. Whatever their faults, the communists were crucial to the defeat of fascism and the only viable revolutionary force in Ireland. As long as those realities remained, he would stay loyal to the Comintern line.[89] 'If Communism', he wrote, 'was the enemy-in-chief in the eyes of the Fascists then it clearly was a fighting formation to which anti-Fascists should rally'.[90] Initially he was confident the fascist revolt would wither in the fire of popular enthusiasm for the Republic. Within months he realised that something was going wrong. Bewildered, he returned to Spain to find out.

Mitchell echoed O'Donnell in many respects in *Storm Over Spain*. As a Bloomsbury-based writer from the west of Ireland, Catholic, liberal, republican and a pacifist, she embraced an unusual combination of globetrotting cosmopolitanism and rooted Irishness. Mitchell visited Spain in the spring and summer of 1936 on being told 'In a few months something is going to happen that will keep you out of Spain for a long time.' For a book published in London for the English market, *Storm Over Spain* is remarkably full of references to Gaelic or radical Irish writers. Like O'Donnell, Mitchell understood Spain through its parallels with Ireland. And like Frank Ryan, she tried to evaluate the protagonists through her understanding of Irish history and politics.

That method broke down when it came to anti-clericalism. There were simply no comparisons. The ruthless elimination of Protestant Spain by Franco's crusaders compounded the perplexity. Mitchell concluded, very like O'Donnell in her explanation of the church burning and her irritation with the British left:

> Had the Church as a whole in Spain been the friend of the poor, had the Catholic priests in general supported the social advancement of the toiling masses, it seems unlikely that the clergy would have suffered in the Civil War as they did... Those English papers of the Left which, in spite of the sufferings of these innocent victims of the Civil War, filled their column with splenetic hate against *all* the Religious in Spain, alienated many fair-minded readers.[91]

Not being of the left, Kate O'Brien was less given to agonising over socialist transgressions or making excuses for the 'corruption' of 'an overwhelmingly wealthy and powerful Church'. Hailing from a wealthy family in Limerick, Kate had worked as a governess in Bilbao and published a novel *Mary Lavelle* (1936) on the back of her experiences. To her great disappointment, for she was proud of her new independent Ireland, the book was banned. Her travelogue, *Farewell to Spain*, was published in August 1937 as the city fell to the Nationalists. She had no illusions about Stalin – 'a rampant Fascist bully' – or 'the Communistic insult to individualism and spiritual freedom', but as a pacifist, agnostic and liberal, she saw the war as one of 'militaristic absolutism against democracy'.

As a cultural Catholic, with a deep admiration for St Teresa of Avila, she denounced Franco from a Castilian perspective for destroying her beloved traditional Spain and 'infecting' it with the detestable Moors. How much of this was genuine and how much was artifice to subvert Franco's appropriation of Catholicism and patriotism is moot. Hanna Sheehy Skeffington gave *Farewell to Spain* a warm welcome in the *Irish Democrat*, applauding Kate's belief that 'it is probable – pace *The Universe* and the *Catholic Herald* – that she [St Teresa] an indomitable fighter, would have been to-day on the side of Valencia and Madrid.'[92] On the other side of the trenches, the intrepid Catholic war correspondent, Francis McCullagh, in despatches to the *Irish Independent* and his *In Franco's Spain* (1937), ignored Nationalist atrocities.[93] The most intriguing Irish voice on the war was Seumus MacKee's *I Was a Franco Soldier* (1938), the story of a disillusioned banderista, published by Charles Duff, an Irish propagandist for the Republic, as a riposte to O'Duffy's *Crusade in Spain* (1938). 'Seumas MacKee' is likely to have been a pseudonym, but Duff insisted that the account was genuine.[94]

### WATERSHED AND AFTER

The anticipated return of O'Duffy's brigade alarmed the ECCI. An International Brigades news bulletin attributed O'Duffy's 'desertion' to the inability to 'find fresh troops to fill the gaps caused by the war', evidently unaware that his bandera had suffered more demoralisation than casualties and would be received at home with embarrassment.[95] When Francis Mooney, chairman of the Dublin branch, arrived in Moscow for May Day in 1937, the ECCI took the opportunity to reassess the popular front formula in Ireland. Comintern analysts expected the Christian Front, augmented by O'Duffy's 'fascist bravos', to mount a serious challenge to Fianna Fáil at the next general election and strengthen 'developments toward fascism in Ireland'. As the CPI was ill-equipped to meet the threat, it was argued that the ECCI should apply to the CPI its broad front prescriptions for the PCE. It proposed that the CPI invite into membership 'proved types' such as Owen Sheehy Skeffington, Roddy Connolly, and O'Donnell, and offer 'assistance and advice' to enable Hanna Sheehy Skeffington 'with her immediate circle of associates' to be enrolled. A new popular front should extend its embrace beyond the rank and file of Fianna Fáil, and to this end 'a small group of influential Fianna Fáil people' should be invited to Russia, and cultural and trade relations opened with Ireland.[96]

A memo to André Marty, secretary of the Comintern and chief political commissar of the International Brigades, concluded: 'The main question in our attitude to the elections must be to do everything possible to prevent the victory of the Cosgraveites and Christian Front clerical reaction and fascism, which is the most pressing danger.'[97] On 23 May Mooney met Marty, Max Raylock and 'Mehring', pseudonym of R. A. Mirring, an ECCI emissary to the CPGB in 1934 and now the Estonian party's representative to the Comintern.[98]

Marty thought Ireland too complicated for immediate decisions and suggested Mooney meet Pollitt to arrange the appointment of a commission to prepare for the general election and O'Duffy's return. Meanwhile, the best Marty could offer was:

> It is advisable for the Irish party comrades to systematically study Lenin and Stalin, but not, of course all their works. They should study, to begin with, Lenin's 'Left Wing Communism', and Stalin's speech to the Red Army graduates of the Military Academy on Cadres. These two things will be sufficient for the time being.[99]

Stalin's speech in May 1935 had proposed – if that is the right word – that the slogan 'technique decides everything' be replaced with 'cadres decide everything.' It was deemed an 'important' speech, and 'the most striking example of the growth of such cadres', according to the Soviet party's history, 'was the Stakhanov movement'. The emphasis on cadres would not help Seán Murray's prospects, but for the moment his leadership was being saved by Spain and the absence of alternatives.

The CPI's election manifesto duly called, not for the replacement of Fianna Fáil, but for 'a vigorous working class and republican opposition' to make Fianna Fáil 'fight'. The campaign turned into a nightmare for Murray. Big Jim Larkin was standing as an Independent Labour candidate in North East Dublin and it was policy to encourage him to come back into the official labour movement, so the party nominated Bill Scott for the less propitious South Dublin. In addition to serving in Spain, Scott was a bricklayer, and 15,000 building workers had been on strike since 13 April. The CPI won no influence over the strike, though Mooney was prominent in the Amalgamated Society of Painters and Decorators and the *Irish Democrat* regularly covered the dispute. Matters worsened when the CPGB declined to advance the deposit for Scott due to Pollitt's differences with Murray. The CPI withdrew Scott in favour of Frank Ryan, who stood as a 'United front against fascism' candidate. Ryan had talked with Tom Barry and Owen Sheehy Skeffington about building an active united front and mounting a campaign against the proposed Bunreacht na hÉireann, but nothing came of it.[100]

Ryan was advertised as the 'Republican standard bearer' and not all Dublin comrades appreciated Murray's gesture of solidarity. Some decided he was too deferential to O'Donnell. Completing the tale of woe, and reflecting discord with *Irish Democrat*, the IRA boycotted the campaign. On 1 July Ryan polled 875 votes and lost his deposit.[101] He had not wished to contest and was already back in Spain on 14 June. Murray succeeded him as editor of the *Irish Democrat*. Fianna Fáil lost eight seats in the election and returned to office with backbench support from the Labour Party. The CPI described the result as 'a victory for the electorate over reaction'.[102] Crucially for Moscow, Fine Gael, too, lost ground and the Christian Front threat failed to materialise. O'Duffy's men had limped home in June, to be received with embarrassment on account of their lacklustre military performance and internal disputes, which suggested some disillusionment with Franco and his war. On all sides, interest in Spain began to abate.

For most, fascism receded into the distance of central Europe. For the far left, it was moving closer to the socialist motherland. Comintern concern with Ireland shifted from Spain to the implications for Soviet Russia of the Anglo-Irish agreements of April that ended the economic war, repatriated the treaty ports and elicited a promise from Éamon de Valera that he would not permit Éire to be used as a base of attack against Britain. Murray had denounced the agreements in *Inprecorr* for ignoring partition and tying Ireland to Neville Chamberlain's policy of appeasement.[103]

The Comintern was more concerned with the emergence of an Anglo-German alliance against Russia and a re-run of the Spanish Civil War in Ireland: if pro-Franco elements backed an anti-Soviet alliance, then Fianna Fáil's defence of neutrality would be progressive. But the CPGB wondered if the CPI in Éire was of any value and its very existence was debated by the CPGB's political bureau in the presence of Murray and Nolan on 18 May 1938. Murray was reduced to pleading for the party's survival. Johnny Campbell, the CPGB's representative to the ECCI and a staunch Moscow loyalist, contended that Murray's major error had been opposition to Fianna Fáil, a 'progressive, national reformist party of the small capitalists, farmers, and workers' that had resisted pressure to recognise the Franco regime and that had steadily eliminated British power over Éire, despite repeated CPI predictions to the contrary. Campbell later drafted a lengthy statement that indicated the degree to which London and Moscow evaluated the CPI for its use in international affairs:

> As a consequence of the policy of our Party we have not yet seriously raised in Ireland the question of the external Fascist menace to the new won rights of the people of Southern Ireland and the role of Eire (Ireland) as an independent state at the league of nations, and in the Conferences of the British Dominions...

The decline of the Communist Party of Ireland is primarily due to the fact that neither in the theory or practice of that Party, nor in the occasional advice given to it by the CPGB, is there any sign of an attempt to apply the policy of the 7th World Congress to Ireland:

> The de Valera government has now reached a stage when it will be more difficult to make any advance against the internal forces of reaction. It will be subjected to increasing pressure from the Church, from the Cosgrave party, from the reactionary wing of the capitalist class.
> The way forward to a broad front of all the democratic forces in Ireland is for our party to rally all the democratic forces to push the de Valera government to the left.[104]

The CPGB's central committee resolved to put the Irish question before the ECCI and recommended that the CPI in Éire concentrate on Dublin, make friends with the Labour Party and the unions, and engage sympathetically with opposition from Catholic workers.[105] It was fortunate for Murray that the final word did not rest with Pollitt. The Comintern was now Stalin's first line of defence. The CPI had played its part on Spain and it could have a role in defending neutrality and shaping an Irish alternative to British perspectives on Anglo-Soviet relations. It fell in step with the new line in January 1939, announcing its support for the Anglo-Irish agreements of 1938 and for Fianna Fáil.[106]

The CPI sustained solidarity with Spain through the *Workers' Republic*, 'a monthly journal of left-wing thinking', issued from May 1938. Outside the party, the main initiatives of 1938–1939 were the Frank Ryan Release Committee and the Irish Foodship for Spain Committee. Chaired by Father O'Flanagan, with Patrick Byrne, Republican Congress, as secretary, the foodship committee was based in the usual haunt of popular front auxiliaries, 14 Sackville Place. Formally, the appeal was humanitarian and non-political. In practice, it was difficult for activists to conceal their sympathies. O'Flanagan told one of the last public meetings on Spain that it was 'the war that the people of Catholic Ireland thought was a war for Christianity. The Italian Cromwell of to-day was murdering in Spain just as the English Cromwell murdered in Ireland, and the descendants of the murdered Irish were applauding his deeds.'[107]

Despite being shunned by the Labour Party and the Trade Union Congress, the committee collected £700 worth of food, clothes and medical supplies, which were pooled with a British foodship project and exported from Belfast via Liverpool in February 1939. Objections from Jacob – a scourge of Anglocentrism – that the Irish effort be independent of the British, were dismissed as 'shocking sectarianism'.[108] The bulk of Irish people were tired of Spain. Efforts by the *Workers' Republic* to generate protests against visits to Dublin by Italian naval vessels generated no response.[109] For once, *TCD Miscellany* captured the public mood:

> The Spanish Civil War is a thing I abhor;
> Admittedly I've learnt a lot I didn't know before;
> From Gibraltar to Madrid
> I know everything they did,
> I've read up on the atrocities and wallowed in the gore,
> And every second day I have seen the papers say
> That the peace of Europe's threatened and it must give way;
> And I don't want to hear no more.[110]

Communist and Republican Congress support for Republican Spain is well known, but not well understood. Far from turning their backs on Irish insularity, so-called socialists took the Spanish Civil War as a signal to dig deeper into our native heritage to tap the springs of revolt. They had no difficulty in reconciling organic Irish anti-imperialism with what they regarded as their international duty. For the CPI, communism was a world party, guided by the Comintern, the general staff of the global revolution. Fascism was not confined to Franco's Spain, and Franco's victory merely heightened the need to defend Soviet Russia, the increasingly embattled socialist motherland.

For the Republican Congress on the other hand, Spain was the end of the road. A tradition of interaction of socialism and republicanism, invented by James Connolly, made flesh by Big Jim Larkin and the Irish Transport and General Workers' Union, and sustained in fits and starts by the CPI and the IRA, had finally run into the ground, expiring with a last hurrah on the battlefields of Spain.

Solidarity beyond the CPI and Republican Congress is easier for a postnationalist Ireland to understand, but not so well known. Extending to diverse elements of the liberal middle-class, it found expression in literature and drama. If small, the engagement was novel. Most remarkable was how much it was shaped by the popular front idea. It was also a portent, prompted by the same forces that would drive the liberal agenda in post-1960s Ireland: opposition to clericalism, social conservatism, conformity and censorship, and a quest for freedom of conscience, secularism and involvement with international affairs. Behind it all was the fear of Ireland going fascist, which was not so fanciful in the first year of the war. When O'Duffy's 'fascist bravos' returned home a busted flush, the menace faded, and the passions over Spain subsided.

NOTES

1. Michael O'Riordan, *Connolly Column: The Story of the Irishmen Who Fought in the Ranks of the International Brigades in the National Revolutionary War of the Spanish People, 1936–1939* (Dublin, 1979), p. 77; Peter O'Connor, *A Soldier of Liberty* (Dublin, 1996), p. 17; Máirín Mitchell, *Storm Over Spain* (London, 1937), p. 217; David Krause (ed), *The Letters of Sean O'Casey, Volume 1, 1910–1941* (London, 1975), p. 656; *Worker*, 26 December 1936; 9–16, 30 January 1937; *Irish Democrat*, 4 December 1937; Commissariat of War, XV Brigade, *The Book of the XV Brigade: Records of British, American, Canadian and Irish Volunteers in the XV International Brigade in Spain 1936–1938* (Madrid, 1938), pp 28–9.
2. See Pete Jackson, '"A rather one-sided fight": the *Worker* and the Spanish Civil War', in *Saothar*, 23 (1998), pp 79–87.
3. *Worker*, 25 July 1936.
4. RGASPI, The national question and the policy of the CPI since the 7 congress CI, 26 May 1936, f. 495, o.14, d.337, ll. 168-171.
5. E. H. Carr, *The Comintern and the Spanish Civil War* (London, 1984), p. 7.
6. R. Dan Richardson, *Comintern Army: The International Brigades and the Spanish Civil War* (Lexington, Ky, 1982), p. 11.
7. *Worker*, 26 September 1936, 6 February 1937.
8. Ibid., 10 October, 7 November, 19 December 1936.
9. Ibid., 22 August 1936.
10. *Irish Democrat*, 24 April 1937.
11. National Library of Ireland (NLI), Rosamond Jacob Papers, diaries, 32,582/1–170, 30 April 1937.
12. *TCD Miscellany*, 4 February 1937.
13. *Irish Independent*, 18, 25 August 1936; *Irish Press*, 16 September 1936.
14. Donal Ó Drisceoil, *Peadar O'Donnell* (Cork, 2001), p. 53.
15. *Irish Times*, 23 September 1936.
16. *Worker*, 15 August, 12 September 1936; RGASPI, letter from Murray, 14 January 1938, f. 495, o. 14, d. 340, ll. 1-2.
17. See the *Derry Standard*, 28 April 1937.

18. University College Dublin Archives, Eithne Coyle O'Donnell papers, P61/45.
19. *Worker*, 21 November 1936; *Irish Press*, 17 November 1936, 6 January 1937.
20. *Irish Press*, 6 November 1936; *Irish Independent*, 6 November 1936.
21. Eimear O'Connor, *Sean Keating: Art, Politics and Building the Irish Nation* (Dublin, 2013), pp 93–4.
22. *Irish Press*, 18 January 1937.
23. Ibid., 25 January 1937; McGarry, *Irish Politics and the Spanish Civil War*, pp 99–100.
24. *Irish Press*, 20, 29 January 1937; McGarry, *Irish Politics and the Spanish Civil War*, pp 99, 153.
25. Stephen J. Brown, SJ, *The Press in Ireland: A Survey and a Guide* (Dublin, 1937), p. 49.
26. Seán Ó hEidirisceoil, 'A personal memoir of the thirties', in H. Gustav Klaus (ed), *Strong Words, Brave Deeds: The Poetry, Life, and Times of Thomas O'Brien, Volunteer in the Spanish Civil War* (Dublin, 1994), p. 198.
27. Seán Cronin, *Frank Ryan: The Search for the Republic* (Dublin, 1980), pp 81–7, 264; *Irish Times*, 14, 18 January 1937; William Burton, 'The Spanish Civil War, Irish newspapers, journals, and periodicals: a thematic examination, 1936–39' (PhD, Ulster University, 2019). On O'Flanagan see Denis Carroll, *They Have Fooled You Again: Michael O'Flanagan (1876–1942), Priest, Republican, Social Critic* (Dublin, 1993).
28. https://medium.com/@stewreddin/irish-citizens-of-basque-origin-the-story-of-ireland-s-basque-refugees-during-the-spanish-civil-war. Accessed 20 February 2019.
29. *Irish Independent*, 2 March 1937.
30. *Irish Times*, 10 May 1937
31. *National Student*, March 1938.
32. *Irish Independent*, 28–30 April 1937; *Catholic Herald*, 30 April 1937.
33. Charlie McGuire, *Roddy Connolly and the Struggle for Socialism in Ireland* (Cork, 2008), p. 161; Sheehy Skeffington, *Skeff*, pp 83–5.
34. *Irish Press*, 1 May 1937; *Irish Democrat*, 8 May 1937; for biographical notes on all Irish brigadistas see Barry McLoughlin, *Fighting for Republican Spain, Frank Ryan and the Volunteers from Limerick in the International Brigades* (Vienna, 2014), pp 170–229; see also www.mcloughlin.at.
35. P. P. Anderson, 'The struggle over the evacuation to the United Kingdom and repatriation of Basque refugee children in the Spanish Civil War: symbols and souls', in *Journal of Contemporary History*, 52:2 (2017), pp 297–318; Ben Edwards, *With God on Our Side: British Christian Responses to the Spanish Civil War* (Newcastle upon Tyne, 2013), pp 239–54.
36. *Sunday Independent*, 10 April 1938; *Munster Express*, 11 June 1937.
37. *Irish Independent*, 4 June 1937.
38. *Irish Democrat*, 15 May, 5 June 1937.
39. https://medium.com/@stewreddin/irish-citizens-of-basque-origin-the-story-of-ireland-s-basque-refugees-during-the-spanish-civil-war. Accessed 20 February 2019.
40. RGASPI, Proposals in connection with the Communist Party of Ireland, 8 May 1937; Annual general meeting of the Dublin branch of the CPI, 21 February 1937, f. 495, o. 89, d. 102, ll. 1-9; f. 495, o. 14, d. 339, ll. 5-17.
41. Seán Byers, 'Seán Murray, the Irish republican left and international communism, 1916–1962' (PhD, University of Ulster, Jordanstown, 2012), p. 169.

42. Andrée Sheehy Skeffington, *Skeff: The Life of Owen Sheehy Skeffington, 1909–1970* (Dublin, 1991), pp 84–5; Seán Cronin, *Frank Ryan: The Search for the Republic* (Dublin, 1980), p.104; Jack Macgougan, 'Letting Labour lead: Jack Macgougan and the pursuit of unity, 1913–1958', in *Saothar*, 14 (1989), pp 114, 22; TNA, KV 2/1185, Seán Murray (PF 399.199).
43. *Worker*, 13 March 1937.
44. *Irish Press*, 27 February, 8 March 1937; Krause, *The Letters of Sean O'Casey, Volume I*, pp 803–4; David Krause (ed), *The Letters of Sean O'Casey, Volume II, 1942–54* (New York, 1980), p. 870.
45. NLI, Rosamond Jacob Papers, diaries, 32,582/1–170, 30 April 1937.
46. Emmet O'Connor, *Reds and the Green: Ireland, Russia, and the Communist Internationals, 1919–43* (Dublin, 2004), pp 222–3.
47. *Irish Press*, 29 March, 1 April 1937; Cronin, *Frank Ryan*, pp 109–12.
48. *Worker*, 30 January, 6 February 1937.
49. RGASPI, J. R. Campbell, The situation in Ireland, 27 February 1939, f. 495, o. 14, d. 340, ll. 10-59; we are obliged to Andrew Boyd for details on Halley.
50. *Irish Democrat*, 8, 22 May 1937; Mike Milotte, *Communism in Modern Ireland: The Pursuit of the Workers' Republic Since 1916* (Dublin, 1984), p. 174; CPI, *Communist Party of Ireland*, p. 28.
51. Byers, 'Seán Murray, the Irish republican left and international communism, 1916–1962', p. 170.
52. Cronin, *Frank Ryan*, pp 105–6, 113; RGASPI, Meeting on the Irish question, 23 May 1937, f. 495, o. 14, d. 339, ll. 27-38; see letter from Halley, dissociating the *Irish Democrat* from the IRA, *Irish Democrat*, 12 June 1937.
53. Cronin, *Frank Ryan*, p. 105.
54. NLI, Rosamond Jacob Papers, diaries, 32,582/1–170, 30 July 1937.
55. Graham Walker, *The Politics of Frustration: Harry Midgley and the Failure of Labour in Northern Ireland* (Manchester, 1985), pp 100–1; *Belfast News-Letter*, 1 November 1937; J. K. Robinson, 'Annual conference of the Northern Ireland Labour Party', in *Inprecorr*, 49, 13 November 1937.
56. *Irish Democrat*, 6 November 1937; Walker, *The Politics of Frustration*, p. 101.
57. Macgougan, 'Letting Labour lead', pp 114, 112; RGASPI, letter from Murray, 14 January 1938, f. 495, o. 14, d. 340, ll. 1-2.
58. McGuire, *Roddy Connolly and the Struggle for Socialism in Ireland*, p. 161; Sheehy Skeffington, *Skeff*, pp 83–5; Swift, *John Swift*, pp 102–3.
59. David Convery, 'Irish participation in medical aid to Republican Spain, 1936–39', in *Saothar*, 35 (2010), p. 44.
60. Sheehy Skeffington, *Skeff*, pp 83, 251; *Irish Democrat*, 2 October 1937.
61. Sheehy Skeffington, *Skeff*, p. 84.
62. Thomas O'Brien, 'The New Theatre Group: to die or not to die', in Klaus (ed), *Strong Words, Brave Deeds*, pp 147–8. See also Joe Deasy, 'Reviving the memory: New Theatre movement', in *Labour History News*, 3 (spring, 1987), pp 3–5.
63. John P. Swift, 'John Swift, 1896–1990: a solitary voice that echoes still', in Francis Devine and Kieran Jack McGinley (eds), *Left Lives in Twentieth Century Ireland* (Dublin, 2017), p. 81; *John Swift*, pp 99–101.

64. NLI, Rosamond Jacob Papers, diaries, 32,582/1–170, 31 October 1936; C. S. Andrews, *Man of No Property* (Dublin, 1982), p. 40.
65. Ó hEidirisceoil, 'A personal memoir of the thirties', p. 206.
66. Klaus (ed), *Strong Words, Brave Deeds*, p.114; cited in East Wall History Group, *In Support of An Ideal: Jack Nalty: From East Wall to the Ebro* (Dublin, 2018), p. 5.
67. Klaus, *Strong Words, Brave Deeds*, p. 147.
68. Ibid., pp 22–33, 35–6, 147–50.
69. Joseph Donnelly, 'A memoir', in Kay Donnelly (ed), *Heroic Heart: A Charles Donnelly Reader* (Belfast, 2012), p. 65.
70. Leslie H. Daiken (comp), *Good-Bye, Twilight: Songs of the Struggle in Ireland* (London, 1936), p. xviii.
71. Donnelly, 'A memoir', p. 70.
72. A quintessentially liberal history, Terence Brown, *Ireland, A Social and Cultural History, 1922–79* (London, 1981), pp 168–9, is uncanny in the way it offers a mirror image of Daiken, whom it does not mention.
73. Daiken, *Good-Bye, Twilight*, p. xii.
74. Ibid., pp xi–xviii.
75. Hugh Thomas, *The Spanish Civil War* (London, 1965), p. 291 n.
76. Katrina Goldstone, 'Leslie Daiken and Harry Kernoff', in Emmet O'Connor and John Cunningham (eds), *Studies in Irish Radical Leadership: Lives on the Left* (Manchester, 2016), pp 201, 208; *Irish Democrat*, 10 April 1937.
77. *Irish Press*, 12 May 1934; Burton, 'The Spanish Civil War'.
78. Charles Donnelly, 'Literature in Ireland', in *Comhthrom Féinne*, 5:4 (1933), p. 65.
79. Eoghan Ó Duinnín, *La Niña Bonita agus An Róisín Dubh: Cuimhní Cinn ar Chogadh Catharta na Spáinne* (Baile Átha Cliath, 1986), p. 106.
80. Joseph O'Connor, *Even the Olives Are Bleeding: The Life and Times of Charles Donnelly* (Dublin, 1992), pp 46–8, 80; Donnelly, 'A memoir', pp 64–5; Gerald Dawe, 'Introduction', in Kay Donnelly (ed), *Heroic Heart: A Charles Donnelly Reader* (Belfast, 2012), pp 13–17. *Heroic Heart* incorporates Joseph Donnelly, *Charlie Donnelly: The Life and Poems* (Dublin, 1987); McLoughlin, *Fighting for Republican Spain*, pp 189–90.
81. Bob Doyle, *Brigadista: An Irishman's Fight Against Fascism* (Dublin, 2006), p. 143.
82. *Irish Democrat*, 17 April 1937.
83. Daiken, *Good-Bye, Twilight*, pp 78–9. For another example, see the poem by Mick McGinley, *Irish Democrat*, 10 April 1937.
84. Peadar O'Donnell, *Salud! An Irishman in Spain* (London, 1937), p. 187.
85. Ibid., pp 8–9.
86. Ibid., p. 124.
87. Ibid., p. 71.
88. Ibid., pp 74–5, 124, 134; Daiken, *Good-Bye, Twilight*, p. xiii.
89. Donal Ó Drisceoil, *Peadar O'Donnell* (Cork, 2001), pp 96–7; Peter Hegarty, *Peadar O'Donnell* (Cork, 1999), pp 227–40; Michael McInerney, *Peadar O'Donnell: Irish Social Rebel* (Dublin, 1974), pp 171–6.
90. O'Donnell, *Salud!*, p. 199.
91. Mitchell, *Storm Over Spain*, pp 59–60.

92. Kate O'Brien, *Farewell Spain* (London, 1937), xx, pp 221–2; Eibhear Walshe, 'Lock up your daughters: From ante-room to interior castle', in Eibhear Walshe (ed), *Ordinary People Dancing: essays on Kate O'Brien* (Cork, 1993), pp 156–7; *Irish Democrat*, 16 October 1937.
93. Francis McCullagh, *In Franco's Spain* (London, 1937); John Horgan, "The great war correspondent': Francis McCullagh, 1874-1956', in *Irish Historical Studies*, Vol. 36:144 (November 2009), pp 542–63.
94. We are obliged to Jason McGeoghan for this point.
95. Marx Memorial Library, London, International Brigade Memorial Archive, box 22, news bulletins and papers of the British battalion, file A: news bulletins of the International Brigades, *News Bulletins of the International Brigades*, I, April to December 1937, no.120, 30 April 1937: 'Ireland: the fascists desert their party'.
96. RGASPI, Proposals in connection with the CPI, 8 May 1937, f. 495, o. 89, d. 102, ll. 1-4.
97. RGASPI, Memorandum on Ireland, 22 May 1937, f. 495, o. 89, d. 102, ll. 5-9.
98. Andrew Thorpe, *The British Communist Party and Moscow, 1920–43* (Manchester, 2000), p. 216.
99. RGASPI, Meeting on the Irish question, 23 May 1937, f. 495, o. 14, d. 339, ll. 27-38; Commission of the Central Committee of the Communist Party of the Soviet Union (Bolsheviks) (eds), *History of the Communist Party of the Soviet Union (Bolsheviks)* (Moscow, 1945), pp 337–8.
100. Cronin, *Frank Ryan*, p.113; *Irish Press*, 24 June 1937.
101. Byers, 'Seán Murray, the Irish republican left and international communism, 1916–1962' (PhD, University of Ulster, Jordanstown, 2012), pp 173–4.
102. Milotte, *Communism in Modern Ireland*, pp 175–6.
103. *Workers' Republic*, May 1938.
104. RGASPI, The situation in Ireland and the crisis in the Communist Party, 2 August 1938, f. 495, o. 20, d. 252, ll. 22-35; Fragen für die Untersuchung in Irland, 9 August 1939, f. 495, o. 14, d. 340, ll. 3-5.
105. RGASPI, Zusammenfassung der Debatte zu dieser Frage auf der ZK-Sitzung der KP Englands am 1. und 2. Juli 1938, f. 495, o. 20, d. 252, ll. 36-49.
106. Milotte, *Communism in Modern Ireland*, pp 177–8.
107. *Irish Times*, 19 January 1939.
108. Leanne Lane, *Rosamond Jacob: Third Person Singular* (Dublin, 2010), pp 273–4; NLI, Rosamond Jacob Papers, diaries, 32,582/1–170, 13 December 1938; Carroll, *They Have Fooled You Again*, p. 221.
109. *Workers' Republic*, July 1938.
110. Elyot Knight, 'Spanish jig-saw', in *TCD Miscellany*, 19 November 1937.

THREE

# THE WAR IN THE NORTH

Following the attack on the Workers' College in her home in 63 Eccles Street during the anti-communist riots in Dublin in March 1933, the veteran socialist republican Charlotte Despard gathered a few of her favourite paintings, handed her crumbling Georgian mansion to the Friends of Soviet Russia and moved to the Newtownards Road. Her relocation to Unionist east Belfast personified the shifting climate in the 1930s.[1] As the Catholic Church flexed its biceps in the Free State, the North became the more liberal part of Ireland.

The specificities of anti-socialism in Northern Ireland have been overlooked, being subsumed into the generic conservatism that pervaded both communities in the six counties in the Stormont years. But the Unionists had their own brand of anti-socialism, and the Spanish Civil War elicited a unique response in the Catholic community. The chronic problems of Northern Ireland's obsolescent industries worsened in the slump that followed the Wall Street crash. Distress sparked incidents such as the outdoor relief strike in October 1932, when the Belfast RWG was instrumental in stimulating agitation for better pay and conditions for unemployed men, and Catholics and Protestants united in battles with the Royal Ulster Constabulary (RUC). For Unionists, the loss of working-class support was an abiding fear, and had prompted the foundation of the Ulster Unionist Labour Association in 1918. The Association's chairman, John M. Andrews, was Minister of Labour between 1921 and 1937. Immediately after the outdoor relief riots, the Youth Evangelistic Campaign brought 20 preachers to Belfast for a three-week mission against communism. A state on permanent alert for subversion had familiar ways of dealing with protest. Arrests of communists increased, and the Ulster Protestant League led violent opposition to communist street meetings. The League had recently been formed 'to safeguard the employment of Protestants', and it was during the slump that Unionist MPs made their most notorious appeals for sectarian solidarity and membership of the Orange Order increased.[2] Communist advances, however marginal, and repeated calls from socialists for a 'united front' between the NILP and the CPI made Unionists more paranoid about the left as a Trojan horse of republicanism.

The Royal Silver Jubilee celebrations in May 1935 ratcheted up the tension. Alderman Harry Midgley, the NILP's chairman and sole MP, found it impossible to hold public meetings. The NILP and CPI offices were attacked by loyalists in June. Sectarian violence in July left 13 dead, dozens injured and hundreds homeless. Once again, Madame Despard's home was considered unsafe. The disturbances prompted an inquiry by the National Council for Civil Liberties in London, which Stormont and Westminster ignored. For Unionists, royalty was the gift that kept on giving. The Silver Jubilee was followed by the celebrations for the coronation of King George VI on 12 May 1937. That summer, the Ulster Protestant League was joined by the Jubilee Defence Protestant Association in disrupting socialist meetings at the Custom House steps.[3]

Conversely, the rise of fascism in Europe and closer contact with British socialists was encouraging a radical subculture in Belfast, whose focal points were the bookshop run by Betty Sinclair for the CPI in Skipper Street and Davy McClean's Progressive Bookshop in Union Street. McClean was Belfast agent for the Left Book Club. In 1937 McClean asked Malachy Gray, 'a Fall's Road red', to become convenor of the Club in Belfast.[4] Gray 'jumped at the chance' as Spain was 'right at the centre' of the Club's activities.

As part of the UK, with an economy based on war-related industries – shipbuilding and engineering and textiles and clothing – Belfast was alert to the European crises and the threat of German rearmament in particular. John Hewitt, poet and 'Labourman', as NILP stalwarts liked to be known, was one of the few in the North who would speak of going *up* to Dublin, and yet could write of the Northern working class: 'Economically we have belonged to the British industrial complex. And then out of the economic involvement grew up the conception of loyalty. They were working for the British market so they were British. It wasn't the Irish market so they weren't Irish.'[5]

The Spanish Civil War made big waves in the rock pool of the far left. Andrew Boyd, a future organiser for the National Council of Labour Colleges, was typical in that his initial encounter with socialism was through John Strachey's pamphlet *Why You Ought to Be a Socialist*, bought at Belfast's Custom House steps at a meeting to protest against the Munich Agreement. Weeks later, his first political act was to attend a reception for International Brigaders in the York Street Labour Hall.[6]

The left in Northern Ireland at this time comprised the NILP, the SPNI and the CPI. Republican Congress membership in the six counties was confined to a few individuals. The three main factions all had their own approach to the

Civil War. Midgley was a bellwether of NILP opinion before losing the run of himself on Spain. A Connollyite during the third Home Rule crisis and vehemently anti-partition in 1921, he gradually abandoned socialist republicanism as Northern Ireland consolidated and by the 1930s was keen to re-orient the NILP from a cross-border to a cross-channel sensibility. Spain was an opportunity to bring it into lockstep with British Labour.

Spain, and Midgley, also exacerbated underlying tensions between Catholics and Protestants in the NILP. Some suspected that Midgley's passion for the cause reflected a latent anti-Catholicism. The SPNI would find itself increasingly at odds with Midgley's come-hithers to the British Labour Party.

Even more than the NILP, the CPI would reflect the shift in orientation from Dublin to Belfast. In March 1935 it dropped the 'Irish' prefix from the *Workers' Voice* to improve sales in Belfast, and its two branches gradually drifted apart. The Belfast branch hoped that Spain would bring about a 'left unity' alliance between the CPI and the NILP, something Midgley opposed and on which the SPNI was sharply divided by what the communists regarded as its Trotskyists.[7] Thanks to Spain and Munich, the CPI quietly consolidated its influence in the unions, and by 1939 it would be prioritising opposition to the Stormont government rather than Stormont itself.

## THE ULSTER INQUISITION

Unionists deplored Republican Spain and all forms of radicalism. It was editorial policy for the *Belfast News-Letter*, the *Northern Whig* and the *Belfast Telegraph* to stigmatise the Labour parties of Britain and Ireland as 'the socialists', lest readers associate them with honest workingmen or think them less menacing or less foreign than their continental counterparts. Spain was never debated at Stormont – which of course did not have a foreign affairs remit – or raised by Unionists at Westminster.[8] Even the fascist fringe of Unionist Ulster said little on Spain.[9] At the same time, Unionists regarded the Catholic Church in Spain as the agent of its own misfortune, a sorry witness for Christianity and the cause of Spain's decline. The 'failure of Romanism' was a theme in speeches on 'Black Saturday' 1936 – the 'fields' of the Royal Black Preceptory on the last Saturday in August – and the Orange assemblies on 12 July 1937.[10]

Wishing a plague on both houses, the Unionist press offered a more balanced reportage of the war than its nationalist counterparts. London's adoption of the non-interventionist policy seemed a sensible way of preventing the conflict from escalating into a European war, and reassuringly Victorian in its echo of 'splendid isolation' from the hot-headed continentals.

Horgan's characterisation of the *Belfast Telegraph*'s line as one of endorsing Whitehall's policy while taking a 'sideswipe at the Catholic Church' was true of the Unionist newspapers at large.[11] But they could vary on detail. Enniskillen's incongruously named *Impartial Reporter*, in reality a sectarian Argus, refused to publish an appeal from the Spanish Medical Relief Committee as it might aid 'the communists and murderers' in Madrid.[12] Each community saw Spain through its own sense of history and identity and Unionists needed no reminding of the approaching 350th anniversary of the Spanish armada. 'The Spaniard', according to the *Belfast Telegraph*, 'has been described as at once the perfect gentleman and the greatest embodiment of cruelty in the world. It was certainly so in the days of the Armada and the Inquisition, and it is much the same today. . . it is a sad reflection on the influence of the Church. . .'.[13] The *Derry Standard*, voice of the city's Presbyterian employers, covered the bombing of Guernica with the headings: 'Spain's Horrors, Huge Toll by German Bombs, 'NO SURRENDER', Basques Echo the Derry Watchword.'[14] An editorial entitled 'Ireland and Spain' opined:

> We believe Government agents committed outrages of an abominable character, but their opponents are certainly not qualified to sit in judgement upon them, even if we overlook the Guernica bombing, of which Franco vigorously protests his innocence. . . In this civil war there have been committed acts as barbarous as any of the Inquisition days, so we may take it that Spain has not advanced very far along the road to civilisation since the dark days of religious persecution in that country which more or less coincided with her preparations to invade Protestant England, and, as one of the leaders of the Armada stated, **to burn the Protestant Queen Elizabeth in the streets of London** [emphasis in the original].[15]

At the other end of the spectrum, there were Unionists who took a savage satisfaction in the spectacle in Spain. The vice-chairman of the Ulster Protestant League told his listeners not to worry about Spain: 'Let them stew in their own juice and exterminate themselves as much as they like – and the more they do it the better'.[16]

Nationalists traditionally looked on Labour as an ally. The last great Nationalist leader, Joe Devlin, who had died in 1934, advised his party to monopolise politics in Catholic areas and to let the NILP have a go at the Unionists elsewhere, giving Labour the possibility of winning mixed constituencies with a combination of blanket Catholic and radical Protestant votes. Labourmen had mixed feelings about accommodating 'Wee Joe'. Jack Beattie, MP was expelled from the NILP in 1934 for refusing to call a by-election in Belfast Central, which might have pitted his party against the Nationalists. Midgley, on the other hand, argued that Devlin's approach amounted to a mirror image of Unionist sectarianism – the Unionists did not contest majority Catholic constituencies. Like Ernest Blythe, he held that the best way to undermine the Unionist Party was to park the partition question pending a nationalist majority; a counsel of perfection that was too subtle for a bluntly divided society.[17]

Clerical fears of socialism, mirabile dictu, arose only when the NILP challenged the Nationalists. In contrast to the Protestant panic, the Catholic Church had little to say in public on the 1932 outdoor relief strike. But discreet clerical pressure would alter the composition of the Belfast CPI by June 1933, causing Dublin to tell the Comintern: 'the best progress is now made in the non-nationalist section.'[18]

Spain brought another turn of the dial. At their annual Lady's Day parades on 15 August 1936, the Ancient Order of Hibernians passed a resolution denouncing the 'campaign of Anti-Christ' in Spain. The Bishop of Down and Connor directed that 6 September should be a 'Day of Atonement and expiation for the sacrileges in Spain'.[19] What Spain did not change was the Northern clergy's jealous control of its flock. It extended no welcome to the Irish Christian Front, which failed to achieve the level of support it enjoyed in the Free State. Rumours that the Front intended to enter electoral politics persisted.[20]

Reports of anti-clerical excesses reinforced the authority of the clergy within the Catholic community, and the nationalist press was entirely pro-Franco. The main nationalist paper, the *Irish News*, had a daily circulation of about 50,000, and was edited by T. J. Campbell, Nationalist MP for Belfast Central and a Christian Front supporter. In the *Irish News*, as in all of the nationalist newspapers, Franco's troops were 'the patriots' and their enemies were 'Reds' and puppets of Soviet Russia.[21] Criticism of the insurgents was quickly taken for anti-Catholicism by a people raw from the taunts of Orangemen, Blackmen, Purplemen and Apprentice Boys with their endless calendar of marches. As an attack on the greatest shield of the Catholic community, it heightened the sense of beleaguerment felt by an abandoned people stuck on the wrong side of the line after 1921 and doomed to the humiliation of being second-class citizens in their own country.

Inevitably, it bared sectarian fangs. When Reverend E. H. Lewis-Crosby told a Church of Ireland synod that assaults on the Catholic Church in Spain were due to its leaders being 'hand in glove with those who have oppressed the peasant classes and others', he was likened by the *Irish News* to Uriah Heep, currying favour through 'groundless allegations against a great Catholic nation in its agony'.[22] Accusations of hypocrisy or double standards against the Unionists, the British, or what the *Derry Journal* called 'the pink press', was a regular defence. 'It is significant', noted the *Journal*, in the wake of the cross-channel furore over Guernica, 'that none of these [English newspapers] made any protest against the torturing and murdering of priests and nuns, the horrible desecration of the dead, and the burning of churches. On the contrary, they either denied or sought to justify these abominable crimes.'[23]

Other tu quoque ripostes to the British included massacres of the French during the Peninsular War, aerial bombing of Wazir tribesmen on the northwest frontier of British India and the starvation of Boer women and children in South African concentration camps, not to mention the curse of Cromwell, transportation to the Barbadoes, the Great Famine, 'souperism', the Black and Tans, partition, sectarian discrimination and the Special Powers Act. The priests were talismans against the Carthaginian sea-monster, as John Mitchel dubbed the British empire, and no people in Ireland were as tightly policed by the clergy as six-county Catholics. But the priests could not control the public sphere in the North as they could in the south.[24]

It was moreover a time when nationalist Ireland still pursued the dream of reviving an integral Gaelic culture and restoring the nation broken at Kinsale in 1601; a time when the *Derry Journal* could editorialise on 'The jazz plague' and fulminate against 'Los Angeles "culture"', the dance hall, and the 'moral consequences of the jazz fever, the infection of the nigger and lounge-lizard schools of melody'.[25] The very internationalism of communism and a cause like the Spanish Republic was itself an alien concept. By the same token, the *Journal* was admitting the popularity of Hollywood and the impact of cosmopolitanism. Ultimately, Northern engagement with Franco's Spain was weaker than the Free State's. The number of Northern volunteers for Eoin O'Duffy's brigade was relatively small, and it has been argued that recruitment owed something to a personal loyalty. O'Duffy was officer commanding the Monaghan Brigade, 5th Northern Division during the War of Independence. Michael Collins had sent him to Belfast at the height of the pogroms in 1921 and his organisation of the IRA's Belfast Brigade in defence of Catholic homes made a lasting impression.[26]

### THE SOCIALIST PARTY

The first Irish party to send men to Spain after the outbreak of the Civil War was the SPNI. With a membership of about 120, the party included some of the NILP's most dynamic personalities. In the manner of British socialist parties, it also had a youth section, a Clarion Rambling Club and a Clarion Cycling Club.[27] The Clarion clubs had emerged in England in the 1890s to foster socialist fellowship through recreation. Their horror at smoky, industrial society and preciousness for the countryside as a place of leisure had no resonance in Ireland, where the countryside was a place of toil and poverty.

By early August the SPNI was pitching into the work for Spain. 'Night and day we were at it', recalled party secretary Jack Macgougan.[28] Its opening discussion on Spain led to a clamour for sending volunteers to fight. It was agreed to lobby the NILP, the League of Nations Union, the Peace League, the CPI and the trade unions in the first instance.

Opposition quickly materialised. A street meeting in west Belfast on 12 August nearly triggered a riot amid shouts of 'Up General Franco'.[29] A second meeting, in the Labour Hall in York Street on 14 August, drew a capacity crowd. After some disturbance, Jack Dorricott rose to speak. An ex-miner from Durham, Dorricott had moved to Belfast in 1929 to become an organiser for the National Council of Labour Colleges, and made the Colleges a significant factor in the politicisation of emerging shop stewards.[30] Though a member of the NILP, he made no secret of his communist sympathies or pro-Soviet views, which were broadly in keeping with the Labour Colleges' Marxist philosophy. It was a time when working-class education was taken seriously. Over the summer of 1930, for example, when inter-war trade unionism in Northern Ireland was at its lowest ebb, Dorricott spoke to 25 union branches.[31] In York Street, over persistent heckling, Dorricott rejected reports of church burning in Spain with incredulity. 'Did anyone really believe,' he asked, 'that the masses in Spain would destroy their own faith?'. Peadar O'Donnell, just returned from Catalonia, offered a more accurate perspective, though it was hardly the whole truth.

> Under [the] Government the Roman Catholic people of Spain attended their churches Sunday after Sunday and lived their normal lives without interference of any kind. Describing a scene of which he was an eye-witness in which, in a provincial town, a score of young men went into a church and threw its contents onto the street, Mr O'Donnell said the reason the inhabitants stood looking on inert and paralysed was that their own priests had adopted an attitude antagonistic to the workers' movements. There was never any fear of the church being burned or the priest being molested, but at the back of people's minds there lurked resentment against the Fascist-minded attitude of the priests.[32]

Midgley and Bill McCullough, Belfast District Organiser of the CPI and secretary of the Belfast no.1 branch of the National Union of Railwaymen, also spoke.

In mid-August the SPNI decided to subvent a medical unit of four doctors, four nurses and eight first-aid men, and the Spanish Medical Relief

Committee was established to 'support the Spanish government and workers in their heroic stand for political liberty'.[33] The scheme was soon modified in favour of funding two drivers for a Scottish ambulance unit being assembled by businessman and Provost of Glasgow University Sir Daniel Stevenson with the patronage of prominent Scottish Liberals. Macgougan felt the route to what would become the International Brigades was precluded by communist hostility. As late as December 1936, George Orwell, whose *Homage to Catalonia* did much to shape the popular British view of the war after 1945, thought he needed approval from the CPGB to join the Republican forces. Once in Barcelona, he used his ILP contacts to avoid the International Brigades. The SPNI shared the ILP's view of communists as authoritarian and manipulative. Forty-five volunteered for the Scottish ambulance unit. The chosen two, elected by ballot, were Joe Boyd and Fred McMahon.[34]

Both were unusual volunteers in being relatively old and in steady, white-collar employment. Born in 1907, Boyd was raised on the family farm near Coalisland. At the age of ten he moved with his family to Belfast and then to New York. Returning to Belfast in the early 1930s, Joe and his brother, John, set up a dairy in Ulsterville Gardens in salubrious south Belfast. Using American pasteurising and bottling techniques, the business flourished and became the leading supplier of bottled milk to Belfast schools. Joe immersed himself in the culture of the contemporary British left, being an atheist – a Protestant atheist – and a member of the Clarion Cycling Club and the Fabian Society, as well as the SPNI. His experience as a trainee pharmacist and truck driver stood him in good stead in the ballot, and as a pacifist he would not have served as a combatant. McMahon, a 25-year-old Catholic, lived with his widowed mother at 30 Ravenhill Street in east Belfast and worked as a clerk in W. J. Jenkins & Co., a clothing and handkerchief manufacturers in Bedford Street. He had been elected SPNI chairman in 1935 and was secretary of the Clarion Cycling Club. Macgougan remembered him as a 'real live wire'. He put his motives bluntly: 'I was an anti-fascist – that's why I went to Spain – I was violently anti-fascist.' Both told the *Belfast Telegraph* that they volunteered for humanitarian reasons and to defend democracy. Both were single, probably a requirement of candidates.[35]

On 17 September, inoculated against typhoid and vaccinated against smallpox, the 19 men of the Scottish medical unit left Glasgow in a convoy of 6 ambulances and a supply lorry, led by Fernanda 'Feddie' Jacobsen. Travelling south from Calais they loaded up provisions, knowing that food was scarce in Spain, and crossed the border into Portbou, one of few places where the Republic could obtain foreign supplies. Boyd had his first direct encounter with Spanish politics in Barcelona, where he met both anarchists and 'fanatics like the Communists – often brave but bigoted individuals' – and the first

British volunteers. Boyd and McMahon had a long conversation with Nat Cohen, who had been cycling to the People's Olympiad, a socialist alternative to the 'Nazi Olympics' in Berlin, due to open on 20 July. Cohen, an East End garment worker and communist, stayed on and hoped to expand his 'centuria', actually about ten compatriots, into a British battalion in one of the militias. The battalion was to be called after Tom Mann, a living legend of British trade unionism and founder of the CPGB.[36] National pride, or using Spain to advance politics back home, was already materialising, even in the most international of contexts.

The convoy then motored on to Valencia and reached Madrid on 1 October. After three days in the capital, they were deployed to Aranjuez, 50 km south, which was to be their base on the Toledo front. But the advance on Madrid under one of Franco's most important and ruthless generals, Juan Yagüe, already notorious as 'the butcher of Badajoz', continued relentlessly. The paramedics found themselves continually falling back. At Parla, on the southern outskirts of Madrid, they were overtaken again, forcing Boyd's unit into a hasty retreat, and compelling him to drive over the bodies of dead children scattered across the plaza. The front stabilised at the gates of Madrid. For Boyd, it was a short respite. He recalled in 1976:

> On November 8 – my birthday – my Belfast friend and I were caught by the Fascists. The war was fought on an open front – holding hills and towns, not a solid line of defence. We were heading for Carabanchel, outside Madrid, and knew that the day before there had been heavy Nationalist shelling in the area and that they had captured the village. But we were told our side had retaken it... Our soldiers warned us in Spanish (which we couldn't then understand) not to venture past them. But we drove on and met two boys with red crosses on their arms... Turning a corner, we ran smack into a Fascist machine gun post. They hauled us out of the ambulance. One of the boys was murdered there and then.[37]

As Boyd and McMahon were taken to the rear they noticed evidence of a mass execution, and were shocked to see that some of the victims were wearing Red Cross armbands. Both feared a similar fate until they bandaged a wounded soldier who spoke English and convinced their captors that they were paramedics and not Russian. Boyd continued: 'At Getafe we were given a gruelling interrogation by a man I believe now to be the Nationalist General Yagüe, who massacred so many people in the building at Badajoz. We weren't shot, but we were sent to Toledo and kept in the cellar of a hotel.' Another guest in the hotel was the nominal President of the Nationalist junta, General Miguel Cabanellas, who appeared in a nightgown to ask Boyd about Madrid and talk generally about the war. Emerging from a further interrogation they noticed a man who looked English and shouted to him their names and a request to contact the British consul. Next day they were given their first meal since capture and were driven to Salamanca and better treatment. Midgley was quick off the mark with a flurry of telegrams to Clement Attlee, leader of the British Labour Party, and Walter Citrine, secretary of the Trades Union Congress. With Provost Stevenson's help he enlisted the British Foreign Secretary, Anthony Eden, to negotiate a release. On 20 November Boyd and McMahon were repatriated via Lisbon. Back in Belfast, they denied seeing any atrocities by government troops and affirmed their intention to return to the war.[38]

The ambulance unit was not without controversy in other respects. Five Scots were sent home in October for 'looting bodies on the field', a charge they described as 'fantastic'. Two others chose to go back with them. The problems were typical. Feddie Jacobsen, a Liberal Party official in Scotland, encountered difficulties with the politics of her medics and complained of communist attempts at infiltration. The unit had an awkward relationship with the more communist influenced Spanish Medical Aid Committee and three members resigned over political differences in 1937.[39] A CPGB investigation of desertion accused Scottish ambulances of being used to evacuate deserters from Madrid to Valencia and home to England.[40] Inexperience, naivety and politics caused the field medical units from Britain to be dogged by misfortune in Spain.[41]

Meanwhile, the SPNI pressed on with meetings every two or three weeks, the great majority of them on Spain. On 20 September it returned to the Custom House steps – the first Labour body to do so for 18 months – and drew 250 people to a meeting of the Spanish Medical Relief Committee.[42] Attendances usually varied between 200 and 400, and Spain was likely to draw the larger numbers. On St Valentine's night, 1937, the SPNI screened *The Defence of Madrid*.[43] The hour-long documentary was regarded as excellent propaganda. The SPNI offered to show it anywhere in the six counties in conjunction with a lecture. The United Patternmakers' Association at least took up the offer.[44] The SPNI's best known action for Spain was a meeting in the Ulster Hall on 24 March 1937. The star turns were Fr Ramón Laborda and O'Donnell, who was billed as a famous author and eye witness on Spain. They were joined on stage by Madame Despard. Midgley, a forceful orator, 'cried off'. 'Many felt it was because of the association with O'Donnell and a Catholic priest,' according to Macgougan.[45] Expecting trouble, the Ulster Hall management asked for a deposit of £150, and were surprised when Macgougan produced the money. Despite the capacity attendance, the trouble was confined to a few university students shouting 'Up Franco' and 'What about the murder of nuns?'. Presiding, Victor Halley said he hoped the meeting would expose the lie that the war was one of Christ and anti-Christ. Laborda then sang a Basque salutation to a pianoforte accompaniment.

After O'Donnell read his speech, Laborda ventured into English to complain about the Irish Church's 'pre-judgement' of events in Spain. 'Not one Irish priest has asked me about the war,' he said. O'Donnell spoke on the role of industrial and land-ownership problems in Spanish politics. He admitted that mistakes had been made, 'but if priests and parsons would keep out of politics, people would no more think of attacking them or their churches than they would a hospital. . .'. The meeting concluded with a repudiation of 'the Fascist followers of General O'Duffy as representing Ireland either north or south. . .'.[46]

Both Laborda and O'Donnell had been prevented from addressing the 'Literific', the debating society in Queen's University, on 8 March, arriving to find the doors locked by the Students' Representative Council.[47] Plausibly, the Council was bothered more by O'Donnell's republicanism than by Fr Laborda. The student body at Queen's was about 20 per cent Catholic. As yet, the Catholic middle-class thought it patriotic to send its sons and daughters to UCD. The Council's organ, the *New Northman,* published several articles on Spain and reflected liberal Unionism in expressing its horror of the war and incredulity at the Catholic endorsement of Franco and his atrocities to be found in the *Irish News* and the Vatican.[48] Queensmen were a little more politicised than their counterparts in Cork and Galway, but less animated than those in Dublin. The *New Northman* struggled to stay afloat. A more accurate reflection of student attitudes is found in the Queen's rag mag, *Pro Tanto Quid,* in the headline: 'The War in Spain – half time scores, Insurgents 3, Government 3.'[49]

The CPI's hopes of a formal popular front were disappointed. There was to be no equivalent in the North to the cooperation achieved through the *Irish Democrat*. However, a degree of unity was reached through the Left Book Club and its offshoots, the Progressive Publications Society and the Theatre Guild. The Guild opened its first production, *Waiting for Lefty*, in December 1937. Other ventures included the SPNI and Left Book Club sponsored Arms for Spain Committee, the Belfast Anti-Fascist Committee and branches of Irish Friends of the Spanish Republic and the International Brigades Dependents' Aid Committee.[50] Some fizzled out after a few meetings. An activist could expect to find himself on several committees and there was only so much the stage army of Belfast socialists could sustain. The NILP certainly, and the SPNI possibly, lost Catholic comrades over Spain.

The most successful humanitarian mission was the London-based National Joint Committee for Spanish Relief, established in late 1936 to coordinate the divers relief efforts. In England, pro-Franco elements denounced it as a political stunt. A Northern Ireland section was chaired by the young and debonair eighth Earl of Antrim. It contributed 100 tons of food, clothes and medical supplies to a ship that called at Belfast in February 1939 en route for Liverpool and Spain. One quarter of the consignment came from Fr Michael O'Flanagan's Irish Foodship for Spain Committee. The southern convoy flew Irish tricolours to the border, where they switched to Spanish colours. With his flair for publicity, Lord Antrim arranged a 'parade of lorries' through the streets of Belfast, led by Midgley in a car with a loud hailer. The cross-channel dockers, who were Protestant and in the ATGWU, gave their services voluntarily and made a collection for Spain. Had the ship been sailing directly to Spain it would have been handled – or not – by the deep-sea dockers, who were Catholic and in the Irish Transport and General Workers' Union. By the time it was dissolved in June 1939, Antrim's committee had raised £1,029, aside from the ship.[51] Another aristocratic intervention came from the 'red Duchess' of Atholl, who spoke for the Northern Ireland Joint Committee for Spanish Relief in Belfast to raise funds for Basque child refugees.[52]

### HARRY MIDGLEY AND THE NILP

The *Irish News* signalled its stance on the Civil War on 23 July 1936 with an editorial entitled 'The communist bid in Spain'. Another editorial, 'For Catholic Spain', followed on 28 July, and a further 27 on Spain between October and December 1936.[53] Midgley was drawn like a moth to a candle. His Christian socialist faith left him no choice, he said. 'Real communism', he told the *Irish News*, in words that merely confirmed Catholic suspicions that communism was the fons et origo of it all, 'simply means the application of the Gospel of Jesus to human society'. Communism was problematic in the Free State. In the six counties, so too was Christianity. Midgley's father was a late convert to Methodism. He died when Harry was seven, and his widow remarried into the austere Plymouth Brethren.

Though a 'gentile' in the Brethren household, Harry was influenced by their sola scriptura theology and aversion to ritual.[54] His first letter to the *Irish News* appeared on 29 July. In increasingly acrimonious contributions, he deplored the paper's reportage for its exclusive concern for Catholics, its use of lurid 'atrocity stories' and its representation of the protagonists as 'Reds' and 'Christian patriots'. Midgley in turn provoked a flood of angry correspondence over the next two months, accusing the Madrid government of being as undemocratic as Stormont, financed by Moscow, and in cahoots with Freemasons. Other letters were more nuanced and raised reasonable concerns about what was happening in Spain. Midgley tended to treat them all as one and to see Catholics as hopelessly single-minded, obsessed with their Church and incapable of understanding the meaning of civil liberty and pluralism.

The exchanges plumbed new depths when J. J. McCarroll, Nationalist MP for Foyle and proprietor/editor of the *Derry Journal*, weighed into the fray. Insulting Midgley personally, he labelled him anti-Catholic, asked why he hadn't supported a Nationalist motion at Stormont against discrimination in employment, wondered why the Belfast socialists had not been so concerned about Catholic victims of the 1935 riots and warned that Midgley's Stormont seat in Belfast's highly marginal Dock constituency depended on Catholic votes. Midgely replied in kind, sneering at McCarroll and his 'puny little sectarian whimperings'. Knowing McCarroll was right about his Stormont seat, he played the martyr. 'If', he wrote, 'I am to be driven out of public life because I proclaim the faith within me and stand for what I believe to be true then I submit that the people who take up such an attitude are unutterable bigots, whether they call themselves Protestants or Catholics.'[55]

Midgley had become a pamphleteer of late and published four since 1933. The most recent was entitled *A Bombshell of Facts on Home and Foreign Affairs*, reflecting the increasingly formative impact of international developments on Midgley's domestic politics. In September 1936 he added a fifth pamphlet, *Spain: The Press, The Pulpit and the Truth*, based on a lengthy letter to the *Irish News*. The prologue indicated the way in which he saw anti-fascism and anglo-centrism as intertwined:

> I am determined that the workers of Northern Ireland shall be warned off the fate which may befall them and the workers of Great Britain if the forces of Democracy and Representative Government are overthrown in Spain by the cruel and arrogant forces of Fascism. A Fascist victory in Spain means new life, hope and inspiration to Mussolini and Hitler; a new menace to Democratic Government in Britain and France, and the inevitability of world war.[56]

The pamphlet centred on the atrocities. Midgley acknowledged that government troops had been responsible in cases, pleading that cruelties were inseparable from war. He denied that the Republican side was exclusively responsible for excesses or that they reflected the policies of the popular front. Giving examples, he argued that reports in the *Irish News* had been exposed as lies in English papers like *The Times* and the *Manchester Guardian*. He also cited cases of atrocities by the Francoists, and questioned the anomaly of using Moslem troops to defend Christianity and the morality of allies who had imprisoned workers in Germany and Italy and used poisoned gas against

Christians in Abyssinia. Playing a trump card, he dared the *Irish News* to explain the roots of Spanish anti-clericalism. Midgley's apologia was more extreme than that of most Unionists, who were quite willing to condemn the church burning unreservedly, and the mask slipped when he appeared to equate the Catholic Church with 'superstition and oppression'. He has, of course, been vindicated in his arguments on atrocities.[57]

The controversy might not have been so serious for Midgley had it not led to confrontations with Catholic clerics. Fr J.P. Burke, preaching in Newry Cathedral, commended Catholics in Omagh for leaving the ATGWU after it donated £1,000 to 'the Reds in Spain'. 'Some of your Labour leaders are openly advocating support for the Communist movement,' he warned. 'Catholics in Omagh have left the Transport Union in protest. Catholic workmen in Armagh have publicly asked for prayers and Masses for the Catholic cause in Spain. What of Newry?'.[58] The epilogue in Midgley's pamphlet referred Fr Burke to the defence of the Spanish government by Monica Whately, founder of the Catholic Women's Suffrage Society, a former ILP'er and an entrant in *The Catholic Who's Who* for 1936.[59] 'Does Fr Burke think he is doing a good day's work by introducing sectarianism into the Trade Union Movement?', asked Midgley.

In October Monsignor Arthur Ryan, lecturer in scholastic philosophy at Queen's University, spoke to a large audience in St Mary's Hall in central Belfast. Before citing lurid examples of anti-clericalism and singling out Labour for its willingness to collude with communists, Ryan referred to bigots 'exulting' in the plight of Spanish Catholicism and pillorying the Church as the enemy of liberty, while ignoring the illiberal suppression of all religions by the Red regime in Madrid. Spanish Catholics had accepted the Republic, according to Ryan, only to have their newspapers suspended and religious buildings attacked by Red mobs, leaving them no choice but revolt.[60] Midgley responded on 25 October in a lecture in the York Street Labour Hall entitled: 'A reply to Dr Ryan'. Three hundred people paid the 3d admission, among them Ryan, who exchanged greetings with his antagonist.

Midgley's own anti-Catholicism allowed him to come closer than other socialists in representing the reality of anti-clericalism in Spain. He deplored the fact that for 450 years the Church had enjoyed 'dominion over the spiritual lives' of the Spaniards and control of 'education, politics, industry, commerce, land policy, and finance'. Obstructing any attempt at reform, it had earned the hatred of a people who were now exacting their revenge. There was talk of persecution today, but had Ryan protested when the Spanish government slaughtered thousands of workers and imprisoned some 30,000 in 1934? The Church in Ireland had blundered in backing tyranny in Spain and one day

Ireland would tell the clergy to stick to religion and leave politics and economics to the people. 'I will probably lose my position in public life as the result of the stand I have taken,' he predicted, 'but I deny the right of any Church to dictate how I should think.'

Invited to reply, Ryan reiterated that Spain's 1931 constitution was unfair to Catholics and that the popular front's anti-clericalism gave them no option but rebellion. Misled by left-wing slogans 'dear to his heart', Midgley was failing to see the facts. Concluding on a personal note, he added that he too was a socialist, and he would be sorry to see Midgley victimised.[61]

Matters worsened after Midgley spoke in Dromore Town Hall on 9 November and argued that as the Catholic Church had controlled education for centuries it was to blame for the high level of illiteracy and the failure of politics in Spain. The atrocities were to be expected in war, the more so as some clergy had taken up arms against the government. Even the genial Ryan turned against him. Deploring Midgley's 'abusive epithets and sneering innuendo', he bracketed socialists and Orangemen as an 'unholy alliance' united in badgering the long-suffering Northern minority.[62] As both sides wrapped themselves in victimhood, the alienation of Catholics from Midgley was complete. But Midgley continued to throw caution to the winds, telling the *Irish News*:

> That the Rebels have been largely composed of Moors (Mohammedans) and Foreign Legionnaires recruited from the scum of the earth, and that part of their campaign consists in ravishing and raping the women of Spain seems to make no difference to [Catholic] clerics who seem more anxious to secure a return of their ancient autocratic power which was taken away from them by the Spanish Constitution of 1931. . . We know that superstition has given us delusions and illusions, dreams and visions. ceremonies and cruelties, faith and fanaticism, beggars and bigots, persecutions and prayers, theology and torture, piety and poverty, saints and slaves. and mummeries, disease and death. Science will put honesty above hypocrisy: mental veracity above blind belief. It will teach the religion of usefulness. It will put thoughtful doubt above thoughtless faith. It will give us philosophers and thinkers, instead of theologians and slaves. Greater, grander, nobler than all else—it will make the world free.[63]

Ryan reckoned he had a 'rosy future' as an orator for the Ulster Protestant League or, as the *Derry Journal* styled it, 'the "Ulster" Protestant League'.[64]

The NILP had no difficulty with Midgley's anti-fascism. Spain was the subject of much attention at its annual conference on 29–30 August 1936, and a motion of solidarity with the Republic was passed.[65] The Ulster Medical Aid for Spain Committee was appointed on Midgley's initiative. Midgley and

Sam Haslett, SPNI, the joint secretaries, would devote considerable time to the project. The name was itself significant. Unionists were pushing the British government to have Northern Ireland rebranded 'Ulster', to the indignation of nationalists, and a few Unionists. The *Derry Journal* referred to it disparagingly as 'the Midgley committee'. Similarly, Midgley referred invariably to 'the Spanish government' rather than 'the Republic'. Most of the SPNI were unhappy with Midgley's efforts to bring the NILP into a British rather than an Irish context. Midgley's supporters made their move against the NILP's traditional ambivalence on identity politics at the 1937 annual conference, calling for cooperation with Labour 'throughout the British Commonwealth'. Midgley himself compared Irish nationalism with 'Hitlerism' and claimed that the people of Northern Ireland, with their centuries of marination in Anglo-Saxon political values, had no desire to follow the Free State down the path of isolation. An amendment from the Armagh branch, proposing collaboration with workers in the south to achieve Irish unity, was heavily defeated on a card vote, as was another SPNI push for left unity with the CPI. Midgley regarded the conference as a triumph and thought he had laid the basis of a new liaison with British Labour that would make the NILP less vulnerable on the constitutional question and address the chronic problem of inadequate funding for the party from the amalgamateds.[66]

But many comrades were uncomfortable with his breach of conventions on talking about religion in Ulster, and were beginning to see him as anti-Catholic. Gray remembered him in 1938 lambasting the Catholic Church when the meeting was supposed to be about Munich: 'I had a lot to learn, particularly from Harry Midgley, on how not to behave in the political life of Northern Ireland.'[67] Precisely because it was so divided along sectarian lines, what might be regarded as acceptably secular or anti-clerical elsewhere was frowned on in liberal circles in the North.

In January 1938 Prime Minister Craigavon called a snap election, saying he wanted a mandate against Éire's new constitution, which claimed jurisdiction over the entire island. The NILP had yet to resolve the question of trade union funding and a hasty appeal from the British Labour Party to assist 'our Irish comrades' did little to help. The sinews of the party were still bruised by the polemics over Spain. Nonetheless there were grounds for optimism. Nationalists boycotted the elections in several constituencies and a novel feature of the hustings was the number of Unionist splinter groups entering the lists on social issues. Instead, the NILP saw its share of the poll fall from 8.7 per cent in 1933 to 5.7 per cent.

Its sole success was a fluke, and ironic in view of Midgley's pro-Union strategy. Paddy Agnew, an anti-partitionist, won South Armagh unopposed because of the boycott by local Nationalists. It was the only time the NILP won a Stormont seat outside Belfast. In Dock, the Nationalists decided to field a candidate, James Collins, and split the anti-Unionist vote rather than see Midgley returned. Collins raised the Monsignor Ryan controversy and Midgley's campaign was harassed by crowds of young people shouting 'Up Franco' and 'Remember Spain', and singing 'Amhrán na bhFiann'. On one farcical occasion Midgley tried to assuage them with a rendition of 'God Save Ireland'. His brake had to be tailed by RUC tenders, after being rushed by angry mobs. At least two Labour meetings were abandoned and Midgley eventually confined himself to the Protestant streets. Dock had about 4,500 Catholic voters. The figures suggest he lost about 3,000 of them.

**Table 3.1:** Dock general election results, 1933, 1938

| | |
|---|---|
| *1933* | H. C. Midgley (NILP) 4,893 (57.0 per cent) |
| | Charles Blakiston-Houston (Unionist) 3,685 (43.0 per cent) |
| | Turnout 77.5 per cent |
| *1938* | G. A. Clark (Unionist) 3,578 (42.6 per cent) |
| | James Collins (Nationalist) 2,891 (34.5 per cent) |
| | H. C. Midgley (NILP) 1,943 (22.5 per cent) |
| | Turnout 82.5 per cent |

Midgley attributed his defeat to the power of the Catholic Church, Spain and 'the [Irish] unity question'. 'The Roman Catholics in Ireland', he said, 'have been, and are still being misled by their leaders with regard to Spanish affairs, but some day they will realise this for themselves and it will be a matter for them to deal with.'[68] Wiping his hands of Dock he embarked on a journey that would take him into the Unionist Party and the Orange Order and earn him the sobriquet 'Lord Linfield' with his former comrades.[69] Midgley's reputation was also thrown at NILP candidates in other Belfast constituencies, notably Oldpark and Falls.[70]

Spain was raised again at the NILP annual conference in October 1938. The conference unanimously expressed its admiration for the Spanish government and deplored the policy designed to prevent it from securing weapons to 'liberate their country from the Fascist invader'. An amendment from Derry proposed to replace the motion with one denouncing atrocities and fascist aggression and hope that democracy would prevail in Spain. E. McGowan said that they were 'up against it owing to the attitude of their people on the Spanish issue. The Labour Party in Derry was really working under a cloak.' 'I am a Catholic', he concluded, 'and I say that we in the Labour movement should cut this Spanish business out.' Midgley had the amendment rejected, reiterating that those who called for tolerance in Spain were intolerant in Ireland and that the theologians should keep out of politics. He added that his services to NILP 'country' branches had frequently been refused because of his stance on Spain.[71]

### TRADE UNIONS

Trade unions were among the few organisations in Northern Ireland that transcended the religious and political divisions. Because industrialising Ulster had an economically integrated labour force, in which Catholics were a subaltern rather than a parallel caste, it produced one, formally secular, trade union movement rather than two confessional ones. With a few exceptions, such as the docks and teaching, where workforces were overwhelmingly from one community, there was little appetite for Irish or 'Ulster' unions. Union officialdom was predominantly Protestant. A survey of 53 unions in 1959 found that of 379 branch secretaries 80 per cent were Protestant; as the results did not include some 'Ulster' unions, the true figure was certainly higher.

Inevitably, unions reflected the religious composition of employment. Taking the two biggest unions, Catholics accounted for 46 per cent of branch secretaries in the mainly unskilled ATGWU, and 12 per cent in the Amalgamated Engineering Union.[72] The bulk of Northern trade unionists were part of the British labour movement and nominally sympathetic to the Spanish Republic. The amalgamateds had extended to all of Ireland in the late 19th century and accounted for about 75 per cent of trade unionists in Ireland in 1900. When Jim Larkin initiated a revival of Irish trade unionism in the south, the North stayed stubbornly with the amalgamateds. About 70 unions represented 80,000 out of 300,000 insured workers in 1937. Less than 5,000 were in Free State-based unions, 62,500 were in British-based unions and the remainder were in Northern Ireland-based unions.[73] Unions were scarcely involved with the Irish Trade Union Congress and there was little incentive for them to have a public voice. The North's provincial status and 'step by step', the government's commitment to duplicate Westminster legislation whether it agreed with it or not, meant that the key decisions on wages, conditions and the economy were made in London. The key function of unions was to track cross-channel wage rates and secure parity, if possible. Only 23,847 members of amalgamateds were 'contracted in' to pay dues into their union's political fund. Envious of the relationship between the British Labour Party and its affiliates, Midgley complained regularly about the lack of trade union support for, and rank and file engagement with, the NILP.[74]

The Spanish Civil War did nothing to improve things. McMahon recalled 'the average trade unionist [as] apathetic' on Spain, with the exception of a few shop stewards. Midgley's own union, the National Union of Distributive and Allied Workers, reported resignations on account of its stand on the war.[75] In 1937 Belfast trades council cancelled its May Day parade and held an indoor meeting on Spain instead. The parade was also dispensed with in 1938 in favour of a rally at the Custom House steps, with resolutions passed condemning the non-intervention pact and the 'open support' given by the British government to the Fascist powers in their conquests of Austria, Spain and China.[76]

The best-known instance of union dissent was the defection of Catholics in Omagh from the ATGWU referred to by Fr Burke in September 1936. Their branch protested that the fight in Spain was between communism and Christianity and that 'the terror' in Spain had been engineered by agents of Moscow. The ATGWU's general secretary Ernest Bevin spoke in Derry's Guildhall in June 1938. Only the hecklers mentioned Spain. In Belfast the most influential union was the Amalgamated Engineering Union, which had been controlled by the Ulster Unionist Labour Association until the mid-1920s, when the Unionists were displaced by socialists. The union's president issued a strong appeal for the Spanish Republic in April 1938, but it was not until 1939 that the union established its own Labour Group in Belfast. Andrew Boyd, then an apprentice in Harland and Wolff, was advised by his own branch secretary that if he wished to 'get on' in the Engineers he should join the Freemasons. Boyd reckoned the masons were well placed throughout trade union officialdom in Northern Ireland.[77] Soon after the trouble in Omagh, a row erupted in the Derry branch of the National Union of General and Municipal Workers over a motion condemning Brother Frank Callaghan for his participation in 'the Midgley committee'. Callaghan explained to the branch that the meeting he had attended was of the NILP executive and dissociated himself from Midgely and his views. He was also quizzed on his attitude to communism. The assembly elicited divided opinions on Spain. September 1936 marked the high point of the disruption, and Callaghan became known throughout the six counties.

Though still in the NILP, Callaghan campaigned in Pottinger in the 1938 Stormont elections, where Beattie stood on an independent Labour ticket. Catholics in the Short Strand made up a crucial part of his vote and Catholic teachers comprised a greater share of his union. Beattie had been appointed an official of the Irish National Teachers' Organisation in 1934, a largely Catholic union in the six counties and instrumental in getting the 'Workers' Republic' reference deleted from the Irish Labour Party's constitution. Coincidentally or not, Beattie stayed quiet on Spain. His collaboration with Callaghan was intended to distance him from Midgley, evidently to some effect: he won the seat. Beattie was also prominent at a rally in the Ulster Hall, intended to impress the trades council's agenda on candidates. There was nothing said on Spain.[78] Protestants were more likely to go with the flow of sentiment in British-based unions. When the UK's Civil Service Clerical Association appealed for subscriptions to send an ambulance to Spain, the *Belfast Telegraph* reported 'singular success' for the scheme in coverage of Northern Ireland members.[79]

Another measure of popular attitudes to Civil War protagonists arose from the arrest of Bilbao-registered merchantmen between July and October 1937. The Valencia government had nationalised all shipping under the Spanish flag, and when one of the captains in Belfast sought to put the edict into effect he was challenged by the vessels' owners. The *Eolo*, *Apolo* and *Cobetas*, with grain and maize from Argentina, were tied up, pending adjudication by the Admiralty Court. The Republicans among the ships' companies made contact with Midgley, who put up some of them in his home. They in turn joined him on political platforms.[80] In Derry three tramp steamers with grain from the River Plate, the *Atalaya*, *Gorbea Mendi* and *Serentes*, were affected. The *Atalaya* and *Serentes* became the subject of litigation. Both continued to fly the Republican flag, though their skippers were Franquistas. While the *Derry Journal* referred to their crews as 'reds' or 'in sympathy with the Red junta', it is equally plausible that they favoured the Republic as they were Basque.

With help from public donations, the men were lodged in the city's seamen's home and local houses, but there was no official support from the Derry Labour Party, trade unions or other sources, and their money ran out within weeks. In October, 40 men from the *Atalaya* and *Serentes* entrained for Barcelona with the help of the Spanish government, leaving skeleton crews of about 50. Amidst great excitement, they were seen off from the Midland Station by over 100 well-wishers, including a few girlfriends. They had made a good impression on the locals as clean-living and educated and their attendance at Sunday mass was a boon to anti-Francoists. One of the remaining Spaniards later married the daughter of a local Italian fascist – the Derry Italian community having its own squad of Blackshirts. Another returned to Spain in the spring of 1938 and died fighting for the Republic.[81]

The ships drew wider interest on the far right. The pro-Nazi Link organisation in Britain championed Franco's claims, though the Ulster branch, run by Admiral Sir Barry Domvile, said nothing.[82] On 6 February 1938, three days before polling in the Stormont elections, over 100 of O'Duffy's followers, some of whom had fought in Spain, took a midnight special train from Dublin to Portadown. Forty-four then peeled off by rail-bus to Derry, while the remainder steamed on to Belfast. All claimed to be certified mariners or stokers and members of the National Sailors' and Firemen's Union. In Belfast, the dockers indicated that they would refuse to cooperate with them.

Also on 6 February, about 50 Spanish republican sailors arrived in Derry, along with an agent of the Valencia government. Both sides were anticipating the release of the boats by the Admiralty Court and intended to seize them immediately. There were moments of tension when O'Duffy's men and Spanish republicans were spotted at the same dance, but order prevailed. The absence of word from the Admiralty and quayside policing deterred action and the Irish fascists returned to Dublin with shouts of 'Up Franco'. In March, 35 Spanish fascist sailors arrived from Belfast to take over the *Serentes*. This too was frustrated, and the legal wrangles continued in the Admiralty Court. The Spaniards endured the idleness stoically, playing cards for hours, whittling wood with penknives and never talking politics with their enemies. The enemies united in August 1938 at a requiem mass in St Eugene's Cathedral for the first officer of the *Gorbea Mendi* who had drowned in Lough Foyle. The Franco junta was represented by a sub-agent from Liverpool. In March 1939 the ships were released by the Admiralty. With the fall of Madrid the Republicans in Derry left for Belfast to seek out Midgley. In July there were still 27 Republican sailors in Belfast living on charity. The Earl of Antrim issued an appeal for assistance. The remaining mariners decorated the flotilla for Franco's victory. In Belfast the crews were supplemented by 40 freshly arrived Spanish 'soldiers', as the *News-Letter* described them. Petitions of locals for work aboard were declined. At the end of April, the *Serentes* and *Atalaya* sailed for home. A large crowd gathered on the docks, waving Papal flags acquired for the Eucharistic Congress. The ships were followed by the *Gorbea Mendi* in May.[83]

On Spain, as on so much else, Northern Ireland was a place apart. While Catholics throughout Europe sided with Franco because of perceptions of the Republic's anti-clericalism, the Catholic response in the six counties was conditioned by the exceptional power of their clergy, the role of religion in defining the minority and the minority's image of itself as a beleaguered people. Protestants too were in an unusual position in loathing both antagonists. If, for Catholics, Spain was saints and Jesuits, for Protestants it was the Inquisition and the Armada. That curiosity allowed the North to be more objective on the war and more tolerant of radicalism than the Free State for the first time since partition.

The left made what it could of the freedom. But it also suffered internal disruption that offset that advantage. The major impact was on the mindset of the left. Northern comrades acquired a more European outlook than their southern counterparts. By the time of the Munich Agreement, Belfast socialists were focused firmly on the threat of another big war, determined that Britain should stand up to Hitler and convinced that they should stand together with Britain.

NOTES

1. Andro Linklater, *An Unhusbanded Life: Charlotte Despard, Suffragette, Socialist, and Sinn Féiner* (London, 1980), pp 241–2, 254.
2. Paddy Devlin, *Yes, We Have No Bananas! Outdoor Relief in Belfast, 1920–39* (Belfast, 1981), pp 138–9; Emmet O'Connor, *Reds and the Green: Ireland, Russia, and the Communist Internationals, 1919–43* (Dublin, 2004), p. 164; Andrew Boyd, *Holy War in Belfast* (Belfast, 1987), pp 205–18.
3. Graham Walker, *The Politics of Frustration: Harry Midgley and the Failure of Labour in Northern Ireland* (Manchester, 1985), pp 75–6; *Belfast Telegraph*, 1 November 1937.
4. Malachy Gray, 'A shop steward remembers', in *Saothar*, 11 (1986), pp 110–11.
5. Ketzel Levine, 'A tree of identities, a tradition of dissent: John Hewitt at 78', in *Fortnight*, 213 (4–17 February 1985), p. 16.
6. Andrew Boyd, *Fermenting Elements: The Labour Colleges in Ireland, 1924–1964* (Belfast, 1999), pp 79, 95. For similar experiences of politicisation see Gray, 'A shop steward remembers'; Jack Macgougan, 'Letting Labour lead: Jack Macgougan and the pursuit of unity, 1913–1958' in *Saothar*, 14 (1989), pp 113–24; and Andy Barr, 'An undiminished dream: Andy Barr, communist trade unionist', in *Saothar*, 16 (1991), pp 95–111.
7. RGASPI, Proposals in connection with the Communist Party of Ireland, 8 May 1937, f. 495, o. 89, d. 102, ll. 1–9; J.R. Campbell, The situation in Ireland, 27 February 1939, f. 495, o. 14, d. 340, ll. 16–31.
8. Fearghal McGarry, *Irish Politics and the Spanish Civil War* (Cork, 1999), p. 178.
9. See James Loughlin, *Fascism and Constitutional Conflict: The British Extreme–Right and Ulster in the Twentieth Century* (Liverpool, 2019).
10. *Belfast Telegraph*, 29 August 1936, 12 July 1937; *Belfast News-Letter*, 31 August 1936.
11. John Horgan, *Irish Media: A Critical History Since 1922* (London, 2001), pp 38–9.
12. *Derry Journal*, 11 September 1936.
13. *Belfast Telegraph*, 31 August 1936.
14. *Derry Standard*, 28 April 1937.
15. Ibid., 5 May 1937.
16. *Irish Press*, 21 September 1936.
17. Walker, *The Politics of Frustration*, pp 85–6.
18. RGASPI, Report from Ireland, undated [July 1933], f. 495, o. 89, d. 91, l. 23.
19. Paul Abraham, 'Midgley, Roman Catholicism, and Spain', in *New Ulster*, 2, winter, 1986.

20. McGarry, *Irish Politics and the Spanish Civil War*, pp 174–5; *Irish Press*, 3 March 1937.
21. John Fitzsimons Harbinson, 'A history of the Northern Ireland Labour Party, 1891–1949' (PhD, Queen's University, Belfast, 1966), pp 88–94.
22. *Irish News*, 6 November 1936.
23. *Derry Journal*, 30 April 1937.
24. John Mitchel, *Jail Journal* (Dublin, 1913); William Burton, 'The Spanish Civil War, Irish newspapers, journals, and periodicals: a thematic examination, 1936–39' (PhD, Ulster University, 2019).
25. *Derry Journal*, 31 August 1936.
26. Raymond J. Quinn, *A Rebel Voice: A History of Belfast Republicanism, 1925–1972* (Belfast, 1999).
27. Ronnie Munck and Bill Rolston (eds), *Belfast in the Thirties: An Oral History* (Belfast, 1987), p. 147; Macgougan, 'Letting Labour lead', p. 122, fn6; Walker, *The Politics of Frustration*, p. 114.
28. Macgougan, 'Letting Labour lead', p. 114; *Belfast News-Letter*, 12 October 1936.
29. *Belfast News-Letter*, 13 August 1936; *Northern Whig*, 15 August 1936.
30. Gray, 'A shop steward remembers', p. 111; Matt Merrigan, 'Socialist trade unionist: Matt Merrigan's political formation', in *Saothar*, 12 (1987), p. 103.
31. Boyd, *Fermenting Elements*, pp 33, 62, 79, 110–11.
32. *Belfast News-Letter*, 15 August 1936.
33. Ibid., 10, 22, 26 August 1936.
34. Ibid., 16 September 1936.
35. Emmet O'Connor, 'Tyrone volunteers in the Connolly Column in the Spanish Civil War', in *Dúiche Uí Néill*, pp 301–11; Macgougan, 'Letting Labour lead', p. 114; John Quinn, *Irish Volunteers for Spain* (Belfast, 2004), pp 78–9; *Belfast Telegraph*, 9 November, 4 December 1936.
36. *Belfast News-Letter*, 12 October 1936; Bill Alexander, *British Volunteers for Liberty: Spain, 1936–1939* (London, 1982), p. 41; R. Dan Richardson, *Comintern Army: The International Brigades and the Spanish Civil War* (Lexington, Ky, 1982), pp 28–9.
37. Liz Shaw, 'Joe Boyd – the last Brigader', in *Belfast Telegraph*, 18 June 2005.
38. Ibid.; *Belfast Telegraph*, 9, 20 November, 4 December 1936.
39. *Belfast Telegraph*, 15 October 1936; Modern Records Centre, University of Warwick, Trades Union Congress deposit, Scottish Ambulance Unit, 292/946/42/79.
40. RGASPI, Report on British deserters, 8 August 1937, f. 545, o. 6, d. 88, ll. 18-19.
41. David Convery, 'Irish participation in medical aid to Republican Spain, 1936–39', in *Saothar*, 35 (2010), pp 37–46.
42. Public Record Office of Northern Ireland, Belfast (PRONI), RUC reports, HA/32/1/558.
43. McGarry, *Irish Politics and the Spanish Civil War*, pp 179–80; *Belfast Telegraph*, 13 February 1937.
44. *Irish Democrat*, 15 May 1937.
45. Macgougan, 'Letting Labour lead', p. 114.
46. *Belfast News-Letter*, 25 March 1937, 18 November 1938; *Northern Whig*, 25 March 1937; *Irish Press*, 25 March 1937.

47. Ken Armstrong, 'The effects of the Spanish Civil War on Ireland' in *Lisburn Historical Society Journal*, 10 (2005–6); *Irish Press*, 9 March 1937; *Worker*, 13 March 1937.
48. Burton, 'The Spanish Civil War'; *New Northman*, summer 1938.
49. *Pro Tanto Quid*, 1938.
50. PRONI, RUC reports on Arms for Spain committee, HA/32/1/559; *Irish Democrat*, 18 December 1937.
51. PRONI, RUC report on NILP meeting on food for Spain, 15 January 1939, HA 32/1/563; *Irish Press*, 5 September 1936; *Belfast News-Letter*, 28 November, 29 December 1938, 3, 9–10 February, 1 July 1939. See also Convery, 'Irish participation in medical aid to Republican Spain, 1936–39', pp 37–46.
52. *Sunday Independent*, 10 April 1938.
53. McGarry, *Irish Politics and the Spanish Civil War*, p. 174.
54. Census of Ireland, 1911; Graham Walker, 'H. C. Midgley', in *Oxford Dictionary of National Biography*, online.
55. *Irish News*, 14 August 1936; *Derry Journal*, 31 August 1936.
56. Harbinson, 'A history of the Northern Ireland Labour Party, 1891–1949', pp 88–94.
57. Paul Preston, *The Spanish Holocaust: Inquisition and Extermination in Twentieth Century Spain* (London, 2012), details atrocities on both sides and concludes that Republican atrocities were grossly exaggerated.
58. *Irish News*, 10 September 1936.
59. Linda Walker, 'Monica Whately', in *Oxford Dictionary of National Biography*, online.
60. *Derry Journal*, 21 October 1936.
61. *Belfast Telegraph*, 24 October 1936; *Northern Whig*, 27 October 1937; Harbinson, 'A history of the Northern Ireland Labour Party, 1891–1949', pp 88–94.
62. *Derry Journal*, 11–13 November 1936.
63. Ibid., 18 November 1936.
64. Ibid.
65. *Belfast News-Letter*, 31 August 1936.
66. Walker, *The Politics of Frustration*, pp 100–1; *Belfast News-Letter*, 1 November 1937; J. K. Robinson, 'Annual conference of the Northern Ireland Labour Party', in *Inprecorr*, 49, 13 November 1937.
67. Gray, 'A shop steward remembers', p. 112.
68. *Derry Journal*, 14 February 1938.
69. PRONI, RUC report on SPNI meeting, 8 January 1940, HA 21/1/560.
70. *Belfast News-Letter*, 2, 7 February 1938; *Northern Whig*, 2 February 1938; Walker, *The Politics of Frustration*, pp 104–7; Connal Parr, 'The undefeated: Radical Protestants from the Spanish Civil War to the 1960s', www.academia.edu/8238959/The_Undefeated. Accessed 13 June 2020.
71. *Belfast News-Letter*, 31 October 1938; *Derry Journal*, 31 October 1938.
72. Denis P. Barritt and Charles F. Carter, *The Northern Ireland Problem: A Study in Group Relations* (Oxford, 1962), p. 141.
73. *Ulster Year Book, 1938* (Belfast), p. 163; Terence Gerard Cradden, 'Trade unionism and socialism in Northern Ireland, 1939–53' (PhD, Queen's University, Belfast, 1988), p. 201; Walker, *The Politics of Frustration*, p. 103.

74. Walker, *The Politics of Frustration*, p. 103.
75. Quinn, *A Rebel Voice*; Walker, *The Politics of Frustration*, p. 110.
76. *Belfast News-Letter*, 5 February, 30 April 1937.
77. Boyd, *Fermenting Elements*, p. 60; letter from Andrew Boyd to the author, 17 June 2009; *Londonderry Sentinel*, 7 April, 25 June 1938.
78. *Derry Journal*, 4, 23 September 1936; *Belfast News-Letter*, 5 February 1936; Walker, *The Politics of Frustration*, p. 105.
79. *Belfast Telegraph*, 6 July 1937.
80. Walker, *The Politics of Frustration*, pp 98–9; *Londonderry Sentinel*, 14 March 1939; *Belfast News-Letter*, 6 October 1937; PRONI, RUC reports on Arms for Spain committee meeting, 25 July 1938, HA 32/1/559.
81. *Derry Journal*, 19, 26 July, 11, 16, 30 August, 4, 11 October 1937; 11 February, 1 April 1938; *Londonderry Sentinel*, 31 March 1938, 25 March 1939; *Irish Democrat*, 16 October 1937.
82. I am obliged to James Loughlin for this point.
83. *Derry Journal*, 7–11 February, 7 March, 1 April, 12, 28 August 1938, 3, 24 April 1939; *Londonderry Sentinel*, 25–27 August 1938; 21, 25 March 1939, 1 April 1939; *Belfast News-Letter*, 6 April, 1 July 1939.

FOUR

# THE INTERNATIONAL BRIGADES AND THE IRISH CONTINGENT

The founding of the International Brigades in October 1936 in Albacete, capital of a province in the region of Castilla-La Mancha south of Madrid, was the final result of long discussions within the Communist International that were coordinated and modified in consultation with the Kremlin.

### SOVIET FOREIGN POLICY ON SPAIN

Spain was hitherto not a priority in Soviet foreign relations and diplomatic relations were only established with Madrid after the victory of the Popular Front in the Cortes elections of February 1936. The intervention of the Soviet Union in the Spanish Civil War came about when Stalin realised that the Non-Intervention Committee was a farce, doing nothing to curtail shipments of arms and men from the fascist powers of Germany and Italy to the insurgent generals.

Soviet foreign policy in the 1930s wavered between some kind of accommodation with the new German regime and the so-called 'Western option', i.e. a defence pact with the democratic powers of France and Britain. As early as 1934 Stalin was using David Kandelaki, Trade Commissioner at the Soviet Embassy in Oslo, to sound out German official representatives on the possibilities of a 'non-aggression agreement' between Berlin and Moscow. His initiative came to naught, despite meetings with Göring and Hjalmar Schacht, minister for the economy, because Hitler, true to his ideological tenets, wanted relations with the Bolsheviks frozen, ordering the cutting of trade to five per cent of its pre-1933 volume. In his speeches at the Nürnberg rally in September 1936 and in the Reichstag in January 1937, Hitler left nobody in doubt concerning his visceral hatred of the Soviet state.[1]

As regards the 'Western option', London was inveterately hostile and only entered into half-hearted negotiations with the Kremlin weeks before the Second World War commenced. The pact of the USSR with France (1935) in the case of aggression by a third party was limited by the proviso that any military steps to be taken had to be approved by the signatories of the 1925 Locarno Pact. Furthermore, no official talks between the Soviet and French military high commands took place. Likewise, the pact with Czechoslovakia of the same year could only become operational when and if France intervened militarily. On the credit side, Moscow believed that the change in international perceptions of the USSR heralded by the 7th World Congress of the Communist International (1935) discarding sectarianism against the socialists and the adoption of anti-fascist alliances of communists, social democrats and liberals had led to major successes of the communist parties at the 1936 national elections of February (Spain) and May (France). In neither case was the CP represented in the respective cabinet. In view of this accretion to Soviet standing, Stalin could not stand idly by and allow a fascist takeover in a country bordering on a major power: France, though heavily polarised, was a key component in his 'western' calculations, and it had borders with his enemies Germany and Italy. And, as self-proclaimed leader of the 'world proletariat', he could hardly leave his Spanish followers at the mercy of Franco and his fascist allies.

### SOVIET AID TO REPUBLICAN SPAIN

Moscow's response to the rebellion in Spain was hesitant at first, initially focusing primarily on the shipment of food and the organisation of public funding and demonstrations in major Soviet cities, followed by the dispatch of journalists, film-makers and a few military experts to the Spanish cockpit. Direct military aid to the beleaguered Spanish Republicans was passed by the Soviet Politburo only on 29 September, roughly coinciding with the shipment of Spanish gold reserves from Cartagena to Odessa, which were to fund arms shipments from the USSR.[2]

The Soviet assistance was considerable and vital, especially between October 1936 and the summer of 1937. The penultimate big delivery arrived in Spain in August 1938, and the very last one, in February 1939, was to a great extent stranded in the French railway system because the border to Spain was closed. This was the case for most of the conflict. Other delays or curtailments of the arms traffic were due to technical difficulties: Soviet freighters had to run the gauntlet of Italian submarines and the naval patrols of the Non-Intervention Committee, and risk capture or sinking by German or Francoist battleships in the Mediterranean.

After the sinking of the Russian freighter Komsomol in December 1936, the Soviets, afraid of an international incident, took precautionary steps, largely avoiding the Mediterranean route for arms shipments save for humanitarian freight (clothing, food) not proscribed by the Non-Intervention patrols. Three Soviet freighters were sunk and ten captured and brought to the Franco zone, but many ships from Russia, changing flags and using other guises on the way, arrived safely in Republican ports. An alternative route, between Murmansk and Bordeaux, was plied by a French shipping line founded by the Parti Communiste Français (PCF) with funds from Madrid between December 1937 and August 1938.[3]

There were other reasons for a decrease in Soviet hardware. First, Stalin's realisation that Republican Spain was a hotbed of left-wing dissent antagonistic to his politics, or that the war was lost by late 1937. Second, he had other preoccupations in 1937–1938, primarily the planning and monitoring of the Great Terror against the general population, party cadres (including political exiles from Poland, Germany and Bulgaria), industrial staff and the Red Army: 1.5 million arrests and at least 681,000 executions.[4] Third, he was also concerned by the danger to his eastern frontiers, when border incidents between the Red Army and the Japanese troops flared up into open warfare in 1939.

The following table gives the extent of Soviet and Axis military hardware shipments to Spain, and from the USSR to China (1937–39). The most exhaustive scrutiny of published and Russian archival sources on this topic was carried out by Daniel Kowalsky of Queen's University Belfast. The figures reveal the superiority of the insurgent Spanish forces in respect of artillery, tanks and aircraft:[5]

**Table 1:** Foreign military aid to Republican and Francoist forces

|  | USSR-Spain | Others-Rep. Spain | Built in Rep. Spain | Germany-Spain | Italy-Spain | USSR-China |
|---|---|---|---|---|---|---|
| Aircraft (combat) | 648–680 | 178 | 316 | 593–655 | 726–1,000 | 985 |
| Tanks and Armoured cars | 407 | | | 250 | 950 | 82 |
| Artillery pieces | 1,186 | | | 700 | 1,930 | 1,317 |
| Mortars | 340 | | | 6,174 | 1,426 | |
| Machine-guns | 20,486 | | | 31,000 | 3,436 | |
| Rifles | 497,813 | | | 157,306 | 240,747 | 480,000 |
| Shells (millions) | 3.4 | | | 1.1 | 7.7 | |

The Spanish Republican army lacked not only arms, because of the Non-Intervention policy of the European democracies and the USA, but often the right kind of weapons. Moscow sent in late October/early November 1936 three modern aircraft to the Spanish theatre. The 'Mosca'('Fly') Polikarpov I-16 monoplane fighter with retractable landing gear and a maximum speed of 390 km/h and four–six machine-guns in the wings. Its sister aircraft, the I-15 'Chato' ('snub-nosed'), was of older design, a biplane and almost as fast. Finally, the Tupolev SB2M-100 'Katiushka', a twin-engined monoplane bomber that had retractable undercarriage, was a novelty because it was an all-metal plane. The fighters seem to have been more than a match for the German (He-51) and Italian (Fiat CR. 32) biplane fighters that escorted the heavy Junkers 52 bombers on raids to Madrid. This relative advantage was lost by mid-1937 with the arrival of modern German aircraft, especially the Messerschmitt BF109 fighter, the Junkers 87 'Stuka' dive-bomber and the new Heinkel 111 twin-engined monoplane bomber.

Fascist air superiority proved to be a decisive factor. The Republic never had enough heavy artillery pieces or mortars: many of its early machine-guns were either unreliable French (Chauchat) or US (Colt) pieces from the First World War. The staple heavy machine-gun in the brigadas mixtas was the 7.62 mm Russian Maxim-1910, which needed a crew of up to eight: gunner, feeder and observer, and five water- and ammunition-carriers (each ammunition case weighed 10 kg) who doubled as riflemen-defenders. With its wheeled undercarriage and shield, the gun had a gross weight of 65 kg.

The standard weapon of the IB infantry, various types of the Russian Mosin Nagant rifle, had been zeroed-in with the chisel-tipped bayonet attached. Most volunteers found the bayonet a nuisance, used it as a tent peg or threw it away at some stage, which meant that the sighting was then askew. The weapon was built for the arctic winter, not for torrid Spanish summers, and the wooden shaft often split in the heat. Its bolt was too short so that clearing the jammed weapon was a problem.[6]

The most prized and efficient Russian weapon in the brigades was the brand-new 45 mm anti-tank gun, and the British battalion had 3 pieces. But these had been disabled or commandeered by other units by April 1938. The Soviet advisers were terrified that the weapon might fall into enemy hands and were just as solicitous about their aircraft or tanks. One of the weaknesses of Republican command was that the Russians decided when and how their aircraft and tanks were to be employed, not the Chief of Staff of the Republican Army Vicente Rojo. All-arms coordination was therefore never attained to a substantial degree.

In the final resort it was not the quality of republican armaments that was decisive but that the amount of heavy weaponry it managed to procure was unable to match the sheer scale of arms shipments from Italy and Germany.

Generally, it was a war of movement, of columns, and there were never enough tanks on either side to use Blitzkrieg tactics.

One lesson learned from the war was the efficacy of anti-tank and anti-aircraft guns, especially the German 88 mm. Leaving the technical questions aside, it is clear that a contributory factor of the Republic's defeat was low morale in the rear, caused on the one hand by the side-lining of the anarchists after May 1937 and the concomitant rise in communist influence and, on the other, the desperate food shortages.

## THE COMINTERN, THE INTERNATIONAL BRIGADES AND THE CONTENTIOUS RULE OF ANDRÉ MARTY

While Soviet military assistance to the Madrid Government was overseen by Klim Voroshilov, Soviet Defence Minister, and managed by Soviet Military Intelligence (GRU), all decisions in relation to the International Brigades were taken under the aegis of Georgi Dimitrov, General Secretary of the Communist International, after consultation with Stalin, other Soviet leaders and his colleagues in ECCI, especially the Russian member Dmitry Manuilsky. In late August 1936, Comintern bodies were discussing 'the lessons from the trial of the Trotskyist-Zinovievist terrorist centre', i.e. the dissemination of the fabricated charges against the defendants in the first of the three great Moscow show trials (1936–38). All sections (CPs) of the Cominitern were directed to print brochures and press material on the sham proceedings.[7] This conspiracy theory became a sine qua non of the communist world-view, and it was sedulously propagated in the International Brigades, primarily by its leader André Marty and by German communists holding key posts in the IB bureaucracy. Towards the end of the war, 'Trotskyist' became a common charge against those who persistently questioned decisions.

The first moves by the Comintern in recruiting volunteers for Spain targeted key military experts, mainly airmen. On 11 August the ECCI Secretariat sent a cipher message to the CPUSA, urging party leader Earl Browder to recruit pilots. He initially sent six. The PCF also began to dispatch aircraft crews, and Harry Pollitt informed the ECCI Presidium that the CPGB had sent three pilots.[8] On 28 August, as Dimitrov noted in his diary, the Soviet Politburo had discussed 'the eventual organisation of an international corps'.[9] The situation in Spain was discussed at a top-level meeting in the Kremlin on 14 September and in the sessions of the Presidium and the Secretariat in ECCI in the following days. The resolution directing the communist parties to begin general recruitment for the Spanish war was passed by the Secretariat on 18 September: 'Volunteers from among the workers from all countries with experience in war service should be recruited to go to Spain.'[10]

Apart from the problems in Spain in providing an infrastructure for foreign volunteers in the air force or the various militias, the recruitment of brigade volunteers in the home country was difficult. The Comintern overestimated the ability of communist parties to find and send suitable men, firstly because the parties in Britain and the USA, for example, were relatively small in 1936–37 (USA 38,000, Britain 15,000)[11] and secondly because the leadership in each case was loath to send full-time officials. The methods of recruitment were extremely haphazard in Britain, as Albacete subsequently complained to the CPGB leadership:

> There should be strict control on all men sent out. Not all men prove suitable for the struggle out here. Drunkards, down-and-outs, criminals and others of this character are not wanted out here. There should be a stop to recruiting in hostels and parks, Embankment etc. We want men from the working-class movement, class-conscious comrades who really know something about the struggle in Spain. [. . .] It is no exaggeration to say that the British have got a bad name in the rearguard. The number of desertions, cases of drunkenness, indiscipline etc. are high.[12]

The first medical examination of volunteers took place in Paris, the clearing house for incoming recruits, if at all. The bulk of the early volunteers came direct from France; they were French-born or Polish political and economic emigrants, Italian anti-fascists in exile or some of hundreds of German communists leading precarious lives in semi-legal asylum in France, Belgium, Holland and Denmark. A special group consisted of heavily vetted German and Austrian political exiles in the USSR, who left for Spain from Leningrad by rail in October, and they were followed by others with special Red Army training (sappers, tank-crew and infantry officers) from April 1937 via the sea route from a Black Sea port.[13] By early November the French party had sent 3,720 volunteers to Spain, and by February 1937 the French contingent had risen to 8,000 out of a total of 14,000 from all countries.

The Comintern was dissatisfied with the recruitment efforts in London and New York. Unrealistically, Manuilsky demanded that Pollitt send 1,000 men; the CPGB leader reduced this first to 500, then cabled in November to say he could only promise 200. The quota set by Manuilsky for the Communist Party of the USA (CPUSA) was ludicrously inflated (10,000) and Browder promised 5,000 within three months. By the end of the year a mere 120 American volunteers had been shipped to France. The problems were largely those of organisation and of the finance solicited from Moscow for funding the transports from Britain and the USA. Told by Dimitrov of the difficulties with the CPUSA, Stalin said on 2 January 1937 that no more recruitment was needed and proposed its cessation. Cables were dispatched in that sense to the main capitals, but André Marty (1886–1956) pleaded for reconsideration, stating that a further 10,000 volunteers were needed. The Soviet Politburo allowed the parties to resume the call for volunteers on 7 January.[14]

A major figure in the history of the International Brigades and their relations with Moscow was Marty, a former sailor who was elected on the communist ticket to the French Chamber of Deputies in 1924. He rose to membership of the French Political Bureau in 1931 and, most importantly, was from 1932 the representative of the PCF at ECCI and a member of its Presidium. When the Comintern was re-organised after the 1935 7th World Congress, Marty became one of the ten permanent secretaries and was responsible for the English-speaking countries. In August 1936 Dimitrov sent him to Spain to supervise the monitoring of the Spanish communists by other Moscow emissaries. Because of his choleric, authoritarian nature and erratic decision-making Marty was in constant conflict with Maurice Thorez, the PCF leader, who on a visit to Moscow in September 1936 complained that Marty was acting arbitrarily in Spain. Stalin was pleased with the electoral advances made by his French comrades, and that positive predicament favoured Marty when he was recalled to report in Moscow. On his return he assumed leadership in Albacete.[15]

The gigantic task of establishing the base in Albacete fell largely on the shoulders of the exiled Italian communist Luigi Longo (Gallo), an ECCI office holder since 1926 who first set up reception centres for incoming brigadistas in Perpignan and Marseilles. By 10 October 500 of them were waiting in the Catalan fortress of Figueras for further transportation. Longo found that in Albacete there was a shortage of everything: buildings had to be adapted (installation of water and toilets) and bedding, billets, food supplies, uniforms (mainly from France) and footwear had to be distributed. The first 500 volunteers disembarked from the train in Albacete on 12 October, only two days after the Italian Commissar had arrived in the provincial capital. Ten days later the Government officially recognised the International Brigades.[16] Longo and two delegates were granted an audience by Premier Francisco Largo Caballero, the austere left-wing Socialist who listened in silence to their request that the International Brigades be placed at the disposal of the General Staff of the Republic's army recently formed. Caballero merely said that they should consult Diego Martínez Barrio, the former Speaker of the Cortes who was now Governor of Albacete Province. Longo was taken aback by the cool reception, but he obviously lacked, because of his communist conceit, the proper psychological insight into Spanish sensibilities. Caballero relied on professional army officers loyal to the Republic and he shared their resentment against self-important, foreign legates of Stalin who had accredited themselves military ranks without any knowledge of the science of warfare. This dislike of communist importunity (shared by many professional officers until the war's end) reached an explosive climax in January 1937, when Caballero told the Soviet Ambassador to get out of his office ('Fuera!') after the latter's demand that the Premier remove his top soldier, General Asensio Torrado.[17]

Longo could rely on Martínez Barrio to iron out the most pressing organisational difficulties, and he also enjoyed the support of the communist 5th Regiment, which had a unit in the town.[18] That was also the experience of Louis Fischer, a non-communist American journalist usually resident in Moscow, who became quartermaster of the base in November 1936. He found Marty to be hysterical, suspicious and jealous of the good relations that Fischer forged with leading Soviet military advisers and journalists in Madrid. Fischer was glad to take up Marty's offer of press work in Valencia after he had witnessed how his Polish storeman and four other volunteers were arrested at gunpoint on charges of 'Trotskyism'.[19] Marty's relations with his own party continued to be strained. He complained in December that 50 members of a French battalion had deserted, and he wanted a portion of those remaining – 'recruited in the bars of Lyon' – to be replaced by new volunteers from Paris. He was chided, in turn, by Dimitrov, for 'lack of coordination, manifestations of individualism and the aggravation of personal relationships [with Maurice Thorez]'.

Marty seemed untouchable because of his good relations with 'la casa' (Moscow), even after José Díaz, general secretary of the PCE, complained to Dimitrov that Marty in Albacete 'is personally interfering and is taking decisions on all issues, including the most trivial ones'. The collective leadership in Albacete that the PCE had recommended only functioned when Marty was in Moscow on ECCI business from February 1937.[20] When he visited Stalin at his datcha in March, he was accorded a warm welcome.[21] Palmiro Togliatti (Ercoli), the new Comintern representative in Spain from the summer of 1937, had the support of the Spanish party when he urged Moscow in November to stop Marty's return to Albacete, quoting his ability to create animosity and the risk of endangering the relationship between the PCE and the Negrín Government. Their recommendation went unanswered, for Marty had the best krycha (Russ: roof, i.e. support) imaginable: Stalin's good-will, if that is the right phrase.[22]

With Marty abroad for most of 1937, the leadership in Albacete became more professional and less arbitrary, and the worst bureaucratic excrescences were removed during the organisation of proper military structures. The International Brigades' 'political wing' was its War Commissariat, headed by Inspector-General Longo with French and German deputies. Its headquarters was in Albacete, with a large section in Madrid's upper-class Salamanca district, at Calle Velázquez 63, where Frank Ryan had an office. There were smaller dependencies (delegaciones) in Barcelona and Valencia manned usually by German communists. Longo's most prominent colleague in the headquarters was another Comintern heavyweight, Franz Dahlem, a former deputy in the Reichstag, a member of the Politburo of the Kommunistische Partei Deutschlands (KPD) who had candidate status on the ECCI panel (1935–1943). Both could use the growing influence of the Soviets in Spain to ensure that the political education and propaganda within the brigades was conducted via the political commissars from company level upwards on strict adherence to Comintern precepts.

That, of course, was against the general thrust of Popular Front politics, and not a few volunteers from Britain and Ireland resented this form of political dictation, which frequently ascribed military defeats to 'sabotage' or a lack of political will and insinuated that the men lacked commitment. It was symptomatic that all political commissars of the British battalion – not those in the companies – were graduates of the Lenin School.[23]

The Commissariat was involved in running battles with the Ministry of Defence before and after the incorporation of the International Brigades in the Republican Army in September 1937. First, there was the wilful ignoring of the edict of Defence Minister Indalecio Prieto (21 October 1937) that forbade statements and meetings of a party-political nature. In each International Brigade the twentieth anniversary of the Russian Revolution was celebrated by order from Albacete. On the other hand, Dahlem and others criticised the preference of Prieto for socialist commanders and political commissars.[24] Second, when appointing military commanders, Dahlem and Longo continued the harmful practice of giving preference to 'good elements' over tried and gifted officers – non-deviation 'from the Party line' was paramount, often with disastrous results. Third, ministerial directives regarding the question of the authority deciding pay, promotions, leave and repatriation were thus ignored by Albacete.[25] Relations between the Defence Ministry and the Commissariat remained strained, with neither side gaining the upper hand, and this baleful stalemate only subsided to a certain degree when the openly defeatist Prieto resigned his portfolio in April 1938.

One dispute that was settled had to do with the dangers – as Marty perceived them – to the hegemony of the French communists at the top level of the brigades. The German units had a high reputation, playing a key role in the defence of Madrid and in all subsequent battles. They were admired throughout the brigades for discipline and smart turnout, and for their officers with First World War experience (e.g. Hans Kahle, Ludwig Renn). Robert

Merriman, chief of staff of the 15th Brigade, remarked during the fiasco of March 1938 that 'the only people who do not run away are the English and the Germans.'[26] Shortly afterwards, when Dahlem was absent, having gone to Paris, Marty had four leading German communists expelled from Spain: Dahlem's deputy Karl Mewis, a cadres officer with the 45th Division, the Political Commissar and the Commander (Heiner Rau) of the 11th Brigade.

In a series of encounters, Marty shouted at Mewis, accusing the Germans of protecting their cadres and withdrawing them to the rear, a colonial attitude towards Spaniards in the 11th Brigade and the general policy of installing German communists in all units of the IB. Marty could use the argument that all communist party relations were to go through the Central Committee of the PCE and that he was in charge of its 'foreign parties commission'. Mewis and Dahlem were representatives of the KPD, once the largest communist party outside the Soviet Union, with a quarter of a million members, and the third-strongest party (17%) at the last free elections in Germany (November 1932).[27] By early 1938 the Party had lost over half of the cadres it had sent to Spanish battlefields.[28] As regards Heiner Rau, the commander of the 11th Brigade, Marty accused him of deserting the front (he was wounded and in hospital for a few days) in Aragon in March and of 'expressing a pessimistic remark about our aviation' because he and other German volunteers had criticised the lack of support from the Republican air force during the retreats. Although Rau was re-instated as brigade commander by General Walter, he had to retire because of his wound and leave Spain in April. Marty also ordered the demotion of German officers and commissars in the various depots and training bases.[29]

Having got rid of his main political rivals in the brigades, Marty persisted in his chauvinistic megalomania towards, compared to the Germans, political 'small fry' with little clout in the Comintern – the British and the Americans. The Frenchman knew Harry Pollitt from Moscow meetings, addressed him cordially ('mon cher Harry'), but was defamatory and dismissive in his dealings with lower-ranked British communists or volunteers. Marty's manic and spiteful micromanagement impulses were shown when in July 1938 he accused Peter Kerrigan, *Daily Worker* correspondent in Spain, of distributing cigarettes at Mataró hospital solely to English comrades. Kerrigan replied that he had given out 30 loose cigarettes to English, American, Canadian and Spanish patients. Marty obviously did not want any foreigner visiting the wounded without his permission.[30]

A serious stand-off occurred when the Welsh miners' leader Arthur Horner intervened on behalf of the families of three Welsh deserters who were held in prison before being interned in a monastery in Puig (Valencia province). The three men – Griffith Jones, Will Hopkins and W. J. Thomas – were arrested in Valencia in mid-September 1937 in the company of the Scottish volunteer James Kempton.[31] Thomas was an early recruit, had suffered wounds that went septic after the Jarama battle and had a nervous collapse at Brunete. His health declined in Valencia and he underwent an operation on his inflamed liver. He received assistance from the British Consulate and his family also approached the Spanish Embassy in London.

When Hopkins escaped from Puig in July 1938 and reached home, the families started a campaign, supported by the South Wales Miners' Federation, to have the volunteers repatriated.[32] Horner travelled to Spain and told the IB leadership in Barcelona that 'the matter has caused considerable difficulty [. . .] and agitation will not cease until the three individuals return home.' In early 1939 they reached Britain.[33] Marty wrote to Pollitt on the case in October 1938 and promised an investigation. His remarks about the agitation in Wales displayed once more his mania for depicting defeats, dissent or desertions as works of the 'class enemy':

> I am sure the Welsh miners, with their old revolutionary traditions, would have very well understood the reason for the arrest of conscious or unconscious agents of Franco who try to break up the People's Army which is holding back the Fascists. [. . .] Why should not the Government of the Spanish Republic have the right to arrest those who provoke desertion and probably organize it in a link with the men of the [British] Intelligence Service or in the service of Franco? [. . .] Twenty years' experience shows that each time the workers' enemy has wanted to attack the Soviet Union he has always done so with the pretext of prisoners.[34]

Marty's last spiteful act in response to a request from Pollitt was not directed against British subjects but former doctors of the International Brigades who in London had set up a 'Chinese Medical Aid Committee' in 1939. They were planning their departure to China to work for the Chinese Red Cross during the war against the Japanese invaders. The initiative came from Dr Fritz Jensen, a Viennese communist since 1929 and a member of the PCE, who was the first head of medical services in Albacete in late 1936. He later served with the 13th Brigade, was wounded at Brunete and ended the war as the head of the medical staff of the 42nd Division on the Ebro.[35] Jensen, strong-willed and fearless, had fought for the rights of his staff and patients in Spain against the bureaucracy of Albacete.[36] Marty was incensed when he heard about the Chinese expedition, complaining to Pollitt that six named doctors with Spanish service, including Jensen, were 'bad elements, Trotskyists, agents of subversion' that did not merit any recommendation.[37] Pollitt must have questioned the harsh assessment since Marty answered in June (Jensen and others had left Britain for China in May) by slandering the Viennese physician, accusing him of 'Trotskyism' and 'systematically disorganizing the IB medical service'. Marty was especially angry that Jensen had the support of Pollitt and the Austrian CP.[38]

The only known dispute reported between Marty and the Irish was with Frank Ryan, whom he reputedly had arrested for loudly condemning the removal of a portion of the Irish volunteers from the British battalion. The incident probably took place in Chincón at a meeting of officers of the 15th Brigade on the eve of the British going into the Jarama battle on 12 February 1937. Ryan was soon released, but the evidence for the clash comes from unreliable witnesses and neither Ryan himself nor any Irish volunteer ever mentioned it in writing.[39] Marty's disputes with the Americans were legion. He criticised the quality of American recruits, held them to be 'cry-babies' and 'arrogant'.[40] Marty remarked to John Gates, the new American commissar of the 15th Brigade in 1938, that the Americans were 'cowards' and 'cowboys'. Gates defiantly defended his countrymen, adding that the French in Spain were prone to 'chronic drunkenness'.[41]

While other sources would support Gates's verdict, Marty's hostility had arguably little to do with politics, but with a general dislike or jealousy of American living standards and the constant bitching of the Americans, used to plain talking, about conditions in Spain. American ire was directed primarily at Vladimir Čopić because of the disastrous attacks on the Jarama front, and in its aftermath all American officers and the CPUSA representatives sought to have the Croat (Commander of the 15th Brigade) removed. The matter came to a dead end in June 1937 when Čopić threatened U.S. battalion commissar Harry Haywood with arrest should he persist in demanding a new chief for the 15th Brigade.[42]

American tempers were assuaged by the fact that by the autumn of 1937 they held most of the key posts in the 15th Brigade. Marty, albeit with defamatory insinuations, could dismiss the CPUSA's request for more repatriations in 1938 because he had the support of the Republican military. His last run-in with the Americans (and Canadians) in June 1938 was ludicrous but typical of his megalomania: complaints in the 15th Brigade were widespread that packages containing cigarettes sent from the North America or Britain had not arrived, i.e. had been stolen in Spain. Marty alleged that a Canadian battalion commissar had blamed him personally for the non-arrival of the post and that 'this campaign against the chiefs of the brigades has at its goal the demoralisation of the Anglo-American volunteers.'[43] Jim Bourne, the American secretary of the Spanish Party in the 15th Brigade, tried to convince Marty that there was no 'campaign', at most gossip in the rear.[44]

There was a growing consensus in 1938 that the IB should be removed, partly because they composed merely five of the over 200 brigadas mixtas, partly because they were 'extremely exhausted' and counted for 'no more than 5,000 soldiers in their ranks', as Manuilsky wrote to Voroshilov and Stalin on 29 August.[45] Spanish communists hoped that their withdrawal might impress the Non-Intervention Committee to pressurise Germany and Italy to follow suit.[46]

In the third week of August 1938 Togliatti, Marty and leading members of the PCE arrived in the Soviet capital to discuss the situation in Spain. At the fifth of such deliberations on 27 August, the inner leading circle of the Comintern (the Russian delegates and Dimitrov) agreed on the dissolution of the brigades and informed the Kremlin. Stalin did not answer or acknowledge the letter but Voroshilov gave his agreement over the telephone. On 1 September, six ECCI members agreed unanimously to the departure of volunteers.[47]

## THE INTERNATIONAL BRIGADES IN THE REPUBLICAN ARMY

Spain having been neutral during the First World War, its army officers lacked experience of modern warfare. If they studied military tactics, they preferred French models of defensive action. An exception consisted of the troops used in the costly Moroccan War (1908–1926), the so-called africanistas of the tercio (Spanish Foreign Legion) and the Spanish commanders of Moroccan mercenaries (regulares). Franco owed his swift career up the military ladder to his exploits in North Africa, and these detachments proved to be his best units in the civil war. It is however open to question if battling in the desert and the mountains against an elusive enemy who was finally defeated only with French help gave the Francoists a clear tactical advantage over Republican forces.

On the mainland, the Army had a surfeit of officers, few modern weapons and two squadrons of antiquated tanks, and the air force relied on about 300 obsolescent aircraft, including British and French biplane fighters.[48] During the 1920s garrison officers were expected to train the yearly intake (*quinta*) of mostly illiterate conscripts for an army that was top-heavy with ageing officers and thus causing promotions to be blocked. With the inception of the Republic in 1931, a reform of the armed forces began, with generous terms for the immediate retirement of commissioned officers on full pay. It had the unforeseen result that most of the 8,000 who took the package were younger officers of a Republican persuasion. There was no purge of rightist officers, but the conservative 1933–1935 government sacked known left-wing sympathisers.[49]

A commission in the army was a career for sons of the lower-middle class and minor civil servants, promising increased social status. General garrison duties were boring and the army was often used to quell civil disturbances, which further antagonised the Left and confirmed the officer corps in their belief that they were the guarantors of public order and the unitary state.

By 1936 the armed forces were deeply politicised, with clandestine organisations of the left and right. UMRA (Unión Militar Republicana Antifascista), for example, trained the militias of the socialists and communists, while UME (Unión Militar Española) was planning the uprising against the Popular Front administration.[50] When the war broke out in July 1936, there was roughly an equal number of officers in the Republican and rebel zones, but five of Spain's eight military districts went over to the rebels. Officers caught in the wrong place were ruthlessly purged: in loyal areas around 4,000 were dismissed because of untrustworthiness, along with 700 officers of the Guardia Civil; an unknown number went into hiding, were imprisoned, executed officially or murdered. Suspected 'Red' officers arrested in the rebel zone in July were usually shot immediately. Only 2,000 of the over 16,000 officers on the Army List in 1936 served in the Republican Army.[51]

The re-organisation of a new People's Army, ERP (Ejército Republicano Popular) after the July 1936 putsch was a considerable achievement but an intricate endeavour: at first to persuade the militias of the trade unions, the anarchists and the anti-fascist political parties to accept conventional army structures (appointment, not election of officers) and the adoption of basic training and battle techniques (drill, digging trenches for cover). The main proponents of a traditional army model were the communists organised in the 5th Regiment in Madrid, which served as a prototype for infantry units. The basic unit was the brigada mixta of four battalions (three rifle and one machine-gun company in each) with associated service units (sappers, cavalry, signallers, supplies and four light batteries of artillery), totalling 3,000 soldiers. The subsequent shortage of artillery had the consequence that it was controlled at divisional level and often did not act in full coordination with the brigades. The same held true for the crews of armoured cars and tanks – Russian or foreign communist volunteers.[52]

Because of the shortage of trained officers and non-commissioned officers on the Republican side, battle tactics were often unimaginative (lack of manoeuvring skills) due to the hierarchical system that was, perhaps, aggravated by communist authoritarian methods. In contrast, on the rebel side there was the German idea of 'Auftragskommando', i.e. a unit has a mission that self-confident professional officers were to carry out without undue interference from above. In the Republican Army, the motto seems to have been, when 'learning by doing', the avoidance of mistakes.[53]

The first brigade of foreign volunteers, later known as the 11th International Brigade (or Thälmann) and mainly Austro-German, was formed on 22 October, the 12th (Franco-Belge) on 9 November, the 13th (multinational) on 1 December and the French 14th (Marseillaise) the day after. The Anglo-American brigade, the 15th, was not inaugurated until 31 January.[54] Their contribution to the Republican war effort has arguably been exaggerated (mainly by Franco's apologists and foreigners) as they made up less than five per cent of the ERP intake in 1936–1939. After Franco could not capture Madrid from the north in the early stages of the war through the Sierra Guadarrama, his forces mounted offensives from the south and the west. From 8 November the International Brigades were thrown into the battle in the western suburbs around the new University City and then to the defence of the suburbs and villages in the west. The contribution of the foreign volunteers was decisive in November, and later in February on the Jarama. Thereafter the International Brigades were seen as battle-hardened troops and deployed prominently in later battles (Guadalajara, Brunete, Aragon, Teruel, Ebro), sustaining high losses.

The exact number of volunteers from abroad fighting in the International Brigades is unknown. Figures are quoted as between 35,000 and 42,000. The Military Control Commission of the League of Nations that monitored the removal of the Internationals from Spain in late 1938 established a total of 32,159 volunteers.[55] The latter statistic tallies with tables compiled within the brigades that Marty presented to ECCI in August 1940,[56] but 35,000 seems more likely. The figures in the Moscow State Archive for Political and Social History (RGASPI) are fragmentary and it is symptomatic of the inefficient administration that Zaisser, commandant of the Albacete Base, wrote at the end of March 1938 that the total intake to date was 31,369, of whom 9,097 brigadistas were at the front from a total of 15,992; the whereabouts of eighteen per cent was unknown, and a further thirty per cent had been killed or repatriated.[57] A German staff officer on an inspection in Albacete in August 1937 estimated that there were between 35,000 and 40,000 index cards with photographs of volunteers in a base office.[58] The exact number will probably never be known. Recruitment trends can be discerned, however, for the English-speaking volunteers.

**Table 2:** Official total number IB volunteers, October 1936–August 1938, by month and country of origin

| Month | UK | US | Can. | Irl. | Global | Month | UK | US | Can. | Irl. | Global |
|---|---|---|---|---|---|---|---|---|---|---|---|
| 1936–Mar. 1937 | 877 | 733 | 173 | 148 | 18,714 | Dec. 1937 | 59 | 23 | 46 | 16 | 738 |
| Apr. 1937 | 53 | 178 | | 6 | 1,089 | Jan. 1938 | 95 | 45 | 35 | 7 | 1,155 |
| May 1937 | 137 | 304 | | 3 | 1,232 | Feb. 1938 | 131 | 78 | 23 | 6 | 1,298 |
| June 1937 | 36 | 363 | | 4 | 1,341 | Mar. 1938 | 58 | 42 | 16 | 6 | 890 |
| July 1937 | 30 | 217 | | 6 | 902 | Apr. 1938 | 66 | | | 6 | 529 |
| Aug. 1937 | 57 | 107 | 71 | 7 | 951 | May 1938 | 21 | 34 | | 4 | 451 |
| Sept. 1937 | 84 | 78 | 54 | 12 | 938 | June 1938 | 11 | 18 | 2 | | 237 |
| Oct. 1937 | 79 | 64 | 61 | 6 | 955 | July 1938 | 4 | 10 | | | 108 |
| Nov. 1937 | 44 | 42 | 31 | 7 | 637 | Aug. 1938 | 1 | 5 | | 1 | 92 |

All: RGASPI          UK, 1,843, US, 2,341, Can, 512, Irl, 245, Global, 32,297[59]
All: Literature      UK, 2,400, US, 2,800, Can, 1,448, Irl, 250, Global, 35,000+[60]

What is clear from the obviously incomplete figures is that the numbers for all nationalities from the first enthusiastic surge (October 1936–March 1937) tapered off in the spring/summer of 1937, declining further in the autumn, with a discernible increase in the first two months of 1938, and a further considerable decline from April.

Based on the official figure of 32,000 volunteers, the percentage per nationality calculated by the given total for the monthly intakes shows the clear dominance of Continental Europeans: France 27.7 per cent, Poland 9.6 per cent, Italy 9.3 per cent, USA 7.2 per cent, Germany 6.9 per cent, Balkans 6.5 per cent and Britain 5.6 per cent.[61] The strength of the 15th International Brigade varied but was persistently below full unit strength (3,700):

**Table 3:** 15th Brigade strength 1937–1938

| Date | Brit. batt. | U.S. batt. | Can. batt. | Brig. Totals | Remarks |
|---|---|---|---|---|---|
| 20 Mar. 1937 | 440 | 350 | – | 2 608 | Incl. Balkan, Spanish and Franco-Belge batts. |
| 1 July 1937 | 441 | 800 | – | 2 144 | as above. |

| | | | | | |
|---|---|---|---|---|---|
| 9 Oct. 1937 | 346 | 343 | 468 | 1 873 | Incl. Spanish batt. |
| 22 Oct. 1937 | 256 | 337 | 425 | 2 205 | Incl. Spanish batt. |
| 6 Dec. 1937 | 423 | 491 | 534 | 2 535 | Incl. all nationalities |
| 20 Jan. 1938 | | | | 3 192 | Incl. Spanish batt. |
| 31 Mar.1938 | 585 | 554 | 604 | 2 329 | Incl. Spanish batt. |
| 6 Apr. 1938 | 211 | 102 | 197 | 1 333 | Incl. Spanish batt.[62] |

Statistics also reveal the sharp drop in numbers following the March retreats and the preponderance of Spaniards in all battalions of English-speakers, already at 61 per cent in December 1937.[63]

### THE IRISH CONTINGENT IN THE INTERNATIONAL BRIGADES

Our knowledge of Irish volunteers is based on personal and other IB files in the RGASPI, files compiled by the British Special Branch and held in Kew (TNA, KV2, KV5), data provided by pestered colleagues, and personal enquiries answered by a score of people. Information was also garnered in Irish archives (Register of Births, Marriages and Deaths, Dublin), the National Archives and National Library and press reports. Data was also found in Marx Memorial Library. Also accessed were internet sources on the volunteers from Canada,[64] the USA[65] and Britain.[66] Canadian immigration records also proved useful.[67] The excellent series of articles on individual volunteers and the reprints from Irish left-wing periodicals provided by Ciaran Crossey (www.irelandscw.com) and the late Jim Carmody were also of great assistance. Various biographical snippets were garnered from books and articles. It should be emphasised that only those for whom there is documentary proof that they served in the International Brigades are taken into consideration, i.e. Irish serving in other units of the Republican forces have not been considered. Another criterion is Irish by birth or residence, with second- or third-generation Irish outside the scope of this study. Confusion arises because some men went to Spain under a pseudonym, or gave inquisitive policemen at British ports other names, false dates of birth or spurious places of origin. At present there are about 20 cases provisionally excluded, whose Irish dates of birth are unclear, or because RGASPI references are fragmentary or non-existent.

The figures given in the following are provisional and updates and new material on Irish brigadistas can be found on: www.mcloughlin.at. As regards the county of origin (birthplace) of the 247 volunteers, Dublin and Antrim dominate:

Antrim 47, Armagh 8, Carlow 1, Cavan 3, Clare 2, Cork 13, Derry 12, Donegal 7, Down 11, Dublin 56, Fermanagh 2, Galway 5, Kerry 6, Kildare 3, Kilkenny 7, Laois 1, Leitrim, 1, Limerick 6, Longford 2, Louth 5, Mayo 5, Monaghan 3, Offaly 2, Sligo 1, Tipperary 7, Tyrone 2, Waterford 11, Westmeath 2, Wexford 2, Canada 1, at sea 1, UK 3, unknown 9 = 247.

Counties Meath, Roscommon, and Wicklow are unrepresented.

What is striking about the flow of Irish volunteers (country of departure) is that only a quarter went direct from Ireland and over half were from the UK. The Irish contingent among the Canadian volunteers is surprisingly high and those travelling from the United States relatively low, presumably because Irish Republican organisations in the USA were not enthusiastic about Irishmen fighting in 'foreign wars':

Ireland 62, UK 134, Canada 31, USA 12, Australia 3, France 1, joined in Spain 1, unknown 3=247.

Concerning recruitment patterns in the twenty-six Counties, it emerges that the great majority left between December 1936 and February 1937. Thereafter enlistment seems to have been discouraged in Dublin, until a smaller, second wave arrived in Spain from late March 1938. Irish volunteers arriving between these dates were recruited primarily in the UK and Canada. Not surprising to experts is the large contingent of at least 82 from the Six Counties. At least four of the volunteers repatriated by Frank Ryan in 1937 returned to the Spanish battlefields after a few months: Jack Nalty, Paddy Duff, Michael Lehane and Jim O'Regan. The date given for arrival in Spain is not always accurate to the day since Moscow files often do not distinguish between registration in Figueras or Albacete, and the date the men joined the British battalion. All Irish volunteers from Ireland or the UK who arrived in Spain after the battle of Brunete (July 1937), were assigned to the British battalion (57th).

Information from Moscow on the early Irish arrivals is scanty because a cadres department was not established in Albacete for the English-speakers until March/April 1937. According to scholars, the proportion of communists among the British volunteers was about 75 per cent;[68] in the US battalions the proportion was roughly the same, between two thirds and three quarters.[69] Internal documents from the brigades (22 Dec. 1937) show that of the 2,471 US brigadistas integrated up to that date, 78 per cent were members of the CPUSA or the Young Communist League.[70] Of the 955 Canadian volunteers in late 1937, half were communists, the same percentage applied to the British contingent of 739.[71] An analysis of party affiliation within language groups found that almost 60 per cent of all Internationals in Spain at the end of 1937 (20,089) were communists, with the percentage highest among the German speakers (70.8 per cent), followed by the Anglophones (63.9 per cent), the Italian-speakers (60.0 per cent) and those speaking a Slavic language (50.7 per cent).[72] In the case of the Irish brigadistas, this figure was lower, totalling 47–50 per cent according to the incomplete data at our disposal. Some volunteers had been members of more than one CP (e.g. Peter O'Connor, Jim Prendergast, Johnny Power, Bob Doyle, Ben Murray):

CPI 34, CPGB 50, Communist Party of Canada 20, CPUSA 14, Communist Party of Australia 1.

The figures collated for political affiliation are underestimates, including membership of an Irish Republican organisation: IRA 47, Irish Republican Congress 25. It seems that the earliest contingent, the one led by Frank Ryan in December 1936, contained a high number of active IRA volunteers. Afterwards, communists predominate in the groups that left Ireland for Spain. However, it is likely that a greater number of the Irish in Spain had been active in the IRA, the CPI and the Congress than listed in these pages.

Many of the Irish who travelled from Britain do not seem to have been politically active beforehand in Ireland. Up to 13 were members of the Labour Party or the Independent Labour Party in Britain or Northern Ireland. Striking is the high number of Irish who were members of the British Communist Party.

As regards previous military experience, this is an under-researched topic for the brigades as a whole. Roughly one third of the Irish had undergone some kind of weapons' instruction: 24 in the British Army, eight in the Irish Free State Army and at least 47 in the IRA. At least 10 had taken part in the Irish War of Independence and 15 in the Irish Civil War. There were also a handful of World War veterans. Two thirds of the Irish who fought in the International Brigades survived the war. Almost all Irish IB volunteers were wounded, many more than once. Fatality rates in Spain were enormous for a 20th century war the British Army figures, in percentage, for men killed in action or who died of wounds or disease in the First World War: was about 13 per cent.[73] This was less than half the proportional losses of the Irish in the Spanish Republican Army (at least 29 per cent). The British fatality rate in Spain was 25 per cent. 165 Irish survived, the fate of ten volunteers remains unclear, and the 72 deaths occurred as follows:

60 killed in action or died of wounds in Spain, 1 died of disease, 2 were killed in accidents, 3 were executed, 6 missing believed dead. The 60 deaths in battle: Madrid front 4, Cordoba front 7, Jarama 16, Brunete 9, Aragon 8, Teruel 3, Ebro 13.

At least 26 Irish-born IB soldiers were taken prisoner by the troops of Franco and his ally Mussolini, mainly during the March retreats of 1938. They were repatriated with the help of the British Government in 1938/1939 and Dublin later reimbursed the British Foreign Office for the travel costs. The majority seems to have stayed in the UK.

The Irish contingent had its share of troublemakers. Many of these, however, had cracked up in the appalling conditions of modern warfare, were chronically ill from wounds or digestive complaints and disease or became demoralised because the promised repatriation was never sanctioned by Albacete. The number of what communists called 'lumpen elements', or what we would call adventurers, is low, between 10 and 20. Three Irish volunteers were rejected at Figueras for reasons of health or bad conduct, and an equal number in Paris. At least two were sent straight back because they were underage. The total for reparations due to illness, wounds, under enlistment-age and political considerations was 46 in 1937.

There seems to have been little animosity between the national groups in the British battalion from July 1937 to the withdrawal of the brigades in September 1938. The initial difficulties at Madrigueras were caused primarily by the treatment of Irish volunteers by British officers and CPGB political commissars. Individuals from a subjected nation generally know more about the conqueror's country than the other way round, and that held true for the 15th International Brigade. The year 1936 was only 14 years after the withdrawal of British forces from the south of Ireland and the armed struggle had shaped patriotic Irish mindsets. The stories of ex-IRA men may have mystified or bored city-bred Britons or Americans, and two members of the British battalion mentioned later their discomfort on hearing, for them, morbid patriotic ballads from their Irish comrades.[74] These critics obviously did not understand Irish political history or why the term 'republic' had a special ring for Irish volunteers: having being defeated in their efforts to secure one in 1919–1923, the politically conscious of the Irish considered the fighting in Spain as a struggle against fascism but also one to keep the country an anti-monarchical democracy. Another specific trait was the keenness of certain Irishmen for soldiering and their competence: Paddy O'Daire, Peter Daly, Jack Nalty and Paddy O'Sullivan were prominent examples. Perhaps previous IRA training eased the transition from civilian to military life because many in the Irish cohort comprehended right from the start the need for discipline and 'got on with the job'.

NOTES

1. Sergej Slutsch, 'Stalin und Hitler 1933–1941: Kalküle und Fehlkalkulationen des Kreml', in Jürgen Zarusky (ed.), *Stalin und die Deutschen: Neue Beiträge der Forschung* (Munich, 2006), pp 59–88.

2. Stanley G. Payne, *The Spanish Civil War, the Soviet Union and Communism* (New Haven and London, 2004), p. 141; Juriy Rybalkin, *Operatsiya 'X': Sovetskaya voennaya pomosh' respublikanskoy Ispanii (1936–1939)* (Moscow, 2000), pp 28–9.

3. Gerald Howson, *Arms for Spain: The Untold Story of the Spanish Civil War* (London, 1998), pp 130–45, 235.

4. J. Arch Getty & Oleg V. Naumov, *The Road to Terror: Stalin and the Self-Destruction of the Bolsheviks, 1932–1939* (New Haven and London, 1999), p. 588.

5. Daniel Kowalsky, *Stalin and the Spanish Civil War*, Chapters 9, 10, especially Tables IV-1 to 6 (Chapter 10), www.gutenberg-e.org/kod01/frames/fkod1mg.html; Rybalkin, *Operatsiya 'X'*, p. 44; Jung Chan, Jon Halliday, *Mao: The Unknown Story* (New York, 2005), p. 205; Rafael A. Permuy López, *Air War over Spain* (Hersham, 2009), pp 25–7; Howson, *Arms for Spain*, pp 302–3.

6. Ian McDougall (ed.), *Voices from the Spanish Civil War: Personal Recollections of Scottish Volunteers in Republican Spain 1936–39* (Edinburgh, 1986), pp 117–68.

7. Fridrikh I. Firsov, 'Dimitrov, the Comintern and the Stalinist Repression', in Barry McLoughlin, Kevin McDermott (eds), *Stalin's Terror: High Politics and Mass Repression in the Soviet Union* (Houndmills, 2003), pp 57–9.

8. Fridrikh I. Firsov, Harvey Klehr, John Earl Haynes (eds), *Secret Cables of the Comintern 1933–1943* (New Haven and London, 2014), pp 86–7; RGASPI, f. 495, o. 2, d. 232a, l. 122.

9. Bernhard H. Bayerlein (ed.), *Georgi Dimitroff: Tagebücher 1933–1943* (Berlin, 2000), p. 126.

10. Antonio Elorza, Marta Bizcarrondo, *Queridos Camaradas: La Internacional Comunista y España, 1919–1939* (Barcelona, 1999), pp 314, 303 (reproduction of decision in English).

11. https://depts.washington.edu/moves/CP_map-members.shtml; accessed 2 October 2017, https://core.ac.uk/download/pdf/12825503.pdf. Accessed 5 October 2017.

12. RGASPI, f. 545, o. 6, d, 87, ll. 39–40.

13. Hans Landauer and Erich Hackl, *Lexikon der österreichischen Spanienkämpfer 1936–1939* (Vienna, 2003), pp 16–17.

14. Firsov, *Secret Cables*, pp 88–90, 99–102.

15. Bayerlein, *Dimitroff Tagebücher*, pp 130–1.

16. Andreu Castells, *Las Brigadas Internacionales de la Guerra en España* (Barcelona, 1974), p. 452.

17. Hugh Thomas, *The Spanish Civil War* (London, 4th edn, 2012), pp 533–4.

18. Luigi Longo, *Die International Brigaden in Spanien*, (West-Berlin, n.d.), pp 43–57.

19. Louis Fischer, *Men and Politics*, (New York, 1946), pp 386–401.

20. Firsov, *Secret Cables*, pp 97–8.

21. Bayerlein, *Dimitroff Tagebücher*, p. 154.

22. Firsov, *Secret Cables*, pp 75–6.

23. RGASPI, f. 545, o. 6, d. 89, l. 37; Alan Campbell, John Halstead, John McIlroy, Barry McLoughlin, 'Forging the Faithful: the British at the International Lenin School', in *Labour History Review*, 1:63, April 2003, pp 99–128.

24. Angela Berg, *Die Internationalen Brigaden im Spanischen Bürgerkrieg 1936–1939* (Essen, 2005), pp 69, 72.
25. Ibid., pp 70–1.
26. John Angus, *With the International Brigade in Spain* (Loughborough, 1983), p. 9.
27. Bert Hoppe, *In Stalins Gefolgschaft: Moskau und die KPD 1928–1933* (Munich, 2007), pp 23–4.
28. Bundesarchiv Berlin-Lichterfelde (BA-L), SAPMO, RY I 2/292, pp 232–41.
29. RGASPI, f. 545, o. 2, d. 39, ll. 32–9.
30. RGASPI, f. 545, o. 1, d. 11, l. 111.
31. RGASPI, f. 545, o. 6, d. 149, l. 54.
32. RGASPI, f. 545. o. 6, d. 87, ll. 11–15.
33. Robert Stradling, *Wales and the Spanish Civil War: The Dragon's Dearest Cause?* (Cardiff, 2004), pp 155–7.
34. RGASPI, f. 545, o. 6, d. 87, l. 20.
35. Eva Barilich, *Fritz Jensen. Arzt an vielen Fronten* (Vienna, 1991).
36. Walter Fischer, *Kurze Geschichten aus einem langen Leben* (Mannheim, 1987), pp 92–9.
37. RGASPI, f. 545, o. 6, d. 87, l. 43.
38. RGASPI, f. 545, o. 1, d. 11, ll. 148a, 148b.
39. Fred Copeman, *Reason In Revolt* (London, 1948), p. 83; Imperial War Museum, London (IWM) Interview 794, Fred Copeman, reel 1; IWM, Interview 810, Peter Kerrigan, reel 3; D. Corkhill, S. Rawnsley, *The Road to Spain: Anti-Fascists at War, 1936–1939* (Dunfermline, 1981), p. 59 (Interview with Kerrigan); Barry McLoughlin, *Fighting for Republican Spain: Frank Ryan and the Volunteers from Limerick in the International Brigades* (Lulu Books, 2014), pp 64–5.
40. Cecil Eby, *Between the Bullet and the Lie: American Volunteers in the Spanish Civil War* (New York–Chicago–San Francisco, 1969), p. 27.
41. Peter N. Carroll, *The Odyssey of the Abraham Lincoln Brigade: Americans in the Spanish Civil War* (Stanford, 1994), p. 194.
42. www.merrimandiary.com/2014/06/15. Accessed 27.09.2016.
43. RGASPI, f. 545, o. 1, d. 35, ll. 105–6.
44. RGASPI, f. 545, o. 6, d. 1, ll. 51–3.
45. Ronald Radosh, Mary R. Habeck, Grigory Sevostianov (eds), *Spain Betrayed: The Soviet Union and the Spanish Civil War* (New Haven and London, 2001), p. 469.
46. Firsov, *Secret Cables*, p. 106.
47. Bayerlein, *Dimitroff Tagebücher*, pp 169–72.
48. Permuy López, *Air War over Spain*, pp 3–10.
49. Michael Alpert, *The Republican Army in the Spanish Civil War, 1936–1939* (Cambridge, 2007), pp 7–10.
50. Ibid., pp 12–16.
51. Ibid., pp 88–91, 312–13.
52. Ibid., p. 315.
53. Michael Alpert, 'The clash of Spanish armies: contrasting ways of war in Spain, 1936–1939', in *War in History*, 6:3 (1999), pp 331–51, here 336–8.
54. Castells, *Las Brigadas*, pp 452–514.

55. I. Nesterenko (ed.), *International Solidarity with the Spanish Republic 1936–1939* (Moscow, 1976), p. 370.
56. RGASPI, f. 495, o. 20, d. 282, l. 171.
57. Rémi Skoutelsky, *Novedad en el Frente. Las Brigadas Internacionales en la Guerra Civil* (Barcelona, 2006), p. 457.
58. RGASPI, f. 545, o. 2, d. 145, l. 172.
59. RGASPI, f. 545, o. 2, d. 108, l. 208.
60. See works by Baxell, Carroll, Beeching, and McLoughlin.
61. RGASPI, 545. o. 2, d. 108, l. 208. These percentages are confirmed by an internal IB document of 18 Oct.1938 (RGASPI, f. 545, o. 6, d. 6, l. 1.)
62. RGASPI, f. 545, o. 1, d. 4, l. 4; f. 545, o. 3, d. 454, ll. 9, 10, 37, 55, 71, 75; f. 545, o. 2, d. 39, l. 111.
63. RGASPI, f. 545 o. 3, d. 454, l. 71.
64. www.web.net/~macpap/volunteers.htm. Accessed 12 April 2019.
65. www.alba-valb.org/volunteers/browse/accessed. Accessed 3 June 2019.
66. www.international-brigades.org.uk/content/roll-honour. Accessed 12 November 2019.
67. www.bac-lac.gc.ca/eng/search/Pages/ancestors-search.aspx. Accessed 19 March 2019.
68. Richard Baxell, *Unlikely Warriors: The British in the Spanish Civil War and the Struggle against Fascism*, (London, 2012), p. 7.
69. Carroll, *The Odyssey of the Abraham Lincoln Brigade*, p. 19.
70. RGASPI, f. 545, o. 6, d. 5, ll. 1, 6, 7.
71. Ibid., ll. 8, 13.
72. RGASPI, f. 545, o. 2, d. 108, l. 54.
73. Denis Winter, *Death's Men: Soldiers of the Great War* (London, 1979), pp 192–3.
74. Fred Thomas, *To Tilt at Windmills: A Memoir of the Spanish Civil War* (East Lansing, Mi, 1996), pp 58–9; Working Class Movement Library, Salford, Bob Clark Ms. p. 41.

FIVE

# THE ROAD TO THE LINCOLNS

It is possible that per capita the Irish accounted for more volunteers in Spain than any other nation. While most fought for Franco, and over half of those on the other side were expatriates, the contribution to the Spanish Republic from Ireland was remarkable for a country with a communist party of about 120 members, confined organisationally to Dublin and Belfast. It is a curiosity overshadowed in the non-Irish historiography by the tragicomic odyssey of General Eoin O'Duffy's 'Irish brigade'. The Irish involvement with the Nationalists was unique. No country provided so many genuine volunteers for Franco. It would be one of two factors that produced the Connolly Column. The fundamental factor was the decision of the ECCI in September 1936 to create the International Brigades.

For the next two years, the brigades became the primary focus of the Comintern and its affiliates. The Comintern determined the ideology and politics of the brigades and put in place procedures for recruitment, assessment and processing of candidate volunteers, transport to Spain, unit formation and dealing with all the demands that went with sustaining an army, such as discipline, pay, housing, medical care, postal services, newspapers and supply of weapons, uniforms and food. This was no mean achievement and while the Comintern is sometimes depicted as an éminence grise, or even a grisly éminence, this could not have been done without regulation and what the communists liked to call 'Bolshevik enthusiasm'. Moreover, the Comintern was remarkably successful in combining party control with the eclecticism that went with the popular front, and in integrating the brigades into the Ejército Popular. One could be cynical and argue that the popular front was just a short-term tactic, but all politics is short-term. The communists were honest in saying their top priority in Spain was to stop fascism.

In age and social background, the Irish volunteers were typical, and the Irish response was just as brisk as that of other anglophone countries. By January 1937, when the formation of the British and American battalions was being finalised, an Irish unit was ready. But which battalion would it join?

Where the Irish differed was in the involvement of a non-communist group, the Republican Congress, in recruitment and leadership and in the relatively high proportion of non-communists in volunteers from Ireland. Those differences in turn would result in a distinctive composition and politics for the Connolly Column in Spain, one that the communists regarded with suspicion initially. Trouble ensued when the Irish objected to fighting with the British and went over to the Americans in the Abraham Lincoln battalion. The incident has been treated as tantamount to a mutiny and is usually taken as an illustration of the abiding tension between republicanism and socialism. Arguably it says more about the CPGB and the persistence of nationalism generally in the International Brigades.

## MOTIVATION AND RECRUITMENT

The CPI was coy about recruitment. Its history of the Connolly Column confined the Comintern to the small print of a footnote and represented the International Brigades as emerging spontaneously from the efforts to defend Madrid in November 1936. It also said that 'the arrival of the International Brigades [in November] and the presence of [comrade] Bill Scott in Madrid quickly raised the question of Irish participation in the military struggle against Franco.' Scott had signed up in London in September and made his way to Nat Cohen's group in Barcelona before joining the mainly German-speaking Thälmann centuria and taking part in the defence of Madrid. In November the Thälmann battalion, as it now was, would become part of the 12th (Garibaldi) International Brigade.[1] Yet Michael O'Riordan's claim that Scott's presence in Madrid 'raised the question of Irish participation' is contradicted by the admission that the CPI decided in September 'that an Irish Unit of the International Brigades should be formed'. The CPI's official history made the same points.[2]

The coyness was entirely in keeping with the Comintern's popular front policy. In the first instance it wished to discourage the perception that the communists were escalating the conflict through Moscow manipulation. *Britons in Spain*, commissioned by the CPGB and published in January 1939, wrote of how 'The idea of the International Brigades arose spontaneously in the minds of men' and had the Brigades developing organically from foreign volunteers in the militias.[3] In April 1938 *Time* magazine reported European speculation about the Lincoln battalion having been created by the Comintern or the CPUSA, but its members boasting it arose casually from solidarity forged round a Spanish campfire on Christmas Day 1936.[4]

The Comintern also wanted to play down the communist input, to maximise recruitment for the brigades and support for the popular front. Communists gave their political affiliation in the Brigades' identification cards as 'anti-fascist'. Initially at least, there was a concern that so unprecedented a project might backfire at any stage, in failing to attract recruits, in problems of military organisation, or when comrades were sent to the front. As the reputation of the brigades consolidated, the communists became less reticent about claiming credit.

The Comintern was drawn gradually into the war. Willi Münzenberg, its propaganda 'wunderkind', organised a European Conference for the Defence of the Spanish Republic in Paris on 13 August. Ostensibly it was convened by another Comintern front, the World Committee Against War and Fascism. Over the coming weeks, more fronts to aid Spain were created, the Soviet diplomatic presence in Madrid increased and the Soviets began covert operations to buy arms for Spain on the international market. As commitment deepened, and the military situation worsened, Moscow agreed to a request from Maurice Thorez, head of the French party, that military units be formed. They would be open to non-communists but the gatekeepers would be senior comrades.[5] Even getting to Spain was difficult for volunteers outside communist-controlled channels.

Within the International Brigades, political control was maintained by the ubiquitous commissar delegates of war, to give them their official title. At each level of command, the military authority was paralleled by a political officer. The system was introduced during the Russian Civil War when the Red Army wished to make use of the skills of former Tsarists but was not sure they could be trusted.

Once it had taken the plunge, the Comintern pulled out all the stops. Affiliates were instructed to provide recruits, and given quotas based on their membership and potential, with the numbers deliberately pitched a little on the side of ambition. The figures for Ireland are unknown. What is known is that its potential was limited. Forty-seven attended the annual general meeting of the Dublin branch in February 1937. Sixteen were excused and 12 were in Spain. The Belfast branch was smaller again, with about 40 members.[6] The CPI had appointed Bill Gannon to organise the Irish contribution.[7] Born in Dublin in 1902, Gannon was a veteran of Michael Collins's squad in the War of Independence and of the Civil War, and suspected of involvement in the assassination of Minister for Justice Kevin O'Higgins in 1927. In the 1930s he was drawn to the left by Jim Prendergast. Both joined the CPI on its foundation, and Gannon's sister, Margaret, would marry Seán Murray.

Emigrating to New Zealand in 1939, Gannon worked on the waterfront and in transport, joining the Communist Party of New Zealand. After returning to Dublin in 1945 he became a founder member of the revived communist party, trading as the Irish Workers' League, and was given a 'red funeral' in 1965. Prendergast's ashes were later buried with Gannon.[8] As a loyal comrade with excellent republican connections, Gannon was an ideal choice.

When and why did the Republican Congress commit to recruiting for the International Brigades? A debate had been rumbling along in the Congress since the outbreak of the war. O'Duffy proposed an 'Irish Volunteer Brigade' for Spain in letters to the press on 10 August. In a side-swipe at the Republican Congress, he attacked 'the Third International' as 'mainly concerned with combatting Christianity' through the '"United Front" which we have heard spoken of in Dublin city at so-called "Anti-Fascist" meetings'.[9] O'Duffy too saw Spain through Irish eyes. '[I]f an Irish Brigade were actually fighting on the Spanish Christian Front', he promised, 'the Irish nation would rally behind it, and communism would never again raise its ugly head in Ireland. . . the fight against Communism in Ireland can be most effectively waged on the Spanish Front.'[10] The Congress applauded the NILP for its stand on Spain on 24 August. Some wanted a stronger commitment. Charlie Donnelly's brother Joseph claimed:

> At a meeting attended by Peadar O'Donnell, George Gilmore and Frank Ryan, a bitter row developed between Charlie and Frank Ryan in which Charlie accused Ryan of betraying the legacy of Connolly unless Congress publicly supported the Republican Government. Ryan's answer was that while Charlie had been writing accusing letters from London, he had been trying desperately to hold the rapidly weakening Congress together in Ireland and in America. The argument was finally settled and the meeting agreed that a message of support should be sent to the Spanish Republican Government. This was to set off a chain of events which would bring Ryan himself to Spain.[11]

The agreed telegram of solidarity was sent on 15 September. Ryan remained opposed to direct intervention. He wrote to Gerald O'Reilly of Clan na Gael on 17 September saying O'Donnell was 'too full of Spain and could think of nothing else', adding 'I wouldn't go to Spain, nor to USA, just now, because I feel I have to stand my ground here and rally our own.'[12] Three days later Joseph Cardinal MacRory called on de Valera to proscribe the Republican Congress for its cable of solidarity to Largo Caballero. MacRory's remarks were made, very publicly, to an assembly of 7,000 pilgrims at the shrine of Oliver Plunkett in Drogheda. They also contained a slip-up: 'We should all pray for Spain and, if able to, we should all help from our purses, help her to obtain war supplies – what I should say is medical supplies. . .'. Ryan responded immediately with a lengthy, considered riposte, accusing His Eminence of selectivity in his condemnation of atrocities. The gravamen was the distinction he drew between religion and politics, and he signed off with the ringing rebuke: 'as a Catholic, I will "take my religion from Rome", but as an Irish Republican, I will take my politics from neither Moscow nor Maynooth.' The sentence was published in the *Irish Times*, but omitted from the *Irish Press* report. Cronin believed that the cardinal 'sent both Frank Ryan and Eoin O'Duffy to Spain'.[13]

Yet Gilmore was designated to lead the Republican Congress contingent in Spain until an air accident en route to Bilbao put him on crutches.[14] The despatch of Gilmore to Bilbao suggests that the Republican Congress, or Gilmore at least, preferred a linkage with the Basques rather than the International Brigades. Rose Jacob noted of the meeting in the Engineers' Hall in Dawson Street on 3 December that Ryan corrected the impression given by Gilmore that they were only concerned for Basque Catholics and dwelt on the importance of Spain to working class organisations internationally. Patently affected by a letter from Bill Scott, he went to speak with violent passion about the Irish fighting in Madrid. Hanna Sheehy Skeffington told Jacob that Ryan was 'going'. Jacob wasn't certain.[15] Nothing was certain. O'Donnell and Ryan were closer to Murray and the CPI, but O'Donnell was not enthusiastic about sending their few precious cadres to Spain.[16] Jacob reckoned that Gilmore shared O'Donnell's reservations and she herself took time to be convinced, writing in March 1937 of how Ryan 'half-converted me when he spoke of the Spaniards and others in Madrid, when they saw the staff sent out by the Medical Aid Committee here, saying to him "Now we see that Ireland is not a Fascist country, as we had thought." That *is* value to Ireland.'[17] Ryan kept his counsel and dithered before eventually throwing his lot in with the CPI's recruitment drive. Its approval was vital for admission to the International Brigades.

He was warmly welcomed. The communists had no problems with volunteers from any background for virtually any reason, and cheerfully admitted that the brigades contained a few adventurers and mavericks. It fitted in with popular front propaganda.[18] Sometimes Ryan suggested that his motivation was to counter O'Duffy. On other occasions he dismissed the idea. Various personal reasons have been put forward for his change of mind, ranging from his zest for action to the pressure from Charlie Donnelly. Tommy Patten had already become the first Republican Congress man to go to Spain when he left from London in October. From his sanguine handling of the *Irish Democrat* in 1937, it is unlikely that Ryan's faith in the Republican Congress was flagging. He gave three reasons for 'the Irish contingent' in December, all of which chimed with popular front thinking: 'to redeem the

Irish honour besmirched by the intervention of Irish Fascism on the side of the Spanish Fascist rebels... to aid the revolutionary movements in Ireland to defeat the Fascist menace at home, and... to establish the closest bonds of friendship between the Republican democracies of Ireland and Spain.'[19] He departed on 11 December, without as much as a goodbye to Rose. In fairness, it may have been to spare her feelings. He also tried to keep the secret from his family – three of his sisters were nuns. Rose wrote, with the exasperation of unrequited love: 'the ruffians. No job, love of excitement & fighting, & the idea of the importance everywhere of the fight in Spain – but they may be more needed here.'[20]

Most communist party secretaries had their quotas to fill. As the war progressed, its lethal consequences became better known, and hopes of victory receded, parties were obliged to put more and more pressure on comrades to enlist.[21] It was not just a question of numbers. The British battalion comandancia in Albacete demanded better quality. Estimating that half the men were demoralised and that 'the British have got a bad name in the rearguard', it told the CPGB: 'There should be a stop to recruiting in hostels and Parks, Embankments etc.'[22] Clearly the CPI did not come under the same strain. Spain was a priority at the CPI's Dublin district annual general meeting in February 1937, with comrades urged to redouble their efforts in leafleting, postering, raising awareness in trade unions and collecting funds for the Irish troops. Nothing was said about enlistment, and no one has ever suggested that they were harangued into volunteering by the CPI.[23] When four New Theatre Group players made a pact to enlist in 1938, Murray persuaded two that they would be more useful at home.[24] Family tradition has it that Murray refused to allow Gannon to go as he was married with children. And Eugene Downing, who left in March 1938, worried about rejection by Murray. Inevitably, there were jibes as to why Murray didn't go himself. He is not known to have addressed the question.[25] At 38, he would have been relatively old, and was running to seed. 'Duine suairc ba ea Seán', Downing recalled, 'agus aghaidh dearglasta, dea chothaithe aige a chuirfeadh easpag i gcuimhne duit'. Back in Dublin in late 1938, Downing felt the war and the loss of so many close comrades had weighed very heavily with him. Andrew Boyd's first impression, in 1941, was of 'a decayed, overweight person, who, I already knew, was too fond of the liquor'.[26] His IRA days were long behind him. It is also likely that the CPI in Dublin would have collapsed without him.

Republican Congress leaders said they could have recruited many more. O'Donnell said he wanted just enough men to make a credible counterpoint to O'Duffy. By mid-September the *Irish Independent* was reporting that 5,000–6,000 had volunteered their services for O'Duffy, and what number

O'Donnell had in mind is unknown. His claim that 'though hundreds offered to go to Spain he selected only 145' was echoed by Ryan.[27] 'Hundreds' may have been an exaggeration, and '145' is obviously an unreliable figure, but there are at least two accounts of O'Donnell trying to prevent men going to Spain, though both appear to date from 1937.[28] Ryan left with a group from Dublin's Westland Row train station on 11 December 1936, following the standard route to Liverpool, London, Paris and Perpignan. The press implied that he commanded 80 men, including 40 from Dublin, led personally, 30 from Belfast and 10 from Rosslare, all departing Ireland for Spain in the week before 14 December.[29] The reports initiated a persistent tendency to exaggerate the numbers who went directly from Ireland. Joe Monks named 'thirteen Irishmen who had travelled with him [Ryan] in the contingent that had crossed the frontier from France on the 14th December 1936'.[30] Of these, two had joined the group in London. No doubt there were others leaving on proximate dates who were inspired by the Republican Congress recruitment drive. What might be called Ryan's cohort, generously defined as those who arrived in Spain from Ireland in December, amounted to no more than 39. It is impossible to be precise on the provenance of their recruitment. Five are known to have been members of the Republican Congress, 11 were in the CPI, four were in both, another four were or had been in the IRA, and 12 were of undetermined affiliation. It was by far the biggest batch from Ireland for any month of the civil war.

The flow of men to Spain from Ireland fell to a trickle in 1937, when the Non-Intervention Committee introduced the additional hurdle of making it illegal to join the war in Spain. Bob Doyle was informed in January by Cora Hughes that Republican Congress recruitment had ceased. Doyle was also in the CPI, but it is possible that, aged under 21, he had been rejected by Murray on account of his youth.[31] Determined to fight, he set off on an odyssey that illustrated the difficulty of getting to Spain for those unable to use the CPI or the CPGB. He had made no less than four trips to Spanish ports, Nationalist and Republican, as a merchant seaman or stowaway before joining the CPGB. Once a trusted comrade, he was shown the well-worn path from King Street in London's Covent Garden to the French party's headquarters in Paris's Place du Combat, a large dilapidated square to the north-east of the city centre.[32] Ryan was certainly against sending more men when he returned to Dublin. From Paris he had enquired with Gerald O'Reilly about a visit to America.[33] Christy Quearney pleaded in March 1937:

> look Frank, what about organising some of us to go back with you; there were at least four of our [IRA] company already serving there... We knew Spain was no

picnic. Anyhow, Frank no; the Army is in a bad way and we are not winning in Spain. Stay behind and reorganise the Army, we may need it yet.[34]

The exchange also reveals Ryan's ready access to the IRA, which for him was still 'the army'. Quearney had previously refused to join the Republican Congress as it had broken with the IRA and, in his mind, the lawfully constituted Republic. Few knew how to get to Spain other than through the choke point of the CPGB in London and knew that that required a letter of introduction from Murray or O'Donnell.

The large number of expatriates incoming in 1937 was affected, from January, by the arrival of volunteers from the US and Canada. Both fought in the Abraham Lincoln battalion until the creation of a second North American battalion, the George Washington, in May, and a Canadian battalion in July.[35] Some expatriates were long out of Ireland and politicised abroad, while others were recent emigrants and still engaged with Irish politics. Canadian and London Irish were at either end of the spectrum. Some 1,680 Canadians served in Spain. Only 245 were Canadian-born.[36] According to Petrou, 39 'ethnic' Irish went to Spain directly from Canada, another one went from the US, a further five were returned emigrants from Canada and went to Spain from London, two other Irishmen served in the MacPaps and an additional three had other Canadian connections. Of course, this was a small number of the total Irish emigration to Canada, which totalled 88,500 for the 1920s and just under 20,000 for the 1930s. But a more significant comparator is the 12 volunteers who went from the US, though over 80 per cent of Irish emigrants to North America went to the US.[37]

The relatively high number of Irish from Canada reflected the strength of the Communist Party of Canada among immigrants and the immigrant experience in Canada. The Canadian contingent had more immigrants than any other country and just half of the immigrants hailed from eastern Europe, giving them a significant over-representation. The typical recruit arrived in Canada between 1925 and 1930, settled around Toronto or Vancouver, was single and unskilled, worked in migratory jobs like lumberjacking, mining, farm labouring or road-maintenance, and was hit by the Great Depression.

Fearful of communism, Prime Minister Richard Bennett introduced a de facto ban on the Communist Party in 1931 and created relief camps in 1932. With no unemployment insurance, 170,000 were driven to seek refuge in the camps, where they lived in barracks and were expected to work on public improvement projects for 20c a day. Instead of isolating unrest, the camps concentrated the discontented, and their spartan conditions led to protests and clashes with the police, most famously in the 'On to Ottawa trek' of 1935, when men in the camps in Vancouver struck, and decided to march on Ottawa. The trek was stopped by repeated baton charges by the Royal Canadian Mounted Police at Regina. Violence at the hands of the authorities was probably a factor in conditioning men for service in Spain. Of 115 Canadians who completed questionnaires on their membership of the International Brigades in May 1937, almost half said they had been arrested or imprisoned.[38]

From the outset, the camps were recruiting grounds for the Communist Party, which was flourishing through fronts like the Workers' Unity League, which led 90 per cent of strikes in Canada between 1933 and 1936. Though the communists were keen to recruit non-party members for Spain, about 76 per cent of Canadian volunteers were communists, which was above average. Similar points could be made about other characteristics. In all countries, volunteers were more likely to be unemployed, low paid, unskilled or in migratory, temporary or insecure employment. These characteristics were more true of the Canadians. Canadians were underrepresented in respect of Jews, intellectuals and white-collar occupations.

Of the 45 'ethnic' Irish volunteers logged by Petrou, we know the Irish address of 35, and 24 of these were residents in Ulster (the nine counties), whereas only about 90 of all Irish volunteers were native Ultonians. Whether the imperial connection was important is not certain, but in at least two instances the passage to Canada was funded by empire settlement schemes. Their known destinations were chiefly Vancouver and the Toronto/Windsor area. Obviously, they headed to the more industrial cities and, in the case of Vancouver, a hotbed of protest against unemployment and the conditions in the relief camps. Their occupations were diverse but most were in insecure, temporary, low-paid employment as lumberjacks, miners, labourers and cooks. One man described his occupation as 'waiter and variety artist'. In occupation, the Irish were like the Canadian volunteers generally, except that they were even more proletarian. Most were probably radicalised in Canada. Five recorded an Irish political affiliation prior to emigration. Four had been in the IRA and one in the Republican Congress. By contrast, at least 19 were in the Communist Party of Canada, one was in the CPUSA and two were in the CPGB. Military service is another common characteristic. In addition to the three IRA men, two had soldiered in the Free State army and four in the Canadian services (army, militia or the Mounties). Four had been arrested by the Canadian police for political activities.[39]

London was unique in having an active branch of an Irish political group outside Ireland and engaged on a week-to-week basis with Irish politics. For working class people, London was the real economic capital of Ireland and the last resort of young, mobile, unemployed men. Nine of the eleven Waterford volunteers, for example, worked on the buildings or in factories and shuttled back and forth to London as economic circumstances dictated.[40] As a terminus of the Great Western Railway, Waterford had a physical link to Paddington. As late as the 1970s one could see men in British Rail uniforms working on the city's quays and buy a ticket locally for the boat-train via Fishguard, symbolically obviating Dublin. Other Irish volunteers from London had been waiters, motor mechanics, or soldiers in the British army. The last of the Connolly Column reported in August 1938 and the roll included one woman, Hannah Ruth Ormesby, originally from Dromore West in Sligo, who arrived in Spain in April 1937 as a nurse in a British ambulance detachment.

The Irish from Ireland, and especially those who went out in December 1936, were distinctive for their below-average proportion of communists and above-average proportion of men who were not merely non-communists, but members of what had once been feared as a competitor, namely the Republican Congress.

### 'COMRADES, WE ARE BEING BLACKGUARDED'[41]

Christopher 'Kit' Conway's response on discovering that his company commander, George Nathan, had been a 'Black and Tan', could be applied equally to the treatment of the Irish decision to leave the British for the Abraham Lincoln battalion in January 1937. Accommodating the Republican Congress required an adjustment of attitudes in Moscow and King Street. Both the Comintern and Harry Pollitt blamed O'Donnell especially for the disaster in Rathmines in September 1934 and for leading the CPI like a will-o'-the-wisp into the forlorn grey mists of left republicanism, compromising its very identity as a Bolshevik party. Pollitt prevented a proposed visit to Soviet Russia by O'Donnell in 1935, citing a dispute over finances. The normally compliant Murray went so far as to protest to the Anglo-American Secretariat, pleading that 'despite all his shortcomings [O'Donnell] is by no means a person to be despised.'[42]

The CPGB held Ryan in greater regard, and he was keen to make an impression. In London, en route for Spain, he had himself kitted out in polished leather boots and a leather greatcoat. Before long, his IRA pedigree had inflated into a legendary reputation as a War of Independence commander, though he had joined the IRA during the Truce. Aside from his more disciplined and military character, the Spanish Civil War put a premium on non-communist and Catholic opponents of Franco. With his association with Ireland, Ryan was a prized propaganda asset.[43] When the Republican Congress made it known that they wished their volunteers to be treated as a separate national unit in Spain, contrary to the formal policy of the Comintern, Pollitt concurred. On 12 December, he wrote to the comandancia of the International Brigades in the Gran Hotel, Albacete about the impending dispatch of 300 men from England, advising: 'les irlandais que vous recevrez seront si possible groupés en sections irlandaises.'[44]

Ryan reached the comandancia on 16 December. Albacete was a small, dusty, industrial city, about 250 km south-east of Madrid, chosen for its rail connectivity. Many Internationals disliked it as a haven of spies, rumour mongers, deserters and fifth columnists. Within days Ryan was told to make ready his 43 Irish effectives. A crisis had arisen in Andalusia, where General Queipo de Llano had launched the Aceituna Campaign, an offensive from Córdoba and Granada spearheaded by Carlist Requetés and Moorish regulars. All anglophones, most with no military training, were pressed into the 145 strong no.1 company, 12th (Marseillaise) battalion, 14th (Marseillaise) International Brigade. The 14th Brigade had been formed with French and Belgians in the main.

Ryan was assured that the Irish would be allowed to form a distinct section and asked Nathan, the no.1 company commander, to arrange it. The two struck up an unlikely friendship, but with his relaxed style, pipe between his teeth and hunting crop for a swagger stick, Nathan was a pleasant alternative to the apparatchiks. The no.1 section of no.1 company was 'Irish'. What 'Irish' meant at sub-battalion level was unclear. Monks, a proud veteran of the 4th battalion, Dublin Brigade, IRA, thought he fought in 'An Irish Unit'. Frank Edwards – in the Republican Congress but inclined to see republicans as dangerously romantic – poured cold water on the idea: 'We were not there as a separate unit, we were part of a British company. Frank [Ryan] was fighting hard for a separate identity, but he was too optimistic. He was outvoted. There was no way we would be made a separate Irish unit.' What both agreed on is that Ryan wanted an Irish formation to make an impression on politics back home.[45] Spaniards would know the no.1 company as 'los ingleses', and it would later be called the Major Attlee company after the British Labour Party leader's visit to the battalion.

If events in Andalusia were serious enough to postpone the formation of an anglophone battalion, Ryan was in no position to stand on ceremony. More surprising was Ryan's announcement that he would not be joining them, as he needed to sort out the position of the Irish in the proposed 15th International Brigade. Various explanations have been offered as to why he was never given a field command, despite his IRA experience in a milieu where there was 'a real shortage of officers'. He was hard of hearing and was wanted for propaganda work. He had no experience of a regular army. But non-party people rarely got far in the International Brigades. Nathan was exceptional in that respect. He knew it and applied, unsuccessfully, to join the party. Unlike Ryan, he was not a member of a rival organisation. Kicking his heels in Albacete left Ryan feeling bewildered, useless and sore at being backwatered. His place at the front was taken by Kit Conway, a distinguished IRA veteran and a communist Domhnall O'Reilly, a graduate of the International Lenin School, was made a political commissar.[46]

The role of the commissars, or 'comic stars' as they were nicknamed by the cynics, varied with their command. It was usually less grand and of more practical value than it sounds. At company level, their duty was welfare and morale. Some likened them to secular padres. They did 'an enormous number of odd jobs', according to British battalion adjutant Tom Wintringham:

> Laundry, and in our last weeks hot baths, and a club with radio and canteen, singsongs, food, news, mail – all these things were up to them. For discipline they were more useful than any number of guard-rooms and orderly officers. In their little meetings, through their wall-newspaper, and more than all through personal contact and argument and example, they strengthened and organised the morale, the political understanding, and determination that was the basis of our discipline.[47]

In formations composed of political activists, most of whom resented traditional ideas of military etiquette, tact and example were important. Edwards summed up his own time as commissar, after Donie O'Reilly was wounded: 'It was my job to keep up morale, to shout "Adelante" (forward), in a charge, "Communisti pirote!" (Communists in front!).'[48]

On Christmas Eve the no.1 company marched to Albacete's railway station and entrained for Andújar, 270 km to the south west. As men were leaving the train the company suffered its first casualties, from 'avions', one of a few foreign words creeping into the battalion's argot. Christmas was celebrated in Andújar with a dinner of cold bully beef. From Andújar the battalion was rushed in 'camions' 20 km to Lopera and thrown into desperate attempts to recover the town in the face of withering fire on 27–29 December. Before Lopera were two hills, a small one and a big one. The Irish gathered together to sing *Off to Dublin in the Green*, and then charged, shouting 'Up the Republic'.

Over two days the Internationals took the bigger obstacle four times, only to be driven back again by machine-gunning 'avions'. It came to be christened 'Calvary Hill'. The traumatic impact on the raw recruits was made worse by their antiquated weapons, inadequate clothing for the biting cold of the nights, basic mistakes causing fatalities from friendly fire and elementary deficiencies such as the absence of field kitchens and rudimentary medical services. The battalion's only machine guns were Chauchats. The Irish took to calling them 'Chau Chaus'. Light and versatile, they were the first machine gun that could be used by one man. They were also cursed as 'the worst machine-gun ever made'. The majority jammed at the first shot. The battalion's Austrian Steyr rifles were even worse: 'many of them blew up in the firers' hands.'[49]

Edwards remembered:

> It was pretty grim. Their fire-power was far greater than ours and their equipment much better. The first shot I fired as I advanced, the rifle broke up in my hands. I did not know what to do. I had no gun. Just at that moment a comrade fell so I grabbed his rifle...[50]

Casualties had to be carried or dragged to safety by their comrades and were then evacuated on farm carts. Throughout the night men lay in the olive groves shouting 'camillero!' and 'brancardier'. André Marty hastened to deal with a breakdown in morale. The Marseillaise battalion's commander, Gaston Delasalle, was arrested for incompetence, accused of treason and executed after a drumhead court martial. Guilty or not, there was no sympathy for him. Marty was present to provide additional evidence against him. He was beginning to acquire the fearsome reputation that would earn him the sobriquet 'the butcher of Albacete'. Monks noted the Irish losses:

> Of the thirteen Irishmen who had crossed the frontier from France with Frank Ryan on the 14th December six had been killed or died of wounds. They were Frank Conroy, Anthony Fox, Leo Green, Michael May, Michael Nolan and Thomas Woods. Gerald Doran, John Goff and myself were wounded and only four – Frank Edwards, Michael Lehane, Jimmy Prendergast and Patrick Smith – were left...[51]

Most of the Irish casualties were due to mistakes made in a tactical withdrawal. Monks had been wounded in the chest on 28 December and was hospitalised in Linares with Seán Goff.

The four surviving effectives soldiered on with Nathan's company and the 14th Brigade at Majadahonda and Las Rozas de Madrid in efforts to stop the encirclement of the capital. There were more Irish casualties at Las Rozas on 10 January. Medical services had not much improved. Edwards wrote home:

We were lying in position on a ridge. Dinny Coady lay near me with another Irishman, Pat Murphy, between us. A shell landed between Coady and Murphy. I immediately felt a sharp pain in my side. Murphy screamed. I glanced towards. He was enveloped in a cloud of smoke and dust. But I could see his face – he was ghastly pale. I got up and walked down to a ravine where our Company Headquarters section was posted, and told them to send up a stretcher at once.[52]

Lifting the blanket on a stretcher, Edwards was stunned to find Coady's corpse staring back at him. Soaked in blood, he himself was helped to an ambulance by Mike Lehane and two Austrians. Once in hospital, his treatment was good, and survival triggered a strange giddiness. 'I felt a seasoned warrior. I had been through it. I had been wounded. I got reckless. I felt that, as I had been hit once, I could not be hit again. Could anything be more silly?'[53] When Nathan's company returned to Madrigueras and a heroes' welcome from the 15th Brigade in January, just 67 men remained. Monks claims that the Irish dead also included Henry Bonar and Jim Foley.[54]

The 15th International Brigade was envisaged as a mixed unit with an anglophone battalion. As more Americans arrived and were given their own battalion, the 15th came to be seen as the brigade for anglophones, though it was not exclusively so. By the end of January it comprised the mainly Slav Dimitrov battalion, the Franco-Belgian 6 February battalion, the American Abraham Lincoln battalion and the 16th battalion, which included Australians, New Zealanders and Cypriots as well as British and Irish. The 16th was established formally on 27 December, with just two companies, and numbered the 57th battalion in the Ejército Popular. It would eventually comprise three infantry companies and a machine-gun company. The no.1 company, normally the shock detachment, was made up of Lopera veterans. There was also a brigade staff, commissariat and specialist details for things like map-making, logistics, engineering and communications.[55] The question of an Irish unit did not arise. For a name, the commissars chose to honour the recently deceased CPGB MP Shapurji Saklatvala.[56] Notwithstanding its utility in obviating an embarrassment, the title never caught on. So, in deference to the Irish within it, the 16th was sometimes called the 'Anglo-Irish' or 'English-speaking' battalion, until everyone settled on the shorter 'British', except the continentals, to whom 'British' was invariably 'English'.[57] As more Irish trickled into Albacete, they were forwarded the 30 km north to Madrigueras, where the 16th was being assembled.

Madrigueras was a destitute pueblo of stoic peasants on the plain of La Mancha. Like Albacete it endured hot summers and cold, wet winters, and the endless drizzle and battalion footfall turned its earthen streets to 'soupy mud'.[58] Between the weather, the monotonous drilling and the cold billets, time passed slowly. The day began with a breakfast of ersatz coffee and bread at 6 a.m. Sometimes there was butter, or the possibility of buying churros. Lunch and dinner were the same every day: each a vile stew of meat, rice and potato scraps all boiled together in olive oil.[59] The ubiquitous olive oil was the bane of the non-continentals. Some saved their pay to buy outrageously expensive eggs on bread in the village café. The complaints were genuine. The Ejército Popular as a whole suffered more from sickness and disease than the enemy, but the British battalion was noted for its tummy troubles. British cooks were no improvement as they were unfamiliar with Spanish cuisine and army methods. The diet worsened as hunger tightened its grip on the Republic. Michael O'Riordan recalled:

> At this late stage in the war, food often consisted of a slice of bread fried in olive oil and a cup of weak coffee, with the main meal being that of 'Garbanzos' (chickpeas). Mess-kits were often an old jam-jar or a tobacco tin, and rudimentary spoons and forks that were self-carved out of wood.[60]

With his customary good humour, Downing saw a funny side to the fare:

> Piseánaigh an príomhbhia a bhiódh again. Thugamar *beans* orthu i mBéarla ach chick-peas an t-ainm ceart. Ba chúis gháire dúinn nuair a chualamar gur thug Bill Rust, comhfhreagraí an *Daily Worker* sa Spáinn, tuairisc ar an gCathlán Briotánach sa *Daily Worker* lena rá go rabhamar *full of beans*. Nuair a fuaireamar feoil, *burro* (nó miúil) be ea é de gnáth.[61]

The clothing situation was no better. As boots wore out, 'alpargatas' or rope-sandals became standard.[62]

For the Irish in Madrigueras there was the additional discomfort of eating in the local church. Like churches in other parts of the Republic, it had been sacked and now served as a refectory and mess hall. Even the British anti-clericals were taken aback by the villagers' hatred of the clergy. Edwards astounded the Spaniards with his knowledge of Latin hymns. "'Ah, you were a Catholic before the war", they would gasp'.[63] Other targets of criticism were the inadequate sanitation (no provision had been made), useless training and incompetent officers (each being in the eye of the beholder) and ancient weaponry and shortages of ammunition (no quibbles there). The billets varied from haylofts to comfortable villas vacated by landlords. Most troops stayed with peasant families. The generosity and warmth of people who lived in abject poverty offset their own grievances.[64]

For recreation there was little except paint-stripper wine or rot-gut anis. Encouraging the men to try the novelty of wine, the water was not safe. One Irish teetotaller was no sooner in Madrigueras than he contracted typhoid fever from drinking the water.[65] Parcels of cigarettes from home were prized, but often pilfered. The acrid Spanish alternatives were known as 'anti-tanks'. Some took to smoking vine leaves.[66] Pilferage too was detected in the commissariat, a generic hazard with all armies. Some memoirs exaggerated these problems; others ignored them. Wintringham offered a rounded, if chipper, summation and a warning on the tendency of memory to dwell on the sensational:

> This chronicle may seem to give the impression that the battalion consisted of drunkards, and a few thieves; of course that is not true. There were not more than half a dozen hard soakers among the first six hundred men to reach us, and only three or four 'real tea-leaves'.[67]

On New Year's Day, Ryan tackled the Irish question in a statement to his compatriots:

> A chairde,
> As most of you will have read in the newspapers before leaving home, an Irish unit of the International Brigades is being formed. It may be necessary to make clear to some why all Irish comrades are not just now together. The fact is that the military situation does not allow the war to be held up so that all Irishmen can be collected and formed into a unit. At the earliest opportunity that will be done. The unit now at the front, the unit now in training, and the other comrades now on their way to us will be united in one unit.
> This unit will be part of the English-speaking battalion which is to be formed. Irish, English, Scots and Welsh comrades will fight, side by side, against the common enemy – Fascism. It must also be made clear that in the International Brigades in which we serve, there are no national differences. We are all comrades. We have come here as soldiers of liberty to demonstrate Republican Ireland's solidarity with the gallant Spanish workers and peasants...
> [A]t the first available opportunity I will, in co-operation with the officers of the English-speaking battalion, re-unite all groups in a distinctive Irish unit. Until then, I ask every man to play his part as a disciplined and eager soldier...[68]

On 3 January, or soon after, Ryan was given work to do with the 12th International Brigade in Madrid.[69] It was in itself peculiar that he should have been assigned to the 'Garibaldis', mainly composed of proud Italians who sported red-neckerchiefs in honour of Giuseppe Garibaldi and his 'red-shirts'.

Shortly after that Ryan's locum, Terry Flanagan, was arrested as a political 'suspect', pending repatriation.[70]

The senior people in the British battalion were Wintringham, his o/c Wilfred Macartney, Peter Kerrigan, the CPGB representative at Albacete and base commissar, and Dave Springhall, the battalion commissar. Unusually for a senior CPGB official, Wintringham was a Balliol man who got on well with almost everyone and attracted no strong feelings one way or the other. By contrast, the cavalier Scottish journalist Wilf Macartney had had a chequered career in the British army, including a spell in the 'Black and Tans'. His ten years in Parkhurst prison for spying for the Soviets impressed the CPGB, while his account of prison life, *Walls Have Mouths* (1936), caused a sensation, partly for its discussion of prison sexuality. But in Madrigueras, suspicions accumulated about his political integrity and military ability.

Kerrigan and Springhall were similar types, dour apparatchiks, on the CPGB's central committee, and trained in the Lenin School. Both were very conscious of the value of Spain to politics at home.[71] On 4 January 1937 Kerrigan urged Pollitt to press their common preference for the creation of an 'English battalion' – oddly, for a Scot, he used 'English' rather than 'British' – and said he would oppose the despatch of more troops to the front lest it reduce his men below battalion strength. He also called for more Welshmen, 'as apart from Scotland and London only Liverpool and the Irish are really showing any great recruitment for the Brigade.'[72] Neither would have wanted heroics in Spain to redound to the glory of the Republican Congress at the expense of the CPI. Both were also grappling with the inevitable problem of negotiating boundaries in a novel formation and of imposing a structure on men with what the communists called 'rank and file tendencies'.

On 12 January, with Ryan in Madrid, Flanagan in jail and many of Ryan's core supporters – those of them left – fighting around Madrid, all Irish volunteers at Madrigueras were summoned to a meeting and asked if they wished to transfer to the Americans, who had begun to arrive at Villanueva de la Jara, a further 30 or so km to the north, in the second week of January.[73] The question itself was at odds with Comintern policy and military discipline. According to Peter O'Connor, who was present:

> About forty-five comrades attended and decided, by a majority of five, to join the Lincoln Battalion. The main reason given by those who voted to join the Americans was the wrongs done to Ireland by the English in the past. They claimed that though they were anti-fascist, they still looked on the English as the enemy. Those of us who were not only class conscious but politically conscious as well [sic: he meant not only politically conscious but class conscious as well]. . . pleaded passionately for a distinction to be made between anti-fascist or working

class comrades from England and British imperialism. British imperialism and international capitalism, we pointed out, was the enemy of both the Irish and British working class. Here was a golden opportunity to show we had something in common with our British comrades...[74]

Kerrigan and Springhall attributed the decision to 'bad elements'. Springhall reported to Pollitt on 19 January:

> Re Irish. In accord with the wishes of the Brigade HQ [Head Quarters] in dealing with national groups, we [illegible] to the Irish Section in our Battalion (not the lot that came out with Ryan) they were given the opportunity to discuss whether they would prefer to go with the American Battalion or stay with us. All the Cds [comrades] who had any connection with IRA or IRC [Republican Congress] or TU [trade union] movement elected to stay with us but they were in a minority of 11 against 23. They have now gone today to the Americans and we are frankly glad. We know that it can be bad politically both in Ireland and England but they were an awful lot of [illegible] Irish exiles from Edgeware Rd [London], petty criminals – hooligan types. So all had to go and again I will say we are glad – and knowing the Americans I am sorry for the Irish.[75]

Kerrigan wrote to Pollitt in a similar vein on 24 January, blaming the vote – which he put as 26–11 – on 'bad elements', and 'very many non [Communist] Party people'.[76] The unpublished official history of the British battalion, deposited in the Comintern archive in Moscow, was more negative still. Noting several problems with drunks and lumpen elements, it concluded that many of the British comrades were glad to see the Irish go.[77] Except that contrary to Springhall's post to Pollitt on 19 January, 'all' did not go, and some of those who stayed were the worst 'hooligans', suggesting that the initiative was not about discipline.

The accounts by O'Connor, and Springhall/Kerrigan, are the only descriptions of the split that are first hand and original. The earliest published CPGB history, *Britons in Spain* (1939) avoided the controversy altogether, and noted simply that 'The Irish divided themselves between the British and American Battalions.'[78] The next CPGB history, *British Volunteers for Liberty* (1982), offered some politically tactful excuses for the Irish – 'a number of Irish agitated to go to the American Abraham Lincoln Battalion... inevitable against the background of Irish oppression' – before citing some of the damning indictments of Springhall/Kerrigan.[79]

One might expect the Irish to take a different view of it. Ryan has become a folk hero on the left, hailed in songs by the likes of Christy Moore, Cruachan, and The Pogues. Yet Irish veterans of Spain and their memorialists have treated the 'mutiny' as an embarrassment. The CPI's *Connolly Column* echoed the CPGB historians in saying that the Irish 'were divided between [the Lincoln] and the British Battalion'. The chapter on Ireland in Ivan Nesterenko's *International Solidarity with the Spanish Republic, 1936–1939*, published by the Soviet Academy of Sciences in 1976, offered the patently deceptive explanation that 'Because of the high rate of casualties the James Connolly Unit was disbanded and the Irish volunteers were divided between the British and American battalions of the newly formed Abraham Lincoln 15th International Brigade [sic]'.[80] The chapter was written by O'Riordan, who later blamed the Liverpool-Irish for the split.[81]

Subsequent histories of the British and Lincoln battalions, while acknowledging Ryan's stature, merely rationalised the conflicting written accounts, surmising that the dispute was sparked by a combination of disciplinary problems, resentment of the British officer types, references in the communist press to the British battalion or a more politically driven anglophobia.[82] Kerrigan published in the *Daily Worker* an article on the Lopera battle, 'How Britons beat Moors', in which he referred repeatedly to the 'English', but which appeared on 18 January. McGarry and Hoar saw in the defection an echo of the schism in Rathmines Town Hall in 1934, which they misread as a conflict between republicanism and socialism. Stradling – who was concerned to debunk what he regarded as the hagiography of the Connolly Column – both accepted anglophobia as a cause of the split and was sceptical of official communist explanations.[83]

Memoirs and recollections should not be discounted as a source of mentalities but are a second set of false friends on facts. Many are in contradiction, or absurdly inaccurate. Fred Copeman's rollicking, self-serving autobiography, *Reason in Revolt*, has long been read with arched eyebrows and, not surprisingly, his version of the dispute could not have happened:

> Punch up between Irish and English around 11 at night. When it had finished, [Frank] Ryan said we have enough of this. At a meeting the next morning Frank said, we are out. He said we're going to join the Yanks...All right, go, but you won't like it, mate, I said. They stayed with the Yanks for a while and then came back to us.[84]

Yet Jason Gurney's *Crusade in Spain*, respected for its honesty if not always for Gurney's tart observations, was just as implausible in claiming that the defection to the Lincolns was caused by the arrest of 'practically the whole of the Irish detachment' after a feud with another platoon.[85]

Other British volunteers recalled tensions with the Irish, but accounts vary as to their importance. In Stradling's summation, veterans who 'had shuffled off political allegiance' played them up for their narrative value, while the 'ever-solids' played them down.[86] It is also likely that memories were coloured *ex-post facto* by the fall-out from the crisis. Moreover, ethnic prejudices were common on all sides in the brigades – a belief that race shaped character was the conventional wisdom before the Holocaust – and taken seriously by the high command. General Walter, nom de guerre of the Polish Karol Wacław Świerczewski, described the 'nationality question' as 'the main hindrance impeding the growth of our potential'.[87] In British eyes, the Germans were officious, the Spaniards were lazy, the French were... well, French and the Irish were either anglophobic drunks or loveable rogues. 'You know you meet Irishmen who seem to be cuddly,' recalled Walter Greenhalgh, from Manchester, describing Frank Ryan.[88] Londoner Fred Thomas, who joined the 16th battalion in May 1937, was surprised that quarrels were so frequent and quick to reflect 'chauvinist prejudices', but thought them 'not overly serious' or peculiar to any ethnicity.[89] Typically, Britons passed off friction with the Irish patronisingly as inevitable and understandable. According to Charles Bloom, a Jewish East Ender: 'The Irish were always in trouble with us, with our officers. . . They had a long standing antipathy towards the British. I can understand that.' Yet Flanagan was 'a good friend of mine. I had many discussions with him.' It was always others who couldn't get on with the Irish, and vice versa. Recollections became more colourful again once the Irish reached the Lincolns.[90]

Why the Irish voted to join the Lincolns is secondary. The key question is why the meeting on 12 January was called. It was, after all, an extraordinary decision, at odds with any sense of discipline or internationalism. There are three possible explanations. The first is that it was brought to a head by routine misconduct. However, in four reports to Pollitt between 4 and 10 January, the commissars made no reference to disciplinary problems with the Irish other than with two London-Irishmen: one had refused to obey an order and the other was described as a drunk and an anti-Semite.[91] By contrast, trouble with the Scots was noted by Kerrigan on 4 January, and Springhall complained on 19 January: 'Glasgow or at least Tounhead so called CP members have been like a plague to me. . . Their reaction [to the Irish vote] was to simultaneously put in written requests to go to the Irish section!'[92] By late January a 'battalion blacklist', probably drawn up by Springhall, logged 33 names, of whom 10 were Irish. Two had their transgressions noted. One was faulted for drunkenness and another for indiscipline.[93] It does not suggest a political problem with the Irish as a whole. Crucially, Springhall sourced the 12 January meeting in 'the wishes of the Brigade HQ in dealing with national groups', and not in problems created by the Irish. Springhall's account of the meeting is worth parsing for its disingenuousness. 'In accord with the wishes of the Brigade HQ in dealing with national groups': International Brigades policy was to avoid divisions along national lines and group volunteers by language merely for operational reasons. And there were some, like Marty and the polyglots of the top brass, who opposed any compromise of internationalism, even for operational efficiency. Why should there be a special position on the Irish? When Springhall spoke of 'the Irish section in our Battalion (not the lot that came out with Ryan)', he implied that only the men sent to the front on Christmas Eve were Ryan's.

It is true that these were disproportionately from Ireland, and the others were more likely to have been resident in Britain before travelling to Spain, but all of the Irish looked on Ryan as their leader. Were the majority of Irish volunteers in Madrigueras apolitical hooligans with no communist, republican or trade union background, a characterisation never repeated in records of the British or Lincoln battalions? Why would the 'criminal-hooligan types' bother about the nationality issue, and all the republicans wish to stay with the British? Plausibly, Springhall seized on the trouble with the two London-Irishmen to play the old trick of depicting dissidents as criminal rather than political. The gratuitous insult to the Americans suggests he was a man under pressure.

The second explanation is that the Irish wanted to go, for nationalist reasons. O'Connor's account has been cited as evidence, but it is evidence on the vote, not on why the meeting was called. O'Connor, a member of the Republican Congress, the CPGB, and a life-long admirer of Ryan, insisted that that there was no demand among the Irish for the meeting. Incensed that it had taken place, he made several enquiries to find out who was responsible. All he could elicit was that some believed it was Springhall and others thought it was Kerrigan, an odd obfuscation in a command structure run on Bolshevik lines.[94] The measure of Irish anglophobia was tested when it emerged that Nathan had not only served in the Auxiliary Division during the War of Independence but had been active in Ryan's native Limerick and implicated in the murder of the Sinn Féin mayor of the city.[95] Nathan was directed, probably by Marty, to explain himself to Ryan and his colleagues. He admitted that he had been an intelligence officer in the Auxiliaries, said that being a Jew he had become implacably anti-fascist and that they were all on the same side now. The defence was accepted and Nathan earned the respect of the Irish as a good man under fire.[96] Ryan, at least, also knew that Macartney had been in the 'Black and Tans' and raised no objections.[97]

The third explanation is Ryan's. On his return to Madrigueras, Ryan was outraged to find his men divided between two battalions. Writing in March from Paris, where his letter was not subject to International Brigade censorship, he had no doubt that he had been removed from the scene deliberately and that 'the representatives of the British CP wrecked the Irish unit.'[98] Unfortunately, he did not say why, other than blaming Macartney and others for failing to appreciate his political strategy of keeping the Irish in the British battalion: 'the English send out the worst officer-type. The leaders of the CP of Great Britain and the rank and file understand our (Irish) position. It just happened that we got the in-between crowd of the swelled-headed adventurer type...'[99] This sounds naïve, but the Comintern archives reveal that Ryan – and O'Donnell – were naïve in presuming the goodwill of the CPGB leaders towards the Republican Congress. Stradling suggests that Marty instigated the split, and McGarry speculates that Marty may have been paranoid about fifth columnists among volunteers from a strongly pro-Franco country, interpretations partly supported by Patrick Keenan. Keenan, who had worked as a mechanic in Albacete before deserting, told the Irish legation in Paris that the Brigades' leadership held the Irish in suspicion and that Irish had demonstrated against the arrest of Flanagan.[100] Springhall, of course, claimed to be acting for Brigade headquarters. On the reasons for the vote – not the meeting – Ryan had two explanations. The first was the arrest of Flanagan.[101] In Ryan's opinion, Macartney had 'framed' Flanagan to provoke the Irish. The arrest is curious. Flanagan was a member of the CPI as well as an ex-IRA man, and Ryan got him released with ease. In April Springhall refused a request from Flanagan to return home.[102] Secondly, Ryan believed, the Irish were irritated by insensitive officers who treated them as 'British'.[103]

The most likely explanation is that the meeting was an over-reaction by Springhall to the considerable problems of welding disparate citizen soldiers, more 'bolshie' than Bolshevik, into a cohesive fighting force, and to a projected problem of political control over a non-party unit. Springhall would not have acted without Kerrigan's approval, but as battalion commissar, the smooth political functioning of the battalion command was his business. He was based in Madrigueras and Kerrigan was half an hour's drive away in Albacete. Bill Alexander, CPGB historian and veteran of Spain, also says that Springhall called the meeting.[104] Springhall had a penchant for conspiracy and a willingness to go solo for the cause. In 1943 he was gaoled for passing British defence secrets to Soviet Russia. Though communists believed that Britain should be doing more to help the Red Army, the CPGB was appalled that he should have gone so far, and he was expelled. A 'hopelessly obtuse and humourless man', in Gurney's opinion, overwhelmed by the task at hand, it's reasonable to conclude that Springhall would not have wanted the British battalion to include a sizable corps of foreigners under non-party command, ever-ready to flaunt their independence.[105]

## THE FALLOUT

The trek to the Lincolns in Villanueva de la Jara took place on 19 January. In a further twist to the tale, not much more than 21 Irish departed, including men who had argued for staying with the British. A greater number remained, some of whom were on Springhall's blacklist![106] The 'mutiny', as it was seen by many in Madrigueras, had a negative impact on the discipline and morale of the trainees.[107] The recriminations persisted. In an attempt to shift the blame, Kerrigan claimed that Ryan demanded the transfer of the Irish to the Lincolns at a 'Burns Nicht' supper on 24 January, and protested so vehemently that he was arrested by Marty and released only after intervention by the British. Another version has Ryan arrested because of a misunderstanding, arising from his deafness.[108] The return of Conway's men from the Córdoba front caused more trouble for Kerrigan, the more so as the untested men at Madrigueras held their battle-hardened comrades in awe. Conway himself spoke out. Kerrigan reported on 1 February:

> The Irish trouble cropped up again yesterday. It was raised very sharply by one of no.1 co[mpan]y who have returned from the front. He accused the military and political leadership of the B[attalio]n of being responsible for it and threatened to raise it in England and Ireland. He was supported by Ryan who was present and he demanded unity of all Irish no matter where they were. At the same time he declared they had been driven out of the Bn and talked of Chauvinism etc.
>
> M (not Macartney) [Marty] who was present proposed a commission and it meets today to finally solve this problem. Springie [Springhall] will present the facts to the commission.[109]

The commission began by interviewing Prendergast, the most senior party man available. A veteran of the RWG, CPI and CPGB, and a student in the International Lenin School in Moscow in 1934–5 – sent home for 'bad work [mauvais travail]' as Springhall quickly informed the commission – Prendergast had been elected a political delegate of the Irish in the 14th Brigade at Las Rozas. His record did not prevent him being accused of being 'critical' or of being 'used' by others such as Donie O'Reilly and Éamonn McGrotty, who was on Springhall's blacklist. O'Reilly would be sentenced to two months in the punishment battalion for disobeying an order on 11 February but reinstated on Ryan's intervention. The commission implied that the trouble caused by the Irish was not their attitude to the British squaddies but more the pointed disagreement with senior British officers, motivated by chauvinism or 'rank and file tendencies'. At the same time, the commission decided on 2 February,

Springhall's response was absolutely wrong and would lead to political complications. The confusion arose from insufficient political education and ought to be resolved through more 'serious' political work on the meaning of the popular front and anti-fascism. It was therefore decided that the Irish 'must stay [doivent rester]' with the British and the Irish in the Lincolns be regrouped with the British battalion. It was also recommended that as the Irish lacked 'military cadres', their section be commanded by a Scot. Ryan, cited as 'Oreins', a transliteration of Ó Riain, was to be the political 'responsable' for the Irish 'formations'. The decision was endorsed by 'General Galle', known also as 'Gal', nom de guerre of the 15th's Hungarian brigadier, János Gálicz.[110]

Ryan could take some consolation from the outcome. From Paris, he informed Gerald O'Reilly:

> And now for confidential news. . .While one Irish section was on the Cordoba Front, & I was 'loaned' (moryah!) to the 12th (Italian and German) Brigade in Madrid for a week which became a month, there was another Irish section accumulating with Scots, English & Welsh at the Base. I had a Dubliner named Terry Flanagan (fresh from Dublin B[rig]de, IRA) in charge of that Section. Flanagan was framed as 'a suspect', believe it or not, by Wilfrid McCartney [sic] Batt[alion] Commander, ex-British officer, author of 'Walls Have Mouths' & ex-Black & Tan (vide Gen Crozier). The Irish Section was shifted off to the Americans. When I came back (end of Jan.) I was told a pack of lies by McCartney. To cut a long story short, I discovered – as a result of my own investigations – that Flanagan was being deported as 'an undesirable' & had reached Barcelona on his way out. I stopped the deportation and got Flanagan back. McCartney framed another of my most important men [Donie O'Reilly] for 'disobeying an order' – which order should not have been given save through me. The man got 2 months imprisonment, without trial. I have since got him released. To the International Brigade authorities I pointed out that Ireland's nearest enemy is British Imperialism; therefore Ireland's nearest ally must be the British working class & that therefore the Ir[ish] and Brit[ish] must be side by side in the Internat[ional] Bdes. I was able to convict the British of having made a grave political error.
>
> McCartney's attitude towards his 'own men' as well as towards ours, caused resentment. As a result of all, he was sent home. And the bastard wounded himself in the left arm with his own revolver, on the day of his departure & got the London 'Daily Worker' to say he was wounded by Fascist rifle-fire near Madrid!![111]

In February, Springhall was replaced as political commissar by George Aitken. Aitken later wrote, in protest to the CPGB politburo about a critical estimation of his work in Spain:

I would remind Comrade Springhall that they do not hide removals in the Int[ernational] Brig[ade]s when they consider them necessary. They did not hide his own removal from the position of Political Commissar of the Brigade because of his grave political mistake in helping the Irish Section of the British Bn to transfer to the American Bn.[112]

Macartney, a ticket of leave man who had to report regularly to the British authorities as he completed his prison sentence, was replaced as battalion commander by Wintringham. Before he could return to England he was accidentally shot in the arm by Kerrigan. Ryan was not alone in doubting the official explanation. Undoubtedly the battalion leaders wanted rid of Macartney at that stage, but why shoot a man who was leaving in any case? Ryan retained the confidence of the International Brigades and was chosen to edit *The Book of the XV Brigade*, the official account of the Brigade up to 1938. He had it subtitled *Records of British, American, Canadian, and Irish Volunteers in Spain, 1936–1938*, though formally the Brigade contained no Irish unit.

Meanwhile the division of the Irish was not undone. Ryan explained to Gerald O'Reilly: 'Unfortunately, owing to the military situation, I could not follow up on the matter. The USA lads were on a war-footing & the Irish Unit was indispensable. . . I just placed myself at the disposal of the new Batt o/c. – Wintringham – to show I could fight as well as talk'.[113]

Franco's army launched an offensive to cut the road from Madrid to Valencia on 6 February and the 15th Brigade was rushed to Jarama. Augmented by a few Irish-Americans, the Irish in the Lincolns formed the James Connolly Centuria. It was accorded a de facto recognition as Irish, and nobody bothered about its de jure status. The Irish seconded to the Marseillaise battalion at Christmas 1936 had stayed with the British and were joined by all incoming Irish recruits. The nationality problem never surfaced again.

NOTES

1. PRONI, RUC report on SPNI meeting, 18 April 1937, HA/32/1/555.
2. Michael O'Riordan, *Connolly Column: The Story of the Irishmen who fought in the Ranks of the International Brigades in the National-revolutionary War of the Spanish People 1936–1939* (Dublin, 1979), pp 46–52, fn7, 55; CPI, *Communist Party of Ireland: Outline History* (Dublin, 1975), p. 63.
3. William Rust, *Britons in Spain: A History of the British Battalion of the XVth International Brigade* (2003 ed, Pontypool), p. 4.
4. R. Dan Richardson, *Comintern Army: The International Brigades and the Spanish Civil War* (Lexington, Ky, 1982), pp 32–3.

5. Ibid., pp 11–15.
6. RGASPI, Proposals in connection with the Communist Party of Ireland, 8 May 1937; Annual general meeting of the Dublin branch of the CPI, 21 February 1937, f. 495, o.89, d. 102, ll. 1-9; f. 495, o. 14, d. 339, ll. 5-17.
7. O'Riordan, *Connolly Column*, pp 49, 55.
8. Irish Military Archives, MSP/34/William Gannon 25776; *New Zealand Tribune*, April 1966; *People's Voice*, 6 April 1966; Christopher Prendergast, 'Diary', in *London Review of Books*, 27:6, 17 March 2005, pp 42–3.
9. *Irish Independent*, 10 August 1936.
10. *Irish Press*, 29 August 1936.
11. Joseph Donnelly, 'A memoir', in Kay Donnelly (ed), *Heroic Heart: A Charles Donnelly Reader* (Belfast, 2012), p. 75.
12. Seán Cronin, *Frank Ryan: The Search for the Republic* (Dublin, 1980), pp 78–9, 82.
13. *Irish Press*, 23 September 1936; *Irish Times*, 23 September 1936; Cronin, *Frank Ryan*, pp 78–9.
14. Grattan Freyer, *Peadar O'Donnell* (Cranbury, NJ, 1973), p. 101.
15. NLI, Rosamond Jacob Papers, diaries, 32,582/1–170, 3 December 1936
16. Freyer, *Peadar O'Donnell*, p. 101.
17. NLI, Rosamond Jacob Papers, diaries, 32,582/1–170, 3, 14 December 1936, 23 March 1937.
18. Rust, *Britons in Spain*, p. 30.
19. Adrian Hoar, *In Green and Red: The Lives of Frank Ryan* (Dingle, 2004), p.152; *Worker*, 19 December 1936.
20. NLI, Rosamond Jacob Paper, diaries, 32,582/1–170, 14 December 1936.
21. Richardson, *Comintern Army*, p. 32.
22. RGSAPI, 'Records in London. Observations'. 22 December 1937, f. 545, o. 6, d. 87, ll. 39–40.
23. RGASPI, Dublin annual general meeting, 27 February 1937, f. 495, o. 14, d. 339, ll. 5–17.
24. David Corkhill (ed), *The Road to Spain: Anti-Fascists at War, 1936–1939* (Fife, 1981), pp 146, 151; Klaus, *Strong Words, Brave Deeds*, pp 19–20.
25. East Wall History Group, *In Support of An Ideal*, p.79; Seán Byers, 'Seán Murray, the Irish republican left and international communism, 1916–1962' (PhD, University of Ulster, Jordanstown, 2012), pp 162–6.
26. 'Seán was a cheerful person, with a red, well-fed face that would remind you of a bishop'. Eoghan Ó Duinnín, *La Niña Bonita agus An Róisín Dubh: Cuimhní Cinn ar Chogadh Cathartha na Spáinne* (Baile Átha Cliath, 1986), pp 11, 100; letter from Andrew Boyd to Emmet O'Connor, 11 August 2009.
27. Michael McInerney, *Peadar O'Donnell, Irish Social Rebel* (Dublin, 1974), p.179; McGarry, *Irish Politics and the Spanish Civil War*, p. 58.
28. Freyer, *Peadar O'Donnell*, pp 101–2; Peter Hegarty, *Peadar O'Donnell* (Cork, 1999), pp 232–3.
29. *Irish Times*, 14 December 1936.
30. Joe Monks, *With the Reds in Andalusia* (London, 1985). The 13 were Monks and Jim Prendergast, recently settled in London, and, from residence in Dublin: Gerald Doran, John Goff, Paddy Smith, Frank Conroy, Anthony Fox, Leo Green, Michael May, Michael Nolan, Thomas Wood, Frank Edwards and Michael Lehane.

31. The claim is made in McGarry, *Irish Politics and the Spanish Civil War*, p. 54, without evidence.
32. Bob Doyle, *Brigadista: An Irishman's Fight Against Fascism* (Dublin, 2006), pp 44–5; 'Bob Doyle', in David Corkhill and Stuart J. Rawnsley (eds), *The Road to Spain: Anti-Fascists at War, 1936–39* (Dunfermline, 1981), pp 147–51.
33. ROR, letter from Ryan to Gerald O'Reilly, 5 March 1937.
34. Uinseann MacEoin, *The IRA in the Twilight Years, 1923–1948* (Dublin, 1997), p. 769.
35. Chris Brooks, 'The making of the Washington Battalion', in *The Volunteer*, 21 March 2014.
36. Michael Petrou, *Renegades, Canadians in the Spanish Civil War* (Vancouver, 2008), pp 69–70, 190–241.
37. David Wilson, *The Irish in Canada* (Ottawa, 1989), p.6.
38. Petrou, *Renegades*, p. 31.
39. Ibid., pp 190–241.
40. Emmet O'Connor, 'Behind the legend: Waterfordmen in the International Brigades in the Spanish Civil War', in *Decies: Journal of the Waterford Archaeological & Historical Society*, 61 (2005), pp 267–85.
41. Quoted in Robert A. Stradling, *The Irish and the Spanish Civil War: Crusades in Conflict* (Manchester, 1999), p. 242, fn 28.
42. RGASPI, 'The Communist Party of Ireland and the Irish Republican Congress', f. 495, o. 18, d. 1059; Murray to the Anglo-American Secretariat, f. 495, o. 14, d. 335, l. 24.
43. Jason Gurney, *Crusade in Spain* (London, 1976), pp 71–2.
44. 'The Irish you receive will be grouped into Irish sections if possible', RGASPI, 'Extraits d'une lettre du PC d'Angleterre en date de 12-12-1936', f. 545, o. 2, d. 39, l. 13.
45. Monks, *With the Reds in Andalusia*, p. 7; Uinseann MacEoin (ed), *Survivors: The Story of Ireland's Struggle as Told Through Some of Her Outstanding Living People Recalling Events from the Days of Davitt, Through James Connolly, Brugha, Collins, de Valera, Liam Mellows, and Rory O'Connor to the Present Time* (Dublin, 1987), pp 11–14; RGASPI, Report on Lopera, f. 545, o. 3, d. 479, ll. 52-57.
46. National Museum of Labour History, Manchester (NMLH), Kerrigan to Pollitt, 4 January 1937, CP/Ind/Poll/2/6; McLoughlin, *Fighting for Republican Spain*, pp 49–50; Hoar, *In Green and Red*, p. 158.
47. Tom Wintringham, *English Captain* (Harmondsworth, 1941), p. 115.
48. MacEoin, 'Frank Edwards', *Survivors*, p. 12.
49. *Daily Worker*, 18 January 1937; RGASPI, Report on Lopera, f. 545, o. 3, d. 479, ll. 52-57; Alvah Bessie and Albert Prago (eds), *Our Fight: Writings by Veterans of the Abraham Lincoln Brigade, Spain, 1936–1939* (New York, 1987), p. 132.
50. MacEoin, 'Frank Edwards', *Survivors*, p. 13.
51. Monks, *With the Reds in Andalusia*.
52. *Worker*, 30 January 1937.
53. MacEoin, 'Frank Edwards', *Survivors*, p. 13.
54. Richardson, *Comintern Army*, p. 72; Sam Lesser, 'Death and confusion among the olive groves' in *IBMT Newsletter*, 43, 3 (2016), pp 17–18; Monks, *With the Reds in Andalusia*.
55. Richard Baxell, *Unlikely Warriors: The British in the Spanish Civil War and the Struggle Against Fascism* (London, 2012), pp 125–6, 132.

56. Wintringham, *English Captain*, p. 40.
57. A word search in the *Daily Worker* between 27 December 1936 and 31 October 1938 produced 191 citations for 'British battalion', 11 for 'English-speaking battalion', four for 'Anglo-Irish battalion', three for '16th battalion', one for 'English battalion', and none for 'Saklatvala battalion'. The Lincoln battalion was given just five mentions over the period.
58. Gurney, *Crusade in Spain*, p. 75.
59. Fred Thomas, *To Tilt at Windmills: A Memoir of the Spanish Civil War* (East Lansing, Mi, 1996), p. 21.
60. O'Riordan, *Connolly Column*, p. 138.
61. 'Pulses were the main meal. We called them beans in English, but chick-peas was the correct name. We laughed when we heard that Bill Rust, correspondent of the *Daily Worker* in Spain, reported in the *Daily Worker* that the British Battalion was full of beans. When we got meat, it was usually burro or mule.' Ó Duinnín, *La Niña Bonita agus An Róisín Dubh*, p. 43.
62. O'Riordan, *Connolly Column*, p. 138.
63. MacEoin, 'Frank Edwards', *Survivors*, p. 13.
64. Baxell, *Unlikely Warriors*, pp 120–8; Richard Baxell, *British Volunteers in the Spanish Civil War: The British Battalion in the International Brigades, 1936–1939* (London, 2004), p. 195, fn 32.
65. Peter O'Connor, *A Soldier of Liberty* (Dublin, 1996), p. 14.
66. Ó Duinnín, *La Niña Bonita agus An Róisín Dubh*, p. 43.
67. Wintringham, *English Captain*, p. 46.
68. Quoted in O'Connor, *A Soldier of Liberty*, pp 16–17.
69. Stradling, *The Irish and the Spanish Civil War*, p. 160.
70. McGarry, *Irish Politics and the Spanish Civil War*, p. 68. Controversy surrounding the arrest may explain grossly exaggerated recollections that the entire Irish section had been arrested, or that the Irish had arrested the British officers.
71. NMLH, Kerrigan ms, CP/Ind/Misc/18/06.
72. NMLH, Kerrigan to Pollitt, 4 January 1937, CP/Ind/Poll/2/6.
73. Stradling, *The Irish and the Spanish Civil War*, p. 155.
74. O'Connor, *A Soldier of Liberty*, pp 14–15.
75. IBA, Box C, file 9/8, Springhall to Pollitt, 19 January 1937.
76. MML, IBA, Box C, special files, 9/11, Kerrigan to Pollitt, 24 January 1937.
77. Baxell, *British Volunteers in the Spanish Civil War*, p. 62.
78. William Rust, *Britons in Spain: A History of the British Battalion of the XVth International Brigade* (Pontypool, 2003, first ed. 1939), p. 37. Rust was then editor of the *Daily Worker*.
79. Bill Alexander, *British Volunteers for Liberty, Spain 1936–1939* (London, 1982), pp 68–9. Alexander was a veteran of Spain and a former assistant secretary of the CPGB.
80. O'Riordan, *Connolly Column*, p. 67; I. Nesterenko (ed), *International Solidarity with the Spanish Republic, 1936–1939* (Moscow, 1976), pp 5–6, 197.
81. 'Corrected notes from the discussion between Mick O'Riordan with Ciaran Crossey and John Quinn, Dublin 21 September 2001', in John Quinn, *Irish Volunteers for Spain: A Short History of the Northern Irish Volunteers who Fought in Defence of the Republican Government of Spain, 1936–39* (Belfast, 2004), p. 110.

82. Alexander, *British Volunteers for Liberty*, pp 68–9; James K. Hopkins, *Into the Heart of the Fire: The British in the Spanish Civil War* (Stanford, 1998), pp 173–6; Baxell, *British Volunteers in the Spanish Civil War*, pp 63–4; Imperial War Museum (IWM), Interview 794 Fred Copeman, reel 1, 1976; Interview 992, Charles Sewell Bloom, reel 2, 1977.

83. Fearghal McGarry, *Irish Politics and the Spanish Civil War* (Cork, 1999), pp 66–7; Fearghal McGarry, *Frank Ryan* (Dundalk, 2002), pp 49–50; Hoar, *In Green and Red*, p. 164; Stradling, *The Irish and the Spanish Civil War*, p.160.

84. IWM, Interview 794, Fred Copeman, reel 1, 1976; Fred Copeman, *Reason in Revolt* (London, 1948).

85. Gurney, *Crusade in Spain*, pp 70–7.

86. Stradling, *The Irish in the Spanish Civil War*, p.242, fn 33; see also Baxell, *Unlikely Warriors*, pp 133–5.

87. Cited in Baxell, *British Volunteers in the Spanish Civil War*, p. 147.

88. IWM, Interview Interview 11187, Walter Greenhalgh, reel two (1992).

89. Thomas, *To Tilt at Windmills*, p. 29.

90. IWM, Interview 992, Charles Sewell Bloom, reel 2, 1977; Cecil Eby, *Between the Bullet and the Lie: American Volunteers in the Spanish Civil War* (New York, 1969), p. 26.

91. MML, IBA, Box C, special files, 9/6, Springhall to Pollitt, 10 January 1937.

92. Ibid., file 9/8, Springhall to Pollitt, 19 January 1937.

93. RGASPI, Battalion blacklist, f. 595, o. 6, d. 93, ll. 23-27a; McLoughlin, *Fighting for Republican Spain*, p.58.

94. Information from Peter O'Connor.

95. Nathan was one of a team that shot dead the mayor of Limerick and two others on the night of 7 March 1921. See Richard Bennett, 'Portrait of a killer', in *New Statesman*, 24 March 1961, and correspondence in the *New Statesman*, 31 March and 9–21 April 1961.

96. Hoar, *In Green and Red*, pp 166–7.

97. ROR, letter from Ryan to Gerald O'Reilly, 5 March 1937, and cited in Cronin, *Frank Ryan*, p.91.

98. Quoted in Cronin, *Frank Ryan*, p. 90.

99. Ibid., p. 91.

100. Stradling, *The Irish and the Spanish Civil War*, pp 156–7; McGarry, *Irish Politics and the Spanish Civil War*, pp 67–8; NA, DFA 10/55, letter from the Irish Legation in Paris to Dublin, 25 February 1937.

101. McGarry, *Irish Politics and the Spanish Civil War*, p. 68. Controversy surrounding the arrest may explain exaggerated recollections that the entire Irish section had been arrested, or that the Irish had arrested the British officers.

102. MML, IBA, Box C, special files, 12/1, Springhall to Pollitt, 21 April 1937.

103. Cronin, *Frank Ryan*, p. 91.

104. Alexander, *British Volunteers for Liberty*, p. 54.

105. Gurney, *Crusade in Spain*, p. 61. Gurney, incidentally, is seriously mistaken in saying that Springhall spied for the Nazis in World War 2.

106. McLoughlin, *Fighting for Republican Spain*, pp 61–2; RGASPI, Rapport du camarade Leemans commissaire politique sur la Commission Irlandaise, f. 545, o. 2, d. 68, l. 139, 2 February 1937.

107. Gurney, *Crusade in Spain*, p. 77.
108. Kerrigan placed the supper in Chinchón, but the battalion celebrated Burns Night in Madrigueras on 24 January. McLoughlin, *Fighting for Republican Spain*, pp 64–5.
109. MML, IBA, Box C, special files, 10/1, Kerrigan to Pollitt, 1 February 1937; see also IWM, Interview 810 Peter Kerrigan, 1976, reel 3.
110. RGASPI, Rapport du camarade Leemans commissaire politique sur la Commission Irlandaise, f. 545, o. 2, d. 68, ll. 139-140.
111. ROR, letter from Ryan to Gerald O'Reilly, 5 March 1937, and quoted in Cronin, *Frank Ryan*, p.91.
112. MML, IBA, Box C special files, 17/1, undated statement by Aitken [probably September 1937. I am obliged to Jim Carmody for this information].
113. ROR, letter from Ryan to Gerald O'Reilly, 5 March 1937, and quoted in Cronin, *Frank Ryan*, p. 91.

# SIX

# BLOOD AND BOREDOM ON THE JARAMA

FEBRUARY–JUNE 1937

Frank Ryan was appalled by the orchestrated removal of some of his best men to the American unit. He hoped that the decision would be reversed, that all Irish be re-united in one battalion. While he was still at the Madrid front in January, Ryan wrote to his spokesman with the Americans, Éamonn McGrotty:

> If your name is down to speak, refer to Marty's plea for unity and say you endorse it. Say you represent one of the Irish sections [platoons] – the section which was at a few hours' notice transferred from the Sixteenth Batt. [British]. The Irish Political Commissar (F. Ryan) was not consulted. The Irish Unit was split through no fault of its own. You and all the Irish comrades want it reunited.[1]

Re-unification never happened because it became clear that there were not enough recruits from Ireland to form a separate entity or because of the heavy casualties at Jarama and Brunete. The machinations of Springhall and Kerrigan were, of course, not forgotten; but as they soon left Spain, the controversy died down. Whether it affected Frank Ryan's confidence in the IB leadership, as distinct from his commitment to the anti-fascist cause, is an open question.

After the controversial meeting in Madrigueras on 12 January, 24 Irish volunteers left the British battalion for the American one.[2] Almost all the transferees were ex-IRA or Republican Congress activists. About 30 Irish decided to stay with the British in training, while a further 10, the survivors of No. 1 Company at Lopera, were fighting on the Madrid front when the confrontation with Springhall took place. The American base was at Villanueva de la Jara, some 60 km to the north of Albacete. A big village rather than a town proper, Villanueva received the first American contingent of 96 in their smart 'doughboy' First World War outfits on 7 January with some trepidation. Their predecessors, a French unit, had alienated the villagers by breaking into wine-cellars, fighting when drunk and accosting some of the local women. The Americans were billeted in the abandoned convent of Santa Clara behind the imposing church. The convent had been left in a filthy state by the French: they clogged toilets and left refuse and turds everywhere, which took the newcomers days to clean up.³ As one wit put it, 'The French shit anywhere and the Spanish shit everywhere.'⁴ The large, cold building was typical for Spain, with only six latrines on the ground-floor for 200–500 men, so a long latrine trench was built.⁵

The Americans were communists to a man, clean and abstemious by European standards: they had only one case of a drunken American volunteer sentenced to the 'brig' (guardroom) before they left for the front on 15 February.⁶ In the Brigades, especially amongst the British, the 'Yanks' soon acquired the reputation of being great at organising themselves. They slowly won over the inhabitants of Villanueva by their exemplary behaviour, film-shows and the installation of a battalion clinic on the Plaza Mayor that was also open to the public.⁷ The villagers reacted by giving their spare mattresses to the volunteers or arranging for fresh food supplies from the surrounding countryside as army rations were meagre.⁸

TROUBLE WITH THE IRISH IN THE AMERICAN BATTALION

When the Irish arrived on 20 January, tales of the ructions in Madrigueras were common currency. Some Americans resisted the transfer, 'claiming that the Irish were a bunch of drunks who spent most of their time fighting among themselves'.⁹ One brigadista from Philadelphia confided to his diary that the Irish, on their first night in Villanueva, were drunk at the village dance. 'We don't like them,' he continued, 'because they are too rough', while noting in his entry of the following day that the 'Irish behaved a little better'.¹⁰ Robert Merriman, a former officer in the reserve of the American army who was commissioned immediately on arrival in Albacete and was to be the battalion's first commander in the field, had a talk with two Irish volunteers on the night of 23 January. He gained the impression that 'they will be a problem.'¹¹ Very few of the men, either American or Irish, had ever travelled outside the English-speaking world and were inclined to inflate the importance of their own nationality and 'revolutionary' credentials. The North Americans were assertive and opinionated and had some self-acclaimed 'tough guys' in their ranks, not least the ex-sailors in the machine-gun company.

The main problem with not a few of the Irish was the cheapness and availability of alcohol. A hard core disgraced themselves by imbibing too much and misbehaving. The main problem with the Irish and the British at Madrigueras and Villanueva was that, after training, there was little to do. The Spanish towns where they were trained or stayed in the early period (Madrigueras, Villanueva, Albacete, Chinchón) were dreary places, unpaved and muddy in the wet and cold early winter of La Mancha, containing half-empty shops. There were 'no smokes' (No hay tabac!) and little in the way of sweets or chocolate. The only commodity that was cheap and abundant was alcohol, not beer but strong, very dry wines or even more potent anis or brandy. The more serious-minded learned Spanish and befriended local families, to whom they brought their rations to be cooked, eating in common with the husband, wife and children.

In the coming two weeks the Irish contingent grew: two arrived after 20 January (Liam Tumilson, Vincent O'Donnell) and another three had come from the United States (Paddy Roe McLaughlin, Pat Hamill, Michael Moran). The Irish unit, soon given the name 'James Connolly Column' by its members, also contained a handful of American-Irish (e.g. the three Flaherty brothers from Boston) and some 'adopted Yanks'. Among the Irish was Jack Hedley, who had been an official of the Irish Transport and General Workers' Union after the First World War and an organiser of the 'creamery Soviets' in 1922.[12] In 1936 he was District Organiser for the CPGB in Liverpool.[13] The Irish and the Cubans formed one platoon each in No. 1 Company of the Lincoln Battalion. At least three Irish (Tumilson, McLaughlin, Paddy Stanley) were posted to the machine-gun section and a few to barracks or kitchen duties.[14] Merriman started a programme of rigorous training 'with classes in street fighting, scouting, map-reading, grenade-throwing and in the use of the bayonet'.[15] Tumilson instructed on street fighting, Stanley on the use of the Chauchat machine-gun.[16] There were few weapons, however, merely some rifles (Austrian Steyr and Canadian Ross) and no ammunition, while both machine-guns (Hotchkiss, Chauchat) had worn-out bores.[17] The American battalion was gravely under-strength before Jarama: 350 instead of 600 in a comparable Spanish unit, and could form three, instead of four, companies.[18] A minority of the Americans had previous military training, but Merriman's main problem was that of the leading personnel, especially the persons the CPUSA had chosen to lead the battalion before sailing to Europe. The commanding officer, James Harris, an ex-seaman of Polish origin, proved to be a drunk and incompetent, and may have been temporarily mentally deranged. He was later demoted and sent as a common soldier to serve with the Polish Dombrowski Brigade. Harris was killed at Teruel in February 1938.[19] The prospective political leader, i.e. political commissar, was Samuel Stember, another 'dud' whose nerve also gave.[20] He was sent home in May 1937.[21]

By February 6, Merriman was confident that the battalion was starting to function.[22] He had effectively side-lined the erratic Harris and two days later removed John Scott (real name: Inver Marlow) from commanding the 136 riflemen in No. 1 Company of Cubans and Irish.[23] The new leader was the Cuban Arturo Corona, and Michael Kelly, a humorous Galway man who had been active in the London Republican Congress, led the Irish platoon. The reason for switching Scott to No. 2 Company is not clear, but perhaps Merriman felt that the Irish volunteers did not want to be led by an Englishman or, more probably, blamed Scott for the ongoing trouble with the indiscipline of the Irish. At a meeting of battalion officers on 8 February, Merriman 'laid his cards on the table', telling the Irish representative to 'either act decently or to leave.'[24]

Trouble with Kelly's men had been simmering for a while. One serial offender was the teenager Colum Cox from Drumcondra, who had been sentenced to seven days' detention by British officers in Madrigueras for drunkenness and was estimated to have 'nil' political understanding and an impudent nature.[25] In Villanueva he was sent to the disciplinary labour unit for five days; he escaped and was caught.[26] Cox then returned at night drunk.[27] He was joined in the 'brig' by Hugh Dooley from Belfast.[28] Four other Irish volunteers had taken a 'holiday', going AWOL (absent without official leave) for a day,[29] and a further two were arrested for drunkenness.[30] Some of Cox's comrades feared he would be sent to Albacete for exemplary punishment and threatened to 'follow him' out of the parade ranks should he be removed. Michael Kelly possibly quelled this mini-mutiny by reporting the rumour to his superior officer.[31] On the following day, 10 February, Jack Hedley convened a 'political meeting' by popular demand of the Cubans and the Irish.[32] No doubt the miscreants, roughly one fifth of the Irish contingent, were excoriated, and the trouble seems to have ceased for the moment. It is likely that some problems were caused by dietary upsets, and the Irish, not used to the oily Spanish food, suffered from gastritis or, because of the lack of potable water, contracted typhoid. Peter O'Connor, a teetotaller, was struck down by enteric fever for the second time and confined to hospital between 9 and 15 February.[33] Shortly before moving to the front, the American battalion had 13 men in hospital, seven had just been released by the doctors and another ten were exempted from drill for health reasons.[34]

## THE US BATTALION HEADS FOR THE JARAMA

The Lincoln battalion, including some New Yorkers who had arrived three days before, left the village on 15 February, heading for the Jarama battlefields in a convoy of 50 trucks. There was a stopover in Albacete and rousing speeches from Marty and Kerrigan. At last they received their rifles – old Czarist Remingtons presented free of charge to Madrid by the Mexican government – as well as 150 rounds for each man, grenades and thin French Adrian helmets that were soon thrown away. The convoy reached the village of Chinchón, where the men dismounted and fired five rounds in the direction of a quarry wall. At dark they arrived at positions near Morata de Tajuña, the last town held by the Republicans at the centre of the Jarama pocket.[35]

One group of three trucks, driven by Frenchmen without maps and travelling without lights, took a wrong turning at a crossroads outside Morata. The mistake was noted by Dr Pike, the battalion physician and a passenger in the third truck, who stopped that vehicle and directed the driver to take the correct, western route. The two lead lorries lumbered onwards in a northerly direction and ran into an ambush in the dark. The first one, carrying battalion records and equipment, overturned, and the second with sick men on board crashed into the first. Many of the men were killed by grenades, it is said, and there were no survivors. At least 16 Lincolns died, including Michael Russell from Ennis, Co. Clare, who had emigrated to Canada just before the Wall Street Crash of 1929.[36] The other Americans were unaware of their fate, but soon realised that they would imminently be part of the desperate struggle to drive back the fascist onslaught aimed at capturing the road between Madrid and Valencia, now the seat of the Republican Government.

### THE JARAMA BATTLE: THE BRITISH ATTACK AND RETREAT, 12–14 FEBRUARY

After Franco's attempts to capture the Spanish capital from the west (Casa de Campo) and villages further to the west (Majadahonda-Boadilla del Monte-las Rozas) had ground to a halt leading to strongly defended trench systems on both sides, his next offensive was to be in the south, driving over the high ground above the Jarama river from the west, crossing it and capturing the Madrid-Valencia highway. If successful, this strategy would have cut communications between the two main Republican nerve-centres and facilitated completing the fascist encirclement of the capital. In the southern sector, roughly astride the road San Martín de la Vega in the west to Morata de Tajuña in the east, the 15th Brigade was detailed to capture the central section of small hills and drive the fascists back to the river, while the Americans, still in training at Villanueva de la Jara, were to attack the heights of Pingarrón south of the British positions some days later.

Few of the men in the battalion or on the staff of the Brigade had substantial military experience. Brigade commander was János Gálicz (General Gal), a Hungarian officer of the Red Army and an ex-prisoner of war (POW) from the First World War, about whom very little is known. He soon left to command a division and was recalled to the Soviet Union in 1937. Like all Russian advisers or appointees, Gálicz had no time for the 'discussion culture' of the British, Irish and Americans, expected orders to be obeyed under pain of death and, to be fair, was probably overwhelmed by the task in hand.[37]

Vladimir Čopić, Brigade Commissar as from 7 February 1937,[38] was soon in charge of the 15th Brigade throughout most of the battles until his recall to Russia in 1938. As a student Čopić was offered a commission in the Austro-Hungarian army. He served for eight months, commanding a platoon in a Jägerbatallion, before being captured in the Carpathians after 15 days of combat in 1915. While a POW in revolutionary Russia, Čopić joined the communists and was a member of the Central Committee of the Yugoslav Communist Party from 1919 onwards and a parliament deputy in 1921. Following the proscription of the party, he spent five periods in prison between 1919 and 1925. After his escape in 1925 he worked as a teacher and party functionary at Moscow's International Lenin School.

Čopić was a model revolutionary: he spoke Serbo-Croat, Russian, German and Czech fluently and could read and make himself understood in English, Italian, Bulgarian and Slovenian.[39] His military capabilities are open to question, but in the last resort he was obliged to act in unison with Soviet advisors who often ordered frontal attacks. Čopić's chief of staff was Claus Becker ('Colonel Claus'), a former sergeant-major with World War experience in the German flying corps. An ex-journalist and KPD-member, Becker is said to have enrolled in André Malraux's flight of antiquated bombers (Escuadrilla España) before being appointed commander of the Chapayev battalion of the 13th International Brigade in October 1936. But he was dismissed from that post one month later for allegedly panicking at the front near Teruel, and for misappropriating funds.[40]

The British battalion was led by two even-tempered individuals, Captain Tom Wintringham as commander and George Aitken as political commissar. Wintringham, son of a liberal-minded, upper middle-class family in Grimsby, was interested in military affairs since childhood. Reaching enlisting age in 1916, he left Balliol College, Oxford, and joined the Royal Flying Corps, but, as his eyesight was defective, he served as a machine-gunner or observer over the western front, and later as a dispatch-rider. Following a short stay in the Soviet Union, Wintringham joined the CPGB in 1923 and was sub-editor of the party's *Sunday Worker*. He became one of the managers of the *Daily*

*Worker*, founded in 1930, and its 'military expert'. He was in Spain for the paper in August 1936 and joined the brigades in November.[41]

Equally imperturbable was George Aitken, a World War veteran, metal worker and founder member of the CPGB, who was one of the first British students at the International Lenin School in 1927 but left early because of his wife's bad health.[42] He knew Čopić from the Lenin School and got on well with him. According to Jason Gurney, cartographer-scout on the Brigade staff and a keen observer of leading personalities, Aitken was 'the only Political Commissar who was effective without being sanctimonious'.[43] Also on Brigade Staff during the crucial days of 12–14 February (but attached to the French 14th Brigade) was the redoubtable George Nathan. The company commanders were, with one exception, also reliable. Christopher (Kit) Conway, from Tipperary had served in the British, Irish and US (National Guard) armies and had been training officer of the IRA before Spain; he was now leading the legendary No. 1 Company. The second company, the machine-gunners, was under the command of Harold Fry from Edinburgh[44], the third under Bill Briskey, formerly a leading trade unionist among London busmen, who was portrayed as 'kindly and conscientious' by his runner.[45] Bert Overton, from Stockton-on-Tees, was an ex-Guardsman wont to boast of his military abilities. He led the fourth company into battle and was to belie that self-acclaimed prowess.[46] Finally, Frank Ryan, acting as assistant to battalion commissar Aitken, took a rifle from a dead man on the first day of the battle (12 February) and stayed in the line.[47] On the way to the front via Chinchón, the men got off the trucks in Villarubia de Santiago and let off a few rounds into the hills. Most of them had never fired a rifle before, and in the machine-gun company, George Leeson, an ex-Royal Navy man, had to show the men in his platoon how to adjust the sights. His group had no idea that the enemy had broken through and crossed the river, or of what was in store for them.[48] Indeed, the forces of Franco were tightening the noose, having crossed the bridge at Pindoque on 11 February and now moving north to south down the Tajuña valley. A grave threat emanated simultaneously also from the west following the successful crossing of the Jarama by Franco's elite troops (Legionnaires, Moors and German Condor Legion machine-gun units), capturing San Martín and now thrusting forward towards the heights beyond the eastern bank. Neither the soldiers of the 15th Brigade nor the staff knew exactly how far that advance had proceeded.

After a 7 a.m. breakfast at a large farmhouse near the front line on 12 February, the men of the British battalion moved forward and were in position by 10 a.m. The weather was fine and the men, generally young and military neophytes, were in good spirits. In reality they were in a good

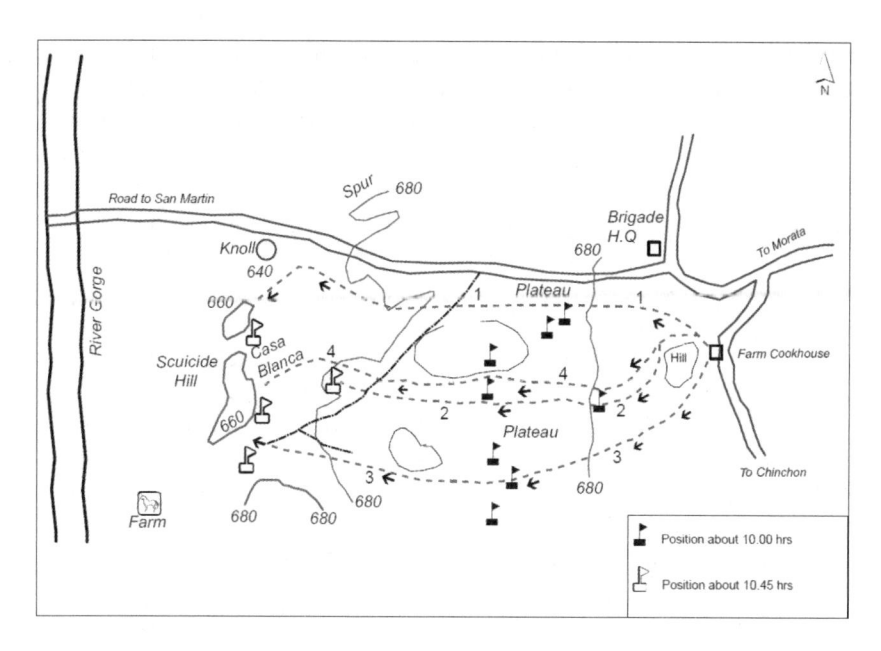

Jarama Front, British attack, 12 February 1937 (courtesy of Diarmuid Duggan)

defensive position on a plateau: the escarpment sloped down on to open ground. In the middle distance the battalion could see three hills, on the left a conical prominence that was devoid of cover and beside it another ('Suicide Hill') capped by a white house (Casa Blanca), with a smaller knoll on the extreme right. In the far distance one could see the cliffs on the further bank of the Jarama river. Only on the morning of the attack did the scouts of the Staff and of battalion commander Wintringham reconnoitre the ground and make crude maps.[49] Gal at Morata could not rely on modern cartography either, for his maps did not contain contours for hills, just brown smudges for elevated ground.[50] He gave the order to advance (without aerial or artillery support) and George Nathan arrived to confirm it, pulling No. 1 Company led by Kit Conway out of reserve. Shortly before 11 a.m. the companies advanced down the escarpment heading towards the hills and passed small olive groves. No. 1 Company was on the extreme right, No. 3 commanded by Bill Briskey on the left and No. 4 under Bert Overton in the middle. All companies reached the objectives without opposition. The sun was shining but the men had no entrenching tools to dig in and there was little natural cover.

The Russians at Brigade headquarters insisted that the battalion advance further, i.e. beyond the hills and towards the river. Gal confirmed the order on the telephone to Wintringham. But then a ferocious artillery and machine-gun barrage started. Overton's men on 'Suicide Hill' were sitting ducks, for the white house they occupied was a natural target for enemy gunners. When the Franco-Belge battalion was forced back on the British right flank around midday, fascist machine-gunners on the knoll on the right could enfilade the valley, forcing the retreat of No. 1 Company and mortally wounding Conway. He received three bullets in the groin and died in hospital that night. Conway had probably advanced too far and was often in prominent view when urging on his men.[51] In mid-afternoon, experienced Moroccan troops started their attacks and also took the two hills on the left. Fleeing infantrymen bunched up in the four-foot deep sunken road and were hit by machine-gun fire and snipers. Wintringham ordered a retreat but Gal countermanded it, the British had to 'hold on at all costs'. Communications between Wintringham and his company commanders under fire broke down: he ordered them to retreat, but the brigade order did reach the companies, so the retreat arguably started too late.

For hours there was no supporting fire from Harold Fry's No. 2 (machine-gun) Company: the machine-gun belts for the Maxims contained the wrong ammunition and the replacement belts did not arrive quickly because the lorry driver was drunk and crashed the vehicle. Fred Copeman, already wounded, and battalion commissar George Aitken located the lorry and had the boxes of bullets retrieved. Filling the belts by hand and positioning the Maxims behind a low stone wall, Copeman directed a devastating fire on the advancing tabor (company) of Moroccans around 7 p.m. These colonial troops were professionals, marksmen who also knew how to infiltrate enemy lines or no man's land by weaving and dipping, using folds in the broken ground. Now it was the turn of Franco's mercenary survivors to flee. That was the last important action of a disastrous day; the battalion was down to a third of its initial strength: 200 shocked and exhausted volunteers. When the stragglers and deserters hiding in the rear were herded together, the battalion numbered about 275, plus a Spanish company.

The fighting on 13 February, the second day, was quite confused. The men were on stand-to at 3 a.m. and a dawn attack on the sunken road by the Moors was beaten off by 20 minutes of accurate machine-gun fire. Wintringham, to his credit, ignored an order issued by the Russians, conveyed to him by Springhall, to advance in the early afternoon. Aircraft and tanks were promised, but their presence could be counted in minutes: a few bombs were dropped on 'Suicide Hill' by Republican Chato biplane fighters on a solitary run and two Russians tanks retired before reaching British positions. A second order to Wintringham to advance at around 3pm from Brigade 'or be escorted back' was ignored by the British captain. His problem was that the flanks were open because the Franco-Belge of the 14th Brigade, the communist soldiers of Enrique Líster and a Spanish cavalry unit had pulled back. The frontline was now the sunken road, and the position to the left of the British battalion was an open space. Wintringham had placed Fry's machine-gunners rather far forward on the left flank with the argument that the position offered a splendid field of fire, and, as added security for the Maxims, had positioned the survivors of Overton's company to the right of Fry's men. But when the fascist artillery barrage recommenced, No. 4 Company, with Overton in the lead, withdrew in haste to the sunken road. Some British machine gunners, expecting Spanish reinforcements on their left, were shot at from the rear, others were duped by Spanish Foreign Legion troops singing the 'Internationale'. Fry's men were soon overwhelmed. At this juncture Wintringham was wounded. In the evening, Joseph ('Jock') Cunningham, returning from hospital, took over the running of the battalion.

On the third day, 14 February, the setbacks continued. Many of the volunteers were now into their third day without food. Enemy crossfire forced Cunningham to give up the sunken road. When fascist tanks appeared, the British and Irish had to retreat further. Then the left flank broke and the withdrawal became a rout. Only after a stiff talk by Gal, who emphasised that the way was now open for Franco's troops to take the Madrid-Valencia road, did the 180 survivors of the battalion take heart and say they would return to the line. In a memorable action, later recounted in a famous passage written by Frank Ryan and included in almost all books about the British and the Irish in Republican Spain,[52] Cunningham and Ryan led the men they had gathered together to retake the lost positions and, singing, they marched off. They were joined by French and Spanish stragglers. This group surprised the enemy, who retreated to the two hills, and the battalion line was re-established near the sunken road. On the next day Frank Ryan was wounded in the left arm by a bullet that went through the head of a man beside him, and shortly afterwards was knocked unconscious by the blast of a tank shell that damaged a tendon in his leg.[53] He recuperated in Elda, one of the fortunate 'walking wounded', and left Spain by air for Toulouse in early March. Nine Irishmen with the British battalion died during the battle or shortly afterwards: John Campbell, Kit Conway, Pat Curley, Leslie Doran, Leo Green, Robert Hilliard, Albert McElroy, Maurice Quinlan and Richard O'Neill. At least 18 of the Irish survivors were wounded.[54] Of the 630-odd men of the British battalion who went into battle at Jarama on 12 February, only 80 were uninjured three days later.[55]

Taken as a whole, the British battalion had fought well against the elite Moorish and Foreign Legion soldiers of Franco. Wintringham had displayed that he understood terrain tactics and the use of firepower, but his soldiers were hampered by their inexperience, lack of equipment (entrenching tools, grenades, anti-tank weapons of any kind) and the failure of Overton's Company No. 4. The February days were arguably the 'finest hour' of the volunteers from Ireland and Britain: never again would they be the last line of defence in the crucial stage of a major battle, never again would there be so many Irish and British in the International Brigades. What soured the men towards the authorities was the original ill-planned advance, and the fact that there were only three or four stretcher bearers in the battalion – the official dressing station was 5 km behind the lines – and many men wounded in no man's land could not be retrieved.[56] Overton's case was discussed at a full battalion meeting two months later. He had added to his obloquy after Jarama by claiming captain's pay (he was a sergeant) while in hospital. There was a unanimous call for a court-martial which, at Brigade level, duly sentenced him to service in a front-line penal battalion. Overton was killed at Brunete in July when bringing ammunition to the front lines.[57]

Only 29 of the original machine-gun company strength of 120 survived to be taken prisoner, including Jack Flynn from Derry, a deserter from the British Army. Fry's second-in-command, Edward Dickinson, was shot on the spot after protesting that two of his companions had been killed by their captors. Others were killed or wounded when crossing open ground. The captives were handed over to a Spanish cavalry unit who made abundant use of rifle-butts and whips to hurry on the laggards, and were then imprisoned in a room in San Martín de La Vega for two days without food, water or medical attention. Two imprisoned French Internationals were taken out and shot. The next makeshift prison was a filthy cell in Navalcarnero, where the men were poorly fed once a day and subjected to serial beatings by the Moors. Roughly one week after capture, ten or so survivors of the machine-gun company were driven to Talavera de la Reina in trucks and locked up in a disused factory where they were visited by British journalists (reports from the *Daily Mail* on the visit were intentionally misleading and spiteful) and a British diplomat. Conditions gradually got better, newsreel teams (*Movietone News*) filmed them doing forced labour and the men's morale improved. A favourite pastime was lice-hunting or a primitive form of baseball in the courtyard. The guards, believing the men had a surplus of energy, forced them to dig mass graves in the cemetery, the last resting place of Spanish Republican troops that the British had befriended who were driven away in lorries by the Foreign Legion and dispatched by firing squad. Working under protest at a munition dump, the British received some pay which they topped up by selling tins of sardines and then bought tobacco and extra food. The prisoners also received occasional gifts of wines and clothes from sympathetic locals.[58]

After interrogation by Don Pablo Merry del Val, the son of a former Spanish Ambassador to Britain, the men were put on trial in Salamanca and sentenced to death or 20 years' incarceration. They were eventually pardoned and left Spain under fascist fanfare at the end of May after they had solemnly signed a pledge that they would not return. For reasons unknown, Clonakilty-born George Leeson was not released until September, and two others not until November.[59] A tragic postscript to the capture of the machine-gunners was that one of the captives, Jimmy Rutherford, returned to Spain under the name of James Small and was captured again, in Calaceite in March 1938, recognised by Merry del Val in San Pedro de la Cardeña concentration camp, and shot in Burgos central prison on 1 June.[60]

### THE AMERICANS ATTACK, 23 AND 27 FEBRUARY

While the British were recovering in primitive trenches, the Americans were to be part of a series of counterattacks by Republican command to recapture lost ground, specifically the area south of the 12–14 February blood-letting and its most prominent feature, Pingarrón (690 m), and the river ford outside San Martín. Both positions were stormed by Spanish Republican troops on 23 February but retaken in fierce fighting by a Moorish tabor from Tetuan.[61] It is likely that the first blooding of the Americans on 23 February was a diversionary attack. In any case, it was to some extent a reprise of the costly 12 February debacle suffered by the British and Irish, and a foretaste of worse disasters. The Americans had relieved the Slav Dimitrov volunteers on 21 February, occupying their trenches. Under the supporting fire of four Maxims, the 450 Americans, with fixed bayonets, scaled the trench wall and ran towards the entrenched enemy on Pingarrón opposite on the afternoon of 23 February. No. 1 Company was the first to advance – its American members, then the Cubans and the Irish.

Under strong machine gun fire from old British positions to the north and from Pingarrón facing them, some of the volunteers covered 500m by skillfully using the scant cover and a few got within grenade-throwing distance of the enemy positions. The Spaniards or Slavs on both flanks had not advanced as planned, and one of the two tanks in support was hit. The early fall of dusk on a winter evening prevented further casualties. Company commander Scott was killed, then replaced by Bill Henry, who had shovels brought up by the machine-gunners and dug in. The engagement was broken off between 10 p.m. and 11 p.m., the Americans were ordered back to the take-off position and had nothing to show for their pluck except 20 fatalities and over 40 wounded. Why the attack was launched with only two hours of daylight remaining was never explained.[62]

The US battalion was re-organised with Bill Henry, a First World War veteran from Belfast, taking over No. 1 Company, assisted by McGrotty as adjutant, while No. 2 Company was given to Martin Hourihan, a teacher of Irish extraction. All officers involved discussed a second attack with Gal and Čopić on 26 February; it was to take place the next morning at 7 a.m. along the whole front of the Internationals, with the Americans as the main attacking force.

As with the British and Irish two weeks earlier, the promised assistance was nugatory: the tanks never arrived, and the armoured cars in their place let off a few belts of heavy calibre machine-gun fire towards Pingarrón and retired; two or three aircraft appeared briefly and flew away after a strafing run, and the ancient French 75 artillery pieces fired shells that fell short, near Republican Spanish units. Rather stupidly, the Americans and the other Internationals had given notice of their intent by firing all weapons at the fascist lines before dawn. That brought a rain of shells and machine-gun fire down on the Republican front. Around 10 a.m. the 24th Spanish battalion on the Americans' flank advanced but soon scurried back under murderous fire. The Dimitrov battalion refused to advance and 12 British who did were picked off. Merriman pleaded with Čopić to call off the attack since the support was not sufficient, but the commissar was adamant. Finally, Brigade Head Quarters (HQ) sent Lieutenant Clifford Wattis, an Englishman from Stockport, and the Londoner Douglas ('Dave') Springhall to ensure that the Americans went 'over the top' just before noon.[63]

It was a slaughter. Merriman was wounded in the shoulder straight away, and Springhall received a bad facial injury when just out of the trench. In the next few minutes all the other officers were killed, first Bill Henry, then McGrotty. On his way to the first-aid post, Merriman insisted on being brought to HQ to see to Čopić, who refused to talk to him. The attack petered out in the afternoon rain. The losses of the Americans were 127 killed and 200 wounded. In the evening, the retrieved corpses were stacked in piles like wood and set on fire.[64] Along with Henry and McGrotty, the other Irish killed on 27 February were Charlie Donnelly (Political Commissar of the Irish platoon) and John Dolan.[65] Michael Kelly crawled back late through the heavy rain, pulling a wounded Cuban comrade behind him, before going out again to rescue a second and being wounded, but not fatally.[66] The men of the British battalion also tried to advance under heavy fire on 27 February but Cunningham and Frank Ryan 'called for a withdrawal immediately after seeing that no support of any kind was being given to the Lincolns and themselves.'[67] There were over 30 fatalities in the British battalion, including Thomas T. O'Brien from Liverpool.⁶⁸

The 80 to 90 survivors in the American battalion were incandescent and vengeful, calling Merriman 'Murderman'. Later, both he and all responsible American officers and political delegates in Spain sought to have Čopić removed, but to no avail because the Croat was a Moscow appointee. The Americans demanded a public meeting with the 'top brass', which surprisingly was granted on 1 March in the courtyard of the cook-house building in the presence of curious British, Irish and other spectators. None of the Americans spoke, only the brigade leadership, who praised the courage of the men and recounted the desperate plight at the front during February, the difficulties of supplies and coordination and the inexperience of all troops involved. John Tisa from New York thought the exercise of 'open democracy' helped to improve morale.⁶⁹ Five from the battalion presented a petition to Čopić, who passed it on 'as evidence of American insubordination and mutiny'.⁷⁰ At least three American deserters from Jarama eventually made it home to the United States.

### THE 'TRIAL' OF CLIFFORD WATTIS

The special ire of the Americans was directed against Lieutenant Clifford James Wattis, who, it was alleged, had forced the not-so-eager out of the trench into the murderous fire on 27 February under gunpoint. Wattis, according to Battalion Staff scout Jason Gurney, had 'an exaggerated military manner' and boasted of the days 'with the Cherry Pickers [11th Hussars], old man' and was treated with some deference by Brigade staff because of his supposed military background.⁷¹ Wattis, though undoubtedly courageous and capable, was a great dissembler. He was not trusted by committed communists right from the outset. R. W. Robson, the CPGB functionary detailed to check the recruits in London, who interviewed Wattis on 22 December, felt that his interviewee 'had arrived in London with very slender recommendations which he could not verify, but him [Wattis] being an ex-army officer he did not want to risk losing him'. Robson took the precaution of warning the leader of the group of 20 heading for Victoria Station to take the Newhaven-Dieppe boat and not to give Wattis any information about the point of contact in Paris. Arriving at Victoria Station in the evening, Wattis confessed he was unsure, stating that Robson did not trust him and that he had forgotten his bag. After he had retrieved it by hiring a taxi to his lodgings, Wattis was perturbed to learn that his fellow-travellers were only going as far as Dunkirk and not Paris. He said he was now booking a sleeper and would meet the men in Paris. He did not turn up.⁷²

Robson's instinct was correct, for Wattis's military career was anything but regular. He joined the Royal Marine Infantry as a 17-year-old in 1921, but was bought out by his father a few weeks later and again the following year.[73] Almost immediately he enlisted in the Royal Warwickshire Regiment in Birmingham but was dismissed with ignominy in late 1926. Wattis also came to grief with the Special Constabulary in Birmingham after less than three years' service – he was dismissed because of fraud. And his sojourn in RAF blue lasted but a few months in 1934, presumably because his past caught up with him.[74] When Wattis arrived in Spain mid-January 1937 he stated he had joined the CPGB in Birmingham the previous December, a dubious claim.[75] He impressed the British at Madrigueras in mid-February with his skills as an instructor and then moved up to the front.[76] On 13 March Wattis was 'tried by his peers' under the aegis of the Juridical Commission. The court-martial body with its impressive title, however, was not a juridical board proper, rather a soldiers' tribunal, and from the outset it had protested at the attempts from Albacete high command or from Kerrigan to interfere in its proceedings.[77] The sitting was stormy and obviously a therapeutic exercise to placate a committee of Americans who had called for the head of Wattis. The IB leadership had limited the number of American witnesses, and the court was chaired by Bert Williams, a Welsh political commissar. Many of the charges against Wattis could not be definitely proved, e.g. that he had ordered the machine-gunners forward instead of allowing them to give covering fire when the men climbed out of the trenches on 27 February, or that he had threatened some soldiers at pistol point or that he arrogated to himself the command of the American battalion after Merriman was wounded. In addressing the court, Wattis said he had been a captain in the British Army until 1934, and closely interrogated his accusers. While many of the charges were based on hearsay, Wattis antagonised everybody by boldly claiming that he had made no mistakes at all on 27 February. He accepted the majority decision that he be degraded to the rank of a soldier but requested that he should not be sent to the Americans, 'where his life would not be safe'. Finally, it was decided that the verdict was temporary pending the hearing of further witnesses.[78]

In reality, the American heavy machine guns broke down after firing off a few belts and the commander Douglas Seacord took a rifle and went with his detachment, 'over the top'.[79] Copeman claimed that Wattis should have crawled into the firing zone in an attempt to establish some order among the scattered groups.[80] As witness statements show, however, Wattis did go out into the killing zone, persuading the men to advance further, 'tapping his well-polished boot with his stagger stick'. Some of the Americans got to ten metres of the fascists' barbed wire.[81] The Juridical Commission found that Wattis had, without justification, taken charge of the American battalion immediately after helping to pull in the wounded Captain Merriman shortly after noon, i.e. before he was officially confirmed in that office by Gal around 6 p.m. It also concluded that the Englishman was an 'adventurer and a careerist' and pleaded for a new trial.[82] Nothing of the sort happened, for Wattis had the support of the Brigade Staff and arguably did what any competent officer would have done when, after speeding to the trenches on a motorbike from Morata with Springhall on the pillion, he ascertained that as the latter and Merriman were wounded, it was time to act. He was shunted out of harm's way on 21 March, being appointed commander of the (penal) Labour Battalion in Morata.[83]

TRENCH WARFARE ON THE JARAMA

After the February battles, the Jarama battleground was transformed into a Western Front scenario: barbed-wire, trenches, trench raids, patrols in no man's land, sniping, lice-infested inhabitants suffering from bad food, lack of sleep, flooded quarters and plummeting morale. In fact, the British and the Irish were worse off than their fathers in Flanders, where food and logistics were incomparably better and each battalion was rotated in or out of the dystopian trenches, usually not spending more than two weeks in any one roster in the front firing line. The 15th Brigade was condemned, by contrast, to spend over four months, with some short intervals, on the static front.

In the American battalion, Martin Hourihan was elected new commander against the wishes of Čopić, who wanted 'someone with military experience like Lieutenant Wattis' to be appointed, a suggestion that was howled down by the American rank-and-file.[84] Hourihan was quiet and efficient, an Irish-American from small-town Pennsylvania with two brothers in the priesthood and a father who wanted him to follow suit. As a seaman, Hourihan joined the Wobblies and, after being discharged with dishonour for his radical views after six years in the US Army, he studied and became a teacher but returned to the seafaring life before leaving for Spain in December 1936.[85]

The first imperative of the Brigade was to build deep, front-line trenches linked by communications trenches of equal depth to the rear and Brigade HQ. By all accounts, the solutions arrived at were fairly makeshift initially, and even when Spanish sapper units or penal battalions joined in the digging, there was a lack of expertise, equipment and material. The soil on the Jarama crumbled easily, so when the rains came, the trench walls collapsed, forcing the men to rebuild what was, at the beginning, no more than a series of linked-up foxholes. Jason Gurney, now with the Americans, praised the engineering skills of his new comrades:

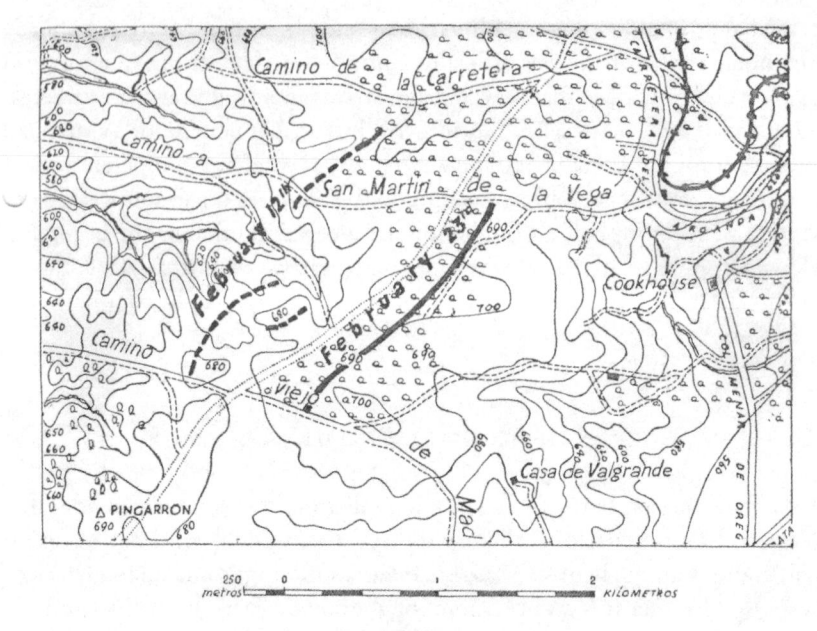

Jarama Front (*Book of the XV Brigade*)

This [the American] was one of the safest trench lines on the whole front as the trenches were deep enough to enable anyone to walk around below the level of fire. The machine-gun positions were well-fortified and there was a truly magnificent system of dug-outs, in marked contrast to the miserable little burrows in which the British survived [...] The trenches nearly all had sufficient head room for standing, with bunks dug into the side lined with mattresses made from mountain brush.[86]

Gurney noted, however, that there were no reserve trenches, so if the front line was captured, there was no prepared position to fall back on. The Americans, he maintained, were sticklers for keeping their trenches and dug-outs clean, and the latrine pits were behind, along the communications trench. This was due to the admonitions of the American battalion medical officer, Dr William Pike.[87] The British did not have a medical doctor at the front, but Dr Walter Fischer ('Dr Langer'), the Viennese communist and Chief of the Medical Services of the 15th Brigade from February to September 1937, visited them and found them incredibly stoical when wounded but arrogant with a sense of their racial superiority. He was especially critical of the British practice of not transferring the wounded by battalion ambulance from the first-aid posts to the brigade hospital near the front, but far further inland to the hospital of the 14th Brigade where they would be cared for by British staff. Fischer also writes of his efforts to enforce hygienic standards: the building of safe, dry toilets, clearing the passages of rubbish and explaining to the volunteers that their skin complaints were linked to lack of personal hygiene. Gradually, he adds, matters improved with the provision of a 'shower-lorry' and disinfectants against the scourge of body lice.[88]

There were two general complaints common to both battalions: the bad food and the appalling weather. Many men suffered from diarrhoea and even dysentery, and were weakened by an inadequate diet and the filthy conditions. Men who were used to the uninspired cooking habits of Britain and Ireland – many of them badly nourished before Spain because of poverty – found it hard to stomach the gooey mess – often cold and consisting of rubbery mule-meat and vegetables with rice – sent up from the cook-house. In most cases the holders of such 'cushy numbers' as cooks had no culinary experience and, although the ingredients were often good, did not know how to cook them, frying everything in olive oil. It was more plentiful in most places in Spain than clean water. As regards the weather, central Spain had one of its wettest springs ever, more than four weeks of intermittent and intense rainfall.[89] Peter O'Connor wrote in his diary that the storm and rain that blew up on 13 March prevented him from standing upright.[90] Life was miserable, as one American volunteer wrote:

> The weather was bad. It rained and there was mud. A cold wind blew down from the Guadarramas and howled around the position of the Brigade, high above the Tajuna valley. The men would get up in the morning to find mud in their dugouts, blankets soaked, clothing wet in varying degrees. The coffee was carried on foot for two kilometers and was cold by the time it reached them. They would sometimes crawl back into the dugouts without bothering to drink the cold coffee, and try to warm up under the wet blankets. The comrades were too tired to dig latrines for a time and hygienic conditions consequently were very bad. There were times, when, in spite of urgent need, there was reluctance to let the pants down in the face of an icy wind, and would try to wait for a momentary let-up in the rain.[. . .] Most of the meals were as cold as the morning coffee. With the soup in his plate, a comrade would try to find a dry place to sit down. Then the wind would come up and whip the food out of his spoon before he could swallow it.[91]

War perforce accelerates learning processes. 'Keep your head down!' was a constant call and many, as on the Western Front, especially in 1914–16, paid the ultimate price by momentarily forgetting it. While most of Franco's crack troops had been replaced by conscripts of dubious commitment, there were enough snipers on call to shoot careless Internationals, usually in the head. There was also a topographical advantage enjoyed by the fascist troops, for they were, like the Germans in the Ypres Salient in the Great War, holding the high ground: the British line stopped at the sunken road and was overlooked by the three hills bloodily contested on 12 February, and the Americans were similarly situated, below Pingarrón.

Generally, however, the front was quiet, apart from two major attacks. The first one, on 14 March, a concentrated effort of Francoist units and aided by tanks, struck at the flank to the left of the American battalion and drove back the raw Spanish recruits in blind panic. They were rallied by American medics and detainees of the labour battalion and returned to the fight, while a few American infantrymen and four from the staff of the British battalion, including the commander Jock Cunningham and his adjutant Fred Copeman, counter-attacked up the disputed trench system, using grenades and shooting the Moors escaping over the top of the parapets. Some ground was thus recovered but about 150 yards of Republican trenches had been lost to the enemy. Cunningham was badly wounded and Copeman dragged him to safety. He was duly appointed his successor.[92] Liam Tumilson, the officer commanding the Lincoln's machine-gun company, was killed outright by a sniper when trying to relocate a machine-gun to quell the breakthrough on his left.[93]

The second major action was a Brigade initiative on 5 April. Chief of Operations in the 15th Brigade from 26 March was Captain Allan Johnson (his real name was Allan McNeil), a regular officer in the US Army and a graduate of the General Staff College on leave of absence from the Massachusetts National Guard.[94] The object of the attack was to retake the trenches captured on 14 March and storm the heights of Pingarrón.[95] The attack was to be spearheaded by the Italian Garibaldi Battalion (fresh from its success at Guadalajara) and aided by the Polish Dombrowski Battalion and tanks. The Americans were in reserve giving covering fire and were only to be moved with the approval of Johnson. The Italians were successful, recapturing the territory lost on 14 March, but their right flank, the Poles, refused to move, although castigated by the crews of Russian tanks lumbering towards Pingarrón. Hostile fire was intense, and the American No. 1 Company was ordered over the top by Čopić without consulting Johnson. For once, republican artillery fire was accurate, but the attack was a failure because of lack of coordination: it was supposed to be launched at 7 a.m. by the Garibaldis, but started three hours late, giving the enemy plenty of time to regroup. The Lincolns were thrown into the fray and until their withdrawal at around 4 p.m. suffered 20 casualties.[96] The only fatality seems to have been Hugh Bonar from Donegal, a veteran of the Irish Civil War who was killed instantly by an explosive bullet to the head when advancing beside Peter O'Connor.[97] Johnson received an attendance with General Miaja in Madrid and explained, as shown above, why the attack failed. Barthel, the French Brigade Commissar, was informed of the attack only late the night before and complained that the men knew it was impending days before he did.[98] Johnson obviously had a flaming row with Čopić, who now as Brigade Commander, together with Gal as head of the 15th Division, had turned an originally well-planned action into yet another cock-up. The Yugoslav accused Johnson of 'working against him'. The American, Čopić noted cynically, 'recognised his fault and promised to continue working legally'.[99]

Discipline in the American battalion was as good as could be expected considering the conditions. Some men went AWOL to Morata, or even Madrid, returning with venereal disease. But there were, as yet, no calls for repatriation, but instead freely expressed discontent and the wish to be taken out of the line, even for a short period. The Irish recovered the bodies of Charlie Donnelly and Eamonn McGrotty from no man's land on 9 March, held a 1916 Rebellion ceremony and concert on Easter Monday, 29 March, and a memorial for James Connolly on 12 May.[100]

Drunkenness was not a major problem, except among some Irish and a handful of 'hard cases' in the machine-gun company.[101] The battalion leadership ordered that any man under the influence of alcohol or possessing same would be sent to the Labour Battalion for ten days.[102] Another measure was the gradual removal of men obviously unfit for service and slated for repatriation, including William Fennelly from Abbeyleix, who had only one lung and was physically weak (he subsequently deserted but returned to Spain) or Denis Holden from Carlow, considered to be too old and too fond of drink.[103] Colum Cox added to his catalogue of infractions by trying to desert from the front for the second time, but was caught and sentenced on 8 March to three months in the Labour Battalion. Most of these sentences were subject to early remission and Cox and John Colman from Cork could have re-joined their comrades had they agreed to the anti-typhoid inoculation.[104] Both were finally released on 17 April.[105] Other breaches of discipline concerned men who had overstayed their short leave in Madrid and were consequently posted as deserters.[106] The most spectacular case of ill-discipline in the American battalion, which must have caused no little chortling in the ranks, was of the New Zealander Lieutenant William McDonald, the battalion secretary. He was sent to Madrid in late April with a hefty wad of notes to purchase items for the battalion, and booked into the Hotel Florida (Hemingway's bolt-hole); there, he went on a spree with an English comrade and the American pilot Frank Tinker, visiting various bars and a brothel. He was surprised when he woke up next morning to find the money still under his bed, but lost it when it was stolen from a lorry on the way back to Morata.[107] McDonald went before the war tribunal but received only two months in the labour unit, presumably because he was 'un bon militant'.[108]

The situation in the British battalion was far worse. The general discontent seems to have been far more corrosive and disciplinary problems were legion. Fred Copeman, officer commanding since mid-March, was a controversial figure. Tall, muscular, a non-drinker and a skilled boxer from his days in the Royal Navy, Copeman brought the rough justice of that service into play, but was arguably a fair and competent commander, at least one who held things together. Copeman's failing was his 'bruiser' attitude, i.e. the propensity to settle arguments with his fists.[109] His language was lower-deck argot full of expletives, uttered in raucous Cockney. Jason Gurney held him to be fearless but always threatening violence,[110] while for Walter Gregory, Fred Copeman was 'a real disciplinarian and his firm, almost authoritarian style was probably one which the battalion needed at that time.'[111] David Crook, an intellectual in the machine-gun section, liked and admired the new commander.[112] Alexander Foote also appreciated the leadership qualities of Copeman, driving him around as brigade transport officer.[113] The battalion Political Commissar, George Aitken, had a good working relationship with Copeman and maintained that he, as the older man, could persuade the highly volatile Cockney to change a hasty decision.[114]

Aitken, a Scottish labour veteran with a calm, laconic manner, was not universally popular, perhaps because, as an old-time communist cadre, he thought in hierarchies and had little to say to those unaccustomed to party jargon or to the fearful youngsters and the 'old soldier' professional gripers. Walter Greenhalgh, a young communist from Manchester and a friend of Frank Ryan's, liked Aitken and was his assistant in bringing out *Our Fight*, a Brigade newssheet.[115] In early April, the English officer of the Cadres Department in Albacete visited the British and formed the impression that Copeman, 'a brave and good comrade', was 'militarily insufficiently developed' and 'too quick-tempered in his handling of the men'. He qualified his remarks by emphasising that any new commander would find it hard to live up to the reputation of Jock Cunningham, who was 'idolised by his comrades'. The visitor was taken aback by the strength of ill-feeling against Aitken, who 'does not seem to have the best manner of approach to the comrades'. He recommended that Aitken be promoted to be Brigade Political Commissar, which happened shortly afterwards.[116]

The first break in the enervating tedium came on 5 March, when the British were transported to Morata de Tajuña for a general clean up (change of underclothes and baths), an interval lasting four days, with sing-songs in the billets and speeches by Cunningham, Aitken and Harry Pollitt, who was on the first of his five visits to the battalion. Aitken held that his biggest disciplinary problem was caused by a group of homesick Glaswegians.[117] Copeman established a daily routine akin to that of a British battalion during the Great War: rifle and billet inspection, digging deeper trenches or saps in no man's land, night patrols in front of the wire, fatigue parties to oversee sanitation and refuse problems, warnings about the spread of scabies etc. A striking difference was his insistence on receiving a discipline report three times daily, an indication of his necessarily tight rule.[118]

Driving a sap (observation post linked to the firing-line) into no man's land was perilous work, usually carried out by members of the Labour Battalion, but regular work parties also went out in the dark to fix barbed-wire obstacles.[119] Far more dangerous, and as unpopular with the rank-and-file as they had been in France 20 years earlier, were trench raids to capture prisoners for interrogation. It was a Brigade order by Gal, carried out for about three weeks without much enthusiasm by Copeman, who feared losses. On one such sortie, a fascist colonel was captured in a latrine and brought back; in another, two of the British raiding party were wounded by the rifle-fire of nervous Spanish sentries when returning.[120] There was little contact with the American battalion, who could quite early in their Jarama sojourn boast of a library, a barber, a canteen shop, a radio set with powerful loudspeakers and a wall newspaper, aptly titled *Daily Manaña*.[121] In weeks of nightly digging, American volunteers dug new trenches with side cuts, eventually joining up the 'Ts' and thus pushing their front line forward. By careful observation during the day (spying from a burnt-out tank in no man's land), the Americans located enemy machine-gun posts and had the new anti-tank battery brought up to knock out the enemy strong-points.[122] The British still had to wait until mid-May before the radio system was working to broadcast the BBC news and the Saturday football results.[123]

Relief from their Jarama purgatory seemed at hand on 29 April when the men of the 15th Brigade were transported by truck to Alcalá de Henares, an old university city and the birthplace of Miguel de Cervantes and the Republican President Manuel Azaña. The predominantly French 14th Brigade took over their trenches. Before leaving, the British battalion held a memorial meeting to their fallen comrades in front of a cairn made in the shape of a pointed star (the IB emblem) and placed flowers on the graves. After leaving the trucks in Alcalá, men went in search of a decent meal and not a few got blind drunk. The French created the most trouble and the majority in the American battalion was soon incapably intoxicated. The military commander of the town, a conservative career officer, did not attend the first of May parade of the brigades on the town square, and had made no provision for their quartering, even refusing straw for the English-speakers, forcing them to sleep on the concrete floors of the dilapidated barracks.[124] As this respite from routine was terminated after four days and the men were sent back to their Jarama trenches – where the French reliefs had transformed the Americans' habitat into a rubbish-tip[125] – calls for a permanent transfer became virulent.

Bill Paynter, a Welsh miner sent by the CPGB to replace Peter Kerrigan as commissar of the British at Albacete in March, complained to the French military commandant there that, although the men had been brought back with the promise that their final removal from the front was only a matter of days, nothing had happened in the meantime. He added that 'this history of broken promises [. . .] only serves to encourage desertion, indiscipline, and a general deterioration of the men.'[126] Such was also the tenor of the meetings between the Brigades' commissars on 10 May.[127] Short (48–72 hour) passes were granted for leave in Madrid to men with good records, but the departure of the whole Brigade did not take place until 17 June, when the British moved to Mondéjar, 60 km west of the capital. Twenty-five battalion soldiers had left earlier to join the officers' training school near Pozorrubio, a hutted encampment in the woods about 150 km north of Albacete. Three taking the sergeants' course were Irish: Paddy Duff and Jack Nalty from Dublin and Gerard Doyle from Limerick.[128] The 40 British and Irish who had joined the new anti-tank battery in March, in contrast, had come straight from the Madrigueras training base. By late June, at the time of their departure from Jarama's unhappy valley, only 12 Irish-born and six Cubans were still on the fighting strength of the American battalion.[129]

## DISCIPLINARY PROBLEMS AMONG THE BRITISH

The voluminous files on breaches of discipline in the British battalion while stationed on the Jarama demonstrate that the punishments meted out were lenient. Most cases involved intoxication, refusal to go to the front or desertion from it, desertion from hospital, disobedience and inveterate grousing. The Brigade 'guard-house' was in the fenced aviary of a luxurious country mansion, now the new Brigade HQ that overlooked the Tajuña valley and the main Madrid-Valencia highway. Men incarcerated there were probably better fed than in the trenches, and they received a daily cigarette ration. Trial was by a prosecutor and the political commissars, but each battalion could send three delegates to ensure that the culprits got a fair hearing. The sentences were light and most of the condemned could return to their battalions after serving one fourth of the sentence.[130] Cases of nervous exhaustion (neurasthenia) were treated with compassion, and the patients were sent home in most cases.[131]

Among the Irish troublemakers, Joe Ryan (Limerick), a teenager who should have been sent back immediately on age grounds, left his post in the line, was arrested in Madrid along with 12 others from the British battalion, and was sentenced in late April to one month in the Labour Battalion. The officers of the British battalion were 'strongly opposed' to Ryan and three others re-joining the battalion as they were 'consistent grumblers' and because their influence in the unit was 'very bad'.[132] Joe Ryan escaped from detention and, together with Joe Moran from Birkenhead, tried to board an English ship in Valencia harbour on 7 May 1937, but they were apprehended.[133] Ryan was allowed to leave Spain in July 1937.[134]

The Commander of the Brigade detention centre on the Jarama, Lieutenant Clifford Wattis, was accused by the Juridical Commission of favouring British detainees, i.e. giving them 'easy jobs' in the courtyard of Brigade HQ. Other strictures in his direction included an unduly lenient regime and outbursts of temper that 'unnecessarily annoyed' his charges.[135] Wattis had slighted the French, who regarded the IB as their fiefdom, by confronting a hostile crowd demanding the release of an imprisoned member of the Franco-Belge battalion on the night of 23 April. Wattis increased the number of guards who lined all approaches to the prison. Order was thus restored, and his account was confirmed in writing by two of his guard, Sid Quinn (Belfast) and an English comrade.[136] Colonel Claus of Brigade staff had brought these charges, but Fred Copeman pursued another line, accusing the purported ex-officer of purloining cigarettes sent from Britain, i.e. distributing only a portion of the shipment to the prisoners.[137] The matter, it seems, was not pursued.

Finally, there were three serious cases that, in another army, would have led to long prison sentences or even the death penalty:

1) A Scottish volunteer attacked his company commander with a rifle, wounding him in the hand, which required stitching. He spent only one month in confinement.[138]

2) The volunteer who, in a drunken state, crashed the lorry bringing the correct Maxim ammunition to the British at the front on 12 February was 'amnestied' after two weeks in detention.[139]

3) A middle-class South African, who stole – and did not 'lose' like his American counterpart – battalion funds received six months in the Labour Battalion, from which he escaped, seeing out the war in a Republican prison.[140]

As the British battalion was a collective with its share of misfits or individuals unsuitable or not properly trained for a military life in exceedingly tough conditions, the tolerant line on infractions practised by Copeman and Aitken was prudent. They could hardly impose the British Army disciplinary code, and it is to their further credit that they absolutely refused, in their entire period in Spain, to countenance the death penalty, a policy urged on them by the Division as early as April 1937.[141]

### THE IRISH IN ANDALUSIA AGAIN

In March 1937, there was also a fascist attack in the southern region of Andalusia, which before 1936 had been the poorest part of Spain and a stronghold of working-class militancy and peasant radicalism. In the bitterly poor mountain areas, many families lived in caves. Apart from farming, the main occupation was in mining (lead, copper, bismuth) but most of the pits, often foreign owned, had closed or were working at low levels. Relations between the miners and agricultural labourers (brazeros) on the one hand, and the Guardia Civil on the other, were poisonous. When Pozoblanco was recaptured by the workers' militia, 170 policemen were executed.[142] That was when most of the landscape fell to Franco's units early in the war, and the capture of Málaga, the main port in the south, in February was an unprecedented disaster for the Republicans that increased distrust in Largo Caballero's direction of the war effort. The March 1937 onslaught on republican positions took place in the extreme west of Córdoba province, a drive to the north-east in mountainous country with the aim of securing the precious mercury mines at Almadén. Franco's troops advanced as far as Pozoblanco, which was well-defended. The garrison held out in the shattered town, and in a counterattack most of the villages captured days before were retaken by anarchist militiamen, militarised police units (carbineros) and the 13th International Brigade.[143]

In order to stabilise the front in the Chimorra mountain range (foothills of the Sierra Moreno), the IB command at Albacete 'lent' the newly formed 20th International Battalion to the 86th Mixed Brigade. The battalion was multinational, with companies of Slavs, French-Belgians, German speakers and an Anglo-American component of 40–50 that formed the 92-man strong 2nd Company with Latin Americans. The leader of the battalion was an astute tactician, the Italian ex-naval officer with experience of the First World War Riccardo Formica, who adopted the pseudonym Aldo Morandi in Spain. The four Irishmen in the battalion were veterans of No. 1 Company of the British battalion, and three had been wounded – Joe Monks, Frank Edwards and Peter Daly. Unscathed to date was Paddy O'Daire, another tactical planner who carried French military manuals in his knapsack to add to the infantry techniques he had acquired during his seven years in the Irish Free State Army.

The first commander of the Anglo-American Company was Robert Traill, a British university-educated linguist who had lived in Moscow; the second was Rollin Dart, a 30-year-old American who had served over three years as a pilot in the army air force. The elected commissar of the company was John Gates, a former CPUSA organiser from New York, who spoke Spanish. When the new battalion was in training in Madrigueras, Gates displayed his gift for public relations by presenting the children of the village with toys and sweets and a slapstick pantomime in the local cinema that included a red-headed Scot playing the bagpipes and the leading of a mule (burro) down the aisles and on to the stage.[144] The battalion moved south on 20 March and first saw action when travelling on the light railway from Pozoblanco to Peñarroya. In a scene worthy of a propaganda film about the Russian Civil War, enemy artillery shelled and damaged the tracks, and the men disembarked and took up defensive positions underneath the peak of El Terrible. A night attack was beaten off and the whole battalion was moved east to the hard-fought terrain around the Chimorra peak (958 m). The battle swayed to and fro, with attacks and counterattacks, interspersed with periods of boredom and bad weather. Traill was promoted to chief of brigade staff, Dart took over the second company and both Daly and O'Daire were given lieutenant rank.

The highpoint of the Anglo-American company's sojourn in the mountains was an attack by Moors on 18 April, which was preceded by aerial bombardment from the Italians, an artillery barrage and by fire from trench mortars and anti-tank guns. The unit withdrew in disarray from a hill, with Edwards holding up some Moors by throwing grenades. Then the men rallied to O'Daire's command 'Form a line!', and the battalion's machine-gunners caught the Moors on the slope. At dusk O'Daire reconnoitred the terrain and, realising that the new positions would be untenable at daylight, organised a counterattack in the mist and won back the trenches.[145] The 20th Battalion, relieved on the night of 29 April, was given a period of rest in Dos Torres before returning to the mountains. The survivors finally left the area by truck for Albacete on 4 July. According to Joe Monks, 8 members of the Anglo-American company had been killed, over 30 were in hospital (including Peter Daly, wounded for the second time in the hip, but who soon re-joined the unit), 2 had self-inflicted wounds and 2 had deserted. His final count was 44 men standing out of the original strength of 92.[146] Gates stayed with the 86th Brigade, but other Americans, Irish and British applied for transfer to their respective battalions of the 15th Brigade. Edwards and Monks were repatriated in the summer of 1937, while Daly and O'Daire rose to prominence as commanders of the British battalion. Gates re-joined the Lincolns in March 1938 and was appointed 15th Brigade Commissar.

NOTES

1. RGASPI, f. 545, o. 3, d. 438, ll. 121–2.
2. Most of the Irish that left Madrigueras had been training with No. 2 Company under Harold Fry (RGASPI, f. 545, o. 6, d. 47, l. 107).
3. Cecil Eby, *Between the Bullet and the Lie: American Volunteers in the Spanish Civil War* (New York–Chicago–San Francisco, 1969), pp 22–3.
4. Richard Baxell, *Unlikely Warriors: The British in the Spanish Civil War and the Struggle Against Fascism* (London, 2012), p. 96.
5. William Herrick, *Jumping the Line: The Adventures and Misadventures of an American Radical* (Oakland and Edinburgh, 2001), pp 146–7.
6. Ibid., p. 147.
7. Eby, *Between the Bullet and the Lie*, pp 28–9.
8. John Tisa, *Recalling the Good Fight: An Autobiography of the Spanish Civil War* (South Hadley, Mass., 1985), pp 29–30.
9. Marion Merriman and Warren Lerude, *American Commander in Spain: Robert Hale Merriman and the Abraham Lincoln Brigade* (Reno, 1986), p. 86.
10. RGASPI, 545, o. 3, d. 468, ll. 15–16.
11. www.merrimandiary.com/2014/01/23. Accessed 14 June 2018.
12. Emmet O'Connor, *Reds and the Green: Ireland, Russia and the Communist Internationals, 1919–43* (Dublin, 2004), p. 32; Mike Milotte, *Communism in Modern Ireland: The Pursuit of the Workers' Republic since 1916* (Dublin, 1984), pp 33, 57
13. RGASPI, f. 545, o. 3, d. 440, l. 6.
14. https://albavolunteer.org/2016/01/jarama-series-the-james-connolly-column/. Accessed 14 June 2020; RGASPI, f. 545, o. 2, d. 262, l. 332; f. 545, o. 3, d. 501, l. 11.
15. Tisa, *Recalling the Good Fight*, p. 29.
16. RGASPI, f. 545, o. 3, d. 501, l. 37.
17. Arthur H. Landis, *The Abraham Lincoln Brigade* (New York, 1968), p. 35; Eby, *Between the Bullet and the Lie*, p. 34
18. www.albavolunteer.org/2016/02/jarama-series-organization-of-the-abraham-lincoln-battlion/. Accessed 14 June 2020.
19. RGASPI, f. 545, o. 6, d. 47, l. 70.
20. For the behaviour of Harris and Stember, see the standard works by Carroll, Eby and Landis.
21. RGASPI, f. 545, o. 2, d. 112, l. 51.

22. www.merrimandiary.com/2014/02/04/. Accessed 14 June 2020.
23. RGASPI, f. 545, o. 3, d. 501, l. 42.
24. www.merrimandiary.com/2014/02/07/. Accessed 14 June 2020.
25. RGASPI, f. 545, o. 6, d. 93, l. 23. This battalion 'Blacklist" contains the names of 14 Irish volunteers.
26. www.merrimandiary.com/2014/01/. Accessed 14 June 2020.
27. RGASPI, f. 545, o. 3, d. 501, l. 4.
28. Ibid., l. 47.
29. Ibid., l. 18.
30. Ibid., l. 77.
31. Ibid., l. 51.
32. Ibid., l. 65.
33. Peter O'Connor, *A Soldier of Liberty: Recollections of a Socialist and Anti-fascist Fighter* (Dublin, 1996), p. 17.
34. RGASPI, f. 545, o. 3, d. 501, l. 73.
35. Eby, *Between the Bullet and the Lie*, pp 36–40; Tisa, *Recalling the Good Fight*, pp 35–8.
36. www.albavolunteer.org/2016/02/jarama-series-the-first-casualty-and-the-lost-trucks/. Accessed 14 June 2020.
37. Jason Gurney, generally very critical of all 'Russians' in Spain, stated Gal had 'a pleasant, easy manner' and was unfairly blamed for the Jarama failures (Jason Gurney, *Crusade in Spain* (London, 1974), p. 93).
38. RGASPI, f. 545, o. 3, d. 452, l. 6.
39. RGASPI, f. 495, o. 277, d. 191; f. 545, o. 3, d. 452, l. 8 (autobiography)
40. RGASPI, f. 545, o. 6, d. 350, l. 14; f. 545, o. 6, d. 359, ll. 59–61; www.merrimandiary.com/2014/02/23. Accessed 14 June 2020; Werner Abel, Enrico Hilbert (eds), *'Sie werden nicht durchkommen': Deutsche an der Seite der Spanischen Republik und der sozialen Revolution* (Hessen, 2015), p. 51.
41. RGASPI, f. 545, o. 3, d. 456, ll. 154–6.
42. RGASPI, f. 495, o. 198, d. 1246.
43. Gurney, *Crusade*, p. 117.
44. RGASPI, f. 545, o. 6, d. 136, ll. 85, 88.
45. Walter Gregory, *The Shallow Grave: A Memoir of the Spanish Civil War* (London, 1986), p. 48.
46. Baxell, *Unlikely Warriors*, p. 126.
47. Seán Cronin, *Frank Ryan: The Search for the Republic* (Dublin, 1980), p. 91.
48. IWM, Interview 803, George Leeson, reel 2.
49. For the details, see Gurney, *Crusade*, pp 99–102.
50. Tom Wintringham, *English Captain* (London, 1941), p. 61.
51. IWM Interview 794, Fred Copeman, reel 2.
52. Originally reproduced in the book edited by Ryan himself, *The Book of the XV Brigade* (Madrid, 1938), pp 58–61.
53. Cronin, *Frank Ryan*, pp 97–8; M. Acier (ed.), *From Spanish Trenches: Recent Letters from Spain* (New York, 1937), pp 116–19.
54. RGASPI, f. 545, o. 6, d. 89, ll. 80–4.
55. Baxell, *Unlikely Warriors*, p. 159.

56. Gregory, *Shallow Grave*, pp 50–1.
57. Bill Alexander, *British Volunteers for Liberty: Spain 1936–1939* (London, 1982), p. 107.
58. RGASPI, f. 545, o.3, d. 473, ll. 147–9.
59. Baxell, *Unlikely Warriors*, pp 174–180; IWM, Interview 803, George Leeson, reel 3.
60. Isaac Rilova Pérez, *Guerra Civil y Violencia en Burgos 1936–1943* (Burgos, 2016), p. 396.
61. Landis, *The Abraham Lincoln Brigade*, pp 70–1.
62. For a succinct account of the 23 February battle, see: Merriman, Lerude, *American Commander in Spain*, pp 100–5; Tisa, *Recalling the Good Fight*, pp 41–45; www.albavolunteer.org/2016/02/jarama-series/. Accessed 14 June 2020.
63. Merriman's report of the 23 and 27 February battles are in RGASPI, f. 545, o. 2, d. 164, ll. 4–7.
64. Tisa, *Recalling the Good Fight*, pp 47–53.
65. www.albavolunteer.org/2016/03/jarama-series-pingarron/. Accessed 14 June 2020.
66. Alvah Bessie, Albert Prago (eds), *Our Fight: Writings by Veterans of the Abraham Lincoln Brigade, Spain 1936–1939* (New York, 1987), pp 133–4.
67. Landis, *The Abraham Lincoln Brigade*, p. 84.
68. Baxell, *Unlikely Warriors*, p. 162.
69. Tisa, *Recalling the Good Fight*, pp 55–6
70. www.albavolunteer.org/2016/03/jarama-series-the-aftermath/. Accessed 14 June 2020.
71. Gurney, *Crusade*, p. 127.
72. RGASPI, f. 545, o. 6, d. 212, ll. 82–4.
73. The National Archives, Kew (TNA), ADM 159/168/21075, 159/199/21543.
74. TNA, KV 5/131, index-card Clifford Wattis.
75. RGASPI, f. 545, o. 6, d. 212, l. 81.
76. RGASPI, f. 545, o. 3, d. 433, l. 1a.
77. RGASPI, f. 545, o. 2, d. 142, l. 2.
78. RGASPI, f. 545, o. 3, d. 499, ll. 96–105.
79. Landis, *The Abraham Lincoln Brigade*, p. 84; Tisa, *Recalling the Good Fight*, p. 52.
80. RGASPI, f. 545, o. 3, d. 499, l. 143.
81. Landis, *The Abraham Lincoln Brigade*, pp 84–5.
82. RGASPI, f. 545, o. 3, d. 449, ll. 132–4.
83. RGASPI, f. 545, o. 3, d. 425, l. 74.
84. Eby, *Between the Bullet and the Lie*, p. 69. The new post was confirmed on 15 March (RGASPI, f. 545, o. 3, d. 425, l. 156).
85. Gurney, *Crusade*, pp 132–7; RGASPI, f. 545, o. 3, d. 453, ll. 35–6.
86. Gurney, *Crusade*, p. 138.
87. RGASPI, f. 545, o. 3, d. 501, ll. 10, 21.
88. Walter Fischer, *Kurze Geschichten aus einem langen Leben: Mit einem Nachwort von Leopold Spira* (Mannheim, 1986), pp 107–9. He titles this chapter 'Die Individualisten'.
89. Robert A. Stradling, *Irish and Spanish Civil War 1936–39: Crusades in Conflict* (Manchester, 1999), pp 69–70.
90. O'Connor, *Soldier of Liberty*, p. 18.
91. RGASPI, f. 545, o. 3, d. 471, l. 41.
92. Fred Copeman, *Reason in Revolt* (London, 1948), pp 103–4.

93. RGASPI, f. 545, o. 3, d. 478, ll. 39–40.
94. RGASPI, f. 545, o. 3, d. 429, l. 108; Eby, *Between the Bullet and the Lie*, p. 6; Landis, *The Abraham Lincoln Brigade*, p. 110.
95. RGASPI, f. 545, o. 3, d. 425, l. 129.
96. Landis, *The Abraham Lincoln Brigade*, pp 161–2; Tisa, *Recalling the Good Fight*, pp 60–1; RGASPI, f. 545, o. 2, d. 164, l. 190.
97. RGASPI, f. 545, o. 3, d. 478, l. 45; O'Connor, *Soldier of Liberty*, p. 23.
98. RGASPI, f. 545, o. 3, d. 471, ll. 52–3.
99. Ibid., l. 58.
100. O'Connor, *Soldier of Liberty*, pp 23–4.
101. RGASPI, f. 545, o. 3, d. 501, l. 193.
102. Ibid., l. 171.
103. Ibid., ll. 155, 238.
104. Ibid., l. 66.
105. RGASPI, f. 545, o. 3, d. 496, l. 45.
106. RGASPI, f. 545, o. 3, d. 501, l. 229 (Patrick Stanley and another comrade)
107. RGASPI, f. 545, o. 3, d. 450, l. 104.
108. Ibid., l. 103.
109. Judith Cook, *Apprentices of Freedom* (London–Melbourne–New York, 1979), p. 78. A Glasgow volunteer had unwisely challenged Copeman to a fistfight and lost.
110. Gurney, *Crusade*, pp 111–12.
111. Gregory, *Shallow Grave*, p. 58.
112. James K. Hopkins, *Into the Heart of the Fire: The British in the Spanish Civil War* (Stanford, 1998), p. 184.
113. RGASPI, f. 545, o. 6, d. 135, ll. 8–9. Foote was later recruited by Douglas Springhall to work for Soviet Military Intelligence (GRU). See his interesting memoir: Alexander Foote, *Handbook for Spies* (London, 1949), pp 14–18.
114. MML, Box c, 17/7, letter by Aitken to Political Bureau of CPGB (September 1937), p. 2.
115. IWM, Interview 11187, Walter Greenhalgh, reel 5.
116. RGASPI, f. 545, o. 6, d. 93, ll. 1–2.
117. Baxell, *Unlikely Warriors*, pp 165, 170; RGASPI, f. 545, o. 2, d. 103, ll. 8–19 (Aitken to Kerrigan, 05.03.1937)
118. RGASPI, f. 545, o. 3, d. 495, 496 (Daily Orders).
119. Brian Lewis, Bill Gledhill, *Tommy James: A Lion of a Man* (Pontefract, 1984), pp 59–62.
120. IWM Interview 794, Fred Copeman, reel 4; RGASPI, f. 545, o. 3, d. 496, l. 17 (battalion report, 10 April 1937).
121. Tisa, *Recalling the Good Fight*, pp 63–4.
122. Steve Nelson, *The Volunteers* (East Berlin, 1958), pp 125–8.
123. RGASPI, f. 545, o. 3, d. 495, l. 7 (battalion orders, 14 May 1937).
124. Baxell, *Unlikely Warriors*, pp 170–1; Gurney, *Crusade*, pp 148–9; RGASPI, f. 545, o. 3, d. 471, ll. 56–7.
125. Gurney, *Crusade*, p. 149.
126. RGASPI, f. 545, o. 2, d. 69, l. 180 (letter to Vidal, 11.05.1937); Will Paynter, *My Generation* (London, 1972), pp 67–70.

127. RGASPI, f. 545, o. 3, d. 435, ll. 43–51.
128. RGASPI, f. 545, o.3, d. 453, l. 12; f. 545, o. 6, d. 89, l. 11.
129. The Irish were: Patrick Hamill and Maurice Moran (both via the USA), Vincent O'Donnell, Thomas O'Brien, Peter O'Connor, Patrick Power, William Power, John Power, James O'Regan, Michael Waters, Thomas Hayes and Michael Kelly.
130. Lewis, Gledhill, *Tommy James*, pp 58–9.
131. RGASPI, f. 545, o. 3, d. 450, ll. 85–6; f. 545, o. 3, d. 449, ll. 79, 87.
132. RGASPI, f. 545, o. 3, d. 450, ll. 94–7.
133. RGASPI, f. 545, o. 3, d. 307, ll. 13–14.
134. RGASPI, f. 545, o. 3, d. 449, ll. 75–6.
135. RGASPI, f. 545, o. 3, d. 451, l. 23.
136. RGASPI, f. 545, o. 3, d. 450, ll. 90–2.
137. RGASPI, f. 545, o. 3, d. 496, l. 73.
138. RGASPI, f. 545, o. 3, d. 450, ll. 138–9; f. 545, o. 6, d. 105, ll. 48, 50–1; f. 545, o. 3, d. 450, l. 136; f. 545, o. 3, d. 451, l. 50.
139. RGASPI, f. 545, o. 6, d. 149, l. 74–8; f. 545, o. 3, d. 450, ll. 78–81.
140. RGASPI, f. 545, o. 2, d. 103, l. 17; f. 545, o. 3, d. 440, ll. 60–5; 545, o. 6, d. 147, ll. 57, 60.
141. Cook, *Apprentices of Freedom*, pp 82–3 (Interview with George Aitken).
142. Franz Borkenau, *Kampfplatz Spanien: Politische und soziale Konflikte im Spanischen Bürgerkrieg, Ein Augenzeugenbericht* (Stuttgart, 1986), pp 188–97. The book was originally published in London in 1938 as *Spanish Cockpit*.
143. Landis, *The Abraham Lincoln Brigade*, pp 137–8.
144. John Gates, *The Story of an American Communist* (New York, 1958), pp 45-7.
145. Alexander, *British Volunteers*, p. 115.
146. Joe Monks, *With the Reds in Andalusia* (London, 1985), p. 36. The account by Monks is the most detailed of the Córdoba operation.

SEVEN

# FIRST OFFENSIVE: BRUNETE

While the 15th Brigade was beginning to cope with trench life on the Jarama in early March, a battle was taking place east of Madrid, Guadalajara: an offensive from the north-east, the first time that regular troops sent from Italy were deployed. Their compatriots in the Garibaldi battalion of the 12th International Brigade, together with the Germans of the 11th, anarchist soldiers and the tanks and aircraft of the Russians, routed Mussolini's prized divisions in a week of sleet and rain. It was seen as the Republic's first major victory but, as at the Jarama and the fighting for the La Coruña road, it ended in a stalemate. In this battle no units of the 15th Brigade were involved.

## BACKGROUND TO THE BATTLE OF BRUNETE

Republican military strategists had been long debating a major offensive, but opinion was divided as to where it should take place. General Asensio Torrado and Prime Minister Largo Caballero favoured a thrust to the southwest in Estremadura, towards the city of Badajoz and the Portuguese border. The area, staff officers in Madrid believed, was lightly held by inexperienced troops and Franco would have faced major logistical problems in reinforcing his garrisons there. The plan was rejected in May because of the primacy of the Madrid sector and its propaganda value, with the addendum that it would be difficult to move troops, artillery and tanks to the south-west undetected. In any case, Soviet advisers refused the use of their aircraft and tanks.

That month the communists increased their influence, succeeding in toppling Prime Minister Largo Caballero after the anarchist-POUM uprising in Barcelona and having him replaced with the pragmatic socialist Juan Negrín. His Government planned new attacks. On 31 May Republican troops struck north towards Segovia in the battle of La Granja, which is the climax of Hemingway's *For Whom the Bell Tolls*. The Republican air force bombed its own infantry, and the Soviet General Walter (Karol Świerczewski) ordered the 14th Brigade into a disastrous frontal attack up the pinewood hillsides. A new attack towards Huesca on 12 June, in which George Orwell, fighting in the POUM division, was wounded, was also a failure.[1] Neither offensive had a serious effect on Franco's ongoing battle for the Basque country.

Colonel Vicente Rojo, chief of staff in the Ministry of Defence, devised an alternative battle scheme: to punch a huge hole in the fascist encirclement 25 km to the west of Madrid with the maximum use of all resources that would simultaneously force Franco to halt operations in the north – Bilbao had fallen on 19 June. Rojo's strategy comprised two simultaneous attacks: from the north, starting from the foothills of the Sierra Guadarrama around Philip II's austere palace of El Escorial and driving swiftly south towards Brunete, with the possibility of advancing further to the important railhead at Navalcarnero; and from Madrid's southern suburbs towards Villaverde. The pincers would have closed between Brunete and Alcorcón, thus encircling fascist divisions to the west of the city, destroying their salient and removing the danger of daily artillery bombardments on the urban population.

The Brunete offensive plan looked well on paper, but it underestimated the speed with which Franco would pour reinforcements into the battle. Rojo's battle plan had, from the beginning, a severe logistical limitation, namely that he could supply his troops by one major road only – from Valdemorillo in the north through villages yet to be captured with the goal of Brunete in the south. Even in the build-up, his tanks and troops were held up by persistent traffic-jams. Finally, the Brunete offensive went off at half-cock because the southern thrust towards Villaverde failed.

The Americans now boasted a second battalion called after George Washington and commanded by Oliver Law. He was the first Afro-American in history to command such a large unit in the field. Brigade Commissar was Steve Nelson, a Croatian-born neo-American who had attended the Lenin School in Moscow and acted as an emissary of the Comintern in India and China. Because of his clear-headedness, courage and humanity, Nelson was to be the most popular officer from the US in Spain. The Irish with the Americans were commanded by Paul Burns, with Johnny Power as commissar.

The Americans left Albares on foot on 3 July, skirting Madrid in a wide arc to the north and camping in a forest on the lower slopes of the Guadarramas. Frank Ryan arrived and agreed with Burns, O'Connor and Johnny Power that the latter's two brothers, Paddy and Billy, should be sent home. They agreed reluctantly.[2] Their comrade Michael Kelly, badly wounded in the side at Jarama, was defiant. He had 'released himself' from hospital and was posted to light duties under Martin Hourihan but managed to cajole his way to the

# First Offensive: Brunete

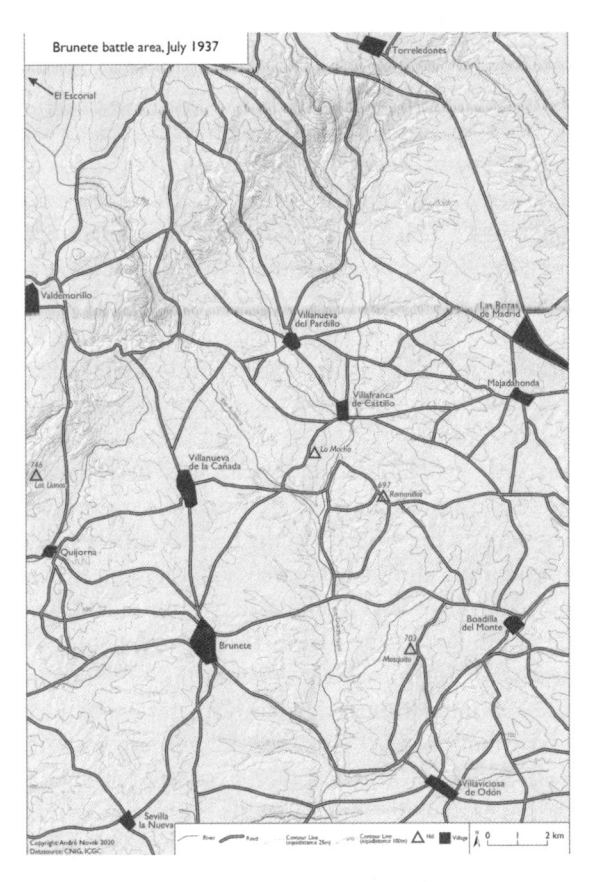

Brunete battle area, July 1937 (courtesy of André Novak)

front,³ confiding to an English rifleman on the battle's eve, that 'I was with the boys when they had to retreat at Jarama and now I mean to be with the boys when they are attacking.'⁴

The 15th Brigade was at its peak in numbers, over 2,500 volunteers, including 370 British and Irish: four companies (524) in the Lincoln and another 300 or more in the Washington Battalion formed at Albacete in June, as well as 445 from the Balkans (mainly Yugoslavs), about 250 Franco-Belge and a Spanish battalion.⁵ It comprised two regiments, the first incorporated the British and the Americans, the second the Dimitrovs, the Franco-Belge and the Spanish 24th battalion. They were commanded, respectively, by majors Jock Cunningham and the Frenchman Gabriel Fort. Vladimir Čopić was still in overall charge of the brigade, with George Aitken as commissar and George Nathan, a prodigal son returning, as chief of operations.⁶ Nathan had left, of his own volition, his position of battalion commanding officer in the 14th Brigade, citing the influence exerted by communist functionaries and Soviet advisers.⁷ The 15th Brigade was in the 15th Division under Gal, within the XVIII Corps. General Miaja oversaw the general direction of the Republican army: 70,000 men, 130–150 armoured vehicles, 217 field-guns, bombers and a fighter aircraft detachment of which only 50 were serviceable.⁸ It should be noted that while the Internationals had experienced battle, their totals comprised 18 per cent of all the Republican units committed to the offensive. Any account, therefore, doing justice to the contribution of the English-speaking volunteers must depict the overall strategy and tactics of the three-week conflict. The battle of Brunete had three distinct phases: 1) 6–11 July, general Republican advance, 150 km$^2$ gained; 2) 11–17 July, stalemate; and 3) 18–26 July, massive counterattacks and fascist advances.

The sister brigade of the 15th in Gal's division was the 13th IB, a battle-seasoned unit who had fought at Teruel, Málaga and on the Córdoba front. Officers of the 13th scouting for billets near Torrelodones found that the area was full of villas and summer houses, refuges for Madrid's better-off in the summer among pinewoods and flowing streams. The officers of the 13th Brigade guided their English-speaking comrades to such comfortable billets. The men of the 13th Brigade felt that they had been systematically ignored: they had served 20 weeks of uninterrupted duty on several fronts, and were long urging their recall from the Pozoblanco sector. Transported hastily north on 29 June and receiving no food for two days, the 13th Brigade was deployed to the attacking forces assembling in the foothills of the Sierra Guadarrama.[9]

Commander of this multinational unit – its Chapayev battalion had men from 21 countries on its muster-roll – was Wilhelm Zaisser, one of the most competent and experienced communist military cadres in Spain. A lieutenant in the German Army in the First World War, Zaisser joined the KPD in 1919, taking a leading part in the communist uprisings in Germany in the early 1920s before receiving military training in Moscow. The Comintern sent him as military advisor to rebels in Syria and Morocco, then to assist Mao's forces in China before appointing him head of the International's highly clandestine military school near Moscow. In Spain, Zaisser assumed the nom de guerre General Gómez and was chosen to lead the 13th Brigade from November 1936.[10]

Once again in Madrid just days before the battle of Brunete began, Zaisser hurried to the War Ministry and pleaded that his men needed time for rest and reorganisation. His request was rejected by Colonel Manuel Metallana, chief-of-staff of the Army of the Centre. Zaisser then lost his command of the 13th Brigade. The 'reason' given for his dismissal was the initial refusal of the commander in the Chapayev battalion to carry out an order by Gal brought by two strange officers because he did not know that Zaisser, his highly popular leader, had been removed.[11] His successor was Vicenzo Bianco (Krieger), a military neophyte with 'good credentials' who had represented the Italian CP at ECCI in Moscow and was a former chief of staff in the 14th Brigade, where he had been Nathan's adversary.

## BRUNETE: THE EARLY DAYS, 6–11 JULY

Moving off before sunrise on 6 July, the British battalion descended towards the plain, marching slowly because of the heavy traffic. There were strict orders for lorries to dim lights, and when Copeman spotted an anarchist transport column travelling under full beams, he and his adjutant Charlie Goodfellow shot out the bulbs of the headlights.[12] The day promised to be searingly hot, the start of a three-week purgatory in an arid cauldron of flying steel, with temperatures frequently over 40°. The two main rivers in the area, the Guadarrama and the Aulencia, were one to two feet deep and soon dried up altogether. Republican aircraft provided a show of strength at the outset, bombing the villages ahead, but from 11 July, apart from bombing sorties, they were generally absent from the skies, giving the German and Italian bombers or strafing fighters a free run. The view to the front was panoramic, the church tower of Villanueva de la Cañada straight ahead, Brunete behind it, and the high buildings of Madrid in the heat-haze in the distance. Today, it is difficult to reconstruct the open terrain between the villages in what is now a built-up area interlaced by major roads. Mosquito Crest (702 m), for example, the heights where the 15th Brigade was bled white, is now part of the El Bosque housing scheme.[13]

But the view then was also deceptive, for the golden wheat fields on the brown plain were interspersed by scrub, small woods, depressions and rushes on river banks; the long ridge of Romanillos on the men's far left was not a verdant slope but a prominence pitted by gullies, defiles, dried-up stream-beds (barrancos), trees and outcrops of rock. The area attacked was about 150 km$^2$, bound on the west by the river Perales and about 15 km to the east by the elevated ground (Romanillos, El Mosquito) before the town of Boadilla del Monte.

The fascist defence was mobile, with patrols between well-fortified garrisons at the villages: in the north of the pocket Villanueva de la Cañada, Villanueva del Pardillo and the hills adjacent to Villafranca del Castillo, and in the west Los Llamos hill and the village of Quijorna. On the eve of hostilities, Franco had only five infantry battalions and 25 artillery pieces in the immediate battle zone, with reserves in Navalcarnero and garrisons in Boadilla (300 men) and Las Rozas, in all about 16,000 soldiers. Events were to show, however, that Franco's logistical experts could send reserves into the struggle at great speed. The Republicans had put the rumour about that they were planning an attack in Aragon; the accounts on a build-up of Republican forces around Valdemorillo were not taken seriously by Franco's officers, perhaps because the preparations were well-concealed, not least the encampment of units in wooded areas.[14]

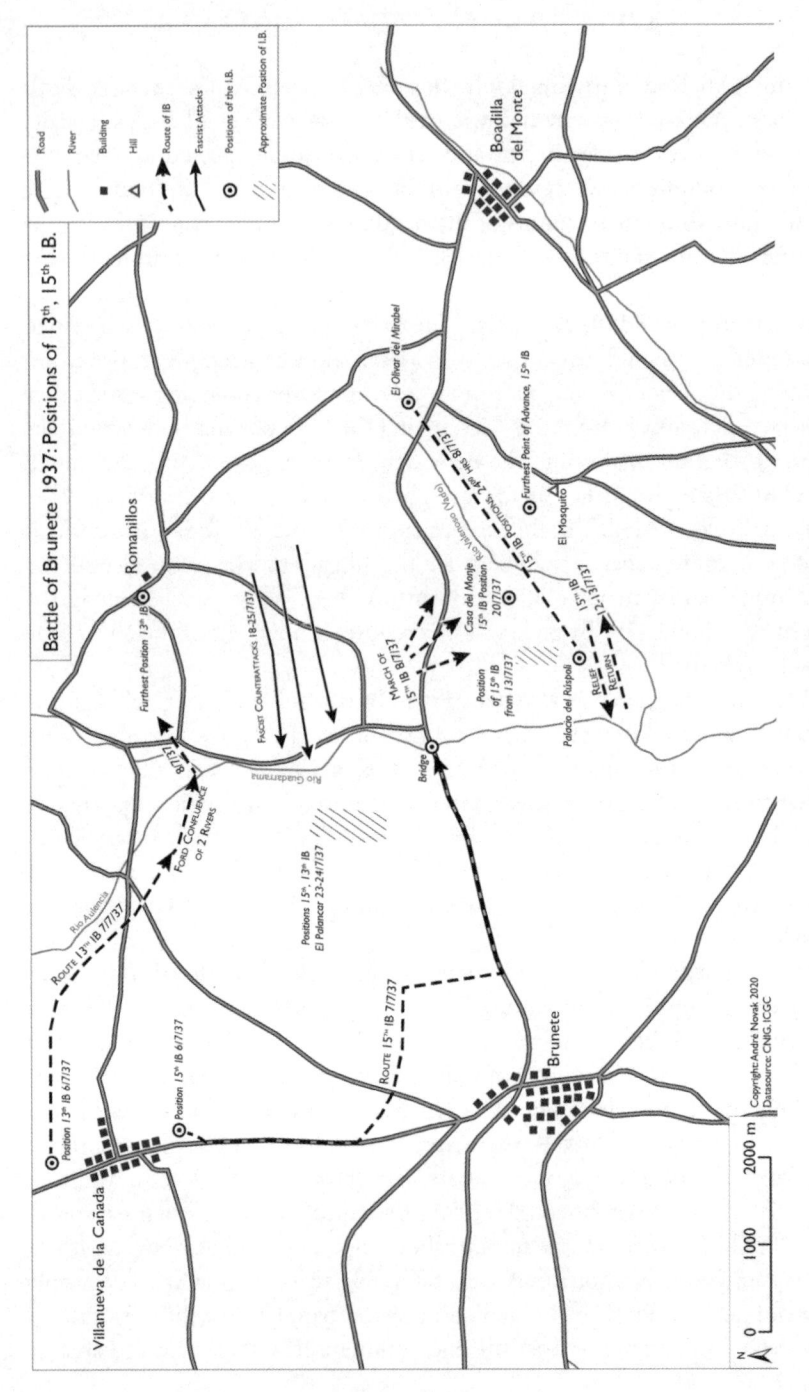

Battle of Brunete, July 1937: Positions of 13th and 15th IB (courtesy of André Novak)

On the night before D-Day (6 July) some fascist commanders, however, took precautionary steps. Franco later admitted that he had not taken intelligence reports of a major Republican offensive seriously.[15]

The corps order to the 15th Brigade foresaw it advancing beside the 34th Division of José María Galán towards Villanueva de la Cañada and, after the capture of the village by the 34th, the plan was to advance with the 13th Brigade on its left flank to the confluence of the rivers Guadarrama and Aulencia, to cross the bridge and to proceed south-eastwards to the position where the Guadarrama cuts the Brunete–Boadilla road, about half way between both villages.[16] That would be the jumping-off point for the storming of Mosquito crest. To the south, Enrique Líster's 11th Division carried out a remarkable coup de main. Months earlier he had formed a scouting and guerrilla company that later grew to battalion strength; using these scouts, who marked out the route, he led his men off from Valdemorillo at 10 p.m. on the night of 5 July. Without aircraft, tanks or artillery, his division reached Brunete on foot at dawn having covered 12 km. The town was lightly held by Falange volunteers who fled to the cemetery during the first attack. Republican bombers devastated the centre, and by noon the small garrison had surrendered. Líster had trumped the over-cautious generals in Madrid, especially Miaja who had earlier told President Azaña that his forces would need four days to take Brunete.[17] Líster did not proceed further, rightly fearing that his lines could be enveloped and his division eventually surrounded because his flanks were wide open.[18] His perspicacity was prompted by the failure of other commanders to capture key villages to his rear: Villanueva de la Cañada and Quijorna.

Since 1937 military historians have argued whether Líster missed a golden chance to attack further south and east, and this sin of omission, it is alleged, was one of the main reasons why the battle plans of the Republic failed at the start. One of the chief Russian advisers, Rodion Manilovski (Colonel Malino in Spain, Soviet Defence Minister 1956–67), gave the non-committal answer to Líster's request to drive on: 'Decide as the situation indicates, but I would not advise it.'[19]

With the villages to the north still in enemy hands, the road south to Brunete was not safe and, in any case, there were no reserve divisions available to be ferried south to boost Líster's second battle phase. Still, some of Líster's detachments advanced some kilometres out from Brunete, south towards Sevilla La Neuva, and east towards Villaviciosa de Odón. His sorties were soon stopped by Franco troops hurrying north – including Moors, who occupied some hills near the Guadarrama river – and by the arrival of two artillery batteries.

By late afternoon, only the road north from Brunete was open; the others were under direct fire from the enemy. Líster's call for reinforcements, he argues, was ignored by the high command. His 'window of opportunity' was between 6 a.m. and 9 a.m. on 6 July, when the bridge over the Guadarrama on the Brunete–Boadilla road, and also the heights above it, the future fighting ground of the 13th and 15th IB, were unguarded. The resources to complete this task were not available at the time, and the high command, taking the cautious view, ordered Líster to consolidate his positions in the afternoon of 6 July.[20]

The second reason often stated for why the new Republican army 'lost' the battle of Brunete was the failure to capture positions in the north of the bulge on the first day: Villanueva de la Cañada, Quijorna and the heights of Las Llanos. Villanueva, which the 15th Brigade was supposed to bypass, was situated on a hill and well-fortified with concrete bunkers linked to basements of houses by tunnels, and barbed wire. It was defended by 800 Falangists from Seville reinforced on 5 July by the arrival of three anti-tank pieces and a German artillery expert. There was little cover on the approaches to the village, and its resolute defenders broke the momentum of the Republican advance.

The Republican artillery barrage started at 5.45 a.m. and some aircraft bombed the centre, missing the defensive positions. The first assault of the 34th Division at 6.45 a.m. failed, as did the second at around 11 a.m. because the infantry did not follow the tanks. Malinovski later stated that the Republican command made the 'adolescent mistake' of allowing too much time between the end of the shelling and the infantry attack, thus giving the defenders time to leave cover and man their machine-guns. Lieutenant-Colonel Jurado, the corps commander in charge, ordered portions of the 13th and 15th Brigades to join the attackers. Assaults at 3 p.m. and four hours later (with one of Líster's battalions) also ended in disaster, so it was decided to attack in the dark. The town finally fell after a bayonet attack by carbineros (militarised customs or police), and the Lincolns and Dimitrovs of the 15th Brigade. Only 200 defenders were still standing, and their commander ordered the evacuation around 10 p.m.; 140 Falangists were taken prisoner.[21]

During the day, the British battalion of the 15th Brigade had been pinned down for hours to the south of the village, taking first casualties when some men were shot down from the church tower that was put out of action only late in the evening when the British anti-tank battery was taken out of reserve. The volunteers had long since emptied their water bottles and had to lie low in the searing heat. Because the 46th Division of El Campesino (Valentín González) was in trouble at Quijorna 7 km to the east, the few tanks near Villanueva trundled off to assist his assault. Around 6 p.m. orders came through that the 15th Brigade had to take Villanueva de la Cañada. General Walter arrived, took Copeman aside and, referring to the camouflaged and underground fortifications, said the village had to be captured because it was 'on the junction of what must be our lateral and direct route of supply for this sector'.[22] Also, on the evening of this first day, the other fascist strongpoints at Quijorna in the west, and Villanueva del Pardillo and Villafranca del Castillo to the north-east, were still in enemy hands.

Copeman tried to ferry his men through the wheat fields towards the southern end of the village, and was then instructed by Čopić to take up positions for attack on the main road between Villanueva and Brunete because the Polish and Slav battalions were to break into the village from the rear. The Americans had suffered heavy casualties moving forward earlier to the northern end of the village. Martin Hourihan, commander of the Lincolns, was severely wounded when the Americans were dug in outside the town just before the general attack order arrived from Gal. Steve Nelson now took over the battalion.[23] Michael Kelly from Galway had dragged Hourihan to safety and was mortally wounded shortly afterwards.[24] At dusk they were withdrawn behind a hill and in the dark the very welcome kitchen lorry arrived with food, water and wine.[25] By then the Dimitrovs, Americans and a Spanish brigade of carbineros had finally entered the village from opposite ends and captured Villanueva. Suddenly, in the fading light, the British saw a group of women and children fleeing down the road and were momentarily caught unawares when a group of fascist troops emerged behind the civilians firing and throwing grenades. Copeman ordered his machine-gunners to clear the road: almost all the cowardly defenders, and some women, were killed.

George Brown, the Kilkenny-born member of the Central Committee of the CPGB, was shot dead by a Falangist in the confusion. He had been sent from Albacete to work with Frank Ryan at the Commissariat in May, but opted for the front and was appointed company commissar with the British at Brunete.[26] Already enraged by the despicable ruse of using civilians as a shield, the British were further infuriated when Bill Meredith, a company commander, was shot dead when trying to help one of the enemy wounded. Fearful that his men would wreak revenge on the prisoners, Copeman withdrew his soldiers, believing that it was better to leave mopping-up to Spanish riflemen. The exhausted volunteers, depleted by 50 casualties, at last had the chance of fresh water and food before sleeping rough in the devastated village.[27]

Four other Irishmen were among the fatalities: the teenager Joe Kelly from Rathmines, Bill Davis, also from Dublin and who had served in the Irish Guards, Bill Loughran (McLaughlin) from Belfast and also ex-Irish Guards, and Stewart Homer ('Paddy O'Neill') from Banbridge, Co. Down, a further veteran of the British Army and a sergeant in the 3rd company of Canadians with the Lincolns when killed.[28] The costs for taking Villanueva were high: in the battalions of the 15th Brigade there were an average of 20 fatalities and 30–

40 wounded. The toll was highest among the Dimitrovs: 60 killed and over 100 wounded.[29]

Franco quickly realised the parlous state of affairs, breaking off an inspection tour to the Santander front, returning to Burgos and sending an aide by plane to survey the battlefield near Madrid. He complained bitterly that 'they have broken my Madrid front', called a halt to hostilities in the north and ordered all aircraft to be sent to the Brunete sector. He later gave General Hugo von Sperrle of the Condor Legion the command over all air operations.[30]

The delay in capturing Quijorna was due to the courage of the defenders and the obtuseness of El Campesino. The village had 500 inhabitants and 200 Falange defenders well ensconced in a circular defensive ring topped by barbed wire, with the main strongpoint in the cemetery overlooking the Brunete road. Their commander was on the alert and received Moorish infantrymen and three anti-tank pieces on the eve of the battle. The attack of El Campesino's 46th Division should have commenced at 4 a.m., but because of traffic delays it was now to start at 5.30 a.m. after half an hour's gun barrage. He 'modified' the orders of his Corps Commander Juan Modesto, sending in merely one battalion to attack from the north. It was a fiasco. A second assault failed at 7 a.m., and in both cases El Campesino had not employed any field guns. He further disobeyed orders by not cutting the road south, which meant that a battalion from Toledo could slip into the town to aid the defenders in the night of 6–7 July. El Campesino's men finally captured Quijorna on 9 July after Juan Modesto had wrested control of the battle from his rival, sending in the German 11th Brigade to capture the graveyard, the key position in the village.[31]

Two valuable days had been lost, but elsewhere the news was good: the important heights of Los Llanos near Quijorna were captured in the night of 7–8 July by the 101st Mixed Brigade, which was led by one of the most prominent of the new communist commanders, Pedro Mateo Merino, who was to be the last divisional commander of the 15th International Brigade, on the Ebro in 1938.[32]

The original timetable of the Republican offensive was long redundant: positions had been captured entailing heavy losses and days later than anticipated. Villanueva del Pardillo, for example, was not conquered until midnight on 10 July. Čopić believed the 15th needed a rest, and the divisional order was changed during the day: the 15th was to cross the Guadarrama on 7 July and take up positions behind the bridge where the river cuts the Brunete-Boadilla road – a cross-country march of 4 km – while the 13th was supposed to advance on their left flank. Brigade staff had been misled by a report, sent back by a cavalry squadron assigned to probe the terrain at the Guadarrama river bridge not far from Boadilla del Monte on 6 July. The riders stated that the bridge had been blown up and that the area was being held by 'important forces'. That was untrue: the bridge was intact and the defenders numbered barely 200 of a Galician battalion posted to the east of the river to repel the advance of the Internationals and give the defenders of Boadilla time to man the heights of both Romanillos and Mosquito. The Galicians were hardly an unsurmountable obstacle for the 15th Brigade, and on the first day there were only two companies of fascist infantry on the heights.

However, the forces arrayed against the Internationals grew exponentially: on 6–7 July reinforcements of nine battalions poured into Boadilla and the slopes in front of it, bringing the total defence force up to 13 battalions, three more than the attackers could muster – six in the 15th and four in the 13th Brigade. By 9 July, Franco's forces had 26 battalions in the front lines and 12 in reserve, 100 field-guns and about 300 aircraft.[33] The ridge was about 5 km long and too extensive for the attackers. Even if the two brigades (13th and 15th) had captured it promptly, it is doubtful whether it could have been held given the air power of the fascists and the lack of field guns and mortars on the Republican side. Northwards, at the confluence of the Aulencia and Guadarrama rivers, an advance group of the 13th Brigade discovered around mid-day on 7 July that the bridge marked on their Michelin map (they had no other) did not exist, the crossing was just a sandy ford, over which engineers soon built a makeshift bridge. A patrol of the Chapayevs went forward to scout. The men arrived at their designated positions on the heights in the afternoon, but the enemy, now ensconced 1,200 m distant, drove them back at the half-way mark under heavy fire.[34]

For the 15th Brigade, speed was now essential, but the going was slow on 7 July, from the early afternoon start over soft, sandy soil without shade in intense heat (over 40°). There was confusion in orders, for Čopić held that Cunningham sent his troops south down the Villanueva-Brunete road instead of towards the Guadarrama.[35] The Brigade moved down the road to Brunete, resting and eating in an olive grove beside the road, out of the sight of enemy bomber aircraft. After two hours the march recommenced, this time across country.[36] The Washington battalion was to the fore, with the British behind, traversing open ground along the dry bed of a rivulet, with stooks of harvested corn to their right and left. The Washingtons marched in bunched formations, despite warnings from the experienced officers of the Lincoln battalion that they should fan out. When four Italian Caproni bombers appeared low over the columns, the British took expert cover, but the men of the Washington battalion, in their tight formation, lost 20 comrades in the hail of bombs. The British now went to the head of the brigade, but the soldiers were soon losing contact with one another, spread out chaotically in disparate clusters. The terrain changed the nearer they approached the Guadarrama, barrancos and patches of forest, where they were ambushed by fascist scouts who soon fled back over the ridge.[37]

According to Brigade orders for the battle on 8 July, the 13th and 15th Brigades were to move off after being fed at 5 a.m. and to ascend and occupy the heights.[38] At 3.30 a.m. on 8 July the 13th Brigade received the assault order personally from Krieger: move up the track from the ford and begin the ascent to Romanillos with the assistance of artillery and tanks, and of an anti-tank battery to the south. The movement was spotted by machine-gunners on the heights, but the advancing groups continued, using dead ground and bushes and protected by their own artillery. Once the Russian tanks rumbled forward and began firing, the fascist troops on the slope retreated. The 13th Brigade was now to swing to the left and occupy the Romanillos ruins, 1,200 m away. To reach it, the Internationals would have to traverse craggy, wooded ground.[39] One group of the Chapayevs, mainly Austrians, advanced too quickly without guarding flanks and was ambushed by Moors. Those who could not retreat were bestially done to death and their bodies mutilated and set on fire.[40]

It was late evening on 7 July when the men of the 15th IB camped in a covered area, sending scouts ahead, passing Republican cavalry on the road and then going into hiding among thick bushes on the riverbank. At 8 a.m. on 8 July, the infantry burst through the rushes, splashing across the river where it cut the Brunete–Boadilla road. In the advance they cleared points of resistance north and south of it and drove the enemy from hastily improvised trenches with the aid of tanks.

As movement was slow through the wheat fields, Brigade officers decided to march on the Boadilla–Brunete road in order to make up for lost time. Strong artillery and machine-gun fire halted the advance after approximately 2 km and the Americans had their first casualties of the day from bombing aircraft.[41] Having overcome a fascist strongpoint in an olive grove, the Americans dug in for the night.[42] The ascendancy of hostile air power now became clear (with the new Heinkel He 111 and Dornier 17 bombers and the modern monoplane fighter Messerschmitt 109Bf), so that the brigades and the main roads were under constant aerial attack; food and water could be brought forward only at night and the wounded carried over long distances of uneven terrain to the ambulances in the valley below. By noon on 8 July Čopić, citing the exhaustion of his men, requested a fresh brigade from divisional commander Gal, but was told that no extra troops were available.[43]

On the slopes, the tanks had overtaken the infantry and, waiting for them to come up, fired off their cannon before retiring. It was a typical uncoordinated attack, a key moment when Mosquito could have been taken, but to advance now over the last few hundred yards to the crest without armour would have been suicide.⁴⁴ At the close of their exhausting, cautious uphill struggle on 8 July through clumps of trees hiding snipers, the battalions of the 15th Brigade covered about 3 km and had reached a secondary ridge running diagonally north-east to south-west, from El Olivar de Mirabal, situated on the outskirts of Boadilla and on to the north of the Brunete–Boadilla road, down to the valley floor around the estate Palacio de Rúspoli. Mosquito was 300–400 m away. While the infantry had been making their strenuous way up to that position, the 15th Division had launched an attack in the south, up the road leading east from Brunete, with tanks and infantry (probably from the 24th Spanish battalion of the 15th Brigade) that broke into Boadilla but was stopped at the cemetery in the south-east of the town. The sortie convinced the Republican command, wrongly, that Boadilla had been captured. So runs the report of a Spaniard serving as political commissar in the 15th Brigade.⁴⁵ It was probably another case of cautious Soviet tankmen going back at the first sign of resistance from a fortified position. One of the defending officers wrote:

> On the eight day [of July] the battle they pushed us. It was the gravest day in the defence of Boadilla. We climbed a knoll dominating the north-east of the town. They [the Republican unit] came up the Brunete road. Then they could have scored an easy victory, and gratis. Nobody came to our aid, save for a group of clerks and farm-hands sent into the front line. I still don't know why the worst did not happen. They seemed to be in battalion strength, accompanied by half a dozen Russian tanks. That was sufficient to grill us in our own juice. The security forces in the town, some Guardia Civil, armed peasants and a few dozen soldiers formed a front to meet them. Instead of driving forward to attack them, they [the Republicans] let off four cannon shells wounding about a dozen of us, and then retired in orderly fashion back down the road.⁴⁶

Most probably such a small attacking force would have been soon engulfed by superior numbers rushed to the town. In any case, such an opportunity would never repeat itself because any attacks eastwards from Brunete in the coming days would encounter dogged resistance from the reinforcements hurried to Boadilla and occupying defensive posts along the ridge. At least three further attempts by Líster's division, aided by tanks, up the Boadilla road were repulsed by strong artillery fire on 8, 9 and 11 July. From the latter date Republican forces officially adopted a defensive strategy.⁴⁷ By evening on 8 July the Chapayevs of the 13th Brigade were exhausted, their Colt machine-guns were all defective and there was a gap of 1,500m between two battalions.⁴⁸

On 9 July, the Chapayev battalion to the north reconnoitred their positions, digging out emplacements for machine-guns and anti-tank pieces. Their officers sensed that the initiative had been lost, reckoning that the defenders 700 m to their front outnumbered them three to one, and so spent the day trying to avoid the strafing fighters periodically swooping down.[49] This day would be a disastrous one for the British and the Americans. The British sustained a two-hour rain of shells. An anti-tank projectile decapitated Charlie Goodfellow, the adjutant, an event that shook his friend Fred Copeman to the core. Earlier, near the riverbed at the base of the slope, enemy aircraft had bombed a supply dump captured by the British, setting the ammunition on fire and causing several to be wounded.[50]

The divisional order was to take the ridge 'at all costs', with the assistance of two Spanish battalions, but the necessary armoured support came hours late at 11 a.m., stopped 1 km from enemy positions, discharged a few rounds and retired.[51] The Americans were about 400 yards from the crest and had to advance over open, sloping ground at 10 a.m. without the support of artillery or aircraft. Harry Fisher and Johnny Power were runners for the commander of No. 1 Company Paul Burns, and Power impressed his American comrades by sharing the content of his water-bottle to the last drop. Minutes later the Lincolns went forward into a storm of steel, men dropping left and right. Power was shot in the ankle and thigh and carried to the rear by Fisher, and Paul Burns was wounded. Oliver Law, leading No. 2 Company, not heeding Power's shouting to get down, was hit in the stomach and died within the hour. The ranks had already been depleted by up to 60 casualties, of whom a third were fatalities. Losses among the Washingtons were even higher, surpassing 100. The Lincolns retired from the slope to a knoll under Nelson's leadership, formed defensive positions and were expecting a counterattack.[52] At least the 15th IB had beaten off two attacks on the El Olivar position, inflicting heavy losses on Franco's legionnaires.[53]

The order of the 15th Division for 10 July was aspirational and contained no tactical directives: with the aid of tanks, the brigades were to capture the height of Romanillos and Mosquito with a battalion of the 86th Brigade, and to advance down the reverse slope into Boadilla del Monte.[54] Gal had obviously no idea of what was happening on the ground, how his soldiers, outnumbered and outgunned, were stuck fast, far from their objectives. At the northern end of the slope, the Chapayev battalion was down to 180 men, and the advance, postponed for hours, was to commence once five light tanks or armoured cars and three large tanks had arrived. They did not show up, but the infantry went forward with the help of sporadic artillery fire, gaining a few hundred metres. They were still 500 m away from Romanillos and now under the intense fire of Condor Legion batteries, which also targeted the supply routes on the far bank of the Guadarrama.[55] Čopić tried to rally the over-cautious tank crews who had not appeared during the day, finding one retreating from the Chapayev's lines in the dusk. He threatened the driver with a pistol, harangued the crews and they promised to advance. But it was too late in any case, and hostile anti-tank fire was intense. Shortly afterwards he received another one of Gal's senseless orders: Mosquito was to be taken without artillery fire. Čopić held a conference with Nathan and Cunningham and was accosted by Gal's adjutant as darkness fell: why had not the advance begun?[56]

11 July was the sixth day of the offensive and the date of the last and most desperate attempt to conquer the ridge. Gal's directive was a repetitive and self-serving admonition: the failure on the tenth was due to 'a lack of pressure from our forces to capture Mosquito and Romanillos but the advance today would recommence with the aid of field-guns and armour from 11 am.' It was postponed at 11.40 a.m. to 12.30 p.m. At 7 a.m. Republican planes bombed Boadilla, and some units attacked with artillery support, not knowing that the assault had been delayed. Three Russian tanks went up in flames and the Internationals were forced back. Mirko Marcovics, the Serbo-American who had been trained in the Red Army and was now commanding the depleted Washingtons, sent a message back to Brigade headquarters:

> The situation of the battalion is very difficult. We cannot get water or munition up to our positions. There is a danger of an enemy counter-attack on our right flank. This can happen at any moment and I cannot do any more than I am trying to do at present.[57]

The 12th Division of Guadarrama led the counterattack of the Franco troops with a squadron of German light tanks. Subject to air raids, the Americans had dug deep, and two anti-tank guns of the British commanded by Malcolm Dunbar were concealed behind their foxholes. About half a kilometre away, eight light tanks rumbled down the incline and were caught on open ground by the anti-tank pieces: one burst into flames, others were disabled and the rest retreated in haste. The six machine-gun teams of the Americans held their fire on the hesitant Moors driven forward by their officers until they had entered the gully in front. The Lincoln riflemen aimed at the enemy still streaming down the slope behind the main group. Their fire at a distance of 100 yards was so devastating that many Americans felt that they had finally avenged their losses of 27 February.[58] The Chapayevs, after an artillery barrage on Romanillos, went forward at 4 p.m. with tanks, but gained little ground because of the intense machine-gun fire and shelling by the German anti-tank batteries. The battalion strength was reduced to just over 120.[59]

## BRUNETE: ON THE DEFENSIVE, 12–27 JULY

During the night of 12–13 July, the 15th Brigade was relieved by the 16th Mixed Brigade and withdrew a few kilometres, seeking shelter on the far side of the Guadarrama river where the willows and bushes offered some cover; there were pools to wash off encrusted grime, and water and food were more accessible. The British battalion had been reduced to half-strength, under 150 men. Copeman was soon sent to Mondéjar to rest, his commissar Bert Williams left because of an aggravated heart condition, and the command devolved on Joe Hinks, an expert machine-gunner, assisted by commissar Wally Tapsell.

Čopić, wounded in the head by a shell-splinter on 12 July, was replaced by his chief-of-staff Colonel Claus.[60] The Americans were also severely diminished, from over 800 to about 500, their two battalions merging under Mirko Marcovics, and Nelson reverted to his commissar role.[61] After their first good meal in days and a welcome bath in the shallow pools beside the rushes, the joint American unit was ordered to assemble during a fierce artillery barrage and re-cross the river to plug a gap to the east left open by retreating troops. It proved to be a false alarm, and the Lincoln-Washingtons returned after the short advance to their riverbank.[62]

The sortie was preceded by a showdown between Claus and Marcovics with Nelson at his side. It was a multilingual altercation: Claus waiting for his order to be translated from German into English, and, to his annoyance, the Yugoslavs began arguing among themselves in Serbo-Croat. The gist of the matter was that Marcovics refused to lead his men forward to help beleaguered Spanish marines, saying to Nelson that he would hold him responsible before the American public for the consequences should he, Nelson, concur with the imperious German. Marcovics then expressed himself in plain English to Claus, calling the order 'disastrous' and its certain outcome a repetition of the Jarama bloodbath. Marcovics was ordered to hand over his pistol to Claus and his command, temporarily, to Nelson, and then report himself to divisional headquarters.[63]

The period of rest afforded the British lasted hardly a day: the 16th Mixed Brigade were forced under severe pressure to cede ground near Mosquito, so Copeman's depleted unit had to cross the river once more and climb, a highly contested order that caused a mini-mutiny led by Tapsell (see below), which was soon quelled. Meanwhile, on the ridge before Romanillos, the 13th Brigade had not been relieved and was under persistent shellfire and air-attack. The resolute German-speakers leading the Chapayev battalion had had enough of Krieger, the luckless brigade chief, who, they believed, had fouled up their march to the front on the first day causing unnecessary delay, had been unable to coordinate the sporadic tank assistance and had appeared drunk and abusive in the front lines before making himself unavailable for 24 hours. Alfred Kantorowicz, the German writer and battalion intelligence officer of the Chapayevs, was 'delegated' by his fellow-officers and those of the sister battalions to make haste to Madrid and plead for the relief of the remnants of the brigade. He passed all cordons and finally arrived at the IB Commissariat in Calle Velázquez, 63.[63] All, including Zaisser, intimated that the men must hold out.[64]

Just as the Republican units went on the defensive and the Franco forces on the offensive, much confusion was caused by the resignation of XVIII Corps commander Lieutenant Colonel Enrique Jurado, purportedly due to heart problems.[65] He had been frustrated by the costly battle for Villanueva de la Cañada and the longer struggle of Gal's 15th Division on the slopes before Boadilla, and was, according to Communist officers of high rank, a vacillator, an old professional unsuited to the rigours of battle and not wishing to be too much in the limelight because he feared for his family held hostage in Morocco.[66] His successor from 12 July was to prove equally controversial – Lieutenant Colonel Segismundo Casado, who in March 1939 led the Madrid coup against the Negrín Government.

The main battles now centred in the triangle formed by the confluence of the Aulencia and the Guadarrama and defensive points, especially the Saracen castle at Villafranca del Castillo and the hills adjacent to it. At this point, Republican strategy was confused: War Minister Indalecio Prieto issued his decision for the army to go into defensive mode in all areas on 14 July; but Rojo, in order to secure a strong defence, still ordered attacks on Villafranca and the hill of La Mocha. Casado, the new corps commander, ordered Manfred Stern (General Kléber) to send his unblooded young troops to launch four suicidal assaults on these bastions. A fifth assault on the well-fortified La Mocha, ordered by Miaja, was rejected outright by Kléber, who offered his resignation; Miaja refused it and there the matter rested. Finally, according to Kléber, Casado ordered a complicated series of unit replacements on the front that destabilised the Republican lines, excused himself as 'sick' and decamped to Valencia.[67] The first round of fascist attacks and Republican counter-moves had proved indecisive, and Franco's generals started a second wave of assaults from 18 July.

The British, Dimitrovs and the Franco-Belge were now positioned on the banks of the Vado, a tributary of the Guadarrama, facing the Romanillos ridge. The Americans were roused from sleep around midnight on 16 July and sent north to stem the gains made by Franco's troops, who had forced their way into the first houses in Villanueva del Pardillo, at the northern end of the pocket. It was considered that travelling on the roads even at night was too dangerous, so the Americans tried to complete the 11 km along the narrow riverbed strewn with rocks before dawn broke. Some men walked in their sleep, stumbled forward in their shredded rope sandals (alpargatas) and arrived too late. Peter O'Connor had to have his raw, sockless feet bandaged before limping on.[68] When the Americans came to the Villanueva de la Cañada-Villanueva del Pardillo road at first light, they were in full view of the enemy. Moving off the road again, the men rested, then moved to a deep barranco shielded by bushes and assembled around their food truck. Then the area was plastered by an artillery barrage and the men dug in; the planes attacked again and again, bombing and then returning to strafe. The casualties were surprisingly light. Hours later, the survivors reached the trenches of the republican 10th Division. The Lincoln Machine-Gun Company beat off an attack by legionnaires in the afternoon; during the night the American second company stopped an attacking tabor of Moors with grenades and rapid rifle fire. In the night of 19–20 July, the US battalion withdrew to their old positions on the far side of the river.[69] On 18 July Moorish troops captured the key position of El Olivar de Mirabel near Boadilla and continued on the next day to gain ground down the slope, pushing the British towards the Guadarrama. The 100 survivors of the battalion under Wally Tapsell and Joe Hinks were nearly surrounded, but they retreated in good order towards Casa del Monje south of the Boadillla–Brunete road and were still to the east of the river. One group under Tapsell positioned themselves near the Valenoso (a tributary of the Guadarrama flowing down from Boadilla); the other, under Hinks, dug in defending the zone to the east.[70] On 20 July Gal ordered a counter-thrust of the 13th and 15th IB to regain lost ground. In a short, fierce engagement, Casa del Monje was captured with the aid of tanks, but the advance of 1 km came to a halt because the armoured vehicles ran out of ammunition. By that stage portions of the 13th IB had lost the will to fight, especially the two Spanish battalions (50th Juan Marco and 51st Otumba), who fled their positions on 18 July after all their machine-gunners were either killed or seriously wounded and followed the headlong retreat of a brigade on their right flank.[71] The gains at Casa del Monje were soon lost to Moroccan auxiliaries and the new defensive line of the 15th Division was a gully just south of the Brunete–Boadilla road. The decimated and exhausted 13th IB was relieved by a Spanish brigade on 23 July, descended the slopes under heavy fire and was pulled back to secondary defensive positions,[72] but the British formed the left flank of the front line, just below the road and with their backs to the river.[73]

The avalanche of fascist attackers gradually pushed the republican troops across the Guadarrama. The balance of the 18–23 July fierce fighting was unmistakably in favour of Franco's more experienced detachments, who captured key heights in the west of the salient and liquidated republican pockets to the north and east of the Guadarrama at great cost, especially in the futile attacks against Merino's 101st Mixed Brigade on Los Llanos, which virtually destroyed two Navarrese brigades. In the south, Líster's men in Brunete were exhausted, subject to artillery fire and German bombing raids. Some soldiers went mad, others killed themselves and Líster left for army headquarters near Torrelodones on 20 July, putting his case for a speedy relief. Rojo promised him that a counterattack was being planned with the 14th Division under the anarchist Cipriano Mera and, if successful, Líster would be able to get his men out. In the meantime, however, he had to hold out for another two to three days.

Líster, the communist, had little confidence in the fighting capacity of Mera's men, and when the relief came it was too late. The transfer of the anarchists on 21 July was botched by the high command, letting them bivouac in reserve positions near Villanueva de la Cañada, and Miaja cancelled their departure south at 9 a.m. on 24 July; two hours later Brunete fell to the fascists with a pocket of last resistance in the cemetery. Modesto admitted at noon that the town was lost and sent in the 14th Division with tanks. The anarchists ran straight into a massed attack, reaching the first ruined houses before being driven back with heavy casualties.[74]

With the fronts crumbling, the remnants of the 13th and 15th IB, aided by a Spanish brigade, dug in on knolls in the El Palancar area on the night of 23–24 July in order to defend the rivers banks of the Guadarrama. They were subject to a devastating air-raid in the dark that hit the medical station and killed Randall Sollenberger, the American doctor from Manchester. The Lincolns arrived from a few hours in reserve and in a counterattack drove back the Requetés from Navarre, stabilising the line.[75] During the night of 25–26 July, two Spanish brigades were dispatched to relieve what remained of the 15th Division: about 300 Americans, 50 British and Irish and over 800 from the 13th IB. The relieving troops refused to dig in and, as a precautionary measure, Nelson ordered his machine-gunners to cover their position. When the Spanish brigades in front fled before another attack of the Navarrese in the early morning light, the Internationals and a few tanks stopped the advance for a few hours. When it had increased in force, causing many Republican troops to retreat in panic, the 15th IB went into the frontline for the last time.[76] The exhausted men of the 13th International Brigade were to go north, to act as a second defence line at Villanueva del Pardillo. A portion of them mutinied (see below). The order to withdraw never reached the British, but they united behind the Guadarrama, about 50 exhausted and emaciated figures. Fighting a tactical retreat helped by French and German machine-gunners, the British came across two apparitions, beer at Cunningham's post, then the battalion postman Tom Richardson bringing food and wine. William Beattie from Belfast, a veteran of Lopera who had served eight years in the Royal Irish Rifles, was killed during the retirement, the last Irishman to die in the battle. Spanish marines reached the British positions, and the 40 or so survivors went as fast as they could to the north, through the ruins of Villanueva de la Cañada, before dawn and the arrival of enemy aviation.[77] The country they traversed was covered in smoke caused by German aircraft dropping incendiary bombs on the wheat fields.

In truth Franco's army was also spent: the offensive had ended, once again, in a stalemate. Franco realised this on 25 July, but his cock-a-hoop generals did not, urging him to continue and capture the capital. He dampened their ardour by stating that defences were to be strengthened and any reinforcements in the area were needed for a renewed attack on Santander, ending with a threat: 'I said stop the advance and the only one here who gives orders is me.' He wanted to complete the war in the north before the autumn rains began and was worried about the diminution of his air power: four German bombers had been downed in the last days of the Brunete campaign.[78]

The shattered remnants of the 15th Brigade were heading for their sylvan retreat near Torrelodones, seeking recovery, rest and recriminations. George Nathan organised the food and billeting arrangements there and, returning to the front lines to assist the withdrawal, he was mortally wounded in an air raid.[79] The survivors of the 15th Brigade were severely under-weight, suffering from lack of food, dehydration, stomach complaints and diarrhoea, if not dysentery. Nelson had lost two stone and slit the seat of his trousers during the torrid three weeks in order to relieve himself in the field.[80] Ronald Liversedge, a newly arrived recruit from Canada, was shocked by the sight of the survivors:

> Thin to the point of emaciation, bloodshot, pus running from their eyes, facial bones sticking out prominently, and in reply to questions, brusque to the point of rudeness [. . .] I could not remember seeing men quite so drained of all vitality in France in the First World War.[81]

On the evening of their second day of recovery in the woods, 28 July, the men could hardly believe the bad news: Quijorna was almost surrounded and the Brigade would have to retrace their steps to relieve the besieged 10 km away. Aitken left immediately to intercede with the Corps commander, who gave him the laconic reply, 'We may all be dead before morning.'[82] Claus knew the order was impossible and was relying on whether the battalion commanders could sway the more committed. Nelson let the other officers have their say before speaking: Mihály Szalvai (known to all by his nickname 'Chapayev'), the leader of the Dimitrovs, and the commander of the Spanish 24th battalion, refused to commit their men; the officer of the Franco-Belge was speechless.[83] Nelson then said that he believed the men would comply if the military situation was explained to them, which prompted a sharp rebuttal from Tapsell. Claus read out the order and Cunningham supported him, outlining the desperate plight of the defenders in Quijorna. Nelson then faced the Americans, arguing that where they sat now was at the mouth of a ravine that could not be defended, so it was a case of marching back down the road to Quijorna tonight or, on the morrow, hurrying north to cover the same distance in order to form a line at El Escorial. Tapsell changed his mind and, addressing the 37 men surrounding him (five were too exhausted to raise themselves), he appealed to their communist discipline: as anti-fascist soldiers they had to obey an order, even if he deplored it. The British and Americans formed a column and marched off in the dark but were intercepted after a few hundred yards by a dispatch-rider with good news: the Quijorna garrison had managed to extricate itself, the relief was unnecessary.[84]

Captain Frank Ryan had celebrated 4 July in the American camp before the battle,[85] and witnessed the storming of Villanueva de la Cañada.[86] On 27 July, Ryan came to visit Peter O'Connor, who, answering his enquiry earlier, wrote that he was the last Irishman standing in the Lincolns. Ryan told the Waterford man that he was going home because he was 'afraid that all the Irish would be killed as at that point' and that he needed 'some survivor or survivors to put the record straight about the Spanish War' in Ireland.[87] It transpired that other Irishmen came through the confusion of the fighting – Jim O'Regan and Michael Lehane.[88] Tom Jones, a stretcher-bearer from Gorey with the British and a hero to the survivors on 'Suicide Hill' on 12 February,[89] was said to have reached safety but British battalion records posted him as missing after Brunete.[90] Ryan had already slotted Jim Prendergast for repatriation and was surprised to find him at the front, badly shaken after two days and two nights in the thick of the Brunete fighting. He sent him immediately to Madrid.[91] A member of the original No. 1 Company (Lopera, Las Rozas, Jarama), and political commissar of the Irish platoon, Prendergast was wounded on 12 February, and after his recovery he joined the officer training school at Pozorrubio where he was attested to have 'no capacity for military leadership'.[92] Still, the training school C.O. Robert Merriman was curious to hear what the Dubliner had to say about the Villanueva attack, bribing him to come out from Albacete on 11 July with packets of Lucky Strikes and a box of chocolates.[93] In mid-July Ryan collected a group for a photograph at the IB base, mainly the veterans of the Pozoblanco front: Frank Edwards, Peter Daly, Paddy O'Daire and Joe Monks, and the graduates from Pozorrubio, Prendergast and Jack Nalty. Daly and O'Daire refused to be sent home and were held in high esteem as valuable officer material, while Nalty spent nine months in Ireland before returning to the British battalion in April 1938.[94]

There were no happy snapshots of the British, who were embittered by the three-week ordeal and the perceived incompetence of the Republican high command. Syd Quinn, an ex-British soldier, criticised the diversion to take Villanueva and, in later years, while admiring Copeman as a leader of men, stated that the commander 'was breaking up ("went off his nut"). We could all see it coming. The poor bugger was on his own [and] didn't know which way to turn.'[95] Quinn was soon allowed to return to Britain. He believed the war was lost at Brunete. He praised the sangfroid of Lieutenant Clifford Wattis:

> The most interesting character [. . .] was Clifford Wattis, ex-RAF, peaches and cream complexion, fair. He said I'll think I'll have a shave. That man doing that little thing showed the men that not all was lost. He had a charmed life. [. . .] Wattis and Copemen were superb.[96]

The greater part of British criticisms revolved around the general conduct of the battle, their inadequate equipment, the strategical and tactical errors, and less on the actions of individual officers whom many believed had been promoted above their level of ability (Copeman, Cunningham). Commissar Tapsell was a scatter-gun critic, an emotional Londoner acting from humane motives but forgetting the exigencies of army life and its strict hierarchies in a desperate battle. One of the most incisive criticisms of Tapsell's conduct during the battle is provided by Walter Greenhalgh, Frank Ryan's periodical co-worker in the Madrid IB Commissariat, a Mancunian communist whose sister had married into the family of George Brown. After his truck was destroyed beside Brigade headquarters on the Guadarrama riverbed, Greenhalgh acted as runner and therefore got to know the front intimately. Shortly after the British had left Mosquito ridge (12–13 July), he met an angry comrade from his city who complained:

> What sort of an army is this? I just left a meeting around a truck where Tapsell is telling the men to walk out of the line and to walk up to brigade headquarters and protest that they are being sent to their deaths for no reason. I am not going to stay in a mob like this.

The brigade commander had Tapsell placed under arrest. 'The upshot', Greenhalgh remembers, was that Čopić and Claus were demanding Tapsell's head. Aitken had pleaded, he told me, that it would be political suicide to take this action against Tapsell because he was a member of the Central Committee of the CP and that kind of scandal should not be allowed, [promising them] to take Tapsell back to England.[97]

Copeman, also angry at the arrest of his commissar, went to headquarters, telling Joe Hinks to bring the machine-gun company there should he not return within two hours. Tapsell justified himself by arguing that the troops were not yet trained to carry out a highly technical form of attack (Mosquito ridge) after overrunning heavily defended positions at Villanueva.[98] According to Aitken, Tapsell at the time was 'beat to the wide, absolutely demoralized and not normal', seeing 'the whole offensive [as] a ghastly failure and a severe defeat, while the new Spanish forces were less than useless'.[99] Tapsell was released and returned to his men.

But the matter did not end there, for Tapsell continued his rantings before the survivors when the shell of the British battalion returned to Mondéjar, alleging that his countrymen 'had been deliberately placed in all the tough spots' and stating 'as a fact' that the battalion 'had been let down' by Spanish auxiliaries 'on every occasion'.[100] Fearing that Tapsell would end up before a military tribunal for mutiny, Aitken detained him in his room in Mondéjar for some days and then packed him off to Valencia out of harm's way. The turbulence within the British battalion during Brunete still awaited a post-mortem session in London and caused little or no reaction within the IB leadership in Albacete.

The fate of the 13th Brigade (Chapayev battalion of Germans and Austrians, the French battalion Vuillemin and the two Spanish battalions Juan Marco and Otumba) produced, by way of contrast, consternation and anger in the higher echelons of the IB. The 13th Brigade was still in the firing line on the valley floor on 23–26 July, hemmed in by attacking forces, under constant shelling and retreating slowly. Krieger (Vicenzo Bianco) ran amok, abusing his Spanish soldiers and shooting one with his pistol for disobeying the order to march to Villanueva del Pardillo. This was the final straw for about one third of the 870 survivors (the 13th had gone into battle with 3,000 men) who mutinied and headed for the rear.[101] Krieger was arrested but soon released, and the brigade itself officially disbanded on 4 August, by the order of Colonel Rojo on the grounds that one battalion had fled their positions. Gal had informed Miaja that the brigade had disobeyed orders and was on its way, armed, to Madrid.[102] In Galapagar, outside the fighting zone, about 300 of the brigade mutineers were surrounded by carbineros and disarmed.

André Marty wrote a long analysis of the affair, including the detail that in the last stages of the battle the Spanish battalion 'Juan Marco' left its trenches, openly defying Krieger and threatening to shoot him. Franz Dahlem, Marty continued, appealed to the men to return to the battle but they refused outright. The only positive feature of the affair was that Wilhelm Zaisser was completely rehabilitated in November by the Spanish CP and went on to execute the timely reform of the bloated bureaucracy at the IB base.[103] The 13th Brigade was later re-established as a Polish-Balkan-Hungarian-Spanish unit.

### THE BALANCE OF THE BATTLE

Only the propagandists could believe that Brunete was a decisive Republican victory. True, there was a gain in ground of about 50 km$^2$, but the costs had been enormous for both sides. Spanish sources estimate the casualties for Franco's troops were about 16,000 (1,000–2,000 killed, 11,000–12,000 wounded and over 1,000 taken prisoner), those of the Republic between 18,000 and 20,000 (the figures are incomplete), with perhaps a higher rate of mortality due to the difficulties of getting the wounded out of the pocket to hospital, through the solitary road, constantly under artillery fire or air attack.[104] The overall plan was too ambitious, the Republic simply did not have the resources to carry it out: few reserves, not enough aircraft to seriously contest the air-superiority of the Franco side, not enough trucks to ferry the men to their fighting positions, not enough field-pieces or mortars to pound enemy positions or break up his attacks, and insufficient tank forces (without radio) gingerly going forward without proper coordination with the infantry. Inadequate tactical experience and training among Republican commanders, often ex-NCOs, played a part, but in the general balance of armed forces, in men and material, the troops of Miaja and Rojo were at a grave disadvantage after the third day of the struggle. There were numerous errors on the part of the Republican generals, confusion about orders and counter-orders against a background of general distrust between the 'professionals' and the young Communist commanders. The loyalty and the decisions of leading figures at HQ are open to question (Jurado, Matallana, Casado), not least because of their hidden sympathies for Franco's cause and alleged sabotage during the Brunete campaign.[105] Even the affable General José Miaja, the acclaimed 'Hero of Madrid', showed little tactical finesse and was generally indolent and hesitant. For Negrín, Miaja was 'a nincompoop, no good for anything, he doesn't know where the front is and can't even keep four soldiers in his mind at once.'[106] For the Prime Minister and Prieto, Minister for War, who followed the battle closely in its planning and execution at headquarters, Rojo was the hero of the hour. After all, his battle plan had halted the fascist advance in the north for five weeks.

The 'butcher's bill' for the International Brigades was horrendous, 33 per cent, from over 13,300 to just 9,000. Almost 800 had been killed, over 2,300 wounded and up to 500, many of them deserters, were missing. The units assigned to take the Romanillos-Mosquito ridge had the highest losses of all brigades. The fatalities were highest in the 15th Brigade (293), followed by the 11th (165) and the 13th (150). The British battalion lost 85 per cent of its strength, the Chapayev 73 per cent.[107] At 167, the number of missing, including deserters, was the highest in the American and British battalions.[108] Eight Irishmen were killed and at least 13 were posted as wounded.[109]

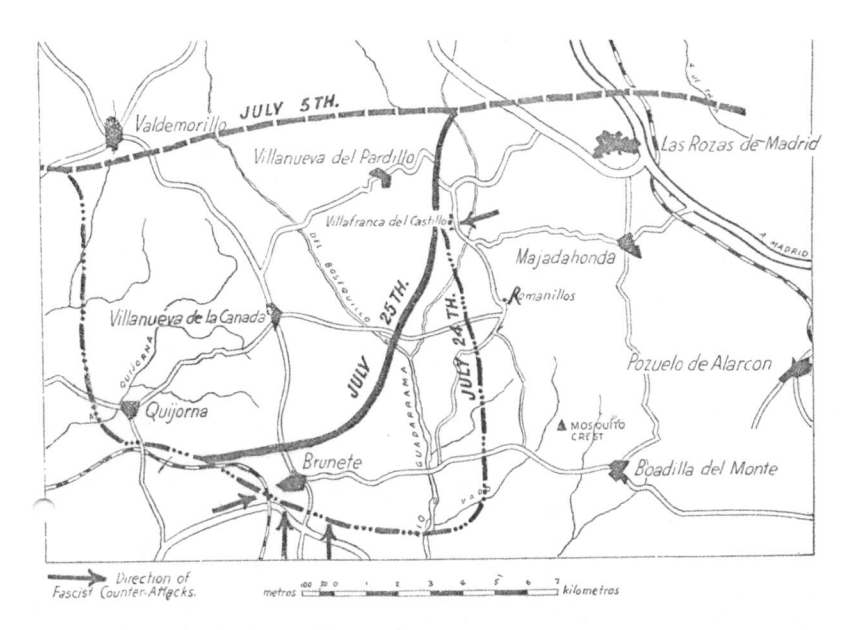

Battle of Brunete, July 1937: Limits of Republican advance (*Book of the XV Brigade*)

At the end of the battle, the leaders of the British battalion drew up a list of 36 deserters, 'some of them with first-class records'.[110] Deserters from the Washington and Lincoln battalions numbered over 100.[111] Considering that the battle, fought under extreme climactic conditions, lasted seven times as long as the intense phase on the Jarama, and that the volunteers were under more sustained and murderous fire of aircraft and artillery than anything undergone hitherto, it is not surprising that so many left the lines for the rear, heading for Albacete or Madrid. At least six Irishmen were among those who absconded, three were arrested and later taken back into the British battalion, while the others managed to depart from Spain illegally. Bill Paynter, the British CP representative at Albacete, began to interview the deserters dribbling into the town. Of the eight he had questioned by 15 July, all had been wounded or sick before the battle, and 'on the whole' had good military records but had 'lost their nerve'. He recommended setting up an isolated centre in the countryside that would not be a prison-camp but an education and rest area to help the men recover their morale, for him the only feasible alternative: repatriation would encourage more desertion, while keeping them in the Guardia Nacional prison in the town would dispirit them further, and allowing them to wander the streets would mean the demoralisation of others.[112]

Little is known about the detention centres in the rural vicinity of Albacete: Camp Lukács (named after the pseudonym of the fallen Hungarian commander of the 12th Brigade, Máté Zalka), a guarded encampment in an olive-grove, was originally conceived for men with a long charge sheet of drinking offences, while Villa Maruja was on an agriculture estate reserved for those who had disobeyed orders.[113] Bill Paynter visited the interned with Arthur Horner, the Welsh miners' leader. The aggrieved men who wanted to go home were not impressed by Horner's political remarks but evinced great interest when he told them about the recent heavyweight bout between Joe Louis and Tommy Farr. 'The Tonypandy Terror' had lost on points to the 'Brown Bomber' in New York on 30 August. Paynter, hard pressed by complainants, explained that alternatives to the detention centre could be worse if the volunteers were subject to the full rigours of Spanish military law.[114]

John Angus, a young middle-class Londoner wounded on Mosquito Ridge, was appointed political commissar of the British at Camp Lucas (as the English-speakers called it) while unfit for the front. When he arrived in November he found that all but a handful of the 60 to 70 he was to 're-educate' were demoralised, and that all had a case: recruited on the promise that their stay in Spain would be a limited one (six months as a rule). They were resentful that there was a repatriation ban in force, especially because they knew that 'the entire British leadership from the battalion right down to company or even lower level had been allowed to go home either on leave or permanently'. Angus viewed the whole enterprise with some distaste, preferring the title 'prison camp' to 'rehabilitation centre' and noting that grim Germans had most of the supervisory jobs. Angus came to the conclusion that the only solution was to remove the British from the canvas compound and to transfer them to their countrymen at the new training base at Tarazona de La Mancha. Captain Allan Johnson, the American commandant of the town, was unwilling at first to accept the lorryloads of men, but relented, and they were rapidly integrated.[115]

## REPATRIATION OF THE IRISH

At least 36 Irishmen were repatriated in the course of 1937, usually after an examination before a medical commission. Two were considered too old for combat (Dennis Holden and Seamus O'Beirne), four were repatriated for family reasons (the Power brothers Paddy and Billy, Maurice Moran and Seamus Cummings), and others for general reasons of weak health, disability or ill-discipline (Joe Ryan, Colum Cox, Hugh Dooley, Sean Penrose and George Boyle). The available data suggests that the remainder of those sent home were considered to 'have done their bit': men who had fought in one or more of the battles and had been wounded.

Frank Ryan was mindful of the concerns of their families in Ireland and felt that the Irish had already contributed enough to the struggle. He was also motivated by the desire to retain a core of left-wing Republican militants in Ireland. He directly intervened to have 15 and more sent home and made Peter O'Connor the treasurer for a smaller group who were to be kitted out with new suits and travel money before leaving Albacete. Four on the list (Johnny Power, Kevin Blake, Vincent O'Donnell and Danny Boyle) were either refused permission to leave, or did not want to.[116] Ryan was inventive in making a good case for 'the lads', stating that Paddy Duff and Jim ('The Farmer') O'Regan were 'being recalled by the IRA'.[117]

## POST-MORTEM IN LONDON

In Britain, the Political Bureau of the CPGB was gathering material for the showdown meeting with the battalion leadership recalled after Brunete. Fred Copeman and Bert Williams left in mid-August,[118] along with Tapsell, who the Spaniards were glad to see leaving: he was described as 'a trouble maker' (French: 'indésirable') in his travel papers and allotted only 50 pesetas travel expenses, while Copeman and Williams were handed the customary amount, three times that figure.[119] Aitken and Cunningham departed in early September, presumably travelling first class with all the fittings, for Albacete requested a reimbursement of the total costs of 5,000 pesetas from the CPGB office at London's 16 King Street.[120] That was an arrangement commensurate with their ranks: Cunningham was a major, and Aitken's patent, as a brigade commissar, entitled him to the status and pay of a lieutenant-colonel. He was thus the highest-ranking volunteer from Britain to serve in Spain, but that did not impress the mandarins of King Street. What the Party had to examine was why the collective leadership of the British battalion had collapsed during the Brunete carnage; they also had to nominate the right people to rebuild it. It seems that there was more than one meeting to solve the crisis. Trouble had been brewing since the trench tedium on the Jarama: Cunningham, courageous but with an explosively choleric disposition, was a difficult man to get on with, a constant trial for the even-tempered George Aitken. Simmering resentments became known early in the battle, as Bill Paynter informed Pollitt as early as 11 July:

> The battalion is still in action and less than half its original manpower. I am hoping by the time I get back up, they will have been taken from the line for rest. When I saw them they were all exhausted but their spirits were still good. The internal position is, however, bad, and a very strained position exists between Jock [Cunningham] and George [Aitken], so much so that I am afraid that when they do come out there will be another show down. I had a short conversation with George, Tappy [Tapsell] and Bert [Williams], and from what I could gather, steps will have to be taken with Jock. He is in a very bad mood and has made public declarations during the battle that can only be described as criminal if they are true. Nothing could be done while I was there since the action was still in progress, and the lads are getting a very heavy bombardment from three different angles. Jock was especially uncommunicative to me, which was a new attitude. All the comrades are very strained and I shall not do anything until some kind of calm has again been established. The short point is that things cannot go on any longer in the present state.[121]

Cunningham was a natural leader but he was obviously out of his depth in conducting the manoeuvring of 1,500 infantry men – nothing strange in the Army of the Spanish Republic. In reality, he was in an impossible situation, subject to the orders of an incompetent (Gal) who, in turn, had to answer to Madrid. The only way to make the best out of a cruel predicament was to cooperate with others, taking their advice and criticism, for which he was temperamentally unfit. Cunningham had 'exploded with rage when charged by the Brigade Command with weakness in his control of the three battalions in his regiment'.[122] Another problem was hubris, generated by the propaganda status given by Pollitt to both Cunningham and Copeman, including eulogies in the *Daily Worker* and membership of the Central Committee. The Political Bureau discussed the statements made on return by all the participants.

The decision arrived at was highly contested and, in retrospect, unfair: Cunningham, Aitken and Bert Williams were to stay in Britain, Tapsell and Copeman to return on condition. The dissenters against the vote were Peter Kerrigan and Johnny Campbell, who thought the duo unsuitable for another stint in Spain.¹²³ Bill Paynter, too, who does not seem to have been part of the discussion round, was against Tapsell being re appointed battalion commissar, arguing that 'he was bound to come to loggerheads with the leadership and react in his usual boisterous style.'¹²⁴ Pollitt summarised the tumultuous meetings in a letter to the CPGB representative at ECCI, Robin Page-Arnot:

> No excuses can be made for some our oldest and most responsible comrades [Aitken, Williams]. Comrade Jock Cunningham has been exceptionally difficult since his return and we have not been able to solve the difficulty yet. It would appear that Jock from his point of view was the only person who was right and this has produced many difficulties since his return.¹²⁵

Cunningham resigned his CPGB membership and lived out his life as a tramp and casual labourer, dying in 1969 from the long-term effects of a chest wound.¹²⁶ George Aitken was shoved off to the post of Party Organiser in the North-East as a replacement for Bill Rust who took over from Will Paynter in Albacete. Aitken believed that he had been dismissed because Springhall was of the opinion that he, Aitken, as 'Party political leader' had not held 'the leading comrades together', so that his work in Spain was a 'failure'. That was archetypical Bolshevik reasoning: as you can't criticise the leadership, you look for a scapegoat lower down in the hierarchy. Aitken's parting shot was the remark that sending Tapsell back was 'madness', coupled with the prediction that Copeman, 'if he is sent back, he will break down again as he did before.'¹²⁷ In the meantime, Steve Nelson and Frank Ryan were re-building the British battalion, proposing Jack Roberts, a CPGB councillor from Wales, as commissar and Peter Daly as the new commander.¹²⁸

### NOTES

1. Antony Beevor, *The Battle for Spain: the Spanish Civil War 1936–1939* (London, 2006), pp 275–7.
2. Peter O'Connor, A *Soldier of Liberty: Recollections of a Socialist and Anti-fascist Fighter* (Dublin, 1996), p. 26.
3. Alvah Bessie, Albert Prago (eds), *Our Fight: Writings by Veteran of the Abraham Lincoln Brigade, Spain 1936–1939* (New York, 1987), pp 134–5.
4. Brian Lewis, Bill Gledhill, *Tommy James: A Lion of a Man* (Pontefract, 1984), p. 68.
5. RGASPI, f. 545, o. 1, d. 4, l. 4.
6. RGASPI, f. 545, o. 3, d. 426, l. 207.

7. RGASPI, f. 545, o. 6, d. 177, ll. 10–11.
8. Beevor, *Battle for Spain*, p. 278.
9. Alfred Kantorowicz, *Spanisches Kriegstagebuch* (Frankfurt am Main, 1982), pp 353–68.
10. Hermann Weber and Andreas Herbst (eds), *Deutsche Kommunisten: Biographisches Handbuch 1918 bis 1945* (Berlin, 2004), pp 891–2.
11. RGASPI, f. 545, o. 6, d. 375, l. 80; Kantorowicz, *Spanisches Kriegstagebuch*, pp 420–1.
12. Copeman, *Reason in Revolt*, p. 122.
13. David Mathieson, *Frontline Madrid: Battlefield Tours of the Spanish Civil War* (Oxford, 2014), pp 185–223.
14. Andreu Castells, *Las Brigadas Internacionales de la Guerra de España* (Barcelona, 1974), pp 235–6.
15. Severiano Montero Barrado, *La Batalla de Brunete* (Madrid, 2010), pp 48–54.
16. RGASPI, f. 545, o. 3, d. 426, ll. 218–9.
17. Ibid., l. 98.
18. Enrique Líster, *Unser Krieg* (East Berlin, 1972), pp 182–4, 197–9.
19. Juan Barceló Luqué, *Brunete. El nacimiento del Ejercito Popular* (Madrid, 2018), pp 116–17.
20. Montero, *La Batalla*, pp 94–7.
21. Ibid., pp 81–90.
22. Fred Copeman, *Reason in Revolt* (London, 1984), p. 125.
23. Steve Nelson, James R. Barrett, Rob Ruck, *Steve Nelson: American Radical* (Pittsburg, 1981), p. 216.
24. Bessie, Prago, *Our Fight*, pp 135–6.
25. Arthur Landis, *The Abraham Lincoln Brigade* (New York, 1968) pp 192–3; Harry Fisher, *Comrades: Tales of a Brigadista in the Spanish Civil War* (Lincoln, Na, 1999), pp 55–8.
26. RGASPI, f. 545, o. 1, d. 36, l. 238; IWM, Interview 11187, Walter Greenhalgh, reel 5.
27. Copeman, *Reason in Revolt*, pp 130–2; Richard Baxell, *Unlikely Warriors: the British in the Spanish Civil War and the Struggle against Fascism* (London, 2012), pp 226–8.
28. Michael Lonardo, 'Under a watchful eye: a case study of police surveillance', in *Labour/Le Travail*, 5 (spring 1995), pp 11–41, here p. 39.
29. Montero, *La Batalla*, p. 109.
30. Ibid., pp 91–4.
31. Ibid., pp 82–3, 104.
32. Ibid., pp 102–3.
33. Ibid., pp 108–9, 214.
34. RGASPI, f. 545, o. 3, d. 333, l. 208; Kantorowicz, *Spanisches Kriegstagebuch*, pp 391–3.
35. RGASPI, f. 545, o. 3, d. 467, ll. 58–9.
36. RGASPI, f. 545, o. 4, d. 480, ll. 5–6.
37. Copeman, *Reason in Revolt*, pp 132–3; Cecil Eby, *Between the Bullet and the Lie: American Volunteers in the Spanish Civil War* (New York-Chicago-San Francisco, 1969), p. 132.
38. RGASPI, f. 545, o. 3, d. 426, l. 220.
39. Kantorowicz, *Spanisches Kriegstagebuch*, pp 391–9.

40. Ibid., pp 403–4; Vereinigung österreichischer Freiwilliger in der spanische Republik 1936 bis 1939 (eds), *Österreicher im Spanischen Bürgerkrieg Interbrigadisten berichten über ihre Erlebnisse* (Vienna, 1986), pp 152–3.
41. RGASPI, f. 545, o. 3, d. 470, l. 13.
42. RGASPI, f. 545, o. 3, d. 480, ll. 6–7.
43. RGASPI, f. 545, o. 3, d. 467, l. 59.
44. Eby, *Between the Bullet and the Lie*, p. 133.
45. Barceló, *Brunete*, p. 157.
46. Montero, *La Batalla*, p. 122.
47. Ibid., pp 99–102.
48. RGASPI, f. 545, o. 3, d. 336, ll. 149, 151.
49. Kantorowicz, *Spanisches Kriegstagebuch*, pp 403–4.
50. Lewis, Gledhill, *Tommy James*, p. 75.
51. RGASPI, f. 545, o. 3, d. 467, l. 60.
52. Fisher, *Comrades*, pp 60–5; Landis, *The Abraham Lincoln Brigade*, pp 203–7.
53. Montero, *La Batalla*, p. 117.
54. RGASPI, f. 545, o. 3, d. 467, l. 60.
55. Kantorowicz, *Spanisches Kriegstagebuch*, pp 404–7.
56. RGASPI, f. 545, o. 3, d. 467, ll. 60–1.
57. Ibid., ll. 61–2.
58. Montero, *La Batalla*, pp 118–21; Landis, *The Abraham Lincoln Brigade*, pp 212–3; Eby, *Between the Bullet and the Lie*, p. 136; Nelson, *Volunteers* (East Berlin, 1958), pp 176–7.
59. Kantorowicz, *Spanisches Kriegstagebuch*, pp 407–11.
60. Bill Alexander, *British Volunteers for Liberty: Spain, 1936–39* (London, 1982), p. 127.
61. Eby, *Between the Bullet and the Lie*, p. 137.
62. Landis, *The Abraham Lincoln Brigade*, p. 217.
63. Peter N. Carroll, *The Odyssey of the Abraham Lincoln Brigade: Americans in the Spanish Civil War* (Stanford, 1994), pp 143–4.
64. Kantorowicz, *Spanisches Kriegstagebuch*, pp 411–26.
65. Barceló, *Brunete*, p. 135.
66. Montero, *La Batalla*, p. 11
67. Ronald Radosh, Mary R. Habeck, Grigory Sevostianov (eds), *Spain Betrayed: The Soviet Union and the Spanish Civil War* (New Haven and London, 2001), pp 338–41; Montero, *La Batalla*, pp 140–3.
68. Peter O'Connor, *A Soldier of Liberty: Recollections of a Socialist and Anti-fascist Fighter* (Dublin, 1996), p. 28.
69. Eby, *Between the Bullet and the Lie*, pp 138–40; Landis, *The Abraham Lincoln Brigade*, pp 218–22; Fisher, *Comrades*, pp 67–9.
70. Montero, *La Batalla*, p. 172.
71. RGASPI, f. 545, o. 3, d. 221, ll. 69–71.
72. Kantorowicz, *Spanisches Kriegstagebuch*, pp 448–52.
73. Montero, *La Batalla*, pp 172–4.
74. Ibid., pp 159–60, 184–90; Barceló, *Brunete*, pp 266–70.
75. Landis, *The Abraham Lincoln Brigade*, pp 228–9; Montero, *La Batalla*, pp 191–2.

76. Montero, *La Batalla*, p. 205.
77. Lewis, Gledhill, *Tommy James*, pp 87–9; Alexander, *British Volunteers*, pp 128–9.
78. Montero, *La Batalla*, pp 201–3.
79. Nelson, Barrett, Ruck, *Steve Nelson*, pp 221–3.
80. Ibid., p. 219.
81. David Yorke (ed.), Ronald Liversedge, *Mac-Pap: Memoir of a Canadian in the Spanish Civil War* (Vancouver, 2013), p. 77.
82. Alexander, *British Volunteers*, p. 130; Baxell, *Unlikely Warriors*, pp 234–5.
83. Landis, *The Abraham Lincoln Brigade*, p. 232.
84. Lewis, Gledhill, *Harry James*, p. 91; Nelson, Barrett, Ruck, *Steve Nelson*, pp 224–5.
85. ROR, letter from Frank Ryan to Gerald O'Reilly, New York, 4 July 1937.
86. ROR, letter from Frank Ryan to Helen O'Reilly, Dublin, n.d. (late July 1937).
87. O'Connor, *Soldier of Liberty*, p. 29.
88. Seán Cronin, *Frank Ryan: The Search for the Republic* (Dublin, 1980), p. 123.
89. Commissiariat of War, XV Brigade (ed.), *The Book of the XV Brigade: Records of British, American, Canadian and Irish Volunteer in the XV International Brigade in Spain 1936–1938* (Madrid, 1938), p. 66.
90. RGASPI, f. 545, o. 3, d. 426, l. 249.
91. ROR, letter from Frank Ryan to Helen O'Reilly, Dublin, 22 July 1937.
92. RGASPI, f. 545, o. 6, d. 187, ll. 3–5.
93. www.merrimandiary.com/2014/07/11. Accessed 25 September 2014.
94. ROR, letter to Helen O'Reilly Dublin, 21.07.1937; Joe Monks, *Reds in Andalusia* (photo).
95. James K, Hopkins, *Into the Heart of the Fire: The British in the Spanish Civil War* (Stanford, 1998), p. 242.
96. IWM, Interview 801, Sydney Quinn, reel 2.
97. IWM, Interview 11187, Walter Greenhalgh, reel 6.
98. Copeman, *Reason in Revolt*, pp 136–7.
99. MML, Box C, file 17/7, letter from George Aitken to Political Bureau, (September 1937), hereafter Aitken Ms., p. 5.
100. Baxell, *Unlikely Warriors*, pp 235–7.
101. Max Schäfer (ed.), *1936–1939, Spanien: Erinnerungen von Interbrigadisten aus der BRD* (Frankfurt am Main, 1976), pp 178–9; Montero, *La Batalla*, pp 242–6.
102. Montero, *La Batalla*, p. 244.
103. RGASPI, f. 545, o. 6, d. 375, ll. 84–5. Werner Abel kindly passed on this document.
104. Montero, *La Batalla*, pp 271–3.
105. See the discussion about Casado and Matallana (Chief of Staff of the Army of the Centre) in Paul Preston, *The Last Days of the Spanish Republic* (London, 2016), pp 34–5.
106. Barceló, *Brunete*, p. 234 (extract from diary of President Azaña).
107. Based on the calculations in: RGASPI, f. 545, o. 1, d. 4, l. 4; 545, o. 3, d. 247, l. 324; f. 545, o. 3, d. 336, l. 191a.
108. RGASPI, f. 545, o. 1, d. 4, l. 29.
109. RGASPI, f. 545, o. 6, d. 51, l. 100.
110. Baxell, *Unlikely Warriors*, p. 238.
111. Carroll, *The Odyssey of the Abraham Lincoln Brigade*, p. 148.

112. RGASPI, f. 545, o. 2, d. 70, ll. 56–7.
113. Peter Huber and Ralf Hug, *Die Schweizer Spanienfreiwilligen: Ein biographisches Handbuch* (Zürich, 2009), p. 43.
114. Paynter, *My Generation*, p. 71.
115. John Angus, *With the International Brigades in Spain* (Loughborough, 1983), pp 1, 6–8.
116. RGASPI, f. 545, o. 2, d, 70, l. 39; f. 545, o. 6, d. 53, l. 14.
117. RGASPI, f. 545, o. 6, d. 53, ll. 20, 22.
118. RGASPI, f. 545, o. 2, d. 113, l. 12.
119. Ibid., l. 6.
120. RGASPI, f. 545, o. 3, d. 39, l. 16.
121. MML, Box 21/13/3c, Paynter to Pollitt, 11 July 1937.
122. Alexander, *British Volunteers*, p. 131.
123. RGASPI, f. 495, o. 14, d. 229, l. 36 (Political Bureau sitting, 14–15 October 1937).
124. TNA, KV 2/1192, Walter Tapsell, Special Branch entry, 3 September 1937.
125. RGASPI, f. 495, o. 14, d. 243, l. 161.
126. Judith Cook, *Apprentices of Freedom* (London-Melbourne-New York, 1979), pp 97–8.
127. MML, Aitken Ms, pp 2, 10.
128. RGASPI, f. 545, o. 3, d. 441, l. 87.

# EIGHT

# FAILED OFFENSIVES: ARAGON AND TERUEL

After Brunete, the men of the 15th Brigade needed time to recover. When resting in the woods near Torrelodones immediately after the three-week ordeal, not a few made scathing comments on the behaviour of Spanish troops during the battle. The English-speakers were demoralised also by what they heard had happened to the 13th Brigade. Some of the arguments against the lack of air cover by the Spanish Republican Air Force (FARE) resembled what the Dunkirk Tommies had to say about the RAF: in Spain the vitriolic comments died down when the men were told that not enough planes were available. When the 15th IB was transferred closer to Madrid, to Hoyo de Manzanares, criticism turned to resignation or realism: that they would die in Spain, or that the war would be long and the casualties enormous. The long-promised leave to Madrid was seen as a sop: 18 hours in the capital.[1]

The mood in the American battalion improved when new levies arrived and men with long records were sent to the rearguard; it improved further still when a delegation from the USA brought a shipment of soap, cigarettes and chewing gum.[2] By the second week in August, Brigade morale was lowest in the British battalion, with men citing the high casualties, the inefficiency of their armament (especially machine guns) and the inconsiderate treatment in hospitals; the general mood expressed itself in the strong belief that the unit was in no state militarily or psychologically 'to go into action'.[3]

When Aitken and Cunningham visited the British on 14 August, Aitken was booed by the men, while Cunningham continued his running argument with Marcovics about mistakes made at Brunete.[4] The British leadership was resentful about its removal from Spain, a feeling compounded by the realisation that the Americans were now far more numerous and would soon be running the Brigade. By mid-August, Frank Ryan and Arthur Olorenshaw had arrived at Mondéjar to assist in the re-formation of the British battalion, which had become augmented by 70 Americans.[5] The Brigade was also strengthened by the formation of the Mackenzie-Papineau Battalion of Canadians, who were now in Spain in some numbers and were training at the new infantry school at Tarazona. Two of the early Canadian arrivals were Jim Woulfe, an IRA veteran from Athea, Co. Limerick, who left Ireland shortly after his release from internment following the Irish Civil War,[6] and Patrick McGuire from Monaghan. Both were training at the sergeants' school in Pozorrubio in May when they were castigated by Merriman after a night of excessive drinking – he allowed them to stay because they apologised.[7] In all, there were 30 Irishmen in the Canadian contingent, mainly from Northern Ireland. Two of the Irish reached officer rank and became platoon leaders – Tom Traynor from Strabane and the ex-miner Joe Kelly from Belfast. The second-oldest Irish volunteer also came from Belfast via Canada, the electrician Tom ('Pop') Cochrane, a father of six children who at the age of 51 joined the Lincolns in April and was repatriated on grounds of age and health (with four wounds sustained at Brunete) in late 1937.[8]

REORGANISATION OF THE INTERNATIONAL BRIGADES

Behind the scenes, a general reorganisation of the brigades was in motion. The result was a 'hispanisation', with at least 50 per cent of the units to be composed of Spaniards, resulting in more Spanish officers, the introduction of Spanish as the lingua franca (it had been French to date) and the reshuffling of the battalions into monolingual brigades (English, French, German, Italian, Slavic). With the incorporation of the IB into the Republican Army by a decree (23 September) of Indalecio Prieto, the Minister of Defence, the Internationals were to fulfil the role of the Foreign Legion founded in 1920 (Tercio de Extranjeros), which was now fighting for Franco. The quasi-autonomy of the IB was over.[9]

Prieto, a centrist in the Partido Socialista Obrero Español (PSOE), had initially admired communist troops for their discipline, but in the course of 1937 he tried to 'depoliticise' the Army and curb the powers of the political commissars. He also clashed with Russian military experts.[10] The International Brigades thus lost their semi-independent role, and the members, hitherto accustomed to slack discipline, would now face the severe military code of the Spanish Army, including execution by firing squad. Prieto aimed at the full subjugation of Albacete (Marty was absent in Moscow on ECCI business), demanding details of volunteer numbers and the keeping of accounts (there were rumours of embezzlement) and sending an investigation team to the town when the information was withheld.[11]

Leading communists, too, realised that the brigades needed a thorough shaking-out. Grigory Shtern ('Grigorovitch'), the top Soviet military adviser, wrote to Moscow as early as 2 July that there were tensions between Spaniards and the International Brigades – low morale, chauvinism between the nationalities (especially the French, Poles and Italians) and the desire for repatriation.[12] Vital Gayman ('Vidal') who was holding the fort in Albacete in the absence of Marty, in his letter of resignation in late July condemned the attitude of professional Spanish officers towards the foreign volunteers ('nothing but a foreign legion, an army of mercenaries fighting for money'), who had put the IB in positions 'to attack the most heavily fortified positions' and refused them leave from long front-line service.[13] Palmiro Togliatti (Ercoli), as new representative of the Comintern, analysed the problems facing the IB, arguing for the repatriation of British, American and Italian volunteers who had joined on the understanding that their service would not exceed six months: they should be replaced by new intakes.

As in all wars, service was for the duration of the conflict and the Republican Ministry of Defence was loath to make exceptions for foreigners. Repatriation thus became more difficult after 1937, but some exceptions were granted, mainly for political reasons or because the volunteer in question was considered unfit for further military duties. Togliatti believed that many Spanish brigades were now on the same level of efficiency of the Internationals and held it to be intolerable that foreigners be given the rank of general when a Spaniard could only attain that of lieutenant-colonel. He was also critical of the interference of 'fraternal parties' in Albacete, the contemptuous attitude in some units towards their Spanish comrades-in-arms and the practice of the Germans to dispose of cadres without consulting the Ministry of Defence. Foreign volunteers were now encouraged to join the PCE. Togliatti also noted the bloated number of officers in the German 11th Brigade – 250 for 2,000 men. By 9 August, he concluded, over 18,000 foreigners had joined the IB, of whom 8,000 were casualties and, because over 4,600 had been repatriated, the fighting strength of the six Brigades (11th–15th, 150th) had fallen to 3,100.[14]

Recruitment proved to be a major problem, because the numbers never again reached the level of the first six months (18,714). Although the British figures are incomplete in respect of national minorities, the monthly average of 80 recruits from the UK for the entire period (October 1936-August 1938) fell sharply in the second half of 1937.[15] The fall-off in new volunteers was compensated by drafts of Spanish recruits. The general reorganisation of the IB headquarters in Albacete from August ended the francophone hegemony, reduced the percentage of desk-bound staff from 14 to 5 per cent, dissolved the offices of the foreign CP representatives and increased the portion of volunteers in training from 40 to 70 per cent.[16] Overall, the professionalisation both of the brigades and of the army was enhanced, but brigade decisions often continued to be taken on political rather than purely military grounds, while in the Army rivalries and incompetence persisted, mainly due to the grave shortage of trained cadres.

THE OFFENSIVE IN ARAGON: THE BACKGROUND

At Prieto's urging, Republican high command launched a new campaign in late August, with the goal of capturing Zaragoza, the capital of Aragon – for Spanish Catholics a sacred city (dedicated to the Virgin Mary and St James) and a stronghold of anarchism until 1936. The area had fallen in the first days of the attempted coup d'état and Republican strategists believed the front was lightly held. The offensive was to be executed by the new Army of the East commanded by General Sebastián Pozas, with the IB units fighting in General Walter's 35th Division. It was hoped that the new east-west thrust would temporarily halt Franco's advance in the north against Santander, but the city fell three days after the Republicans began their attack on 24 August.

Franco did not take the bait this time, and any reinforcements he did send into Aragon were dispatched from the trenches around Madrid. In retrospect, one could argue that the decision to launch the Aragon attack was highly questionable in military terms, so soon after the immense bloodletting around Brunete. But as so often in the war, the Republican initiative, apart from the hope of slowing down the Italo-Francoist conquest of the north, was partially due to internal politics. In July the Government had finally moved against the anarchist Consejo (Council) de Aragón, a system of collectivised agricultural holdings, and dissolved it – a highly controversial measure still debated among historians. The Council was a thorn in the side of the Government, the communists and centrist socialists, and the arguments for its abolition centred on the charges that many peasants had been forced to join the collective farms and hand over their animals and implements. In any case, Prieto was not unduly embarrassed to use his enemies, the communists, to break up the anarchist bastion, commissioning Enrique Líster's 11th Division with the task.[17] By now launching a massive push into Upper Aragon, the Republican authorities sought to remove the bad impression caused by the dissolution of the Council, to ensure the continued presence of anarchist units at the front and to reinforce them with units more loyal to the Government.[18]

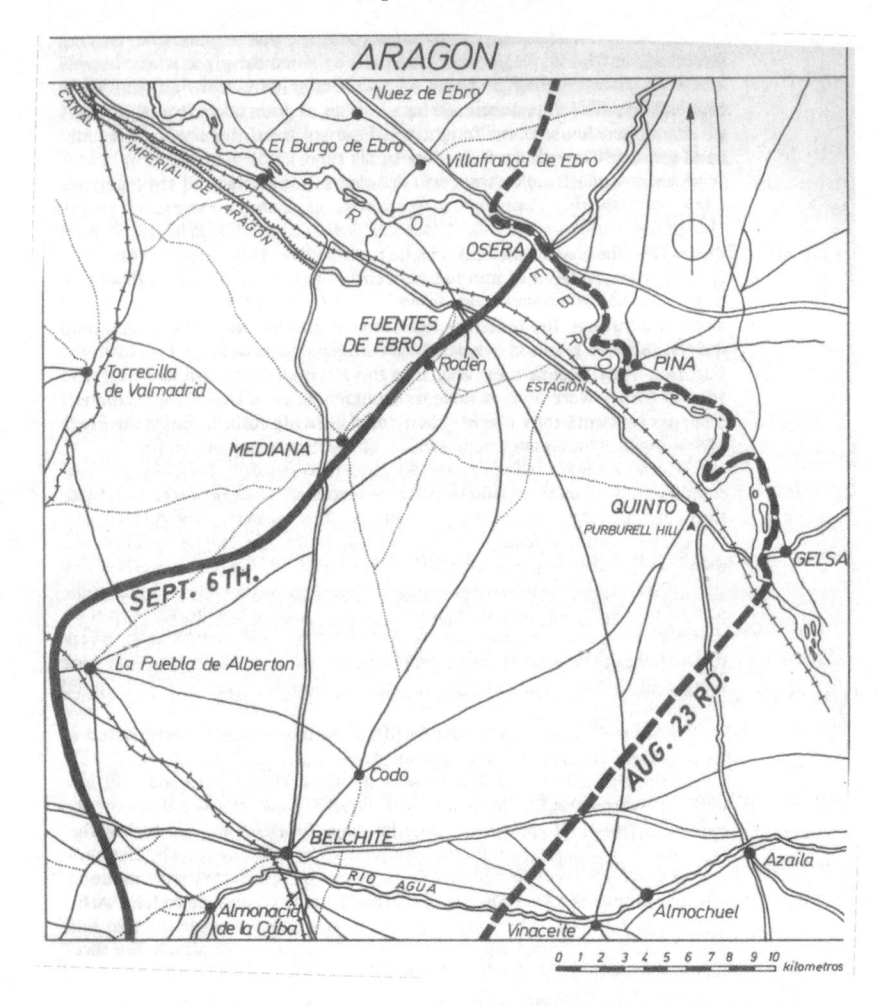

Aragon Offensive, August–October 1937 (*Book of the XV Brigade*)

For the first time in the war, the Republican forces had superiority in men, tanks and aircraft. The offensive mirrored that of Brunete and stuttered on after initial successes into October: a lack of manoeuvring skills and coordination among commanders, delays caused by stubborn defence of fascist strong-points and mutual recriminations. The main fighting took part in the south (Lower Aragon) around the Ebro. In the north, the Poles of Kléber's 45th Division took Villamayor de Gállego on the outskirts of Zaragoza in a night raid, other units captured some hillside forts; but two battalions of the Italian 12th Brigade, in approaching a hill-fort during the night, took a wrong turning and found themselves at dawn between two hills and subject to withering fire. Kléber's men lost nearly all the points taken and he stopped his part of the offensive on 29 August.[19]

Further south, Líster rushed forward with a squadron of Russian BT-5 tanks towards Fuentes de Ebro, but he came up against strongly defended positions on the plain before the town. He lost a cavalry unit and almost all his tanks in the frontal assault. Corps Commander Modesto blamed him personally for the disaster, which deepened the animosity between the two. Soviet advisers held Líster to be at fault because he did not want to subordinate himself to Modesto's orders.[20] In the lunar landscape south of Zaragoza, Walter's 35th Division had more success, with battle honours going to the 15th Brigade.

### THE CAPTURE OF QUINTO

Its units left their bases near Madrid on 18 August, riding in railroad box cars to Híjar. The men received new uniforms and the first issue of the Degtyarev light machine gun at a stopover in Valencia. Their first objective was Quinto, a town on the Ebro and the Barcelona–Zaragoza railway line. The plain west from Quinto was arid, semi-desert, treeless, insufferably hot and dusty. Approaching it from Azaila in the south, the soldiers could not see the town set in a depression on the plain, only the tower of its parish church and a prominence on the outskirts overlooking the Ebro, Purburell. The American battalion was led by Hans Amlie from North Dakota, a member of the American Socialist Party, a rarity in the Lincolns. His commissar was the seamen's union activist John Quigley Robinson from Belfast. Both had served in World War One. Lieutenant Wattis now commanded a company of Spaniards in the American battalion. Although Gal had been recalled to Russia and the 15th Division abolished, Vladimir Čopić was still Brigade Commander, Steve Nelson Brigade Commissar. On his staff were Robert Merriman (Chief of Staff) and Tom Wintringham of Jarama fame.

The attack went in at 6 a.m. on 24 August, with the Dimitrovs to the fore. They withdrew under heavy fire and swung north of the town. The British under Peter Daly stayed in reserve, and the Americans pulled back on encountering strong firing. One key point was the cemetery west of the church, which was captured by the Lincolns and the 11th Brigade following an air attack, with the aid of tanks and accurate artillery fire, in the early afternoon. The fighting continued into the evening and the next day, when bombing squads finally took the church with the aid of the anti-tank battery and nitroglycerine bombs, dragging away the wounded Wintringham. Infantry later winkled out the snipers in desperate house-to-house combat. On the afternoon of 25 August, the British were ordered to take the last bastion of the fascists – Purburrell. Daly was told it was lightly held by Merriman who ordered the assault.[21] Contrary to this unfounded supposition, typical of Čopić, the mound was topped by concrete bunkers, trenches and machine-gun nests constructed by German engineers, but no artillery support was summoned. The men went forward and were met by a hail of bullets from the hill and from snipers still active in the town. Commander Peter Daly was hit in the stomach and died in Benicasim hospital on 5 September. When darkness came, the British withdrew.

During the night, two Americans cut the water pipe leading to the hilltop, and a patrol descending to take water from the Ebro was captured, confirming the strength of the defenders and the desperation of the water supply. At dawn on 26 August, the attack was renewed with the help of the Spanish 24th Battalion and the Americans. The fighting went on all day: the anti-tank guns smashed numerous machine-gun nests, and Italian airmen, thinking the hill was in Republican hands, bombed the garrison. The trenches were taken in a classical charge at 6 p.m. Čopić, obtuse and as careless of men's lives as ever, criticised O'Daire for pulling back his troops after the first failed assault on the hill fort. The wily Donegal captain took a copy of British Army Field Regulations from his pocket, proving to his Croatian commander that he was correct in taking the decision to wait for artillery (Part III).[22]

As the Dimitrovs had captured the railway station and the cement factory in the meantime, the conquest of the town was complete. Over 500 prisoners were taken on the hill; others had earlier surrendered at the church.[23] There were spontaneous killings of fascist snipers by Americans; some officers were shot after being questioned by Merriman, others on orders of General Walter.[24] Many Americans, including Lieutenant Pat Read of the telephonists, were uncomfortable with the revenge killings, but were told that the order came from above; in any case, the fascists killed all Internationals after capture, so the justification ran.[25]

### THE CAPTURE OF BELCHITE

The momentum of the campaign was slowing to a stop. Líster's men were stuck before Fuentes, Kléber's near Zaragoza. Modesto then changed course, concentrating attacks on Mediana and Belchite south of Zaragoza on the road to Teruel and discarding the original plan of the Internationals who were to drive on to Zaragoza in lorries protected by tanks and armoured cars. After the spectacular victory at Quinto, Merriman feared a mutiny because logistics were breaking down, leaving the men without food or transport for two days.[26] Speed was of the essence to bring the impasse at Belchite to a conclusion. The British were directed to stop hostile reinforcements coming south from Mediana on their way to assist the defenders in Belchite. They were under 100 men after the fighting at Purburrel and some refused the order at first, recalcitrant and unhappy foot soldiers with fresh memories of Mosquito Hill.

O'Daire appealed to their communist loyalty and they reluctantly went forward.[27] The British formed a cordon on the hills around Mediana, successfully beating off fascist movements and forcing the enemy back into the town.[28] The German 11th Brigade played a key role in stopping Franco's troops from

Belchite attack, August–September 1937 (*Book of the XV Brigade*)

moving reinforcements to Belchite by defending the highest point in the arid landscape, Sillero (695 m), which overlooked Mediana and the railroad to Zaragoza.[29] The Lincoln, Dimitrov and 24th battalions moved towards Belchite, a town of symbolic significance for Franco, a battle site in the independence struggle against Napoleon – his Marshal Louis Suchet routed the Spaniards near the town in 1809 who then closed the town gates against him. Now it was being attacked once again by foreigners.

The region around the old settlement had been dominated by a conservative agricultural syndicate for decades and generally voted for the Right. Catholic influence in the town of 3,800 inhabitants was strong: three imposing churches built in the Baroque era along the main street: the parish church of San Martín de Tours, San Juan (Torre de Reloj) and San Rafael and its Dominican nunnery. The fourth, San Agustín of the Augustinian monks, was in the northwest corner beside the main town gate (Arco de la Villa).

The February 1936 elections brought change, and a Socialist mayor. He was shot by Falangists in July 1936, along with his wife, brother and over 170 sympathisers of the Republic.

Belchite was devastated in the August-September fighting of 1937. It was given martyr status by Franco, who visited it when it was recaptured in March 1938. Many of the ruins were subsequently knocked down for security reasons, as the townspeople did not move to the nearby Belchite Nuevo until 1964. Three Spanish brigades began their assault on 24 August, capturing the railway station and completing the encirclement of the town in the next two days. The ancient borough was under constant attack by artillery and Russian fighter planes. The defenders had built numerous tunnels, steel and concrete emplacements, street barricades and machine-gun nests in the churches and repelled the initial attacks.

On 1 September, the 15th Brigade (minus the British) marched from Codo towards Belchite. The Spaniards of the 24th stayed in reserve, the Slavs moved to the northwest, and the Lincolns passed through an ancient forest of olive trees before beginning a slight ascent through walled terraces in the late afternoon. They stopped within sight of San Agustín and its high bell-tower, and came under heavy fire from the church and the houses around it on the plaza. Captain Amlie ordered a retreat to a prepared trench but a number of his men did not hear the order and were pinned down when daylight broke on 2 September.

The exact geographical layout is difficult to reconstruct today because of the razed buildings. To the north a road ran west to Azaila, which the Americans had to cross, and south of it was a lane with an olive-oil factory or barn (accounts differ in the designation) on the left. The track continued into the courtyard of the Augustinian church and adjoining monastery of the monks, ending on the Plaza San Agustín. This complex of buildings and narrow streets had to be captured, as snipers and machine-gunners dominated the approaches. It was evidently the key point of the defence.

The second day was supposed to be the decisive one. The seminary at the other end of the town fell, the Dimitrovs had occupied the first houses near the main town gate and the British anti-tank battery shelled sniper positions around the church. The Americans were detailed to capture the Baroque edifice at all costs. The men were hungry and thirsty (the kitchen lorry did not arrive) and moved south over the terraces towards the Azaila road. They came under heavy fire, many were wounded, one platoon was virtually wiped out and a company commander killed.

Amlie refused to advance further, supported by Quigley Robinson, who told Nelson on the phone that they were also being shelled by their own artillery.[30] Steve Nelson scouted a way into the town on 2 September when he negotiated a dry gully (acequia de Becú) and reached the olive-oil factory at the back of the church, which was unoccupied.[31] It was soon filled by Americans who radiated out in separate attacks, skirmishing with the enemy. The defenders in the church ran out when the shells landed on the nave and apse and, when the barrage was lifted, rushed back through the main door on Plaza San Agustín to man their parapets and doorways. On 3 September Jim Woulfe from Co. Limerick, attacking in the church courtyard, was mortally wounded in the face and right shoulder by a grenade blast, and died that night in the hospital at Híjar.[32] His friend, Lieutenant Piet Nielson, adjutant of No. 1 Company, remembers the incident:

> Him and I stuck close together during the tough going in the years '33-37. We roomed together in Vancouver and helped each other out when we were able to get a bit of work. I tell you, it struck me pretty hard when Jim got it [...] War seemed completely to stun Jim up until the attack on Quinto. There he appeared to make up his mind to fight in the first ranks at every opportunity. During the attack on Belchite he was fatally wounded. He got it in the courtyard of the Belchite church when our group was engaged in the first assault for position of this stronghold (September 3rd).[33]

The following day the church finally fell into Republican hands, after immense pressure from General Walter and from the Government. Defence Minister Prieto had announced on 3 September that the town had been captured solely by Spaniards, and instructed General Pozas and Army Chief of Staff Rojo to issue bulletins with this 'fake news'. He was courting the professional officers and the anarchist military leaders, who were equally antagonistic towards communist units.[34] By 4 September, the Lincolns had already lost half their effective strength and, temporarily, their commander Amlie, who soon returned from hospital. The final assault was planned jointly by Wattis and squad leaders. It was launched by three groups.[35] The sixteenth-century San Agustín church had three entrances, east, west and south (main door), and above the nave on both sides were balconied galleries that led to the cloisters and the monks' quarters. The groups started a concerted assault, timing their arrival at the church when a barrage of shells and tank projectiles would cease, thus surprising the defenders. One group ran out from the olive-oil factory and was decimated by machine-gun fire. Another bunch of about 20 Lincolns emerged from a trench about 40 yards from the church and jumped into the Becú gully. The parapet on the other side was unoccupied because of the shelling and the Americans vaunted it, going in through San Agustín's west entrance and throwing hand-grenades at the fascists returning through the main door. Many of the IB attackers were hit defending the entrance because snipers were posted in the houses on the plaza. Later, a machine gun was brought up, which gave the Lincolns control of the church porch.[36] The third group also entered the church by a side door into a corridor. A machine-gun crew at the opposite end of the passage near the main door fired at once, bringing down three Lincolns. Their comrades went upstairs, broke through a wall leading to the gallery using picks and destroyed the machine-gun emplacement.[37] All three entrances were now manned by Internationals behind sandbags.

Savage fighting house-to-house continued for a further two days. All the Brigade staff joined the bombing parties. Most of the garrison finally surrendered (many had escaped through tunnels) on 6 September after Commissar Dave Doran had commandeered a propaganda truck with a loudspeaker. His message to the garrison was unequivocal: surrender now or die. His threat worked. Those who escaped in arms were hunted down in the olive groves and shot, but the majority realised that resistance was futile and crossed the barricades with hands raised. Belchite was a charnel house with up to 5,000 dead, their bodies either doused with petrol and burned for fear of epidemics, or afterwards interred in pits or under one of the pillars of the San Agustín church. The Americans shot snipers and officers, but the final killings were carried out by the 24th Battalion of the 15th IB. Carlist or Falange officers, hiding behind a human wall of terrified inhabitants, tried to escape, throwing grenades at the approaching mopping-up detail. It was a repeat of Villanueva de la Cañada. Not one of Franco's officers is said to have survived the desperate hand-to-hand fighting.[38]

The losses incurred by the 15th Brigade in the old municipality were heavy: 471 casualties, including 112 dead and 271 wounded.[39] On the last day of the battle, Nelson was hit by a sniper when he passed the open window in the olive-oil factory, and Lieutenant Wattis suffered multiple wounds from a hand-grenade when on a bombing sortie.[40] Both survived. Frank Ryan visited the charred town, collecting material for the battalion monthly newssheet *Our Fight*, and departed for Barcelona to have it printed there.[41]

Merriman was promoted to major for the Brigade's achievement at Belchite. He was contemptuous of Čopić ('scared stiff during air raid and the time we went into the town but he slanders Americans'),[42] and unduly harsh in judging the humane and hesitant Amlie, also holding O'Daire to be 'weak' and some of the British, expecting repatriation, to be 'watching themselves'.[43] Amlie was given indefinite sick leave and sent back to the States at the end of the year; likewise his commissar Robinson.[44] It seems that any officer who opposed the orders of the Brigade leadership, i.e. crossed swords with the martinet Čopić, was sooner or later removed. Merriman was learning how to play Brigade politics. Recriminations abounded in the wake of the failed offensive. On 6 September, to much publicity, General Pozas visited Belchite to confirm that the anarchist 153rd Mixed Brigade (24th Division, XII Army Corps) had taken the town on 3 September. Anarchist sources stated that the 15th Brigade had been withdrawn during the fighting for 'looting'. A bulletin issued by the Ministry for the Interior on 6 September praised a police brigade for the attacks on the seminary in Belchite but did not waste a single word on the Internationals.[45] Pozas blamed General Walter for the fiasco in Aragon: he had concentrated on secondary objectives and not the main one.[46] Walter countered with protests about the slanderous anarchist comments on the behaviour of the Internationals, and Modesto telegraphed a personal protest to Rojo. Russian advisers, it seems, stayed on the sidelines of the internal controversy.[47]

The Americans finally left Belchite on 9 September. On trucks or marching to and fro to improvised billets, the survivors of Belchite were disgruntled about the food and the high blood toll in their last action, and were asking why the good coordination of all arms at Quinto had not been replicated. They had marched off in a bitingly cold wind and dust storms. Their bivouac camp was later swamped after torrential rain in the hamlet of Almochuel, 'a tiny hideous village of about twelve or fourteen houses situated on the edge of a bleak, empty mesa.'[48] Merriman and Doran called battalion and company meetings to hear the complaints and General Walter gave a tough talk to the Americans.[49] Discontentment in the British battalion was more pronounced because a hard core of the depleted unit (under 100) wanted to return to Britain with Aitken and Cunningham. Eighteen riflemen refused to move off with the Brigade, and relented only when Čopić threatened them with arrest and transfer to an all-Spanish unit.[50] In mid-September the Brigade bade farewell to the tough Dimitrovs, who were sent to Kléber's 45th Division and later became part of the 129th Brigade.

## THE DEBACLE AT FUENTES DE EBRO

The 15th International Brigade moved constantly about Aragon in cold, wet weather before returning to Quinto to prepare for the attack on Fuentes de Ebro, the key to taking Zaragoza, in the second week of October. The operation was hastily prepared and proved to be one of the greatest self-induced disasters in the history of the Republican Army. The 15th Brigade was now a seasoned battle unit but was let down this time by the incompetence and bad staff-work of General Walter and his Russian advisors. Fuentes was 16 km upstream from Quinto, but about 4 km from the river, a town on a hill about 200 m above the plain. Once the brigades had taken it, so the unrealistic plan went, the men would move on to El Burgo de Ebro upriver. The approaches to Fuentes were pitted with deep gullies and were well fortified. The IB battalions were placed in a semi-circle south of the town: the British were to move into positions between the Ebro and the railway line, the Americans were to straddle it and the Canadians were to face the town from the south, separated from it by a wide plain and a deep gully in front of the first streets. This was the first engagement of the newly formed Mackenzie-Papineau battalion. American CP representatives in Spain had insisted that the recruits be given several months training at Tarazona before a baptism of fire.[51] They were commanded by the American Robert Thompson, with his fellow-countryman Joe Dallet as commissar.

The plan saw the involvement of about 40 Russian tanks (including the new heavy model BT-5) advancing over the plain, each carrying six members of the 24th Battalion on the hull, smashing the barbed wire and trenches that the bomb-wielding Spaniards on board would clear of the enemy. Unfortunately, no reconnaissance of the terrain had been carried out and Malcolm Dunbar of the anti-tank battery warned in vain that artillery fire had destroyed the water channels on the plain, making it muddy and unsuitable for tanks.[52]

On the evening of 12 October, a major from the division told Merriman that the attack would begin at noon the following day. Later, the Russian commander of the tank squadron arrived and conferred all night with the officers of the 15th Brigade. Robert Merriman 'felt bad about using the 24th in such a dangerous and complicated undertaking'.[53] His premonition was well-founded because the young Spaniards had not been trained for such a manoeuvre. The attack was so hastily prepared that company commanders were not issued with maps indicating enemy strongpoints.[54]

Traffic jams delayed the battalions reaching their trenches in the early hours of 13 October. The British were lucky to enter their positions in darkness, but the Americans were seen at dawn and subjected to heavy machine-gun fire. The Canadians were last to arrive, in full view of the enemy, and suffered severe casualties before the attack had begun at all. Their late arrival was due to a ridiculous decision by Dave Doran, the new Brigade Commissar, who had organised a meeting of the Mac-Paps to discuss the role of battalion commissar Dallet. He had been a stickler for discipline in Tarazona and was therefore highly unpopular. This meeting, on the eve of battle, went on all night. The chastened and rueful Dallet was given absolution.[55]

Around noon, a flight of R-5 Polikarpov Russian biplane light bombers flew over the Internationals and bombed the fascist lines. The tanks, which should have attacked immediately afterwards, were 90 minutes late, driving forward much too fast. Their bombing squads bounced off or were shot at by adjacent Spanish Republican troops who had not been informed of this new tactic. It was failing because the infantry now 'going over the top' were far behind the tanks and exposed on the open plain.

In the British battalion, Paddy O'Daire had been sent to Officers' Training School and the new leader was Harold Fry (who had returned to Spain after being captured at Jarama), assisted by commissar Eric Whalley. Both Fry and Whalley were killed just yards from their trench. The new American commander Phil Detro wisely pulled back his men, who had been advancing under heavy fire towards the barbed wire.

The Canadians suffered worst, Joe Dallet was killed instantly, his men falling around him like skittles. There was no natural cover and the survivors tried to dig in, scooping the hard Aragonese soil with their tin mess plates. They could see over two dozen Soviet tanks on fire near the trenches in front of the town and their crews being picked off as they jumped out. In the evening, some of the Canadians moved right to trenches on the rim of a ravine. They realised they could never enter the town for the ground rose steeply on the other side. Platoon leader Sergeant Andrew Molyneaux (Belfast) was wounded trying to cross the ravine.

A squad of Canadians went forward to guard the Austrian crews trying to repair the stalled tanks, but most of the vehicles were abandoned because of Moors on patrol. When enemy fire abated at dusk, the jumbled remnants of the Canadian and American battalions retreated to shallow trenches. When dawn broke and the firing on their positions resumed, the men hugged the ground, thirsty and hungry and using their mess plates to get down deeper. In the coming days Spanish sappers and labour battalion soldiers improved the trench systems.[56] On 19 October the action was called off, after the last unsuccessful attack, this time by an anarchist brigade. The Soviet tanks had received a severe mauling, not least by breaking into the narrow streets where they could not manoeuvre and were easy prey. Franco's officers alleged that 17 tanks had been captured and another half-dozen destroyed by anti-tank and grenade fire.[57] Several tanks never got that near the enemy trenches, getting stuck in the silt marshes near the river after ploughing through fields of maize.[58]

After the battle, the headquarters of the 15th Brigade gave their losses as about a quarter.[59] The 24th Battalion was virtually extinct: the Canadians had lost one third of their muster roll of 468 (60 fatalities and over 100 wounded), and American losses were 18 dead and 52 wounded.[60] At least eight non-Spaniards in the British battalion died.[61] A post-mortem was held shortly afterwards at Lécera, with separate meetings for officers and commissars. The commissars' assembly broke up after Doran had been escorted out of the building following a fiery 'political' speech. The word that went down the line was that 'the failure of artillery and airplane preparation had been caused by the sabotage of the Tank Corps commander.' That was true 'Bolshevik' reasoning, linking the responsibility for the catastrophe with adherents of the tank expert Marshal Tukhachevsky, who had been shot on Stalin's orders four months earlier.[62] In reality, the mistakes committed at Brunete were repeated during the thrust into Aragon and compounded by hasty and insufficient preparation: inability to control large formations of troops, bad coordination between tanks and infantry, inadequate artillery, lack of reserves and miserable logistics.

### TARAZONA TRAINING BASE

Still, the Brigades were gaining in proficiency, and a degree of professionalisation was attained by the autumn of 1937. Officers were now to be saluted and to eat separately from the men, which was annoying for some old-timers among the English-speakers used to addressing their superiors on familiar terms. The first 'casualty' of the new ruling was Ron Liversedge, a Yorkshireman wounded three times in World War One and newly arrived from Canada. When training with the American battalion at Tarazona, Liversedge was appointed lieutenant of the all-Canadian company by Merriman, first commander at the new training base, but handed back his command and reverted to the ranks because he disapproved of separate eating arrangements for commissioned officers.[63]

Tarazona was a drab town of 6,000 inhabitants on the plain of La Mancha 40 km north of Albacete. The peasants left for their strips of land on the outskirts at dawn and returned at dusk with their mules. They were dignified and friendly and there seems to have been little trouble between them and the 5,000 foreigners who underwent basic training between June 1937 and the closure of the base in April 1938. When Merriman went on the staff of the 15th Brigade, Major Allan Johnson took over. The consensus is that he was a strict and efficient commander. Training in the recruits' companies (now including Spaniards) lasted two to four months, but there were also specialist schools for non-commissioned officers, cartographers, machine-gunners, snipers, etc.

One rule causing much ridicule was Johnson's insistence that the men salute the Republican colours in the town square every time they passed the flag. Twenty-four men were put on a charge for disobeying the order in November, but the regulation was soon dropped.⁶⁴ The main billet was an unheated convent, others slept on the concrete floor of the school and all ate in the town cinema. Apart from the Irish from Canada, another 20 of their countrymen, new volunteers who had lived in Britain, drifted in during the second half of 1937. Reveille was at 5.30 a.m., followed by breakfast (coffee and a hunk of bread), parade, four hours of instruction, lunch, siesta, a further four hours of training (including Spanish classes), evening meal and lights out at 9 p.m.⁶⁵

Paddy O'Sullivan from Dublin, who had served in the Irish Army Volunteer Reserve and been wounded at Brunete, was put in charge of the recruits' company.⁶⁶ He was promoted to lieutenant in January 1938.⁶⁷ With constant new intakes, the number of men in training swelled to almost 900, organised in two battalions, by the end of November.⁶⁸ At the end of the year there were 28 Irish at Tarazona.⁶⁹ They could count on Johnny Power, who was promoted to lieutenant in October, as a sympathetic political commissar.⁷⁰

THE BRITISH AT REST AND THE BOOK OF THE XV BRIGADE

At the onset of winter, which coincided with a typhoid outbreak, the British were back in Mondéjar. After short leave O'Daire returned as battalion commander in November, but Frank Ryan, ever mindful of sparing Irish lives, insisted that O'Daire be sent to a school for higher officer training.⁷¹ He probably had to leave for other reasons. Čopić resented him since Purburrell, and O'Daire also had 'problems with the Commissar',⁷² but he was 'immensely popular' because of his 'rank and file' reflexes.⁷³ The main cause of his removal was the return of Fred Copeman. Harry Pollit wanted Copeman to be given a top job on the staff, but the proposal was rejected.⁷⁴ So the volatile Jarama commander took over the battalion on 23 November, and the controversial Wally Tapsell was appointed Battalion Commissar, temporarily.⁷⁵ O'Daire was sent as second in command to the training depot, describing his role there as the 'Tarazona rubber-stamp'. After two months on a senior staff course, O'Daire returned to the battalion as company commander in April 1938.⁷⁶

This reshuffling of cadres in Mondéjar rekindled old animosities. Bill Rust, the new representative of the CPGB in Spain, alleged that Copeman had an 'anti-Brigade' attitude, a general feeling among the 105 British and Irish, with Tapsell dissenting. Copeman therefore treated him with open contempt.⁷⁷ Walter Greenhalgh shared his commander's opinion of Tapsell, and got intentionally drunk so that he would not be able to give the address of welcome for the return of the commander and his commissar. With the memory of Tapsell's conduct at Brunete still fresh, Greenhalgh explained his dissatisfaction about the changes in the British unit, especially the retention of Aitken in Britain, to Frank Ryan, for whom he had collected material for *The Book of the XV Brigade*. Ryan concurred, adding, 'Yes, I know that, but you lost the battle in London. I'll think about it.' He was as good as his word, shortly afterwards securing captain's bars for Greenhalgh and his transfer as political commissar to the auto-park in Albacete.[78] Ryan himself was busy in compiling the book about the English-speaking volunteers, leading a team that included John Tisa and Lon Elliott (both editors of *Volunteer for Liberty*, the 15th Brigade newspaper) and Sandor Voros.[79] The Hungarian exile to America had been sent by Commissar Doran to assist Ryan and he had been assiduous since the summer in collecting American testimonies. He describes meeting Ryan and the political complications of their joint task:

> Frank Ryan was unmistakably Irish in the proud way he carried his bushy, gray-haired head, from his ruddy face and large hooked nose, and his six-foot-and-some robust figure... He gave me a rousing welcome and took me out 'to wet our gills' before we got to work.

They had several problems to solve: first, deal with the list of 'worthies' Dave Doran wanted prominently placed, and then string the missing chapters and the narrative together.[80] Second, the text had to please the brigades' top brass, not least Gallo, who wanted the Canadians highlighted.[81] Finally, the book, which stops at Fuentes, could have been printed before the end of 1937 were it not for the shortage of paper in Madrid. Oliver Green, a lithographer from Birmingham and a member of Ryan's staff, was sent to Barcelona to find high-quality paper.[82] That the book was completed in record time is also suggested by the fact that Ryan planned to be with his parents in Dublin for Christmas 1937, and that he intended to go to America afterwards.[83] The propaganda tour of the United States had been suggested by Dave Doran in a letter to Bill Lawrence, the CPUSA representative in Albacete, as early as October.[84] The printing delay kept Ryan in Madrid, and when the Brigades were rushed to Teruel on New Year's Eve, Voros convinced his Irish superior 'that he had seen enough action already and that it was my turn now; he was to stay in Madrid and see the book through the printshop while I was to return to the Brigade, which was fighting around Teruel.'[85] Ernest Hemingway called into the Commissariat to take Ryan and Voros out for a drink in December.[86] It was not all carefree entertainment, as Ryan confessed in a letter to Dublin:

> I think Hemingway is away. Haven't seen him since before Christmas. We had a few wild nights together. One night we were being shelled at the hotel. He wouldn't move to relatively less dangerous quarters downstairs. He went down

once, that night, to collect a dud shell, which he subsequently fitted up as a reading lamp! On such occasions I can't give any such exhibitions of courage. I've a standing objection to being under fire when I'm away from the front. At the front you get used to taking your chances. Behind the lines, I just can't take chances. The result is that in comparative safety my nerves are usually at their worst.[87]

Ryan got chilblains in the bitterly cold Madrid winter and gave another talk on Madrid radio, where the announcer introduced him as 'commander of the English battalion', only later to correct himself by saying that Ryan was leading the 'English brigade', a mistake Ryan took with ironic humour.[88] While hoping to see his family and friends in Dublin soon, Ryan had to await publication of his book. He was as committed as ever, as he wrote to Ireland in late February:

> I'd stop this war and all wars if I could. But I haven't got the power. Meanwhile, I'm under orders. And when I say that my orders will probably lead me home within a month, let no one try to panic me running away before then. I came to do my share of the job. When I'm told my share is done, and that I am to do something else, at home or elsewhere, I'll do it. But while I'm here, under orders, it's not helpful to be worrying unduly. More especially, when my present job is an easy one – compared with what others do.[89]

In Mondéjar, training was strenuous and the British battalion reached a complement of 150 when the Brunete casualties re-joined. There was a bout of spit-and-polish and general cleaning when it was announced that a delegation from the Labour Party was to visit. General Walter brought Clement Attlee, Ellen Wilkinson and other MPs to the hillside village on the evening of 6 December, where they were met in torchlight by a guard of honour and the local band on the square. The Labour leader got a rousing reception when he accepted that the famed No. 1 Company would carry his name.[90] The following weekend the battalion organized a fiesta with music, boxing and football (the British lost twice) for the villagers.[91]

In the preparatory phase of the Battle of Teruel, the British battalion left Mondéjar for the last time on 10 December and travelled to Alcañiz by train, but had to march the next 40 km into the mountains, to Mas de las Matas, north-east of Teruel. When that city fell on 17 December, spirits rose in the battalion, and a parade was held the following day, followed by a dance. During the festivities, the small figure of Harry Pollitt moved through the throng. He was on his third visit to the battalion, this time bringing letters, food parcels and much craved-for Player's cigarettes.

The Christmas dinner was truly Lucullan, with pork, wine and nuts, followed by British chocolate and plum pudding, deftly organised by the resourceful quartermaster Lieutenant 'Hooky' Walker. The 55 men of the closely knit Anti-Tank Battery pooled their funds and sat down to a meal of 'four big turkeys, five chickens with suitable garnishing', followed by champagne and plum pudding.[92] Some hardened fighters disliked the fact that the officers ate separately from the men, and noticed the even more opulent fare served up at Brigade Headquarters.[93] There was also a boisterous 'theatrical' evening, offering sketches and songs. When some of the latter were veering towards the obscene, an Irish singer was called for. He was on guard, but soon relieved, climbed the stage and sang 'The Death of James Connolly' and as an encore 'The Boy from the County Clare'.[94] The festivities over, the 15th Brigade was rushed to the Teruel front on New Year's Eve.

### BATTLE IN THE SNOW: TERUEL

The brigadistas associated Jarama with rain and storms, Brunete and Aragon with insufferable heat and thirst, but their defensive battle around Teruel was in the coldest weather they ever experienced in Spain. The city of 14,000 in the south of the poor and thinly populated province of the same name was traditionally the coldest spot in Spain, and the winter of 1937/38 was the severest for 20 years. This austere city, 930m above sea level, was divided by a long viaduct over the deep gorge of the Turia river and dominated by several hills: La Muela de Teruel to the south-west, and two to the north, El Muletón and Santa Bárbara, the latter of which was topped by a cemetery.

Once again, the reasons for the Republicans to attack it were partly strategic, partly political. To capture a provincial capital in the Francoist zone would be a propaganda coup, but the more compelling argument was the value of a pre-emptive strike against Franco's new Army of Manoeuvre, which was planning another thrust against Madrid from the north-east, starting from Zaragoza through Guadalajara. Furthermore, the territory in fascist hands west of Teruel was in Guadalajara province. The Guadalajara front was guarded by the Republic's IV Corps, commanded by the anarchist Cipriano Mera. One of his men crossed the lines and reached Aragon where he learned that there was a massive troop build-up between Zaragoza and Catalayud, i.e. on the highway going south-west to Gualdajara and Madrid. Mera duly reported to Miaja in Madrid, prompting Rojo to drop his revived plans of an offensive in Estremadura.

Rojo's plan, employing 40,000 soldiers and four army corps, was to encircle Teruel as soon as possible. He believed it was lightly held, predicting an 'offensive-defensive' battle and hoping to gain a foothold for further attacks.[95] It was a high-risk undertaking because Franco's Army of Manoeuvre was not far away and his forces had superiority in artillery and aircraft. The town-dwellers – most were escorted out of the embattled city to Valencia on Prieto's orders – were cowered even before the fighting started. In the early months of the war the western part of Teruel province fell to the rebel military. The fascist reign of terror between July 1936 and the early post-war years claimed over 1,000 lives in the town. One of the first mass-executions was on Plaza del Torico, the main square, in late August 1936: a Falangist danse macabre to musical accompaniment.[96]

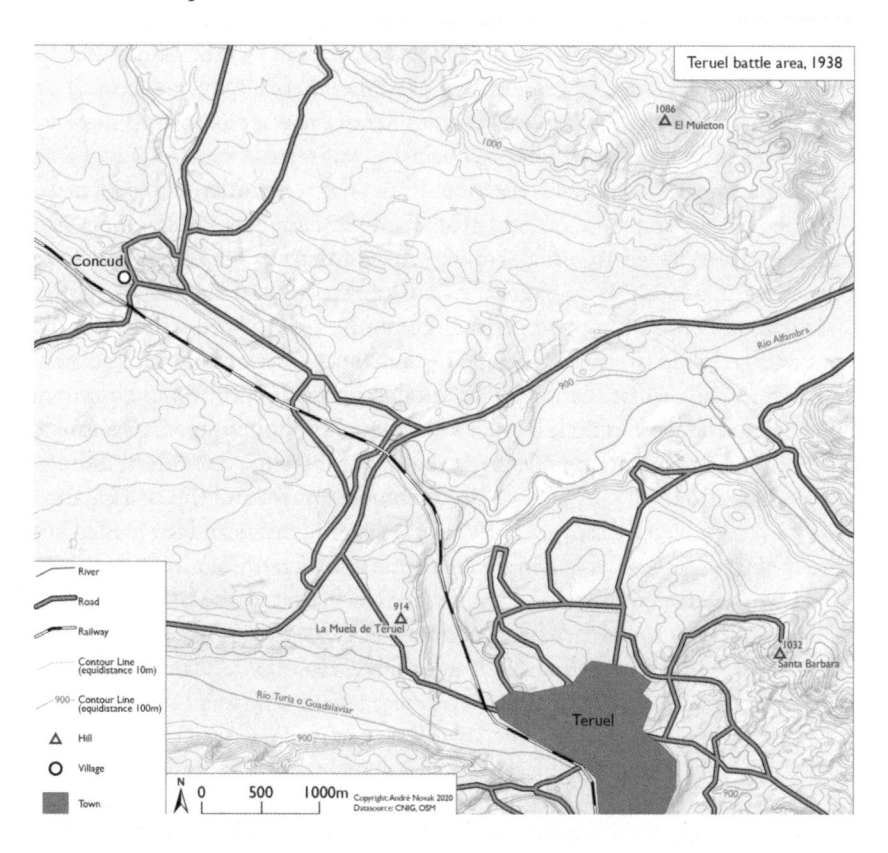

Teruel battle area, 1938 (courtesy of André Novak)

The Republican forces commenced the assault in snow flurries on 15 December 1937, gaining the element of surprise because neither aircraft nor artillery were used. The encirclement was completed by the evening. La Muela fell on 18 December and the next day Prieto and Rojo arrived with a convoy of foreign journalists, making the city a feature of international press headlines. Fighting was now concentrated in the city centre, by street and house, attacks led by dinamiteros, while the core of the 4,000 defenders were holed up, with hostages, in the main municipal and ecclesiastical buildings.

The Republican Government claimed the city had fallen on Christmas Eve, but Colonel Rey d'Harcourt, the town commandant, did not officially surrender until 7 January. By that time Franco's counter-offensive was well under way. The dictator dithered until 23 December: he was counselled by his Italian and German advisers to go ahead with the Guadalajara offensive, but although Teruel was of little strategic value, as the main road through it went from Zaragoza to Valencia and not to Madrid, his amour propre had been offended and he was not prepared to allow his enemies to take, and hold, one of his provincial seats. Bad weather prevented rebel movement until 29 December, when the biggest artillery barrage of the war to date was directed at Republican positions. When La Muela was retaken by Navarrese troops on the last day of the year, the International Brigades were ordered to the front.

They started out in a blizzard that was to last four days, travelling over winding, ice-covered mountain roads where trucks broke down and were pushed over precipices to break the 60 km traffic jam on the way from Valencia to Teruel. Dropped off at different half-destroyed hamlets, some Internationals had to sleep in the open, others on the back of open trucks or in ruins or, in the case of the fortunate ones, in barns. Frostbite was common, and the men converted their blankets into ponchos, hoping to keep warm by constant movement. It was a defensive battle for them from the start, often in exposed positions on cliff faces. The machine-gunners and the British anti-tank battery proved their proficiency, while the Americans and the Canadians used their scouting skills to disturb enemy positions in night raids.

The first action of the Internationals was an attack by the 11th Brigade on La Muela on 5-6 January. The elevation was shaped like a round cake with sheer cliffs. The Germans and Austrians gained a foothold, storming trenches with the bayonet and taking 240 prisoners. With the 11th under extreme pressure from counterattacks, the 15th IB was sent to their aid on 14 January. The Canadians placed themselves on La Muela and adjoining hills, their machine guns on a cliff; the British Maxim crews also sought an advantageous position over one of the precipices of Santa Bárbara. The Americans were posted within the town, where Commissar Fred Keller, a non-Communist and a Catholic, persuaded the nuns to vacate the lunatic asylum and climb on the trucks to Valencia with their charges.[97] It was still relatively quiet on the front to the north of the town, save for the sniping over long distances. One sniper hit and wounded the US commander Phil Detro, a lanky, languid Texan who professed no left-wing views other than admiration for FDR. He died in hospital in Murcia some weeks later.

The 15th Brigade was under strong fire from 17 January. The weather had cleared for Franco's air force to bomb and strafe, and his gunners now had a clear view. The Canadian and British Maxim teams and Dunbar's anti-tank men broke up attacks, but the enemy persisted, foolishly sending cavalry towards the railway tunnel near the confluence of the Guadalaviar and Alfambra rivers on the valley floor. Many Moorish riders went down in murderous fire from machine guns manned by the Mac-Pap HQ staff, others wheeled and retreated, only to then come under a hail of bullets from the Maxims of the Mac-Paps and the British.[98] The 11th Brigade was literally blasted off El Muletón the next day. When Spanish marines fell back, leaving the valley open, the three British infantry companies descended from Santa Bárbara, crossed the river and plugged the gap on the open flank of the Mac-Paps. The British spent the night digging in, and suffered heavy losses from artillery fire on 20 January. Bob Clark from his machine-gun emplacement had a bird's eye view:

> Suddenly what looked like black ants came crawling up the valley evidently intent on occupying those forward positions but they had forgotten about us. [. . .] The blowing of whistles which the enemy officers used as a kind of signal, made it all too real. We suddenly sprang to life on the orders of Cornwallis and in a few seconds had a perfect bead on the advancing enemy. Our heavy gun opened fire and a hail of lead hit the ground a few yards in front of the advancing Fascists, a slight movement of the gun sights and dozens of men collapsed and died. The enemy staggered. At the same time the Canadians on the valley heights opposite opened up with all they had. In a few minutes the valley was completely deserted except for a few score of black objects to testify to the enemy's terrible mistake. We kept on firing for quite a long time. How exhilarating it all was. I felt almost ashamed of myself when I remembered afterwards how full of joy I felt, how exalted, how terrible. How near we all are to animals. . .Yet when I thought of what happened to our lads [British No. 1 Company] earlier in the day, I excused myself. This war was like all wars: kill or be killed. Dead silence followed.[99]

About half of the Spaniards in the Canadians' Second Company deserted, but the fragile frontline held until the 15th Brigade was relieved on 3 February by El Campesino's division. The British had lost about a third of their strength through death, wounds and sickness. Twenty-one men of the battalion (now named the 57th) had died, thirteen alone from No. 1 Company.[100] Among the 18 men killed on 20 January were Patrick Glacken from Donegal and Sergeant David Walsh, originally from Ballina, Co. Mayo, mortally wounded by a shell-burst in his trench. The losses of the Canadians (60th) were the highest in the Brigade at 250, and both the American (58th) and the Spanish (59th) battalions suffered about 80 casualties.[101]

The battalions of the 15th Brigade, on their way to bases near Madrid, were called back to the Teruel area to stem the fascist onslaught – the last Republican troops left the town on 22 February. The English-speakers and the remnants of the 11th Brigade, with the Spanish battalions, were sent over 70 km north to carry out a diversionary attack around Segura de Los Baños, a Republican-held village of stone houses surrounded by oak and pine woods over a river valley. A series of hills dominated the valley to the south and the approaches to Vivel de Rio Martín, the next village in fascist territory. There three roads met, and its capture, so it was hoped, would draw enemy forces away from the Teruel pocket.

The operation was hastily conceived and executed in appalling cold weather. Discontent in the Brigade arose because of chaotic transport arrangements, especially among the Canadians who felt Commissar Doran expected them, once more, to sleep in the open. There was no hot food, and the men consumed their iron rations.[102] When the units finally got into position, they hid in stone barns and stayed out of sight during the day. With the help of local peasant guides, the Americans were to climb and capture Pedigrossa, the Canadians Atalaya, while the British were to move south to heights dominating Vivel.

On the night of 16 February the men crept forward in a snowstorm. The Canadians captured their objective in the manner of a Western Front trench raid. The resistance to the Americans was fiercer, but they, too, took the enemy trenches. An assault of the Mac-Paps on a third hill failed. Counterattacks followed the next day. Bombing from the air produced few casualties among the men dug in on the wooded slopes, but wrecked the back area where divisional and Brigade staff were posted. As at Teruel, well-positioned machine-gun crews stopped attacks of Franco's infantry. Bob Clark witnessed the shooting down of a Caproni bomber by Republican fighters and was cheered by the troves of food, clothing and equipment left when the 130 prisoners were led away.[103]

On the night of 19 February, the Brigade was rushed away to Teruel, but the men saw no more action and were finally sent to Lécera, near Belchite, where they tried to keep warm in their stone-built quarters. At the end of the Segura action all four battalions were in line and could have captured Vivel, but the order was not given because there were no reserves to hold it. In one of the counterattacks of the British battalion, Sergeant Frank Duffy O'Brien from Co. Louth was killed.[104] The losses incurred in this near-forgotten diversion were not inconsiderable: 31 mortalities and almost 100 wounded. The capture of three trench mortars and seven machine guns, rifles, grenades and shells was hardly recompense for the sacrifice during an attack that, in the end, changed nothing.[105]

## NOTES

1. RGASPI, f. 545, o.3, d. 435, ll. 72–4.
2. Ibid., ll. 73–4; www.merrimandiary.com/2014/08/03/. Accessed 15 June 2020.
3. RGASPI, f. 545, o.3, d. 435, l. 75.
4. www.merrimandiary.com/2014/08/13/. Accessed 15 June 2020.
5. www.merrimandiary.com/2014/08/15. Accessed 15 June 2020.
6. RGASPI, f. 545, o. 6, d. 575, l. 122.
7. www.merrimandiary.com/2014/05/21. Accessed 15 June 2020.
8. RGASPI, f. 545, o. 6, d. 545, ll. 4, 10.
9. The English translation of the decree is published in Michael O'Riordan, *Connolly Column: The Story of the Irishmen who Fought in the Ranks of the International Brigades in the National-Revolutionary War of the Spanish People* (Dublin, 1979), pp 217–20.
10. Hugh Thomas, *The Spanish Civil War* (London, 2012) pp 775–7.
11. Andreu Castells, *Las Brigadas Internacionales de la Guerra en España* (Barcelona, 1974), pp 263–5.
12. Ronald Radosh, Mary R. Habeck, and Grigory Sevostianov (eds), *Spain Betrayed: The Soviet Union and the Spanish Civil War* (New Haven and London, 2001), p. 240.
13. Ibid., pp 241–8.
14. Ibid., pp 253–9.
15. Based on the figures in: RGASPI, f. 545, o. 2, d. 108, l. 208.
16. RGASPI, f. 495, o. 205, d. 229, ll. 147–75 (report of Wilhelm Zaisser).
17. Líster maintains that it was an oral command because Prieto did not want to put it in writing (Enrique Líster, *Unser Krieg* (East Berlin, 1972), pp 204–6).
18. Thomas, *Spanish Civil War*, pp 723–5; Líster, *Unser Krieg*, pp 204–20.
19. Radosh, Habeck, *Spain Betrayed*, pp 353–7; Castells, *Las Brigadas*, pp 275–7.
20. Antony Beevor, *The Battle for Spain: the Spanish Civil War 1936–1939* (London, 2006), p. 298.
21. Bill Alexander, *British Volunteers for Liberty: Spain 1936–39* (London, 1982), p. 149; Arthur Landis, *The Abraham Lincoln Brigade* (New York, 1968), p. 272.
22. Alexander, *British Volunteers*, pp 148–9.
23. Landis, *The Abraham Lincoln Brigade*, pp 276–80.
24. www.merrimandiary.com/2014/08/25/. Accessed 15 June 2020; Baxell, *Unlikely Warriors*, p. 269.
25. Peter N. Carroll, *The Odyssey of the Abraham Lincoln Brigade: Americans in the Spanish Civil War* (Stanford, 1994), pp 155–6; Harry Fisher, *Comrades: Tales of a Brigadista in the Spanish Civil War* (Lincoln, Ne, 1999), p. 77.
26. www.merrimandiary.com/2014/08/27/. Accessed 15 June 2020.
27. Richard Baxell, *Unlikely Warriors: the British in the Spanish Civil War and the Struggle against Fascism* (London, 2012), p. 269.
28. Walter Gregory, *The Shallow Grave: A Memoir of the Spanish Civil War* (London, 1986), p. 81.
29. Hanns Maaßen (ed.), *'Brigada Internacional ist unsere Ehrenname': Erlebnisse ehemaliger deutscher Spanienkämpfer. Ausgewählt und eingeleitet von Hanns Maaßen*, Bd. 2 (Berlin, 1974), pp 44–6, 53–4.

30. Arthur Landis, *The Abraham Lincoln Brigade* (New York, 1968), pp 288–9.
31. Steve Nelson, *The Volunteers* (East Berlin, 1958), pp 212–3; Cecil Eby, *Between the Bullet and the Lie: American Volunteers in the Spanish Civil War* (New York-Chicago-San Francisco, 1968), pp 161–2.
32. Victor Howard (with Mac Reynolds), *The Mackenzie-Papineau Battalion: The Canadian Contingent in the Spanish Civil War* (Ottawa, 1969), p.137; William C. Beeching, *Canadian Volunteers. Spain 1936–1939* (Regina, 1989), p. 68.
33. RGASPI, f. 545, o. 3, d. 469, ll. 36–7.
34. Castells, *Las Brigadas*, p. 282.
35. www.merrimandiary.com/2014/09/03/. Accessed 15 June 2020.
36. RGASPI, f. 545, o. 2, d. 164, ll. 54–58; f. 545, o. 3, d. 469, ll. 6–8.
37. Howard, *Mackenzie-Papineau Battalion*, p. 137.
38. Landis, *The Abraham Lincoln Brigade*, pp 300–3.
39. RGASPI, f. 545, o. 3, d. 454, l. 30.
40. Landis, *The Abraham Lincoln Brigade*, p. 299.
41. www.merrimandiary.com/2014/09/07/. Accessed 15 June 2020.
42. www.merrimandiary.com/2014/09/29/. Accessed 15 June 2020.
43. www.merrimandiary.com/2014/08/31/. Accessed 15 June 2020.
44. Eby, *Between the Bullet and the Lie*, pp 165–6.
45. www.merrimandiary.com/2014/09/09/. Accessed 15 June 2020.
46. Beevor, *Battle for Spain*, pp 299–300.
47. Radosh, Habeck, and Sevostianov, *Spain Betrayed*, pp 481–2.
48. Marion Merriman, Warren Lerude, *American Commander: Robert Hale Merriman and the Abraham Lincoln Brigade* (Reno, 1986), p. 167.
49. www.merrimandiary.com/2014/09/11. Accessed 15 June 2020. See also entry for following day.
50. www.merrimandiary.com/2014/09/15/. Accessed 15 June 2020.
51. Eby, *Between the Bullet and the Lie*, p. 169.
52. Castells, *Las Brigadas*, pp 284–5.
53. www.merrimandiary.com/2014/10/12/. Accessed 15 June 2020.
54. Eby, *Between the Bullet and the Lie*, p. 179.
55. Ibid.
56. Ronald Liversedge (edited by David Yorke), *Mac-Pap: Memoir of a Canadian in the Spanish Civil War* (Vancouver, 2013), pp 87–96.
57. Landis, *The Abraham Lincoln Brigade*, p. 318.
58. Maaßen, *Brigada Internacional*, pp 46–9.
59. RGASPI, f. 545, o. 3, d. 454, l. 42.
60. Ibid., l. 37; Landis, *The Abraham Lincoln Brigade*, p. 320.
61. RGASPI, f. 545, o. 3, d. 488, l. 192.
62. Howard, *MacKenzie-Papineau Battalion*, p. 151.
63. Liversedge, *Mac-Pap*, pp 74,78.
64. RGASPI, f. 545, o. 2, d. 259, l. 199; Harry Fisher, *Comrades: Tales of a Brigadista in the Spanish Civil War* (Lincoln, Na, 1999), p. 88.
65. RGASPI, f. 545, o. 2, d. 261, l. 131.
66. RGASPI, f. 545, o. 3, d. 257, l. 341.

67. RGASPI, f. 545, o. 3, d. 264, l. 20.
68. RGASPI, f. 545, o. 3, d. 263, l. 217.
69. RGASPI, f. 545, o. 3, d. 262, l. 303.
70. RGASPI, f. 545, o. 3, d. 265, l. 212.
71. Alexander, *British Volunteers*, p. 159.
72. RGASPI, f. 545, o. 6, d. 444, l. 21.
73. Ibid., l. 29.
74. Alexander, *British Volunteers*, p. 159.
75. RGASPI, f. 545, o. 3, d. 428, ll. 90, 103.
76. RGASPI, f. 545, o. 6, d. 444, l. 21; 545, o. 6, d. 89, l. 43.
77. Baxell, *Unlikely Warriors*, pp 275–6.
78. IWM, Interview 11187, Walter Greenhalgh, reels 6 and 7.
79. John Tisa, *Recalling the Good Fight: An Autobiography of the Spanish Civil War* (South Hadley, Mass., 1985), p. 7; RGASPI, f. 545, o. 1, d. 61, l. 5.
80. Sandor Voros, *American Commissar* (New York, 1961), pp 368–9.
81. RGASPI, f. 545, o. 1, d. 5, l. 12.
82. RGASPI, f. 545, o. 3, d. 436, ll. 64–6; f. 545, o. 6, d. 142, ll. 20, 101.
83. ROR, Frank Ryan to Helen O'Reilly, 27 October 1937.
84. RGASPI, f. 545, o. 3, d. 441, ll. 95–6.
85. Voros, *American Commissar*, p. 369.
86. Ibid., p. 404.
87. ROR, Frank Ryan to Helen O'Reilly, 20 February 1938.
88. ROR, Frank Ryan to Gerald O'Reilly, 2 November 1937.
89. Seán Cronin, *Frank Ryan: The Search for the Republic* (Dublin, 1980), pp 129–30.
90. Alexander, *British Volunteers*, p. 160.
91. Bob Clark, *No Boots to My Feet: Experiences of a Britisher in Spain, 1937–38* (Stoke-on-Trent, 1984), p. 33; Baxell, *Unlikely Warriors*, pp 276–7; William Rust, *Britons in Spain: The History of the British Battalion of the XVth International Brigade* (London, 1939), pp 101–2.
92. Fred Thomas, *To Tilt at Windmills: A Memoir of the Spanish Civil War* (East Lancing, Mi, 1996), p. 61.
93. Baxell, *Unlikely Warriors*, pp 278–9.
94. Labour History Museum, Manchester, CP/IND/Poll/2/5.
95. Beevor, *Battle for Spain*, pp 313–6.
96. Paul Preston, *The Spanish Holocaust: Inquisition and Extermination in Twentieth Century Spain* (London, 2012), pp 449–53.
97. Landis, *The Abraham Lincoln Brigade*, pp 366–8.
98. Howard, *Mackenzie-Papineau Battalion*, p. 168.
99. Clark, *No Boots*, pp 51–2.
100. Baxell, *Unlikely Warriors*, pp 283–4.
101. Landis, *The Abraham Lincoln Brigade*, p. 382.
102. Ibid., pp 389–91.
103. Clark, *No Boots*, pp 54–7.
104. O'Riordan, *Connolly Column*, p. 111.
105. RGASPI, f. 545, o. 3, d. 488, ll. 200–3.

# NINE

# RETREAT AND CAPTURE

Their withdrawal from the Teruel pocket on 22 February 1938 left the Republican forces in a sorry state: they had suffered around 60,000 casualties (Franco's detachments lost 40,000) and a grave loss of equipment (lorries, artillery, armoured cars and tanks) that they could not replace. The Republican pilots were outnumbered and outfought and faced further decline when the Soviets removed many of them for Chinese operations and did not replace aircraft losses.[1] That over 7,000 Republican soldiers were captured, and over 500 square miles of territory lost, also had a demoralising effect on the best units in the People's Army.[2] The 15th Brigade returned to rest and regroup in familiar territory, the lower Aragon, just south of the Ebro in Azaila and within short distance of the battlefields of the previous autumn: the small towns and villages near Belchite.

The weather improved and a deceptive sense of security prevailed; prominent officers such as Čopić (Brigade Commander) and Doran (Brigade Political Commissar) went on leave, as did leading figures in the American battalion. On 6 March the Americans entered ruined Belchite, sleeping in wrecked buildings still exuding the stench of unburied dead. Republican high command expected a new offensive of the fascists 70 miles to the south around Teruel. Robert Merriman, Chief of Staff of the Brigade, was led to believe his men were part of a third or fourth defensive line.[3] No serious fortification work had been carried out in the period since the capture of Belchite in September and, as that town had sacrificial icon status for Franco, it was a high priority in his planned offensive. The front itself was held by Spanish conscripts and there were no reserve units in place.

### THE FASCIST BREAKTHROUGH TO THE SEA

Lower Aragon is largely bleak and flat (now dotted with wind turbines) and provided good ground for tanks. The massive assault launched by Spanish insurgent units and Italian troops on 9 March had two prongs: one north of the Ebro thrusting towards the area around Lérida, the second south of the river downstream to the Mediterranean near Tortosa. Franco had 150,000 troops at his disposal, nearly 700 artillery pieces and 600 aircraft.[4] The Republicans could muster only about 35,000 dispirited and badly armed soldiers, 60 planes and under 100 field guns.[5] The Internationals were directly in the path of the southern thrust, which first broke Republican lines at Fuendetodos, 20 km west of Belchite. The 15th Brigade battalions were rushed in from Lécera and placed in defensive positions: the British astride the Belchite–Mediana road, the Canadians at Azuara and the Americans on

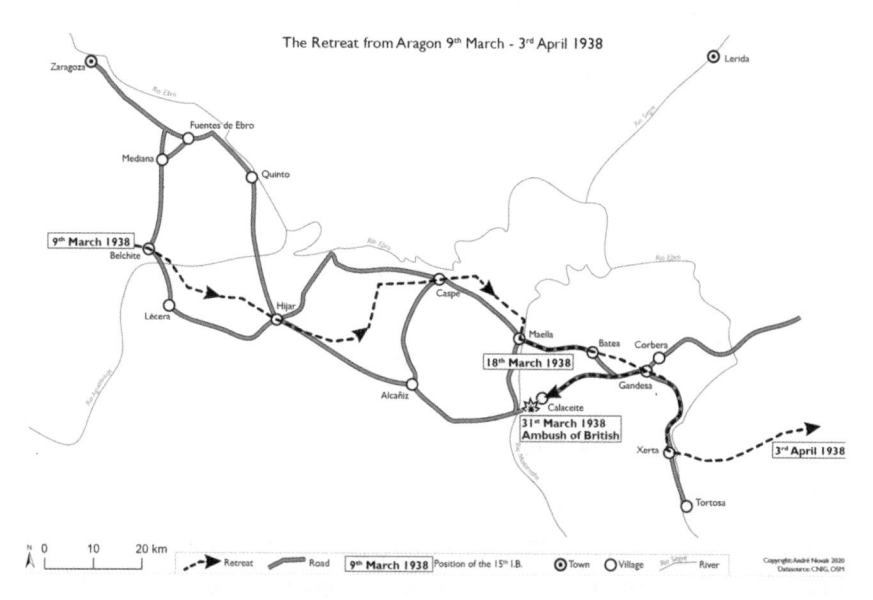

The March Retreats, 1938 (courtesy of André Novak and Diarmuid Duggan)

commanding hills to the west of Belchite. Because of the immense fire power of the attackers and the constant stream of Republican units moving to the rear, the 15th Brigade units realised they were the last flimsy defence. The Americans placed their command post in a monastery on a hill to the west of Belchite (Santuario de Nuestra Señora del Pueyo), where a direct hit killed or seriously wounded leading cadres of the battalion, and another shell sent the unit's arms dumps skywards. Driven back into Belchite, the Internationals had to fight off infiltrating Moorish troops. The town was soon vacated, with the British being the last to leave, hurrying eastwards.

Typical of the headlong retreat was that all communications broke down the Republican army did not possess radio sets. The ferocious barrages destroyed telephone lines so that for days the Brigade's units lost contact with division and corps, their own headquarters and even other battalions. Kitchen lorries did not appear, nor did munition supplies. The Brigade soon lost its three anti-tank pieces, numerous Maxim machine guns were destroyed or had to be abandoned in the gruelling trek; men lost their units and were never seen again, others turned up unexpectedly after slipping through fascist encirclement. The retreat was intercepted by delaying actions, usually short, sharp encounters when the Internationals, under constant attack by strafing Fiat and Messerschmitt fighters and artillery, fired from higher positions, albeit merely with rifles and a few Maxims. The next defensive stand was supposed to be the town of Híjar but it was already in enemy hands, and so too was the next position, the fortress-like Alcañiz towering over the Guadaloupe river. At this stage a number of English-speaking Internationals struck south in the direction of Gandesa, the gateway through the mountains to the sea, but the main group headed for Caspe and arrived there on 15 March. Many of the men had not slept for three nights and were glad to rest and receive some food and weaponry.

The American Brigade Commissar Dave Doran assumed command on the orders of Luigi Longo (Head of the IB Commissariat). This was a telling comment on how the Brigades were run, seeing that Doran, erstwhile organiser for the Young Communist League, had no military experience. Because of his autocratic manner he made enemies easily.[6] In Caspe, however, he proved a rallying-point, believing the town could be held. There was fierce street fighting against enemy infantry and tanks, but the IB men were forced once more to fall back. In the general confusion, lieutenants Sam Wild, Bobby Walker and some others from the British battalion were taken prisoner but, using their fists, boots and elbows, managed to escape.[7] The fighting strength of the British battalion was now down to 20, but was soon boosted again to over 600 with the arrival of recruits (the Albacete and Tarazona bases were closed down) and volunteers curtailing their recuperation in mid-March. The British battalion could rest in Batea for ten days and on 26 March they moved to Corbera, a village 5 km east of Gandesa, and Wild, now promoted to captain, went on short leave to Barcelona. A further batch of 626 recruits from Tarazona arrived in the town.[8]

Doran provoked his antagonists in Corbera. At an early stage in the retreats he had the Irishman Pat Read, a highly popular and former leader of the Brigade's telephonist and linesmen squad (transmisiones) from October 1937, dismissed from the 15th Brigade.[9] After Belchite the previous September, Read had been commended for bravery – 'many comrades owe him their lives because of his intelligence and courage.'[10] During the Teruel battle he lost his command and was degraded to private soldier status for not complying with an order.[11] Doran's directive was not because Read was suffering from tuberculosis and spitting blood, but on account of the strong anti-Stalinist views he expressed as an old 'Wobbly' (American syndicalist). He was, said Doran to Harry Fisher, Read's friend, 'doing a lot of harm, always talking against the Communist Party'.[12] A second incident was a result of the widespread criticism levelled at the Brigade leadership because of the military fiasco and the hellish privations the men had suffered since 9 March. Doran called a meeting in Corbera's cinema, hoping to stage his own show-trial of purported cowards and deserters who deserved the firing squad. Jack Cooper, a young Communist from Cleveland, Ohio (later decorated for his leadership on the Ebro and given officer rank), was now accused of abandoning his machine gun, and Doran was calling for his death and that of others. Cooper had brought the sorry remnants of his unit to Corbera – bearded, emaciated and disorientated figures still holding the barrels of their disabled Maxims. There followed violent protests from the floor. Sandor Voros, adjutant to Doran, who had encountered Cooper during the long flight from Belchite, objected to the farce and was told he would have to witness the executions at divisional headquarters. The yelling match was terminated by their superior Vladimir Čopić, who, mindful of the good press the brigades enjoyed among some leading American journalists – Herbert Matthews of the *New York Times* and the writer Ernest Hemingway often visited the battalion at the front – argued that any executions would damage their cause in America and France. Doran was thus overruled, and the arraigned men were given a 'second chance'.[13]

Frank Ryan, having put *The Book of the XV Brigade* 'to bed' with the printers in Madrid, now arrived and 'nearly had a row' with the dictatorial Doran. The American tried unsuccessfully to prevent Ryan from talking to Čopić and, when the audience took place, the Commander absolved the editor from any blame in not submitting the proofs first. His only objection was that the book 'didn't state the correct I.B. line'. Ryan refrained from remarking that he had not been informed that 'the line' had changed since Christmas and was cheered by the promise that Čopić would talk to Gallo (Luigi Longo) to speed up publication. Ryan now attached himself as assistant commissar to the British Battalion, which 'was doing their best to invent little jobs to keep me going'.[14] On their way to the front in mid-March, some Irish volunteers tried to persuade Frank Ryan to stay at the base in Albacete:

> Before leaving for the front a number of the lads which included Jim Regan of Cork known as 'The Farmer' and myself [probably Johnny Power] went on a deputation to Frank to appeal to him to stay back, as he had been advised to do so

by the doctors. We pointed out to him the value he would be at home in Ireland; we argued with him for over an hour, pointing out the loss he would be politically in Ireland, where a few months previously he had been successful in uniting all sections of the people of Dublin in a mighty Anti-Imperialist demonstration. It was no use, his final reply was, 'wherever the lads are I will be with them'.[15]

Ryan, however, was unarmed and remained so; he had no executive function in the battalion but was probably seen as a boost to morale in a unit that badly needed it. He was highly popular and a good man to have in a tight situation.

### DISASTER AT CALACEITE

The second round of the fascist offensive in Aragon started on 30 March. The British were detailed to march through Gandesa on the road to Alcañiz, beside Líster's 11th Division. The Americans and the Canadians attacked north and west of Batea.[16] The British with Ryan (the battalion now tallied 585 officers and men but the majority was Spanish)[17] did not know where the front was and moved carefully towards the town of Calaceite situated on a rocky hill topped by a church. They camped in olive groves a kilometre and a half to the east of the first houses on orders of the Corps. George Fletcher, commander in place of Wild who did not return until 2 April, received an order by dispatch rider at 2.30 a.m. on 31 March to move west, but neither Fletcher nor Battalion Commissar Tapsell could find the point on the map. Ever the careful soldier, Fletcher (with the experience of 15 years in the Lancashire Fusiliers) sent his cartographer Lieutenant Bee into Calaceite to gather more precise information from Líster's 100th Brigade. As the Spaniards were vague about the front line, Fletcher went to talk to them in person. The Líster officers were uncooperative, also refusing to supply Fletcher with a runner to bring him to the front trenches. So Lieutenant Bee was sent to corps HQ and returned with a guide who said that the British were to continue through Calaceite and halt 4 km to the west and occupy some trenches behind a river bridge. The enemy, the corps lieutenant said, were about 1 km beyond the trenches. The bitter truth was that the Líster had retreated with tanks and artillery and had not informed the high command. The front was wide open and the British were walking into a trap as Mussolini's units were hurrying from Alcañiz in the west. They avoided the main roads, finding their way towards Calaceite over agricultural tracks.

As it was now approaching 5 a.m. and enemy aircraft could be expected at the break of day, Fletcher roused the men and placed No. 1 Company at the

Frank Ryan in the kitchen of R. M. Fox and Patricia Lynch, no date (courtesy of National Library of Ireland)

Showers at Jarama, March 1937. Facilities like these were rare and Brigadistas complained regularly about living conditions at the front (courtesy of Peter O'Connor)

The CPGB's suspicion of the IRA was set aside for the war and the *Daily Worker* lionised the Irish Brigadistas (courtesy of Emmet O'Connor)

Clockwise from the top left: Paddy O'Daire (Donegal); John O'Shea (Waterford); Richard McAleenan (Down); Bob Clark (Liverpool). The Brigadistas saw themselves as a citizen army, but in public perception abroad, the motley dress of Republican troops contrasted unfavourably with the uniform appearance of the Fascists (courtesy of RGASPI)

Jim Woulfe (courtesy of Amina Parkes)

San Agustín Church, Belchite, after the battle. Woulfe was mortally wounded in the cloisters on the right (courtesy of Belchite Tourist Office)

Zaragoza, 4 April 1938. Fascist officers and propagandists talk to the captured members of the International Brigades (courtesy of Archivo Capúa)

Zaragoza, 4 April 1938. A foreign journalist (possibly Kim Philby) talks to the captured members of the International Brigades (courtesy of Archivo Capúa)

San Pedro de Cardeña monastery near Burgos today (courtesy of Barry McLoughlin)

8 July 2004. Unveiling the Waterford IB memorial: Mayor Cllr Seamus Ryan, Michael O'Riordan and Jack Jones (British Batt.), and Moe Fishman (Lincoln Batt.) (courtesy of John Power Photography

Zaragoza, 5 April 1938. Frank Ryan, photographed on the orders of the Francoist High Command (courtesy of Archivo Capúa)

**IRISH FRIENDS OF THE SPANISH REPUBLIC**
(Women's Aid Committee)

# A MEMORIAL MEETING
for

## JACK NALTY and LIAM McGREGOR

Who fell fighting for Liberty and Democracy on the Ebro Front on September 23, the eve of the Demobilisation of the XVth (Internaional) Brigade, Spanish Republican Army.

WILL BE HELD ON

## SATURDAY, OCTOBER 15, at 8 p.m
IN THE
### Banba Hall, Parnell Square

Collection in aid of those returning from the Irish Unit

Spain created the first rallying point for liberals in independent Ireland, and women were prominent in organising support for the Republic in Dublin (courtesy of East Wall History Group)

Madrid, 10 April 1939. Minister Kerney refusing the fascist salute when handing over his credentials to Franco (courtesy of Kerney family)

front with the Spanish officer as guide. Fletcher himself marched in the main body of the battalion 500 yards behind, and the machine-gun company took up the rear.[18] Rounding a bend in the half-light about a kilometre westwards from Calaceite, the first column of the British Battalion was confronted by Italian tanks, while other tanks and charging infantry emerged through trees on the side of the road. Scouts had gone forward to warn of danger, but were delayed by the rough nature of the terrain or captured by the Italians.[19] There was a bloodbath on the highway, the men had no hand grenades and many ran for their lives. The machine-gunners and some riflemen managed to gain high ground and fire on some tanks, which withdrew. Captain Frank Ryan initially thought the tanks were friendly ones. So did Wally Tapsell, Battalion Commissar, who was shot dead by one of the drivers. About 140 Internationals were captured (including at least 8 Irishmen) and 150 killed or wounded; the great majority were recruits sent to the front from Tarazona training camp.[20] Three Irishmen, Bob Doyle, Eddie Vallely ('Peter Brady') and Jackie Lemon were carrying their Degtyarev light machine gun, ammunition and spare parts in the column beside Frank Ryan. They were surrounded and captured with him. In his tunic, with his Sam Browne belt, breeches and leggings, he was obviously an officer. Marching off into captivity, Ryan said to Doyle, 'My book comes out today.' Lined up against a barn, the captives were asked who their officer was. Despite the protests of his comrades, Ryan stood up and gave his name and rank. An execution squad of the Guardia Civil drove up and intended to shoot the prisoners against a wall, but Italian officers argued with the dreaded police, who left. It was now late morning and the prisoners were kept in a wired compound. Ryan was again questioned by an Italian officer and, refusing to give further information, was struck in the face. Lemon and Doyle had to restrain Frank Ryan from retaliating.[21]

The British and Irish prisoners were fortunate that their captors were Italians of the 23rd (Blackshirt) Division,[22] eager to exchange these 'Reds' for Italian aviators or soldiers taken prisoner in one of the few Republican successes of the war – the battle of Guadalajara a year previously. So the Calaceite prisoners were spared summary execution, unlike 140 Americans captured by Spanish units.[23] One of these unfortunates was Andrew Delaney from Co. Louth, the son of an RIC man. He emigrated to America in 1930 and was a seaman based in Oakland, California, before arriving in Spain in late 1937. The 25-year-old Delaney was one of the recruits training in Tarazona rushed to the front in March. He was captured with over 90 other volunteers of the American battalion in the vicinity of Gandesa on 3 April.[24] Those members of the British battalion not captured moved in groups across country to Gandesa but, finding the town occupied by the fascists, struck south and, under the orders of Malcolm Dunbar (chief of operations in the 15th Brigade), took up position over a narrow defile on the road leading south out of Gandesa towards El Pinell de Brai and the lower Ebro. Like Fletcher, Dunbar had been wounded twice in the Calaceite encounter. After a holding action the group met Wild, who resumed command of the battalion, and were able to cross the Ebro at Cherta or at Móra de Ebre into Republican territory.[25] As the bridge at Móra de Ebre-Móra la Nova was dynamited on 3 April, many Internationals still caught on the other side swam across the swollen Ebro (the dams had been opened) or were drowned in the attempt. On the last day of March, 15th Brigade strength was just over 2,500, with 585 in the British battalion.[26] On 6 April those figures read 1,333 and 211.[27] Brigade headquarters computed at the end of April that 40 men were posted as deserters and 1,088 soldiers were unaccounted for: 296 from the British, 415 from the American and 236 from the Canadian battalion – the dead, deserters or captives of Franco.[28]

### CAPTAIN WATTIS CHARMS THE COMMONS

The most prominent British deserter was Captain Clifford James Wattis (Chief of Supplies, 15th Brigade), the self-styled ex-officer of the British Army who had led 'the brigade in the field' on 2–5 April and was with Dunbar and Wild on the last stage of the trek from Gandesa to Cherta.[29] Wattis enjoyed fleeting fame in Britain after he was feted for his manoeuvring skills over the hills by Sefton Delmer of the *Daily Express* who met him ('a tall, red-faced Army type of Englishman [. . .] not so long ago an officer in the Warwickshires') and over 60 British and French Internationals in Tortosa on 4 April.[30] The British Communist Party's *Daily Worker* also mainly credited Wattis with the successful outcome of the last leg in the retreat across the Ebro.[31] Delmer cabled soon afterwards that the holding action of Wattis, Dunbar and Wild in the mountain terrain between Gandesa and Tortosa had enabled Republican shock troops to rush to the front and form defensive lines.[32] The journalist also arranged for Wattis, still in Barcelona, to speak to his wife, a secretary-typist in Birmingham, on the telephone.[33] Čopić, commander of the 15th Brigade, like many others, valued Wattis's military ability but held him to be 'politically very backward' and someone who 'could become a danger to us'. What deepened the Croat's suspicion was that Wattis, on reaching Reus near Tarragona with brigade officers, argued in favour of carrying on towards Barcelona and Portbou, the last town on the Spanish side of the French border, i.e. desertion. Nevertheless, Čopić agreed with Harry Pollitt and Bill Rust (representative of the CPGB in Barcelona) that Wattis should be facilitated to return to Britain.³⁴ It later became known that Wattis had stated that he had lorries organised to take the stragglers to Barcelona, but Wild and Cooney demurred and stayed in Spain for all their misgivings about the Republic's chances after the unprecedented flight from Aragon.³⁵ For Pollitt, Wattis was still a comrade who had influence in certain circles in Britain and could be of assistance to the movement. In addition, the British CP leader emphasised, Wattis 'must return to prevent his pension from being cut off'.³⁶ Rust was more sceptical, maintaining that the ex-British Army leader of men ('brave [...] and an excellently trained officer') 'has had enough and cannot be strongly trusted'. But Rust, having talked seriously to Wattis, believed he had 'him where I want him just now'.³⁷ Both communist functionaries were deluding themselves, and subsequent events proved Čopić's assessment to be correct.

The Republican authorities believed that Wattis had been smuggled to Britain on board the English steamer *Thorpeness* between 24 April and 1 May.³⁸ Once in Britain, Wattis made his agenda clear: to discredit the Republican forces by exaggerating Soviet influence in the brigades. He gave an interview to the *Daily Express* and contacted Sir Henry Page Croft, MP for Bournemouth and a leading figure in the pro-Franco pressure group Friends of Nationalist Spain. On 24 May, Captain Wattis addressed a gathering of right-wing MPs in the House of Commons, overstating the importance of the Internationals in the Republican war effort and ventilating some ridiculous theories, e.g. that Stalin would soon be 'liquidated' by Voroshilov, his War Minister, or that Jesús Hernández, the communist Minister for Education in the Madrid Government, was 'really in control in Spain'. His remarks on Soviet advisors, the state of morale in the 15th Brigade or the question of the shooting of insurgent troops after the capture of Quinto by the Internationals (late August 1937) were factually correct.³⁹

Wattis was the kind of Briton that appealed to many ex-officers in the Commons, an apparently doughty fighter with traditionalist views of Britain's place in the world. Page Croft arranged a second meeting in the House for 31 May and this time invited all MPs to attend. Wattis was introduced to his listeners as having 'long service as commanding of a division of the International Brigade', a point that was challenged in the debate and later corrected by the speaker.⁴⁰ To a large extent Wattis confined himself to remarks about the British Battalion, praising the men ('fought magnificently'). As for the battalion officers, Wattis had a good word for but a few (Wintringham, Alexander, Tapsell) and was absolutely scathing about others (Macartney, Copeman, Cunningham, Aitken, etc.)⁴¹ He obviously admired fighting spirit, but was critical about people being promoted because of their political affiliation to positions way behind their ability – an attitude one could expect from a professional soldier. The assembly had one moment of disorder after Ellen Wilkinson, the left-wing Labour MP who had visited the British battalion with Clement Attlee the previous December, accused Wattis of 'certain financial defalcations', a reference to the cheques made out to Wattis for his two articles in the *Daily Express*. In reply Wattis said that, of course, he had cashed the *Daily Express* cheque, which prompted some MPs to shout 'Why not?'[42]

For a while Wattis was courted by the authorities, visiting the War Office, speaking to army brigade officers at Tidworth near Salisbury and propagandists of the British Empire Union. The pamphlet he was planning with the help of his Francoist friends in Britain never saw the light of day as the risk of libel suits seemed likely.[43] Wattis had definitely 'gone over to the other side' and everything he said or wrote was transmitted by the Duke of Alba, Franco's agent in London, to Burgos and shared with the Italian and Portuguese ambassadors to Britain.[44] Wattis's 'disclosures' had no long-term effect on British attitudes to the Spanish war because of his brazen espousal of the Franco regime. His betrayal of former comrades was compounded by what he said in private to one of the Duke of Alba's informants, namely that Frank Ryan ('a leader in the Irish revolt and a political commissar') and four other officers supposedly captured in Aragon should 'under no circumstances [. . .] be repatriated or allowed to get away'.[45]

Not long afterwards Wattis, too, was to see the inside of a prison – albeit a British one. Ellen Wilkinson's accusation was correct, for Wattis had cashed two cheques for a total of £30 from the *Daily Express* although he had received £15 in cash in lieu of the second one. Charged with defrauding that newspaper, a credulous landlady and shopkeepers with cheques that bounced, Wattis jumped bail in March 1939, but was arrested in Bristol and sentenced at Bow Street Police Court in late April 1939 to 12 months' hard labour.[46] The adventurist career of Wattis had strong parallels to that of Wilfred Macartney, another 'professional' trusted by Pollitt.

### POWS MEET THE PRESS AT ZARAGOZA

In the late morning of 31 March 1938 Max Parker from New York was Ryan's interpreter as they marched against the flow of hostile troops and their transport. Ryan tried to keep spirits up, shouting encouragement and insisting to the Italian officers that the prisoners be given food and water. While the parched men were drinking, a German officer approached. He asked why

Frank Ryan was fighting in Spain and not in Ireland. He received the answer that it was the same fight in both places. The men were loaded on to trucks and driven to Alcañiz and kept in a church overnight.[47] Over 600 captured Internationals, including over 150 British and Irish, and other Republican prisoners, arrived at Zaragoza on 3 April 1938. They were marched across the parade ground of San Gregorio Military Academy and held in separate halls for classification.[48] The men of the British battalion were ordered to form lines and give the fascist salute. Frank Ryan, the most senior IB officer present, stated this was against prisoners' rights. Because of the delay in translating back and forth, there was time to discuss the matter among the assembled. Some British communists supported Ryan's stance, but the majority, fearing a beating or worse, wanted some form of compromise based on the British military salute. This was carried out twice in such a bizarre fashion that the fascist officer desisted.[49] On 4 April the British prisoners were marched out to the barrack square and inspected by Spanish officials, including Lieutenant Colonel Lorenzo Martínez Fuset, Franco's military assessor. He was the man responsible for overseeing death sentences. Pablo Merry del Val, head of the foreign section of Franco's Press Department, 'chaperoned' the bevy of foreign journalists to view the defeated Internationals.

Later in the afternoon two journalists were allowed to interview an American prisoner. Max Parker, the brigader who had translated for Frank Ryan earlier, spoke to Kim Philby of *The Times*. William Carney of the *New York Times*, not introducing himself because of the hostility engendered by his reporting, listened in the background.[50] His dispatch, though biased, mentioned the names of six American prisoners, including that of Max Parker, and drew international attention.[51] Parker was able to disclose to the Spanish and foreign journalists that Ryan's life was in danger.[52] Another source was the indiscretion of Víctor Ruiz Albéniz who was in a group of Spanish journalists permitted to meet Ryan, now held apart from the other prisoners. Ruiz Albéniz spoke openly of the identity of the prominent captive.[53] Merry del Val complained to Ryan's gaoler that the Irishman should have been shot. Franco's pressman, on good terms with Hodgson and the Irish fascist Thomas Gunning, demanded Ryan salute him, which the prisoner refused.[54] Ryan maintained later that a journalist from the Catholic *Universe* in London had intervened in his favour.[55] Hearing on the radio that an Irish journalist had been arrested by the insurgents in Spain, Eilís Ryan, Frank's youngest sister, on the advice of Peadar O'Donnell, visited de Valera's residence with her brother and parents. The Taoiseach telephoned the Irish Minister to the Spanish Republic, Leopold Kerney, in France and set in motion a widespread campaign for clemency.[56]

### KERNEY STARTS HIS CAMPAIGN

On Monday, 4 April, Kerney sent an urgent telegram to Burgos, pleading for clemency, and dispatched a letter immediately to Franco's headquarters, requesting information and stating that the fate of the prisoner could have repercussions in Ireland.[57] The Duke of Alba, Franco's agent in London, telegraphed Burgos the same day following representation from the Irish Department of External Affairs.[58] Also on 4 April Carney was accorded the privilege of interviewing Frank Ryan in Zaragoza in the presence of Lieutenant Colonel Fuset. The American's version of the encounter given to Kerney on 12 April – seems plausible, namely that he and Ryan had argued violently: Carney, in Ryan's eyes, was a purveyor of 'fascist propaganda', and the accused retaliated by calling Ryan 'an atheist and anti-religious'. The *New York Times* journalist was told afterwards by Fuset that Ryan had documents of 'a compromising nature' on his person when captured, including jewellery of a fascist officer killed by the Republicans at Brunete the previous July. Carney added that Ryan had 'frequently killed prisoners', and finally another fiction, namely that military trials in the Franco zone 'were public'.[59] The accusation that Frank Ryan had killed or looted prisoners, obviously an idée fixe of Fuset's, had short traction and did not figure in the indictment. Nevertheless, Carney went public with Fuset's diatribe, writing in the *New York Times* at the end of May that:

> Captain Frank Ryan, Irish Communist commander of the Major Attlee Battalion [. . .] when the Republicans captured and held Brunete for a short time last Summer he is alleged to have commanded firing squads of Internationals that executed Nationalist prisoners without giving them any sort of trial and to have shot down with his own pistol a number of Nationalists who were surrounded and offered to surrender.[60]

A riposte followed two days later in the newspaper, signed by seven former members of the Irish unit in the American battalion of the 15th Brigade. They stated that they had fought under Ryan's command at Brunete, that he was attached to Brigade staff and could not have had anything to do with prisoners as he 'speaks only English and Gaelic'.[61] From Zaragoza the first batch of IB prisoners were transported in trucks and arrived in San Pedro de Cardeña Concentration Camp in the vicinity of Burgos at 2 a.m. on 8 April. Ten Irishmen were in the contingent of 290: Frank Ryan, Jackie Lemon, Eddie Vallely ('Peter Brady'), Joseph Leo Byrne, Archibald Bailie, Bob Doyle, David Kennedy, Maurice Levitas, Michael McGrath and Patrick Byrne.[62] As more Internationals were rounded up or transferred to San Pedro from other places of detention, the number of Irishmen interned in the disused monastery soon grew to 20.

## INCARCERATION IN SAN PEDRO DE CARDEÑA

The 625 Internationals in San Pedro de Cardeña camp were initially in a state of numb misery. Uncertain of their fate, dressed in ragged uniforms and sick from undernourishment, dysentery or wounds, they needed time and solidarity to recover from the disillusionment caused by the chaos of the March retreats. Not a few raised questions about the quality of the Republican military leadership, and all were subject to frequent beatings and appalling living conditions. The 157 Irish and British held in the decrepit buildings in early May – other comrades joined them up to and after the last battle of the Internationals on 23 September – knew that they were not summarily shot because they had been captured by Italian troops.[63] By 1 May, 74 Americans and 21 Canadians had been registered as POWs in San Pedro.[64] The British and Irish stood a good chance of being exchanged for Italian soldiers taken at the Battle of Guadalajara (March 1937), or for airmen shot down over Republican territory. Thirteen of the Irish captives were subsequently released because they were on a British list. John O'Beirne from Balbriggan, Co. Dublin, suffering from a troublesome leg wound and arthritis, assumed another man's identity and was released into France in the second week of October 1938 with 13 Americans.[65] The two Irish in the Canadian contingent, Jim Haughey (Armagh) and William McChrystal (Derry) were freed in April 1939, but rested and recuperated in Le Havre for three weeks before being shipped to Canada via London and Liverpool.[66] That left four POWs, who declared themselves the responsibility of the Irish Government. That decision came about presumably when British diplomatic representatives visited the camp, as Bob Doyle remembers:

> Three of the Irish – myself, Maurice Levitas, a Dublin Jew, and Jackie Lemon from Waterford – approached Frank Ryan and asked him would he declare himself British or Irish. Frank stated that he would never hide behind the Union Jack. So we decided to declare ourselves Irish, although we knew that because of the hostility and the hysteria in Ireland, our exchange might be delayed.[67]

The men lived on two floors of an old building, in which the three primitive wash-hand basins and three dry closets were situated downstairs.

The toilets were constantly blocked, so a roster of prisoners was arranged to clear them by diving in naked.[68] The prisoners had neither blankets, soap, towels nor any utensils for eating and drinking. The two meagre meals of the day, at noon and at dusk, consisted of a bread roll and a bowl of 'soup', usually water coloured with a few beans and the gutted portions of fish. As in all Spanish gaols, the prisoners were supposed to spend the day in the courtyard, where they were fed. At the beginning there was a rush to the soldier at the cauldron doling out the 'soup', but the secret communist cell leadership reached an agreement with their comrades that they were to queue up and thus preserve their dignity.[69] On the way down to the courtyard, or from there into the dormitories, the Internationals had to run the gauntlet of stick-wielding military warders, who were also wont to burst into the sleeping spaces at night to beat the prisoners or stage mock executions in the yard.[70] Frank Ryan was recognised as leader and had to adjudicate in disputes. Garry McCartney described his role:

> In the beginning Frank Ryan was prone to working on his own, and apt to be hasty in imposing his will on others, even to the extent of using his fists. After Danny Gibbons and Jack Jones had a long talk with Ryan and Louis Ornitz, an American, they readily agreed to the Party's general proposals to our form our organization, and to the need of our collectively getting the best of the comrades. Frank Ryan and Danny Gibbons were mainly responsible for imposing punishment on two [names omitted by BMcL] for stealing 100 pesetas from another prisoner. Frank's standing as an officer was used to the full, and he worked in consultation with the party members.[71]

Once Frank Ryan chaired a 'court' to try a prisoner caught stealing a bread roll. Ryan said that if he were in Dublin judging a similar case, he would be defence counsel:

> [. . .] but here in the hands of the fascists [. . .] we have to stand together, fully united. It is because stealing a small piece of bread threatens this all-important unity we treasure so highly that this court has been convened. The object is not so much to punish the guilty as it is to preserve and strengthen our unity as we face our fascist jailers.[72]

The prisoners received pre-printed postcards from the International Red Cross in late April to sign, the British and Irish on 6 May, but the only text allowed over the signature was 'Notificándoles que me encuentro bien' ('Notifying you that I am well'), which must have caused incipient puzzlement among the relatives who received the mail weeks or months later.[73] The British Agent in Burgos, Sir Robert Hodgson, requested permission on 4 June for members of his staff to visit the monastery. He argued that some of the lists of British citizens previously provided were incomplete or unclear, and that the intention of the visit was to see under what conditions the prisoners lived in order to reassure the relatives. He wrote that he fully understood that his envoys would be submitted to the all regulations the camp authorities thought fit to impose and announced a visit by an interpreter and the military attaché Lieutenant Colonel Martin.[74] Edward de Renzy Martin had been a POW during the First World War and was later seconded as Inspector of the Gendarmerie to Albania (1927–34).[75] He left London by car for his new posting (Honorary Attaché) at the British Agency in Burgos in mid-May 1938.[76] Martin visited his compatriots in San Pedro on 11 June, 10 September and 1 November.[77] He was the first foreigner to speak to the POWs, and on his initial visit he took their particulars and announced that 100 British inmates would be released the following day. Martin was looking for details regarding the recruitment of the men in the UK and wished all to sign an undertaking that they would repay their transports costs home. He was largely unsuccessful on both counts. Martin was naturally mistrusted as an envoy of the Chamberlain Government and on account of his insistent questioning.[78] However, Hodgson's attaché did pass on a report about the appalling conditions in the camp. Hodgson wrote to Franco's diplomatic corps that his missive was not to be considered as a complaint, as he fully understood the difficulties the camp commandant faced, but that he would welcome if the situation could be possibly rectified. The camp commandant was reminded shortly afterwards in detail what Hodgson's staff had observed in the camp:

1) Lack of ventilation and light in overcrowded prisoners' quarters.
2) Vermin (fleas, lice and rats) in the dormitory which is so crowded that it is impossible to wash the floor, no fresh straw for the mattresses.
3) Insufficient sanitary arrangements, three toilets for 300 prisoners, no paper or sand, three wash hand basins for 300 men.
4) No towels, underwear or shoes for the prisoners.
5) Lack of medicine and milk for the sick.
6) No facilities for writing letters, and that few letters from outside had been received.[79]

Ryan's health suffered in this environment, and he spent much time lying down to alleviate his heart problem.[80] As early as April Franco's Chief of Staff had ascertained that Frank Ryan was in a good state of health, 'save that he is suffering from chronic cardiac high blood pressure'.[81] When 100 British POWs left San Pedro on Sunday, 12 June, Frank Ryan was also ordered to pack his belongings. On hearing the good news from Martin the day before, Ryan wrote to the International Red Cross to say that 99 British and Irish were to be sent to a camp for exchange on the morrow.[82] His comrades believed that Ryan, too, was going home. Bob Doyle and Jackie Lemon gave him notes to post to their families in Ireland. However, he was separated, handcuffed and driven off in a jeep under armed guard.[83]

There were to be no significant improvements in the infrastructure of the camp, which also contained 2,000 Republican soldiers segregated from the Internationals. The beatings continued. While in the courtyard the prisoners had to eat their meagre meals standing up. One hot day in early July, Bob Doyle sat down to eat and two others followed suit. A notorious guard nicknamed 'Sticky' spotted the transgression and had Doyle, Bob Steck, an American, and the South African Jack Flior taken down into the cellar, to the so-called sala de tortura. Doyle was the first to be pushed in and be subjected to a ten-minute beating by four guards, two wielding heavy sticks, a third a heavy strap and 'Sticky' his usual weapon – a bull's penis.[84]

When William Carney visited the camp on 9 July, he talked freely to the prisoners and was taken aback when Doyle and Steck pulled up their shirts, revealing the welts on their backs. The camp commandant had put on a show, showing the journalist the nutritious meal being prepared for his prisoners (red beans, the Spanish red pepper sausage chorizo, and bread), a one-off repast as Carney's visit was arranged beforehand. Knowing that Carney was about to visit them, the prisoners elected a committee to talk to him led by Louis Ornitz from New York and including Bob Doyle.

In his report in the *New York Times* Carney depicted the concentration camp as a tolerable place for POWs, alleging that some Internationals were working in the fields and kitchen, and as barbers or gardeners. This was untrue, for he reported what the commander had said, also that the prisoners were 'sulking' and 'provocative'. Any beatings that had occurred were, according to Carney, administered because prisoners had refused to kneel down during the compulsory Catholic mass. Prisoners were expected to sing the Falangist anthem *Cara al Sol* and give the fascist salute before the priest. Carney was obviously most interested in naming those who were members of the communist party and who had recruited them in the USA. He mentioned that Frank Ryan 'the Irish Communist used to make speeches to his comrades here daily.' The visit had the advantage that the names and addresses of over 60 American prisoners were now in the public domain. That evening Louis Ornitz was pulled out of the queue by the commander, who repeated the complaints he had made to the *New York Times* man. Ornitz was severely beaten and placed on half-rations for several days.[85]

An orgy of violence followed the escape of a group of Internationals in late July.[86] The men's quarters were wrecked by the guards, who confined their charges to the dormitory for days, and prisoners were taken out at random and beaten. One was David Kennedy from Ballycastle, Co. Antrim, whose back was badly bruised after the bludgeoning.[87] The six escapees were all Germans, some of whom had stated they were Dutch because of the rumour that all German IB men were executed at some stage. Hiding by day and marching at night, the two groups of three reached the French border but were caught and brought back to San Pedro. They spent three months in the dungeons, were subjected to daily beatings and later transferred to the stone quarry in the ruins of Belchite.[88]

A series of eerie encounters leading to much speculation occurred during the summer – the interrogations by a German team of psychologists. They were acting on the remit of Antonio Vallejo Nájera, head of the psychiatric services of Franco's army. An officer in the medical corps since 1910, Vallejo had spent World War I attached to the Spanish Embassy in Berlin, where he had the opportunity to examine French and Belgian prisoners of war. Vallejo came to align himself with a specific field of German eugenics, biotypology, by means of which he tried to reconcile German doctrines of racial hygiene with the requirements of Catholic moral doctrine. He thus became an advocate of examining genetic profiles, which over time could serve as a guide for a policy of pre-marital classification and orientation that would produce 'a slow but sure improvement in the Spanish nation's psychological genotype'. He therefore had to localise 'the Red gene' in order to eradicate it, and the Internationals, along with four other groups of Republican captives, were to be his guinea pigs.

Vallejo established a bureau with two doctors and a criminologist in Burgos. His cooperation with the German scientists sent to San Pedro was presumably a result of the widening of police cooperation between the Gestapo and Franco's forces, an agreement suggested by Himmler in April 1938 and signed three months later.[89] The guidelines for the joint psycho-project were: the relationship between a certain biopsychic personality and the constitutional disposition to Marxism, the 'high incidence of Marxist fanaticism in the mentally inferior' and the 'presence of antisocial psychopaths in the Marxist masses.' Vallejo was disappointed in the results of his 'analysis' of the American prisoners' motives in San Pedro: almost 80 per cent maintained their beliefs, 11 per cent did not express any and only one tenth had changed them.[90] Of the British prisoners his study stated that 58 per cent of the English 'were single men with sexual experience outside prostitution'. Vallejo's conclusions as to their beliefs are revealing: 'The immense majority remain firmly attached to their ideas.'[91]

Having received completed questionnaires, the two Germans in civilian attire showed the members of the British battalion pictures of the devastation wrought on Spanish towns, including gruesome pictures of dismembered bodies. The interrogations centred on why the men had volunteered to fight in Spain. Bob Doyle was asked if his first sexual encounter was with a prostitute, while Garry McCartney wasn't sure which eye Admiral Nelson had lost during the Napoleonic wars. When asked to name the planets in the solar system, George Wheeler, a keen amateur astronomer, confounded the Germans by stating they were wrong in omitting Pluto, discovered by an American in 1930.[92] Later all the English-speaking POWs were taken to a field and told to strip. They were photographed naked and had their shorn skulls calibrated by the German eugenicists.[93]

The British prisoners were given permission to write home and some soon received Red Cross parcels or money with which they could buy food and soap in the camp shop. An 'Institute of Higher Education' was established, and 'its faculty included an Indian who lectured on fakirs and gave lessons in palmistry, and an English zoologist; the syllabus prescribed courses in eleven languages, mathematics, bridge and chess.'[94] The 100 British prisoners released in June 1938 were first transferred to an Italian camp in Palencia, 90 km southwest of Burgos. The Italians treated them reasonably well, but the men were sent to the far grimmer and overcrowded Ondarreta prison in San Sebastian in October, when the number of Italian soldiers in Republican hands due for exchange was agreed upon. Forty British were handed over at the French border and reached England on 25 October. Among the arrivals in Newhaven, dressed in khaki Spanish uniforms, were Gerard Doyle (Limerick), Hugh O'Donnell (Donegal) and Joe Murray (Dublin).[95] The last 75 British and Irish in San Pedro were transported to Ondarreta in late January 1939 and had to await the finalisation of the handover arrangements.[96] Most of them reached London on 7 February, including Eddie Vallely ('Peter Brady', Cavan), Victor Barr (Belfast), Thomas Heaney (Galway), Jackie Lemon (Waterford), Bob Doyle (Dublin) and Maurice Levitas (Dublin).[97] The last three had been under guard of the gendarmerie on the train to Paris and were taken to the Irish Legation. There they were given their fare to Dublin via London somewhat reluctantly – they stated that neither they nor their relatives would 'foot the bill'.[98] The last ten to leave Spain were only released after the war, in April 1939, when the Irish brigader Patrick Byrne from Crampton Court, off Dame Street, Dublin, and Dublin-born Joseph Leo Byrne (Liverpool) reached home.

## NOTES

1. Antony Beevor, *The Battle for Spain: The Spanish Civil War 1936–1939* (London, 2006), pp 314, 322.
2. Hugh Thomas, *The Spanish Civil War* (London, 2012), p. 793.
3. Cecil Eby, *Between the Bullet and the Lie: American Volunteers in the Spanish Civil War* (New York–Chicago–San Francisco, 1969), pp 205–7.
4. Beevor, *The Battle for Spain*, p. 324.
5. Arthur Landis, *The Abraham Lincoln Brigade* (New York, 1968), p. 412.
6. See a portrait of Doran by someone who knew him well: Sandor Voros, *American Commissar* (New York, 1961), pp 372–6
7. Bill Alexander, *British Volunteers for Liberty: Spain 1936–39* (London, 1982), pp 175–6.
8. RGASPI, f. 545, o. 2, d. 108, l. 132; Richard Baxell, *Unlikely Warriors: The British in the Spanish Civil War and the Struggle against Fascism* (London, 2012), pp 312–4.
9. RGASPI, f. 545, o. 3, d. 451, l. 61.
10. RGASPI, f. 545, o. 3, d. 433, l. 103.
11. RGASPI, f. 545, o. 3, d. 429, l. 2.
12. Harry Fisher, *Comrades: Tales of a Brigadista in the Spanish Civil War* (Lincoln, Ne, 1999), pp 118–19.
13. Voros, *American Commissar*, pp 411–12; Eby, *Between the Bullet and the Lie*, pp 227–8.
14. RGASPI, f. 545, o. 6, d. 129, l. 18. This information is from a letter sent by Ryan to Alonzo Elliot, his English colleague at the Commissariat in Madrid.
15. National Library of Ireland (NLI), Rosamond Jacob Papers, 33,132.
16. RGASPI, f. 545, o. 2, d. 164, l. 68–9; 545, o. 3, d. 475, l. 14 (map).
17. RGASPI, f. 545, o. 3, d. 454, l. 10.
18. RGASPI, f. 545, o. 3, d. 497, ll. 32–3.
19. Baxell, *Unlikely Warriors*, pp 314–16.
20. Alexander, *British Volunteers*, p. 179.
21. Bob Doyle, *Brigadista: An Irishman's Fight Against Fascism* (Dublin, 2006), pp 62–5.
22. Landis, *The Abraham Lincoln Brigade*, p. 449.
23. Carl Geiser, *Prisoners of the Good Fight: The Spanish Civil War 1936–1939* (Westport Ct., 1986), pp 263–6. His brother Charles Delaney wrote to External Affairs in early 1939, requesting news of Andrew Delaney's fate (NA, DFA 10/1/30, Delaney to External Affairs, 10 February 1939).
24. RGASPI, f. 545, o. 6, d. 851, l. 4; Geiser, *Prisoners of the Good Fight*, p. 265.
25. RGASPI, f. 545, o. 3, d. 497, ll. 17–18 (Report by Bob Cooney), ll. 23–4 (Report by Sam Wild); Walter Gregory, *Shallow Grave: A Memoir of the Spanish Civil War* (London, 1986), pp 108–12.
26. RGASPI, f. 545, o. 3, d. 454, l.10.
27. Ibid., l. 75.
28. RGASPI, f. 545, o. 3, d. 488, l. 204.
29. RGASPI, f. 545, o. 3, d. 497, ll. 23–4 (Report by Sam Wild). In late April Dunbar and Fletcher were praised in dispatches by the 35th Division for their skill and courage during the retreats (RGASPI, f. 545, o. 3, d. 429, l. 233).

30. *Daily Express*, 6 April 1938.
31. *Daily Worker*, 9 April 1938.
32. *Daily Express*, 11 April 1938.
33. Ibid., 25 April 1938.
34. RGASPI, f. 545, o. 6, d. 212, ll. 85 and reverse.
35. Baxell, *Unlikely Warriors*, p. 319. This refers to a letter from Will Paynter to Pollitt (8 April 1938), which stated that Wild 'was for refusing to go into the line again and Bob [Cooney] was wobbly'.
36. RGASPI, f. 545, o. 6, d. 212, l. 86.
37. James K. Hopkins, *Into the Heart of the Fire: The British in the Spanish Civil War* (Stanford, 1998), p. 277.
38. RGASPI, f. 545, o. 6, d. 212, l. 88.
39. Archivo General del la Administración, Alcalá de Henares (AGA), 54/16857, memorandum by the Marqués del Moral to Duke of Alba, 26 May 1938. On the shootings in Quinto, see: Baxell, *Unlikely Warriors*, p. 268; Peter N. Carroll, *The Odyssey of the Abraham Lincoln Brigade: Americans in the Spanish Civil War* (Stanford, 1994), pp 155–6; Fisher, *Comrades*, p. 77.
40. AGA, 54/16857, protocol of the meeting in Parliament on 31 May, signed by C. J. Wattis, 1 June 1938, pp 1, 9. The Communist MP Willie Gallacher had contradicted Page-Croft on this point.
41. Ibid., pp 5–6, 17–18.
42. Ibid., p.9.
43. Ibid., memorandum by del Moral to Alba, 2 July 1938.
44. Ibid., Alba to Gómez Jordana, Burgos, 8 June 1938; Alba to the Portuguese Ambassador, 8 June 1938; Italian Embassy to Alba, 14 July 1938.
45. Ibid., del Moral to Alba, 30 May 1938.
46. *Dunston Times* (New Zealand), 1 May 1939, p. 6, https://paperspast.natlib.govt.nz/newspapers/DUNST19390501.2.43. Accessed 15 June 2020.
47. Geiser, *Prisoners of the Good Fight*, pp 62–3.
48. AGA, 82/4768, Campo de Concentración de Prisioneros de San Pedro de Cardeña, 01 May 1938 (625 POWs present, of whom 149 gave their nationality as British and 8 as Irish).
49. Ian MacDougall, *Voices from the Spanish Civil War: Personal Recollections of Scottish Volunteers in Republican Spain 1936–39* (Edinburgh, 1986), p. 250 (Garry McCartney). See also McCartney's report of 10 August 1976, deposited in the Marx Memorial Library (MML), Catalogue 1994, Box C, Special Files, esp. p. 6.
50. Paul Preston, *We Saw Spain Die: Foreign Correspondents in the Spanish Civil War* (London, 2009), pp 186–7.
51. *New York Times*, 4 April 1938. Carney wrote untruthfully that the Americans had been abandoned by their Spanish officers, and that the Committee to Aid Spanish Democracy in New York had recruited the men to fight.
52. Geiser, *Prisoners of the Good Fight*, p. 97.
53. NA, DFA, 244/8, Kerney to Walshe, 7 June 1938.
54. NA, DFA, 19/1/32, Kerney to Dublin, 7 May 1940.
55. DIFP, *Vol. 5, 1937–1939*, p. 472, Kerney to Walshe, 17 June 1939.

56. Aodh Ó Cannain, 'Eilís Ryan in her own words', in *Saothar*, 21 (1996), p. 137.
57. AGA, 82/4333/233, telegrama oficial, 4 April 1938 San Sebastian-Burgos; Kerney to General Jordana, Franco's foreign minister, 4 April 1938.
58. Ibid., Alba to foreign affairs Burgos, telegrama oficial, 4 April 1938.
59. DIFP, *Vol. 5*, pp 267–9, Kerney to Walshe, 13 April 1938.
60. *New York Times*, 29 May 1938.
61. Ibid., 1 June 1938. The letter was signed by Joseph A. Whalen, Paul Burns, James Murphy, Charles Flaherty, Frank Flaherty, Edward Flaherty and Philip Haydock.
62. AGA, 82/4768, Relación Nominal, 8 April 1938.
63. Ibid., list of 625 prisoners by nationality, 1 May 1938; list of prisoners of English nationality, with names and home addresses, 1 May 1938.
64. Ibid., list of prisoners by nationality, 1 May 1938.
65. Geiser, *Prisoners of the Good Fight*, pp 156–7, 172.
66. William C. Beeching, *Canadian Volunteers, Spain 1936–1939* (Regina, 1989), p. 181.
67. Doyle, *Brigadista*, p. 80.
68. Judith Cook, *Apprentices of Freedom* (London–Melbourne–New York, 1979), p. 120 (Bob Doyle).
69. MacDougall, *Voices*, pp 254–5 (Garry McCartney), p. 283 (George Drever).
70. Baxell, *Unlikely Warriors*, p. 366.
71. MML, catalogue 1994, Box C, file 3, biographical notes written by W.G. McCartney.
72. Geiser, *Prisoners of the Good Fight*, pp 113–14.
73. Ibid., p. 120. The Red Cross representative was not permitted to meet the prisoners.
74. AGA, 82/4768, Hodgson to foreign affairs Burgos, 4 June 1938.
75. MacDougall, *Voices*, p. 350.
76. AGA, 54/06896, British Foreign Office to foreign affairs Burgos, 13 May 1938.
77. Geiser, *Prisoners of the Good Fight*, pp 128, 160, 178. In his interview with Ian MacDougall in the 1980s, Garry McCartney said he believed that Martin visited San Pedro four times (MacDougall, *Voices*, p. 254).
78. Doyle, *Brigadista*, pp 80–2; Baxell, *Unlikely Warriors*, p. 369.
79. AGA, 82/4768, foreign ministry to Col. de Martín-Pinillos, 22 June 1938.
80. Doyle, *Brigadista*, p. 80.
81. AGA, 82/4333/233, general headquarters Burgos to foreign affairs Burgos, 22, 26 April 1938.
82. Seán Cronin, *Frank Ryan: The Search for the Republic* (Dublin, 1980), p. 145.
83. Cronin, *Frank Ryan*, p. 145; Doyle, *Brigadista*, pp 81–2.
84. Doyle, *Brigadista*, pp 74–5.
85. Geiser, *Prisoners of the Good Fight*, pp 138–40; *New York Times*, 11 July 1938.
86. Geisner, *Prisoners of the Good Fight*, p. 152.
87. George Wheeler, *To Make the People Smile Again: A Memoir of the Spanish Civil War* (Newcastle upon Tyne, 2003), pp 151–3, 184.
88. Max Schäfer, *1936–1939 Spanien. Erinnerungen von Interbrigadisten aus der BRD* (Frankfurt am Main, 1976), pp 259–61.
89. Paul Preston, *The Spanish Holocaust: Inquisition and Extermination in Twentieth-Century Spain* (London, 2012), p. 490

90. Javier Bandrés-Rafael Llavona, 'Psychology in Franco's Concentration Camps', in *Psychology in Spain*, 1:1 (1997) pp 3–9, www.psychologyinspain.com/content/reprints 1997/1.pdf?q=concentration-camps. Accessed 16 June 2020.

91. Giles Trimlett, 'Marxist are Retards', in *The Guardian*, 1 November 2002, www.theguardian.com/world/2002/nov/01/spain.gilestremlett. Accessed 15 June 2020.

92. Doyle, *Brigadista*, p. 81; McDougall, *Voices*, p. 258 (McCartney); Wheeler, *To Make the People Smile*, p. 145.

93. Geiser, *Prisoners of the Good Fight*, pp 145–6.

94. Victor Howard (with Mac Reynolds), *The Mackenzie-Papineau Battalion: The Canadian Contingent in the Spanish Civil War* (Ottawa, 1969), p. 203.

95. *Daily Telegraph*, 25 October 1938.

96. Baxell, *Unlikely Warriors*, pp 369–74.

97. *Daily Worker*, 8 February 1939.

98. NA, DFA, Paris 10/55, Repatriations, Irish Legation Paris to External Affairs, 8 February 1939; Doyle, *Brigadista*, pp 87–93; *Irish Press*, 10 February 1939 (interview with Doyle and Lemon).

TEN

# ENDGAME ON THE EBRO

When Italian troops reached the Mediterranean at Vinaròs on 8 April 1938, the Republic was cut in two. Most observers saw the massive breakthrough in Aragon as the beginning of the end for the Spanish Republic. Yet Franco made a grave strategical mistake that gave the Republicans breathing space to organise strong defences: instead of pushing his troops north to capture Barcelona, the heartland of industry, separatism and republicanism, the dictator decided to swing his forces south against Valencia, another important port and industrial centre. His troops suffered heavy losses in repeated attacks on the XYZ line of intricate trench and concrete networks east and west of Viver in the Sierra de Espandán. Franco ordered a halt to regroup on 23 July, some 60 km north of Valencia.[1]

This is the background to the Battle of the Ebro (25 July–16 November 1938), the longest and most costly battle of the whole war. It was to be another diversionary attack designed by Rojo, a desperate push north to south across the river into territory his soldiers had lost four months previously. Prime Minister Negrín hoped that the offensive would relieve the pressure on Valencia and produce a kind of stalemate that would be terminated by a greater crisis that summer: the danger of a major international conflict over Czechoslovakia. If Britain and France were to go to war with Germany, Franco would lose an ally and the Republicans would gain one across the Pyrenees. Negrín could not foresee that the Czechs would be shamefully abandoned by Chamberlain and Daladier, but he knew that he had no other choice than to offer further resistance: Franco was not interested in a compromise peace but hell-bent on grinding down his Republican foes, at the front and in the rear.

The opening of the French border between March and June compensated the Republicans to a certain extent for the massive losses of equipment in the March retreats, but most of the new arms went to the troops desperately fighting in the Levante. The 15th Brigade alone had lost 30 trucks during the flight east,[2] and a large depot of stores and equipment of the IB in Gandesa fell to Franco's army on 2 April. That was a result of the panic in the Ministry of Defence, which ordered the evacuation of Albacete and all bases in that province and their transfer to Barcelona. The new brigades' depot was at Las Planas (now a western suburb), a barracks at Olot (north-east of Girona) and a recruits' training centre at Montblanc near Tarragona. There was a clearing station for recovered or demobilised Internationals in Badalona just north of Barcelona, where the men vegetated, badly fed and housed and virtually ignored.[3] Wilhelm Zaisser, commander in Albacete, managed the transfer of 8,000 soldiers and equipment between 6 and 10 April to Barcelona but was himself 'demobilized' the following month: a victim of internecine army politics between professional Spaniards and communist commanders.[4]

Čopić and other Brigade officers began to gather the demoralised survivors of the 15th Brigade in villages on the northern bank of the Ebro, putting them to digging fortified positions and patrolling the riverbanks. Lieutenant Walter Gregory of the British battalion felt there was 'a lack of buoyancy' among his compatriots, and Sam Wild told him he felt another successful attack by the Francoists would break the men's will to resist. Food was very scarce and most of the volunteers were in poor physical shape, dysentery being a common complaint. The general mood improved over time, with the delivery of new weapons (especially Czech and Soviet light machine guns) and visits by Harry Pollitt and the journalists Bill Forrest (*News Chronicle*) and Sefton Delmer (*Daily Express*) in mid-April.[5] The British numbered 140, and their Spanish comrades 80, by 10 April, with the battalion gaining daily in strength due to the closure of the camps in the south, the slimming down of Brigade staff and the arrival of a large contingent of new men (and returnees) from Britain and Ireland.[6]

In the second week of April the Lincoln battalion, comprising 40 Americans and 35 Spaniards, assembled before Milton Wolff, the new commander. Four hundred of their March muster had been killed or captured, or were missing or in hospital. The Canadians were even more attenuated, with only 20 in Móra la Nova after their escape across the river.[7] Sixteen Irish boosted the numbers in the British battalion to the end of May: Jack Nalty, Michael Lehane, Paddy Duff and Jim ('The Farmer') O'Regan returned after repatriation by Frank Ryan; seven volunteers, all members of the CPI, arrived from Ireland (Eugene Downing, Hugh Hunter, Alex Digges, Tom O'Brien, Bill McGregor, James F. O'Regan, Michael O'Riordan); George Gorman, Jim Haughey, James Lord and James Domegan travelled from Britain, and Albert Fulton from Australia. Eugene Downing sat in the same railway carriage through France with Nalty and Paddy Duff:

Jack was on his way back to Spain as was his close friend Paddy Duff. Given that I had no experience of war, I didn't understand how brave these men really were. It is easy for the new recruits starting out as he is blind to the perils of the battlefield and to the terrible injuries and wounds that people suffer. Both Jack and Paddy were more than aware of the dangers and hardships that awaited them, yet they were still keen to return to battle. They had already witnessed their own comrades dying at Cordoba and on the Jarama [. . .] They had already played their part and they could have given up at this point, And yet, despite all this, they returned. That's real and true bravery. Jack was very similar to Frank Ryan. He was a strong-willed man and devoted to the cause – someone you could always rely on.[8]

### POSTED TO 'SHANTYTOWN'

In mid-May the Brigade moved to Marçà, a village in Tarragona province 30 km from the sea. A picturesque spot with pinewoods nearby and mountains in the distance, it was to be the base for the Brigade for ten weeks of rest and training, the longest break from combat that the volunteers were to enjoy during the war. South of the village was a secluded vale where the men built shelters from pine posts and branches, christening their new dominion 'Chabola Valley' after the Spanish word for 'shack'. There was a severe shortage of clothes, boots and rifles and a further challenge was the integration of hundreds of Spanish recruits (quintas), some of whom were nicknamed 'baby-bottle soldiers' (quinta del Biberón) because of their youth. They comprised up to 70 per cent of the Brigade.[9]

Life in the sunny settlement was overshadowed by the general food scarcity, lice, scabies and intestinal complaints that played havoc with men's bowels. Cigarettes were in such short supply that some denizens of shantytown took to smoking the leaves from hazel trees. Albert Charlesworth from Oldham, who had gone to Spain with Sam Wild in December 1936, was so undernourished that he was covered in over 100 boils and sent to hospital, taking a long recuperation and missing the Battle of the Ebro.[10] Relations with the desperately poor villagers were good because the Brigade quartermasters distributed food to the hungry, and local women often helped to cook the meals for the volunteers. A series of medical stations set up in large houses in the vicinity also treated Spanish families.[11] The men underwent rigorous military instruction, rising at 5.30 a.m., training morning and afternoon for a total of eight hours with 'lights out' at 9 p.m.[12] The men could go to the cinema in Falset once a week, keep libraries and take part in discussions and sing-songs. Morale among the Americans was unstable, primarily because the belief persisted that men who had served six months were due for repatriation. John Gates, the Brigade Commissar, dismissed such hopes at a battalion meeting: 'You are not going home.' He was respected, but not liked because of his abrasive, authoritarian manner.[13] But why should Marty show favour to the anglophone volunteers when the Poles, Germans, Austrians or Yugoslavs had to remain because they faced prison or worse in their home countries?

Steve Fullarton and Michael O'Riordan attended the corporals' school in the main square of Marçà village. Both became light machine-gunners. O'Riordan was a close friend of Lieutenant Paddy O'Sullivan, who led No. 1 Company for a while during the March Retreats before being wounded.[14] O'Sullivan was a punctilious but fair officer, warning recruits after Brunete of the dangers of marching in close formation or digging shallow trenches.[15] He took Fullarton, an 18-year-old Glaswegian who had lied about his age in Spain, under his wing. Fullarton was afraid of the Dublin man at first, but later came to appreciate his martial bearing and competence.[16]

There were two initiatives to raise morale ('political consciousness') in Marçà. In the British battalion the Welsh communist Billy Griffiths started to build a party organisation at company level. He drove some of the older volunteers 'barmy with his lectures on Marxism' (Fred Thomas) and earned scorn from his commander, Jack Nalty, commander of the machine-gun Company (No. 4). The Dublin IRA veteran 'felt the party was a waste of time' and gave the Welsh volunteer tasks that left him little opportunity for sermonising. Only after he was transferred to the Brigade Staff could Griffiths proselytise unhindered.[17] The other attempt was the creation of an 'activist' movement in early July. Among the Americans, it was seen as 'scoutmasterish', causing some satirists to call themselves 'The FONICS' (Friends of the Non-Intervention Committee), i.e. adherents of the withdrawal of all volunteers from Spanish soil.[18] Even the orthodox communist Bill Alexander, an 'official' chronicler of the British in the 15th Brigade and their commander at Teruel, believed both attempts to 'politicise' the infantry men to have been to no avail: Griffiths was seen by some to be undermining the military hierarchy, while the activism drive 'never really caught on: it was simply not needed, for the spirit was already there.'[19] Eugene Downing stated in his memoirs that the 'activism' movement was detrimental because it was perceived as a scheme to monitor dissension in the ranks, a form of 'spying behind people's backs' that greatly angered most volunteers.[20]

The commander of the British battalion since February 1938 was Sam Wild, a 30-year-old Mancunian with a Mayo mother, who grew up in a household steeped in Irish nationalist lore. Like Copeman, he had been in the Royal Navy, but he jumped ship in South Africa in 1932, served his punishment and returned home. He had a distinguished record in the Spanish war, being wounded at Jarama and Brunete.[21] Wild's 'laddish' attitude (settling scores with his fists, for example), together with his sang-froid under pressure, gave him some popularity. On the other hand, his conduct was erratic and his superiors had their doubts about his leadership qualities: 'Not very good attitude towards Spanish comrades. Needs political development, drinks too much.'[22] Fred Thomas, who wrote one of the best memoirs of the war, held Wild to be 'a bit of a roughneck, elemental in his nature'.[23] Wild's leadership was put in question when he banned drinking in the battalion because of drunken antics of the volunteers in a nearby village. The Spaniards in the battalion, and most of the English-speakers, considered vino (they were stationed in an area where wine was cheap and plentiful) as part of their midday rations, and rebelled. At a meeting of party members Wild was accused of 'getting drunk most nights and being brought home in a lorry', and he was threatened by the party zealots with loss of command. So he rescinded the order, a sign that the political commissars were gaining in authority.[24]

Considering that Wild had 'virtually no knowledge of military tactics', choosing him as officer commanding was questionable, despite his fearlessness and Party membership.[25] When Čopić was recalled to Moscow in the second week of June 1938, he was replaced by Major José Antonio Valledor, an Asturian who had fought in the north.[26] Valledor did not believe that Wild had 'the necessary talent for his command to accomplish the tasks at hand', citing his drinking, ruthlessness in giving orders and swearing at Spanish soldiers.[27] The opinion of Brigade Commissar Gates was also negative:

> Little military theory and his work had deteriorated. While his political work is in order, his treatment of his soldiers is not good, for he swears loudly at them due to his character and bad health. He also drinks too much and has a chauvinist attitude towards Spaniards [. . .] He won't be able to develop any further here, on the contrary.[28]

Visitors from abroad were a welcome distraction from the intense training in high temperatures. The Indian independence leaders Krishna Menon and Jawaharlal Nehru, and Nehru's daughter Indira, came up from Barcelona in the company of the Republican Foreign Minister Julio Álvarez del Vayo and visited the Brigade base. The British battalion showed them the firing power of their Maxims. Maurice Ryan of Limerick, an accomplished machine-gunner since Teruel, cut down a tree on the other side of the valley in a concentrated burst.[29] A five-man student delegation from Britain that included the future Prime Minister Edward (Ted) Heath (Chairman of the Federation of University Conservative Associations) visited the British battalion. They were presented with a copy of *The Book of the XV Brigade*, autographed by the men of No. 1 Company. That meeting was the basis for the mutual respect in later years between Heath and Jack Jones, head of the Transport and General Workers' Union between 1968 and 1978 and the commissar under O'Daire in the Major Attlee (No. 1) Company.[30]

Memorable also were the festivities carried out by the national contingents of the battalions. The Canadians celebrated 'Dominion Day' on 1 July, the Americans their 4 July, with parades and fiestas for all. The Irish were not to be outdone, celebrating Wolfe Tone's birthday (20 June) and treating their guests to a meal of black rice bread, mule meat and vino tinto. There were speeches, IRA songs, Cuban ballads and even a flamenco, or was it a Cossack dance by the young Londoner Max Nash?[31] The last such day of festivities ended in disaster. The British (57th) Battalion of the brigade organised a special day on 18 July, the second anniversary of the generals' uprising. The men marched off at 8 a.m. and assembled with the other battalions on the football field (now the site of a school) in Marçà to listen to speeches and then watch sporting competitions (football, boxing, high jump). The midday meal was comparably generous: stew and beans, followed by the distribution of chocolate, cigarettes and bottles of champagne.

The main attraction of the day was to be a machine-gun competition between two crews: who could mount the barrel on the wheeled carriage, load it, sight the target and pretend to fire the first shot in the minimum amount of time. George Fletcher, battalion adjutant, was backing Maurice Ryan and his No. 2 (unknown), Wild the Gordon brothers from Walsall, Gordon ('Dusty') on the gun and Donald feeding it. When the competition ended shortly before 5 p.m., the soldiers rushed forward to congratulate the teams, but two bullets had been left in the lock and somebody pressed the firing button of the Maxim. A young Spaniard was mortally wounded in the stomach and John Whittle, a veteran from Bury, injured. It was never established why the accident happened, but alcohol may have been in play. It certainly soured relations with Spanish battalion members, who refused to let any English attend the funeral of el soldado Marciel Rodrigo Valero.[32] Fred Thomas's attitude to the incident was probably typical:

> What a lousy way to go. Somebody was at fault and in my opinion it was the first and second in command of the Battalion and the chap in charge of the gun for the careless way they allowed loaded machine-guns to be handled. But I suppose it's easy to judge. Anyway, that finished the fiesta.[33]

A few days later the Brigade was alarmed and set off on a series of marches that led them to the banks of the Ebro near Vinebre. There they were told that they were to cross the river in a new offensive.

## THE FIRST TWO DAYS OF THE EBRO BATTLE, 25–26 JULY

Overall conduct of the operation was in the hands of the commander of the new Army of the Ebro, Colonel Juan Modesto, and comprised three corps: the 5th under Líster, the 12th under Etelvino Vega and the 15th under the 25-year-old physicist Manuel Tagüeña. In his command lay the 35th Division of Pedro Mateo Merino, equally young and a fellow scientist from Madrid University General Walter had returned to the USSR in May. Merino had to manoeuvre three International Brigades, the German 11th, the Slavs of the 13th and the Anglo-American 15th – in all about 12,000 soldiers of whom roughly a quarter were Internationals. The front was 60 km wide, between the riverside towns of Fayón in the north to Cherta in the south; and although Modesto had about 80,000 men at his disposal, there was an acute shortage of ack-ack guns, field pieces, mortars, grenades and aircraft. The 15th Brigade was to traverse the swollen torrent of the Ebro in boats, capture Ascó and drive on about 20 km inland to the towns of Corbera and Gandesa. The divisions of Líster and El Campesino were to attack from the south to take the village of El Pinell de Brai on the far bank and proceed to gain footholds in the Sierra Pandols, the rugged mountain range between Gandesa and the southern stretch of the river. Further downriver, the hapless French and Belgians of the 14th Brigade (Lopera, la Granja) tried to cross the Ebro at Amposta very near the sea and were destroyed, suffering 1,200 casualties in 24 hours, and were forced back over the river.[34] The offensive had been minutely planned: pontoon bridges were constructed in Catalonia or bought in France and, once again, Franco did not take the threat seriously, merely ordering his most capable field commander, Lieutenant Colonel Juan Yagüe, to maintain the alert. When notified of the crossing, El Caudillo sent troops on a forced march to Gandesa and over 100 bombers and an equal number of fighter planes to zero in on the pontoon bridges.[35] The much weakened Republican Air Force – the Soviet pilots had been repatriated – was rarely seen in the coming weeks.

In the early hours of 25 July, the crossings began in boats rowed by locals who knew the currents. Mules laden with the equipment of the machine-gunners swam alongside. Scouts from the 11th and 13th Brigades stifled resistance on the far bank, establishing a bridgehead. A plank footbridge was thrown across and the Polish-Slav battalions passed over shortly before 5 a.m., followed by the Germans and Austrians. The footway was soon destroyed by shelling so the Canadian 60th Battalion and the Spanish 59th were the first of the 15th Brigade to make the crossing in rowing boats, joining up with the German-speakers on the far bank to attack Ascó. They soon captured it, along with Flix, 6 km upstream. Mounting the horses of a cavalry unit that had surrendered together with the garrison battalion in Ascó, a squad of Canadian machine-gunners rushed to the military depot in Flix and divided the spoils (blankets, boots, tinned fish) among their comrades and the local population near Corbera in the late afternoon.[36] When the British 57th battalion crossed, they numbered just over 280 English-speakers, and at least 27 were Irish.[37] Including the Spanish conscripts or volunteers, the unit totalled 558.[38] They were badly equipped, having lost their three Soviet anti-tank guns in the March flight (El Campesino's men 'commandeered' two),[39] and were now relying on one puny looking anti-tank gun,[40] rifles, machine guns and the odd mortar. There was also a shortage of hand grenades. For at least three days

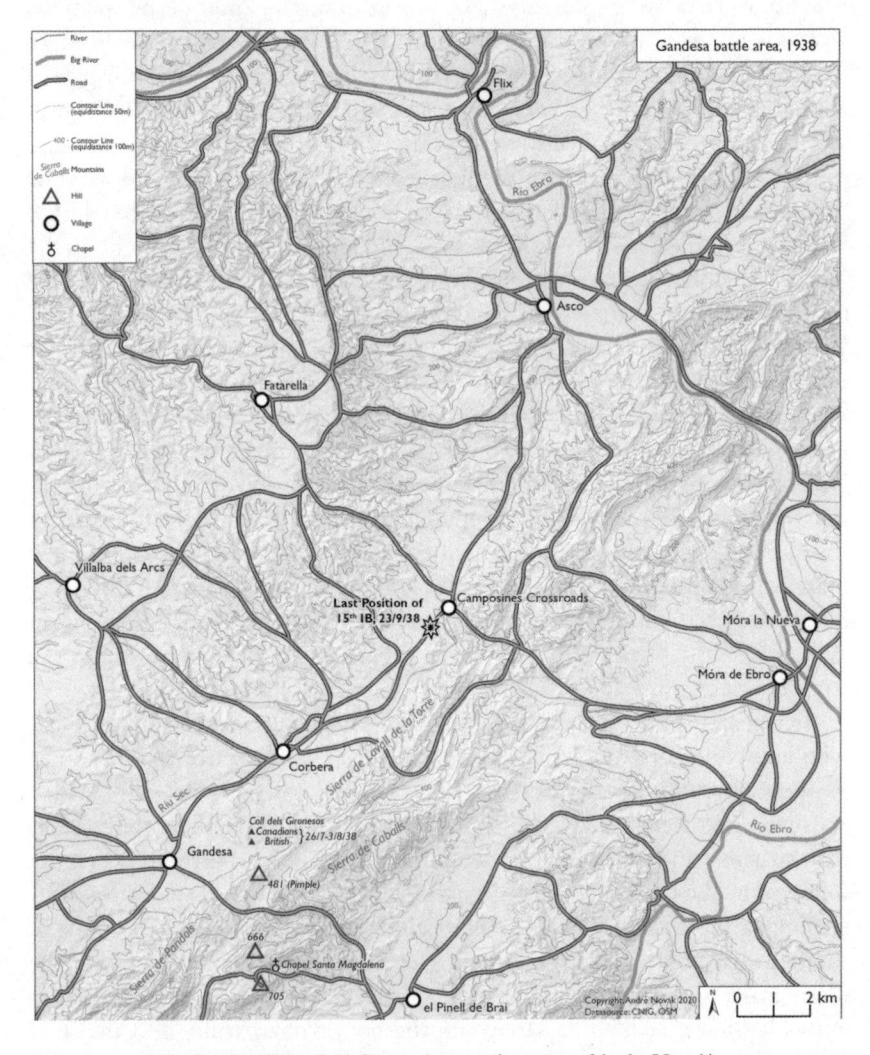

Battle of the Ebro, July–September 1938 (courtesy of André Novak)

they were forced 'to live off the land' (mainly captured stores) because the terrific aerial bombardment of the river crossing, commencing on the first day, held up ambulances, food trucks and vital equipment. On the road south to Corbera, Michael O'Riordan carried the Catalan flag and Bob Clark remembers a peasant kissing it.[41]

The day was a scorcher and many of the troops, exhilarated by their swift advance but now tiring in the afternoon heat, took off their shirts and went onwards in their torn trousers and rope sandals. They could see the church tower of Corbera in the distance, and to the south-east, looming on their left, a formidable mountain chain, a granite spine with sparse vegetation called the Sierra Pandols y Caballs. The high elevations were the key to dominating the area: the Caballs overlooked Corbera, the Pandols Gandesa, and the road leading south from Gandesa to the lower Ebro was the dividing line between the ranges. On the right of the marching British, north of the Ascó–Corbera road, were many small hills that stretched north to Ribaroja on the upper Ebro. It was clear from the start that taking Gandesa and the high ground south of it was the key to victory, for the countryside west of the town of 3,400 inhabitants was relatively flat, and the road open to Calaceite, scene of the disaster on 31 March in lower Aragon.

The British, forming the left flank of the 13th IB, linked up with it about 2 km short of Corbera at around 3 p.m. The Slavs were designated to take the town but were detained by enfilading fire of Moors hiding on hills and in caves nearby. Paddy O'Daire sent his men out on a successful mopping-up operation that ended after night had fallen.[42] Morris Davies's Fourth Company was ordered to attack a hill directly in front at dusk, but darkness intervened and the men rested. The sudden fall of night was fortunate, for the hill in question was already in the hands of the Americans – at least one cock-up was thus avoided.[43] Ted Smallbone, assistant to Commissar Johnny Power, surmised that the bad coordination between units on the march was due to the lack of maps or the inaccuracy of hand-drawn ones:

> One Company HQ would take decisions and action on the basis of its information while another HQ might be taking action on quite different information. So, for example, one Company might be expecting us alongside them and would look around: 'Where's the British battalion, we can't see them anywhere?', while we might be looking around, 'Where's the Mac-Paps or the French or the Garibaldis?' You were never sure who was on your flanks, left or right. So in that sense we were pretty well disorganized.[44]

The Americans of the 58th battalion, on landing on the Ebro's western bank under attack from Italian bombers, struck inland, moving due west towards La Fatarella village. Infiltrating groups drove out the defenders before dawn on 26 July and, having consumed their iron rations, were cheered to discover an abandoned quartermaster's store (intendencia), a veritable treasure trove of Italian tinned food, tobacco, uniforms and welcome boots. There was an unseemly row with the neighbouring 3rd Division about ownership of the booty, but the Americans were first takers and terminated the heated exchanges. They hurried off to help the Spanish 59th Battalion to the south-west in its efforts to cut the road between Gandesa and the town to its north, Vilalba dels Arcs.

Franco's troops were surrendering in droves, even to individuals, providing the 35th Division with valuable equipment, including some heavy guns drawn by tractors. The 13th Brigade used the latter to bombard fascist positions in Corbera on the morning of the second day. The surviving defenders surrendered or fled, and the brigade pushed on 2 km westwards, entering the northern outskirts of Gandesa. Approaching the first houses, the Poles realised that their successful advance stopped here: reinforcements were arriving in the garrison and the streets were blocked by barricades, with rolls of barbed wire placed in circles around machine-gun nests.[45] Some Canadians fighting with the 13th Brigade were in sight of Gandesa's soccer field, but withdrew because of the strength of its defences.[46] When another Canadian company entered the now deserted Corbera on the morning of the second day, they discovered a cornucopia equal to that of the Americans at La Fatarella: Italian-made boots, cigars and all kinds of food, which the locals and the transport trucks of the 15th Brigade carried off after the Canadians had left with their overladen 'cavalry'.[47] Speed was now of the essence for the sky was full of enemy aircraft, 40–60 machines, that soon razed Corbera (it has been left a ruin, like Belchite), and Gandesa had to be taken before even more reinforcements were rushed there by the alarmed command of Franco.

The Internationals advanced up the valley in extended lines through olive groves and vineyards: on the left the entire British battalion, companies of Mac-Paps in the middle, and to the right some Americans and the 13th IB. Both the Canadians and the British were now under the orders of 13th Brigade staff. Two kilometres short of their goal, both brigades came under intense fire from the ridges to their left and from the town itself.[48] The British suffered their first of many casualties inflicted by snipers on the heights above them. Maurice Ryan climbed up on a knoll to position a Maxim to spray the area where he thought enemy marksmen were hiding. Gordon Bennett as No. 2 and his brother Donald as No. 1 on the Maxim were firing from behind a wall when the protective shield of the gun slipped out of alignment. Don Bennett could not see over the sights, and when his brother rose to adjust the plate he was hit in the chest and fell dying.[49]

The British were now scrambling up the knolls on the valley floor (Coll dels Gironesos) and returning the fire from the peaks opposite. Eugene

Downing was struck by a bullet that went through his left leg, and James F. O'Regan helped him down to the medics.[50] On the other side of the slopes towards the Ebro, the divisions of Líster had taken the villages of Miravet and El Pinell de Brai and were advancing up the southern ridges of the Pandols–Caballs. The northern face of the range had therefore to be captured, especially Puig de l'Àliga (481 m), the high point in the ridge overlooking Gandesa, strongly fortified with barbed wire, entrenchments and bunkers. The British were ordered to storm it, an impossible task without artillery, anti-tank guns, air support or mortars.

### THE BLOODBATH ON HILL 481

Six days of assaults would severely reduce battalion numbers, and the men could often neither advance nor retreat because of withering fire from three sides, and were therefore forced to lie flat in scant cover as long as daylight lasted, without food, water or medical aid. The first assault was in the early morning of 27 July, over dipping ground and coming to a sharp halt before the steep incline to the barbed wire on the ridge. No. 1 Company was on scouting duties, No. 4 was the machine-gun company, and so the first assaults fell to companies No. 2 and 3. The first attack soon petered out, and Steve Fullarton was tending to a wounded comrade when he heard Paddy O'Sullivan calling to him. The Irish lieutenant had been wounded in the right leg and left arm. Applying tourniquets to his limbs, Fullarton promised to fetch him at nightfall. But Fullarton was wounded in the right side shortly afterwards and believed that O'Sullivan was killed by counterattacking Moors.[51] At least 20 were wounded, including Jack Jones. Bill Bailey of the Lincolns, posted on a hill to the right, remembered the attack:

> We could see the whole [panorama], like watching a TV set [. . .] The British came out of their trenches [. . .] They were now trying to work their way up the hill. They got half way up the hill – the Fascists just waited. Then they rolled out hand after hand grenade, just rolled it down the hill at them. It was a massacre.[52]

On 28 July, the third company under the Spanish lieutenant Cipriano got to within 20 metres of the enemy trenches before withdrawing. On 30 July No. 2 Company was cut to pieces after advancing a few yards. Their leaders fell in turn: Lieutenants Angus and Gregory and Sergeant Harrington were wounded, and Corporal Harkins was killed.[53] Johnny Power, lieutenant and commissar, took command of No. 2 Company. The following day, 31 July, a desperate charge by No. 3 Company brought the men to within 15 m of the enemy, who drove them off with a shower of hand grenades and machine-gun fire. A night attack, with the help of riflemen from the Lísters and the 13th Brigade, was similarly repulsed.[54]

August 1, a Bank Holiday Monday in Britain, was the date for the presumed last assault on the cursed 'Pimple'. The men were soon under fire and had to lie still in the searing heat before the assault could be resumed at 10 p.m. The British and Irish reached grenade-throwing distance of the enemy trenches, but were beaten off by superior firepower.[55] By then the 57th was a battalion only in name, and Johnny Power took over the amalgamated second and third companies.[56] A coordinated attack in the direction of the cemetery in Gandesa with a Canadian company on 1 August broke down because of enfilading fire.[57]

The great majority of the Mac-Paps, however, were thrown into the cauldron under Hill 481. They defended the dried-up water course ('Valley of Death') that led up to the jumping-off point for the assaults on 'The Pimple', then left it to join the British in the deadly ascent in the last days of July. The German 88mm anti-aircraft and 'tank buster' guns drove off Republican 'Mosca' fighters. Modesto had, from the start, urged the use of aircraft to bomb Gandesa and although supported by Colonel García Lacalle, the commander of the fighter squadrons, the request was initially turned down by Lieutenant Colonel Martínez Visiedo, the chief of operations in the air ministry.[58] On 1 August, when the Republican bombers finally arrived and dropped their loads over Gandesa three times, the German 88s were again deadly accurate, destroying three tanks supporting the Canadian–British assault on 'The Pimple'.[59]

The British were withdrawn from the front line around midnight on 1 August and relieved by Poles, but Wild's surviving men remained close by and were under artillery and air bombardment. The depleted unit was recalled to launch the very last assault on the heights on 3 August, which was unsuccessful and marked the failure of the Ebro campaign.[60] The battalion roll call now stood at 150.[61] The official casualty figures for the International Brigades up to 4 August totalled 2,616. According to records of the 35th Division, the losses were highest in the 15th: 878, of which 218 were from the British unit – 19 dead, 190 wounded and 9 deserters.[62] This is an underestimation, for data from the Moscow files would indicate that Jim Carmody's figure of at least 40 mortalities in the British unit on Hill 481 is accurate.[63]

Six Irishmen died on the slopes of 'The Pimple' or in the vicinity: Danny Boyle, James Straney, Paddy O'Sullivan, James Jones in the assaults, and William Keenan and Edward (Jackie) Patterson (both Mac-Paps) in air raids. At least nine were wounded: Eugene Downing, Michael Lehane, James McKeefrey, Tom O'Brien, William O'Hanlon, Michael Waters, James F. O'Regan, David Thornton and Michael O'Riordan. Lehane was cited for bravery after leading a group of 25 men to within yards of the barbed wire and refusing the aid of stretcher-bearers because of heavy fire. Michael O'Riordan, who brought him to safety, was later wounded in the shoulder and refused to leave with his light machine-gun after the withdrawal of his company 'until ordered to by the Commander and Commissar'. Johnny Power was praised for his courage and for leading the amalgamated companies; he took part 'in all the actions and was an example to all his men'.[64] The operation had foundered within a week, one reason being that the tanks could not cross the Ebro on time, and another being the lack of activity of their airmen. The Lincoln battalion encountered strong resistance on 27 July, the third day, against a new defence line manned by Moors on the hills east of the Vilalba–Gandesa road. After initial successes, the attacks turned to a desperate holding action after the refusal of the quintas to go forward and the wounding of the experienced company commander Larry Lamb. Three further assaults by the Lincolns on the hills near the road failed the following day: the quintas were still reluctant to move even after an irate American officer had shot two of them, and some American volunteers deliberately lagged behind. They had run out of grenades and food and were obviously exhausted. July 29 was a day for regrouping the American companies, and on 30 July two Spanish battalions attacked through the Lincoln positions and were decimated. Wolff called off the attacks, the Americans went into reserve and the food lorry finally arrived.[65] The Lincolns' muster at the beginning of the campaign was about 700, by 1 August it had shrunk to 400, 50 were dead, 250 wounded, and 2 companies contained barely 100 riflemen in all.[66]

### SIERRA PANDOLS: HILL 666

At midnight on 6 August the 15th Brigade was relieved by a Spanish division. They took the road through Corbera, which, like the blighted slopes they had left, stank of unburied dead, and settled down in olive groves near the river about 3 km short of Móra d'Ebre. The British got their first hearty breakfast in weeks, fried bread and sardines, washed down with coffee. Food remained pitifully scarce and foraging parties spread out. John Dunlop and his friend George Wheeler bought vegetables and exchanged them with a peasant family for cooked meals, scarce bars of soap being the currency for later visits of the duo and their 'mates'.[67] On one occasion there was mass-bathing in the Ebro, and new, threadbare cotton uniforms were handed out. This was no sunny retreat because air raids and artillery duels were daily occurrences. Gates was still receiving repatriation requests from the disaffected, which he rejected in toto, while in the British battalion the rumour went the rounds that men who had served at least 14 months in Spain would get home leave. This was confirmed in the essence, but not in the detail: only for six days and only for 30 men from the entire Brigade.[68] The sojourn away from the front line lasted a week. In the meantime, Franco's forces had destroyed the Republican pocket on the upper Ebro between Mequinenza and Fayón, and in a second phase launched a major push to drive the men of Líster off the Sierra Pandols. If the fascists gained the heights around the hermitage of Santa Magdalena southwest of the Gandesa–Tortosa road, they could shell the river crossings at Móra and thus prevent the Republicans from retreating across the Ebro. That was the background for sending the 15th Brigade once more into battle in the afternoon of 14 August.

It was a long, exhausting march along back roads, through the blasted village of El Pinell de Brai, then up a steep path flanked by a precipitous drop. The last stretch took three hours uphill and ended near Hill 666, just down from the highest point Cota 705 (now the site of monuments to the British Battalion and the Quinta de Biberón). To the front were secondary ridges above the Gandesa–Corbera valley, and to their rear downhill the hermitage. The rugged peaks and knolls had been burnt free of all vegetation by incendiary shells and bombs dropped by the Italians and the Condor Legion. In a word, the positions were in a desert of rock, with no possibility of digging in or building proper trenches. The battalions were now subject to *aplastamiento*, an incessant plastering of the area by highly accurate shelling and armadas of aircraft dropping scores of bombs that blew men to pieces, while others were often wounded by whirring shards of steel or splinters of rock.

It was hellish: no ground to dispose of the dead, and all supplies, including water and food, had to be brought up a long winding track. The wounded were evacuated down the same route, a tortuous downhill hike of 4–5 km at night to the ambulances. In some positions no fortifications had been built, so the men constructed shaky piles of calcite rock for cover. The rocks reflected the heat, but at night the soldiers froze when the wind rose. The bloated mule cadavers or the bodies of friend and foe killed in the previous two weeks' fighting let off such a nauseating stench that the medical staff issued the IB volunteers with bags of camphor to hang around their necks. Many Internationals also had pieces of wood to chew to steady their nerves when the terrifying bombardments started. They were to spend 11 days and nights in this mountain inferno.

The 15th Brigade took up posts around a series of three overlapping hills known generally as 666: the Lincolns on the right, Canadians in the centre and the Spanish 59th behind the Americans. The British were in reserve nearby. They could see the dreaded Hill 481 ('The Pimple') in the distance to their front. Because a knoll beneath the Lincolns' ridge was occupied by the enemy, a hastily planned attack was launched to capture it on 17 August. The supporting artillery fire was insufficient, with the Chato fighters machine-gunning Republican positions in the afternoon. The companies then waited for the order to attack, which came when the light had failed. The Americans were driven back by a torrent of bullets, likewise the British just before dawn.[69] Two days of the heaviest artillery and air bombing of the war to date were followed by mass attacks of Franco's infantry. They were repulsed with high losses. The front line of the Americans and British, who had relieved them on 24 August, held. During the night of 26 August, the 15th IB were relieved. Desertions now became a problem, with the young Spaniards surrendering to the enemy in groups, and some Internationals heading for the river. Four from the British battalion deserted two nights later, and two were Irish – Paddy Tighe and James Domegan.[70]

### SIERRA DE LAVALL DE LA TORRE

At their encampment in olive groves off the Ascó–Corbera road, the British battalion could at least wash, shave and sleep in peace. Wild went to hospital because of a wounded hand and was replaced by George Fletcher, while Captain Paddy O'Daire, the battalion secretary Ted Edwards and two Labour councillors (Jack Jones and Tom Murray) were finally repatriated on 1 September.[71] Harry Pollitt, on his fifth and last visit, spoke to the shrunken unit and then travelled inland to visit the wounded. He was obviously moved by their plight and wrote to the Spanish Communist Party and Luigi Longo of the IB Commissariat, urging the immediate return of the 'dead tired' fighters to Britain on leave and posed for discussion a general withdrawal, not least because he feared the loss of 'our very best local and district cadres'.[72] The commissars tried to 'lay down the law': all talk of extended leave or mass-repatriation undermined morale, and although the Ebro offensive was a success, the Internationals were still needed.[73] Gates blamed Pollitt in part 'because he had contributed to fomenting such ideas, which makes it necessary to clarify the matter.'[74]

The fourth part of Franco's offensive in the Ebro pocket was directed against Col de los Gironesos in the valley east of Gandesa under Hill 481, and onwards up to the Gandesa–Corbera road towards Venta de Composines. After the fall of Corbera on 4 September, most of the fighting took place to the east and south of that road, around Sierra de Lavall de La Torre, a northern continuation of the Sierra Caballs, but lower in height and wooded. It overlooked the road north to Ascó, more precisely the stretch Corbera–Camposines.

The defensive clashes and counterattacks of the 15th IB in September happened here, probably to the north, but exact geographical data is not available and many of the references to place and elevation are vague. On 7 September the Brigade was rushed by truck to close a breach in the front. The Americans' Third Company launched a night attack on a hill but was outflanked the next morning. Fighting desperately at close quarters, the Americans retreated in disorder. Only eight of the 70 men escaped.[75] At least 14 were taken prisoner and summarily shot.[76] The ground was less rocky here, and the battalions dug deep trenches and logged bunkers for machine guns. The British captured a hill and clung to it for a week. Hostile air activity was now intense, the Brigade HQ was bombed, but relief arrived around 14 September.[77] Lieutenant Gregory noted at the time that of the 150 men who had crossed the Ebro with him only 24 remained.[78] When the men came out of the line, the British No. 1 and No. 2 companies were amalgamated under Johnny Power, with Bill McGregor, a Lenin School graduate from Dublin, acting as his commissar.[79]

Morale and fighting spirit were declining rapidly. Many of the men were sick from stomach complaints, others were almost barefoot because neither boots nor rope sandals were available.[80] A commander of scouts in the Spanish 59th battalion deserted to the enemy; E. Cecil Smith, commander of the Canadian 60th, wounded himself, intentionally, so the majority believed, while cleaning his pistol; and the American Machine-Gun company, it was alleged, retreated in panic in the face of an enemy attack.[81] Five from the British battalion disappeared on 19 September, three Spaniards and two English sergeants. In all, 22–25 English-speakers deserted from the battalion during the Ebro campaign, but some came back into the line after a few days.[82] The chances of getting out alive were diminishing fast, for the Republic had no answer to the relentless juggernaut of Franco and his allies; only dogged resistance with insufficient means to delay its progress. The fifth phase of the fascist counter-attack, to capture the road junction of Camposines to Fatarella, finally finished off the Internationals as a fighting force. There were now no more recruits from abroad, only a motley collection of unmotivated conscripts and other Spaniards released from penal battalions.

### DISASTER ON THE LAST DAY OF ACTION

On 21 September at 6 p.m., the 15th Brigade was positioned north of Pont dels Bassiols bridge on the Corbera–Camposines road, the British on the left, the Americans in the middle and the Canadians on the right.[83] On the British left flank and south of the road were the 13th and 11th Brigades. Late that night the 15th IB battalions were rushed to help the Poles, whose trenches had been flattened in a storm of shells. The new positions the British entered were highly unsatisfactory: the engineers had constructed shallow trenches on a forward instead of a reverse slope. Furthermore, this sector was lower than the enemy's.[84] None of them knew as yet that on the same day Premier Negrín had announced at a sitting of the League of Nations in Geneva the withdrawal of all volunteers from Republican Spain. Early next morning, some American positions were spotted by an observation plane, and it was followed by waves of JU-52 and Heinkel 111 bombers that unloaded tons of explosives in accurate drops across the brigade's front. During the night Wolff informed his commissars of Negrín's decision, adding that the men had to fight one more day. An American commissar was sent to Divisional HQ to stop both the mail and the Barcelona newspapers, and the British battalion commissar Bob Cooney instructed the commissars not to inform the men. The news filtered down to the Lincoln and Mac-Paps riflemen, but in the British battalion Lieutenant Walter Gregory of No. 2 Company and his 20 or so soldiers knew nothing about it.[85]

The very last day, 23 September, started with an encouraging prelude: Republican fighters strafing the rebel lines and desultory fire from the heavy guns of the 35th Division. Shortly afterwards a terrific barrage rained down on the Brigade, supplemented by over 200 fascist aircraft on bombing and strafing runs. Owing to a breakdown in communication, American machine-gunners never reached the hill to protect the Lincolns' right flank.[86] This proved disastrous, for the attackers came through that gap from a wooden slope on the right, using the cane cover of the barranco of the Vimenoses rivulet behind Gregory's men. He and six others were captured, including Jim Haughey from Armagh.[87] The line broke, all was confusion. The British and the Canadians fell back through the barranco, crossing the road. Many Spanish recruits went over to the enemy, and then five tanks came down the road from Corbera. Three were knocked out by machine-gunners, but the other two, with waves of infantry in their wake, came up through the dry watercourse behind No. 1 Company. Many British were killed or captured, only Johnny Power and a handful of men managed to fight their way out. The massed attackers were now among the machine-gun company. Bill Feely and Syd Booth were letting off bursts from their Maxim and noticed that there was no support firing. Booth left the trench and realised that the hill was deserted. Just as they were breaking down the gun, Jack Nalty ran up:

> 'Come on, you two. I've had to come back for you'. I got the wheels, Feely had the barrel and Nalty the case. Down the hill we went and just as we got to the bottom

we met Johnny Lobban and one or two more. We had only a few yards to go and would have been with the battalion. The fascists had got to the top [of the hill] by then and sprayed us [. . .] Jack Nalty got shot through the head, got killed. I was wounded in the leg, Lobban and Cliff Lacey were killed, and Feely got wounded.[88]

Fletcher and Cooney organised the stragglers and formed a line on a ridge 300 yards back and they were soon joined by the survivors from the other battalions. The attacks subsided, and just after midnight units from El Campesino's division relieved the 15th International Brigade. The losses were appalling, akin to the blood toll of Jarama or Brunete, but on a single day: when the men went into action on 22 September, the roll call was 377, of whom 106 were British or Irish; at withdrawal the survivors numbered 173, including 58 English speakers, i.e. 200 casualties. In all, the losses in the Ebro campaign amounted to 80 per cent of the men from Britain and Ireland who had gone into battle with such high hopes on 25 July. That equalled the casualty ratio at Brunete. Five Irishmen lost their lives on the last day: Jack Nalty and Bill McGregor from Dublin, James Domegan and Henry McGrath from Belfast and Tom O'Flaherty of the Lincolns. While recuperating in Mataró hospital, Eugene Downing asked Sergeant Cornwallis of news of the last day in combat:

> 'How's Jack Nalty anyway?' He gave me a shocked look. 'Nalty's dead', he says. I was so shocked I couldn't say anything. 'He was shot a number of times at close range. He died three hours later.' I couldn't understand it fully and a great wave of sadness passed through me on hearing this. Other people whom I knew had been killed and I was devastated on hearing of their deaths. For some reason this was worse than any of them and I felt physically sick in a way that I'd never had before. We kept talking for another while but about other things, but I didn't hear anything anymore.[89]

For the Canadians, 23 September was equally bitter and traumatic: only 35 were still on their feet when they left the firing zone.[90] When the Americans formed lines on the soccer field in Marçà some days later, 61 stepped forward.[91]

### THE LONG DEPARTURE

The 70-odd survivors of the British battalion soon moved to Guiamets near Marçà. Their feelings were very mixed: they were glad to have survived but were mourning their dead comrades and realising that the war was finally lost. In Marçà, hungry families waited outside the church, the battalion dining hall, for any leftover scraps of food. Men granted short leave to Barcelona found the food situation even worse there.[92] When the series of parades and festivities began, the estrangement between Spanish troops and the Internationals was palpable: after all, the Spaniards were going back into action across the Ebro to probable death or mutilation, and the foreigners were celebrating their own salvation and departure.[93]

News of the 30 September Munich Agreement was but a depressing confirmation that the cause of Spanish democracy was doomed and that a major war was more likely than ever. Several parades were held in the village, a large one before the commanders of the 35th Division, marching columns of the battalions of the 15th Brigade photographed by Robert Capa, and a fiesta for the villagers and toys for the children. Hours afterwards, the men moved off in trucks during a violent thunderstorm and headed north for Ripoll, a town in the north-west of Gerona province, some 25 miles from the French border. On the way the volunteers disembarked in Poblet, north of Tarragona, for speeches by Juan Modesto, President Azaña, Premier Negrín and André Marty. Citations for bravery in the Ebro battle were read out, as well as promotions, including Johnny Power's new rank of captain.[94] The last parade, in Barcelona on 28 October, was a memorable march through crowded streets, the 'Last Hurrah' of the Internationals.

The six-week sojourn in Ripoll was miserable. The weather was cold and wet, the buildings unheated and food supplies scarce. There was little for the men to do, and the shelves of the shops were virtually denuded of most articles, except clothes. The Control Commission of the League of Nations arrived in early November, noting the men's particulars and departed. The members of the commission, almost all military men, were held to be unnecessarily inquisitive, if not downright hostile, like the Canadian commissioner Colonel O'Kelly.[95] The British battalion sent emissaries throughout the Republican zone to seek out compatriots in other units (e.g. the predominantly Slav 129th IB, the Heavy Machine-Gun Battalion, and artillery units) and those in hospitals. Stragglers were sent straight to Ripoll ahead of the main battalion group, which numbered 60 on 30 September and 145 (12 Irish) two weeks later.[96] At least 100 wounded and sick British and Irish were recovering in the hospitals.

A second visit of the Control Commission on 24 November raised hopes, but bureaucratic difficulties continued, and only after a newspaper campaign and lobbying by MPs was the deadlock broken. Three hundred and twenty British and Irish left Ripoll on 6 December and received a rapturous welcome at London's Victoria Station on the evening of the following day. The first Americans also left in early December, but when they landed in New York their passports were confiscated.[97]

The Canadians had the hardest lot. Their Government was initially hostile as the Royal Canadian Mounted Police urged banning their re-entry. Fortunately, as in the case of the Lincolns, the Spanish Government underwrote their repatriation costs, and the representatives of the Canadian Pacific Railway were sympathetic and efficient. Having left Ripoll with their departure undecided, the Canadians were moved to the hill town of Castellar de la Selva near Gerona. They were still there in late January when the fall of Barcelona seemed imminent and the call went out for Internationals to support defensive lines near the city. Over a 100 Canadians volunteered for what is known by Austrian and German volunteers as the disastrous zweiter Einsatz (second deployment), but were not needed. Marty visited them shortly afterwards, and in a red-faced rant called them 'cowards' and 'rabbits'. When one man lit a cigarette, Marty screamed for his arrest, alleging he was a spy signalling to the fascists! The Canadians laughed him off the platform.[98] They left at the end of January and travelled through France and England to the Liverpool–Halifax boat in sealed trains. Some wounded Canadians left later, tagging on to the endless lines of refugees heading for the French border, where they were arrested and put in an internment camp. They were rescued by the British Consul, who was probably also the Good Samaritan for Paddy Duff, discharged from the hospital in Figueras, and held behind barbed wire in St Cyprien camp. Duff did not get home until February 1939.

NOTES

1. Henry Buckley, *The Life and Death of the Spanish Republic: A Witness To The Spanish Civil War* (London, 2014), pp 377–9.
2. Arthur Landis, *Lincoln Brigade* (New York, 1968), pp 490–1.
3. Fred Thomas, *To Tilt at Windmills: A Memoir of the Spanish Civil War* (East Lansing, Mi, 1996), pp 99–105.
4. RGASPI, f. 495, o. 205, d. 229, ll. 161–8.
5. Walter Gregory, *The Shallow Grave: A Memoir of the Spanish Civil War* (London, 1986), pp 113–14.
6. Bill Alexander, *British Volunteers for Liberty: Spain 1936–39* (London, 1982), p. 199.
7. Victor Howard (with Mac Reynolds), *The MacKenzie-Papineau Battalion: The Canadian Contingent in the Spanish Civil War* (Ottawa, 1969), pp 205–7.
8. Eoghan Ó Duinnín, *La Niña Bonita agus An Róisín Dubh* (Baile Átha Cliath, 1986), p. 15.
9. Cecil Eby, *Between the Bullet and the Lie: American Volunteers in the Spanish Civil War* (New York–Chicago–San Francisco, 1969), p. 273; Landis, *The Abraham Lincoln Brigade*, pp 516–7; Angela Jackson, *At the Margins of Mayhem: Prologue and Epilogue to the Last Great Battle of the Spanish Civil War* (Pontypool, 2008), pp 19–21, 32–5.

10. Corkhill, Rawnsley, *Road to Spain*, pp 42–6.
11. Jackson, *At the Margins*, pp 44–8.
12. Ibid., p. 40.
13. Peter N. Carroll, *The Odyssey of the Abraham Lincoln Brigade: Americans in the Spanish Civil War* (Stanford, 1994), pp 190–1.
14. RGASPI, f. 545, o. 6, d. 89, l. 39.
15. RGASPI, f. 545, o. 3, d. 456, l. 140.
16. Ian MacDougall, *Voices from the Spanish Civil War: Scottish Volunteers in Republican Spain 1936–39* (Edinburgh, 1986), pp 292–5.
17. James K. Hopkins, *Into the Heart of the Fire. The British in the Spanish Civil War* (Stanford, 1998), pp 300–1.
18. Jackson, *At the Margins*, p. 91.
19. Bill Alexander, *British Volunteers for Liberty: Spain 1936–39* (London, 1982), pp 201–3.
20. Ó Duinnín, *La Niña Bonita*, p. 52.
21. Greater Manchester International Brigade Memorial Committee (ed.), *Greater Manchester Men Who Fought in Spain* (Manchester, 1983), pp 55–68.
22. RGASPI, f. 545, o. 6, d. 215, l. 30.
23. Thomas, *To Tilt at Windmills*, p. 177.
24. Hopkins, *Into the Fire*, pp 304–5; Jackson, *At the Margins*, p. 37.
25. Hopkins, *Into the Fire*, p. 248.
26. RGASPI, f. 545, o. 3, d. 430, l. 189.
27. RGASPI, f. 545, o. 6, d. 215, l. 19.
28. Ibid., l. 26.
29. Jackson, *At the Margins*, p. 90; Walter Gregory, *The Shallow Grave: A Memoir of the Spanish Civil War* (London, 1986), p. 116.
30. Max Arthur, *The Real Band of Brothers: First-Hand Accounts of the Last British Survivors of the Spanish Civil War* (London, 2009), pp 137–8.
31. O'Riordan, *Connolly Column*, pp 124–5; Ó Duinnín, *La Niña Bonita*, pp 52–4.
32. RGASPI, f. 545, o. 3, d. 8, l. 77; George Wheeler, *To Make the People Smile Again: A Memoir of the Spanish Civil War* (Newcastle upon Tyne, 2003), pp 59–60; Jackson, *At the Margins*, pp 101–4.
33. Thomas, *To Tilt at Windmills*, p. 112.
34. Antony Beevor, *Battle for Spain: The Spanish Civil War, 1936–1939* (London, 2006), pp 350–1.
35. Ibid., pp 351–2.
36. Victor Howard (with Mac Reynolds), *The MacKenzie-Papineau Battalion: The Canadian Contingent in the Spanish Civil War* (Ottawa, 1969), pp 214–15.
37. MML, IB archive, Box C 24/2, letter from Kerrigan to Pollitt, 2 August 1938. We are grateful to the late Jim Carmody for these figures (email, 29 September 2013).
38. Richard Baxell, *Unlikely Warriors: The British in the Spanish Civil War and the Struggle Against Fascism* (London, 2012), p. 334.
39. RGASPI, f. 545, o. 3, d. 434, l. 139 (Dunbar to Walter, 11 April 1938).
40. Thomas, *To Tilt at Windmills*, p. 104.
41. Bob Clark, *No Boots to My Feet: Experiences of a Britisher in Spain. With a Foreword by Jack Jones* (Stoke-on-Trent, 1984), p. 100.
42. Clark, *No Boots*, pp 101–2; Gregory, *Shallow Grave*, pp 123–4.

43. Ó Duinnín, *La Niña Bonita*, p. 60.
44. Howard Williamson, *Toolmaking and Politics: The Life of Ted Smallbone – An Oral History* (Birmingham, 1987), pp 58–9.
45. Landis, *Lincoln Brigade*, p. 528.
46. Eby, *Between the Bullet and the Lie*, p. 290.
47. Landis, The Abraham Lincoln *Brigade*, p. 533.
48. Howard, *MacKenzie-Papineau Battalion*, p. 215; RGASPI, f. 545, o. 3, d. 475, ll. 187–8.
49. www.expressandstar.com/news/2011/07/08/black.country-brothers. Accessed 3 December 2013. The article is based on an interview with Don's grandson Paul. Another, somewhat inaccurate, account is given by a witness, Steve Fullarton, in MacDougall, *Voices*, p. 297.
50. Ó Duinnín, *La Niña Bonita*, pp 61–3.
51. MacDougall, *Voices*, pp 300–1.
52. Hopkins, *Into the Fire*, p. 307.
53. Gregory, *Shallow Grave*, pp 125–6.
54. RGASPI, f. 545, o. 3, d. 475, l. 190; Baxell, *Unlikely Warriors*, pp 331–2.
55. Alexander, *British Volunteers*, pp 207–8.
56. RGASPI, f. 545, o. 3, d. 475, l. 190.
57. Ibid., l. 196.
58. Thomas, *Spanish Civil War*, pp 841–2.
59. Landis, *The Abraham Lincoln Brigade*, pp 541–4.
60. The actual location of the 15th Brigade battalions during the Ebro battle has been extrapolated from maps in Julian Henriquez Caubin, *La Batalla del Ebro: Maniobra de una División* (Mexico City, 1944). I thank Anna Martí for copies of the maps.
61. Baxell, *Unlikely Warriors*, p. 333.
62. RGASPI, f. 545, o. 3, d. 10, ll. 209–10.
63. Email from Jim Carmody, 29 September 2013; RGASPI, f. 545, o. 6, d. 100–216.
64. MML, IB archive, Box 21/B/76, List of Recommendations, 57th Battalion, Ebro Crossing.
65. Eby, *Between the Bullet and the Lie*, pp 288–92.
66. Landis, *The Abraham Lincoln Brigade*, p. 539.
67. Wheeler, *To Make the People Smile*, pp 81–7.
68. Eby, *Between the Bullet and the Lie*, p. 293; Baxell, *Unlikely Warriors*, p. 335.
69. RGASPI, f. 545, o. 3, d. 475, ll. 204–5; Landis, *The Abraham Lincoln Brigade*, pp 553–5.
70. RGASPI, f. 545, o. 3, d. 475, ll. 206–23; f. 545, o.3, d. 435, l. 128.
71. Baxell, *Unlikely Warriors*, p. 337.
72. RGASPI, f. 545, o. 1, d. 11, ll. 112–15.
73. Howard, *Mackenzie-Papineau Battalion*, p. 220.
74. RGASPI, f. 545, o. 3, d. 435, l. 141.
75. Landis, *The Abraham Lincoln Brigade*, pp 566–8.
76. Carl Geiser, *Prisoners of the Good Fight: The Spanish Civil War 1936–1939* (Westport, CT, 1986), pp 226–7.
77. Baxell, *Unlikely Warriors*, pp 338–9.
78. Gregory, *Shallow Grave*, p. 131.
79. RGASPI, f. 545, o. 3, d. 435, l. 157.
80. Ibid., l. 159.

81. RGASPI, f. 545, o. 3, d. 475, ll. 228–32.
82. Based on the volunteers' files: RGASPI, f. 545, o. 6, d. 100–216.
83. Caubin, *La Batalla del Ebro*, Fig.31a
84. Baxell, *Unlikely Warriors*, pp 341–2.
85. Landis, *The Abraham Lincoln Brigade*, pp 576, 582; Gregory, *Shallow Grave*, p. 132; Baxell, *Unlikely Warriors*, pp 340–1.
86. Landis, *The Abraham Lincoln Brigade*, pp 580–4.
87. Wheeler, *Make the People Smile*, pp 118–9; Gregory, *Shallow Grave*, p. 134.
88. WCML, transcription of an interview with Syd Booth, p.49. The names of the volunteers have been corrected by the author.
89. Ó Duinnín, *La Niña Bonita*, p. 102.
90. Howard, *Mackenzie-Papineau Battalion*, p. 223.
91. Landis, *The Abraham Lincoln Brigade*, pp 590–1.
92. Thomas, *To Tilt at Windmills*, p. 163.
93. Jackson, *At the Margins*, p. 127.
94. Baxell, *Unlikely Warriors*, p. 347.
95. Thomas, *To Tilt at Windmills*, p. 166; Beeching, *Canadian Volunteers*, pp 190–1.
96. RGASPI, f. 545, o. 6, d. 47, l. 59; f. 545, o. 6, d. 89, ll. 31–2.
97. Eby, *Between the Bullet and the Lie*, p. 308.
98. Ronald Liversedge (edited by David Yorke), *Mac-Pap: Memoir of a Canadian in the Spanish Civil War* (Vancouver, 2013), pp 147–8; Howard, *MacKenzie-Papineau Battalion*, pp 230–6.

ELEVEN

# DISCIPLINE, DESERTION AND PUNISHMENT

The ferocity of the Spanish Civil War is reflected in the estimation (the figures are still highly contested in modern Spain) that while 200,000 soldiers were killed in action or died of wounds, an equal, if not slightly higher, number (mainly civilians) were executed in the respective zones during or after the war.[1] As in all major fratricidal conflicts within states, unlawful killings (termed 'unofficial executions') of combatants on both sides took place, but were in Spain far more commonplace as the victim was seen as an ideological enemy.

The murder of prisoners, especially officers and commissars, was widespread on the fascist side. On 9 March 1937 Franco issued the order that all foreigners caught under arms were to be executed.[2] A common occurrence in the Spanish Republican forces was the shooting of deserters or officers held to be 'foreign agents' or 'fifth columnists', Stalinist shorthand for purveyors of defeatism or organisers of retreats or flight from the front lines. On the eve of the Brunete battle, El Campesino threatened his men: 'There can be no retreat. The captain who does not know to advance his company, I'll shoot him. If a battalion commander does not achieve the objective set him, I'll shoot him as well.'[3]

On the first night, General Walter reported to Moscow, 18 soldiers were shot by orders of a tribunal for attempting desertion, and a day later Líster pronounced the death sentence on a divisional commissar and a brigade commander for refusing to obey orders.[4] Soviet adviser Grigory Shtern, apprising the last day of combat of Líster's 11th Division in the ruins of Brunete, alleged that 400 of his fleeing troops were rounded up and shot out of hand – surely an exaggeration.[5] Other scattered references would suggest that the incidents were not confined to the Republican side and that they occurred, as in all wars, in desperate combat conditions. Graham Seton Hutchinson, a Scottish colonel who co-founded the British Machine-Gun Corps, was unusually explicit in describing the drastic measures he took during the German 1918 Offensive towards Hazebrouck, the key rail junction to the Channel ports, during the Battle of Méteren in mid-April 1918:

> After an hour of the action [14 April 1918], we discovered in the Belle Croix estaminet beside the mill a crowd of stragglers, fighting drunk. We routed them out, and, with a machine-gun trained on them, sent them forward towards the enemy. They perished to a man. [. . .] So critical was the situation that I issued orders to my sergeants in charge of gun teams that at any time they saw British troops retiring they were to fire on them; and from near the mill I saw one of my gunners destroy a platoon of one battalion which in its panic had taken to flight.[6]

The Spanish war was unusual for the high number of desertions to the other side because individual soldiers found themselves in the wrong zone and showed, as conscripts, only 'geographical loyalty' until an opportunity arose at the front to go over to the enemy lines. Infringements of discipline among English speakers up to the summer of 1937 were treated leniently by the Juridical Commission, primarily because the harsh punishment or execution of soldiers from the democracies would severely damage recruitment and confront the communist party with unwelcome controversy. Proponents of tighter military discipline won the argument, and a decree issued by President Azaña and Defence Minister Prieto on 18 June 1937 enumerated severe punishments: soldiers not present without good reason at three consecutive roll-calls could face between six and 20 years in a labour camp, or the firing squad in exceptional circumstances. Officers and men who abandoned their posts or positions without permission or who practised self-mutilation were subjected to 20 years' incarceration or the death penalty. Running away from the enemy brought a mandatory capital sentence. Finally, those who insulted or struck an officer on active service or refused to obey an order at the front were subject to 20 years in prison, or execution.[7] Capital sentences were rare in the International Brigades. There were a few executions by tribunal, usually in a crisis. A handful of individuals in the 15th Brigade considered a danger to general morale were dealt with summarily in the last months – not tried but shot out of hand by an officer.

The problem with analysing the countless cases of ill-discipline is the haphazard manner of their prosecution. Minor offenders were set to digging latrines or trenches. Prisoners not kept for short detention near the front or sent to 're-education camps' like Camp Lukacs could be detained for months in the Guardia Nacional barracks in Albacete, in the makeshift prison in a church nearby (La Iglesia de la Purísima Concepión) or in the fortress of

Chincilla 20 km to the south. Temporary detention centres were also installed in the regional offices of the IB in Murcia, Barcelona and Valencia.[8] Recalcitrant soldiers could also end up in a labour/disciplinary battalion or in a work camp. Arrests were often arbitrary, especially in Albacete, and it was not until November 1937 that Wilhelm Zaisser, the base commander, imposed some sort of order as regards arrests and proper detention procedures in the hitherto grossly overcrowded gaols of the town in cooperation with Servicio Investigación Militar (SIM), the military intelligence branch of the Republican Army.[9]

### IRISH DESERTERS

In the British contingent almost 300 individuals (15 per cent) are recorded as deserters;[10] among the Americans the total was around 100 (4 per cent).[11] The Irish figure is at about 40 (16 per cent). One must differentiate, however, between short-term deserters who were later re-integrated into the British battalion following 're-education', recidivist offenders who were caught at ports and imprisoned in the Republican rearguard and, finally, those who 'made it home' – at least 24, seven or more of whom were helped by diplomatic staff in Spain and France. There is no documentary evidence on how others left Spain illegally, probably as stowaways on British ships. Among the deserters, one was killed in action shortly afterwards, another was repatriated by Frank Ryan and the third was later taken prisoner by the Italians. A handful could leave the country with the permission of the Republican authorities because they were incorrigible offenders or were expelled in disgrace. Desertions peaked after gruelling battles such as Jarama, Brunete, the March retreats of 1938 and the long Ebro attrition.

Many of the deserters would have been in grave trouble in any professional army for persistence drunkenness, disobedience and general obnoxious behaviour. A contributory factor may have been that punishment for infringements in the English-speaking units, at least before the summer of 1938, was incomparably lighter than the regime of the 'glasshouse' of the British Army, not to mention the rigours of its 'Field Punishment No.1' on the Western Front in the First World War. The presence of a 'discussion culture' and addressing officers by their first names made it difficult to crack down on 'comrade' delinquents. Any attempt to impose stricter disciplinary criteria on volunteers based on ideological grounds came across as politically motivated if the man had a good military record. Furthermore, battalion officers knew they had to make do with the dwindling numbers of the countrymen to hand, who were volunteers, not conscripts.

A common motivation for desertion concerned the general conditions of service: unsuitable or insufficient rations, inferior equipment and a conviction that the Republican high command was losing the war. Many felt that battalion officers were incompetent amateurs. Others had been plagued by ill-health (diarrhoea, dysentery, enteric fever, scabies, etc.) or had come to believe that the medical attention they received after wounding fell far short of what could be expected in a hospital at home. 'Battle fatigue', shell shock and sheer terror, especially from aerial or artillery bombardment, were common motives to flee from 'the colours'. An unknown number had grown tired of the communist dominance in the Brigades and of the accompanying sloganising, or had rejected that hegemony from the outset. A minority of about one tenth in the British battalion were true 'ne'er do wells', addicted to drink and allergic to military discipline.

An overriding motive for absconding from the front, however, was the broken promise of repatriation. Some American and British volunteers stated that they had enlisted on the understanding that service would be of six months' duration. While from the Spanish point of view such a belief was deleterious to the general conduct of the war, arguments about its legitimacy (there is no documentary evidence on how it originated) were compounded by the view that many of those actually repatriated after Brunete, apart from veterans and the badly wounded, had been given preference, either because they were communists or leading cadres. Those verbally promised repatriation but subsequently denied it populated the bases, the 'lame and the halt', often walking wounded whose demoralisation grew infectiously in a community of 'lost hopers'.

The first Irish deserter was Charlie McGuinness, the legendary mariner, adventurer and IRA gun runner. He was given to believing he could use his maritime skills to smuggle armaments to Republican ports. McGuinness's interest in Bolshevism, gained from a stay in Leningrad, soon turned to disgust and disillusionment after enlisting in Albacete in late October 1936. The desecration of churches and executions in the town, where he met Tommy Patten and Bill Scott, coupled with the disorganised state of the militias fighting on the Madrid front, prompted his early departure with the help of the British consulate in Barcelona and the Irish Legation in Paris.[12] Whereas McGuinness had travelled to Spain with the sanction of the CPGB, the next Irish deserter, Patrick Keenan, an unemployed metal worker from Dublin, seems to have made the journey 'under his own steam'. Seeking repatriation at the Irish Legation in Paris in February 1937, Keenan professed that he had been politically inactive in Ireland and had worked as a mechanic at the truck depot of the Albacete base. There, he continued, he was discriminated against by the French commanding officers, accused of 'sabotage' over a pay dispute and arrested. He escaped from custody after four days, made his way to Valencia with a Canadian comrade and thence to France.[13]

Another supplicant at the Irish diplomatic post in Paris was Robert Hepburn, a 25-year-old Dubliner who had suffered a nervous breakdown after the Jarama battle. Hepburn 'did time' in a labour battalion for repeatedly refusing to go to the front and was again arrested when he tried to board a British ship at Alicante in June 1937. Returned to the 15th Battalion, he fought at Brunete, was confined for a period in Camp Lukacs and escaped from hospital in Valencia before finally boarding *SS Wisconsin*, leaving Spain for Marseilles in July 1938.[14]

The next two visitors to J. A. Belton, the Irish Legation First Secretary, and Art Ó Briain, Minister Plenipotentiary, in Paris, were voluble storytellers, cloaking their dishonourable motives in the diction of orthodox Catholicism or right-wing prejudice – Harry Kennedy and Brendan Moroney. Other deserters, at least in the technical sense, left Spain for health reasons. John Tierney, a sailor from Dublin domiciled in London, abandoned the struggle with his friend Fred Clarke because of their wounds. Both had been hit at Brunete (Clarke in the legs, and his vision was affected; Tierney in the arm) and were less than happy with the treatment in the Madrid hospital, where they met Frank Ryan and Jim Woulfe. Sent back from Quinto for further medical treatment, both men exited Spain with the help of the British Barcelona consulate in November 1937.[15] A final group of deserters (four Irish) landed in the infamous Castelldefels prison in an ancient coastal fortress 25 km south of Barcelona. It was first populated by the prisoners evacuated from gaols in and around Albacete and was in operation between March 1938 and January 1939. Its first commandant was Vladimir Čopić's brother Emil (Milan), who had previously been in charge of the IB prison in Albacete. The prisoners, kept in the fort's chapel, were routinely mishandled and tortured, and at least two were murdered. Čopić was reputedly sentenced to death by Catalan authorities – his guards had threatened the local population – because of his inhumane rule. His French successor from May 1938, Marcel Lantez, and six accomplices who had embezzled funds and confiscated cash sent to prisoners, were arrested by SIM in August 1938. Confronted by several testimonies from warders, Lantez was sentenced to death by a tribunal, but as in the case of his predecessor, he would escape into France.[16] Of the four Irish, William Haire and Gerald Ward were released and reached Britain with the main body of volunteers in December 1938,[17] while Charles Mitchell ('John Doyle') and Joseph Magill, both incorrigible deserters, did not reach home until 1939.[18]

OFFICIAL EXECUTIONS

Desertions from the front line carried, as shown above, the death penalty. This was rarely exercised in the 15th Brigade and was usually after the battalion commander called a general meeting of the men to decide the issue. The first of such battalion assemblies took place in October 1937, after a rash of desertions in Aragon. Dave Doran, Brigade Commissar, demanded the death penalty for 12 deserters (one from the British, four from the Canadian and seven from the American battalion), four of whom had stolen an ambulance in order to reach the French border. Company commissars acted as prosecution counsel and picked men from the ranks formed the jury. Although two were sentenced to death, none were shot and men were eventually re-instated, presumably because some wished to redeem themselves in battle or because the command feared repercussions in the Brigade and bad publicity at home.[19]

The next such case occurred in the British battalion during the battle of Teruel. Two men attempted to cross over to the fascist lines on 4 January 1938 but had been intercepted by a cavalry patrol. Sergeant 'Allan Kemp' (he had enlisted under that pseudonym) and his younger confederate Corporal Paddy Glacken (from Greenock but born in Donegal) were found guilty. Kemp, the older man, was captured with a sketch showing British machine gun positions. He was shot by his comrades on 10 January, but Glacken's sentence was commuted to an unspecified spell in the labour battalion. He was killed at the front ten days later. It is possible that Glacken's youth (24), and his confession to commissar Bob Cooney, played a role.[20] The tribunal had been put together from officers and other ranks of the British battalion, and the sentence was based on a general order on tribunals issued by Vicente Rojo, the chief of staff of the Army of the Centre, on 31 December.[21]

It is not surprising that commanders exercised the supreme penalty again during the panic and disorganisation of the March 1938 retreats. A prominent victim was a Spanish major who sped off to the rear with his artillery teams during the defence of Caspe.[22] When the remnants of the brigades had crossed the Ebro to safety, stragglers were being classified (re-integration, punishment battalions or Castelldefels) in Vilaseca west of Tarragona, when three Finnish Internationals (one was a nationalized American) broke out of the compound and caused drunken disturbances in the town. Arrested by the local police and handed over to the military, the trio faced a court-martial and received the death sentence. They were driven to the beach at dusk on 22 April, where they were dispatched by firing squad.[23]

Four days later, four volunteers of the 15th Brigade were shot at dawn for cowardice and desertion: two from the Spanish battalion, a Canadian and the American Paul White.[24] The ex-sailor had been a trustworthy transport officer under Merriman before panicking during the retreats and stealing an ambulance. White stopped short of the French border, met a fellow American soldier and returned with him to throw himself at the mercy of the Brigade. White was unfortunate because, although he was fully repentant and wished to recover his reputation in battle, that very day a divisional order had reached

Brigade Commissar Gates that all deserters were to be shot. His execution caused such consternation and anger in the American battalion that the general execution order was soon rescinded by divisional headquarters.[25]

Death sentences carried out after due process were also relatively rare among the German speakers (11th Brigade). A lieutenant, KPD member and resident in Spain since 1933 was executed after a tribunal hearing. He was accused of 'Trotskyism and provocation', ciphers for a dissident opinion: he had tried to apply Prieto's ban on party political propaganda in his unit.[26] One deserter was shot in Aragon, another during the retreats and a third man faced the firing squad during the Teruel battle after it had emerged that he had disclosed information to the Gestapo in the Rhineland about fellow communists.[27]

In summary, documents at our disposal strongly suggest that court-martials in the field pronouncing capital verdicts were isolated incidents in the International Brigades, where the participatory process (battalion meetings) had to take account of general morale and repercussions at home. The secret murdering of 'troublemakers', however, was another matter, to a great degree attributable to the dire situation at the front and the increasing politicisation of the brigades through the reformation of Party cells (PCE) and the accretion in power to political commissars who, having access to the censored mail of 'suspects', reported to divisional SIM officers.

### SURVEILLANCE AND THE PUNISHMENT OF DISSENT

The first counter-intelligence, or surveillance, body to examine foreigners sympathetic to the Republic or men arriving to enlist in the International Brigades was set up by German communist emigrants resident in Spain who were attached to the foreign department of the Partit Socialista Unificat de Catalunya (PSUC), the Catalan CP. Having internalised paranoid Soviet 'images of the enemy', which entailed labelling the dissenting or dissatisfied as 'Trotskyists', the interrogation teams in Barcelona and Valencia, with their 'private' prisons and torture chambers, gained widespread notoriety in the aftermath of the 'May Days' in Barcelona. Apart from hunting down German anarchists, dissident KPD members and suspected 'Gestapo spies', the centres came under international scrutiny for their persecution of the POUM. That also entailed the observation and arrest of foreign, and especially British, members of the POUM division on leave from the Aragón front and present in Barcelona – Eric Blair (George Orwell) and his wife Eileen, the ILP intellectual Fenner Brockway, and others.[28] Such arbitrary police methods were curtailed in autumn 1937 by the Republican security service, a move welcomed even by Marty, who believed the German Communists in Spain had maintained their own spying organisation. In future, the control and surveillance of IB members would be coordinated by the central committee of the PCE.[29]

In early 1937 the prominent Yugoslav communist Gustav Fejn installed a Servicio de Control, a predecessor to SIM, in Albacete, working closely with NKVD operatives and providing the Soviets with brigadistas who acted as couriers or bodyguards. When the SIM was founded by the Socialist Minister Prieto in August 1937, it soon fell under the influence of PCE police cadres and NKVD personnel. The branch of SIM installed in the International Brigades, however, was a separate entity, relatively weak in numbers and overburdened with case work because it had absorbed the cadres departments at the Albacete base. Led by Karel Htac, a Hungarian cadre sent from Moscow with the alias 'Moreno', the IB-SIM had about 30 monitoring officers behind the front, mainly French or central Europeans, and only two English speakers: Conrad Kaye (Barcelona) and Tony de Maio (Figueras).[30] Through its agents at divisional and battalion level, IB-SIM could monitor the morale and dissenting opinion in the ranks on the basis of reports sent by their agents or the political commissars from the companies upwards. These were supplemented by the information supplied by the cells of the PCE installed in the brigades from late 1937.

In the British battalion, the CPGB was openly organised at Madrigueras in early 1937 but 'this had a bad effect on the non-Party people who felt that they were being excluded from something.' The Party cells were thus dissolved, also because of tension between the commissars and the military leaders (Copeman, Cunningham).[31] During the rest phase in Marçà before the Ebro battle, the Welsh communist Billy Griffiths resurrected party structures. Parallel to propagandising the 'activist movement', the party zealots strove to portray many complaints as political transgressions, in particular criticism of the battalion leaders. 'Lack of political consciousness', on the other hand, was the title often bestowed on rank-and-file complainers. Men were now sent to detention on 'political charges', hitherto a novelty in the British companies.

An exemplary case is that of Alec Marcowich, a communist orator from the Gorbals with a history of dissident behaviour in Party circles in Britain. He voiced criticism of most aspects of life in the Brigades (privileges for officers, bad food, repatriation promised after six months' service, etc.) until Bob Cooney, battalion commissar, got rid of the Glaswegian ('has shown an anti-Party attitude') by Brigade order of 28 June 1938. Marcowich was separated from his fellow soldiers to serve several terms of imprisonment before he was confined to detention for the remainder of the war in Castelldefels.³²

Many who shared some or all of Marcowich's complaints thought it better to wait until after demobilisation, when filling out a questionnaire, to air them, in particular their opinion of the contribution of the IBs' political and military organisations to the Republican war effort. David Wickes was suspected at the start because he initially came to Spain on a delegation of the ILP – a 'Trotskyist' apostasy in the eyes of CPGB ideologues – but then joined the British battalion as an interpreter and assistant paymaster. His first 'action' was in the firing squad on the beach at Vilaseca, but he refused to discharge his rifle at the Finnish deserters. Wickes felt that 'both military and political organization left much to be desired, particularly the latter. Political "pull" was too much in evidence in the choosing of the military command.'³³ David Melville, a Londoner wounded on the Ebro, stated that in the later stages the political and military commands were 'isolated from the men and unpopular with the great majority'.³⁴ The cook and armourer Charles Palmer was pungent: 'the system of commissar is unacceptable to me as a non-Party member.' He also criticised the 'lack of military training for officers'.³⁵ James Nixon was a 43-year-old member of the Labour Party from St Helens, injured in an aircraft attack on 29 July. In Ripoll he wrote that 'the political organization was not sufficiently elastic to allow the airing of grievances without fear, and too rigid to be regarded by some as anything other than dictatorship.'³⁶ Finally, Edward Updale, a former British Army electrician, who 'deserted to the front' from Tarazona and found the American battalion more to his liking than soldiering with his fellow British, made some incisive comments:

> In the military field political leaders are not necessarily military leaders. While a military leader must be sound politically, the knowledge of what a man is fighting for is not sufficient justification for entrusting to him the lives of men and the conduct of an important operation [. . .] The political organisation was often biased against the men with no political background, giving preference to inferior men on account of their previous political affiliations. Many expert soldiers served in the ranks on this account, and their value ignored, with unhappy results, for these men became disgruntled and prejudiced, and lost enthusiasm.³⁷

Similar criticism came from somebody with military experience in the Canadian battalion: Jack McElligott, born in Annascaul on the Dingle peninsula in 1905, had eight years' experience in the IRA before he emigrated to Canada in 1929. As a communist activist in a mining community in British Columbia, McElligott volunteered for Spain, joining the brigades in October 1937, and was promoted to sergeant training recruits in Tarazona. He was decorated for bravery during an attack at Caspe in March and is said to have shot down an enemy reconnaissance aircraft flying low over Canadian positions. Like many Canadians, McElligott openly disliked the predominance of American commissars patronising 'Canucks', losing his rank of sergeant during the Ebro battle because he argued with his superiors in the Special Machine-Gun Battalion on the siting of a Maxim. Abe Lewis, the American cadre chief, attested, without knowing the Kerryman, that McElligott had a 'Trotskyite tendency'. Alec Donaldson, the British cadres supervisor who had been long seeking repatriation and refused to go to the front with all available men in March 1938, judged from afar that McElligott tended to 'rank-and-file-ism' but should be helped by the Canadian comrades to 'overcome his individualism'.[38]

### EXECUTED WITHOUT TRIAL

In the 1930s the verb 'disappear' was used only in the active voice. Nowadays, however, it is employed in the passive sense – someone is 'disappeared', i.e. killed in secret but posted as having 'died in combat' or 'missing'. Such assassinations were not a major phenomenon but happened in probably a handful of cases in all IB language groups. Heinz Prieß, a political commissar in Spain from Hamburg, recounts that years later in the German Democratic Republic he was told by two ex-comrades (SIM officers) on separate occasions that 'backsliders' (Abweichler) and presumptive 'Trotskyists' were taken for a fatal stroll: 'We went into the woods with them and came out without them.'[39]

We know of two notorious cases in the American battalion that were subject to Congressional inquiries. Albert Wallach had deserted at Brunete and Quinto and was picked up in Barcelona after he (and two fellow countrymen) had received no help from the American consul in that city. Incarcerated in Castelldefels, Wallach was allegedly starved and badly beaten before being shot dead in the courtyard around 1 May 1938. Tony de Maio was said to have been his executioner, but he denied the charge.[40] At the same time, the American officers decided to 'disappear' the thrice deserter Bernard Abramofsky with the argument that he was a danger to morale, badly shaken by the March retreats. At first, as no officer wanted to carry out the grisly task, one asked Harry Fisher, who did not personally know the culprit but remembered he was a popular singer and entertainer at concert evenings. Fisher refused indignantly and never forgot 'the offer', learning later that his 'buddy' John Turra had also dismissed the 'proposal'. While the shocked friends conversed in the dark on 30 April, a shot rang out nearby. It seems probable that Milton Wolff, the battalion commander, had pulled the trigger and shot Abramofsky in the back of the head.[41]

There were at least two similar cases in the British Battalion in the last days of the Ebro battle. Policy towards deserters hardened following a meeting of all political commissars of the 15th Brigade in early September: it was urged to pass resolutions in the battalions 'to demand the maximum penalty' as 'these deserters are not the true representative of the International Brigades but adventurers, criminals and cowards, and we have to separate ourselves from these elements.'[42] Sam Wild 'urgently requested' of brigade commander Valledor at the end of August that the maximum penalty be imposed on Reuben Lewis for falling asleep while on duty at a listening post near Hill 666, losing entrenching tools and part of the company rations, returning after 36 hours during a search for water and, most damningly, for having deserted after the companies had been relieved in the Sierra Pandols.[43] Lewis, a young tailor from London's East End, argued that he missed the departure of his rifle company, and while he was climbing down with machine-gun teams his shoes disintegrated so that he had to walk many kilometres in his bare feet before stopping a lorry that brought him to the HQ of the 35th Division. From there he was shown the way to the new British divisions the following day.[44] He was immediately arrested and spent the next two months in confinement.[45]

Lewis was fortunate in that he, probably a bad soldier, had not been long enough in Spain to acquire a disreputable reputation. Neither did he possess a 'suspicious past'. By contrast, for SIM staff, Michael 'Poona' Browne had a very questionable background. He said he was the brother of Felicia Browne, the young Englishwoman killed fighting with the militias in Aragon in August 1936, and that he abhorred fascism. Browne had attended the best public schools before completing military training and gaining a commission in the reserve of the 2nd Battalion, the Worcestershire Regiment. He joined the Imperial Police (in Palestine, North Rhodesia, Bermuda) but was dismissed for insubordination. Afterwards he had lived in a series of countries and was a polyglot. The authorities in Figueras urged that Browne should be watched because of his 'adventurous past'. We have no record of how he performed in battle, but he was posted as a deserter.[46] One veteran told interviewers from the Imperial War Museum decades later that Browne had been shot for that offence by his company commander 'Taffy' Evans.[47]

The fate of Lieutenant Alexander ('Alec') Cummings remains a conundrum that Robert Stradling has examined at some length. Cummings left the Welsh Guards after three years' service, gaining the rank of sergeant in 1931 and was active subsequently in the CPGB in Wales and Liverpool. Arriving in Spain in February 1937, he soon gained command over a company and led it at Brunete, where he was badly wounded on the first day. That experience broke his spirit and he served in the rear in the cadres section in Albacete but was finally posted to the battalion at Marçà in June 1938 and appointed platoon leader in a Spanish company. Cummings threatened desertion if sent into action, which prompted his fellow officers to discuss his future: Harry Dobson, also Welsh, and the 'true believer' Billy Griffiths pleaded for the death sentence by a military tribunal; Commissar Cooney and acting commander George Fletcher were against it. Still, the Brigade was informed. Arrested for being drunk in the lines in mid-September, Cummings was sent back under armed guard. He was demoted to sergeant and ordered to return to the front. On the last day in action of the brigades, Cummings was either killed in battle or executed for cowardice, as one source suggested to Stradling. On his Moscow file the laconic entry reads 'missing 23.9.1938'.[48]

### THE KILLING OF MAURICE EMMETT RYAN

Maurice Emmett Ryan was shot without trial by his commander Sam Wild, but it is unclear when and where exactly it happened. Orthodox communist chroniclers of the British and Irish volunteers concealed the truth for years by stating that Emmett Ryan had been 'killed in action' on the Ebro.[49] Born in Limerick in 1915, known to his family as Emmett and inevitably dubbed 'Paddy' in the British battalion, Ryan grew up in comfortable conditions as the fourth of six sons born to Limerick hotel-owners. When the Desmond Hotel in Lower Catherine Street was sold in 1929, the father went into the furniture business. All of Emmett's brothers emigrated (three to America, one to Canada and the youngest to Australia), and seem to have enjoyed a good education, rugby-playing scions of Limerick's prosperous middle class, but sent to boarding schools at an early age. Emmett attended the Jesuit Crescent College in the academic year 1928/29.

Young Ryan seems to have left Ireland under a cloud, and his parents paid his expenses when he lived in Spain, France and Portugal from 1933. Emmett's departure was probably due to his obstreperous behaviour, which drove his conservative parents to take desperate measures. His father, Edward Ryan Snr, was county organiser for Cumann na nGaedheal in early 1932,[50] and branch officer in the Limerick South Rural Ward.[51] His banished fourth offspring got into trouble when living in Lisbon. He was arrested, fingerprinted and fined in July 1935 for the offence of 'not obeying the order of the police guard'.[52] This was, perhaps, due to his heavy drinking which, in the end, would be his downfall. About a year later it seems that his parents cut off his allowance. In the summer of 1937 Maurice Emmett Ryan worked as an assistant steward on liners. His seafaring career did not exceed two months, as he returned to Southampton in late August.[53]

Ryan arrived in Spain on 5 November 1937, at the assembly point in the fortress of Figueras.[54] He entrained for the IB base at Albacete four days later.[55] At Figueras he was scrutinised by Lieutenant Tony de Maio. Ryan immediately aroused de Maio's suspicion when he stated that he was sent over on his own from London. De Maio learned subsequently that Ryan had been 'picked up' in Paris, i.e. Maurice Emmett, living now in France, had probably gone straight to the assembly centre at Place du Combat for incoming volunteers. A second point of suspicion was the statement that Ryan had served as officer in the Irish Free State Army but had been 'thrown out'.[56] He then said he was an officer in the IRA, a claim de Maio dismissed because Maurice said that he had never heard of Frank Ryan, the leader of the Irish in Spain. Having established that Maurice Emmett Ryan had 'no working class affiliation', de Maio sent a report on the same day to his SIM superior with the request, 'Please notify me further on what is done with this person.'[57]

Ryan was an unusual addition to the British ranks because of his knowledge of Europe and proficiency in foreign languages (Spanish, Portuguese, French), which endowed him with the self-confidence that comes from fending for oneself in foreign environments. His height (6 feet, 2 inches) and manly appearance would also have boosted his self-confidence. However deep his sympathies for the Spanish Republic were, he was a constant 'piss-taker' about conditions in the 15th Brigade. By constantly 'messing' (drunken escapades, ridiculing superiors), and by inventing and exaggerating his past and origins, he only aggravated the enmity towards him harboured by commanders and commissars. That feeling was mutual. At a subconscious level, class prejudice came into play. Narrow-minded British communists suspected left-wing sympathisers from the middle-classes and distrusted intellectuals from that quarter, while simultaneously making a fetish of a proletarian background. Ryan, for his part, reciprocated, making no secret of his opinion that his battalion leaders were working-class bumblers, self-important communists playing at soldiering.

Over time, Ryan won the men's affection because of his wit, courage and efficiency – even his enemies cited him as the best machine-gunner in the British Battalion. But he brought additional suspicion on himself by loose talk about his allegedly rich and fascist family, and especially, that he had a brother fighting in Spain with O'Duffy's unit, which was not true. He was posted to the machine-gunners in Mondéjar with their Russian 1910 Maxims.[58] John Dunlop, a trainee accountant from Edinburgh, remembers the explosive encounter there between Emmett Ryan and battalion C.O. Fred Copeman:

> He disliked Copeman, the commander of the battalion of that time – not only disliked him but hated him. And Copeman thoroughly reciprocated. One time when Ryan was up on a charge for being drunk and disorderly he annoyed Copeman so much that Copeman jumped over the Orderly Room table and felled him with a blow to the jaw. I was on guard on the small cell where Ryan was incarcerated for a while, and all he could do was to nurse his jaw and spit oaths at Copeman [...] And yet the man, although he was such a rogue, was an extremely likeable rogue. He could be extremely amusing, highly diverting at times.[59]

Ryan was gaoled for ten days, with ten days' loss of pay for 'insulting the commanding officer when drunk'.[60] On 10 December 1937 the battalion entrained for the north to southern Aragon in anticipation of the Republican offensive against Teruel. On the train ride to Alcañiz Ryan had a dispute with Commissar Tapsell because the voluble Irishman got off for a chat with the 'Lincoln boys'. He was arrested but no charges were proffered. After a long march from the railhead, the battalion reached the anarchist village of Mas de la Matas in the province of Teruel. It was here that Bob Clark from Liverpool, another machine-gunner, got to know 'Paddy' Ryan better:

> Among the volunteers in the village was a huge Irishman, altogether a rather amazing character and fond of claiming his aristocratic lineage. Most of the lads believed him as he was well educated and spoke three or four languages fluently. He was very popular, but too fond of the booze. In half a joking way he was fond of saying that his brother was a major in Franco's army and the only real reason why he had joined the Republicans was (he being the black sheep of the family) was to shock his aristocratic relations.[61]

Emmett Ryan was wounded at Teruel on 23 January in somewhat unusual circumstances, as John Dunlop relates:

> He himself told me that before he came to Spain he was a gigolo in the South of France. He was in our machine gun team that I was detailed to, on the Teruel front. He was sitting up on the wall of the trench one day delousing his shirt. A sniper's bullet from the other side passed through his chest and tore a big flap of

flesh away from his shoulder blade. He was extremely annoyed about this because it left a huge scar on his shoulder and spoiled his beauty for the ladies on the beaches of the Mediterranean.[62]

It was here that Maurice Ryan showed his proficiency with the Maxim and gained his reputation as an expert machine gun crew member, No.1 on the gun. Despite his valour in the field, Ryan was still a suspect, according to the English Section of the Cadres Department at the headquarters in Albacete:

> Ryan Maurice. English. Aged 22. No occupation, secondary education. No Party. From England 11.11.1937. Bourgeois extraction. Says has brother Officer on Fascist side. Family Fascists. Had fascist leanings himself once. Went to British battalion 18.11.1937. Jailed for disruption. Present whereabouts unclear, probably in jail.[63]

While recuperating from his flesh wound in the hospital of the Internationals beside the sea in Benicasim on 24 February 1938, the Limerick man strolled into one of the cafés in the resort frequented by trainee policemen (Guardia de Asalto), whose school was nearby.[64] A row developed with a police officer and Ryan was felled with a blow from a rifle-butt. He was placed under arrest and sent in disgrace to Vladimir Čopić, who transferred him to the Tarazona training base where he soon earned the displeasure of the commandant Major Johnson.

Ryan probably resented being posted to a company of recruits, and was disinclined to go on parade, so Johnson put him in the lock-up. He was then interviewed by an unknown IB officer, to whom he told some unlikely tales, spiced with accurate details of his bad disciplinary record since enlistment. The 'facts' stated did not add up in a chronological sense: from Blackrock [Co. Dublin], law student at Oxford, joined the Free State Army at 17, spent two years as a 2nd Lieutenant and left the army for religious reasons, then adding he had been 'thrown out'; October 1934 in Barcelona, 1933 in Portugal, again in 1935, Côte d'Azur, gentleman of leisure 1933–35, allowance from parents stopped when he came to Spain; never interested in politics; five brothers, one fascist, O'Duffy captain, officer, back in Ireland already; religious question in family; himself 'trying to help the weaker side', came to Spain because 'he dislikes Fascism for unnecessary slaughter'.[65] The report also included the damning addendum that Ryan, since coming to Tarazona, 'has continued in a similar manner'. Howard Goddard, acting for Johnson, recommended 'that he be thoroughly investigated by your Service [SIM].'[66] After arrival under guard in Albacete, Ryan was supposed to be sent to a labour battalion but soon took ill and was in the hospital in Albacete two days later.[67] 'Should be very closely watched' was the entry in his cadre file, which included new incriminations, obviously untrue: that he had never worked for a living and that his father owned 20 hotels in Ireland.⁶⁸ Eugene Downing, a member of the CPI and a recent recruit to the British Battalion, had a soft spot for Maurice Emmett, and 60 years later he offered a plausible interpretation of the Limerick man's personality:

> Actually he was too bright, too independent-minded and too outspoken, he could see that things weren't well organized and would say so, point out what should be done, so the left-wing working class British running it [the battalion] resented him. He got up their noses, and didn't care if he did. He could run it better than they were doing. He was the best machine-gunner, but as he said himself, it didn't take much brains to work a machine-gun.⁶⁹

In his Irish-language memoir of the war, Downing recounts in his typical wry style Maurice's battle with his two worst enemies – vino and the battalion command. One night Eugene was on sentry duty at battalion HQ when he saw Ryan and two comrades returning to their chabolas, dancing on the road and singing 'Nellie Deane'. They must have woken Jack Nalty, who, as the officer commanding Ryan's machine-gun company, had Ryan brought under guard to Downing. Such was the charm of the prisoner that he wheedled Downing next morning to get him his mess tin near Nalty's billet so that he could have his breakfast. Maurice also had at least one confrontation with battalion C.O. Sam Wild, who asked the large Irishman menacingly if he was calling him a liar. Ryan denied the accusation but won the staring contest.⁷⁰

Ryan was being watched. Captain George Fletcher, battalion adjutant, had been influenced by Ryan's record at Teruel – so it was alleged by SIM informers – and remained under 'his influence'.⁷¹ The Limerick man was also friendly with a 'suspicious element', Joseph Cryer, a man older in years but also a well-travelled polyglot who had been a lecturer in English at the Egyptian University in Cairo. He had strong reservations about separate messing for officers.⁷² Cryer was Sergeant Paymaster of the battalion with an excellent record, but a SIM informant thought his social origins 'very suspect', further that he was a friend of Emmett Ryan, and the informant advocated that he be 'made paymaster in another unit and placed under constant vigilance'.⁷³

During the first setbacks of the Ebro offensive the decision was taken to kill Maurice Ryan. At this time he was still viewed by SIM as a 'very bad and suspicious individual'.⁷⁴ There are no documents about the execution, only oral evidence. The story entered the public sphere when Ian MacDougall published his *Voices from the Spanish Civil War* in 1986 and included the reminiscences of John Dunlop. The Scot thought there was something suspicious ('not the clean tattie') about Maurice Ryan when he and Harold Horne, a graduate of the International Lenin School, watched Ryan 'capering about' and disturbing the drill of a Spanish unit in Tembleque, a rail junction in Toledo province. Both concurred that the silly intrusion was the work of a 'fascist'.[75] Dunlop's version of the cause of Ryan's final and fatal arrest has been accepted by historians:

> But later on, in the attack across the Ebro in the summer of 1938, he was in charge of one of the machine guns and he was found guilty of firing on our own men as they were advancing down a valley and up towards the crest that the enemy was occupying. I myself was under that fire and we knew that a gun from our side was firing on us but we did not know which one it was.[76]

Dunlop gave a longer version of the incident during one of the attacks on Hill 481 in an interview to the Imperial War Museum:

> I was just at the edge of a small hill. Right above my head, just inches above my head, there was a long burst of machine-gun fire but it was coming in the wrong direction. It was not coming from in front of me, it was coming from behind me and it was just hitting the top of this ridge, just above my head. I looked back and I could see this gun, one of our own machine-guns, actually firing. It appeared to be firing on us, so that more or less ended our attack. He [Emmett Ryan] was flaying drunk – I don't know how many of our blokes had been hit and wounded by this gun, but he was overpowered and arrested. I was told later that Sam Wild, the commander of the battalion, and George Fletcher, the second in command, took Ryan for a walk and told him to go ahead of them and then they shot him in the back of the head. I also heard that George Fletcher was in tears over that.[77]

Ted Smallbone refers to Ryan without naming him:

> What happened exactly I am not sure [. . .] The story went that this 'Fascist' lost the rest of his team – I don't know whether part of his team had been hit or whether he had deliberately lost them – and when our lads caught up with him he was well in advance of our lines and had mounted his machine gun and pointed it in the opposite direction – against us. Anyway, he forthwith disappeared. Whether he was taken out and shot I don't know.[78]

There is the strong likelihood that Ryan was not firing the gun at all but enjoying a siesta with a bottle of wine. Jim Brewer from the Rhondda was a member of Ryan's company. Brewer obviously disliked Ryan and resented the Irish predominance (two company commanders and two company commissars) in the battalion:

The following day the enemy was attacking us and we were giving covering fire to our troops. This fellow goes away [. . .] he been put back in charge of the gun now, he just walks away. He'd got a full bottle of wine and presumably went off and found a quiet spot and drank it, you see. In the meantime this chap Thompson took over as No. 1 and a shell landed nearby. I think it blinded him, it definitely blinded him temporarily [. . .] When he was gone [for medical attention], I took over on this gun. Fletcher came along and he said, 'Where is so and so?' I said, 'We haven't seen him all the afternoon'. And he said, 'And this battle going on'. 'He just wandered off', I said. So Fletcher went in search of him and he found him in a drunken sleep under a nice little boulder.[79]

Neither in the files containing divisional orders nor in commissars' reports held in Moscow is there any mention of Ryan's offence, his killing or that he was tried and sentenced to death. The last evidence found to date from an eyewitness is from Tom Murray, a Labour councillor in Edinburgh and a clandestine member of the CPGB.[80] He had very little military experience, having served only three weeks in the British Army at the end of the First World War, and arrived in Spain in March. Because he was a trusted 'comrade', Murray was posted as political commissar to Jack Nalty's machine-gunners and arrogated to himself executive functions in battle. For some inexplicable reason his description of Ryan's demise does not mention the charge of 'firing on his own' or of being drunk during the battle. The 'final straw' for Murray, a hardline communist, was a furious row about the siting of a machine gun in the heat of battle, possibly the incident on 26 July when 'Dusty' Bennett was killed. Tom Murray's version of the killing of Maurice Ryan, given 50 years later, suggests that time was running out for the Limerick man in a contest of wills:

Well, there was one bad character. When we were up at the front there was a member in my Company. I won't mention his name. He was Irish, he came from the Free State, he came from the South. And he was quite a capable bloke, too. It was an unsavoury business. But we decided on a certain move, and he resisted it. He was in charge of one of the machine gun crews, and he resisted it. And we could not understand why on earth he was resisting it. And he wanted to place the machine-gun and his crew in a situation which we thought was extremely vulnerable. I said to him, 'Look here now, you are going to do what you are told [. . .] 'We are at the blooming front, we are not playing around in the rear. We are at the front. The enemy is over the dyke more or less.' And he said, 'To hell with you. I'll so-and-so so-and-so.' He picked up a hand grenade and was about to throw it at me. I jumped out of the way and we took him to the rear. However, we were sure that there was something radically wrong before he was taken back and quizzed.

And of course he was boiling with hostility by this time because we had dragged him back from the front, from the front line and demoted him, as it were [...] And we dragged him back and of course he was very angry with us. There wasn't much of a court martial but there was established information, and his conduct of course was reprehensible at the front, his carry-on, you see. You couldn't stand for that sort of thing [...] I won't tell you who did it. I didn't do it and I won't tell you who did it. But there was a decision taken to get rid of him because of what we had discovered about him. We were suspicious of this customer. Just as we had of course infiltrators on the other side they had infiltrators on our side. Well, at any rate, it was decided to let him have it, as we had discovered that he had a brother in the Fascist ranks. He had a very strong anti-Soviet background and anti-socialist background. At any rate he was got rid of, just shot in the back of the neck. [81]

Emmett Ryan could hardly plead extenuating circumstances before officers he had provoked time and again, and it seems certain that he was blind drunk during the action, either asleep or firing the Maxim inaccurately, possibly in the wrong direction. In any case, as a sergeant, he was in charge of the gun. The incident happened during the assaults on Hill 481. The fatal walk took place either on 2 August, when the battalion drew back a few hundred yards but was still in the battle zone, or around 6 August, when the battered remnants were taken out of the line during the night.[82] Shortly after the Spanish war, Sam Wild informed Jim Prendergast about that gruesome deed. Prendergast, on his return to Dublin in 1941 as CPI organiser, confided to Eugene Downing:

Sam Wild and George Fletcher had taken Ryan for a walk and informed him of the decision that had been taken. He responded calmly, 'You wouldn't do that, Sam, would you?' But he was wrong. He was shot in the back of the head.[83]

Eugene Downing heard about the execution while in hospital in Spain. He was of the opinion that drink was the downfall of Maurice Ryan, a man who 'unfortunately was always kicking against the pricks, in a manner of speaking'.[84] Bob Clark, who lost an eye attacking Hill 481, summed up in old age what Maurice had meant to him:

Paddy, remarkably handsome, educated, of a wealthy family, a great linguist, about the best machine-gunner the British Battalion ever produced, with a supreme contempt for the enemy for which he was to pay with a bullet wound quite early in his part in the war, yet not to be killed by the enemy. Even after his execution nobody could really hate his memory.[85]

Mary Ryan, Emmett's mother, was living in Rush, Co. Dublin, in 1941 when she approached Jim Prendergast about the circumstances of her son's disappearance. The International Brigade Association (IBA) in London informed her that 'it is unquestionable that he was shot by the Franco forces immediately after his capture during the Battle of the Ebro.'[86] She was not convinced; neither was her son Edward, who visited the London offices of the IBA five years later, making the same enquiry. In a written reply he was told a different version, namely that 'Sam Wild and Bob Cooney are able to certify that your brother was killed and buried during the battle of the Ebro.'[87]

From an early age Ryan kicked against the traces. It is not an attitude that goes unpunished in any army. If a soldier, drunk on duty, fired on his comrades, there is every likelihood that he would have been shot out of hand by an officer in the Allied armies in both world wars. Swift retribution to 'steady the troops' had to be seen to be done. Victor Silvester, the dance-band leader popular with BBC listeners for many decades, witnessed such an incident as a 16-year-old in France in 1916 during a German raid: a fellow soldier who did not desist from urging his comrades to run back was shot on the spot by an officer.[88] There would be no paper trace relating his ignominious end, no mention in a battalion diary or divisional dispatches and no punishment for his assassin. The entry in his file would have read 'missing believed dead' or 'killed in action' and his service medals duly sent to his family.

On the other hand, Maurice Emmett Ryan could have been pulled out of the battle zone and sent to the rear to face trial. But the commissars wanted the supreme penalty, and we do not know what the leading Irish volunteers (Paddy O'Daire, Jack Nalty, Bill McGregor, Johnny Power) thought of the matter, or if they intervened one way or the other. In any case, the killing of Ryan was a stain on the British battalion record, and the reasons given for it were based as much on political paranoia as on military procedure, irregular or otherwise.

NOTES

1. Hugh Thomas, *The Spanish Civil War* (London, 2012), pp 900–1.
2. Richard Baxell, *Unlikely Warriors: The British in the Spanish Civil War and the Struggle Against Fascism* (London, 2012), pp 356–7. The order was rescinded two years later because Mussolini needed republican prisoners to exchange for his men captured at Guadalajara.
3. Severiano Barrado Montero, *La Batalla de Brunete* (Madrid, 2012), p. 66.

4. Ronald Radosh, Mary R. Habeck and Igor Sevostianov (eds), *Spain Betrayed: The Soviet Union and the Spanish Civil War* (New Haven and London, 2001), p. 481.
5. Montero, *La Batalla*, p. 188.
6. Lieut-Colonel G. S. Hutchinson, *Machine Guns: Their History and Tactical Deployment. Being also a History of the Machine Gun Corps, 1916–1922* (London, 1938; Uckfield, 2004), pp 246, 250.
7. RGASPI, f. 545, o. 1, d. 64 (Bulletin of the Commissars of the International Brigades, No. 1, 15 July 1937).
8. Andreu Castells, *Las Brigadas Internacionales de la Guerra en España* (Barcelona, 1974), p. 256.
9. Peter Huber, Michael Uhl, 'Politische Überwachung und Repression in den Internationalen Brigaden (1936–1938)', in *Forum für osteuropäische Ideen- und Zeitgeschichte*, 5. Jahrgang, (2001), Heft 2, pp 144–5.
10. James K. Hopkins, *Into the Heart of the Fire: The British in the Spanish Civil War* (Stanford, Ca, 1998), pp 254–6.
11. Peter N. Carroll, *The Odyssey of the Abraham Lincoln Brigade: Americans in the Spanish Civil War* (Stanford CA, 1994), pp 147–8.
12. TNA, FO371/20587, p.19; *Irish Independent*, 4–8 January 1937.
13. NA, DFA 10/55, Paris Repatriations, Irish Legation to Dublin (with enclosures, 25 February 1937), 6 March 1937.
14. Ibid., Irish Legation, Paris, to Dublin, 21 July 1938 (with enclosures); RGASPI, f. 545, o. 6, d. 147, ll. 52–4.
15. RGASPI, f. 545, o. 6, d. 115, ll. 6–7; f. 545, o. 2, d. 64, l. 237. I am grateful to Des Ryan of Limerick, who gave me copies of his correspondence with Fred Clarke.
16. Huber and Uhl, 'Politische Überwachung', pp 146–7; RGASPI, f. 545, o. 2, d. 150, ll. 1–62 (SIM investigation report).
17. RGASPI, f. 545, o. 6, d. 145, ll. 16–17, 28; f. 545, o. 6, d. 212, ll. 16–17, 28.
18. RGASPI, f. 545, o. 6, d. 167, ll. 8–10; f. 545, o. 6, d. 441, ll. 47–57.
19. RGASPI, f. 545, o. 3, d. 345, ll. 81–2, Carroll, *The Odyssey of the Abraham Lincoln Brigade*, pp 164–5.
20. D. Corkill, S. Rawnsley (eds), *The Road to Spain: Anti-Fascists at War*, (Dunfermline 1981), pp 120–1 (Interview with Bob Cooney); Alexander, *British Volunteers*, pp 163–4; Baxell, *Unlikely Warriors*, p. 258.
21. RGASPI, f. 545, o. 3, d. 3, l. 103.
22. RGASPI, f. 545, o. 3, d. 7, l. 8. He was attached to Walter's 35th Division.
23. Cecil Eby, *Between the Bullet and Lie: American Volunteers in the Spanish Civil War* (New York-Chicago-San Francisco, 1969), pp 271–2; RGASPI, f. 545, o. 3, d. 7, ll. 24–5.
24. RGASPI, f. 545, o. 3, d. 429, l. 245; f. 545, o. 3, d. 434, l. 165.
25. Carroll, *The Odyssey of the Abraham Lincoln Brigade*, pp 181–3.
26. Michael Uhl, 'Die Internationalen Brigaden im Spiegel neuer Dokumente', in *Internationale Wissenschaftliche Korrespondenz* (IWK), Heft 4, 1999, pp 486–518, here p. 507.
27. Uhl, 'Die Internationalen Brigaden im Spiegel neuer Dokumente', pp 508–9; Dokumentationsarchiv des österreichischen Widerstandes (DÖW), Vienna, Sammlung IVVdN, Erich Frommelt, Heinrich Lief, Norbert Rauschenberger.
28. Huber and Uhl, 'Politische Überwachung', p. 156; RGASPI, f. 545, o. 2, d. 145, ll., 166–8, 261–3.

29. Huber and Uhl, 'Politische Überwachung', pp 123–8.
30. Ibid., pp 148–52.
31. RGASPI, f. 545, o. 6, d. 1, ll. 43–5.
32. RGASPI, f. 545, o. 3, d. 168, ll. 5–13; f. 545, o. 3, d. 340, l. 275; James K. Hopkins, *Into the Heart of the Fire*, pp 259–64.
33. RGASPI, f. 545, o. 6, d. 215, ll. 1–10 (quotation l. 3 a.).
34. RGASPI, f. 545, o. 3, d. 172, l. 12a.
35. RGASPI, f. 545, o. 3, d. 183, l. 6a.
36. RGASPI, f. 545, o. 3, d. 178, ll. 54–6.
37. RGASOI, f. 545, o. 3, d. 209, ll. 5, 5a.
38. William Beeching, *Canadian Volunteers: Spain 1936–1939* (Regina, 1989), p. 113; RGASPI, f. 545, o. 6, d. 559, ll. 40–6 (McElligott); f. 545, o. 6, d. 125; f. 545. o. 6, d. 61 (Donaldson).
39. Heinz Prieß, *Spaniens Himmel und keine Sterne: Ein deutsches Geschichtsbuch. Erinnerungen an ein Leben und an ein Jahrhundert* (Berlin, 1996), pp 312–13.
40. Carroll, *The Odyssey of the Abraham Lincoln Brigade*, pp 185–6; Sandor Voros, *American Commissar* (New York, 1961), pp 393–4. For a portrait of de Maio, see: Harry Fisher, *Comrades: Tales of a Brigadista in the Spanish Civil War* (Lincoln, Ne, 1999), pp 135–6.
41. Carroll, *The Odyssey of the Abraham Lincoln Brigade*, pp 186–7; Fisher, *Comrades*, pp 140–1, 187.
42. RGASPI, f. 545, o. 3, d. 435, ll. 144–5.
43. RGASPI, f. 545, o. 6, d. 162, l. 145.
44. Ibid., l. 144 rev.
45. Ibid., ll. 144, 146–8.
46. RGASPI, f. 545, o. 3, d. 111, ll. 72–4.
47. Baxell, *Unlikely Warriors*, p. 260.
48. Robert A. Stradling, *Wales and the Spanish Civil War: The Dragon's Dearest Cause?* (Cardiff, 2004), pp 145–50, 226; RGASPI, f. 545, o. 6, d. 121, ll. 3–33.
49. William Rust, *Britons in Spain: The History of the British Battalion of the XVth International Brigade* (London, 1939), p. 197; Michael O'Riordan, *Connolly Column: The Story of the Irishman who fought in the Ranks of the International Brigades in the National-Revolutionary War of the Spanish People 1936–1939* (Dublin, 1979), pp 127, 163; Bill Alexander, *British Volunteers for Liberty: Spain 1936–39* (London, 1982), p. 274. For a more detailed account of Emmett Ryan's life and death, see Barry McLoughlin, *Fighting for Republican Spain: Frank Ryan and the Volunteers from Limerick in the International Brigades* (Lulu Books, 2014), pp 133–63. Stradling, McGarry and Baxell have also dealt with the case at less length (see bibliography).
50. *Limerick Chronicle*, 19 January 1932.
51. Ibid., 7 December 1933.
52. NAI, DFA 4/44/79, Maurice Emmett Ryan.
53. Merchant seamen's papers acquired from cityarchives@southampton.gov.uk, 2013. See also the BT index at www.nationalarchives.co.uk. I am grateful to Des Ryan (Limerick) for documents on Emmett Ryan's return to Britain.
54. RGASPI, f. 545, o. 6, d. 35, l. 169.
55. RGASPI, f. 545, o. 2, d. 303, l. 108.

56. There is no record of a Maurice Emmett Ryan having served in the Irish Army as an officer cadet in the 1930s. Information from Michael Keane, Irish Military Archives, 10 March 2014.
57. RGASPI, f. 545, o. 6, d. 195, l. 58.
58. For details of the training in Mondéjar, see Bob Clark, *No Boots to My Feet. With a Foreword by Jack Jones*, (Stoke-on-Trent, 1984), p. 31.
59. Ian MacDougall, *Voices from the Spanish Civil War: Recollections of Scottish Volunteers in Republican Spain 1936–39* (Edinburgh, 1986), pp 145–6.
60. RGASPI, f. 545, o. 6, d. 195, l. 59 (reverse).
61. Working Class Movement Library (WCML), Salford, Interview script 946.081 CLA, p. 29. I am indebted to John Halstead (Sheffield) for making the journey to Salford and taking copious notes at my unashamed bidding. It is noteworthy that Clark does not mention Maurice Ryan or his subsequent fate in his published memoir *No Boots to My Feet*.
62. MacDougall, *Voices*, p. 145.
63. RGASPI, f. 545, o. 6, d. 99, l. 3.
64. We thank Guillem Casan for information on Benicasim.
65. RGASPI, f. 545, o. 6, d. 195, l. 59a.
66. Ibid., l. 59.
67. RGASPI, f.545, o. 3, d. 39, l. 35.
68. RGASPI, f.545, o. 3, d. 195, l. 62.
69. Notes of talks between Harry Owens and Eugene Downing, n.d. We are grateful to Harry Owens for this material.
70. Ó Duinnín, *La Niña Bonita*, p. 46.
71. RGASPI, f. 545, o. 6, d. 134, l. 37a.
72. RGASPI, f.545, o. 3, d. 120, ll. 102a.
73. Ibid., l. 105a.
74. RGASPI, f. 545, o. 3, d. 451, l. 140.
75. MacDougall, *Voices*, pp 146–7.
76. Ibid., p. 146. See Baxell, *Unlikely Warriors*, pp 258–60 and also Robert A. Stradling, *The Irish and the Spanish Civil War, 1936–1939: Crusades in Conflict* (Manchester, 1999), pp 190–3. Stradling calls Ryan a 'mad Irishman' and a possible 'fascist saboteur'.
77. IWM, Interview 11355, John Dunlop, reel 10. This script is not yet online and we are indebted to Richard Baxell for his notes of the recording.
78. Howard Williamson, *Toolmaking and Politics: The Life of Ted Smallbone. An Oral History* (Birmingham, 1987), p. 51.
79. South Wales Miners' Library (SWML), James Brewer Interview, p. 22. He also intimates that while Ryan had been protected for a long time by his commander Nalty, Irish officers were 'very stern with their own fellows. . . and [felt] superior to the rest of us'.
80. The following account is taken from two interviews given by Murray to Ian MacDougall 'Tom Murray: Veteran of Spain', in *Pencrastus* (Edinburgh), 18, 1984, pp 16–19; MacDougall, *Voices*, pp 306–30.
81. MacDougall, *Voices*, pp 323–4.

82. Rust, *British Volunteers*, p. 180, wrote that the battalion went into reserve on the night of 6 August. In Ryan's file two dates are given for his death: 'missing 30.07.1938' and beside it in pencil 'killed' (RGASPI, f. 545, o. 6, d. 195, l. 60) and 'missing believed killed Ebro 1.8.38' (RGASPI, f. 545, o. 6, d. 195, l. 61).
83. http://irelandscw.com/ibvol-EDInterview1.htm. Accessed 16 June 2020.
84. Ibid.
85. WCML, Interview Bob Clark, p. 43.
86. We thank Ger McCluskey for providing a copy of this letter.
87. MML, Box 41, File A 43, letter to Edward Ryan, 17/19 Stratford Place, London W1, 21 March 1946.
88. Peter Liddle (ed.), *Captured Memories 1900–1918: Across the Threshold of War* (Barnsley, 2010), p. 258.

TWELVE

# THE TRIAL AND IMPRISONMENT OF FRANK RYAN

JUNE 1938–JUNE 1939

Wattis's denunciation of Frank Ryan in London had far less influence on the fate of the Irish leader than those expressed by two hostile newspaper men in Spain: the extreme right-wing journalists Thomas Gunning and William P. Carney. Gunning was the son of a policeman-turned-farmer who had settled near Boyle in Co. Roscommon. After schooling at a diocesan seminary in Ireland, Gunning studied for the priesthood in Freiburg before turning to journalism and Cumann na nGaedheal politics. He was one of the few in the Blueshirt movement and its successor, the National Corporate Party, who was a doctrinaire fascist.[1] Gunning worked as an editor for the *Catholic Standard* before becoming O'Duffy's personal secretary (1933–35). An intriguer par excellence, he plotted to have O'Duffy assassinated by rivals in the declining Blueshirt movement and stated to the Danish novelist Signe Toksvig in Dublin in 1935 that 'four to five hundred people would have to be shot in order to put the country right.'[2]

Gunning, one of the few Spanish speakers in in the Irish Brigade and holding the rank of captain, was O'Duffy's adjutant. He alienated the rank-and-file Irishmen by his intriguing and profligacy, staying away from the Jarama trenches and living it up in Salamanca.[3] He was also at daggers drawn with Fr Mulrean, the Irish Brigade chaplain who afterwards befriended Frank Ryan in Burgos prison.[4] Complaints were also made by the rank-and-file about O'Duffy, and both he and Gunning were sedulous in denouncing one another to Franco's officers.[5] When Gunning absconded he took with him funds that the men had entrusted to him for postage costs, and also took many of their passports.[6] After O'Duffy's ignominious departure from Spain, Gunning remained in the Franco zone as a propagandist and freelance journalist for English-language press agencies. An indicator to his ultimate destination was his friendship in Salamanca (the initial site of Franco's headquarters) with two future Nazi radio propagandists, the American Jane Anderson and John Amery, the wayward scion of a noted Tory family, who was hanged in London in December 1945.[7] By the summer of 1938 Gunning had left Spain, travelling to Baden-Baden with his wife Kathleen for treatment of advanced tuberculosis.[8]

Equally ardent in his sympathy for Franco was William P. Carney who, like Gunning, was to peddle lies about Frank Ryan. Carney, born in Texas in 1898, was assigned to the Paris office of the *New York Times* in 1928, covering Spanish affairs after the declaration of the Republic in 1931. His dispatches from Spain were treated preferentially by the cable desk in New York, a unit of sub-editors ('bull pen') composed of Franco supporters, who, on the other hand, butchered the reports of Ernest Hemingway's friend, Carney's colleague Herbert L. Matthews.[9] Before violently arguing with Ryan and other captive brigaders in Zaragoza on 4 April 1938, Carney had earned the soubriquet 'General Bill' for his mendacious and biased reporting. In a notorious report printed in the *New York Times* on 7 December 1936, he gave the readers details of Madrid's anti-aircraft defences and thought it politic to assign himself to the Nationalist zone thereafter.[10] He was later to announce, prematurely, the recapture of Teruel by Franco's forces,[11] and gave a paid broadcast on Italian radio from Salamanca.[12] Carney lied about the infamous bombing of Guernica, alleging that the Basques themselves had dynamited their sacred site.[13]

By way of contrast, Leopold Kerney, the Irish Minister Plenipotentiary to Spain, occupied himself with Ryan's predicament to an inordinate degree. Born in Sandymount, Dublin, into a Protestant family in 1881, Kerney terminated his studies at Trinity College, Dublin and travelled throughout the Continent from 1911, earning his living as an accountant in the haute couture salons of Paris. He gave his services to the Sinn Féin delegation in Paris from 1919, but was sacked by the Irish Free State Government because he supported de Valera during the Irish Civil War. He represented Sinn Féin again in the French capital from 1923 to 1925, then sided with de Valera's new parliamentary policy and was re-instated to the Irish diplomatic corps by the incoming Fianna Fáil administration in 1932. Kerney's new post was Commercial Secretary to the Paris Legation before being appointed as Minister to Spain in 1935, which he held until retirement age in 1946.[14]

Kerney, as a political (re-)appointee, was viewed with some reserve at the Department of External Affairs in St Stephen's Green, but many of his problems with Dublin were shared by his Irish colleagues in legations and embassies: the hyper-secretive nature of Joseph P. Walshe, Secretary in External Affairs, who had unique access to the near-blind Taoiseach (who was also Irish Foreign Minister) but was prone to leave staff abroad in the dark as to what exactly Government policy entailed and often kept files to himself.[15] Infuriating for Irish diplomats was the penny-pinching attitude in Dublin – 'all overseas missions were underfunded, understaffed and their employees poorly paid.'[16]

During his 11 years as Irish Minister to Spain, Kerney was 'a one-man-show', not having any diplomatic staff (for example, First Secretary or Cultural Attaché) at his disposal and even his office typist, Elizabeth ('Maisy') Donnelly, was employed merely on a weekly basis. Kerney contracted polio in May 1936, taking extended sick leave until February 1937, when he re-opened the Legation in St Jean de Luz on the French side of the Spanish frontier. He found many colleagues from democratic states ensconced there. When the civil war broke out in July 1936, most accredited diplomats, as was the custom, were enjoying the maritime climate in San Sebastian, away from the torrid heat of Madrid. They moved the short distance north into France when the resort fell under Franco's control. Most states then put their missions in the Spanish capital in the hands of a chargé d'affaires. Ambassadors like Chilton (Great Britain) or Bowers (USA) conducted their business from St Jean de Luz, a pleasant seaside town now teeming with spies and rich, right-wing Spaniards who had fled from the Republican zone.[17]

The Irish state chose not to re-open the Madrid Legation under a chargé d'affaires, for relations with the Republican Government in Madrid (which moved to Valencia in November 1936 and to Barcelona in March 1938) were practically non-existent. The Caballero-Negrín Republican cabinets refused to appoint a liaising mission in St Jean, and the Irish twice declined the appointment of a representative of the Spanish Republic to Dublin after the former Minister had changed sides. The Irish affront was due to strong clerical pressure, perceptions that Franco was very likely to win and that the elected Spanish administration was ultimately responsible for the chaos and terror prevailing in Republican areas from July 1936 into the early months of 1937.

Kerney was in favour of recognising the Franco regime in 1937, primarily because it would restore some kind of order,[18] but later pursued a wait-and-see policy in tune with Dublin.[19] He let Franco's entourage know that its alignment with fascism would clash with the 'very strong democratic spirit in Ireland'. As late as August 1938, when it seemed the defeat of the Republic was only a matter of months away, Kerney advocated the status quo: non-recognition of the generals' regime and the upholding of diplomatic relations with the democratic government now based in Barcelona.[20]

The contribution made by Sir Robert Hodgson in attempting to secure the liberation of Frank Ryan by virtue of his direct contact to Franco's staff was highly ambiguous, if not downright counterproductive: as a diplomat he had to follow the instructions of the Foreign Office, but his interventions were arguably tempered by his reactionary views. In order to protect British investments in the Francoist zone and to promote the influence of the UK in Burgos, Hodgson was appointed (ostensibly as 'commercial agent') to liaise with the insurgents in late 1937. This was, in reality if not in law, recognition of the military regime.[21]

Hodgson had just retired from Head of Mission in Albania at the age of 62 when the civil war broke out in Spain. The British Ambassador Sir Henry Chilton invariably referred to the Republican Government – until September 1936 composed entirely of politicians representing various shades of bourgeois Republicanism – in contemptuous tones as 'Reds'.[22] Sir Robert Hodgson in Burgos fitted into the same bracket, not least because of his experiences in Siberia during the Russian Civil War as British Consul to the anti-Bolshevik forces in Omsk, and on account of his marriage to a White Russian.[23] In his first dispatch to London from Burgos, Hodgson painted the military dictator in glowing terms, remarking that his eyes 'have a marked kindliness of expression' and repeating Franco's implausible and cynical statement that 'the first legislative plans of his new government would harmonize with English ideas.'[24] Hodgson did not change his opinion that Spanish fascism was a safeguard against international Communism, putting his thoughts in print in 1953 when he published a volume in praise of the Franco regime.[25]

Meanwhile, Kerney's efforts to obtain information about Ryan did not relent. Not being accredited to the regime in Burgos, the Irish Minister's only channel of communication with Franco's entourage was through Viscount de Mamblas, an Oxford-educated former head of the cultural relations section of the Spanish foreign ministry. He was responsible for liaison with the British and Irish diplomats in St Jean de Luz from February 1937.[26] When Kerney met the Viscount on 14 April, he was disturbed to learn that Sir Robert Hodgson, whose involvement in the Frank Ryan affair he had suggested to Dublin the day before,[27] had given credence to Fuset's fulminations that the Ryan case was 'a bad case or a very bad case' because of the looting accusation.[28]

Hodgson shortly afterwards stated to the Burgos authorities that he had shown interest in Ryan not because of instructions from London but on the basis of a plea from Kerney who avowed that the accused had never been a communist; now, however, having been apprised by the Francoists of Ryan's 'true past', Hodgson would make only a verbal gesture that was not of great import.[29] In the summer of 1939 Kerney heard confirmation of Hodgson's malign influence from the American journalist Carney, who said that that 'he [Hodgson] had done his best to see that Ryan was kept in prison, and that he was a close relative of Somerville, who had been assassinated in Ireland.'[30] The

Irish Minister also learned of Hodgson's machinations from his contact in the military, Walter Meade, a serving officer of Irish extraction: General López-Pinto, Commander of the 6th Military District in Burgos, had confided in Meade that 'Hodgson had expressed himself in a manner entirely unfavourable to Ryan, alleging that he was guilty of crimes in Ireland.'[31]

### GUNNING PROVIDES THE INDICTMENT

Evidence for the case against Ryan was being collated in Burgos. It would transpire that details of his career in Ireland formed the core of the prosecution case because Franco's military jurists knew very little of Ryan's activities in the Republican forces: his military book (carnet), confiscated upon capture, had no entries after July 1937, i.e. the period when Ryan was assistant battalion commissar with the British and busy collecting material for *The Book of the XV Brigade*.[32] Although requesting information on Ryan from Colonel Francisco Martín Moreno, Franco's Chief of Staff, leading officials in the foreign department had already made up their minds, informing de Mamblas that the Irish Government was not interested in Ryan because of the personal prestige he enjoyed but on account of his criminal past; Viscount de Mamblas was requested to obtain information from Kerney even if the Nationalist administration could not countenance according any official status to the interventions of the Irish Minister.[33] Domingo de las Bárcenas, later Franco's legate at the League of Nations in Geneva and Spanish Ambassador to the Vatican, received on request from Pablo Merry del Val of Franco's Press Office a one-page summary of Ryan's political career to date. The highly coloured account was provided by Thomas Gunning, who by his own account wanted Ryan executed:

> There's one man, an International, that was captured at Gandesa; he had seven murders to his name outside the country and he was a scoundrel; for two months I have been trying to get him shot; I've gone to them with tears in my eyes to get them to shoot him, and they won't shoot him.[34]

Subsequently Gunning told Kerney that he had talked both to Merry del Val and to de las Bárcenas about Ryan, and that he had communicated with sources in Ireland about the prisoner, for example, Gertrude Gaffney, the pro-Franco propagandist of the *Irish Independent*, and Major Patrick Dalton, the former second-in-command of O'Duffy's brigade.[35] According to de Mamblas, Gunning 'had prejudiced the case by going from one person to another in Burgos denouncing Ryan'.[36]

The summary signed by de las Bárcenas on 26 April 1938 stated that a trial was being prepared against Ryan accusing him of being in charge of commanding execution squads; however, he had scant details on the captain's military career in Spain, merely his membership of the 14th and 15th International Brigades and his participation in the battles of the Jarama and Guadalajara and the retreats of March 1938 leading to his capture outside Calaceite. The data provided on his political activities in Ireland identified Ryan as a leading figure of the left movement and as a journalist urging incitement to murder politicians and policemen, for which he had been found guilty in court. While this was partially correct, the charge that 'Ryan and his accomplices' had murdered Justice Minister Kevin O'Higgins in 1927, or that he had received subsidies in 1928 from the Soviet Embassy in Berlin for 'his communist activities' were inventions.[37] Equally untrue were the claims that Ryan had been expelled from the IRA (he resigned in 1934), that de Valera had banned the Republican Congress that Ryan had co-founded, that Ryan had carried out propaganda meetings in London, Liverpool and Glasgow while convalescing in Ireland (March–June 1937) and, finally, that he brought more recruits with him on his return to Spain. In fact, he was the only Irishman in the group of 35 volunteers (including six Americans) who climbed the Pyrenees and entered Republican Spain on 14/15 June 1937.[38]

De las Bárcenas recommended to Foreign Minister Francisco Gómez Jordana that, as there were more than sufficient grounds to execute Ryan, it would be necessary to prepare for the foreign press a text that would justify the sentence imposed and that would be formulated so as to obviate any campaign launched against the Nationalists' treatment of prisoners. Such a communiqué was also to highlight the fact that charges for committing common crimes were being prepared against only three of the Internationals captured recently. If Ryan's sentence of death by the military tribunal were to be commuted by Franco, de las Bárcenas continued, this was not to be communicated to the Irish Legation, not only because Ireland did not recognise Franco, but also to damage Ryan's reputation in Ireland: in view of the prisoner's fierce aversion to Great Britain throughout his political career, his name in Ireland would suffer 'a mortal blow' if it became known that he owed his life to the intervention of the British Agent. The document ended with two recommendations:

1) To inform the Military Assessor Fuset and Franco's Chief of Staff Martín Moreno that the Foreign Ministry has no political interest in Ryan's fate; that it was confident that the War Council would examine the case in the light of the accusations formulated above and on the basis of the facts provided; but that the diplomatic staff at Burgos should be informed of the sentence before it became general knowledge in order to formulate same in an adequate form.

2) That it be made known to the competent authorities that the Foreign Ministry intends to inform the Irish Legation only, and the press, if Ryan is shot, and the British Agent and the press if the death sentence is commuted.[39]

Carney confirmed to Kerney in May that this strategy had been sketched out by Gunning:

> It appears that Gunning – who is on very close terms with Jordana, Sangroniz, Hodgson and others, and is considered by them to be an authority on Irish matters – was very much in favour of Ryan being shot, but recommended that, failing that, he should be handed over not to me but to the British – a fate which it is supposed Ryan would resent more than shooting. The intention is apparently to act on that advice.[40]

A somewhat longer version of Ryan's Irish career was compiled by Franco's diplomats a few days later. The addendum surely came from an Irish 'hostile witness', as the new accusation referred to Dáil Debates in which Frank Ryan had figured, in exchanges on 14 October 1931 in connection with the new Public Safety Act that set up the Military Tribunal to judge subversion. William Cosgrave, President of the Executive Council, made a lengthy speech. He quoted almost verbatim the text of an interview given to the *Daily Express* by Frank Ryan and Geoffrey Coulter in the office of *An Phoblacht*, the IRA weekly. Ryan referred to two recent murders committed by the IRA: the shootings of police Superintendent Curtin in Tipperary and Patrick Carrol in Dublin. His remarks were implacably hostile to the plain-clothes detectives, demonstrating his firm belief that such killings were acts of war against someone who exceeded his duty (Curtin) or was a paid police informer (Carrol). Ryan grimly added that 'military organizations cannot tolerate spies or traitors.'[41] This second draft of the indictment ended with a blistering denunciation of Ryan, a vindictive distortion shared by many Irish reactionaries:

> He is the most violent, dangerous and embittered of Irish Communists now living, and the only reason why he has not been sentenced to a long term in prison is because the [Irish] Government, which is leftwing, is so weak that it is dependent to a great degree on assistance from the Left.[42]

On the same day that de las Bárcenas compiled the dossier on Ryan, Viscount de Mamblas wrote from Biarritz to the foreign department about Kerney's supplications. He saw the Irish Government's appeals as 'platonic' calls to Franco for humane treatment. As to Ryan's politics, de Mamblas had gathered from Kerney that he had a revolutionary past in Ireland but not a criminal one, had taken de Valera's side in the Irish Civil War and was in Spain largely because of his hostility to Eoin O'Duffy. De Mamblas warned that the execution of Ryan would make him a martyr in his native country. Finally, he advised Burgos to talk to Gunning, who was, he believed, working for Reuters in Salamanca, and 'who should know more about Ryan's past than anybody else, even if his opinion will not change the motives behind the Irish Government's call for clemency'.[43]

### SUPPORT FOR RYAN IN IRELAND

In Ireland a groundswell of solidarity for Frank Ryan had commenced in the meantime. In early May motions were passed for clemency by the executive of the Gaelic League (Conradh na Gaeilge), the Students' Representative Council of UCD, Limerick Co. Council and the East Limerick Brigade of the Old IRA.[44] On 4 May Kerney transmitted to Jordana a list of the resolutions addressed to Franco and passed in favour of Ryan by the Gaelic League, the National Union of Journalists, the Gaelic societies at UCD and Trinity College, the Association of Secondary Teachers, the Irish National Teachers' Organisation and various other trade union bodies.[45] It is doubtful whether such appeals impressed any of Franco's coterie.

Of more interest, at least initially, was the short biography of Ryan furnished by Kerney. The single page could have been a column in de Valera's *Irish Press*, succinct and pro-Republican in an Irish context, mentioning Ryan's military experiences in 1922–23, periods of detention before 1932, the fact that he was a practicing Catholic, with three sisters in religious orders, and ending with the most important and true statement that Frank Ryan had 'never, at any time' been a member of the communist party.[46] De Mamblas passed the communication to Burgos with the comment that 'this is far the most favourable evidence to date on this individual, and, if true in all detail, suggests that Ryan belongs to a very respectable and very Catholic family.'[47]

It seems that Franco's foreign policy advisers remained unimpressed, repeating their description of Ryan as a left-wing extremist and advising once more that in case Ryan were to be spared the death penalty this should be attributed in a press statement to the activities of the British Government, in order to discredit Ryan at home.[48] An appeal to Franco from de Valera transmitted by the Papal Nuncio in Dublin via the papal representative in San Sebastian received short shrift. Burgos replied that Ryan was in good health and awaiting trial 'for commanding firing squads in the Red Zone', further that the British Agency in Burgos had expressed interest in the case, and after detailing Ryan's activities against the Nationalist cause, concluding with the remark that the authorities had confidence that all the tribunals of the regime would operate 'according to the strict spirit of justice'.[49] An appeal for clemency telegraphed by the Cork genealogist Eoin O'Mahony (a Knight of Malta) to the Duke of Alba in London elicited the same response.[50] A hardening of attitude can also be seen in the instruction from Burgos to de Mamblas to communicate verbally to Kerney that his original plea to Franco of 4 April had been brought to the attention of the competent authority, but that Ryan was under judicial investigation because he taken part in, and commanded, firing squads in the Republican zone.[51] At least Kerney was given permission to send a packet of clothing and illustrated magazines posted from Dublin for Ryan in the San Pedro concentration camp.[52]

Leopold Kerney, unaware how advanced the prosecution against Ryan had proceeded but suspecting who had assisted in its compilation, was once more dependent on Carney for information from the Franco camp. On 23 May the American recounted his conversation with Merry del Val who, he said, believed it 'extremely likely' that Ryan would not be shot but handed over to Hodgson. Carney reported that Hodgson had received instructions from London to intervene in favour of Ryan because of petitions from Catholic bodies in Britain and from Irish personalities, further that 'because he had many other matters to attend to', Hodgson had said 'this Ryan case was a nuisance.' Kerney correctly surmised that there was a group of foreigners in Burgos (Carney, Hodgson, Gunning and officials of the foreign ministry) conspiring actively against Irish interests:

> The intention appears to be to give as much publicity as possible to the release of Ryan and to the fact that he is being made a present to the British authorities as a British subject, and not handed over as an Irish citizen to my care.[53]

Kerney could not be sure that Gunning's contrite revelations to him in St Jean de Luz on 3 June were dissembling or not. In any case, Gunning was adamant that Ryan would not be shot but handed over to Hodgson or the Irish Minister.[54] Kerney attempted to deflate Gunning's standing in Burgos by writing a note verbale to the effect that Dublin had authorised him to state that Gunning's accusation that Ryan had committed seven murders in Ireland, for which the journalist believed he should be shot, was without foundation and furthermore that Ryan was never found guilty of such a crime so that the charge was contrary to the truth.[55]

The last appeal to Franco before Ryan was put on trial on 15 June was probably decisive: a visit made by Pascal Robinson, an Irish-American Franciscan and now Papal Nuncio to Ireland, to the Duke of Alba in London on 8 June. The nuncio conveyed a plea for clemency from de Valera, who requested that Ryan be spared a capital sentence in consideration of the propaganda in his favour waged in Ireland and among the Irish in America, for his death would make him a martyr for his beliefs and produce an enormous reaction against the positive attitude that Nationalist Spain was attempting to engender in the Irish Free State.[56] Alba was informed by Jordana that the telegram from London was receiving favourable attention from Franco.[57]

### EVIDENCE FOR THE PROSECUTION: JANE BROWN

In the second week of May 1938 the military censor in San Sebastian informed Franco's headquarters that he had received two letters from an 'English woman'. The first, sent some months before, had contained a sketch of buildings in an undisclosed town, but the second was to inform 'Your Excellency that an Irish prisoner in Spain is a thorough undesirable and a criminal who does not warrant compassion.'[58] The woman had attached a cutting of a report from the *Irish Independent* of 2 May concerning discussions in the executive (Coisde Gnótha) of Conradh na Gaeilge about passing a motion in favour of clemency for Frank Ryan whose family and friends had written that 'his life was rumoured to be in danger'.[59] The enclosed three-page letter in English to Franco was to play an important role during the trial of Frank Ryan. Not surprisingly, when the letter was read out at the military tribunal the identity of the correspondent was not revealed. It was a devastating denunciation, full of invective and spite, a gratuitous act against a person whom the letter-writer had never met.

In the years after independence, Irish girls and young women of slender means or none sought jobs as governesses in Spain, usually through the offices of the church. One governess, Bridget Boland, originally from Youghal, Co. Cork, was killed by anarchists during the siege of Bilbao in June 1937.[60] The young women she had brought to Spain from her home town were evacuated from the city, but Boland chose to remain with her employers, the family of Count Zubiria.[61] Perhaps the best known of these young Irish female emigrants to Spain apart from the Limerick novelist Kate O'Brien was the Kildare-born Maura Laverty, a literary all-rounder whose cookery books are still found in many Irish homes. She wrote successful plays, and her 'Tolka Row' stage drama was adapted for television and became RTÉ's first highly popular soap-opera of the 1960s. She published a novel, *No More Than Human*, in 1944, relating her impressions of Spain in the 1920s. While remaining a fervent Irish nationalist and a practising Catholic, Laverty criticised the gross inequalities of Spanish society and despised the attitude of upper-class Spaniards towards the poor, even evincing some sympathy with anarcho-syndicalism.⁶²

Being a single female with good references and strong religious convictions were presumably the criteria for the employment of Irish females by rich, often aristocratic, Spanish families. The woman who blackened Frank Ryan's name and strengthened the case of Franco's implacable prosecutors fitted into these categories – Jane Brown from Co. Kildare. She was born in September 1905 in Howth, Co. Dublin, where at the time of the 1911 Census she is recorded as the second youngest in a family of six children. Her parents were servants and moved with the family later to Co. Kildare and became tenants of a small holding. Miss Brown, a trained nurse, emigrated to Spain in 1935 to take up employment with an ennobled family in Chiprana, a village on the Ebro in the province of Zaragoza, the capital of the Aragon region. Her younger sister Christina found a post around the same time with a family in San Sebastian. Both women hoped to remit part of their income to help parents struggling to pay the rent and rates on a small farm.⁶³

Presumably because of the fighting in the first days of the civil war, the aristocratic household, including Jane Brown, moved to Caspe (population 20,000), the nearest town, on 22 July.⁶⁴ In Aragon the anarchists had many strongholds, but in Caspe itself the Socialist trade union UGT was predominant. The area was split between Left and Right on the questions of land distribution, minimum wages for agricultural labourers and the secularisation of education hitherto in the hands of the church. After the victory of the Popular Front at the February 1936 elections the polarisation became more marked but there were no disturbances in the town before Franco's putsch. Trouble was to come from outside when General Miguel Cabanellas, a key figure in planning the coup d'état, declared a state of military law in Lower Aragon from his base in Zaragoza. When the declaration reached Caspe on 20 July, Capitán José Negrete, commander of the local Guardia Civil (paramilitary gendarmerie), abolished the town council and replaced it with a junta of local right-wing businessmen. Numerous Socialists and anarchists fled south, others were detained by Negrete's patrols. Negrete recruited under pain of death all available men, armed them with rifles sent from Zaragoza and carried out a punitive expedition in the countryside, including Chiprana village. His rule of terror did not last long. A column led by Buenaventura Durruti, Spain's most famous anarchist, arrived from Barcelona in an effort to retake Zaragoza and reached Lower Aragon on 25 July, entering villages near Caspe where it destroyed parochial records and burned church ornaments and paintings.

Reinforced by loyalist military with artillery pieces from Catalonia, the anarchists took up battle with the insurgents barricaded in Caspe's old quarter. Dozens of anarchist milicianos fell in the narrow streets, as well as over 20 members of the Guardia Civil and civilians. Negrete had killed at least a dozen civilians and was himself shot down when he tried to escape the encirclement by moving out behind a human shield of local Republicans, women and children. With the town at last in their hands, the anarchists hunted down 'the class enemy', shooting out of hand the town's leading conservative politician and over 30 supporters of the Right. In all, 55 were executed in July and 17 in August.[65] The reign of anarchist terror was largely the work of a detail driving around in their 'death's head' bus and led by Pasqual Fresquet Llopis from Barcelona, a convicted criminal with a violent temper. His men flushed out 'enemies' in other towns, killing at least 300 before being stopped in Reus near Tarragona by a coalition of armed communists, socialists and anarchists in October. By now even the anarchist trade union CNT began to clamp down on desperados like Fresquet because his deadly peregrinations were bringing the organisation into disrepute.[66]

Jane Brown tended to the wounded Guardia Civil in Caspe.[67] She fled afterwards with her employer and his family to a peasant household in the poorer part of the town, but was discovered. All her belongings, including clothes, two birth certificates and her Irish passport, were confiscated by the anarchist militia.[68] Her family in Kildare was naturally worried and asked a Dublin friend to make enquiries with the Department of External Affairs as early as 31 July.[69] In September her mother, also Jane Brown, informed the Department that she had received a letter from her daughter Jane with the news that she was safe and still with the family that employed her.[70] She remained in Caspe for some months, finally reaching Barcelona in early December. With the assistance of the British Consul she sailed to Marseilles and received a train ticket to Paris from his colleague in the French port. The Irish Legation in Paris paid all her further costs, and she arrived in Dublin on 13 December.[71] Not knowing that her daughter was on her journey home, Mrs Brown contacted Liam Burke, secretary of Fine Gael, who in the name of the party leader William Cosgrave asked Joseph Walshe of External Affairs for assistance in the repatriation. Burke was given a reference of Miss Jane Brown's good character ('a really good sort') by the solicitor Gerard Sweetman from Naas, who was afterwards to become a prominent Fine Gael politician.[72]

That Jane Brown wrote the denunciation of Frank Ryan at the behest of, or because she was encouraged by, others of her pro-Franco persuasion is very likely. Deeply religious and traumatised by her experiences of the terror in the Republican zone, she had motivation enough to abhor Spanish revolutionaries. In any case, she received no monetary reward from any quarter for her fierce denunciation, and partially deaf and broken in health, did not work for many years, if ever again.[73] On her return Jane was in debt to the Department of External Affairs for £5.7.4, which she could reduce by only £2 as her employer in Spain, who owed her one and a half year's wages, was unable to remit the amount because of currency restrictions.[74] Only after the return of her sister from Spain in 1946 could she settle the outstanding sum.[75] Jane Brown's denunciation, a good example of the difference between politicised Catholicism and humane Christianity, commenced with a statement that she had received a letter of thanks from Franco for providing information on the situation in Caspe. She then got down to the matter in hand:

> I wish to place a statement before you and ask you to convey to General Franco the seriousness of the matter. [I wish] he would give it his full consideration before settling anything or bringing it to any definite conclusion. Yesterday 2nd May our daily paper, The Irish Independent, published a statement saying that the friends and members of the Gaelic League, of which Frank Ryan, now your prisoner, was a member, have appealed to General Franco for the release of this head and leader of Communism in Ireland. I wish to state on my own behalf, those of my family and a large circle of Catholic friends that to release and send back to Ireland an influential leader of Communism would indeed be a great crime against God, and Ireland.

According to her lights Frank Ryan was:

> […] no innocent offender, driven to crime by circumstances he could not help. He is an unscrupulous man and offender of Christian rights and charity. Before going to Spain to join the 'Reds' he spoke daily in our capital Dublin with *his colleagues O'Donnell and Gilmore, during the entire time the 'Reds' were carrying out their campaigns he, and those who helped him, were collecting money and all types of assistance. His sister, a nun, intervened openly on several occasions, saying that she and Frank were not afraid to speak and give his point of view and that he had had honoured his word going to join up with the Russians in the struggle with them against the Catholics of Spain. Whenever he spoke in Dublin his platform had to be guarded by a strong force of police, otherwise he would have been attacked by his fellow countrymen. Our last President, de Valera, had to do that for him.*

She continued, alluding to her confederates:

> *In the name of the 'Irish Brigade' and others of our nation, I ask you to consider deeply this business and talk about Frank Ryan in accordance with your fine sentiment of justice and right, and give him what he deserves. Why should he escape the punishment he*

> merits? Is he afraid of dying? Why? And they say that there is nothing after this world, etc. etc. Bah! Cowards, rabble all of them. I have never seen him nor met him. I carry no personal animosity towards him but have a profound love of my religion and my county. I suffered in Spain, alongside the Catholics. I tended the sick and dying Guardia Civil in Caspe. I got to know their beliefs and had sympathy for their problems. I love them all. And those who are Catholic and loyal; those who were forced to become Communists through hunger and want all have my pity and sorrow, but with Frank Ryan I would mete out to him, and his class, stern justice only.

Brown, in conclusion, intimated that not all in Kildare shared her views, before once more confirming her admiration for El Caudillo:

> I cannot send this letter in the ordinary way by post as there are too many of Frank Ryan's class in our post office, therefore I enclose it in sister's letter trusting that the Censor will convey it safely to headquarters. My sister sent me a lovely picture postcard of General Franco through the post some time ago, and it was disfigured and marked over, a thing which happened before. So you see we also have them in our midst (?). My greatest wish in life is one day to meet General Franco personally and shake him by the hand.[76]

Miss Brown obviously had been given or had gathered information on Ryan from the O'Duffyites. How could she have known about the political views of his sister, a nun in Tralee, who had died of tuberculosis?

### THE INTERROGATION AND TRIAL OF FRANK RYAN, 13 AND 15 JUNE 1938

The military jurist investigating the case against Ryan had concluded his work by 4 June.[77] The judicial farce began on 13 June in Burgos, when Ryan was interrogated for nine hours[78] by one Arañaz Munido, a temporary judge and ensign of infantry. Of equally lowly rank was the secretary – a cavalry sergeant. The cavalry lieutenant Ignacio Montobbio acted as interpreter. The script before the judge was a copy of the indictment cobbled together by Franco's diplomats at the end of April. Asked about when he came to Spain and who he had recruited to fight in the 'Red army', Ryan replied that 'he is a Republican and came to serve Republican and not Red Spain and only when General O'Duffy had recruited 600 volunteers for Nationalist Spain, and that he himself had recruited nobody.'[79] As to Ryan's journalistic career and his incitement to violence against politicians and policemen, for which he had been sentenced, Ryan replied 'that at the beginning of 1932 he [Ryan] initiated a press campaign to bring down the Irish Government then in power and aimed it especially at the removal from office of the then chief of police, General O'Duffy, who was indeed dismissed later for abusing administrative procedures in order to prevent de Valera from winning office.' When interrogated about his participation in the murder of Kevin O'Higgins and others, in the intimidation of jurors and in carrying out armed robberies, Ryan gave the reply that O'Higgins, as the majority in Ireland believed, was not killed by Republicans, that he had no part in it and that those Republicans arrested on suspicion were soon freed.

It became clear that the interrogators had difficulty in differentiating between Fianna Fáil, the Republican Congress and the IRA. When questioned about the 'Government's dissolution of the Republican association of which the accused was one of the three most prominent leaders' Ryan answered correctly that the Republican Congress had never been proscribed. When faced with the accusation that he had received funds from the Soviet Embassy in Berlin in 1928 in order to initiate communist activities in Ireland and that this point had been proved by a debate in the Irish parliament, the prisoner said that these claims were 'completely inaccurate', that his name was often mentioned in parliamentary exchanges but never in connection with the charges produced here; in connection with the specific debate alluded to in the question, he said that it was part of a campaign by O'Duffy, assisted by a letter from the Irish bishops, to 'discredit the Republican party of de Valera'. Asked if it were true that de Valera's Government had set him free in 1932 and that he then became a hero of the Left, Ryan admitted that the question was correct, that he had always been popular in Ireland and that his extremism was political, not social, having to do exclusively with his struggle for the Republic and its separation from the British Empire. In sum: that he had always been a soldier for the independence of his country.

The next question demonstrated how the strands of Republicanism in the Irish context were deliberately conflated by Ryan's adversaries at home and in Francoist Spain, namely whether he had been expelled or had detached himself from the Republican party because of 'his communist tendencies and then established a communist group known as the Republican Congress'. Ryan admitted that there had been a deep split within the Republican movement because 'it had separated itself somewhat from the people', but that the Republican Congress was not communist, as there already existed a CPI of which he was not a member and had not co-founded and, finally, that the rupture in the Republican Congress was caused by personal differences.[80]

Asked about the policies of Congress, the prisoner replied that it would be necessary to delve deeper into the details of Irish politics, but its policy was 'to put before the people above all the possibility of an armed conflict between nations, and even more to prepare them for a war in order to gain finally the independence of Ireland'.

Frank Ryan was then once again confronted with the question that the Republican Congress had set out to persecute the Church, the Government and the entire social system and to erect a proletarian state, and that it had gone so far in its extremism that de Valera had deemed it necessary to dissolve it and that Congress had been involved in the murder of a police inspector, about which Ryan was said to have boasted. He said that was a huge lie, that many policemen had been killed or wounded in Ireland, but not one since the accession to power of de Valera in 1932. He was then asked about his participation 'in the murder of the British Admiral Sommerville [sic], a relative of the British Agent Sir Robert Hodgsons [sic], murdered at night in the street, as in the previous assassinations'.[81] That was a reference to the assassination of the retired Vice-Admiral Henry Boyle Townshend Somerville, shot by the IRA in Castletownshend, Co. Cork, on 24 March 1936, an outrage that was to induce de Valera to ban the IRA three months later. Somerville, it is said, was killed because he had given letters of references to local boys who wished to join the Royal Navy. In all probability, the prominent sailor's murder was an 'official job gone wrong': as the IRA leader Tom Barry revealed years later, Somerville was to be kidnapped in order to put pressure on de Valera, perhaps to release Republican prisoners. But Barry's order to 'get him' was taken literally by a veteran IRA fighter from Inniskean who put a bullet through the heart of the 72-year-old.[82]

Ryan, of course, had nothing to do with the crime, having left the IRA two years earlier; he was then pursuing policies at variance with those of his erstwhile militarist comrades. Interestingly, there is no mention of the Castletownshend outrage in the long list of crimes attributed to Ryan that had been serving as a draft indictment since April 1938. Neither has any reliable evidence surfaced to date that Hodgson was a close relative of the murdered Royal Navy oceanographer. The British diplomat had married a Russian, Somerville an Australian. The admiral left a widow and an unmarried daughter, three brothers (two colonels and a vice-admiral) and two sisters, his unmarried novelist sister Edith and Hildegard who had married into the local Coghill family. Hodgson did not feature in the list of mourners at the funeral.[83] How he was related (as he alleged) to the prominent west Cork ascendancy family is unknown. Ryan roundly denied the charge, insisting that he had had no part in the murder, and posed a riposte: if it were true, why was Sir Robert Hodgson seeking to have him set free?

The judge then changed tack, questioning him on the circumstances of his joining the 'Red Army'. Ryan answered that he had arrived in December with 'four or five' and had discouraged others from coming. His journey was undertaken to fight for the legitimate Government of the Spanish Republic and not 'the Red cause'. He added that the understanding of the Spanish war in Ireland was that the military had risen in arms against the state but that the navy and the air force had remained loyal. While some Irish newspapers asserted that the Spanish church or, to be more exact, religion was in peril, they also wrote that Germany and Italy were assisting the rebels under Franco by supplying him with aircraft and all kinds of armaments; and as he believed that democracy was in danger, especially because of German and Italian intervention, and on account of his pro-Government sympathies, he had decided to intervene in favour of Madrid.

The prosecuting officers then argued that as one of the aspirations of the nationalist cause was to emancipate Spain from British tutelage, and as it was confronted by a conglomeration of states calling themselves democracies that sought to limit the economic and political independence of Spain, why did the accused, who as an Irishman had fought against the hegemony of the British Empire, not come to fight with those who confronted the British Empire but chose to enrol in the army 'in which the Empire had its more powerful defenders'? This was a gross distortion of foreign relations but reflected the paranoia of the Francoists against Britain, the home of democracy, liberal values, Free Masonry and Protestantism that had not yet recognised the Burgos junta fully in international law. It was also a grotesque portrayal as the British Government was anything but pro-Republican.

Ryan was nonplussed, it seems. He replied that he had not yet seen the problem from this angle and that by reading the press had come to the conclusion that democracy was jeopardised in Spain, otherwise he and others would have done nothing. However, his decision to fight on the Republican side came about because O'Duffy, 'an agent of British interests and the imperialist aspirations of the conservative masses in Ireland' had sailed to Spain with his volunteers. He then said he suspected that O'Duffy's involvement was but a ruse 'in order to return from Nationalist Spain as a champion of religion and that under this slogan he hoped to topple the Irish Government, a tactic, which as it turned out [O'Duffy's brigade returned to Ireland in June 1937], was nothing more than a purely political manoeuvre of the said General in order to recover the prestige he had already lost.'[84]

The next query pertained to his movements after crossing the border. Ryan gave an imaginative reply: he had gone to the offices of the Irish-Iberian Trading Company in Valencia, one of the owners of which was his friend

Ambrose Martin. An employee, Ryan averred, told him that foreigners were enlisting in Albacete. When questioned about André Marty, the head of the International Brigades in Albacete and their overtly communist nature, Ryan replied that he had been directed to the English unit led by the 'liberal, not communist Nathan' and had then proceeded to the front; up to the time of his return to Albacete in late January he had not noticed such a communist tendency, but that the soldiers wore red stars.[85] The accused expanded his explanation by describing how Marty had directed him to the English speakers, suggesting he might become one of their leaders. Ryan continued that he could not take up such a command as he was sent to the front with 140 men. His appointment was not official even though he was granted the rank of lieutenant and that of captain, his present status, after the battle of Brunete in July 1937.

The first stage of the interrogation terminated with questions about his sojourns at the front. In listing the engagements, he omitted to mention Madrid or any military action after Brunete, admitting that he had been wounded and returned to Spain from Ireland in June 1937. Ryan was then asked to explain to the court why he had not noticed during all his time in Spain that the war was 'a struggle for Russia and with Russia, and not for democracy and liberties'. The prisoner gave an indirect answer, avowing that his campaign in Ireland during his sick leave was limited to defending the Madrid Government, that he had held meetings in halls, but never in the open air and not travelled to British cities for propaganda purposes. As to the charge that he had recruited more volunteers in Ireland, Ryan said, as was the case, that 'he had indeed gained adherents but that they did not come to Spain because he believed Irish lives were sacred and were needed for the Irish cause in future.'[86]

Ryan's declaration was stopped at this point and the judge drafted a preliminary judgement: that the actions of the accused amounted to the 'crime of military rebellion, according to articles 237 and 238 of the Military Code'.[87] This was the run-of-the-mill charge heard by hundreds of thousands of Republican soldiers in fascist hands in summary trials, a cynical reversal of military law clauses since it was the adherents of Franco who had rebelled against the state.

Having held officer rank and been a commander of fighting units, Frank Ryan was in grave danger; had his prosecutors known that he was also a commissar, his life would have been even more jeopardised. The constant references to his political past in Ireland, furnished eagerly and added to constantly by his Irish enemies, was an additional motive for his captors not to release him. Ryan was probably the highest-ranking IB volunteer tried in Spain. His comrade of higher rank, Major Robert Merriman, chief of staff of the 15th Brigade, was shot or summarily executed during the March retreats near Gandesa: his group walked into a fascist camp in the dark.[88] After the adjournment Ryan was again led in and asked if he had any corrections to make to the typed record. He challenged some secondary details, explained others in more depth and admitted that the charges proffered in respect of his military career in the charge sheet were correct. Asked if had anything else to say Ryan declared the following (as recorded by the secretary):

> That if they had expounded the objectives of Our Cause to him when he was a free man and in the form that they were expounded here today, that would have definitely modified his attitude [...] but he was a vanquished prisoner and did not want to give the impression of being a deserter from his cause; that he came to Spain to counteract O'Duffy's political campaign in Ireland, opposing him for a cause that was just and that he believes that Our Movement was protected by England by virtue of its adoption of Non-Intervention which prevents the Madrid Government from purchasing armaments; that he said he was, before all and above all, an Irish Republican, whose ideal is the security and independence of the island of Ireland from England and that it follows logically that the enemies of England are his friends; that he rejected as false the evidence presented here in respect of his political career and the political activities.

After the statement and its translation had taken up 90 minutes of the court's time, the judge cut the Irishman short, and all present, including Ryan, confirmed the accuracy of the day's transcription.[89] For the military it was an open and shut case, even if Franco's military intelligence service possessed next to nothing in respect of Ryan's role in the brigades, merely that he had been a captain, or that he was twice portrayed in January and February 1937 in the communist daily *Mundo Obrero*.[90]

The trial commenced at 9 a.m. on 15 June in the infantry barracks in San Marcial 22, Burgos. On the bench sat five officers. Their questions went over the ground Ryan had encountered two days earlier. He admitted that he carried out propaganda in Ireland in favour of the Madrid Government before coming to Spain and that he was a Catholic; he went on to state that he did not believe that the Republican Army was completely communist, and denied that he had received any money for his first journey to Spain, travelling at his own expense. He contested the opinion of the court that Britain was an enemy of Burgos, arguing that, on the contrary, it was protecting Franco with the Non-Intervention Agreement. He also rejected the idea, as his judges alleged, that Britain was sending any material to the Republicans. When queried about his time at the front the prisoner replied that he had received the pay of a private soldier at first, and later that of captain, and further that he had been a company commander and that once, during a battle, had led a battalion. The president of the court then desisted from any more questions and stated that 'the facts presented amounted to the crime of adherence to the rebellion and requested that the death penalty be imposed on the defendant.' Ryan's defender, Guillermo Escribano Uceley, declared that the he did not believe that the facts before the court constituted adherence to military mutiny and entered a plea that the judges should impose a sentence of 12 years and one day in prison. Ryan, asked if he had anything to add, made a short speech that could have been his last:

> That he was not a criminal killer and to demonstrate that, the judges could contact the representative of Ireland in San Juan de Luz [St Jean de Luz] and also the British commercial envoy in the Franco zone, who, he believed, was the brother-in-law of one of those murdered, in whose death they were trying to implicate him; and, in his own defence, he would like to state that he had acted in good faith and if he had known that the ideals being defended in nationalist Spain were those of his country he would have made himself familiar with them here; but now that he was defeated and vanquished he did not wish to make any more protests to justify his wrong conduct [su equivocada conducta].[91]

The death sentence was duly signed by the five judges and confirmed by the military prosecutor of the 6th Military Region. When Ryan was led out, the civil guards and soldiers saluted respectfully. Back in the Central Prison he was kept handcuffed for nine hours.[92] Two years later Ryan provided Leopold Kerney with a retrospective opinion on the trial:

> I was interrogated on June 13 [. . .] by a military judge named Araña [recte: Arañaz Munido]. I was not interrogated on the 14th. On the 15th June, I saw my defender for the first and last time. We had only a few minutes' conversation when the Court began [. . .] he was genuinely interested in me [. . .] The interpreter, a Cavalry Lieut., acted at the interrogation and at the Court Martial; he was apparently in touch with some people who were in my favour. [. . .] At my trial I wasn't interested much in my life, believing it already forfeit. I took up the attitude that I was a prisoner of war, if they wanted to shoot prisoners of war O.K., but I objected to being shot on the evidence of an anonymous letter. When he told me I was a 'bad man' in the eyes of the Irish Govt., I asked them summon you, the representative of the Govt. They answered: 'The Irish Govt. has no representative here'. When they told me I had assassinated Vice-Admiral Somerville 'father-in-law of the present British Ambassador in Burgos', I suggested that the might at

least bring that gentleman as a witness. In the end, I told them I didn't want any clemency or mercy – as the defender had asked – that I had observed the rules of war, such as they are; that I'd done nothing of which I was ashamed, and that I was a soldier in the army of the Govt., which the Govt. of my country recognized. At one stage, the anonymous letter was being used only as 'evidence of my character'; at another time they said 'there are documents before the court'. [. . .] Only one thing I said at the C.M. that may be of use to you: I was asked why I, who was an enemy of the British Govt., fought against Franco who was also its enemy. I remarked that was the first time I had heard such an argument, and that I was very glad to hear it. I also remarked that O'Duffy – their friend in Ireland – was regarded by us Irish as a British agent and that I was first and foremost anti-British.[93]

That Frank Ryan had been tried, never mind sentenced to be shot, remained a secret for some time. Kerney was relieved in late June to hear that 99 British from San Pedro, and Ryan, had left the camp to be exchanged for Italian servicemen held by the Republicans. As he deemed Ryan to be the most prominent of the exchange contingent, Kerney was convinced that he would be well treated by the Italians and that 'the intention to court-martial Frank Ryan' had been 'definitely abandoned'.[94] Sir Robert Hodgson also enquired about the whereabouts of Ryan because he did not seem to be among the British prisoners under guard at the Italian camp in Palencia.[95]

### ENEMIES OF RYAN IN IRELAND

During the summer of 1938 there were publicly aired criticisms of the steps taken by the Irish Government and Irish organisations to appeal to Franco for clemency. The petition signed by the leaders of the Gaelic League drew the ire of a Galway member, Fr O'Dea, who alleged that Ryan 'had received promotion for his services to the international communists in Spain'.[96] A reader of the *Irish Independent* believed the Nationalists did not shoot prisoners out of hand and added that 'if Mr Ryan has not committed any atrocities, he has nothing to fear.'[97] Furthermore, when 400 veterans of O'Duffy's brigade met for their AGM in Dublin's Ormond Hotel on 2 July, they passed a resolution protesting 'against the action of Limerick County Council and of the headquarters of the Gaelic League in petitioning General Franco for the release of Frank Ryan, now a prisoner in Spain'.[98] Shortly afterwards, Timothy Lenihan, Fine Gael TD for North Cork, was more explicit in the Irish parliament:

I say that if there are Irish nationals who have chosen to go out and take the part of the Red Government in Spain and find themselves in trouble because they have taken the part of the Red Government and the Communists, the money of the taxpayers should not be used to get these people out of their trouble. We have not any great pity for anyone who is in danger because he has taken part in the Civil War in Spain on the side of the Reds.[99]

Frank Ryan wrote to his family on 29 June in French – he was allowed to write only in Spanish or French – and informed them of his needs (clothes, money, etc.) and that he still did not know the results of the trial. His closing line was a plea from the death cell in Gaelic code: Deireadh le [end of], Baolbáis [danger of death], and Sílim [I think].[100] Leopold Kerney's letter to Burgos enquiring about Ryan's fate went unanswered, perhaps because the diplomats at Franco's base believed that the Irishman had been exchanged for an Italian and asked the dictator's chief of staff if this were true.[101] In early August Hodgson requested information about prisoners, including Ryan, from the military assessor Fuset, adding that he was aware of the rumour that the death sentence had been suspended.[102] Two weeks later Hodgson was officially notified that Ryan had not been shot and that his sentence was 'under review'.[103]

### HOPES OF A PRISONER EXCHANGE

About 370 servicemen of Mussolini were in Republican captivity.[104] They were eventually exchanged for British POWs in San Pedro. Initially, in April 1938, El Caudillo offered to exchange 18 San Pedro inmates of British nationality (including the Ulsterman David Kennedy) for a similar number of Legion Condor aircrew shot down over Republican territory.[105] Not surprisingly, the Negrín Government was not prepared to hand over highly prized German airmen for foot soldiers.[106] Official Irish sources hoped that Ryan could be exchanged for an Italian POW of the same rank. The Republican Government in Barcelona offered an Italian sergeant, which Kerney rejected, deeming it worthless since he was of the opinion that Ryan was a major. Instead, Kerney suggested to Barcelona that he could accept a captain of the Italian air force or an unspecified number of Italian soldiers.[107] It transpired that there were no Italian officers of Ryan's reputed rank held in the Republican zone. Then an American journalist suggested that Ryan could be exchanged for José López-Pinto, the son of the general commanding the 6th Military district with headquarters in Burgos. The Francoists naturally assented.[108] However, José Giral, Republican foreign minister, rejected the Irish offer, stating that young Pinto was to be exchanged for Félix Miaja Isaac, a son of the famous general in the Republican Army.[109]

The exchange of prisoners connected with efforts to suspend executions on both sides of the Spanish conflict. The International Red Cross and the British Government were active in the negotiations. London sent a commission under Field Marshall Sir Philip Chetwode, a former Chief of General Staff of the British Army in India, to Spain in March 1938. Chetwode was frustrated by Franco's dilatory and deceitful tactics, as the dictator often reneged on agreements, sent common criminals instead of political prisoners and never relented in his policy of executing perceived enemies. Once Franco's victory was obvious to all, British mediation more or less stopped.[110] His admirer, Sir Robert Hodgson, admitted years later:

> But as time went on, enmity between the adherents of the two groups had become ever more intense and an incredibly tiresome and obstinate Spanish official with whom I had to deal, supported by a Colonel on Franco's staff, had evidently made up his mind that not a single one of the unfortunate folk whose names figured on the interminable lists submitted to me should regain his liberty. And none did, despite my efforts.[111]

In the autumn of 1938, however, all of that was in the future, and Kerney could be mildly optimistic on two grounds. First, Viscount de Mamblas informed him on 8 October that Ryan was alive and had narrowly escaped death although the captain had 'a very bad background' that, in the opinion of the Irish Minister, 'justifies a death sentence where Franco holds sway'.[112] Nine days later, the Viscount informed Kerney that he was 'no longer welcome' in Nationalist territory.[113] Second, despite this considerable drawback and the rebuff from Barcelona, Kerney still harboured hopes of an 'officer swop'.[114] Burgos was in favour of an exchange (canje) because of General López-Pinto's interest.[115] Hodgson, too, sought information on Ryan, mentioning that he had learned in early August that 'his case was under examination.'[116]

Kerney saw himself obliged to intervene as well for the egregious Gunning, who, he believed, was under sentence of death for espionage activities in the Franco zone. The Irish Minister was previously of the opinion that Gunning was treating his tuberculosis in a Bavarian sanatorium while on full pay from Reuters.[117] The rumour about Gunning was unfounded and, in the view of Burgos, amounted to one of the many claims spread by the 'Reds to create doubts in Our Cause'. As regards Ryan, the Marqués de Rialp of the prisoner exchange delegation in San Sebastian could not agree to handing over 'the said individual on account of the special circumstances, because it was not a case of a prisoner of war but of a criminal who had carried out the most repugnant crimes'.[118]

Hodgson was again to request information 'regarding the case of Frank Ryan' in January 1939, perhaps unaware that in the meantime the Franco authorities had reverted to their hard line (no exchange).[119] The new argument from the dictator's Chief of Staff in February, transmitted to Hodgson, was that 'His Excellency has received hundreds of telegrams from the Catholics of Ireland asking him not to pardon this prisoner, and because these petitions came from our adherents who assisted us so much in the Crusade, we are obliged to ponder on the decision to be taken in regard to this prisoner.'[120]

This claim was in all probability a gross exaggeration, for although the campaigning of the 'Frank Ryan Release Committee' in Ireland in 1939–40 did prompt some clerics to write to Franco, no evidence for a flood of mail from Ireland to El Caudillo has been found in the archives of the Spanish Foreign Ministry, nor in Franco's private archive.[121] Sir Robert Hodgson, now chargé d'affaires at the British Embassy after Britain's recognition of Franco on 27 February 1939, penned his last letter of intercession to Burgos on behalf of Ryan in flowery language:

> The Embassy has no wish to minimize the importance of the offence committed by Ryan in taking up arms in a cause which was no concern of his, and in which he should never have participated. On the other hand, they submit that he possessed to a high degree a quality which must necessarily appeal to Spaniards, even though misused, namely, that of great personal courage. They trust that this quality may be taken into account when Ryan's case comes up for settlement and that his possession of it may be allowed to militate in his favour.[122]

That was short of requesting his liberation. Hodgson had probably changed his opinion of the Limerick Republican late in the day, after having denounced him at a decisive juncture in 1938. In his memoir of Spain published 14 years later, the retired diplomat paid Ryan a glowing tribute, perhaps recalling what Colonel Martin had told him about the visits to San Pedro:

> Frank Ryan, who had been a member of the I.R.A., became a prisoner in the P.O.W. camp at San Pedro de Cardena and was sentenced to death by a court martial for fighting against Spaniards in Spain. Three times he was taken out under escort to be shot and three times, when he was on the point of being despatched by the firing-party, a remission of sentence arrived. In the first place

the Vatican intervened on his behalf; in the second, the Government of Eire through its representative with Franco [sic]; in the third, I in my capacity as British Agent under Foreign Office orders. Ryan never turned a hair. Moreover, in the P.O.W. camp he was a model, taking a warm interest in his fellow-prisoners, bucking them up and being as helpful to them as possible.[123]

With the war won, Franco had even fewer motives to accommodate a state he considered unfriendly (Britain) or one who recognised his regime very late in the day (Ireland). Considering the primitive state of communications – telephone calls to Dublin were exorbitant (£3 per minute),[124] telegrams could be read by others and post by diplomatic bag was slow and unsafe – Kerney had a much higher degree of autonomy on a day-to-day basis than modern Irish envoys. Instructed by F. H. Boland from External Affairs on 11 March 1939 to make 'a strong and urgent appeal to Gen. Franco for Mr. Ryan's release' during his first official visit to Burgos, Kerney sent three urgent letters to that city beforehand. He received the standardised brush-off: the prisoner was under the jurisdiction of the military authorities and would be treated on the same basis of the military code of justice as all prisoners of war.[125] Kerney's request for a deadline in regard to Ryan's release from captivity merely provoked a response that referred to earlier communications from Burgos.[126] At least his enquiry into the state of health of the Irish captain met with a positive response: the prisoner was 'in a perfect state of health, save that he is suffering from chronic damage to the heart.'[127] Kerney was to elicit nothing substantial from the inscrutable Franco for some months, but he had been assured by Walter Meade, a captain of Irish extraction in the Spanish Foreign Legion and former personal interpreter to O'Duffy, that his efforts of the previous summer 'had undoubtedly prevented the carrying out of the [death] sentence'.[128]

### THE 'FRANK RYAN RELEASE COMMITTEE'

Another factor was the establishment of a 'Frank Ryan Release Committee' in Dublin in early March 1939.[129] Its proponents were a roll call of the Republican elite. President was Aodoghan O'Rahilly, the four vice-Presidents were Patrick Pearse's sister, Maude Gonne, the labour veteran P. T. Daly and Pádraig Ó Ciamh, President of the Gaelic Athletic Association. Joint secretaries were Mollie Hall (daughter of the Dublin Brigade quartermaster during the 1916 Rising), Tom Barry, Roddy Connolly, Donal O'Reilly, Ryan's comrade-in-arms in Spain, and Flann Campbell, son of the famous poet Patrick Campbell.[130] Soon co-opted on to the committee were Con Lehane, a close friend of Ryan, T. B. Rudmore-Brown, Professor of French at Trinity College,

Jim Prendergast and Aileen ('Bobby') Walshe, the wife of Frank Edwards. An appeal had already been signed by 'fifty public representatives and some thousands of citizens' and was sent out for distribution to the Labour Party branches in Dublin.[131]

The most active members of the Committee were Rosamond Jacob and Hannah Sheehy Skeffington. Other frequent attenders at the meetings were Charlie and Nora Harkin, and Linda Kearns, the nurse and ex-Senator for Fianna Fáil. Jacob was from a Quaker family in Waterford, had joined Sinn Féin before the 1916 Rising and was an inveterate Anglophobe, while at the same time being inwardly dismissive of men going to war, a point of view that was not changed by meeting volunteers repatriated from Spain in April and September 1937, and the last returnees in December 1938.[132] Still, she was committed to the cause of Spanish democracy, a regular in solidarity or discussion circles. In October 1936 she was shocked by Thomas Gunning, whom she obviously did not know, when he espoused the cause of fascist dictators in the presence of Seán Murray and Peadar O'Donnell at the Contemporary Club.[133] She saw little of Frank Ryan during his sojourn in Ireland between March and June 1937. Jacob was also involved in the short-lived *Irish Democrat*, going on a door-to-door canvas in the working class estates of Crumlin, for her a new experience.[134] She was also a close friend of Eilís Ryan, who usually stayed in the background and invited Rosamond frequently to her house in Inchicore after she had brought her parents, Vere Francis and Anne, up from Limerick to live with her in late 1937.

Franco's advisers, in ascertaining official Irish attitudes to the dictatorship, now had a 'second opinion' in the presence of the new Spanish Minister to Ireland, Juan García Ontiveros. He and the system he represented were praised profusely by the *Irish Independent*, but the new Minister had problems coming to terms with the right of assembly, association and free expression in his new posting, constantly complaining to External Affairs about the 'Frank Ryan Release Committee' and consorting, almost exclusively, with Fine Gael notables, which ultimately did his standing little good. The Spanish Minister met de Valera for the first time in late May. It was an amicable exchange of views replete with well-worn clichés about the age-old bonds of friendship between two Catholic nations, until at the close of proceedings de Valera asked about Ryan. The Taoiseach emphasised Ryan's 'heroic status' but described his conduct as 'irresponsible'. Ontiveros accorded little importance to de Valera's view that the release of Ryan would be the proof of friendly relations between the states.[135]

The Release Committee had written to Ontiveros pressing for a response.[136] The diplomat had unwanted visitors to his home in Shrewsbury Road, when on the evening of 1 June, Hanna Sheehy Skeffington (for him the 'soul and leader' of the CPI) and Eilís Ryan ('an insipid Miss') stood on his doorstep. He gave them a peremptory hearing before insisting that it was not in his competence to make any intervention for a person whose death sentence had been commuted and was now under sentence for a fixed period.[137] According to Sheehy Skeffington, the delegation conversed in French with the Minister, who seemed to take notice when he was told that Frank Ryan's three sisters were nuns.[138] Minister Ontiveros became unnerved by the constant articles in the press and letters seeking his intercession, and he protested to External Affairs. The officials persuaded the Release Committee to call off the public meeting scheduled for Cathal Brugha Street on Sunday, 11 June.[139]

### KERNEY REBUFFS THE BRITISH FOREIGN OFFICE

The Government in Dublin, Kerney and Frank Ryan himself wanted his release to be processed under the auspices of the Irish Legation, primarily for reasons of sovereignty and because Hodgson was not trusted. In the age of the United Nations and the European Union, it is commonplace for two or more states or a confederation to intervene in favour of a prisoner held by a dictatorship. Such an approach was unknown in the 1930s, except through the International Red Cross. Had Dublin and London acted in tandem in respect of Frank Ryan, the Francoist state could have played one off against the other, now possessing the excuse to do nothing because it did not know which state was responsible for the prisoner. George Strauss and other Labour MPs raised the question of Frank Ryan's release – it had been widely reported that Ryan's death sentence had been commuted to 30 years' imprisonment – in the House of Commons on 15 February 1939. R. A. Butler, the junior foreign minister, promised to 'continue my investigations into the case of Mr. Ryan'.[140] In mid-March, Butler was more specific: 'The case of Frank Ryan has recently formed the subject of further representations to the Spanish Government, which will, I hope, result in his early release.'[141]

Leopold Kerney let it be known in Burgos that 'it would be neither in their own interests nor in ours if they were now to deal with Ryan as a British subject rather than an Irish citizen.'[142] When Kerney first met Jordana, Franco's Foreign Minister, on 10 April, he was told that release after commutation was difficult. Kerney emphasised the good effect that the release would have on Hispanic–Irish relations. He referred to a House of Commons debate on Frank Ryan in the belief that the Irishmen 'had been placed on a list of prisoners whose release was expected shortly by the British', adding 'that it would be a fatal blunder to hand him over to the British rather than myself'.[143] The Irish Government now harboured hopes that the arrival of Ontiveros, the new Spanish Minister to Dublin, would accelerate matters.[144] Irish insistence that Ryan was 'their' prisoner had been registered in London, which Butler underlined in the House of Commons on 17 May: 'There is this other prisoner, Frank Ryan, who is a citizen of Eire and whose case is being looked after by the Eire Minister in Spain. He is reputed to be detained on a civil charge.'[145]

At the end of June, George Strauss, MP again raised the case of Ryan's imprisonment in parliament. He received the standard answer from Butler: that the affair was being looked after by the Irish Minister in Spain, but that the British Ambassador, Maurice Peterson, had offered his assistance.[146] Official British statements on the case of Frank Ryan were prompted by appeals from liberal and left-wing circles in the UK, or by the approach of J. W. Dulanty, Irish High Commissioner in London to the Foreign Office. Peterson, the British Ambassador to Madrid, was willing to help, not taking cognisance of proper diplomatic procedure: Dulanty should have gone through External Affairs first.[147] Peterson's offer was dismissed in no uncertain terms by the Irish Minister:

> If I were to take advantage of your kind offer [...] I would be guilty of creating fresh doubts as to whether Mr Ryan is an Irish citizen or a British subject; such doubts as existed in this regard when your predecessor, Sir Robert Hodgson, appeared to be taking a friendly interest in this case have long been dispelled by me.[148]

Kerney explained his attitude to Walshe, not hiding his annoyance that he had received a message from an Irish colleague [Dulanty] 'through British official channels' and stating that Peterson was 'powerless to help'. He underlined that he would reject courteously any written offer of British assistance in the matter because he believed that 'any "assistance" from or interference of the British Ambassador only weakens my efforts.'[149]

Despite his determination to emphasise the reality of Irish sovereignty when talking to Spanish or British officials, Kerney was no Anglophobe, helping Colonel Martin of the British Embassy to gain access to the three or four British POWs held in Burgos Prison, or conversing with Martin's successor who visited the penitentiary in 1940.[150] In Britain, too, the friends and sympathisers of Frank Ryan had started an extensive campaign for clemency. Ellen Wilkinson, a prominent Labour MP, requested Lord Halifax in June to intercede on Ryan's behalf with the Duke of Alba. Halifax demurred, arguing that the case 'had been taken over' by the Irish Minister in Spain.[151]

## NOTES

1. John M. Regan, *The Irish Counter-Revolution, 1921–1936* (Dublin, 1999), p. 368.
2. Ibid., p. 434.
3. Fearghal McGarry, *Irish Politics and the Spanish Civil War* (Cork, 1999), p. 38.
4. Fearghal McGarry, *Eoin O'Duffy: A Self-Made Hero* (Oxford, 2005), p. 295.
5. McGarry, *Irish Politics and the Spanish Civil War*, p. 42. For a portrait of Gunning in the Nationalist zone, see Robert A. Stradling, *The Irish and the Spanish Civil War, 1936–1939: Crusades in Conflict* (Manchester, 1999), pp 19, 40–1, 118.
6. McGarry, *Eoin O'Duffy*, p. 309.
7. Judith Keene, *Fighting for Franco: International Volunteers in Nationalist Spain during the Spanish Civil War 1936–1939* (London and New York, 2001), pp 121, 260–4.
8. *Irish Independent*, 15 July 1938.
9. Julie Prieto, *Partisanship in Balance: The New York Times Coverage of the Spanish Civil War, 1936–1939*, pdf. pp 15–17, https://alba-valb.org/resource/partisanship-in-balance-the-new-york-times-coverage-of-the-spanish-civil-war-1936-1939/. Accessed 17 June 2020.
10. Paul Preston, *We Saw Spain Die: Foreign Correspondents in the Spanish Civil War* (London, 2009), p. 65–7.
11. Ibid., pp 148–9.
12. Ibid., p. 185.
13. Ibid., p. 186.
14. See Barry Whelan, *Ireland's Revolutionary Diplomat: A Biography of Leopold Kerney* (South Bend, IN, 2019).
15. Aengus Nolan, *Joseph Walshe: Irish Foreign Policy 1922–1946* (Cork, 2008), pp 7–12.
16. Barry Whelan, 'Ireland and Spain 1939–55: Cultural, Economic and Political Relations from Neutrality in the Second World War to Joint Membership of the United Nations' (PhD, NUI Maynooth 2012), pp 189–90. A more generous attitude became apparent only after Walshe's posting as Irish Ambassador to the Holy See in May 1946 and the reforms initiated by Sean McBride, foreign minister in the First Interparty Government. http://mural.maynoothuniversity.ie/4075/1/BW_Thesis.pdf. Accessed 3 June 2020. See also Barry Whelan, 'Ireland's Minister to Spain – L. H. Kerney's diplomatic efforts to secure the release of Frank Ryan", *Saothar* 37, 2012, pp 73–83.
17. For an interesting insight into the atmosphere in St Jean, see Claude G. Bowers, *My Mission to Spain: Watching the Rehearsal for World War II* (New York, 1954), pp 288–303.
18. McGarry, *Irish Politics and the Spanish Civil War*, pp 217–23; DIFP, *Vol. 5, 1937–1939*, pp 76–7, Kerney to Walshe, 7 June 1937 (Kerney's meeting with Republican representative Francisco Ayala).
19. Whelan, 'Ireland and Spain', pp 104–6.
20. Whelan, *Ireland's Revolutionary Diplomat*, p. 120.
21. Tom Buchanan, *Britain and the Spanish Civil War* (Cambridge, 1997), pp 37–62.
22. Bowers, *My Mission*, p. 291.
23. Keene, *Fighting for Franco*, p. 47f.
24. Paul Preston, *Franco: A Biography* (London, 1993), p. 198.
25. Sir Robert Hodgson, *Spain Resurgent* (London, 1953).

26. McGarry, *Irish Politics and the Spanish Civil War*, p. 216.
27. DIFP, *Vol. 5*, p. 269, Kerney to Walshe, 13 April 1938.
28. Ibid., pp 270–1, Kerney to Walshe, 16 April 1938.
29. AGA, 82/4333/233, Memorandum by de las Bárcenas, 26 April 1938.
30. NA, DFA 10/1/31, Kerney to Dublin, 6 July 1939.
31. Ibid., 7 June 1939.
32. NA, DFA, 10/1/33, letter from Ryan to Kerney, n.d. (early January 1940).
33. AGA, 82/4333/233, foreign affairs Burgos to Martín Moreno, 21 April 1938; foreign affairs Burgos to de Mamblas, 21.04.1938.
34. NA, DFA 244/8, Kerney to Walshe, 2 June 1938 (emphasis in original).
35. Ibid., 8 June 1938.
36. NA, DFA 10/1/32, Kerney to Dublin re 'Conversation with de Mamblas', 23 November 1939.
37. The identities of the assassins of Kevin O'Higgins, who acted on their own initiative, became known only in 1985 Bill Gannon, Archie Doyle and Tim Coughlan. See: Uinseann Mac Eoin, *Harry. The Story of Harry White as Related to Uinseann Mac Eoin* (Dublin, 1985), p.106.
38. RGASPI, f. 545, o. 6, d. 35, l. 15.
39. AGA, 82/4333/233, Memorandum by de las Bárcenas, 26 April 1938.
40. NA, DFA 24/22, Kerney to Dublin, 24 May 1938.
41. 'The inside story of the Irish killings', in *Daily Express*, 24 August 1931; Dáil Debates, 14 October 1931, www.oireachtas.ie/en/debates/debate/dail/1931-10-14/33/. Accessed 4 June 2020.
42. AGA, 82/4333/233, undated memorandum, probably by Bárcenas, April 1938.
43. Ibid., de Mamblas to foreign affairs, 26 April 1938.
44. Ibid., In order of the resolutions passed by the bodies named above: *Irish Press*, 2 May, 23 May, 3 May, 9 May 1938.
45. AGA, 82/4333/233, Kerney to Jordana, 4 May 1938.
46. Ibid., Frank Ryan biography attached to Kerney's visiting card for de Mamblas, 2 May 1938.
47. Ibid., de Mamblas to foreign affairs Burgos, 4 May 1938.
48. Ibid., foreign affairs Burgos to chief of staff Burgos, 7 May 1938.
49. Ibid., papal nunciature, San Sebastian, to Jordana, 9 May 1938; foreign affairs Burgos to Spanish papal nunciature, 12 May 1938.
50. Ibid., telegram from Eoin O'Mahony to Alba (copy, n.d.); Alba to foreign affairs Burgos, 11 May 1938; foreign affairs Burgos to Alba, 18 May 1938.
51. Ibid., foreign affairs Burgos to de Mamblas, 21 May 1938.
52. Ibid., Alonso Lara, St Jean de Luz, to foreign affairs Burgos, 29 May 1938; foreign affairs Burgos to St Jean de Luz, 2 June 1938.
53. NA, DFA 244/8, Kerney to Walshe, 24 May 1938.
54. Ibid., 7 June 1938.
55. AGA, 82/4333/233, Kerney to foreign affairs Burgos, 3 June 1938. Kerney was referring to the drunken rantings made by Gunning in the presence of American journalists in a bar in St Jean de Luz on 1 June, a conversation overheard by his secretary Elizabeth Donnelly (NA, DFA 244/8, Kerney to Walshe, 2 June 1938).

56. AGA, 82/4333/233, telegrama oficial, Alba to foreign affairs Burgos, 8 June 1938.
57. Ibid., telegrama oficial, foreign affairs Burgos to Alba, 10 June 1938.
58. Archivo Intermedio Militar Noroeste, El Ferrol (AIMNOR), Causa 1695–38, head of military censorship, San Sebastian, to the secretary of Franco, 9 May 1938.
59. *Irish Independent*, 2 May 1938. See also the *Irish Press* of the same date for details of the discussion.
60. *Irish Times*, 28 June 1937.
61. Ibid., 30 June 1937.
62. Ute Anna Mittermeier, '*No More Than Human*' by Maura Laverty: Impressions of a Reluctant Governess in Spain', in *Estudios Irlandeses*, 2, 2007, pp 135–50, www.estudiosirlandeses.org/2007/03/no-more-than-human-by-maura-laverty-impressions-of-a-reluctant-governess-in-spain/. Accessed 17 June 2020.
63. NA, DFA, 210/155, Repatriation of Miss Jane Brown, letter by Miss Jane Brown to Dept of External Affairs, 28 March 1939.
64. NA, DFA, 10/51 (2), handwritten note, Irish Legation Paris, 9 December 1937.
65. José Luis Ledesma Vera, *La guerra civil y la comarca del Bajo-Aragón-Caspe (1936–1939)*, pp 153–9.
66. Paul Preston, *The Spanish Holocaust: Inquisition and Extermination in Twentieth-Century Spain* (London, 2012), pp 229–31.
67. AIMNOR, Causa 1695–1938, letter from Miss Jane Brown, dated 3 May 1938.
68. NA, DFA, P10/51 (2), handwritten note, Irish Legation Paris, 9 December 1937.
69. NA, DFA, 210/155, Repatriation of Miss Jane Brown, handwritten note, 31 July 1936.
70. Ibid., Mrs Jane Brown to Dept of External Affairs, 11 September 1936.
71. NA, DFA, P10/51(2), Irish Legation Paris, Jane Brown signed questionnaire and handwritten note by official, 11 December 1936; Customs and Excise, Dun Laoghaire, to Dept of External Affairs, 13 December 1937.
72. NA, DFA, 210/155, Repatriation of Miss Jane Brown, Burke to Walshe, 9 December 1936; Walshe to Burke, 10 December 1936; Sweetman to Burke, 9 December 1936. Sweetman sat in the Senate 1943–4, in the Dáil 1948–73 for Kildare, was chairman of Kildare Co. Council 1949–51 and Minister for Finance, 1954–7. He was killed in a car crash in Monasterevin in 1970.
73. Ibid., Miss Jane Brown to External Affairs, 28 March 1939; Mrs Jane Brown to External Affairs, 23 June 1938.
74. Ibid., External Affairs to Miss Jane Brown, 23 January 1938; handwritten note External Affairs, 14 April 1938; memo External Affairs, 9 July 1940.
75. Ibid., External Affairs to Kerney, 19 April 1946; Miss Jane Brown to External Affairs, 27 June 1946, 6 August 1946; External Affairs to Miss Jane Brown, acknowledging the payment of £3.7s.4d, 9 August 1946.
76. AIMNOR, causa 1695–38, p. 4–5, letter from Jane Brown to Dear Sir, 3 May 1938. The passage in italics is a re-translation from the Spanish because one page of the original is missing.
77. Ibid., Región Militar, Estado Mayor, Sección de Justicia to Juez Instructor Número 4 in Burgos, 4 June 1938.
78. DIFP, *Vol. 6*, p.124, extracts from report Kerney to Walshe, 27 December 1939.
79. AIMNOR, causa 1695–38, Statement of the accused, p. 8.
80. Ibid., p. 8a.

81. Ibid., p. 8b.
82. Meda Ryan, *Tom Barry: IRA Freedom Fighter* (Cork, 2003), p. 218. See also the article written by a nephew of the killer: www.theguardian.com/books/2001/feb/10/books. guardianreview. Accessed 3 June 2020.
83. *Irish Times*, 28 March 1936.
84. AIMNOR, causa 1695-38, p. 8b.
85. Ibid., p. 9.
86. Ibid., p. 9a.
87. Ibid.
88. Peter N. Carroll, *The Odyssey of the Abraham Lincoln Brigade: Americans in the Spanish Civil War* (Stanford, 1994), p. 174.
89. AIMNOR, causa 1695-38, pp 10, 10a.
90. Ibid., pp 11-3.
91. Ibid., pp 18-19.
92. DIFP, *Vol. 5*, p. 474, Kerney to Walshe, 17 June 1939.
93. NA, DFA 10/1/33, Ryan to Kerney, received at the Irish Legation, 4 January 1940. Ryan wrote a brief summary of the trial three weeks after sentencing to the International Red Cross (Seán Cronin, *Frank Ryan: The Search for the Republic* (Dublin, 1980), pp 145-6).
94. DIFP, *Vol. 5*, pp 316-7, Kerney to Walshe, 29 June 1938.
95. AGA, 82/4768, Note Verbale by Hodgson, 27 June 1938.
96. *Irish Press*, readers' views, 24 June 1938. See the reply from Dónal O Buachalla, *Irish Press*, 1 July 1938. O'Dea had also criticized the motion of the League in the *Connacht Sentinel*, 17 May 1938.
97. *Irish Independent*, 12 May 1938, letter to the editor from J.N.R. McNamara, Youghal.
98. *Irish Press*, 4 July 1938.
99. Dáil Debates, Finance Vote, External Affairs, 13 July 1938, www.oireachtas.ie/en/debates/debate/dail/1938-07-13/29/#spk_89. Accessed 3 June 2020.
100. NA, DFA, 244/8, Ton frère Frank to ma chère soeur (copy), 29 June 1938; Eilís Ryan to Walshe, 7 July 1938. For the English translation, see Cronin, *Frank Ryan*, p. 146.
101. AGA, 82/4333/233, foreign affairs Burgos to chief of staff Burgos, 6 July 1938.
102. AGA, 82/4768, Hodgson to Fuset, 6 August 1938, based on his handwritten note in French, 4 August 1938.
103. Ibid., Fuset to foreign affairs Burgos, 23.08.1938; foreign affairs Burgos to Hodgson, 29 August 1938.
104. Politisches Archiv des Auswärtigen Amtes, Berlin (PAAA), R. 251.158, report of visit of Italian Ambassador, Berlin, 11 October 1938.
105. PAAA, R. 103.202, List, Burgos 17 April 1938; AGA, 82/4768, List of same date.
106. PAAA, R. 103.203, telegram Geneva-Berlin, 5 July 1938.
107. AGA, 82/4333/233, telegram from Kerney to Barcelona, 10 August 1938.
108. DIFP, *Vol. 5*, pp 338-339, Kerney to Walshe, 16 October 1938. See also the *Irish Press*, 27-8 September 1938.
109. AGA, 82/4333/233, Giral to Kerney, 6 September 1938. One of Miaja's sons, José, was exchanged for Miguel, brother of José Primo de Rivera, the founder of the Falange, in March 1939. Pierre Marqués, *La Croix-Rouge pendant la Guerre d'Espagne (1936-1939): Les Missionnaires de L'humanitaire* (Paris-Montreal, 2015), p. 342.

110. Peter Anderson, 'The Chetwode Commission and the British diplomatic responses to violence behind the lines in the Spanish Civil War', in *European History Quarterly*, 42:2 (2012), pp 235–60.
111. Hodgson, *Spain Resurgent*, p. 130.
112. DIFP, *Vol. 5*, p. 357, Kerney to Walshe, 10 October 1938.
113. McGarry, *Irish Politics and Spanish Civil War*, p. 230.
114. AGA, 42/4768, Kerney to de Mamblas, 21 November 1938.
115. AGA, 82/4333/233, de Mamblas to foreign affairs Burgos, 8 October 1938; foreign affairs Burgos to delegation for prisoner exchanges, San Sebastian, 11 October 1938; de Mamblas to foreign affairs Burgos, 21 November 1938; foreign affairs Burgos to Marqués de Rialp (prisoner exchanges delegation), 24 November 1938.
116. Ibid., Hodgson to foreign affairs Burgos, 28 November 1938.
117. NA, DFA, 10/55, Paris, Repatriations, Kerney to Irish Legation, Paris, 15 December 1938, 28 December 1938; AGA, 82/4768, Kerney to de Mamblas, 17 December 1938; de Mamblas to foreign affairs Burgos, 17 December 1938.
118. AGA, 82/4768, foreign affairs Burgos to de Mamblas, 20 December 1938.
119. AGA, 82/4333/233, Hodgson to foreign affairs Burgos, 24 January 1939.
120. Ibid., chief of staff Burgos to foreign affairs Burgos, 6 February 1939.
121. Whelan, 'Ireland and Spain', p. 83.
122. AGA, 82/4333/233, Hodgson to foreign affairs Burgos, 14 March 1939.
123. Hodgson, *Spain Resurgent*, p. 55.
124. Leopold H. Kerney, Frank Ryan out of Jail, p. 2, www.leopoldhkerney.com. Accessed 3 June 2020.
125. DIFP, *Vol. 5*, p. 415, Boland to Kerney, 11 March 1939; AGA, 82/4333/233, Kerney to foreign affairs, Burgos, 28 March 1939, 29 March 1939, 4 April 1939; foreign affairs Burgos to Kerney, 4 April 1939.
126. AGA, 82/4333/233, chief of staff Burgos to foreign office Burgos, 24 April 1939.
127. Ibid., foreign affairs Burgos to Kerney, 28 April 1939.
128. Stradling, *The Irish and Spanish Civil War*, p. 52; DIFP, *Vol. 5*, pp 457–8, Kerney to Walshe, 1 May 1939.
129. *Irish Press*, 2 March 1939.
130. Ibid., 15 March 1939.
131. Ibid., 24 March 1939.
132. NLI, Rosamond Jacob Papers, 32,582/81, diary entry 30 April 1937; 32,582/82, diary entry 3 September 1937; 32,582/85, diary entry, 13 December 1938.
133. Ibid., 32,582/80, diary entry 31 October 1936.
134. Ibid., 32,582/82, diary entries 30 July, 20 August 1937.
135. Whelan, 'Ireland and Spain', pp 20–2.
136. AGA, 82/4333/233, Frank Ryan Release Committee to Ontiveros, 13 May, 7 June 1939.
137. Ibid., Ontiveros to foreign affairs Burgos, 2 June 1939.
138. NLI, Rosamond Jacob Papers, 32,582/87, diary entries 30 May, 1 June 1939.
139. AGA, 82/4333/233, Ontiveros to foreign affairs Burgos, 12 June 1939; *Irish Press*, 10 June 1939.
140. *Irish Press*, 16 February 1939.

141. Hansard, 13 March 1939, https://api.parliament.uk/historic-hansard/commons/1939/mar/13/spain. Accessed 3 June 2020.
142. NA, DFA 101/1/30, Kerney to Walshe, 22 March 1939.
143. DIFP, *Vol. 5*, pp 434–5, Kerney to Walshe, 11 April 1939.
144. Juan García Ontiveros arrived in Dublin on 1 May 1939 and presented his credentials on 27 July (Whelan, 'Ireland and Spain', pp 20, 23).
145. Hansard, R. A. Butler to George Strauss, 17 May 1939, https://api.parliament.uk/historic-hansard/commons/1939/may/17/spain. Accessed 3 June 2020.
146. Hansard, 21 June 1939, https://api.parliament.uk/historic-hansard/commons/1939/jun/21/spain. Accessed 3 June 2013; *Irish Press*, 22 June 1939.
147. NA, DFA 10/1/31, Peterson to Kerney, 4 July 1939.
148. McGarry, *Irish Politics and Spanish Civil War*, p. 228.
149. NA, DFA 10/1/30, Kerney to Walshe, 5 July 1938; DFA 10/1/31, Kerney to Walshe, 10 July 1939.
150. NA, DFA 219/2, Kerney to Walshe, 4 July 1939; DFA 10/1/32, Kerney to Walshe, 23 March 1940.
151. *Reynolds News*, 11 June 1939.

THIRTEEN

# FRANK RYAN: RELEASE ATTEMPTS, JUNE 1939–JULY 1940

A campaign to put pressure on the Chamberlain Government to secure the liberation of Ryan gained momentum in Britain and climaxed with a mass-meeting in Hyde Park on 18 June 1939.[1] The demonstrators (with Bob Doyle as banner-bearer) then marched to the Foreign Office. At Hyde Park, Jim Prendergast presided, and Desmond Ryan, the writer, historian and participant in the Easter Rising, spoke of his friendship with his namesake.[2] The campaign was directed by the Connolly Club, Republican left-wing Irish emigrants that included the poet Ewart Milne, a close friend of Charlie Donnelly, and Michael McInerney, later one of Ireland's leading journalists.[3] They were supported by the CPI, the CPGB, numerous Labour Party branches, the International Brigade Association and a cross-section of British liberal opinion.

Sean O'Casey, J. B. Priestley, the communist writer A. L. Morton, the historian and war I veteran Guy Chapman, the socialists H. N. Brailsford and Ellen Wilkinson, and other sponsors, supported the collection of the signatures of 72 MPs for a petition to Alba, Franco's Ambassador in London. The delegation that secured the signatures comprised Milne and three Irish International Brigade veterans, Jim Prendergast, Eugene Downing and Michael Waters.[4] The petition called for 'the release of Major Frank Ryan, who, although the Spanish war is officially ended is still being held as a prisoner-of-war'. Alba received the deputation of the parliamentarians, viewing their visit as an inappropriate interference in the judicial system of another country and asking them how they would react in the opposite case.[5] The Ambassador claimed untruthfully that Ryan was being held 'on a civil charge.'[6] A second rally for Ryan's liberation took place in Hyde Park on 27 August.[7] In Ireland the campaign for the Irish prisoner was entering its most intensive phase. At an open-air meeting on 2 July in Middle Abbey Street, Dublin, friends and sympathisers of Ryan voiced their concerns, not least his friend Con Lehane, who described the Limerick native as 'the most chivalrous and brave man that ever walked Dublin's streets'.[8] It was a nationwide endeavour supported by over 50 TDs and Senators and 60 members of the Bar, with the largest number of petitioners coming from the ranks of the Old IRA.[9] Ex-members of the Irish Citizen Army demanded an 'Irish boycott of everything coming from Spain' until Ryan was released.[10] A branch of the Labour Party in Castlecomer, Co. Kilkenny, wrote to the Spanish Legation, enclosing a resolution demanding that 'the Government of Eire refuse to receive the representative of Franco until Frank Ryan was released'.[11]

Appeals to the Government to intercede with Franco also emanated from Fianna Fáil branches in Athlone (13 April) and Dublin Townships (9 June), from Clare Co. Council (1 August) and from the Irish Trade Union Congress (14 April), and from Labour leader William Norton (21 April) and Dublin Trades Union Council (8 September).[12] Juan García Ontiveros presented his credentials in Dublin Castle on 27 July. The official ceremony, due to security fears, had been delayed and was kept secret to the last minute.[13]

There were few dissenting voices, even Eoin O'Duffy invited Eilís Ryan for coffee and afterwards, in her presence, sent a telegram to Franco from Dublin's General Post Office pleading for clemency.[14] The public meeting for Ryan in Dublin on 2 July, however, prompted an inhabitant of Castleisland, Co. Kerry to make disparaging remarks about the speakers, describing Ryan in absurd hyperbole as destined to 'be Generalissimo of the Irish Civil War for a Workers' Republic'.[15] His letter was transmitted to the Dominican Retreat House in Tallaght, Co. Dublin, where Ambrose Coleman, OP posted it to the Spanish Legation, claiming that Ryan 'was condemned for murder, wholesale murder of prisoners', and expressing the hope that 'the Spanish Government will show firmness and not release him'.[16] Eight years earlier, another Tallaght Dominican had assured W. T. Cosgrave that the Special Powers Tribunal inaugurated in 1931 that was to sentence Frank Ryan was 'consonant with canon law'.[17] A further critic of the public efforts to demonstrate solidarity with Ryan was Richard Anthony, a former Labour TD. He dissented strongly from the resolution of the Irish Trade Union Congress at its 1939 annual meeting on Ryan's incarceration, which was forwarded to the Government. He was also on his own in voting against a motion condemning the fascist powers.[18] Franco's regime cared not a whit for public opinion in the democratic states, and it is arguable that it viewed the widespread campaign for Ryan's release in Ireland, Britain and America as nothing more than an irritant. The only international sources to whom the Spanish dictator might defer were states with economic power, his fascist allies abroad and the Vatican.

## MINISTER KERNEY PULLS OUT THE STOPS

Leopold Kerney believed that Republican and left-wing activity in Ireland 'could only prejudice the case, because their agitation would only reinforce the regime's conviction of Ryan's culpability'.[19] He was also perplexed that Ryan's enemies in Ireland were so vindictive as to want him dying in a fascist prison. Kerney did not share the political views of Frank Ryan, but he had seen him traduced as a communist and a criminal. A source of disappointment was that Ryan did not feature on a list of foreigners to be liberated and published by the Spanish Government in August.[20] The freed men were Americans and French.[21] Kerney was already pursuing a different avenue: to conclude a trade agreement with Madrid and use it as leverage to get Ryan out of Burgos prison. In June 1939 he met Franco's Minister for Commerce in Bilbao, who, with Jordana, was willing to start negotiations. Kerney wired home for instructions at the end of August and received them in October. Owing to bureaucratic delay in Dublin, no progress in the trade talks had taken place by the end of March 1940.[22] Food exports to starving Spain were the only small trump the Irish had, but Walshe missed the opportunity.

Just before the Second World War, Kerney again travelled to Burgos and consulted with Franco's new foreign minister, Juan Beigbeder. He disclosed his affection for Ireland and was in favour of stronger trade links, but was evasive about the possibility of Ryan's release – the commutation of the death sentence precluded further legal steps for the moment. Kerney also met Meade, who was now plying his links to the military's inner circle, for example, Franco's former Chief of Staff or an aide-de-camp to Jordana.[23] Kerney again called on Beigbeder in November, and noted that the file on Ryan to be shown to Franco contained press-cuttings he had given to the Duchess of Tetuan. Beigbeder was not optimistic: to date Franco had deferred any decision about Ryan, the 'justice system' was overwhelmed with pending cases, and there was 'no unanimity' in Ireland on the question. The Irish Minister posited the argument that, if Ryan was politically dangerous, then he would be an opponent of the Irish state and de Valera should be his gaoler, if the need arose, and not General Franco. Kerney rightly felt that the opposition to Ryan being freed emanated from Ireland ('secret underhand nature') and was partly fuelled by the activities of the publicity 'resorted to by Ryan's friends'.[24]

Confirmation of the prosecution case against Ryan reached the Irish Legation on 20 December 1939, when Antonio Michels Jaime de Champourcin, the Legation's aristocratic lawyer with links to Franco's secret service, provided Kerney with a summary of the indictment. Kerney learned of Jane Brown's denunciatory letter (he believed she had received a medal from the dictator for her efforts) and rightly surmised that the key passage in the charge sheet was the allegation of propaganda against Franco during Ryan's convalescence in Dublin in 1937. If it were true, the Minister reasoned, an appeal was futile, but External Affairs might make a declaration, based on press reports, that 'no activities of a public nature' had ensued.[25] Any definite proof would have been open to interpretation, but there was a more general problem: Franco tarred all republicans with the same brush, not knowing or not caring about the difference between fervently Catholic Irish republicans and their anti-clerical (and often Masonic) Spanish counterparts. Finally, the document showed that Franco had commuted the death sentence on 12 November – 17 months after it had been pronounced.[26] Ryan had now to serve 30 years, a death sentence by any other name considering his state of health. The following day Kerney had an audience with the Foreign Minister, who evinced interest in the trial summary ('something new to show Franco').[27] The main points of the indictment were published in Ireland at the end of January 1940.[28]

By early 1940, Ryan's hopes of leaving the prison alive were waning and he discussed plans of escape, all soon discarded, with his Welsh comrade Tom Jones.[29] In wartime Ireland, beset by economic problems, rationing and strict censorship, a form of 'donation fatigue' had set in – the Release Committee in Dublin appealed for funds for the food parcels sent regularly via Eilís Ryan to supplement her brother's diet.[30] Answers to questions in the House of Commons (December 1939, April 1940) also signalled lack of progress, producing the stock reply that the Irish Minister was in charge of the case, with the British Ambassador in Madrid willing to support representations.[31]

The Irish Minister learned from a British diplomat, who had visited Ryan and Jones in Burgos on St Patrick's Day 1940, that the four British prisoners would be released in a few days – Jones would be pardoned, and the others expelled from the country. Their liberation was the result of a trade agreement finalised between Franco's office and the British Embassy on 18 March, another occasion for Kerney to advocate, once again, 'a little economic pressure' – an approach that Walshe rejected.[32] The gates had also opened in San Pedro and Cárcel Central in Burgos for American Internationals. In fact, three of the eight liberated US citizens had been held in the prison, namely Larry Doran, Rudolf Opara and Anthony Kerhlicker, and were freed on 18 February, reaching New York one month later.[33] Ryan had informed Kerney immediately, commenting that they had been handed over because of Franco's dependence on American cotton.[34] Doran and Kerhlicker met Gerald O'Reilly, Ryan's close friend and secretary of the American Frank Ryan Committee.[35] The ex-prisoners said:

Frank is idolized by the other prisoners. He is always the leading spirt to keep up the morale [. . .], the lads see no reason to hope for Frank's early release. On one occasion a Spanish official made the remark that L.H. Kerney is a Mason, that Ireland should get rid of all Masons, [the] same as in Spain. [36]

Letters from O'Reilly's committee in New York to Ontiveros, or from Kerney to Beigbeder, referring to the liberation of the Americans as an encouraging precedent, went unanswered.[37] The release of the American Internationals was used by the Irish Government to impress upon Ontiveros that Ryan, the only English speaker still in a Franco prison, should now be freed.

At a lunch with the Papal Nuncio in May, Joseph Walshe expressed the hope to Ontiveros that Ryan would be liberated in the next three months, which was probably a reference to the expected amnesty on the third anniversary of the fascist uprising. Ontiveros's account elicited the response from Franco's office that 'it might be convenient to review what had been done in the Ryan case up to now following the recent letter from the widow of the famous Lord Mayor of Cork.'[38] Franco's officers would have been less impressed had they known that the writer, Muriel MacSwiney, was an avowed secularist and member of the CPGB.[39]

By late April 1940 Kerney was trying to rationalise the total impasse in the Ryan case. He was no longer concerned about the significance of Ryan's enemies at home, preferring the phrase 'occult influences' working against the prisoner. The Irish Minister was very close to the truth with the reference that 'there is secret opposition from another country', which he did not specify. On the other hand, he emphasised the friendlier attitude shown him by Franco's diplomats, and had been apprised, in Franco's army, of the favourable attitude – as expressed by General López-Pinto – that Ryan was 'not guilty'.

The other approach of the Minister was his oblique hint to an old recommendation of some preferential trade deal with Spain, or of some monetary settlement, both of which Walshe had dismissed out of hand.[40] Thoughts on a reappraisal of Ryan's sentence were also the result of Kerney's last intercession of 4 May, in which he described the prisoner as 'fully repentant', petitioning for a full pardon and the extradition of Ryan.[41] The Minister now believed the key to liberation was the Ministry of War, and advised Dublin that he anticipated Ryan's release within '2 or 3 weeks'.[42] The Ministry for the Army did not raise any problems and suggested that military justice authorities should remit a summary of the sentence to Madrid in order to determine if it were possible to agree to a pardon as requested: 'If there are political or international interests which would advise urgency in the matter, normal procedures could be ignored because the exercise of pardon is nowadays a sovereign right.'[43] A copy of the trial summary was duly sent by the military jurists of the 6th Military Region (Burgos) to the Foreign Ministry in Madrid.[44]

KERNEY'S VISITS TO BURGOS CENTRAL PRISON, 1939–40

In his first year in Burgos prison, Ryan had received four parcels of clothing, cigarettes and monthly payments of 150 pesetas (ca. £3) via Kerney and the International Red Cross (IRC).[45] Eilís Ryan prepared the parcels and collected funds, transmitting them to the IRC or the Dept of External Affairs to recompense any outlays by Kerney in Spain. Petrol was expensive on the black market, and many foodstuffs Ryan requested were unobtainable and were purchased by Kerney in France (butter, cheese, chocolate, tea and sugar).[46] It was forbidden to send parcels of foodstuffs through the post from abroad, but Minister Kerney could send or bring such foodstuffs as he wished.[47]

Ryan used the funds at his disposal to purchase items in the prison. He refused, however, to avail himself of the opportunity of having food sent in from outside on a daily basis, obviously a concession to prisoners from wealthy backgrounds. The main diet was completely inadequate (coffee and bread for breakfast, cups of soup for lunch and dinner, four in all), but the Irishman had the means of exchange, bartering coffee and tea for meat and having his meals in the infirmary. After two years' imprisonment, Ryan's weight had dropped nine kilos.[48] He also had a major dentistry job done, losing four molars and receiving 15 artificial teeth.[49]

The first meeting between the Irish emissary and the POW in Cárcel Central in Burgos was on 16 June 1939. The penitentiary was a modern structure opened in 1932 during the liberal era after the dissolution of the monarchy. Originally planned to house 800–900 prisoners in 96 cells, its population swelled to 4,500 by the end of the civil war. During the conflict over 3,000 were killed by the Francoists in the province of Burgos; there is documentation (tribunals files, etc.) on over 1,100 victims, while the remainder fell prey to extrajudicial killers, often Falangistas, who shot perceived enemies after house raids and had them buried at sites not yet discovered.[50] Between 1936 and 1941, 293 inmates of the prison were shot 'legally', more than 370 'disappeared' when removed in a saca ('taken for a ride' in gangster parlance) and about 400 died from natural causes. 'Official' prison executions for 1938 and 1939 totalled 30 and 80.[51]

Minister Kerney learned that the complex housed 4,500 enemies of the regime who slept in large dormitories and spent from sunrise to sunset in the open courtyard, mixing freely. He was surprised by the friendly reception and was told he could visit Ryan whenever he liked. Ryan was handed a parcel of clothes, 300 cigarettes, insecticide powder and money. The Irishmen chatted about the trial and Ryan's health, which, save for palpitations, was not, he said, disturbing, for he was now allowed to spend much time in the infirmary. Ryan joked that his high blood pressure would hardly be affected by the bad prison diet. He mentioned some Polish Internationals anxious for a diplomatic visit, and the presence of a Welsh fellow-Brigader, Tom Jones. For Kerney the long drive to Burgos over bad roads had been worthwhile; he was now of the opinion that the only charge against Ryan was 'evidence of character' based on a letter from Ireland. He planned to talk to General José López-Pinto, commander-in-chief of the army in the Burgos district, about 'the desired measure of clemency' in the knowledge that his goodwill was essential. Pinto, he hoped, might tell him why Hodgson had used any influence he possessed against Ryan.[52]

The Irish Minister was not Ryan's first 'official' visitor. In July–August 1938 Ryan was questioned in Burgos prison on seven occasions by Dr Antonio Vallejo Nájera, the 'Red gene' specialist. He did not make any promises to Ryan, saying the interviews would be used 'neither in favour nor against'. With death peering over his shoulder, Ryan felt he had nothing to lose in describing the motivation for his Spanish involvement, arguments he had not wished to present to the tribunal. There is no documentary evidence to contradict the essence, if not the detail, of Ryan's succinct summary:

> I didn't bring a battn. to Spain. I could have done so. In fact, I prevented many from coming. I was satisfied just enough to offset the O'Duffy propaganda.
> I came back to Spain [mid-June 1937] just when the return of O'Duffy was foreshadowed (in letters from his disgruntled men). I considered my mission to Spain ended when he was leaving Spain; I came back to pull out men, and so to save lives. The number of my men who returned to Ireland June to October 1937, is evidence. After October the Irish unit existed only in name.
> Why did I remain in Spain? (i) It was slow and difficult work repatriating men. (ii) When I was getting men home, I was getting the responsibility of their lives off my shoulders, and becoming more of a free agent, i.e. more of an individual than a representative. (iii) Then pride kept me here; after the fall of Asturias and then after Teruel I couldn't pull out and be considered 'a rat who left the sinking ship'. (Contradictory reasons perhaps, but taken in sequence, related to the events of the war, you will see there is some coherence).[53]

After the interviews, Vallejo concluded that the Irishman was 'a born revolutionary of the romantic type', but that the conversation 'did not disclose any information of a particularly useful character'. Vallejo regretted that had not been 'shot within 24 hours of his capture because his case could only be a thorn in the side of everyone'.[54] Frank Ryan had another unexpected visitor on 12 September 1939: Blanca O'Donnell, Duchess of Tetuan, who was interested in her historic homeland. She undertook the journey to Burgos at the behest of the Irish Minister and with the permission of Foreign Minister Beigbeder. As an aristocrat, the Duchess had access to members of Franco's inner circle. She was grateful to the Irish and understood the concern in Ireland about Ryan's fate, not least because she had been able to leave Madrid in the early part of the civil war with the help of Peadar O'Donnell, Frank Ryan's close friend.[55] Beigbeder provided her with an official car for her journey from Madrid to Burgos, confiding to the Duchess that he had brought the case of the Irish captive to Franco's attention several times without success. She hoped to be able to speak to Franco himself through the intercession of the Foreign Minister. Blanca O'Donnell formed a positive impression of Ryan who told her, in confidence, 'that he had made a mistake in going to Spain, but that he could not make any confession of that kind before a Tribunal'.[56]

Ryan had been buoyed up by the Duchess's visit, as he told Kerney on 25 September. To the Minister the prisoner seemed philosophical about his situation, expressing more concern about his family than himself and saying that one food packet a month (paid for by his sister Eilís by reimbursing Kerney) sufficed. His only wish was for condensed milk, a commodity unobtainable in Franco's Spain.[57] In the period immediately following his sentencing, Ryan shared a cell with 17 others, nine of whom were taken out daily at dawn to be shot or garrotted; their places were taken by nine others.

At the war's end, conditions improved and Ryan could receive letters and books without restrictions, including an Irish Bible given to him years before by Thomas Derrig, de Valera's Minister for Lands.[58] Ryan was popular with the other prisoners, a morale-booster and by now a fluent speaker of Spanish. He was often in the infirmary where he could sleep until 8 a.m. and had the privilege of a milk ration. Ryan taught English for two hours a day to 200 Spaniards, and was learning Italian as well as German. His appearance shocked many, for he looked like an old man and had lost weight in confinement. Apart from his cardiac problems, Ryan also suffered from rheumatism.[59]

Prisoners in Cárcel Central were counted four times a day, which often necessitated standing for hours on end. The dormitories were grossly overcrowded, with only 18 inches of sleeping space for prisoners, who were tormented by lice and protected from the concrete floor by only a thin blanket.[60] Ryan's closest comrade in adversity was the ex-coalminer Tom Jones from Wrexham in North Wales, who had joined the brigades in May 1937. A member of the anti-tank battery, Jones became detached from his unit during the March 1938 retreats and was suspected of attempting to desert from Spain with a fellow gunner, Edward Byrne from Dublin.[61] While Byrne was allowed to leave Spain at the end of April 1938, Jones stayed and was later posted to a special heavy-machine-gun battalion.[62] During the Ebro battle Jones was captured on 17 September, literally with his pants down for he was wounded and suffering from diarrhoea. After recuperation in Bilbao, Jones was brought for trial to Zaragoza and faced a court-martial twice in January 1939. The sentence was death but, like Ryan, the Welshman was spared the firing squad, receiving a sentence of 30 years and being sent to Burgos prison in April.[63]

Ryan and Jones, sometimes conversing to one another in Welsh, discussed world affairs. Ryan was appalled by, and strongly condemned, the bombing campaign of the IRA in Britain in 1939, classifying the perpetrators as irresponsible lunatics. His views on the Hitler–Stalin Pact of 23 August 1939 were of a similar tenor, and he was strongly of the opinion that the USSR was 'going fascist and that this was the reason for the deal'. Jones replied by saying that it was as unlikely as Germany becoming communist, and Ryan seemed satisfied.[64] On 11 November a judge visited the gaol and announced to Ryan and 13 others that their death sentences had been commuted to 30 years.[65] Ryan was the only officer left in the prison who had not been shot – those officially killed by firing squad were told only four hours before the execution.[66] In the meantime Kerney had befriended Fr Mulrean, formerly the chaplain to O'Duffy's brigade and later to the Requetés (Carlists), who evinced an interest in Frank Ryan. Mulrean spoke freely to the Irish Minister of his time with O'Duffy's men and the scandalous behaviour of Gunning.[67] Kerney had a gift for finding confederates, first Meade and now Mulrean, who was on good terms with the Papal Nuncio: just before Christmas, the Irish priest told him, the Papal legate had met foreign minister Jordana at the behest of the Vatican to enquire about Frank Ryan.

When the Minister and Fr Mulrean visited Ryan in Burgos on Christmas Eve 1939, they found the prisoner in good fettle: the cold weather, he maintained, was better for his high blood pressure than the sultry summers. The warder had stacks of mail for Ryan, cards and letters from all over the world, and his visitors presented him with a hamper of food, socks knitted by Mrs Kerney, cigarettes and the scholarly books sent by Eilís, including a German grammar.[68] The prisoner and the Minister went through the trial summary in detail, with Ryan emphasising that the only demonstration he had taken part in during his sojourn at home between March and June 1937 was the anti-coronation rally on 12 May ('on which occasion he had his nose broken'), that he had paid no visits to London, Glasgow or Liverpool for propaganda purposes, and that the two private meetings in Dublin to commemorate the fallen Irish had been all-ticket affairs.[69]

One major bone of contention for all prisoners was compulsory mass on Sundays and the fulminations of the Jesuit chaplain, Fr Marcellino Bolinaga. The altar was adorned with large pictures of Franco, Hitler, Mussolini and the Virgin Mary. On one occasion he berated the prisoners so much that they loudly protested. Two hundred of their number were taken out, beaten and put on half rations in solitary confinement for two months.[70] Frank Ryan had an unpleasant visit from the chaplain's brother, also a Jesuit, who said he had been contacted by the Irishman's parents. The priest was a fervent Franco supporter and told him he would write to Dublin saying that the prisoner was 'happy and contented', stating that Ryan could expect a pardon after serving 12 years. Ryan listened in sullen silence and was alarmed to hear that the visitor would return soon to hear his confession. Ryan wished to avoid what could be a confrontation and asked Kerney to have another visit from Fr Mulrean to ward off the inquisitive Jesuit.[71] When Mulrean next visited Ryan with Kerney on 1 February he heard his confession and received permission to visit the prison in future on his own. The visitors viewed the prisoners in the yard, underfed and badly clad figures, some of whom were very young. By then, Mulrean had arranged for the removal of the objectionable chaplain. The Irish priest also saw Tom Jones and took notes of his case because he had had no visitors from the British Embassy for five months.[72]

When Tom Jones was released on 20 March 1940, tears rolled down Ryan's cheeks, and he requested his friend to talk to his family and friends in the IRA in Dublin. Jones hid the names of the IRA contacts, written on cigarette paper, in the sleeve lining of his coat.[73] On arrival in London Jones talked at length to journalists about Ryan.[74] The Irish Minister visited Ryan again on 5 April, receiving photographs for Eilís and noting that Ryan now had six assistant teachers for his English classes.[75]

True to his promise, Tom Jones travelled to Dublin in May, staying with Ryan's parents and visiting the Department of External Affairs. He praised the assistance of Leopold Kerney, mentioned the interviews he had carried out with leading liberal and socialist personalities in England and stated that 'public agitation and outcry' were the best weapons left, save for the pressure that could be exerted at the conclusion of a trade deal between Ireland and Spain.[76] Kerney was dismissive of the usefulness of any approach from English anti-fascists, preferring his good relationship with both the heads of Franco's diplomatic service and military, but was now aware of what would be, in the final resort, the main stumbling-block: 'I have made the big discovery that Franco himself gave special instructions some considerable time ago that, in this particular case of Frank Ryan, nothing should ever be done in the way of reducing his sentence without his personal consent.'⁷⁷ Kerney's last visits to Ryan were on 5 May, 24 June and 12 July, but a wire from the Legation sent to the prisoner on 24 July went unanswered.⁷⁸ He had probably left the prison.

### GERMANY INTERVENES

German interest in Frank Ryan finally led to his release, with disparate actors and changes of course. The Foreign Office (Auswärtiges Amt), Military Intelligence (Abwehr) and German Army High Command (Oberkommando der Wehrmacht – OKW) were involved in initiatives for or against Ryan, steps undertaken largely during, and because of, the international campaign to gain freedom for the Irish captain. In mid-June 1939, John A. Holden, from an address in Crumlin, wrote to Eduard Hempel, the German Minister to Dublin. He sought his assistance in forwarding a personal letter to Hitler and mentioned he was 'identified with the Fianna Fáil movement'.⁷⁹ In his letter to the dictator, Holden stated he was acting as an individual member of de Valera's party, stressed his pro-German sympathies and his friendship with Ryan's family. While requesting Hitler to intercede with Franco to release the Burgos prisoner from captivity, Holden emphasised that he was 'entirely in disagreement with Ryan over Spain', believing England to be 'an open enemy of this country' and making the questionable claim that 'we are proud of you beyond description.' The writer also referred to his memories of the Ypres battlefield, so he was probably a World War veteran.⁸⁰ Hempel invited Holden to the Legation and made it clear that he could do little, seeing that it was an Irish–Spanish matter. He duly informed Ontiveros and wrote to his superiors in Berlin in the accompanying report to Holden's enclosure about the widespread support for the release of Ryan in wide sections of Irish society (not only on the Left), and as seen in the demonstrations held in Dublin and London. Hempel concluded that he was not recommending that any action should be taken but his dispatch, he surmised, might give others the possibility to contact the Auswärtiges Amt via different channels.⁸¹ That is exactly what happened.

The Abwehr was not interested in Irish contacts after 1933 because official policy was positive towards de Valera, including his suppression of the IRA.⁸² When bombs started to detonate in British cities from January 1939, German military intelligence saw the potential of collaboration with Republican diehards and arranged for the author of the campaign (S-Plan), Jim O'Donovan, to visit Germany on four occasions between February and August 1939. The Abwehr agent Oskar Pfaus had been sent from the Hamburg office

(Abwehrstelle-Ast) to Ireland in February 1939 to forge links with the Republican underground. He knew obviously very little about Irish politics, first visiting Eoin O'Duffy, a hate-figure for IRA men since 1922, and then travelling the country, usually under the shadow of Garda surveillance, visiting persons he thought sympathetic, i.e. O'Duffy's adherents. He also managed to meet the IRA 'chemical experts' O'Donovan and Sean Russell in Dublin in early February and made arrangements for the former's first visit to Hamburg.[83]

There seems to have been no mention of Frank Ryan in these preliminary meetings, but one of Pfaus's contacts in Ireland did raise the International Brigader's imprisonment in a letter to the Abwehr agent. The writer was Patrick Cavanagh from Ballinrobe, Co. Mayo, a former corporal in O'Duffy's bandera.[84] He claimed he was acting on the remit of his fellow veterans in requesting German authorities to assist in ensuring that Ryan would not be pardoned – otherwise Ryan 'would resume his communist activities in Ireland following his liberation and bring ruin upon the country'.[85] Ast-Hamburg informed the OKW of Cavanagh's intervention, and the military dispatched the correspondence to the Auswärtiges Amt. Berlin then instructed the Madrid Embassy in late September 1939 to approach Franco's regime with the view of halting any steps to allow Ryan being pardoned.[86]

The Nota Verbal of Nazi Germany's Madrid Embassy of 18 October 1939 stated that Ryan's liberation was being sought by the governments of Ireland, Britain and the USA against the wishes of the former members of the Irish Brigade who had fought for Franco; they had requested His Excellency not to pardon the prisoner, who, they feared would return to Ireland and reassume his communist activities. Now, the dispatch continued, these people had also approached the German Government with the same request, so that the Embassy, in view of the common bonds of friendship between Germany and Spain and their struggle together against international communism, now acceded to the demand of these Irish and expressed the aspiration that the Spanish Government would not be disposed to issue any pardon to Ryan.[87] This letter from the power that bombed him to victory must certainly have made an impression on El Caudillo. The German Foreign Office, however, was to change its mind because the IRA lobby in the USA (Clan na Gael, James Connolly Club) approached Hans Thomsen, the German chargé d'affaires in Washington, in February 1940. Clan Secretary Michael McSwiney detailed Ryan's prominence in the Republican movement and the international campaign for his liberation in his request to German diplomats to intercede on the prisoner's behalf.[88] Thomsen merely acknowledged receipt of the letter, but suggested to Auswärtiges Amt that it should support McSwiney's appeal.[89] Berlin complied, instructing the Embassy in Madrid to ascertain if Ryan had been released and, if this was not the case, leaving it free for its diplomats in the Spanish capital to accede to Irish wishes for Ryan's release.[90] They were hesitant, obviously not wishing to explain the German volte face, but were instructed at the end of April to do just that: the outbreak of the war had changed everything, and the German Government now supported Ryan's liberation. The Madrid Embassy informed Berlin in late May that it soon intended to contact the proper Spanish authorities to lodge the intervention.[91] Leopold Kerney, who knew nothing of these developments, now had the German Foreign Office and Franco's army on his side. What he also did not know was that, as is often the case with competing bureaucracies in totalitarian states, the secret service (Abwehr) had its own plans, which would stymie the efforts of Berlin's diplomats eager to curry favour with Irish sentiment worldwide.

### FRANK RYAN'S GERMAN FRIENDS: ABWEHR OFFICERS HELMUT CLISSMANN AND JUPP HOVEN

Josef (Jupp) Hoven was born in 1904 in Kornelimünster near Aachen, the second of four sons of a prosperous lime-kiln owner. At the second congress of the International League against Imperialism (a front organisation of the Communist International) in Frankfurt in 1929, Jupp and his brother Viktor met the IRA leaders Peadar O'Donnell and Sean McBride.[92] The motivation of Hoven (and his brothers Viktor and Heinz) to agitate against the 1919 Treaty of Versailles was the highly contested annexation of the 'lost cantons' of Malmedy, Eupen and Sankt Vith to Belgium. The area, just south of Aachen, had been Prussian since 1815. The League of Nations plebiscite in 1920 in the three cantons was a farce – opponents of Belgian annexation had to register with the authorities and were thereafter intimidated from questioning the incorporation of the area into the Belgian state (1925).[93]

An interest in European minorities was what drew the German friends to Ireland and led to their friendship with Ryan. This orientation was also a protest against the First World War victor states, hence the enthusiasm of the young Germans for Breton and Flemish separatism and their fascination with the Irish revolution and its most implacable proponents in the illegal IRA. Jupp Hoven, seven years older than Helmuth Clissmann, was arrested twice by the Belgian authorities for propaganda smuggling in the 1920s, and after a series of unskilled jobs he studied at Frankfurt University from 1930 and completed his sociological doctorate on the Prussian officer corps in the 18th century at Leipzig University in 1936.[94]

Clissmann and his sister grew up in a comfortable middle-class Protestant family in Aachen and, at the age of ten, Helmut joined a gymnastics association and later hiking groups with a pronounced 'Greater Germany' and racist ideology. While still at school, Clissmann was persuaded by Viktor Hoven to join the Schill Bund, an ultra-nationalist movement with origins in the counter-revolutionary paramilitary bodies active in the early years of the Weimar Republic.[95] Jupp Hoven later founded the Jungpreussischer Bund, a grouping that positioned itself at the end of the Weimar Republic on the left, 'anti-Nazi but not unfriendly to the Communists'.[96] Clissmann was involved in political brawls at Frankfurt University and, together with the Hoven brothers Jupp and Viktor, was arrested in November 1932 on suspicion of subversion. Still under the observance of the political police in Frankfurt after Hitler's accession to power, all three, together with communists and other left-wingers, were suspected in 1934 by the Gestapo of links to the left-wing splinter group Sozialistische Arbeiterpartei (SAP).[97] The Hovens and Clissmann can best be described as radical Prussian nationalists with left-wing sympathies who rejected Nazi racialist theories.

Through an English friend of his family who had lived in Aachen before the First World War, Clissmann first visited Ireland and England in the summer of 1930. In the following year he returned with the three Hoven brothers and arranged a hiking tour through Geoffrey Coulter of *An Phoblacht*. They also met Sean McBride, Peadar O'Donnell and Frank Ryan. Clissman, Hoven and two comrades from the Jungpreussicher Bund spent their summer holidays in Ireland again in 1932. They took part in the funeral cortège of Captain James Dowling, formerly of the Casement Brigade, from Westland Row church in Dublin on 6 August. The group must have raised some eyebrows for they were clad in field-grey greatcoats and wore Glengarry bonnets adorned with the black Prussian eagle.

Clissmann studied history at Trinity College, as an exchange student, in the academic year 1933/34, and was attached to the German Department as an unpaid teaching assistant. He was the head of the German Academic Exchange Programme (DAAD) in Ireland from January 1936, a teacher of German in Dublin and a member of the Nazi party since 1934.[98] Clissmann was extremely hard-working and knew many leading Irish personalities through organising exchange programmes for Irish teachers, school pupils and students. He was now comfortably off and married Elizabeth ('Budge') Mulcahy from Sligo in December 1938. Like Hoven in Northern Ireland, Clissmann was under constant Special Branch observation but does not seem to have been involved in spying for the Nazis while in Ireland during 1936–39.[99]

Jupp Hoven, however, carried out espionage for the German armed forces while posing as a student of anthropology in 1937/38 in Ulster, acting on the remit of Büro Jahnke, a sub-unit targeting European minorities. Jahnke worked in the Berlin headquarters of the NSDAP and his office was absorbed into the Abwehr in 1940.[100] Hoven even enrolled at Queen's University, Belfast, to write a sociological thesis on the 'Ulster Problem' in early 1939.[101] Moreover, Hoven accompanied the IRA Chief of Staff Tom Barry to Germany in 1937.[102] Brian O'Neill, a prominent communist at the time, remembers the young men from Aachen:

> Jupp and his friends were only youths when I first knew them, youths with harmlessly vague right-wing ideas, a real affection for Ireland, and fascinated by the IRA. But when they arrived a couple of years after Hitler gained power there was a change. We were discussing the world situation in the St. Anthony's Place printing works, and Jupp asked what we thought about the danger of a war. Frank [Ryan] and I agreed that it seemed a real danger, and I added, 'If you don't get rid of Hitler he will destroy Germany.' Jupp apparently misheard me in the clacking of the flatbed machine and almost shrieked 'So you say Germany must be destroyed to get rid of Hitler.' We [O'Neill and Ryan] heard enough to know where they stood, and later the young men admitted that they had gone over to the Nazi Youth. [103]

When war broke out in 1939, Hoven had some problems attaining a commission in the German army because of his left-wing past, but was posted after some difficulty to a sabotage company that later became the Brandenburg Regiment, a commando unit attached to Abwehr II (sabotage and subversion). Hoven pointed out to his superiors in October/November 1939 that the liberation of Ryan would make a good impression in Ireland and that he might be used in some capacity to the advantage of Germany.[104] He told his friend Clissmann at Christmas 1939 of his efforts, fruitless to date, and Clissmann could reply that he had tried to interest the German Legation some years earlier in Dublin to the same end, but nothing came of it.[105] Clissmann, head of the German student exchange service in Denmark until his call-up in July 1940, was also posted to the Brandenburg regiment but it is not clear that he was in a position to influence Abwehr officers before that, i.e. in the negotiations leading up to Ryan's departure from Burgos in 1940.

### THE 'RELEASE' OF FRANK RYAN

An Abwehr colleague of Hoven and Clissmann, Oberleutnant Kurt Haller, summarised their successful efforts in his interrogation by British officers in 1946:

Towards the end of 1939 the Hoven-Clissmann circle attempted to intervene of Ryan's behalf, on the grounds that they would guarantee his collaboration with Abwehr. When Major Diebitsch became Gruppenleiter I [of Abwehr II], Jupp Hoven and Clissmann gained his confidence, and he backed their request. In May 1940, Abt. II requested the release of Ryan by the Spanish government. As a preliminary measure Wolfgang Blaum [leading Abwehr officer at the German Embassy] was instructed to obtain information about Ryan; this he procured through Champourcin, the Spanish legal adviser to the Irish Legation in Madrid. He found out where Ryan was held, and made it clear that Ryan would only be released at the intervention of the highest German government circles. Canaris [head of Abwehr] intervened personally and Ryan's release was granted on condition that it should appear as a successful escape.[106]

Minister Kerney's cryptic handwritten notes in the last days of April 1940 suggest that the Legation's lawyer, de Champourcin, has misled the Minister, not mentioning that the initial idea had originated in Germany and not in Spain:

a) The 'Spanish' initiative had come from de Champourcin.
b) His German 'friends' were awaiting an interview with their Spanish counterparts.
c) Franco's intelligence service agreed to the German proposal.
d) Neither de Champourcin nor Kerney could impose any conditions.
e) Kerney held the transfer of Frank Ryan to Germany to be 'inadvisable and out of the question, but USA, perhaps'.
f) De Champourcin planned to visit Ryan in Burgos with 'a German "colleague"', using Kerney's car.[107]

The lawyer and Paul Winzer, head of the Gestapo in Spain, visited Ryan in Burgos at some date in July.[108] Winzer asked what Ryan thought were well-prepared questions, making clear that he asked no commitment from the Irish prisoner. Frank Ryan then made the interesting comment, 'I've been waiting for this visit for two years.'[109]

Kerney was not kept up to date of the 'release' developments on a regular basis, which is understandable, seeing that all sides were aware that no suspicion should arise about the Irish Legation being 'an accessory after the fact'. The Irish Minister visited Ryan on 12 July, his last round trip of over 400 km from Madrid to the penitentiary at Burgos. Kerney persuaded Ryan that neither had any choice in the matter – 'sometimes a remedy can be more annihilating than the disease.' They discussed IRA leaders – the prisoner knew from Gerald O'Reilly that Russell was already in Germany[110] – and Kerney warned him about getting involved in violent politics once more in Ireland. Ryan replied that if he got to Ireland he would thank de Valera personally for all he had done on his behalf, while retaining his right to oppose Government policy.[111]

Matters seemed to be going well until the inscrutable Franco dithered; he did not definitely say 'Yes' until 3 July, then changed his mind and said he could not issue a pardon (indulto), before then finally relenting to the plan of Ryan's 'escape'. The Legation paid for the hire of car by de Champourcin and for petrol for the journey from Madrid to Burgos, for the lawyer, and not the Irish Minister, was to be witness to the handover.

At 2 a.m. on 25 July, two cars parked outside the prison. The first contained Franco's chief of police and a German (Blaum); the second contained two armed Falangistas. They emerged with Ryan 20 minutes later and passed de Champourcin's Packard. Kerney's lawyer reached the border at Irun at 7.30 a.m., before the others. He parked the car in the town and went by foot to the international bridge. At 8.30 a.m. the two cars crossed the barrier into France. Ryan gave de Champourcin a quick glance showing that he recognised him. According to Eamon C. Kerney, the son of the Irish Minister, his father, not trusting anyone involved in the transfer, followed de Champourcin's car in his own vehicle and witnessed, from a distance, how Ryan was driven across the frontier bridge. Later that day in San Sebastian, de Champourcin was handed a note by 'a German friend'. It was from Ryan, who wrote to Kerney that everything had gone off without a hitch but that he was not returning immediately to Ireland but 'going on a journey that would take some weeks'.[112] De Champourcin gave his opinion that his destination might be the USA via Siberia. Kerney heard nothing more until 22 August, when de Champourcin said 'the friends' allowed him to say that Ryan had escaped with American help.[113] Part of this deception plan was a letter by Ryan to Kerney, sent at the instigation of the Germans and posted from Estoril, Portugal to the Irish Legation in Madrid in late August. It was clear from the valedictory note that the former prisoner was not on his way to the New World:

> I regret that under the circumstances it was impossible to notify you and thus spare you the worry that personally as well as officially you must have had on my account. But, my American friends were in a hurry and could give me no time for leave-taking (I even had to leave all my luggage behind me!). Although it's liberty, although I can at least do what I like and only what I like, it is unfortunately impossible for me to get home until the war is over. I can only hope that my folks won't worry too much and that's about the only worry I have left in the world [. . .] Many thanks again to you – and to all the other good friends – for all the help you have given me. Someday – soon, let's hope – we'll meet to celebrate, in the old Irish way![114]

Kerney rightly saw the operation as a concession to Germany and not to Ireland. Only then did he send Dublin a blow-by-blow account of Frank Ryan's 'escape'.[115] Germany, and not the US, was to be Ryan's final, and fatal, destination. Irish Military Intelligence (G2) learned from Kerney in October 1941 when he was on leave in Dublin, that

> [He] had no means of getting a decision on that matter from the Department of External Affairs so he took it upon himself the responsibility of telling his Spanish friend to go ahead, but instructed him to keep the name of the Irish Minister in Spain out of it. The Spanish friend returned very jubilant, and said, 'Yes, they are interested, they have been authorized to do something from Berlin.' The Clissmanns [...] had apparently been taken steps on behalf of Ryan and whatever steps they were taking coincided with the request from Berlin.[116]

It is doubtful if de Valera would have agreed to this in 1940, seeing as he refused Ryan's repatriation four years later. Holding the picture of Ryan's health to be 'overdrawn and suspicious' in 1944, the Taoiseach ruled that his homecoming was 'quite out of the question': It would be impossible to bring him home without his falling into the hands of the British at one stage or other and this would entail all sorts of complications.[117]

In July 1940 Kerney found himself in an abnormal situation in time of war, and he had to act 'on his feet' for any delay might have jeopardised the handover in Burgos. In any case, he was, because of his status, in no position to be part of, or to influence, the Spanish–German arrangement. Eilís Ryan was informed by Joseph Walshe at the end of August that her brother had been released and that he had allegedly reached America. As Kerney had no official confirmation of the release, Miss Ryan was requested to keep the matter to herself.[118] A month later newspaper readers learned merely that Ryan was free and had left Spain.[119] Kerney and the British Embassy asked Franco's diplomats repeatedly whether Ryan was alive and of his whereabouts.[120] The Spanish ministries involved (foreign affairs, justice and the military) had to come up with a concoction that did not compromise their secret service, so the Irish Legation received the communication that Frank Ryan had escaped from the penal colony at El Dueso on 20 July 1940, having been sent there five days earlier from Valdenoceda prison.[121] After many letters from the Irish Minister, the contents of Frank Ryan's luggage left behind in Cárcel Central in Burgos were brought to the Legation in May 1942.[122] The valise contained clothing, teaching notes, an Irish Bible, grammars and dictionaries.[123] In 1942, the overworked military jurists examined Frank Ryan's prosecution file for the last time. Franco's semi-judicial system had broken down under its own weight: there were commutations/releases in 1942 and the tribunals ceased operating at the end of the Second World War.[124] Ryan's dossier was duly processed by the bureaucratic apparatus: his 30-year sentence was 'commuted' to 15 years in November 1942, two years after his 'escape'.[125]

### 'LIBERATED' BY THE ABWEHR: LEOPOLD KERNEY'S DILEMMA AND FRANK RYAN'S ACQUIESCENCE

Why did Frank Ryan, a popular figure in Republican and left-wing circles, agree to work for the fascist German State? In the first place, if he did not want to die in prison from his serious cardiac illness, the handover to German intelligence was the only escape route left. Secondly, in the context of summer 1940, with most of mainland Europe under German rule, Ryan conceivably reckoned with the collapse of British power and the chance of Irish unity. The dire straits in which Britain found itself in 1940 could be interpreted as the opportunity for a new 'war of liberation' as the revolutionaries had done at Easter 1916.[126] Finally, Ryan, like Gerald O'Reilly in New York, while sincerely espousing left-wing causes, had not totally abjured the physical force Republicanism of the old school despite his condemnation of the bombing campaign in Britain in 1939–40.

His support for the illegal IRA during his stay in Dublin in the spring of 1937 demonstrates that his old loyalties ran deep. Like many from his political background, he was a committed anti-imperialist and, in concord with even more Irish, still intrinsically hostile towards British power, with memories of Black and Tan or Civil War atrocities still relatively fresh. Britain's lone stance against international fascism in 1940 has a romantic ring in retrospect, but in July 1940, anti-fascists could not exclude the possibility that the British Cabinet, with arch-appeasers like Chamberlain, Halifax and 'Rab' Butler still in office, might sign a 'compromise peace' with Hitler.[127] Most of Ryan's Irish friends in the Spanish trenches, while sharing his paramilitary past, had seen that violent Republicanism was a dead end and they tended towards, or joined, the communist party. Ryan did not.[128] He remained, in essence, a soldier – his 'speech from the dock' at the military tribunal was dissembling only in part.

Leopold Kerney perceived his foremost task in Spain to be the protection of Irish citizens, hence his commitment to Ryan, or to ex-members of O'Duffy's brigade also at the mercy of Franco's ruthless military: securing the release of the young Dubliner Andrew O'Toole, who deserted from the Spanish Foreign Legion, or assisting John J. Madden, a demobilised legionnaire, who had his fare home paid by the Irish Legation.[129] The Minister had exhausted all avenues to have Ryan handed into his care by mid-1940, and took note of the Abwehr plan, which he did not initiate, because he saw no other alternative. It would have gone ahead anyway had he dismissed the proposal. By accepting that it was going to happen, he can hardly have believed, as distinct from hoping, that Ryan was destined for the United States: the Germans wanted him as a contact to the IRA, not as a freelancer who would expose Franco's savage repression by pen and microphone throughout North America. As regards being repatriated on a British 'ticket', Ryan rejected that solution from the start and it is improbable, on account of Ryan's high status in the brigades and his chequered Irish past, that Franco would have acceded to entreaties from London. In any case, Frank Ryan was an Irish citizen, so Kerney was responsible for his safety.

A final question in respect of Ryan's removal from Burgos gaol is why the Spanish dictator had refused his liberation much earlier. True, he wished to accede to the interventions launched over the years by Ryan's spiteful enemies in O'Duffy's expeditionary force and their associates, but two further factors in Franco's psyche overrode any considerations of repercussions abroad: his relentlessly vengeful nature and his world view.

In his first interview with a foreign correspondent (Jay Allen of the *Chicago Daily Tribune*) after the start of the military rebellion, Franco did not hide his intentions, rejecting any compromise or truce and maintaining that the advance on Madrid would continue and that he would 'save Spain from Marxism at whatever cost', even if that meant shooting half the population. He drew Allen's attention approvingly to some magazines on his desk, the bulletins of L'Entente Internationale contre la Troisième Internationale, an anti-Semitic, fascist propaganda organisation based in Switzerland.[130]

Franco later expressed his sociocidal intentions in apocalyptical terms: his struggle was 'a crusade', the war a religious one against 'atheism and materialism' an interpretation that was supported by many in Ireland.[131] Frank Ryan represented everything Franco hated, and El Caudillo had little cause to pardon or liberate him, seeing that he was extremely reluctant to release foreign prisoners (godless mercenaries in his eyes). He only did so when economic pressure was exerted (Britain, USA). The chance to use a trade deal with Franco's devastated country as a lever to get Ryan out of Burgos was dismissed by the obtuse Dublin bureaucracy. From the time of his capture into 1940, Frank Ryan's enemies in Ireland 'did for him', a motley coterie of fascists like Gunning, extreme right-wing clerics and authoritarian Catholics. Franco therefore could always refer to their interventions when refusing all calls for a pardon that, in the end, was supported even by his own army and diplomatic service due to Kerney's indefatigable lobbying.

## NOTES

1. *Daily Worker*, 10, 13, 17 June 1939.
2. *Irish Press*, 19 June 1939; *Evening Mail* (with photo of the 'Release Frank Ryan' banner), 19 June 1939; *Irish Times*, 19 June 1939.
3. Joseph Donnelly, *Charlie Donnelly: Life and Poems* (Dublin, 1987), pp 44–7. McInerney wrote an interesting series on the life and times of Frank Ryan for the *Irish Times* in April 1975. See also: Michael McInerney, *Peadar O'Donnell: Irish Social Rebel* (Dublin, 1974).
4. *Daily Worker*, 17 July 1939.
5. AGA, 82/4333/233, Alba to Madrid with enclosed petition, 2 August 1939.
6. *Irish Press*, 5 August 1939. The delegation reminded him also of the continuing detention of three Britons (*Daily Worker*, 3 August 1939).
7. *Daily Worker*, 23 August 1939.
8. *Irish Press*, 3 July 1939.
9. Ibid., 13 July 1939.
10. Ibid., 17 July 1939.
11. AGA, 54/11731, Moneenroe, Castlecomer, Labour Party branch to the Spanish Embassy, 26 June 1939.
12. NA, DFA 10/1/30, 10/1/31.
13. Barry Whelan, 'Ireland and Spain, 1939–55: Cultural, economic and political relations from neutrality in the Second World War to joint membership of the United Nations' (PhD, NUI Maynooth, 2012), pp 23–4.
14. Aodh Ó Canainn, 'Eilís Ryan In Her Own Words', in *Saothar*, 21 (1996), p. 138.
15. Timothy M. Donovan (b. 1863) was a noted local historian of east Kerry and author of *Revolution: Christian or Communist* (1937).
16. AGA, 82/4333/233, Ontiveros to foreign office Burgos 15 July 1939, with enclosures.
17. Ronan Fanning, *Independent Ireland* (Dublin, 1983), p. 104.
18. *Irish Press*, 6 August 1939; *Irish Independent*, 5 August 1939.
19. Whelan, 'Ireland and Spain, 1939–55', p. 8.
20. *Irish Press*, 24 August 1939.
21. Carl Geiser, *Prisoners of the Good Fight: The Spanish Civil War 1936–1939* (Westport, CT, 1986), pp 222–6.
22. Kerney Family Archive, L. H. Kerney's annual report to Dublin, year ending 31 March 1940. I am grateful to Barry Whelan for a copy of this document.
23. NA, DFA 10/1/31, Kerney to Walshe, 1 September 1939.
24. DIFP, *Vol. 6*, pp 98–9, Kerney to Walshe, 21 November 1939.
25. Ibid., pp 122–3, Kerney to Walshe, 23 December 1939
26. I am grateful to Michael Kennedy of the Royal Irish Academy and the main editor of DIFP for an English-language summary. Correspondence on the commutation can be found in: AIMNOR, causa 1695–98; Archivo General Militar Guadalajara (AMGu), 14/034, Condenado Frank Ryan.
27. DIFP, *Vol. 6*, pp 122–3, Kerney to Walshe, 23 December 1939.
28. Letter from the Dept of External Affairs to Senator D. L. Robinson, *Irish Independent*, 26 January 1940. Fr James A. Cleary of St Joseph's, Dundalk, Co. Louth, sent the cutting to Ontiveros and mentioned his own pro-Franco articles in Catholic journals.

He stated his disbelief that Ryan had been sentenced *merely* for fighting in the International Brigades (AGA, 82/4333/233, Ontiveros to Foreign Ministry, 28 January 1940, with enclosed letter by Fr Cleary, n.d., emphasis in the Cleary letter).

29. Interview with Tom Jones in North Wales, February 1975, no pagination, www.irelandscw.com/docs-RyanByJones.htm. Accessed 4 June 2020.
30. *Irish Press*, 27 May 1940.
31. https://api.parliament.uk/historic-hansard/written-answers/1939/dec/14/spain-mr-frank-ryan; https://api.parliament.uk/historic-hansard/commons/1940/apr/24/clearing-office-spain-amendment-order. Accessed 17 June 2020.
32. NA, DFA 10/1/32, Kerney to Walshe, 23 March 1940.
33. Geiser, *Prisoners of the Good Fight*, pp 227–32.
34. NA, DFA 10/1/33, extract from Kerney report, 11 March 1940.
35. From 1938 onwards, Kerney acted as 'postman' for the O'Reilly–Ryan letters.
36. NA, DFA 10/1/33, extract from letter by Gerald O'Reilly (New York) to his wife Helen (Dublin), 26 March 1940, as intercepted by Irish Military Intelligence.
37. AGA, 82/4333/233, the Irish American Committee for Release of Frank Ryan to Ontiveros, 11 March 1940; Kerney to Beigbeder, 26 March 1940.
38. Ibid., Ontiveros to foreign affairs Madrid, 11 April 1940. Note in red pencil on margin is the translation of the sentence quoted. Muriel McSwiney is obviously the letter-writer in question.
39. Muriel MacSwiney, *Letters to Angela Clifford* (Belfast, 1996), pp 88–9.
40. DIFP, *Vol. 6*, pp 186–7, Kerney to Walshe, 23 April 1940.
41. AMGu, 26/70, Kerney to foreign affairs Madrid, 4 May 1940.
42. NAI, DFA 10/1/32, Kerney to Walshe, 7 May 1940.
43. AMGu, 26/70, Chief Assessor, Justice Dept, Ministry of the Army, memorandum, 16 May 1940.
44. Ibid., Chief Assessor, Justice Dept, 6th Military District, to Ministry for the Army, 21 June 1940; Justice Dept, 6th Military District, to foreign affairs Madrid, 25 June 1940.
45. NA, DFA 10/1/30, Walshe to Miss Ryan, 9 May 1939.
46. NA, DFA 10/1/32, Kerney to Walshe, 3 April 1940.
47. NA, DFA 10/1/31, Ryan to Kerney, 5 September 1939.
48. NA, DFA 10/1/32, Kerney to Walshe, 8 April 1940.
49. Ibid., Walshe to Frank Ryan Release Committee, 31 May 1940.
50. Isaac Rilova Pérez (ed.), *75 años 1932–2007. Centro Penitenciario de Burgos. La Prisión en la Historia. Exposición Retrospectiva* (Burgos, 2007), pp 19–20.
51. Isaac Rilova Pérez, *Guerra Civil y Violencia política en Burgos (1936–1943)* (Burgos, 2016), pp 283–95, 389–416. See also: www.josesaralegui.blogspot.co.at/2012/02/1938-la-prision-central-de-burgos.html. Accessed 17 June 2020.
52. DIFP, *Vol. 5*, pp 470–5, Kerney to Walshe, 17 June 1939.
53. NA, DFA 10/1/33, undated letter from Ryan to Kerney, handed in at the Irish Legation in Madrid on 4 January 1940. Underlined passage in the original.
54. NA, DFA 10/1/32, report of a telephone conversation between Kerney and de Champourcin (the Legation lawyer), 31 January 1940.
55. NA, DFA 10/1/34, extract from letter by Gerald O'Reilly (New York) to his wife Helen (Dublin), 26 March 1940, as intercepted by Irish Military Intelligence; Seán Cronin, *Frank Ryan: The Search for the Republic* (Dublin, 1980), p. 152.

56. DIFP, *Vol. 6*, pp 26–7, Memorandum from Kerney to Walshe, 14 September 1939.
57. Ibid., pp 63–4, Kerney to Walshe, 5 October 1939.
58. *Irish Times*, 10 April 1975, Frank Ryan Profile-4 by Michael McInerney.
59. NA, DFA 10/1/33, Gerald O'Reilly letter to his wife Helen, 26 March 1940.
60. *Irish Times*, 10 April 1975.
61. RGASPI, f. 545, o. 2, d. 302, l. 16.
62. RGASPI, f. 545, o. 6, d. 155, ll. 71, 78.
63. Geiser, *Prisoners of the Good Fight*, pp 233–5.
64. Interview with Tom Jones in North Wales, February 1975, no pagination, www.irelandscw.com/docs-RyanByJones.htm. Accessed 6 June 2020.
65. NA, DFA 10/1/32, Kerney to Walshe, 9 December 1939
66. Ibid., 5 December 1939, 2 December 1940.
67. NA, DFA 219/2, Kerney to Walshe, 19 December 1939; DFA 10/1/32, Kerney to Walshe, 19 December 1939.
68. NA, DFA 20/1/32, Kerney to Walshe, 27 December 1939; Walshe to Miss Ryan, 10 January 1940.
69. DIFP, *Vol. 6*, pp 123–6, extract from report Kerney-Walshe, 27 December 1939.
70. *Irish Times*, 10 April 1975, Frank Ryan Profile, 4, Interview of Tom Jones by Michael McInerney.
71. NA, DFA 10/1/32, Extract from letter from Ryan to Kerney, 1 January 1940.
72. Ibid., Kerney to Walshe, 2 February 1940.
73. Interview with Tom Jones in North Wales, February 1975, no pagination, www.irelandscw.com/docs-RyanByJones.htm. Accessed 6 June 2020.
74. *Daily Worker*, 28 March, 2–3, 9 April 1940 (photo of Burgos prisoners including Jones sitting beside Ryan, p. 4); *Irish Press*, 2 April 1940.
75. NA, DFA 10/1/32, Kerney to Walshe, 3 April 1940; Walshe to Miss Ryan, 19 April 1940.
76. Ibid., F. H. Boland to Kerney, 9 May 1940.
77. Ibid., Kerney to Walshe, 23 May 1940.
78. Ibid., Kerney to Walshe, 7 May, 27 June, 29 July 1940.
79. PAAA, R. 103.027, Holden to Hempel, 13 June 1939.
80. Ibid., Holden to Herr Hitler, 13 June 1939.
81. Ibid., Hempel to Berlin, 6 July 1939.
82. John P. Duggan, *Neutral Ireland and the Third Reich* (Dublin, 1989), p. 59.
83. David O'Donoghue, *The Devil's Deal: The IRA, Nazi Germany and the Double Life of Jim O'Donovan* (Dublin, 2010), pp 115–17; Eunan O'Halpin, *Defending Ireland: The Irish State and its Enemies since 1922* (Oxford, 1999), pp 147–50.
84. Fearghal McGarry, *Irish Politics and the Spanish Civil War* (Cork, 1999), p. 250; Robert A. Stradling, *The Irish and the Spanish Civil War: Crusades in Conflict* (Manchester, 1999), p. 254.
85. PAAA, R. 101.136, AST Hamburg, Aktennotiz über eine Besprechung mit X-Stier, 8 August 1939.
86. Ibid., Berlin to Germany Embassy, Madrid, 29 September 1939.
87. AGA, 82/4333/233, German Embassy in Spain to Spanish Ministry for Foreign Affairs, 18 October 1939. The Germans were of the mistaken belief that Ryan had been sentenced to 10 years' forced labour.

88. PAAA, R. 103.238, McSwiney to Thomsen, 27 February 1940.
89. Ibid., Thomsen to Berlin, 29 February 1940.
90. Ibid., Berlin to German Embassy, Madrid, 21 March 1940.
91. Ibid., Madrid Embassy to Berlin 11.04.1940; Berlin to Madrid Embassy, 24 April 1940; Madrid Embassy to Berlin, 27 May 1940.
92. Joachim Lerchenmüller, *Keltischer Sprengstoff: Eine wissenschaftliche Studie über die deutsche Keltologie von 1900–1945* (Tübingen, 1997), p. 323; TNA, KV 6/79, Hoven, notes for interrogation, 30 April 1945.
93. Ina Schmidt, Stefan Breuer, Ernst Jünger, Friedrich Hielscher (eds), *Briefe von Ernst Jünger 1917–1985* (Stuttgart, 2005), pp 386–7.
94. TNA, KV 6/79, Hoven, notes for interrogation, 30 April 1945.
95. TNA, KV 6/81, Clissmann, personal history, 12 February 1946; supplement to FR 41, 12 February 1946.
96. TNA, KV 6/79, Hoven, notes for interrogation, 30 April 1945.
97. Bundesarchiv Berlin-Lichterfelde, RS 38, 10574, police reports 20 March, 10, 20 April, 30, 31 May 1934.
98. O'Donoghue, *The Devil's Deal*, p. 296.
99. This was the view of G2, Irish Army Intelligence (Lerchenmüller, *Keltischer Sprengstoff*, pp 364–5); TNA, KV 6/80, Clissmann, Dept of Defence, Dublin, memorandum, June 1943.
100. Horst Dickel, *Die deutsche Aussenpolitik und die irische Frage von 1932 bis 1944* (Wiesbaden, 1983), p. 232; TNA, KV 6/79, Hoven, note on Kurt Jahnke, n.d.
101. Robert Fisk, *In Time of War: Ireland, Ulster and the Price of Neutrality, 1939–1945* (London, 1987), p. 89.
102. Dickel, *Deutsche Aussenpolitik und die Irische Frage*, pp 77–8.
103. *Irish Press*, 22 June 1979, Brian O'Neill, 'Frank Ryan – the Laughing Cavalier of republicanism'.
104. Enno Stephan, *Spies in Ireland* (London, 1965), pp 143–4.
105. TNA, KV 6/81, Clissmann, Second Supplement on FR, 30 May 1946.
106. TNA, KV 2/679, Kurt Haller, interrogation 7 August 1946.
107. DIFP, *Vol. 6*, p. 190, handwritten minutes of Kerney, 29–30 April 1940.
108. Winzer is very much a mystery figure. A summary of his career can be found in the following German-language audio: www.youtube.com/watch?v=iuu-bksTQTY. Accessed 6 June 2020.
109. DIFP, *Vol. 7*, p. 140, memorandum by Dan Bryan, 20 October 1941.
110. O'Reilly had arranged Russell's transatlantic voyage (Cronin, *Frank Ryan*, p. 185).
111. DIFP, *Vol. 6*, pp 312–4, Kerney to Dublin, 29 July 1940.
112. www.leopoldhkerney.com/p/2-frank-ryan-out-of-jail.html. Accessed 6 June 2020.
113. DIFP, *Vol. 6*, pp 339–43, Kerney to Dublin, 26 August 1940.
114. Cronin, *Frank Ryan*, p. 237 (Ryan to Kerney, 20 August 1940, received at Legation 18 September 1940).
115. DIFP, *Vol. 6*, pp 339–43, Kerney to Dublin, 26 August 1940.
116. DIFP, *Vol. 7*, p. 139, Memorandum by Col. Dan Bryan of an interview with Leopold H. Kerney, 20 October 1941.
117. NA, DFA 10/1/35, report by F. H. Boland, 8 July 1944. Boland was instructed not to answer Kerney's request.

118. DIFP, *Vol. 6*, pp 346–7, Walshe to Miss Ryan, 27 August 1940.
119. *Irish Press*, 25 September 1940; *Daily Worker*, 28 September 1940.
120. AGA, 82/4333/233, Kerney to foreign affairs Madrid, 11 September, 5, 18, 30 October 1940; foreign affairs Madrid to sub-secretary of justice, 10 October 1940.
121. Ibid., foreign affairs Madrid to Kerney, 6 November 1940.
122. Ibid., Kerney to foreign affairs Madrid, 10 March, 22 April, 1 June 1942.
123. Ibid., Burgos prison to foreign affairs Madrid, 23 May 1942, with enclosed list of items.
124. Paul Preston, *The Spanish Holocaust: Inquisition and Extermination in Twentieth-Century Spain* (London, 2012), pp 506–10.
125. AMGu, 14/034, Condenado Frank Ryan.
126. Fearghal McGarry, *Frank Ryan: Historical Association of Ireland. Life and Times Series, No. 17* (Dundalk, 2002), pp 64–6.
127. British peace-feelers to Mussolini and Hitler after September 1939 were well-kept secrets for decades. See Clive Ponting, *1940: Myth and Reality* (London, 1990).
128. Ryan told Fr Mulrean that he had been asked to join the PCE, but had declined (*Irish Times*, 10 April 1975, Tom Jones interview by Michael McInerney)
129. AMGu, 27/42 (Madden); Kerney Family Archive, annual report by Kerney, year ending 31 March 1940.
130. Paul Preston, *We Saw Spain Die: Foreign Correspondents in the Spanish Civil War* (London, 2009), pp 350–1. The article was printed on 28 and 29 July 1936.
131. Paul Preston, *Franco: A Biography* (London, 1993), p. 290.

EPILOGUE

# WITHDRAWAL, HOMECOMING AND THE POLITICS OF COMMEMORATION

But had I lived four score and ten
Life could not've had
A better end.[1]

On 21 September 1938, Spanish Prime Minister Juan Negrín told the League of Nations that his Government wished to repatriate all non-Spanish combatants to comply with the aims of the Non-Intervention Committee. There was little chance of Germany, Italy and Portugal reciprocating by withdrawing their divisions. The prospect of victory was long gone, and the Spanish Government's last hope was to stay in the fight long enough to ally with Britain and France when the anticipated world war broke out. It was thought the crisis over the Sudetenland would be the powder keg. Instead it was defused by the Munich Agreement on 30 September.

A League of Nations commission to oversee the repatriation process arrived in Republican Spain on 16 October. Both the US and Canadian Governments also sent immigration and police agents to the 15th International Brigade assembly point at Ripoll to determine whether applicants were entitled to American or Canadian citizenship and to gather intelligence on potential subversives. Omitted in many accounts is another series of interviews and form-filling conducted by the War Commissariat of the International Brigades and the leading party committee of the 15th Brigade to assess the calibre of returnees and indicate their value to the party in their home countries.[2]

Repatriation proved to be more protracted than expected. Men had to be collected from various fronts, hospitals and rest homes, and arrangements for documentation, transport and fares home made with Governments of the democracies. At least they had homes to go to. Comrades from right-wing dictatorships were stranded. André Marty told Harry Pollitt that their position was 'getting more difficult every day' and begged him to see about getting as many as possible admitted to England and the dominions.[3] Most would end up in grim French internment camps.

Fortunate as the Irish were, most would face an arduous return to civilian life, the choice of crushing poverty or economic exile, and the disappointment of the Caudillo's endurance long after the death of the Duce and the Führer. Frank Ryan had a singular and controversial demise that calls for special attention. None could have imagined how they would be remembered at the close of the century.

THE ROAD BACK

The Connolly Column had been drifting home since late 1936. Those with an honourable discharge would be given credentials and a few pesetas, which would scarcely get them to the French border. Paddy 'Roe' McLaughlin, going home in February 1938, was assisted in Perpignan by Friends of Spanish Democracy, who lent him pocket money and a ticket to Paris. The Irish Legation in Paris regarded McLaughlin's treatment as exceptionally good, and surmised that he was a special agent, on a propaganda mission.[4] Months later John O'Reilly was stuck in Marseilles, explaining in a letter to his father that the plummeting peseta meant the Spanish Government could not afford to pay his way home. O'Reilly would settle in New York and become best known for marrying Salaria Kee, whom he had met when working as an orderly in the American hospital at Villa Paz.

As a Catholic, an African American and an anti-segregation activist, Kee was lionised by the American left and the subject of a pamphlet by the Negro Committee to Aid Spain, *A Negro Nurse in Republican Spain*. She had taken some persuasion to accept O'Reilly's offer, feeling he knew little of the problems that would attend an interracial marriage in the US, though he himself was apprehensive about the reaction in Thurles.[5] Celebrity status by no means eliminated the discrimination against Kee, and it was with difficulty that, in 1940, she finally secured approval for her husband to join her in the US.

In seven cases, those departing unofficially, as it were, sought travel documents or expenses from the British consuls in Valencia, Barcelona, or Marseilles, and the Irish Legation in Paris. The Irish Legation in Madrid had closed in early August 1936 after the Minister Kerney returned to Ireland on sick leave. On resuming his duties in January 1937, he joined the diplomatic community in St Jean de Luz, spending two busy years in the Golf Hotel.[6]

The first out was also the first to seek Irish consular assistance. Charles J. 'Nomad' McGuinness, having obtained an emergency passport from the British Consulate in Barcelona in November, made his way to the Irish Legation in Paris, and received expenses for the onward journey to Dublin. Back in

Ireland, he was effusive: 'Art O'Brien, a courteous and worthy representative of Ireland, did all in his power to help a fellow soldier of the Anglo-Irish war days... my passing through Paris will forever remain a pleasant memory.'[7]

Ó Briain was Irish Minister to France and Belgium from June 1935 to September 1938, when he was succeeded by Seán Murphy. The rank of minister, a grade lower than ambassador, was deemed suitable for small diplomatic missions and lessened the possibility of objections from London, which did not regard Ireland as a foreign country entitled to an independent foreign policy until it left the Commonwealth in 1949. Technically, Ó Briain and Murphy were appointed by King George V. On 17 December 1937, on foot of press reports about Irish volunteers leaving to fight on both sides in Spain, Ó Briain wrote to the Department of External Affairs requesting advice on what to do in further cases like that of McGuinness.[8] Henceforth, brigadistas would be questioned closely by Legation staff to glean intelligence on conditions in Spain.

There were instances too of men moving in the other direction. In December 1936 William McCarthy, from Youghal, and John McGowan, originally from Sligo, landed at Dunkirk, got drunk and lost their money, papers and luggage. Though both claimed to have been motivated by communist sympathies, they were proceeding independently, and told Ó Briain they had now changed their minds on Spain because of 'religious scruples'. Ó Briain doubted their story and it is probable they in turn reckoned the Legation was more likely to pay their way back to Ireland rather than on to Spain. MI5 reported that McGowan subsequently spoke at a CPGB meeting, posing as a brigadista and former prisoner of war. If not pro-Franco, the Irish diplomats in Paris were certainly not sympathetic to the Spanish Republic. Ó Briain was used to making fine distinctions. As a vice-president and de facto linchpin of the Irish Self-Determination League of Great Britain during the War of Independence, he had worked with British leftists while insisting that the League should keep out of British party politics, despite the membership's Labour leanings. The Department of External Affairs approved the loan of fares home for McCarthy and McGowan, as was usual in the circumstances.[9] Where applicants were proposing to travel to a permanent residence in England, they were told to seek help from the British consulate, which was willing to assist Irish nationals normally domiciled in the UK.[10]

The proclivities of the Legation and the Department of External Affairs on Spain are suggested in the cases of Harry Kennedy, Brendan Moroney and Pat Read. Kennedy called to the Legation on 3 February 1938, claiming to be a refugee from the red terror in Spain. A housepainter from Waterford, Kennedy had joined the International Brigades on 6 August 1937, serving on brigade staff as an instructor under Major Allan Johnson of the Lincoln battalion.[11] It was an odd appointment for one with a vague military or political background, the more so as Johnson was the highest-ranking veteran of the US army in the war, and a 'stalwart party man'.[12] It is tempting to conclude that Kennedy had invented his IRA background and was soon found out. On 1 September he enlisted in the British battalion, deserted, and was sent to a penal detachment. He claimed to have taken part in 'many engagements' and was certainly at Teruel in January 1938, a battle fought in blizzards that produced numerous incidents of frostbite. After a short time in hospital at Valencia, recovering from 'an illness... contracted during the battle', he made friends with British seamen who smuggled him onto a Greek ship bound for Algiers.

Another friendship in Algiers, this time with a Scandinavian sailor, secured him a free passage to Marseilles, where the British consul loaned him his train fare to Paris.[13] Kennedy then appealed to Ó Briain for his fare to London. On going to Spain, he told Ó Briain, he discovered that the struggle was 'in reality a war between Italian and German fascism on the one side and Russian communism on the other', and that the Republicans were anti-clerical and controlled their troops and territory with a 'reign of terror'. Kennedy also made ludicrous assertions about Soviet plans to deploy the International Brigades in China after the war in Spain. With his talent for making useful acquaintances, he stayed the night in Paris at a 'good hotel' in the salubrious Avenue Wagram, where a retired British army captain entertained him 'lavishly' in return for 'a recital of his experiences in Spain'. Subsequently he travelled to London at the expense of the British Charitable Fund in Paris.[14] In Ó Briain's opinion, 'Kennedy's tale was just a little too good... he deceived everybody.' Clearly he regarded him as an adventurer, suggesting 'It is not beyond the bounds of possibility that he may later on decide to try his fortune in the Far East on behalf of some cause or other.' He also wrote that he had detailed the case so that the Department of External Affairs might 'appreciate the type of Irish national that is engaged on the side of the Valencia government'.[15]

In a similar vein, the Legation sent Dublin a detailed debriefing of Brendan Moroney, originally from Ennis. Moroney said he knew nothing of communism and had gone to Spain as a democrat and anti-fascist, only to find the government forces to be Soviet controlled. A former Irish Guardsman, he had learned to play the old soldier and became an inveterate troublemaker in the British battalion, managing to desert after malingering in hospital in April 1938. In Barcelona, the British consul placed him on HMS *Vanoc*, a destroyer of the non-intervention patrol, which took him to Marseilles, where the British consul general gave him papers, 50 francs and directions to the Irish Legation in Paris. Proceeding tardily, Moroney arrived at the Legation in June.

His description of life in Spain was unrestrained. The International Brigades were comprised of the 'scum of the earth', discipline was maintained by summary executions, the Spanish people were pro-Franco, civilians were 'massacred wholesale' on the slightest suspicion of fascist sympathies, anti-clericalism was rampant (this was true) and Frank Ryan was a red murderer who 'deserved to be shot'. His interlocutor was sceptical – Moroney would acquire a reputation for being 'colourful' – but emphasised the 'marked resemblance' with Kennedy's statement regarding 'the character of those engaged in the service of the International Brigade'. As Moroney intended return to London, the Legation requested the British Consulate to help him.[16]

Pat Read applied for an Irish passport at the Legation in 1938, claiming he had lost his British passport in Spain and wished to return to the US. Read had been recklessly critical of the communists to the point that friends feared for his life. He was fortunate to be in the Lincoln battalion. Brigade Commissar Dave Doran removed him to the rear in March 1938 and he was subsequently discharged. His origins were equally unorthodox. Born on a ship sailing from Dublin to London in 1899, Read's family had settled in London, Liverpool and then in Canada. Read himself moved on to the US. Though both his parents were Dubliners, and Read had lived in Ireland from 1921 to 1924, fighting with the CPI's 'red guard' in the Battle of Dublin in June 1922, the Department of External Affairs denied him a passport.[17] Read managed to make his way to America and died in Chicago in 1947.

In fairness to Ó Briain, he acted promptly on repeated appeals from two distraught Cork mothers to have their sons, James Francis O'Regan and Michael O'Riordan, stopped from going to the front in Spain, writing to the French Minister of Foreign Affairs and Kerney in St Jean de Luz. O'Riordan had slipped away leaving a note to assure his 'sincere' Catholic parents that he was bound for a job 'hundreds of miles' from the front. The French authorities promised to assist Ó Briain by preventing the two Corkmen from entering Spain, if possible. Mrs Lucy O'Regan also had a Capuchin friar write an appeal for her son. As Ó Briain explained gently to Mrs Julia Riordan, as she signed herself, there were several such cases and there was little the Legation could do, having no channel of communication to anyone in Spain. O'Riordan was the second-last Irishman to join the International Brigades.[18] Both he and O'Regan would see front-line service.

With the dissolution of the International Brigades, the Legation dealt with two other types of cases. On 6 December 1938, on 'a dry and frosty morning', the remnant of the British battalion at Ripoll – some 300 – and a few Canadians, climbed aboard a goods train that would take them to the border crossing at Puigcerda/Bourg-Madame. The first batch of Americans had entrained for France on 2 December and the bulk of the Mackenzie–Papineau battalion would follow in January. They didn't trouble the Irish Legation in Paris. In the British contingent however, seven men identified as Irish: Michael O'Riordan, John Power, James Francis O'Regan, Tom O'Brien, Mick Waters, Eugene Downing and John O'Shea. The Legation agreed with the Dominions Office that British officials should shepherd all the evacuees from the frontier, where they were given food and passports and loaded onto a sealed train, bound for Dieppe. They were also issued with forms promising to repay the cost of their food and travel. On foot of a protest from the Department of External Affairs, the British agreed to distribute Legation forms to the Irish, to obviate the Irish having to sign as 'British subjects'. Seven other Irishmen – Philip Boyle, William Burgess, Sean Dowling, John Kelly, Michael Lehane, James O'Regan and Patrick Tighe – who were also repatriated with the British battalion were not handled by the Paris Legation, and came to its attention through applications for financial help to the Irish High Commission in London. They were given tickets home. A further two, Alex Digges and Paddy Duff, remained in Spanish hospitals. Barcelona fell on 26 January 1939 and Duff left his hospital in Figueras to join some 450,000 refugees trekking into France. Demoralised by the gathering crisis in Europe, the French authorities gave them a bleak reception. Duff became one of 90,000 interned in inhumane conditions in the St Cyprien camp, 40 miles from the border. He was repatriated in February.[19]

The second category processed by the Legation were prisoners of war. Michael McGrath and Hugh O'Donnell, both captured during 'the retreats', probably in March 1938, were incarcerated in the disused monastery of San Pedro de Cardeña, near Burgos, and included in the first release of prisoners in October 1938. Bob Doyle, Thomas Heaney, Jackie Lemon and Maurice Levitas were captured in the disaster at Calaceite on 31 March 1938, and also spent time in San Pedro. In brutal conditions, they endured beatings by the camp guards and the 'obsession of wondering if we might ever emerge from there alive'. On 6 February 1939, Doyle was among 67 mainly British prisoners exchanged for 70 Italian Fascists, released from San Sebastian prison, and escorted from Hendaye to Paris.[20]

> After delousing, we were taken by the Spanish Civil Guard to the borderline on the International Bridge and handed over to the French gendarmerie. We three [sic] Irish were put on the rear of a train with a gendarme and travelled under guard to Paris, where we were taken to the Irish consul. He tried to make us sign a statement saying we would pay for our fare from Spain to Dublin; this we refused to do. He then asked us to sign on behalf of our parents so that they would foot the

bill; again, we refused, stating that we would be quite happy to go back to join the Republican forces. Reluctantly, he gave us a ticket to Dublin via London.[21]

HOMECOMINGS

The British battalion received an ecstatic reception from 20,000 friends, relatives, and Labour leaders at London's Victoria Station on 7 December 1938. There followed welcoming parties around Britain, notably in Scotland, south Wales and Tyneside in hotels, union halls and cooperative societies. Stragglers, mostly wounded, continued to trickle home over the coming weeks. The support systems for the former combatants were sparse, but they did at least exist. A Dependants' Aid Committee had been established in June 1937, and by October 1938 it had raised £41,847 with the help of MPs, trade unions, clerics, and writers. One member of the committee was Seán O'Casey. The money was distributed in maintenance grants to the families of volunteers or to men incapacitated by the war: some 1,200 Britons had been wounded in Spain. The committee also arranged with the Spanish Medical Aid Committee and sympathetic doctors to provide pro bono medical care and undertook to assist with finding suitable employment for disabled veterans. Following the return of the British battalion, it launched a National Memorial Fund Appeal for £50,000. Grants from the Fund were usually between £80 and £100.[22] Rising employment with the expansion of war-related industries after Germany broke the Munich Agreement also helped.

The story was much the same in the US and Canada. People thronged New York's West Side docks to greet the Lincolns, and Friends of the Abraham Lincoln Brigade organised a parade in mid-town Manhattan. 'Brigade' was adopted to include veterans of the short-lived George Washington Battalion. For the Mac-Paps there were speeches in Toronto's Union Station. The welcomes were not universal, of course, and one thought the crowds contained 'more cops than people'. In all three countries the security services continued to hold brigadistas in deep suspicion.[23]

In Ireland, the picture was rather different. The most formal of receptions was that accorded to the seven volunteers who had travelled to London with the British battalion. On 10 December 1938 they landed at Dún Laoghaire and entrained for Westland Row, where they were greeted by Irish Friends of the Spanish Republic. O'Riordan remembered the low-key arrival:

> A curious crowd of onlookers at the station watched as the returning volunteers and the welcoming party formed up in marching order, and led by a single piper,

set out for Abbey Street corner [the usual venue for CPI street meetings], where on a lorry in the midst of a downpour of rain stood Father Michael O'Flanagan. To the small audience he spoke words of welcome to those back from Spain. The meeting over, the participants adjourned to the Oval Bar to drink, relax and exchange all the news that had built up both in Spain and Ireland.[24]

A little later there was a rare ceremony in the provinces to mark the homecoming of Power, O'Shea, and Jackie Hunt:

> About twenty of us met them off the Dublin train at Waterford. We formed into a line, marched across the bridge, along the Quay, and turned into Henrietta Street to the old Cathal Brugha Sinn Féin Hall, where about fifty people gave them an enthusiastic reception. A party of tea, cakes and sandwiches had been prepared by ex-members of Cumann na mBan and the IRA.[25]

The last man home was Lemon, who reached Waterford on 27 February.

Those who returned during the war were most likely to encounter hostility. Peter O'Connor, just back from Spain in October 1937, was appalled to see a Movietone newsreel 'showing the Reds in Spain firing at a statue of Christ and digging up skeletons of nuns and dragging them through the streets'. Incredulous, he stood up and told the cinema audience that the Spanish Republic's army 'had better use for its rifles' and he had seen men go into battle empty handed.[26]

In truth, it's likely that the newsreel was accurate, if selective. He recalled a 'mixed reception', with some old acquaintances avoiding him in the street and others remaining on good terms. Mixed, with subdued political scepticism offset by personal admiration, was the aggregate experience of brigadistas. As the public fatigued of Spain, and the threat of fascism in Ireland receded, popular attitudes mellowed. Frank Edwards, who was sent home in July 1937 to undertake propaganda work – Ryan's usual alibi for men he felt had 'done their bit' – felt comfortable enough to move on from Dublin to Waterford, where he had clashed with the bishop in 1934:

> Fellows came over to me in the street to shake my hand. 'I don't blame you for going out to have a bash at them', one said, thinking I had gone to Spain to have a crack at the Church. I found however, a complete change. The Christian Front was gone, so too were the last fragments of the Republican Congress. All of my old friends were retired to the side lines.[27]

The change was not due solely to Spain. The revolutionary forces generated by the dislocation of 1916 to 1923 were near exhaustion and the new conservative consensus forged by Fianna Fáil ensured that there would be no renewal of radicalism until the next world war.

The campaign to repatriate Ryan provided a valedictory rallying point for brigadistas and was the swansong of the politics of the Spanish Civil War. Several Frank Ryan Release Committees were formed in Ireland and England. The campaign helped to mend fences as it enjoyed broad support within the Labour movement and Fianna Fáil and in the *Irish Press*. Having shied away from Spain during the conflict, the Irish Trade Union Congress executive lobbied the Taoiseach on Ryan and, on receiving a vague response, pressed harder. Similarly, Jim Larkin, who had stopped Workers' Union of Ireland officials from speaking publicly on the war, raised the issue persistently at the Congress's annual conference in August 1939. He eventually secured the suspension of standing orders, which required a two-thirds majority, and, never one to let a fact detract from a good speech, made a plea for a brave man whom he had 'know[n] as a boy'.[28]

The outbreak of war on 1 September created a new context. O'Riordan was bribed with a commission in the army by a senior member of Fianna Fáil. Declining the carrot, he got the stick. Having moved back into the IRA, he had become quartermaster of Cork city's 1st battalion and took part in an aborted plan to rescue Tomás MacCurtain, who was to be tried for shooting a detective. With two other comrades of the Connolly Column, Power and Patrick Smith, O'Riordan was among 2,000 republicans interned in the Curragh between 1940 and 1943. That his arrest followed the national outrage over the hanging of Peter Barnes and James McCormack for their indirect role in an IRA bombing in Coventry suggests the Government's chief concern lay with the brigadistas' IRA links and the IRA's potential to trigger a British invasion.[29] The CPI prioritised neutrality in what the Comintern deemed an imperialist war, until all arguments were trumped by the German invasion of the 'socialist motherland' on 22 June 1941. The arrival of Neil Goold-Verschoyle in 1942, taken out of circulation with doubtful legality for disruption during a rent strike in Cabra, brought to 'Tintown' an exotic, well-versed Anglo-Irish Marxist didact, who encouraged the formation of a communist faction – the Connolly Education Group. To the IRA command's disgust, it attracted about 200 republicans.[30] A life-long Stalinist, though his brother Brian had been arrested in Spain for suspected Trotskyism and would die in a Soviet gulag, Neil pressed the Education Group to adopt an essentially pro-Allied manifesto on May Day 1942 and produce a monthly paper, *An Splannc*.[31]

With his gift for political elision, O'Riordan ignored the CPI's policy during the Molotov–Ribbentrop pact and wrote of the Connolly Column trio: 'their political task was to explain to the other prisoners of the Irish Republican Movement the anti-national character of Fascism and the relationship between the anti-Hitler war and the cause of Irish national liberation.' It was not a view that commended itself to straightforward anti-British elements, and there were intense rows between the internees on the correct position on the war. One of their guards was Terry Flanagan, Ryan's second in command in Madrigueras. Flanagan had been invalided home in August 1937 and was now a lieutenant in the army.[32]

For the bulk of veterans, the urgent problem was not prison or the lack of support services, but the difficulty of finding work. A handful tried self-employment. Joe Boyd was able to go back to his milk business. The other SPNI medic, Fred McMahon, opened a stationery, toy and fancy goods shop at 47 Donegall Street in Belfast, now headquarters of the Irish Congress of Trade Unions Northern Ireland Committee.[33] Life was harder in the depressed economic conditions of Emergency Ireland. Downing and Tom O'Brien set up lending libraries and O'Brien supplemented his income by writing cowboy novels under the pseudonym 'Harry Mancher'. Waterford was unique in that all of its volunteers had strong connections to their locality before Spain and had worked there in the 1930s, but of the ten survivors from Waterford, only three made a living for themselves in Ireland. England, desperately short of war-workers between Dunkirk and D-Day, offered a tempting prospect. One Waterford man despaired of finding a job and took the boat to Holyhead in May 1942. After an interrogation by special-branch men about his time in the IRA and in Spain, he was put on the next ferry to Dún Laoghaire. An appeal to the CPGB MP Willie Gallacher got the deportation order rescinded.[34] The British party was well-connected once the Red Army entered the war. Suspicion and victimisation of brigadistas was renewed by the Cold War. In 1978 Seán Penrose wrote to Taoiseach Jack Lynch, protesting that he had been dismissed from the US radio station, Armed Forces Network, for having fought in Spain.[35]

The world war created obvious employment outlets. Twenty-four Irish brigadistas served in a range of units including the Irish Marine Service, the Irish army, the British army, navy, air force and merchant marine, London Fire Brigade, the Norwegian merchant navy, the Royal Canadian Air Force, army and merchant navy and the US army and merchant navy. Two more applied to join the Home Guard and two applied for work in the Navy, Army and Air Force Institutes, which ran canteens and recreational centres for British servicemen. Boyd was given a revolver by the RUC and expected to be part of a resistance network should the Nazis occupy Belfast. He was the only one of the Belfast volunteers who could be considered middle class. Captain Jack White's offer to join the Ulster Defence Volunteers (later the Ulster Home Guard) was rejected by the RUC 'in view of your record'. With his trademark artless chutzpah, White protested to Prime Minister J. M. Andrews that he was 'Red. . . never Green'.[36] To avoid arming Catholics, Unionists ensured that the Ulster Home Guard was virtually synonymous with the B Specials. By contrast, MI5 had 'no objections' to Patrick Power, brother of John, enlisting in the Home Guard in England. Agnes Olive Beamish, originally from Cork and a one-time militant suffragette who spent two weeks in Spain in January 1937 with a trade union delegation, joined the women's branch of the British army, the Auxiliary Territorial Service.[37] Paddy O'Daire had the most distinguished career, rising to the rank of major in the Pioneer Corps of the British army. Aside from O'Riordan, James Francis O'Regan also joined the IRA and was given 12 years' hard labour for active service in wartime Britain. Two merchant seamen, Michael Lehane and Joseph Ryan, were lost with their torpedoed ships, as was Jim Haughey when his Wellington bomber crashed in north Devon in 1943.

Politically, the brigadistas ceased to exist. Apart from the handful of survivors in the 1980s and 90s, they never functioned as a symbolic elite of the left. There was no 'Sean-Óglaigh Cholúin Uí Chongaile' to enjoy a privileged place in parades and demonstrations in the manner of Veterans of the Abraham Lincoln Brigade. A few turned Turk, beginning with McGuinness. Eager to advance his ambition to be a writer, 'Nomad' penned five fantastic articles for the *Irish Independent* in January 1937, each with lurid accounts of red barbarity. It was an easy path to publication. Delighted with its convert to the cause, the *Independent* billed the series as 'A true story that will thrill you!' and 'A sensational document'. Nomad planned to follow the series with another exposé on his days in Russia, *Behind the Red Curtain*.[38] Some copies of the 124-page book did appear between 1937 and 1939 but were almost certainly produced by the vanity press.

Frustrated as an author, and unable to secure a commission in the new Irish Marine and Coastwatching Service, McGuinness reluctantly joined the service as a Chief Petty Officer, but conspired with the IRA in 1942 to smuggle the German spy Gunther Schuetz to occupied France in a fishing smack and come back with Frank Ryan. It was typical of McGuinness that he was happy to switch sides to the extent of helping the man widely regarded as the symbolic commandant of the Connolly Column. Schuetz was recaptured before the plan could be effected and McGuinness spent the rest of the Emergency in prison. Captain McGuinness was lost off Wexford with the schooner *Isallt* while skippering a load of fertiliser to Waterford in December 1947. His body was never found, and speculation persists that he was secretly bound for buried treasure in the Cocos Islands.[39]

Moroney, too, intended to write up his Spanish war for the press.[40] On returning home he penned a blisteringly anti-communist account for the Irish Catholic journal *Hibernia*, which also appeared in the pro-Franco periodical

*Spain* in New York. 'If ever I fight in Spain again', it concluded, 'it will not be for the Reds and tyranny but for "Franco and Freedom!"' He lived afterwards in London and reinvented himself as a good brigadista, praising Frank Ryan in letters to the *Irish Post* between 1979 and 1985.[41] He was fortunate that no one challenged his credentials. If Moroney turned with one tide, Ewart Milne, poet, intellectual and a driver for the London-based Spanish Medical Aid Committee, turned with another. In the 1970s he would write of having been 'taken-in by Stalin' and agree with Aleksandr Solzhenitsyn that 'Leninism was Satanism.'[42] 'I certainly repent my mistaken attitude in the Thirties,' he told Downing, who concluded that he was against not only the Soviet Union but the French revolution too.[43]

Relatively few veterans continued in the CPI. O'Riordan's *Connolly Column* cites a mere two, Jim Prendergast in Dublin and Hugh Hunter in Belfast, modestly omitting his own leadership of the Irish Workers' League and the CPI, and Bill Scott, who resigned from the CPI, not over the Molotov–Ribbentrop pact but the Comintern's consequential designation of the war as 'imperialist' and its direction to affiliates to cease anti-fascist propaganda.[44] O'Connor and Edwards remained fellow travellers. MI5 kept tabs on 18 Irish brigadistas who were active in the CPGB in the 1940s, together with a further three who cannot be confirmed as brigadistas. Others were involved in trade unions – two as officials in the Workers' Union of Ireland and the National Union of Railwaymen – and a variety of radical organisations such as Frank Ryan Release committees, the Republican Congress, the IRA, the Labour Party, the NILP, the Ireland-USSR Society and, in England, the Connolly Association, the Independent Labour Party and the International Brigade Association. Olive Beamish became vice-president of the Association of Women Clerks and Secretaries.[45]

Intelligence on how veterans coped with the psychological and physical consequences of the war is sparse and uneven. The first brigadista in an Irish play, Francis in *The Wise Have Not Spoken* (1947), is a maimed and tortured soul who wishes he had died in Madrid.[46] It was a rational conjecture. The Connolly Column had endured very testing conditions of service, made worse by incompetence, returned to a society more conservative than the one they had left and gotten little support from their erstwhile comrades. Above all, they had lost. A few were scathing about the politics or efficiency of the International Brigades. Nobody complained about the personal impact of the war.[47] Complaint was not manly, and whatever trauma they experienced was offset by pride in their service and a sense that Hitler's war validated their choice. Frank Ryan is the best documented case and it's clear that he bore his deteriorating health stoically. Most men discharged on 'medical' or 'health' grounds or because of wounds were logged as such without elaboration. Exceptions were cases of repatriation because of a 'nervous condition', 'shell-shock' and for being 'thoroughly demoralised'. Lemon was scarred, physically and mentally, by his time in San Pedro, but held down a job in the National Board and Paper Mills outside Waterford.[48] Kennedy, who was raised around the corner from Lemon, was arrested for an assault on his sister at her King's Road address in London in February 1938, fined 40 shillings and bound over for six months.[49] Doyle broke down in tears as he walked though blitzed Liverpool and thought of Spain. He faced continual harassment in the Royal Navy and in civvy street whenever his superiors discovered his Spanish background and he developed an ulcer.[50] Less is known of the consequences of physical impairment. Three amputations were recorded, involving the loss of a finger, an arm, and a leg below the knee. Johnny Larmour, who had a 'wasted hand and injured left arm', was given a job managing a CPGB bookshop. One hopes that all had the resilience of Downing, who worked for Middlesex County Council, a film distribution company, and British Gas, despite having 'one foot in the grave'.[51]

With Bolshevik propriety, few went rogue. Irish-Canadian Cormac McCarthy was arrested in Paris in April 1938 for burglary, and Patrick McElroy and Joseph Haines were detained for the robbery and attempted murder of a Great Northern Railway paymaster in Dublin in 1943. The juxtaposition of poverty and a revolver he had bought in South Africa unhinged McElroy, who had a history of militant activism in the republican movement. Haines bumped into his old comrade in arms in Amiens Street, opposite the Great Northern terminus, and hissed 'Don't be a fool', but it was too late. 'Spanish war men on hold-up charge' ran the headline in the *Irish Press*. Their barrister was Seán MacBride. McElroy pleaded that he had been badly wounded in Spain, necessitating two operations, and then suffered from bombing in Egypt, probably when working as a civilian fitter for the Royal Navy. The judge accepted that McElroy 'had some abnormality' after Spain but could not regard it as a defence and sentenced him to seven years in jail. MI5 also believed McElroy to be mentally affected. Haines was acquitted. He too had been wounded in Spain, taking a bullet in the knee.[52]

On balance, the brigadistas coped or sorted themselves out, as contemporary war veterans were expected to do.

## ENDSTATION DEUTSCHLAND: THOMAS GUNNING AND FRANK RYAN

Two significant Irishmen in wartime Spain ended their days in Germany. Frank Ryan's nemesis, Thomas Gunning, was 31 when he succumbed to protracted lung disease in Germany in 1940. Gunning left Spain with his wife in 1938 and stayed in correspondence with Sir Richard Hodgson, the British Agent in Burgos, after he had entered a well-known sanatorium in Sankt Blasien in the Black Forest. His private affairs were soon in turmoil. His wife had left him and he took up with a fellow patient and moved with her to Berlin after his discharge from the sanatorium in August 1939. Gunning's job with the Exchange Telegraph News-Agency was terminated at war's outbreak and he attempted to move to the agency's office in Switzerland. The Swiss police turned down his request as neither they nor Gunning could locate in Zurich the agency manager named by the Irishman. Irish diplomatic staff in Geneva and Berlin attempted to help, but as Gunning also wished his German-born 'secretary' to join him in Berne or Zurich and still could not name his contact there, both were refused an entry visa. Irish diplomats, doubting that Gunning was a 'persona grata', declined to assist him any further and he died on 11 June 1940 in hospital in Breslau. He had been moved there from a Silesian sanatorium after tuberculosis had spread to his bowels and brain.[53]

Frank Ryan's sojourn in Germany was revisited by us at length in 2014.[54] Scarce benefit would accrue from retracing in detail that over-written topic of attempts of Abwehr officers to land Irish-born agents, Frank Ryan included, in Ireland during the world war. In any case, it is outside the remit of our work. Little of substance, if not detail, has emerged since 1980. In that year Seán Cronin published his biography of Ryan and reproduced in full the eight letters transmitted from Ryan to Kerney between 1940 and 1942 that showed that the former captain of the International Brigades fully supported de Valera's policy of neutrality.[55] It is obvious that Ryan, who owed his liberation to the Germans, was expected to reciprocate. None of his reports remain extant in the German Foreign Office files that survived the war and were examined by us twice, in 1976 (Bonn) and 2019 (Berlin). While in the French capital, Ryan, according to Clissmann's statement to his British interrogators in 1946, was asked by Abwehr II to go to Britain to spy for the Germans. He refused.[56] Ryan was then brought to Berlin from Paris by Clissmann on 4 August 1940, ten days after his 'release' from Burgos.[57] Two days later, Ryan and Sean Russell, in the company of two Abwehr officers and Eduard Veesenmayer ('Irland-Experte' in the Auswärtiges Amt) travelled by train to Wilhelmshaven.

On 8 August a U-Boot with Russell and Ryan on board left for Ireland, but returned a week later to Lorient.[58] Russell, who had been given a free hand by his German collaborators, did not confide any details of his plans to Ryan, and his illness (a perforated ulcer) led to his death and burial at sea after a few days.[59] Before that, any conversations aboard the submarine would have been difficult due to Ryan's hearing impediment and the noise of the engines. The mission was aborted because Ryan refused to land on his own, a decision he later regretted. He made it because he would have been almost certainly interned, and he would have had considerable difficulty in explaining Russell's demise to Irish Military Intelligence – and to his fellow internees from the IRA – or that he had had no part in it.

Once the Germans invaded the Soviet Union in June 1941, interest in Ireland waned; two attempts to land Ryan (with Clissmann) in Ireland (on a lake in Roscommon, or on the coast of Kerry) were postponed and later dropped altogether.[60] From early 1942 onwards, Ryan was at a loose end and, following his first stroke in January 1943, not suitable for active service. In his last three years in Germany, Ryan was dogged by ill-health: dental problems (steel teeth inserted in Burgos), rheumatism, an ulcer that necessitated an operation, a traffic accident in Denmark and his cardiac insufficiency, which led to his death in June 1944. The Irish expertise of Clissmann and Hoven was also dispensed with over time: the former was sent on commando missions to Tunisia and Denmark, the latter to a paratrooper regiment in Poland and France.[61] In conclusion, we believe that Frank Ryan was not a collaborator but rather an adviser to German foreign office experts.[62] His importance to the Nazis diminished mainly for geopolitical reasons: the drive east to Moscow was Hitler's top priority.

### 'VIVA LA QUINTA BRIGADA'

Ernst Toller's observation that 'history is the propaganda of the victors' is ultimately true of the Spanish Civil War. Yes, the Republic lost militarily, but in the long run the anti-fascists would win politically. At the close of 2019, there was nothing to commemorate Eoin O'Duffy's bandera except a small plaque on a pew in Dublin's Pro-Cathedral, dedicated to one who died 'fighting with the Christian forces'.[63] By contrast, there were 45 memorials to the men and the one woman of the Connolly Column, with an additional two in Spain on the battlefield of Jarama. Identification with the International Brigades went well beyond the far left. Memorials in Belfast and Dungannon were commissioned by the local councils and others were erected with the blessing of local authorities.⁶⁴ Tributes have been paid to the Connolly Column by Presidents of Ireland and lord mayors of Dublin and Belfast. In 2001 O'Riordan was invited to address the Labour Party's annual conference and hailed by party leader Ruairi Quinn as a champion of democracy in the 1930s. When O'Connor died in 1999, his death was the lead item on the 6.01 news on RTÉ 1. The same RTÉ commissioned a seven-hour television history of the state, *Seven Ages*, broadcast in 2000, which never once mentioned labour. So, what is the celebration of the Connolly Column about?

The key to this question lies in the power of the Catholic Church in Ireland from the 1930s to the 1960s, and the way in which the Church made anti-communism an expression of that power. The climate of hostility extended to even the mildest forms of social democracy, and would intensify during the height of the cold war, when any expression of socialism or left-wing internationalism was taboo.⁶⁵ Given the weakness of the left, it beggars belief that the rationale was political. Arguably, it was not theological either. Plausibly, it was clericalism, and a means of establishing loyalty to clerical authority.

Attitudes relaxed in the 1960s. And whereas the liberalism of that decade was often justified with references to the reforming pontificate of John XXIII and the Second Vatican Council, the 1970s saw the growth of secularism, and the emergence of demands for reform of legislation on sexuality, public morality and control of education: a socio-political force that the media labelled 'the liberal agenda'. The Catholic hierarchy won some tactical battles against 'the liberal agenda' in the 1970s, but by the mid-1980s it was patently losing the war. By the 1990s, secular liberalism was the new hegemon. The Spanish Civil War served as a reminder of how things were, and how much had changed. The Connolly Column became re-imagined as a prophetic forerunner of modern, pluralist Ireland. Just as the clergy had exploited fear of communism to demonstrate its imperium, so the left now flaunted its newfound freedom to exorcise the ghosts of its submission to clericalism. As O'Riordan observed on his invitation to address the Labour Party in 2001, it 'revers[ed] the role of that Party during the War itself'.⁶⁶

The first Irish memorial of the Spanish Civil War was erected in 1984. It required co-funding from the US. Others were unveiled in 1989, 1991, 1994, 1996, 1997 and each year from 2003. The first two were in a well-worn tradition of republican remembrance and were dedicated to two republicans. Subsequent projects were led mainly by radicals of various persuasions and trade unionists, who had the advantage of access to organisation and finance. The commemorations reflected the generational gap between the 'authenticist' mentality of the Irish left in 1936 and the 'modernist' mentality of its successors. With a rooted mindset acquired from republicanism, the 'authenticists' understood Spain through the prism of Irish history. Spain was an extension of Ireland, a second front. For the 'modernists', on the other hand, Spain was (and is) an escape from the shackles of Irish history, and internationalism is a huge part of the attraction of the Connolly Column. Typically, the speeches at commemorations have focused on Catholic reaction at home, anti-fascism, and international solidarity, and have represented the war as a conflict of good and evil that drew, almost magnetically, the best men to fight the good fight. Republicanism is treated as coincidental to the background of volunteers, rather than the fundament of their politics; Spain is the focus.

Belfast offers the most acute example of selective, 'present centred' commemoration, and has seen a scramble among its divers political forces to appropriate the Spanish Civil War. The 12 memorials that appeared in the city between 2006 and 2015 fall into two categories. Those commissioned by the Workers' Party, Sinn Féin, the Irish Republican Socialist Party or Republican Ex-Prisoners are dedicated to particular brigadistas presumed to be identified with the sponsoring tendency, or, where no such brigadistas can be found, make a generic connection between the sponsor and the anti-fascism. Those erected by the Belfast Unemployed Resource Centre, Unite the Union, the International Brigades Commemoration Committee and Belfast City Council are pointedly cross-community. That Belfast volunteers were Catholic and Protestant makes them rather precious in a divided city, and these memorials emphasise the diversity of their backgrounds more than anything else. The inscription on the International Brigades Commemoration Committee's splendid monument in the centre of Belfast's arts quarter uses the mincing language of Northern Ireland's peace and reconciliation industry: 'Dedicated to the people of Belfast, the island of Ireland and beyond who joined the XV International Brigade to fight Fascism in the Spanish Civil War 1936–39, and to those men and women from all traditions who supported the Spanish working people and their Republic.' The stained-glass window in Belfast City Hall bears the caption: 'With the agreement of all political parties, this window was commissioned to reflect the contribution of citizens from Belfast to the fight against fascism in the Spanish Civil War between 1936 and 1939.' Another memorial was 'Unveiled as part of Belfast's annual Anti-Racism World Cup amateur soccer tournament.'[67] Arguably, the overall effect is to illustrate how fractured the city is, and how different the mentality of radical activists and the bien pensants. Elsewhere, memorials have been commissioned chiefly by Friends of the International Brigades, the CPI, trade unions and local history societies. More recent sponsors have included Anti-Fascist Action.

The definition of the Connolly Column as anti-fascists had the added advantage of eluding the collapse of the Soviet bloc. *Pictures of Tomorrow*, one of two Irish plays about veteran brigadistas to appear in 1994, was exceptional in tackling the disillusionment that went with the 'fall of the wall'. More typical was its sideswipe at nationalism. Written by Belfast playwright Martin Lynch, its central character is at the edge of the grave, physically and ideologically:

> There is no future. We're living at the end of hope. When we were young, we could dream great dreams. Now, what have the kids got? Materialism and nationalism. Bosnia, Northern Ireland. We have to sit back and watch narrow-minded men fight over lines on the map. Nationalism is scrumpy compared to the vintage bottle of wine that socialism was. All those wasted years.[68]

The other play, *The Guernica Hotel* by Jim Nolan, discounted the 'fall of the wall' to pit the implacable idealism of a brigadista against the grubby gombeenism of traditional Ireland. 'There is', said Nolan, 'a certain moral stature which screams for social justice, and it doesn't go away when East Germany collapses.'[69]

What would the Connolly Column make of it all? The best insight into the mind of Irish brigadistas is found in the socialist republican values of the *Irish Democrat* and in Daiken's introduction to *Good-Bye Twilight*, where he addressed the dichotomy of 'modernists' and 'authenticists'. For Daiken, 'modernism' was flight: 'traditionalism' was fight. 'Modernists' had tried to escape from Irish reality; their bourgeois aesthetic, cosmopolitanism, and 'fashionable anti-clericalism' amounted to a self-indulgent excuse for politics. However, according to Daiken, the sharpening economic crises were pushing the middle-classes to the left and bringing the 'modernists' into the organic struggle never abandoned by the mainly republican 'traditionalists'.[70] Public opinion on the Spanish Civil War turned turtle too late for veterans to speak as they would have spoken in the 1930s. Peadar O'Donnell's edited memoir in 1974 featured a cursory chapter on Spain. Tellingly it began: 'The Spanish War of 1936-39 would seem to be a subject far removed from that of Peadar O'Donnell and the Irish Left. . .'.[71] As O'Donnell himself had written *Salud! An Irishman in Spain* in 1937, it can be surmised that he too had reached that conclusion. When O'Riordan's *Connolly Column* appeared in 1979, it was produced in the German Democratic Republic for want of an amenable printer in Ireland. The 50th anniversary of Franco's revolt marked a turning point. Harry Owens was overwhelmed by the response to an evening of history, politics and music that he convened in Dublin.[72] A stream of publications began to flow, including biographies, souvenirs, local and general histories, poems, plays and songs – Christy Moore's 'Viva la Quinta Brigada' becoming near universally known. However, there were only five memoirs by combatants, those by: Joe Monks (1985), Eoghan Ó Duinnín [Eugene Downing] (1986),

O'Connor (1996) and Doyle (2002 and 2006). To the five recollections can be added oral history interviews with Edwards (1980) and O'Riordan (1990), and O'Riordan's *Connolly Column* itself, which, if informative and factual, is a eulogistic CPI version of events.[73]

These six veterans and their memoirs have a number of characteristics in common. All went into print as a contribution to radicalism, most at the prompting of younger admirers with a romantic view of Spain. All, apart from Ó Duinnín, were communists to the last. Possibly because he left the party for activism 'in an individual kind of way', or possibly because he wrote in Irish, his second language, which provided a sense of distance from the text and concealment from all but the few who read it fluently, Ó Duinnín offered the most candid account, peppered with amusing anecdotes showing comrades to be more human than the stainless heroes of legend.[74] Monks excelled in describing front-line service, with a taut, gripping narrative.

All the autobiographers leave the reader wishing they had written more or had been challenged by what we know of the CPI since the opening of the Moscow archives. The memoirs said little on life within the party, on their authors' understanding of communism or on the Comintern and communist politics internationally. Glossing over the fractiousness of the Irish left in the 1930s, and the sharp shifts in Comintern policy, they portrayed the authors in relatively bland terms as idealistic radicals and victims of Catholic intolerance. On Spain, they dealt with military life more than politics and depicted the war as simply a struggle of democracy against fascism. All were republicans, and their 'authenticism' is evident to the trained eye, but it is also overlain with the 'modernism' of the post 1970s. Veterans who spoke at public meetings on the International Brigades from the 1980s said little on republicanism and presented themselves as anti-fascists more than communists, ever ready to support contemporary causes, and vindicated by the restoration of liberal democracy in Spain.

There was a consistency here in that in the 1980s, as in the 1930s, they were reflecting the impact of globalisation. Irish mentalities in the 1930s were deeply interested in Catholicism, nationalism, fascism or anti-fascism and communism or anti-communism because that's what being a European meant at a time when Europe was a Europe of the nations.

The Connolly Column had a nationalist heart and internationalist eyes. It was the product of the CPI and the Republican Congress, and the last hurrah of a socialist republicanism that can be traced to the foundation of the Irish Transport and General Workers' Union by Larkin in 1909. When Labour abandoned republicanism in 1922, the communists stepped in and the Comintern persuaded a section of the IRA to adopt its *Weltanschauung*; but from the separatist tradition the 'communist republicans' acquired a rooted approach to the world. They saw the war in Spain not simply as a clash of global ideologies but as a struggle of people like themselves – small holders, farm labourers and workers – against very familiar enemies: bishops, the army, and big landowners. Spain was the swansong of a politics throttled by clerical intolerance at home, and equally, an effort to sustain that politics in Ireland.

This 'authenticist' mentality has been lost sight of in the commemoration of the Connolly Column. The image of pre-European Union Ireland – a station on the highway between Europe and America, speaking the most global of languages, practising the most catholic of religions, with a large and far-flung diaspora touching almost each of its families – as introspective and isolated endures in public perceptions. And the Connolly Column, one of the great examples of Irish extroversion, has become subsumed into the myth. It's a common phenomenon when history becomes public property. Jewish brigadistas from Palestine were incorporated into an Israeli national narrative in the 1970s and 1980s; old representations of them as reds or renegades from the Zionist project yielded to reverence for the first Jews to resist the Holocaust.[75] Ireland differs in degree. Not even the rehabilitation of Veterans of the Abraham Lincoln Brigade in the US compares with the re-discovery and lionisation of the Connolly Column. Like the Lincoln Brigade, which has been invoked by such as President Ronald Reagan, who compared the doubtful legality of his help to the Contras with their aid to Spain, the Column's history has been appropriated by some implausible friends.[76] In the process, its communist republicanism has been sloughed off. Its published veterans did not deny their political pedigree, but those who celebrate them often have other values and other agendas. And agendas evolve. The rise of the new right has given a fresh significance to the International Brigades and seen them mobilised against fascism once again. Conversely, in Spain, conservatives continue to vilify the International Brigades as red assassins and seek to equate communism and Nazism. On 30 October 2019, at the instigation of Vox, Madrid City Council endorsed the designation of 23 August as a Day of European Remembrance of the Victims of Stalinism and Nazism. On 25 November, the council removed plaques in Madrid's East Cemetery bearing the names of 3,000 victims of Franco. The response was renewed cries of 'No pasarán'.

The Connolly Column would not object to being recycled. Times change and causes with them. If the brigadistas made history, they were political activists, not historians. The historian's job is to search for the truth. The activist wants to be relevant.

## NOTES

1. Langston Hughes, in Alvah Bessie and Albert Prago (ed), *Our Fight: Writings by Veterans of the Abraham Lincoln Brigade in Spain, 1936–1939* (New York, 1987), p. 360.
2. D. P. (Pat) Stephens, *A Memoir of the Spanish Civil War: An Armenian-Canadian in the Lincoln Battalion* (St John's, Nfl, 2000), p. 118–19; party characterisations are in RGASPI, f. 545, o. 6 files.
3. Marty proposed sending 1,500 to New Zealand, 1,000 to Australia, 500 to South Africa and 500 to Canada. RGASPI, Marty to Pollitt, undated, f. 545, o. 6, d. 13a.
4. NA, DFA, Art Ua Briain to Dublin, / February 1938, P10/55.
5. Ibid., John O'Reilly to his father, 5 October 1938, P10/55; Negro Committee to Aid Spain, *Salaria Kee: A Negro Nurse in Republican Spain* (New York, 1938).
6. *Irish Press*, 21 August 1936 gave prominence to the 'heroic' efforts to keep open the Irish legation in Madrid for two weeks after the outbreak of the civil war. The *Irish Independent* ignored it. Barry Whelan, *Ireland's Revolutionary Diplomat: A Biography of Leopold Kerney* (Notre Dame, In, 2019), pp 118, 122.
7. *Irish Independent*, 8 January 1937.
8. NA, DFA, Irish Legation, Paris, to Secretary, Dept of External Affairs, Dublin, 17 December 1936, P10/55. For Ó Briain's private papers on his time in Paris see NLI, Art Ó Briain papers, MS 8,449/7.
9. NA, DFA, Irish Legation, Paris, to Secretary, Dept of External Affairs, Dublin, 23, 28 December 1936; 29 December, Dept of External Affairs, Dublin, Irish Legation, Paris, P10/55; TNA, The International Brigade Association and Friends of Republican Spain: list of persons who fought in Spain, 1936–1939, KV5/127; Pádraig Manning, 'The Irish Self-Determination League of Great Britain (ISDL), 1919–31'; 'A mixing of social and national aspirations', in *History Ireland*, 27:6, (2019), pp 40–3.
10. NA, DFA, letter from Irish Legation, Paris, 17 June 1938, P10/55.
11. Ibid., Irish Minister, Paris Legation, to Secretary, Dept of External Affairs, Dublin, 5 February 1938, P10/55. Kennedy's military pay-book gave his employment as an 'instructor' under Major Johnson. RGASPI, f. 545, o. 6 files list Kennedy as attached to brigade staff.
12. Peter N. Carroll, *The Odyssey of the Abraham Lincoln Brigade: Americans in the Spanish Civil War* (Stanford, Ca, 1994), p. 137.
13. Information from Jim Carmody; NA, DFA, Irish Minister, Paris Legation, to Secretary, Dept of External Affairs, Dublin, 5 February 1938, P10/55.
14. NA, DFA, Irish Minister, Paris Legation, to Secretary, Dept of External Affairs, Dublin, 5 February 1938; Ua Briain to the British Consulate General, Marseilles, 8 February 1938, P10/55.
15. NA, DFA, British Consulate General, Marseilles to Irish Legation, Paris, 3 February 1938, and annotation, 4 February 1938; Irish Minister, Paris Legation, to Secretary, Dept of External Affairs, Dublin, 5 February 1938, P10/55.
16. NA, DFA, Irish Legation, Paris, 17 June 1938, P10/55; *Irish Post*, 14 July 1979.
17. NA, DFA, Irish Legation, Paris, C. C. Cremin, to the Dept of External Affairs, Dublin, 5 November 1938, P10/55.

18. NA, DFA, An tAthair Mícheál, OFM Cap, to Irish Legation, 4 April 1938; Irish Minister, Paris Legation, to French Minister of Foreign Affairs, 7 April 1938; Irish Minister, Paris Legation, to L. H. Kerney, 4 May 1938; Mrs Riordan [sic] to Irish Legation, undated [3 May 1938]; Irish Minister, Paris Legation, to Georges Bonnet, 3 May 1938; Irish Minister, Paris Legation, to Mrs Julia Riordan, 6 May, 27 June 1938, P10/55; Manus O'Riordan, '1939 Greaves-O'Riordan conversations in Cork', in *Irish Political Review* (November, 2010).

19. NA, DFA, Repatriation of volunteers from Spain, 3, 5 December 1938; Volunteers from Éire repatriated from Spain, undated; letter from Dublin to Paris Legation, 2 June 1939, P10/55; Michael O'Riordan, *Connolly Column: The Story of the Irishmen who fought in the Ranks of the International Brigades in the National–Revolutionary War of the Spanish People 1936–1939* (Dublin, 1979), pp 136–9; Arthur H. Landis, *Death in the Olive Groves: American Volunteers in the Spanish Civil War, 1936–39* (New York, 1988), p. 219.

20. Manus O'Riordan, 'Irish and Jewish volunteers in the Spanish Anti-Fascist war', lecture, Irish Jewish Museum, Dublin, 15 November 1987. Bob Doyle, *Memorias de un Rebelde sin Pausa* (Madrid, 2002*)*; *Brigadista: An Irishman's Fight Against Fascism* (Dublin, 2006), pp 71–86. Lemon was so often cited as 'Lennon' that it is tempting to conclude he may have been using it as a cover name, or simply tired of correcting people.

21. Doyle, *Brigadista*, pp 90–1.

22. H. Gustav Klaus, *Strong Words Brave Deeds: The Poetry, Life and Times of Thomas O'Brien, Volunteer in the Spanish Civil War* (Dublin, 1994), pp 24–5; Bill Alexander, *British Volunteers for Liberty: Spain 1936–39* (London, 1982), pp 242–4; William Rust, *Britons in Spain: The History of the British Battalion of the XVth International Brigade* (London, 1939), pp 208–10.

23. Carroll, *The Odyssey of the Abraham Lincoln Brigade*, p. 211.

24. O'Riordan, *Connolly Column*, p. 139.

25. Peter O'Connor, *A Soldier of Liberty: Recollections of a Socialist and Anti-Fascist Fighter* (Dublin, 1996), pp 31–2.

26. Ibid., pp 30–1.

27. Uinseann MacEoin (ed), *Survivors: The Story of Ireland's Struggle as Told Through Some of Her Outstanding Living People Recalling Events from the Days of Davitt, Through James Connolly, Brugha, Collins, de Valera, Liam Mellows, and Rory O'Connor to the Present Time* (Dublin, 1987), p. 14.

28. NLI, Irish Trade Union Congress, *Annual Report* (1939), pp 181–3.

29. Uinseann MacEoin, *The IRA in the Twilight Years, 1923–1948* (Dublin, 1997), pp 760, 811–12.

30. Seán Ó Maolbhríde, 'The Curragh communists', in *Irish Times*, 16 June 1971; Manus O'Riordan, 'The spy who grew up with the bold: the Irish republican education of Sir John Betjeman', in *Irish Political Review*, March–April 2010, pp 15–17, 12–14, 15–20.

31. On the Goold-Verschoyles, see Barry McLoughlin, *Left to the Wolves: Irish Victims of Stalinist Terror* (Dublin, 2007).

32. O'Riordan, *Connolly Column*, p. 139; John Quinn, *Irish Volunteers for Spain: A Short History of the Northern Irish Volunteers Who Fought in Defence of the Republican Government in Spain, 1936–39* (Belfast, 2004), p. 111; Tim Pat Coogan, *The IRA* (London, 1995), pp 147–8.

33. We are obliged to Douglas McIldoon for these details.
34. See Klaus, *Strong Words, Brave Deeds*; O'Connor, *A Soldier of Liberty*, p. 35.
35. Military Archives, Military Service Pension, MSP34REF34150.
36. Leo Keohane, *Captain Jack White: Imperialism, Anarchism, and the Irish Citizen Army* (Dublin, 2014), pp 239–40.
37. TNA, The International Brigade Association and Friends of Republican Spain, KV5/118, KV5/129.
38. MML, IBA, Box D-7: Material from the Imperial War Museum, A/2, list of Irish in the British battalion; TNA, British Consul General, Barcelona, report, 24 November 1936; FO 371/20587, p. 19; John McGuffin and Joseph Mulheron, *Charles 'Nomad' McGuinness: Being a True Account of the Amazing Adventures of a Derryman, Pirate, IRA Man, Gun Runner, Polar Explorer, Adventurer, Mercenary, Rogue, Escaper and Hero* (Derry, 2002), pp 137, 150–59; *Irish Independent*, 2–8 January 1937.
39. McGuffin and Mulheron, *Charles 'Nomad' McGuinness*, pp 150–218; 'Pax Ó Faoláin' in MacEoin, *Survivors*, pp 142–3.
40. NA, DFA, Irish legation, Paris to Dublin, 17 June 1938, P10/55.
41. Brendan Moroney, 'Twenty months in the International Brigade', in *Hibernia*, September 1938, pp 23–5; *Irish Post*, 14 July, 11 August 1979, 13 October, 28 November, 12 December 1981; 23 October, 4 December 1982, 14 May, 1 October 1983; 2 November 1985; *Clare Champion*, 21 December 1979.
42. *Irish Times*, 13 April 1976.
43. Eoghan Ó Duinnín, *La Niña Bonita agus An Róisín Dubh: Cuimhní Cinn ar Chogadh Cathartha na Spáinne* (Baile Átha Cliath, 1986), p. 115. See also Anna Kathryn Kendrick, '"On guard with the Junipers": Ewart Milne and Irish literary dissent in the Spanish Civil War' (Senior thesis, Harvard, Ma, 2009).
44. O'Riordan, *Connolly Column*, p. 139.
45. TNA, The International Brigade Association and Friends of Republican Spain, KV5/117–131.
46. Paul Vincent Carroll, *The Wise Have Not Spoken: A Drama in Three Acts* (London, 1947), p. 6.
47. Among British volunteers, the closest to an embittered memoir is Jason Gurney's *Crusade in Spain* (London, 1974), which stands out for that very reason.
48. Interview with Mick Barry, Waterford, 10 July 2004.
49. Emmet O'Connor, 'Behind the legend: Waterfordmen in the International Brigades in the Spanish Civil War', in *Decies: Journal of the Waterford Archaeological & Historical Society*, 61 (2005), pp 267–85; information from Jim Carmody.
50. Doyle, *Brigadista*, pp 104–5.
51. TNA, The International Brigade Association and Friends of Republican Spain, KV5/126; *Irish Times*, 9 August 2003.
52. *Irish Press*, 3, 10 April, 24–5 June 1943; *Irish Independent*, 24–6 June 1943; TNA, The International Brigade Association and Friends of Republican Spain, KV5/127.
53. NA, DFA 244/22, Thomas Gunning.
54. McLoughlin, *Fighting for Republican Spain*, pp 115–31.
55. Seán Cronin, *Frank Ryan: The Search for the Republic* (Dublin, 1980), pp 237–47.

56. TNA, KV 6/81 Clissmann, interrogation, 30 May 1946.
57. Cronin, *Frank Ryan*, p. 188.
58. Abwehr-Tagebuch, entries 3-8 August 1940 (copy in the possession of Barry McLoughlin).
59. Ibid., entry 3 August 1940.
60. Her Majesty's Stationery Office (eds), *Documents on German Foreign Policy, D: 13* (London, 1954), pp 363–6.
61. TNA, KV 6/79, Hoven; KV6/80, 81, Clissmann.
62. Ryan is labelled a collaborator in Fearghal McGarry, *Frank Ryan* (Dundalk, 2002), pp 58–73.
63. The plaque reads: 'In memory of Gabriel Lee who died fighting with the Christian forces in Spain on 23 March 1937 RIP', https://comeheretome.com/2018/08/21/gabriel-lee-1904-37-and-eoin-oduffys-irish-brigade/. Accessed 24 November 2019.
64. The Irish memorials (with date of erection and dedication, if specific) are located in Achill Island (1984 to Tommy Patten); Kilgarvan, County Kerry (1989 to Michael Lehane); Liberty Hall, Dublin (1991); Unite Hall, Waterford (1994 to the 11 local brigadistas); Unite hall, Dublin (1996); Unite hall, Clonmel (1997 to Amalgamated Transport and General Workers' Union solidarity with Spain, 1936–9); Coalisland (2003 to Charlie Donnelly); Dungannon District Council Offices (2004 to Charlie Donnelly); The Mall, Waterford (2004 to the 11 local brigadistas); Burncourt, County Tipperary (2005 to Kit Conway); the John Hewitt bar, Belfast (2006); Milltown cemetery, Belfast (2006 to 'Irish republicans who fought against fascism' in Spain); Leeson Street, Belfast (2006 to Paddy McAllister); Writers' Square, Belfast (2007); Inistioge (2007 to the four Kilkenny brigadistas); Inistioge (2008 to George Brown); Unite Hall, Belfast (2009); Republican Memorial Garden, Short Strand, Belfast (2010 to Liam Tumilson and Jim Stranney); Wexford (2011 to Peter Daly); Connolly Books, Dublin (2012); Slieve Foy, Louth (2013 to the seven local brigadistas); Aughnacloy (2013 to Ben Murray); Falls Road, Belfast (2013); Inchicore (2013 to the six local volunteers); Derry (2013 to north west volunteers); Falls Road, Belfast (2013 to Dick O'Neill and William Beattie); Limerick (2014 to local brigadistas); Shankill Road, Belfast (2014 to seven local brigadistas); Omeath (2014 to seven local brigadistas); Falls Road, Belfast (2014); Belfast City Hall (2015); Derry (2015); Dundalk (2016 to seven local brigadistas); Bottomstown, Limerick (2017 to Frank Ryan); Castlebar Peace Park (2018 to Tommy Patton [sic] and David Walsh); Dromore West, Sligo (2018 to Ruth Ormesby); Dublin (2018); UCD (2018 to Charlie Donnelly); Inchicore (2018); Dublin (2018 to Jack Nalty); Dublin (2019 to Bob Doyle); Kildare (2019 to Frank Conroy); Ennis (2019 to Michael Russell).
65. Emmet O'Connor, 'Anti-communism in twentieth century Ireland', in *Twentieth Century Communism: A Journal of International History*, 6 (2014), pp 59–81.
66. O'Riordan, *Connolly Column* (2005 ed.), p. 4.
67. www.international-brigades.org.uk/memorials. Accessed 8 June 2020.
68. Martin Lynch, *Pictures of Tomorrow* (1994), published in *Pictures of Tomorrow and Rinty* (Belfast, 2003), p. 61.
69. *Irish Times*, 3 January 1994; 'A drama inspired by the Irish Brigaders', in *The Volunteer*, Vol. XV:1, 2, Fall 1994; Pat McEvoy, 'Minister and minstrel: a critical analysis of the plays of Jim Nolan' (MA, Waterford Institute of Technology, 2014), pp 67–77.

70. Leslie H. Daiken (comp), *Good-Bye, Twilight: Songs of the Struggle in Ireland* (London, 1936), xi–xviii.
71. Michael McInerney, *Peadar O'Donnell: Irish Social Rebel* (Dublin, 1974), p. 171. The book is based 'almost entirely' on interviews with O'Donnell.
72. Doyle, *Brigadista*, pp 140–7.
73. For the extensive range of publications, varying from detailed scholarly studies to short appreciations, see www.geocities.com/IrelandSCW/. The memoirs are Joe Monks, *With the Reds in Andalusia* (London, 1985); Ó Duinín, *La Niña Bonita agus an Róisín Dubh*; O'Connor, *A Soldier of Liberty*; Doyle, *Memorias de un Rebelde sin Pausa* and *Brigadista*; 'Frank Edwards' in MacEoin, *Survivors*, pp 1–20; and 'Michael O'Riordan of Cork City and the International Brigade', MacEoin, *The IRA in the Twilight Years, 1923–1948*, pp 751–66. O'Riordan has also been interviewed in newspapers and written for CPI journals on Spain.
74. The quote is from McInerney, *Peadar O'Donnell*, p. 181.
75. Raanan Rein, 'A belated inclusion: Jewish volunteers in the Spanish Civil War and their place in the Israeli national narrative', *Project Muse*, https://muse.jhu.edu/article/460757/summary. Accessed 17 June 2020.
76. Carroll, *The Odyssey of the Abraham Lincoln Brigade*, pp 374–5.

## Appendix: List of the Irish in the International Brigades

| Name | Born | Born in Co. | Came from | Politics | Arrival | Fate | Remarks |
|---|---|---|---|---|---|---|---|
| ANDERSON Samuel | 1904 | Down | Canada | CPCan | 23.10.1937 | Survivor | Repat. 1938 |
| ASH Francis | 1909 | Down | UK | CPGB | 11.01.1938 | Open | Reported as deserter March 1938 |
| BAILIE Archie | 1912 | Antrim | UK | | 02.10.1937 | Survivor | POW |
| BAMBRICK Arthur | 1915 | Longford | Canada | CPCan | 18.10.1937 | Survivor | Sergeant, repat. 1938 |
| BARR Victor | 1916 | Antrim | UK | YCL | 12.01.1938 | Survivor | POW |
| BARRY William | ? | ? | Australia | CPAUS | 1936 | KIA | Madrid fatality |
| BEATTIE William | 1908 | Antrim | UK | CPGB | 10.12.1936 | KIA | Brunete fatality, July 1937 |
| BLACK William | 1913 | Antrim | UK | | | Survivor | Repat. 1937 |
| BLAKE Patrick | 1916 | Dublin | IRL | IRC | 03.01.1937 | Survivor | Repat. 1938/39 |
| BONAR Henry | 1897 | Dublin | UK | | 07.01.1937 | DOW | Madrid fatality |
| BONAR Hugh | 1907 | Donegal | IRL | | 14.12.1936 | KIA | Jarama fatality, 05.04.1937 |
| BOURNE Edward J. | 1908 | Antrim | IRL | LP | 10.11.1936 | Survivor | Repat. 1937 |
| BOYLE Daniel | 1906 | Antrim | IRL | IRA, CPI | 07.12.1936 | KIA | Ebro fatality |
| BOYLE George | 1900 | Antrim | UK | CPGB | 21.12.1936 | Survivor | Repat. 1937 |
| BOYLE Philip | 1903 | Donegal | UK | CPGB | 20.09.1937 | Survivor | Normal repat. 1938 |
| BRADY Patrick | 1904 | Limerick | UK | CPGB | 07.01.1937 | Survivor | Repat. 1937 |
| BRENNAN Michael | 1910 | Kilkenny | IRL | CPI | ? | Survivor | No further data |
| BRENNAN Michael | 1919 | Kilkenny | IRL | | 11.02.1937 | Survivor | Repat. 1937 |
| BROWN George | 1906 | Kilkenny | UK | CPGB | 31.01.1937 | KIA | Brunete fatality |
| BROWN Michael | 1900 | Kilkenny | UK | CPGB | 03.12.1936 | Survivor | Deserted early 1937, home. |
| BROWN Samuel | 1912 | Antrim | Canada | | 20.01.1937 | Survivor | Repat. July 1938. |
| BURGESS William | 1910 | Cork | USA | CPUS | 24.08.1938 | Survivor | Normal repat. 1938 |
| BURKE Patrick | 1897 | Mayo | UK | | 21.01.1937 | Survivor | Repat. 1937 |
| BYRNE Edward | 1914 | Dublin | IRL | | 09.09.1937 | Survivor | Repat. 1938 |
| BYRNE J.J. | ? | ? | ? | | ? | KIA | Jarama fatality |

| Name | Born | Place | Country | Affiliation | Date | Status | Notes |
|---|---|---|---|---|---|---|---|
| BYRNE Joseph Leo | 1913 | Dublin | UK | CPGB | 02.02.1938 | Survivor | POW |
| BYRNE Patrick C. | 1899 | Dublin | Spain | CPI | 06.12.1937 | Survivor | POW |
| CAMPBELL James | 1902 | Derry | UK | | 27.01.1937 | Survivor | Expelled from Spain |
| CAMPBELL John | 1910 | Antrim | UK | | 22.01.1937 | KIA | Jarama fatality |
| CARBERRY Dominic | 1905 | Dublin | Canada | | 26.12.1937 | Survivor | Repatriated 1938, returned to Ireland |
| COADY Denis | 1903 | Dublin | IRL | | 08.12.1936 | KIA | Madrid fatality |
| COCHRANE Vincent | 1913 | Dublin | UK | CPGB | 17.02.1937 | Survivor | Repat. 1937 |
| COCHRANE Thomas | 1885 | Antrim | Canada | CPCan | 15.06.1937 | Survivor | Repat. 1938 |
| COFFEY Patrick | 1911 | Longford | IRL | | 14.04.1938 | Survivor | Rejected at Figueras |
| COLMAN John Charles | 1906 | Cork | IRL | IRA | 22.12.1936 | Survivor | Repat. 1937 |
| COLEMAN John | 1909 | Antrim | UK | | 18.11.1937 | Survivor | Normal repat. 1938 |
| COLLINS William | 1911 | Antrim | UK | | 14.01.1938 | Survivor | POW |
| CONROY Frank | 1914 | Kildare | IRL | IRA, CPI | 16.12.1916 | KIA | Cordoba fatality |
| CONWAY Christopher | 1899 | Tipperary | IRL | IRA, CPI | 12.12.1936 | DOW | Jarama fatality. Company C.O. |
| COX John Colum | 1917 | Dublin | IRL | IRC | 17.01.1937 | Survivor | Repat. 1937 |
| CULLEN Hugh O'Brien | 1915 | Down | UK | | 18.11.1937 | Survivor | Deserted, home, left Spain May 1938 |
| CUMMINGS James | 1899 | Dublin | IRL | CPI | 13.12.1936 | Survivor | Repat. 1937 |
| CURLEY Patrick | 1890 | Dublin | UK | | 22.12.1936 | KIA | Jarama fatality |
| CURTIN Edward | 1909 | Tipperary | UK | | 05.01.1937 | Survivor | Possible deserter |
| DALY Peter | 1903 | Wexford | UK | IRA | 16.12.1936 | DOW | Captain, C.O. British battalion. Aragon fatality, died 05.09.1937. |
| DAVIS William | 1909 | Dublin | UK | CPGB | 1936 | KIA | Brunete fatality |
| DELANEY Andrew | 1912 | Louth | USA | CPUS | 12.1937 | Executed | POW, executed by fascists |
| DELANEY Thomas | 1919 | Kilkenny | IRL | | 11.02.1937 | Survivor | Repat. 1937 |
| DEVITT Thomas | 1903 | Dublin | Canada | CPCan | 30.03.1938 | Survivor | Repat. 1939 |
| DIGGES Alexander | 1914 | London | IRL | CPI | 14.04.1938 | Survivor | Repat. 1939 |
| DOLAN John | 1897 | ? | UK | | 12.1936 | KIA | Jarama fatality, 27.02.1937 |
| DOMEGAN James | 1916 | Antrim | UK | CPGB | 14.04.1938 | KIA | Ebro fatality |
| DONALD James | | Derry | UK | | 30.01.1937 | KIA | Aragon fatality, March 1938 |
| DONNELLY Charles | 1914 | Tyrone | UK | IRC | 25.12.1936 | KIA | Jarama fatality, killed 27.02.1937 |
| DONOVAN Tom | 1914 | Cork | UK | | 10.12.1936 | Survivor | 11th Brigade; ILP detachment, Huesca front |

| Name | Born | Born in Co. | Came from | Politics | Arrival | Fate | Remarks |
|---|---|---|---|---|---|---|---|
| DOOLEY Hugh | 1910 | Antrim | UK | | 01.01.1937 | Survivor | Repat. 1937 |
| DORAN Gerry | 1911 | Antrim | IRL | | 12.1936 | Survivor | Repat. 1937 because of wounds |
| DORAN Lester A. | 1913 | Louth | UK | | 01.01.1937 | KIA | Jarama fatality |
| DOWLING John | 1909 | Kilkenny | IRL | CPI | 11.02.1937 | Survivor | Repat. August 1938 |
| DOWNING Eugene | 1913 | Dublin | IRL | IRC, CPI | 30.03.1938 | Survivor | Repat. 1938 |
| DOYLE Gerard | 1907 | Limerick | UK | CPGB | 11.02.1937 | Survivor | Sergeant, POW |
| DOYLE Lawrence | 1902 | Dublin | IRL | | 21.01.1937 | Open | Possible deserter |
| DOYLE Robert | 1916 | Dublin | UK | CPI | 08.12.1937 | Survivor | POW |
| DRURY-FULLER Geo. | 1918 | Kerry | UK | CPGB | 24.02.1937 | KIA | Medical services, runner, Ebro fatality |
| DUFF Patrick | 1902 | Dublin | IRL | CPI | 08.12.1936 | Survivor | Sergeant, repat. 1937, returned to Spain March 1938, repat. 1939 |
| EDWARDS Frank | 1907 | Antrim | IRL | IRA, IRC, CPI | 15.12.1936 | Survivor | Platoon leader, repat. 1937. |
| FENNELLY William | 1897 | Laois | UK | IRA | 1936 | Survivor | Repat. 1937, returned, deserted |
| FINNEGAN John | 1909 | Monaghan | Canada | CPCan | 21.07.1937 | MIA | Missing in action 03.04.1938 |
| FLANAGAN Terence | 1912 | Dublin | IRL | IRA, CPI | 21.12.1936 | Survivor | Repat. 1937 |
| FLYNN Jack | 1914 | Derry | UK | | 07.01.1937 | Survivor | POW, captured at Jarama, released May 1937 |
| FOLEY James | 1903 | Dublin | UK | | 23.01.1937 | KIA | Cordoba fatality |
| FOX Anthony | 1914 | Dublin | IRL | IRA | 1936 | KIA | Cordoba fatality |
| FULTON Albert | 1905 | Antrim | Australia | CPAUS | 28.04.1938 | Survivor | Repat. 1938 |
| GALLAGHER Edward | 1898 | Derry | UK | | 1936 | Survivor | Repat. 1939 |
| GIBSON Patrick | 1906 | Dublin | IRL | IRC | 16.05.1937 | Survivor | Lieutenant, repat. 1939 |
| GLACKEN Patrick | 1913 | Donegal | UK | LP | 29.09.1937 | KIA | Desertec, later Teruel fatality |
| GOFF John (Sean) | 1910 | Dublin | IRL | | 11.11.1936 | Survivor | Repat. 1937 |
| GOLDING Patrick J. | 1904 | Offaly | UK | CPGB | 24.02.1937 | Survivor | Repat. 1938 |
| GORMAN George | 1900 | Derry | UK | | 03.05.1938 | KIA | Ebro fatality |
| GOULDNEY Fredrick G. | 1909 | Dublin | IRL | | 28.12.1936 | Survivor | Left Spain 1937 |
| GREEN Leo | 1909 | Dublin | IRL | | 16.12.1936 | KIA | Jarama fatality, killed 12.02.1937 |
| HAINES Joseph | 1915 | Dublin | IRL | | 28.12.1936 | Survivor | Repat. 1937 |

# Appendix

| Name | Born | County | Country | Affiliation | Date | Status | Notes |
|---|---|---|---|---|---|---|---|
| HAIRE William | 1902 | Armagh | UK | | 02.01.1937 | Survivor | Deserted, caught, repat. 1938 |
| HALL Patrick | 1912 | Down | UK | IRA | 14.01.1937 | Survivor | Deserted after Brunete to UK |
| HAMILL Patrick | 1905 | Cavan | USA | CPUS | 04.01.1937 | Open | Repat. 1937 |
| HAUGHEY James | 1919 | Armagh | UK | | 16.05.1938 | Survivor | Lieutenant, POW, released, repat. 1939, killed WW2 |
| HAYES Frederick | 1888 | Offaly | UK | | 03.12.1936 | Survivor | Repat. 1937 |
| HAYES Thomas | 1893 | Dublin | IRL | IRA | 19.12.1936 | Survivor | Repat. 1937 |
| HEANEY John | 1913 | Antrim | Canada | | 20.09.1937 | Survivor | Deserted, caught, repat. 1938 |
| HEANEY Thomas | 1919 | Galway | UK | | ? | Survivor | POW, captured March 1938 |
| HENRY William | 1896 | Antrim | IRL | NILP, CPI | 19.12.1936 | KIA | Jarama fatality |
| HEPBURN Robert | 1913 | Kildare | UK | | 06.02.1937 | Survivor | Deserted to France July 1938 |
| HILLEN James Isaac | 1906 | Greenock | IRL | CPI | 10.12.1936 | Survivor | Lived in Ireland. Repat. 1937 |
| HILLIARD Robert | 1904 | Kerry | UK | CPGB | 22.12.1936 | DOW | Jarama fatality. |
| HOLDEN Denis | 1891 | Carlow | UK | | 19.12.1936 | Survivor | Repat. 1937 |
| HUNT John | 1911 | Waterford | UK | IRA, IRC, CPGB | 21.12.1936 | Survivor | Repat. August 1938 |
| HUNT Vincent | 1906 | Tipperary | UK | | 11.1936 | KIA | Ambulance driver, Brunete fatality |
| HUNTER Hugh | 1904 | Antrim | IRL | CPI | 30.03.1938 | Survivor | Repat. 1938 |
| JOHNSON William | 1903 | Down | UK | | 05.01.1937 | Survivor | Repat. 1937 |
| JOHNSTONE John | 1900 | Antrim | UK | CPGB | 10.03.1938 | Survivor | Repat. December 1938 |
| JONES James J. | 1905 | Dublin | UK | CPGB | 27.01.1937 | KIA | Ebro fatality |
| JONES Thomas | 1910 | Wexford | UK | | 1936 | MIA | Brunete fatality |
| KEENAN Patrick | 1908 | Dublin | IRL | | 22.12.1936 | Survivor | Deserted February 1937, home |
| KEENAN William | 1901 | Down | Canada | | 04.12.1937 | KIA | Ebro fatality |
| KELLY Christopher | 1906 | Dublin | USA | | 24.08.1937 | Open | Deserted, fate unknown |
| KELLY John | 1914 | Waterford | UK | | 12.08.1937 | Survivor | Normal repat. 1938 |
| KELLY Joseph | 1898 | Donegal | Canada | CPCan | 27.03.1937 | Survivor | Lieutenant, repat. 1938 |
| KELLY Joseph M. | 1918 | Dublin | UK | | 20.12.1936 | KIA | Brunete fatality |
| KELLY Michael | 1905 | Galway | UK | IRA, IRC | 15.12.1936 | KIA | Brunete fatality |
| KENNEDY David | 1915 | Antrim | UK | LP | 27.02.1938 | Survivor | POW |

| Name | Born | Born in Co. | Came from | Politics | Arrival | Fate | Remarks |
|---|---|---|---|---|---|---|---|
| KENNEDY Harry | 1909 | Waterford | UK | | 06.09.1937 | Survivor | Deserted, home |
| KERR Thomas | 1910 | Antrim | UK | SPNI | 08.12.1937 | DOS | Deserted, died of typhoid |
| LARMOUR James | 1910 | Antrim | UK | CPGB | 18.12.1936 | Survivor | Repat. 1937 |
| LAUGHRAN William | 1903 | Antrim | UK | | 10.12.1936 | KIA | Brunete fatality. |
| LEESON George | 1907 | Cork | UK | CPGB | 07.01.1937 | Survivor | POW, released Sept. 1937 |
| LEHANE Michael | 1908 | Kerry | IRL | CPI | 12.12.1936 | Survivor | Repat. 1937, returned, killed WW2 |
| LEMON John | 1918 | Waterford | UK | | 12.08.1937 | Survivor | POW, repat. 1939 |
| LEVITAS Maurice | 1917 | Dublin | UK | CPGB | 18.01.1938 | Survivor | POW, repat. 1939 |
| LORD James | 1916 | Antrim | UK | | 23.03.1938 | Survivor | Normal repat. 1938 |
| LOWRY Joseph | 1906 | Armagh | UK | | 10.12.1936 | Survivor | Repat. 1937 |
| LYNCH John Joseph | 1917 | Derry | UK | | 15.01.1937 | Survivor | Repat. 1937 |
| LYNCH Patrick J. | 1918 | ? | UK | | 28.12.1937 | Survivor | Deserter |
| LYNCH Thomas | 1913 | Dublin | UK | | 22.12.1936 | Survivor | Repat. 1937 |
| MADERO Alex | 1911 | Louth | UK | | 22.12.1937 | DIA | Shot in accident |
| MAGILL Joseph | 1907 | Armagh | Canada | CPCan | 10.01.1937 | Survivor | Deserted caught, repat. 1939 |
| MALONE John | 1912 | Dublin | Canada | CPCan | 01.12.1937 | Survivor | Repat. 1939 |
| MARTIN Chris | 1907 | Cork | UK | | 25.01.1938 | Survivor | Normal repat. 1938 |
| MARTIN Samuel | 1912 | Antrim | IRL | IRA, CPI | 14.04.1937 | Open | Deserted at Brunete |
| MAY Michael | 1916 | Dublin | IRL | CPI, IRC, IRA | 1936 | KIA | Cordoba fatality, 28.12.1936 |
| MC ALEENAN Richard | 1909 | Down | UK | | 16.12.1937 | Survivor | Normal repat. |
| MC ALISTER Patrick | 1909 | Antrim | Canada | CPCan | 02.12.1937 | Survivor | Normal repat. 1938 |
| MC CABE John | | Louth | UK | | ? | Survivor | Rejected Figueras |
| MC CALLEN James | 1914 | Antrim | IRL | | 13.10.1937 | Survivor | Rejected Figueras |
| MC CARTHY Cormac | 1893 | Canada | Australia | | 04.06.1937 | Survivor | Deserted to France, April 1938 |
| MC CHRYSTAL William | 1905 | Derry | Canada | CPCan | 14.08.1937 | Survivor | POW, repat. 1939 |
| MC CLURE George | 1894 | Down | UK | CPGB | 27.01.1937 | Survivor | Normal repat. 1938 |
| MC DADE William | 1897 | Antrim | UK | | 22.12.1936 | Survivor | Adjutant to Tom Wintringham at Jarama. Repat. 1937 |

## Appendix 385

| | | | | | | | |
|---|---|---|---|---|---|---|---|
| MC ELLIGOTT John | 1905 | Kerry | Canada | CPCan | 21.10.1937 | Survivor | Repat 1939 |
| MC ELROY Albert | 1915 | Fermanagh | IRL | | ? | KIA | Jarama fatality |
| MC ELROY Patrick | 1911 | Dublin | IRL | IRA | 05.01.1937 | Survivor | Repat. 1937 |
| MC GOVERN Bernard | 1914 | Leitrim | ? | | 10.01.1937 | Survivor | Probable deserter |
| MC GRATH Henry | 1902 | Antrim | UK | CPI | 10.11.1936 | KIA | Ebro fatality |
| MC GRATH Michael | 1898 | Cork | UK | IRA | 23.01.1938 | Survivor | POW, repat. 1938 |
| MC GREGOR William | 1914 | Dublin | IRL | IRA, CPI | 14.04.1938 | KIA | Co. Commissar, Ebro fatality |
| MC GROTTY Eamonn | 1911 | Derry | UK | | 22.12.1936 | KIA | Jarama fatality |
| MC GUINNESS Chas. | 1893 | Derry | IRL | | 1936 | Survivor | Deserted 1936, home |
| MC GUINNESS Patk. | 1910 | Dublin | UK | CPGB | 18.11.1937 | Survivor | Deserted, caught, repat. 1938 |
| MC GUIRE Patrick | 1900 | Monaghan | Canada | | 25.04.1937 | Survivor | Repat. 1939 |
| MC KEEFREY James | 1912 | Antrim | UK | | 05.05.1938 | Survivor | Repat. 1938 |
| MC LARNON Alan | 1907 | Armagh | UK | IRC | 23.12.1936 | Survivor | Repat. 1938 |
| MC LAUGHLIN Matthew | 1910 | Derry | Canada | CPCan | 21.06.1937 | KIA | Aragon fatality, March 1938 |
| MC LAUGHLIN Ml. | 1890 | ? | USA | CPUS | 08.04.1937 | Survivor | No further data |
| MC LAUGHLIN Patk. | 1902 | Donegal | UK | CPUS | 01.01.1937 | Survivor | Repat. Feb. 1938 |
| MC PARLAND Eugene | 1915 | Armagh | UK | | 25.07.1937 | Survivor | Repat. August 1938 |
| MEEHAN John | 1912 | Galway | IRL | | 17.09.1936 | DOW | Cordoba front fatality |
| MITCHELL Charles | 1914 | Dublin | UK | | 22.12.1936 | Survivor | Deserted, caught, repat. 1939 |
| MOLYNEAUX Andrew | 1906 | Antrim | Canada | CPCan | 11.07.1937 | Survivor | Sergeant, repat. 1939 |
| MONKS Patrick Jos. | 1914 | Dublin | UK | CPI | 15.12.1936 | Survivor | Repat. 1937 |
| MORAN Maurice | 1910 | Mayo | USA | CPUS | 06.01.1937 | Survivor | Repat. 1937 |
| MORONEY Brendan | 1913 | Clare | UK | | 10.12.1936 | Survivor | Deserted, home 1938 |
| MORRISON William | 1910 | Antrim | UK | | 22.12.1936 | Survivor | Repat. 1938 |
| MURPHY James | ? | ? | UK | | 15.09.1937 | KIA | Aragon fatality 1938 |
| MURPHY John | 1902 | Derry | UK | | 29.08.1937 | Open | No further data |
| MURPHY John(Liverpool) | 1909 | ? | UK | | 15.01.1937 | Open | No further data |
| MURPHY J.Pat. | 1914 | ? | UK | | 07.01.1937 | Open | |
| MURPHY Patrick (Cardiff) | 1897 | ? | UK | | 15.09.1936 | Survivor | Repat. 1938 |
| MURPHY Patrick | 1915 | Antrim | UK | | 04.02.1937 | Survivor | Deserter, allowed leave Spain May 1938 |
| MURPHY Thomas | 1903 | Monaghan | UK | CPGB | 04.02.1937 | Survivor | Repat. 1938 |

| Name | Born | Born in Co. | Came from | Politics | Arrival | Fate | Remarks |
|---|---|---|---|---|---|---|---|
| MURRAY Ben | 1895 | Fermanagh | UK | CPI, CPGB | 09.02.1937 | KIA | Aragon fatality, March 1938 |
| MURRAY Joseph | 1886 | Antrim | UK | CPGB | 23.12.1936 | Survivor | Repat. 1937 |
| MURRAY Joseph | 1911 | Dublin | UK | CPGB | 02.12.1937 | MIA | Missing Aragon, March 1938 |
| NALTY Jack | 1902 | Galway | IRL | IRA, IRC, CPI | 16.12.1936 | KIA | Lieutenant, repat. 1937, returned to Spain in March 1938. Ebro fatality, 23.09.1938 |
| NOLAN Michael | 1910 | Dublin | IRL | IRC | 12.12.1936 | KIA | Cordoba fatality |
| O'BEIRNE James | 1887 | Cavan | IRL | IRA | 05.12.1936 | Survivor | Repat. 1937 |
| O'BEIRNE John | 1899 | Galway | USA | CPUS | 06.09.1937 | Survivor | POW, repat. 1939 |
| O'BOYLE Patrick | 1894 | Antrim | USA | CPUS | 19.11.1937 | Survivor | Repat. 25.10.1938 |
| O'BRIEN Francis D. | 1909 | Louth | UK | CPGB | 09.09.1937 | KIA | Sergeant, Teruel fatality, March 1938. Ebro fatality, |
| O'BRIEN John | 1910 | ? | UK | IRA | 03.12.1936 | Survivor | Repat. 1937 |
| O'BRIEN Thomas | 1914 | Dublin | IRL | IRC, CPI | 14.04.1938 | Survivor | Normal repat. 1938 |
| O'BRIEN Thomas | 1909 | Dublin | UK | | 16.12.1936 | Survivor | Deserted, caught, repat. 1938 |
| O'BRIEN Thomas T. | 1911 | Dublin | UK | CPGB | 16.12.1936 | KIA | Jarama fatality |
| O'CONNOR James | 1905 | Dublin | Canada | CPCan | 14.08.1937 | KIA | Aragon fatality 17.03.1938 |
| O'CONNOR Peter | 1912 | Waterford | UK | IRA, IRC, CPI, CPGB | 21.12.1936 | Survivor | Repat. 1937. Sergeant |
| O'DAIRE Patrick | 1905 | Donegal | UK | CPGB | 05.12.1936 | Survivor | Captain, C.O. British Battalion, repat. Sept. 1938 |
| O'DONNELL Vincent | 1904 | Dublin | UK | CPGB | 26.01.1937 | Survivor | POW |
| O'DONNELL Hugh | 1899 | Donegal | UK | CPGB | 12.08.1936 | Survivor | POW |
| O'DONNELL John | 1915 | Tipperary | UK | | 22.12.1937 | Survivor | Deserted, left Spain April 1938 |
| O'DONNELL William | 1913 | Tipperary | UK | | 11.08.1937 | Survivor | Repat. 12.05.1938 |
| O'DONOVAN Michael | 1914 | Westmeath | UK | | 22.12.1937 | Survivor | Repat. 1937 |
| O'FARRELL Thomas | 1902 | Dublin | UK | | 20.12.1936 | Survivor | Deserted, caught, POW |
| O'FLAHERTY Thomas | 1914 | Kerry | USA | CPUS | 20.02.1938 | KIA | Ebro fatality |
| O'HANLON Wm. | 1913 | Antrim | UK | IRA, IRC | 16.09.1937 | Survivor | Normal repat. 1938 |
| O'NEILL Richard | 1910 | Antrim | UK | NILP, CPI | 10.12.1936 | KIA | Platoon leader, Jarama fatality |
| O'NEILL Homer Stewart | 1900 | Down | Canada | CPCan | 30.03.1937 | KIA | Brunete fatality, real surname Homer |

## Appendix 387

| Name | Birth | County | Country | Party | Date | Status | Notes |
|---|---|---|---|---|---|---|---|
| O'REGAN James F. | 1916 | Cork | IRL | IRA, CPI | 30.03.1938 | Survivor | Normal repat. 1938 |
| O'REGAN James | 1911 | Cork | IRL | IRC | 18.12.1936 | Survivor | Repat. 1937, returned to Spain, normal repat. 1938 |
| O'REILLY Domhnall | 1903 | Dublin | IRL | CPI | 01.12.1936 | Survivor | Political Commissar, repat. March 1937 |
| O'REILLY John | 1908 | Tipperary | UK | | ? | Survivor | Repat. Oct. 1938 |
| O'RIORDAN Michael | 1917 | Cork | IRL | IRA, CPI | 05.05.1938 | Survivor | Normal repat. 1938 |
| ORMESBY Hannah | 1901 | Sligo | UK | | 18.04.1937 | DIA | Killed in fire, Barcelona |
| O'SHEA John | 1903 | Waterford | UK | IRC | 17.02.1937 | Survivor | Sergeant, normal repat. 1938 |
| O'SHEA John | 1904 | Kerry | Canada | CPCan | 28.05.1937 | MIA | Platoon leader Canadian Co. with Lincolns. Missing in Aragon March–April 1938 |
| O'SHEA Peter | 1913 | ? | UK | | 15.12.1937 | Survivor | Deserter |
| O'SULLIVAN John | 1908 | Cork | USA | CPUS | 11.11.1937 | MIA | Believed killed, March–April 1938 |
| O'SULLIVAN Patrick | 1914 | London | IRL | CPI | 08.02.1937 | KIA | Lieutenant, Ebro fatality |
| PATTEN Thomas | 1910 | Mayo | UK | IRC | 10.10.1936 | KIA | Madrid fatality |
| PATTERSON Edward | 1904 | Armagh | Canada | | 07.01.1938 | KIA | Ebro fatality at Gandesa |
| PENROSE John | 1905 | Dublin | IRL | IRA | 24.02.1937 | Survivor | Repat. 1937 |
| PLAIN David | 1909 | Armagh | UK | | 14.04.1937 | Survivor | Deserted, caught, repat. 1938 |
| POLLOCK Herbert | 1899 | Derry | Canada | CPCan | 29.07.1937 | Survivor | Repat. Canada 1939 |
| POWER John | 1908 | Waterford | UK | CPGB, CPI, IRC, IRA | 21.12.1936 | Survivor | Captain |
| POWER Patrick | 1909 | Waterford | UK | IRC, CPI | 21.12.1936 | Survivor | Repat. November 1937 |
| POWER William | 1912 | Waterford | IRL | CPI | 04.02.1937 | Survivor | Repat. 1937 |
| PRENDERGAST Jas. | 1915 | Dublin | IRL | CPI | 12.12.1936 | Survivor | Repat. 1937 |
| PRITCHARD David | 1906 | Down | Canada | | 28.10.1937 | MIA | Missing or captured March 1938 |
| PYPER Robert | 1906 | Antrim | UK | | 09.02.1938 | Survivor | Deserted, home May 1938 |
| QUINLAN Maurice | 1911 | Waterford | UK | IRA, IRC, CPI | 21.12.1936 | KIA | Jarama fatality |
| QUINN Sydney | 1909 | Antrim | UK | CPGB | 02.12.1936 | Survivor | Repat. 1937 |
| READ Patrick | 1899 | At sea | USA | | 17.03.1937 | Survivor | Repat. 1938 |
| ROE Michael A. | 1908 | Westmeath | IRL | | 07.01.1937 | Survivor | Repat. 1937 |

| Name | Born | Born in Co. | Came from | Politics | Arrival | Fate | Remarks |
|---|---|---|---|---|---|---|---|
| ROBINSON QUIGLEY John | 1897 | Antrim | USA | CPUS | 10.01.1937 | Survivor | Commissar, repat. 1937 |
| RUSSELL Michael | 1909 | Clare | Canada | CPUS | 19.02.1937 | Executed | Captured and killed by fascists 16.02.1937 |
| RYAN Frank | 1902 | Limerick | IRL | IRA, IRC | 15.12.1936 | Survivor | Captain, POW, died Dresden 1944 |
| RYAN Joseph | 1917 | Limerick | UK | LP | 28.12.1936 | Survivor | Deserted, repat. 1937. Killed WW2 |
| RYAN Maurice | 1915 | Limerick | France | | 05.11.1937 | Executed | Shot by Sam Wilde, CO British Battalion, August 1938 |
| SCOTT Willoughby | 1908 | Dublin | IRL | CPI | 20.07.1936 | Survivor | Repat. 1937 |
| SHEEHAN Thomas | 1904 | Cork | UK | CPGB | 15.02.1938 | KIA | Aragon fatality 1938 |
| SIMS Thomas | 1904 | Tipperary | Canada | CPCan | 08.09.1937 | Survivor | Ambulance driver. Repat. Canada |
| SMITH Patrick | 1910 | Dublin | IRL | IRA | 09.12.1936 | Survivor | Repat. 1937 |
| STAFFORD William | 1905 | Cork | UK | | 08.08.1937 | Survivor | Deserted March 1938 |
| STANLEY Patrick | 1916 | Dublin | IRL | IRA | 09.12.1936 | Survivor | Deserted, caught |
| STEELE George | 1914 | Antrim | UK | | 14.01.1937 | Survivor | Deserted, caught |
| STOKES Edward | 1907 | Kilkenny | IRL | | 10.11.1936 | Open | Probable deserter |
| STRANNEY James | 1915 | Antrim | UK | IRA, IRC | 16.09.1937 | KIA | Corporal, Ebro fatality, |
| TAYLOR Albert E. | 1901 | Kildare | UK | | 11.02.1937 | Survivor | Repatriated 1938 |
| THORNTON David | 1905 | Antrim | Canada | | 04.12.1936 | Open | |
| TIERNEY Frank | 1911 | Antrim | Canada | | 27.07.1937 | Survivor | Repat.1939 Canada |
| TIERNEY John | 1902 | Dublin | UK | CPGB | 16.05.1937 | Survivor | Deserted, home Nov. 1937 |
| TIGHE Patrick | 1914 | Dublin | UK | IRA | 08.12.1936 | Survivor | Deserted, normal repat. 1938 |
| TRAYNOR Thomas | 1897 | Tyrone | Canada | CPCan | 29.04.1937 | Survivor | Platoon leader, repat. 1939 |
| TUMILSON William | 1904 | Antrim | UK | IRC, IRA | 21.01.1937 | KIA | C.O. MG Co. Lincolns. Jarama fatality |
| VALLELY Edward | 1910 | Cavan | UK | | 22.12.1937 | Survivor | POW, repat. 1939, aka "Peter Brady" |
| WALSH David | 1904 | Mayo | UK | | 16.09.1937 | KIA | Teruel fatality |
| WARD Gerald | 1909 | Dublin | UK | CPGB | 12.06.1937 | Survivor | Deserted, normal repat. |
| WATERS Michael | 1913 | Cork | IRL | IRA | 06.01.1937 | Survivor | Normal repat. |
| WOOD Thomas B. | 1919 | Dublin | IRL | | 15.12.1936 | DOW | Cordoba fatality |
| WOULFE James | 1899 | Limerick | Canada | IRA, CPCan | 05.03.1937 | DOW | Aragon fatality, Belchite 03.09.1937 |

# Bibliography

### PRIVATE PAPERS AND COLLECTIONS

Andrew Boyd, Public Record Office of Northern Ireland
Eithne Coyle O'Donnell, UCD Archives
Rosamond Jacob, National Library of Ireland
Seán MacEntee, UCD Archives
Barry McLoughlin, Vienna
Correspondence between Gerald O'Reilly (donator) and Frank Ryan, 1935–37
Abwehr Ireland Diary, 1939–44 (donated by the late Prof. T. D. Williams)
Joseph Cardinal MacRory, Cardinal Tomás Ó Fiaich Memorial Library and Archive, Armagh
Art Ó Briain, National Library of Ireland

### PUBLIC RECORDS

**Ireland**
Military Archives, Dublin
    Military Service Pension files
National Archives, Dublin
    Department of Foreign Affairs
    Department of Justice
    Department of the Taoiseach
National Library of Ireland, Dublin
    Irish Trade Union Congress, annual reports
Public Record Office of Northern Ireland, Belfast
    RUC reports

**Russia**
State Archive for Social and Political History (RGASPI), Moscow
    Fond 495, Communist International
    Fond 534, Profintern
    Fond 545, International Brigades (IB):
    Opis' 1: Documents of IB War Commissariat
    Opis' 2: Documents from headquarters of IB at Republican Ministry for Defence
    Opis' 3: Documents of 35th, 45th Division (10th–15th and 129th International Brigades)
    Opis' 6: Personal files of volunteers

**Britain**
The National Archives, Kew
    Admiralty (ADM)
    Foreign Office (FO)
    Government Code and Cypher School decrypts (HW)
    War Office (WO)
    Secret Service (KV)
Imperial War Museum, London
    Interviews with IB veterans
        Accessed online: Charles Bloom, Syd Booth, Jim Brewer, Fred Copeman, Walter Greenhalgh, George Leeson, Tom Murphy, Sydney Quinn
Marx Memorial Library, London
    International Brigades Memorial Archive
Modern Records Centre, University of Warwick
    Trades Union Congress deposit
National Museum of Labour History, Manchester
    CP/Ind/Misc./18/6; CP/Ind/Poll/2/5 and 6
South Wales Miners' Library, Swansea
    Manuscripts of interview with Jim Brewer
Southampton City Archives
    Merchant navy papers of Maurice Emmett Ryan
Working Class Movement Library, Salford
    Manuscripts of Bob Clark; Manuscripts of interview with Syd Booth

**Germany**
Politisches Archiv des Auswärtigen Amts, Berlin
    R. 29.888, Bureau Veesenmayer, Ireland 1941–2
    R. 101.336, Spanien (imprisonment of Frank Ryan)
    R. 101.850, Abwehr Irland, 1941–44
    R. 103.027, Correspondence on Frank Ryan
    R. 103.238, Correspondence on Frank Ryan
    R. 103.201, 202, 203, 204, 205, Correspondence on POW exchange, Spain, 1937–39
    R. 251.158, report of visit of Italian Ambassador, Berlin, 11.10.1938
Bundesarchiv, Berlin-Lichterfeld
    RS. 38.10574, Staatspolizei Frankfurt (Hoven brothers and Clissmann, 1934)
    SAPMO, RY1/I 2/292, German IB correspondence

**Spain**
Archivo General de la Administración, Alcalá de Henares
    54/11729–11731, Spanish Legation Dublin-Madrid, 1936–39
    54/6857/16, Material on Ireland; Francoist propaganda in *Cork Examiner*; disclosures of Clifford Wattis in London
    82/4333/233, folder Frank Ryan
    82/04768, IB POWS, exchange and imprisonment

Archivo General Militar, Guadalajara
    Comisión Central de Examen de Penas, folder 14/034 Frank Ryan
    Extranjeros, Folder 26/70, Frank Ryan
Ministerio del Interior, Madrid
    Burgos Prison File 364/37, 1938–40, Frank Ryan
Archivo Intermedio Militar Noroeste del Ferrol
    Causa 1695-38, Frank Ryan's interrogation and trial transcripts

**Austria**
Dokumentationsarchiv des österreichischen Widerstandes, Vienna
    Sammlung IVVdN, files on German IB volunteers

NEWSPAPERS & JOURNALS

*An Phoblacht*, 1933
*Belfast News-Letter*, 1935–9
*Belfast Telegraph*, 1936–7, 2005
*Catholic Herald* (London), 1937
*Cencrastus* (Edinburgh), 1984
*Clare Champion*, 1979
*Comhthrom Féinne*, 1933
*Cork Examiner*, 1938–40
*Daily Worker* (London), 1930–45
*Derry Journal*, 1936–8
*Derry Standard*, 1937
*Fortnight*, 1985
*Inprecorr*, 1937
*Irish Democrat*, 1937
*Irish Independent*, 1936–7, 1943
*Irish News*, 1936
*Irish Post* (London), 1979
*Irish Press*, 1931–8, 1943
*Irish Times*, 1933–9, 1971, 1975–7, 2003
*Irish Workers' Voice*, 1933
*Limerick Chronicle*, 1932–3
*Limerick Leader*, 1936–7
*Londonderry Sentinel*, 1938–9
*Munster Express*, 1936–7
*National Student*, 1938
*Nationalist and Leinster Times*, 1938
*New Northman*, 1938
*New Statesman*, 1961
*New Ulster*, 1986

*Northern Whig*, 1936–8
*Pro Tanto Quid*, 1938
*Republican Congress*, 1934
*Standard*, 1937–8
*Sunday Independent*, 1938
*TCD Miscellany*, 1937
*Worker*, 1936–7
*Workers' Republic*, 1938

IRISH VOICES OF EXPERIENCE OF SPAIN

Doyle, Bob, *Memorias de un Rebelde sin Pausa* (Madrid, 2002)
——, *Brigadista: An Irishman's Fight against Fascism.* Notes and Additional Text by Harry Owens (Dublin, 2006)
'Frank Edwards', Uinseann MacEoin, *Survivors: The Story of Ireland's Struggle as Told Through Some of Her Outstanding Living People Recalling Events from the Days of Davitt, Through James Connolly, Brugha, Collins, De Valera, Liam Mellows, and Rory O'Connor to the Present Time* (Dublin, 1987), pp 1–20
MacEoin, Uinseann, 'Michael O'Riordan of Cork City and the International Brigade', *The IRA in the Twilight Years, 1923–1948* (Dublin, 1997), pp 751–66
MacKee, Seumas, *I Was a Franco Soldier* (London, 1938)
McCullagh, Francis, *In Franco's Spain* (London, 1937)
McGuinness, Charles, 'The story that will thrill you'; 'Adventures in war-torn Spain'; 'Foul war on religion'; 'Massacre in a cemetery'; 'Under fire by the enemy'; 'Among those about to die'; *Irish Independent*, 2–8 January 1937
Mitchell, Máirín, *Storm Over Spain* (London, 1937)
Monks, Joe, *With the Reds in Andalusia* (London, 1985)
Moroney, Brendan, 'Twenty months in the International Brigade', *Hibernia* (September 1938)
O'Brien, Kate, *Farewell Spain* (London, 1937)
O'Connor, Peter, *A Soldier of Liberty: Recollections of a Socialist and Anti-fascist Fighter* (Dublin, 1996)
O'Donnell, Peadar, *Salud! An Irishman in Spain* (London, 1937)
O'Duffy, Eoin, *Crusade in Spain* (Dublin, 1938)
Ó Duinnín, Eoghan, *La Niña Bonita agus An Róisín Dubh: Cuimhní Cinn ar Chogadh Cathartha na Spáinne* (Baile Átha Cliath, 1986),
O'Riordan, Michael, 'Corrected notes from the discussion between Mick O'Riordan with [sic] Ciaran Crossey and John Quinn, Dublin 21 September 2001', in John Quinn, *Irish Volunteers for Spain: A Short History of the Northern Irish Volunteers who Fought in Defence of the Republican Government of Spain, 1936–39* (Belfast, 2004)

# Bibliography

BOOKS AND ARTICLES

Abel, Werner, and Enrico Hilbert (eds), *"Sie werden nicht durchkommen": Deutsche an der Seite der Spanischen Republik und der sozialen Revolution* (Hessen, 2015)

Acier, M. (ed.), *From Spanish Trenches: Recent Letters from Spain* (New York, 1937)

Abraham, Paul, 'Midgley, Roman Catholicism, and Spain', in *New Ulster*, 2, winter, 1986

Adibekov,G. M., Ye N. Shakhnazarova and K. K. Shirinya, (eds), *Organizatsionnaya Struktura Kominterna 1919–1943* (Moscow 1997)

Adibekov, G. M. (ed.), *Politbyuro TsK RKP (b) i Komintern 1919–1943. Dokumenty* (Moscow 2004)

———, *Politbyuro TsK RKP (b) – VKP (b) Povestki dnya zasedanii. Tom II. 1930–1939. Katalog* (Moscow 2001)

Alexander, Bill, *British Volunteers for Liberty: Spain 1936–39* (London, 1982)

Alpert, Michael, *The Republican Army in the Spanish Civil War* (Cambridge, 2007)

———, 'The clash of Spanish armies: contrasting ways of war in Spain, 1936–1939', in *War in History*, 6:3, 1999, pp 331–52

Anderson, Peter, 'The Chetwode Commission and the British Diplomatic Responses to Violence Behind the Lines in the Spanish Civil War', in *European History Quarterly*, 42:2, 2012, pp 235–60

Anderson, P. P., 'The struggle over the evacuation to the United Kingdom and repatriation of Basque refugee children in the Spanish Civil War: symbols and souls', in *Journal of Contemporary History*, 52:2, 2017, pp 297–318

Andrews, C. S., *Man of No Property* (Dublin, 1982)

Angus, John, *With the International Brigades in Spain* (Loughborough, 1983)

Armstrong, Ken, 'The effects of the Spanish Civil War on Ireland', in *Lisburn Historical Society Journal*, 10, 2005–6, unpaginated

Arthur, Max, *The Real Band of Brothers: First-Hand Accounts of the Last British Survivors of the Spanish Civil War* (London, 2009)

Artisov, A. N (ed.), *RKKA y Grazkdanskaya voina v Ispanii 1936–1939gg. Sborniki informatsionnykh materialov Razvedyvatel'nogo upravleniya RKKA. Tom 1, Sborniki No. 1–15* (Moscow 2019)

Bandrés, Javier, and Rafael Llavona, 'Psychology in Franco's concentration camps', in *Psychology in Spain*, 1:1, 1997, pp 3–9

Barceló Luqué, Juan, *Brunete: El Nacimiento del Ejercito Popular* (Madrid, 2018)

Barilich, Eva, *Fritz Jensen: Arzt an vielen Fronten* (Vienna, 1991)

Barr, Andy, 'An undiminished dream: Andy Barr, communist trade unionist', in *Saothar*, 16, 1991, pp 95–111

Barritt, Denis P. and Charles F. Carter, *The Northern Ireland Problem: A Study in Group Relations* (Oxford, 1962)

Baxell, Richard, *British Volunteers in the Spanish Civil War: The British Battalion in the International Brigades, 1936–1939* (London, 2004)

———, *Unlikely Warriors: The British in the Spanish Civil War and the Struggle Against Fascism* (London, 2012)

Bayerlein, Bernhard H. (Ed.), *Georgi Dimitroff: Tagebücher 1933–1943* (Berlin, 2000)

Beeching, William C., *Canadian Volunteers: Spain 1936–1939* (Regina, 1989)
Beevor, Antony, *The Battle for Spain: The Spanish Civil War 1936–1939* (London, 2006)
Bell, J. Bowyer, *The Secret Army: A History of the IRA 1916–1970* (London, 1970)
Bennett, Richard, 'Portrait of a killer', in *New Statesman*, 24 March 1961
Berg, Angela, *Die Internationalen Brigaden im Spanischen Bürgerkrieg* (Essen, 2005)
Bessie, Alvah and Albert Prago (eds), *Our Fight: Writings by Veterans of the Abraham Lincoln Brigade, Spain 1936–1939* (New York, 1987)
Bowers, Claude G., *My Mission to Spain: Watching the Rehearsal for World War II* (New York, 1954)
Borkenau, Franz, *Kampfplatz Spanien: Politische und soziale Konflikte im Spanischen Bürgerkrieg. Ein Augenzeugenbericht* (Stuttgart, 1986)
Boyd, Andrew, *Holy War in Belfast* (Belfast, 1987)
——, *Fermenting Elements: The Labour Colleges in Ireland, 1924–1964* (Belfast, 1999)
Brenan, Gerald, *The Spanish Labyrinth: An Account of the Social and Political Background to the Spanish Civil War* (Cambridge, 1960)
Brooks, Chris, 'The making of the Washington Battalion', in *The Volunteer*, 21 March 2014
Brown, S. J., Stephen, *The Press in Ireland: A Survey and A Guide* (Dublin, 1937)
Brown, Terence, *Ireland, A Social and Cultural History, 1922–79* (London, 1981)
Buchanan, Tom, *Britain and the Spanish Civil War* (Cambridge, 1997)
Buckley, Henry, *The Life and Death of the Spanish Republic: A Witness to The Spanish Civil War* (London, 2014)
Campbell, Alan, John Halstead, John McIlroy and Barry McLoughlin, 'Forging the Faithful: the British at the International Lenin School', in *Labour History Review*, 1:63, April 2003
Carr, E. H., *The Comintern and the Spanish Civil War* (London, 1984)
Carroll, Denis, *They Have Fooled You Again: Michael O'Flanagan (1876–1942), Priest, Republican, Social Critic* (Dublin, 1993)
Carroll, Paul Vincent, *The Wise Have Not Spoken: A Drama in Three Acts* (London, 1947)
Carroll, Peter N., *The Odyssey of the Abraham Lincoln Brigade: Americans in the Spanish Civil War* (Stanford, 1994)
Castells, Andreu, *Las Brigadas Internacionales de la Guerra en España* (Barcelona, 1974)
Chan, Jung and Halliday Jon, *Mao: The Unknown Story* (New York, 2005)
Chubar'yan, A. O. (ed.), *Istoriya Kommunisticheskogo Internationala 1919–1943: Dokumental'nie ocherki* (Moscow 2002)
Clark, Bob, *No Boots to My Feet: Experiences of a Britisher in Spain 1937–38*. With a Foreword by Jack Jones (Stoke-on-Trent, 1984)
Commissiariat of War, XV Brigade, *The Book of the XV Brigade: Records of British, American, Canadian and Irish Volunteers in the XV International Brigade in Spain 1936–1938* (Madrid, 1938)
Commission of the Central Committee of the Communist Party of the Soviet Union (Bolsheviks) (eds), *History of the Communist Party of the Soviet Union (Bolsheviks)* (Moscow, 1945)
Communist Party of Ireland, *Outline History* (Dublin, n.d. [1975])
Connolly O'Brien, Nora, *We Shall Rise Again* (London, 1981)
Copeman, Fred, *Reason in Revolt* (London, 1948)

Convery, David, 'Irish participation in medical aid to Republican Spain, 1936–39', in *Saothar*, 35, 2010, pp 37–46
——, 'Ireland and the fall of the Second Republic in Spain', in *Bulletin of Spanish Studies*, vol. LXXXIX, nos. 7–8, 2012
Coogan, Tim Pat, *The IRA* (London, 1995)
Cook, Judith, *Apprentices of Freedom* (London/Melbourne/New York, 1979)
Cooney, John, *John Charles McQuaid: Ruler of Catholic Ireland* (Dublin, 1999)
Corkill, D. and S. Rawnsley (eds), *The Road to Spain: Anti-Fascists at War* (Dunfermline, 1981)
Cronin, Mike, 'The Blueshirt movement, 1932–5: Ireland's fascists?', in *Journal of Contemporary History*, 30, 1995, pp 311–32
——, Cronin, *The Blueshirts and Irish Politics* (Dublin, 1997)
Cronin, Seán, *Frank Ryan: The Search for the Republic* (Dublin, 1980)
Daiken, Leslie H. (comp), *Good-Bye, Twilight: Songs of the Struggle in Ireland* (London, 1936)
David, Deacon, *British News Media and the Spanish Civil War: Tomorrow May Be Too Late* (Edinburgh, 2008)
Dawe, Gerald, 'Introduction', in Kay Donnelly (ed), *Heroic Heart: A Charles Donnelly Reader* (Belfast, 2012)
Deasy, Joe, 'Reviving the memory: New Theatre movement', in *Labour History News*, 3, spring, 1987, pp 3–5
Degras, Jane (ed.), *The Communist International, 1919–1943: Documents, Volume 3, 1929–1943* (London, 1965)
Deighton, Len, *Blood, Tears and Folly: In the Darkest Hour of the Second World War* (London, 1993)
Devine, Francis, *Organising History: A Centenary of SIPTU, 1909–2009* (Dublin, 2009)
Devlin, Paddy, *Yes, We Have No Bananas! Outdoor Relief in Belfast, 1920–39* (Belfast, 1981)
Dickel, Horst, *Die Deutsche Aussenpolitik und die Irische Frage von 1932 bis 1944* (Wiesbaden, 1983)
Donnelly, Charles, 'Literature in Ireland', *Comhthrom Féinne*, 5:4, 1933, p. 65
Donnelly, Joseph, *Charlie Donnelly: The Life and Poems* (Dublin, 1987)
——, 'A memoir', in Kay Donnelly (ed), *Heroic Heart: A Charles Donnelly Reader* (Belfast, 2012)
Donnelly, Kay (ed), *Heroic Heart: A Charles Donnelly Reader* (Belfast, 2012)
Douglas, R. M., *Architects of the Resurrection: Ailtirí na hAiséirghe and the Fascist 'New Order' in Ireland* (Manchester, 2009).
Duggan, John P., *Neutral Ireland and the Third Reich* (Dublin, 1989)
Dundas, Lawrence, *Behind the Spanish Mask* (London, 1943)
East Wall History Group, *In Support of An Ideal: Jack Nalty: From East Wall to the Ebro* (Dublin, 2018)s
Eby, Cecil, *Between the Bullet and the Lie: American Volunteers in the Spanish Civil War* (New York-Chicago-San Francisco, 1969)
Edwards, Ben, *With God on Our Side: British Christian Responses to the Spanish Civil War* (Newcastle upon Tyne, 2013)
Elorza, Antonio, and Marta Bizcarrondo, *Queridos Camaradas: La Internacional Comunista y España, 1919–1939* (Barcelona, 1999)

English, Richard, 'Socialism and republican schism in Ireland: the emergence of the Republican Congress in 1934', in *Irish Historical Studies*, xxvii, 195, 1990, pp 48–65

Enzensberger, Hans Magnus, *Der kurze Sommer der Anarchie. Buenventura Durrutis Leben und Tod. Roman* (Frankfurt am Main 1980)

Fanning, Ronan, *Independent Ireland* (Dublin, 1983)

Firsov, Fridrikh I., 'Dimitrov, the Comintern and the Stalinist repression', in Barry McLoughlin and Kevin McDermott (eds), *Stalin's Terror: High Politics and Mass Repression in the Soviet Union* (Houndmills, 2003)

Firsov, Fridrikh I., Harvey Klehr, and John Earl Haynes (eds), *Secret Cables of the Comintern 1933–1943* (New Haven and London, 2014)

Fischer, Louis, *Men and Politics* (New York, 1946)

Fischer, Walter, *Kurze Geschichten aus einem langen Leben. Mit einem Nachwort von Leopold Spira* (Mannheim, 1987)

Fisher, Harry, *Comrades: Tales of a Brigadista in the Spanish Civil War* (Lincoln, Ne, 1999)

Fisk, Robert, *In Time of War. Ireland, Ulster and the Price of Neutrality, 1939–1945* (London, 1987)

Fleming, Lionel, *Head or Harp* (London, 1965)

Foote, Alexander, *Handbook for Spies* (London, 1949)

Freyer, Grattan, *Peadar O'Donnell* (Cranbury, NJ, 1973)

Gallagher, Michael, *The Irish Labour Party in Transition, 1957–82* (Manchester, 1982)

Gates, John, *The Story of an American Communist* (New York, 1958)

Geiser, Carl, *Prisoners of the Good Fight: The Spanish Civil War 1936–1939* (Westport Conn., 1986)

Geoghegan, Vincent, 'Cemeteries of liberty: William Norton on communism and fascism', in *Saothar*, 18, 1993, pp 196–9

Getty, J. Arch, and Oleg V. Naumov, *The Road to Terror: Stalin and the Self-Destruction of the Bolsheviks, 1932–1939* (New Haven and London, 1999)

Goldstone, Katrina, 'Leslie Daiken and Harry Kernoff', in Emmet O'Connor and John Cunningham (eds), *Studies in Irish Radical Leadership: Lives on the Left* (Manchester, 2016)

Grant, Adrian, *Irish Socialist Republicanism, 1909–36* (Dublin, 2012)

Gray, Malachy, 'A shop steward remembers', in *Saothar*, 11, 1986, pp 109–15

Greater Manchester International Brigade Memorial Committee, *Greater Manchester Men Who Fought in Spain* (Manchester, 1983)

Gregory, Walter, *The Shallow Grave: A Memoir of the Spanish Civil War* (London, 1986).

Griffiths, Richard, *Fellow Travellers of the Right: British Enthusiasm for Nazi Germany* (Oxford, 1983)

Gurney, Jason, *Crusade in Spain* (London, 1976)

Haffner, Sebastian, *Defying Hitler: A Memoir* (London, 2003)

Hamill, Jonathon, 'Saor Éire and the IRA: an exercise in deception?', in *Saothar*, 20, 1995, pp 56–66

Hanley, Brian, 'The Storming of Connolly House', *History Ireland*, 7:2, summer 1999, pp 5–7

——, *The IRA 1926–1936* (Dublin, 2002)

——, 'The Irish Citizen Army after 1916', in *Saothar* 28, 2003, pp 37–47

Hegarty, Peter, *Peadar O'Donnell* (Cork, 1999)

Henriquez Caubin, Julian, *La Batalla del Ebro: Maniobra de una División* (Mexico City, 1944)
Her Majesty's Stationery Office (eds), *Documents on German Foreign Policy*, D:13, (London, 1954)
Herrick, William, *Jumping the Line: The Adventures and Misadventures of an American Radical* (Oakland and Edinburgh, 2001)
Hoar, Adrian, *In Green and Red: The Lives of Frank Ryan* (Dingle, 2004)
Hodgson, Sir Robert, *Spain Resurgent* (London, 1953)
Hogan, James, *Could Ireland Become Communist? The Facts of the Case* (Dublin, 1935)
Hopkins, James K., *Into the Heart of the Fire: The British in the Spanish Civil War* (Stanford, Ca, 1998)
Hoppe, Bert, *In Stalins Gefolgschaft: Moskau und die KPD 1928–1933* (Munich, 2007)
Horgan, John, *Irish Media: A Critical History Since 1922* (London, 2001)
——, '"The great war correspondent": Francis McCullagh, 1874–1956', in *Irish Historical Studies*, 36:144, 2009, pp 542–63
Howard, Victor (with Mac Reynolds), *The Mackenzie-Papineau Battalion: The Canadian Contingent in the Spanish Civil War* (Ottawa, 1969)
Howson, Gerald, *Arms for Spain: The Untold Story of the Spanish Civil War* (London, 1998)
Huber, Peter, and Ralf Hug, *Die Schweizer Spanienfreiwilligen: Ein biographisches Handbuch*, (Zürich, 2009)
Huber, Peter, and Michael Uhl, 'Politische Überwachung und Repression in den Internationalen Brigaden (1936–1938)' *Forum für osteuropäische Ideen- und Zeitgeschichte*, 5. Jahrgang, 2001, Heft 2
Hutchinson, Lieut.-Colonel G. S., *Machine Guns: Their History and Tactical Deployment (Being also a History of the Machine Gun Corps, 1916–1922)* (London 1938, Uckfield, re-print 2004)
Jackson, Angela, *At the Margins of Mayhem: Prologue and Epilogue to the Last Great Battle of the Spanish Civil War* (Pontypool, 2008)
Jackson, Pete, '"A rather one-sided fight": The *Worker* and the Spanish Civil War', in *Saothar*, 23, 1998, pp 79–87
Kantorowicz, Alfred, *Spanisches Kriegstagebuch* (Frankfurt am Main, 1982)
Keene, Judith, *Fighting for Franco: International Volunteers in Nationalist Spain during the Spanish Civil War, 1936–1939* (London and New York, 2001)
Kennedy, Michael, et al. (eds), *Documents on Irish Foreign Policy (DIFP), vols 5 to 8 (1937–1948)* (Dublin, 2006–2012)
Keohane, Leo, *Captain Jack White: Imperialism, Anarchism, and the Irish Citizen Army* (Dublin, 2014)
Klaus, H. Gustav (ed), *Strong Words Brave Deeds: The Poetry, Life, and Times of Thomas O'Brien, Volunteer in the Spanish Civil War* (Dublin, 1994)
Klehr, Harvey et al. (eds), *The Secret World of American Communism* (New Haven and London, 1995)
Knight, Elyot, 'Spanish jig-saw', in *TCD Miscellany*, 19 November 1937
Komolova, N. P. (ed.), *Komintern protiv fashizma. Dokumenty* (Moscow 1999)
Kolpakidi, Aleksandr, and Dmitrii Prokhorov, *Imperiya GRU. Ocherki istorii rossiiskoi voennoi razvedki. Kniga vtoroya* (Moscow 2001)

Krause, David (ed), *The Letters of Sean O'Casey, Volume I, 1910–1941* (London, 1975)

——, *The Letters of Sean O'Casey, Volume II, 1942–54* (New York, 1980)

Landauer, Hans and Erich Hackl, *Lexikon der österreichischen Spanienkämpfer, 1936–1939* (Vienna, 2003)

Landis, Arthur H., *The Abraham Lincoln Brigade* (New York, 1968)

——, *Death in the Olive Groves: American Volunteers in the Spanish Civil War, 1936–39* (New York, 1988)

Lane, Leanne, *Rosamond Jacob: Third Person Singular* (Dublin, 2010)

Lee, J. J., *Ireland, 1912–1985: Politics and Society* (Cambridge, 1989)

Lerchenmüller, Joachim, *Keltischer Sprengstoff: Eine wissenschaftliche Studie über die deutsche Keltologie von 1900 bis 1945* (Tübingen, 1997)

Lesser, Sam, 'Death and confusion among the olive groves', in *IBMT Newsletter*, 43:3, 2016, pp 17–18

Levine, Ketzel, 'A tree of identities, a tradition of dissent: John Hewitt at 78', *Fortnight*, 213, 1985, p. 16

Lewis, Brian, Gledhill, Bill, *Tommy James: A Lion of a Man* (Pontefract, 1984)

Liddle, Peter (ed.), *Captured Memories 1900–1918: Across the Threshold of War* (Barnsley, 2010)

Linklater, Andro, *An Unhusbanded Life: Charlotte Despard, Suffragette, Socialist, and Sinn Féiner* (London, 1980)

Líster, Enrique, *Unser Krieg* (East Berlin, 1972)

Liversedge, Ronald (edited by David Yorke), *Mac-Pap: Memoir of a Canadian in the Spanish Civil War* (Vancouver, 2013)

Lonardo, Michael, 'Under a watchful eye: a case study of police surveillance', in *Labour/Le Travail*, 5, spring 1995, pp 11-41

Longo, Luigi, *Die Internationalen Brigaden in Spanien* (West Berlin, n.d.)

López, Carlos Barciela, Xavier Tafunell, and Albert Carreras, *Estadísticas Históricas de España Siglos XIXXX, Vol. I* (Bilbao, 2005)

Loughlin, James, *Fascism and Constitutional Conflict: The British Extreme-Right and Ulster in the Twentieth Century* (Liverpool, 2019)

Lynch, Martin, *Pictures of Tomorrow and Rinty* (Belfast, 2003)

Lyons, F. S. L., *Ireland Since the Famine* (London, 1971)

Maaßen, Hanns (ed.), *Brigada Internacional ist unsere Ehrenname': Erlebnisse ehemaliger deutscher Spanienkämpfer. Ausgewählt und eingeleitet von Hanns Maaßen*, Bd. 2 (Berlin, 1974)

Manning, Maurice, *The Blueshirts* (Dublin, 2006)

Manning, Pádraig, 'The Irish Self-Determination League of Great Britain (ISDL), 1919 31: "A mixing of social and national aspirations"', in *History Ireland*, 27:6, 2019, p. 403

Márquez, José Maria, Pablo Vico Gil and José Luis Ledesma (eds), *Violencia roja y azul. España, 1936–1950* (Barcelona 2010)

Mathieson, David, *Frontline Madrid: Battlefield Tours of the Spanish Civil War* (Oxford, 2014)

Matić, Igor-Philip. *Edmund Veesenmayer. Agent und Diplomat der nationalsozialistischen Expansionspolitik* (München, 2002)

MacDougall, Ian, 'Tom Murray: Veteran of Spain', *Cencrastus*, 18, 1984, p. 1619
——, *Voices from the Spanish Civil War: Personal Recollections of Scottish Volunteers in Republican Spain 1936-39* (Edinburgh, 1986)
MacEoin, Uinseann (ed), *Survivors: The Story of Ireland's Struggle as Told Through Some of Her Outstanding Living People Recalling Events from the Days of Davitt, Through James Connolly, Brugha, Collins, De Valera, Liam Mellows, and Rory O'Connor to the Present Time* (Dublin, 1987)
MacEoin, Uinseann, *Harry: The Story of Harry White as Related to Uinseann Mac Eoin* (Dublin, 1985)
——, *The IRA in the Twilight Years, 1923-1948* (Dublin, 1997)
Macgougan, Jack, 'Letting Labour lead: Jack Macgougan and the pursuit of unity, 1913-1958', in *Saothar*, 14, 1989, pp 114-22

MacSwiney, Muriel, *Letters to Angela Clifford* (Belfast, 1996)
Marqués, Pierre, *La Croix-Rouge Pendant la Guerre d'Espagne (1936-1939)* (Paris-Montreal, 2015)
McGarry, Fearghal, *Irish Politics and the Spanish Civil War* (Cork, 1999)
——, 'Irish newspapers and the Spanish Civil War', in *Irish Historical Studies*, 22:129, 2002, pp 68-90
——, *Frank Ryan* (Dundalk, 2002)
——, *Eoin O'Duffy: A Self-Made Hero* (Oxford, 2005)
McGuffin, John, and Joseph Mulheron, *Charles 'Nomad' McGuinness: Being a True Account of the Amazing Adventures of a Derryman, Pirate, IRA Man, Gun Runner, Polar Explorer, Adventurer, Mercenary, Rogue, Escaper and Hero* (Derry, 2002)
McGuire, Charlie, *Roddy Connolly and the Struggle for Socialism in Ireland* (Cork, 2008)
McInerney, Michael, *Peadar O'Donnell: Irish Social Rebel* (Dublin, 1974)
——, 'Frank Ryan Profile – parts 1-5', in *Irish Times*, April 1975
McMahon, Cian, 'Eoin O'Duffy's Blueshirts and the Abyssinian crisis', in *History Ireland*, 2:10, summer 2002, pp 36-9
McLoughlin, Barry, and Kevin McDermott (eds), *Stalin's Terror: High Politics and Mass Repression in the Soviet Union* (Houndmills, 2003)
McLoughlin, Barry, *Left to the Wolves: Irish Victims of Stalinist Terror* (Dublin, 2007)
——, *Fighting for Republican Spain: Frank Ryan and the Volunteers from Limerick in the International Brigades* (Lulu Books, 2014)
Merrigan, Matt, 'Socialist trade unionist: Matt Merrigan's political formation', in *Saothar*, 12 1987, pp 94-106
Merriman, Marion, and Warren Lerude, *American Commander in Spain: Robert Hale Merriman and the Abraham Lincoln Brigade* (Reno, 1986)
Mitchel, John, *Jail Journal* (Dublin, 1913)
Milotte, Mike, *Communism in Modern Ireland: The Pursuit of the Workers' Republic Since 1916* (Dublin, 1984)
Mittermeier, Ute Anna, '*No More Than Human* by Maura Laverty: Impressions of a reluctant governess in Spain', in *Estudios Irlandeses*, 2, 2007, pp 135-50
Montero Barrado, Severiano, *La Batalla de Brunete* (Madrid, 2010)

Moradiellos, Enrique, 'The origins of British Non-Intervention in the Spanish Civil War: Anglo-Spanish relations in Early 1936', in *European History Quarterly*, 21:3, 1991, pp 339–64
——, *Franco: Anatomy of a Dictator* (London, 2018)
Munck, Ronnie, and Bill Rolston (eds), *Belfast in the Thirties: An Oral History* (Belfast, 1987)
Negro Committee to Aid Spain, *Salaria Kee: A Negro Nurse in Republican Spain* (New York, 1938)
Nelson, Steve, *The Volunteers* (East Berlin, 1958)
Nelson, Steve, James R. Barrett and Rob Ruck, *Steve Nelson: American Radical* (Pittsburgh, 1981)
Nesterenko, I. (ed.), *International Solidarity with the Spanish Republic 1936–1939* (Moscow, 1976)
Nolan, Aengus, *Joseph Walshe: Irish Foreign Policy 1922–1946* (Cork, 2008)
O'Brien, Mark, '"In war torn Spain": the politics of Irish press coverage of the Spanish Civil War', in *Media, War, and Conflict*, 10: 1, 2017, pp 1–14
O'Brien, Thomas, 'The New Theatre Group: to die or not to die', in H. Gustav Klaus (ed), *Strong Words Brave Deeds: The Poetry, Life, and Times of Thomas O'Brien, Volunteer in the Spanish Civil War* (Dublin, 1994)
Ó Canainn, Aodh, 'Eilís Ryan In Her Own Words', in *Saothar*, 21, 1996, pp 129–46
O'Connor, Eimear, *Sean Keating: Art, Politics and Building the Irish Nation* (Dublin, 2013)
O'Connor, Emmet, *A Labour History of Waterford* (Waterford Council of Trade Unions, 1989)
——, *James Larkin: Radical Irish Lives* (Cork, 2002)
——, *Reds and the Green: Ireland, Russia and the Communist Internationals, 1919–43* (Dublin, 2004)
——, 'Behind the legend: Waterfordmen in the International Brigades in the Spanish Civil War', in *Decies, Journal of the Waterford Archaeological and Historical Society*, 61, 2005, pp 267–85
——, 'Mutiny or Sabotage? The Irish Defection to the Abraham Lincoln Battalion in the Spanish Civil War', in *Working Papers in Irish Studies*, Winthrop University, South Carolina 2009, working paper 093, 2009
——, *A Labour History of Ireland, 1824–2000* (Dublin, 2011)
——, 'Anti-communism in twentieth century Ireland', in *Twentieth Century Communism: A Journal of International History*, 6, 2014, pp 59–81
——, *Big Jim Larkin: Hero or Wrecker?* (Dublin, 2015)
——, 'Tyrone volunteers in the Connolly Column in the Spanish Civil War', in *Dúiche Uí Néill*, 2017, pp 301–11
O'Connor, Joseph, *Even the Olives Are Bleeding: The Life and Times of Charles Donnelly* (Dublin, 1992)
O'Connor Peter, *A Soldier of Liberty: Recollections of a socialist and anti-fascist fighter* (Dublin 1996)
O'Donoghue, David, *Hitler's Irish Voices: The Story of German Radio's Wartime Irish Service* (Belfast, 1998)
——, *The Devil's Deal: The IRA, Nazi Germany and the Double Life of Jim O'Donovan* (Dublin, 2010)

Ó Drisceoil, Donal, *Peadar O'Donnell* (Cork, 2001)
O'Halpin, Eunan, *Defending Ireland: The Irish State and its Enemies since 1922* (Oxford, 1999)
Ó hEidirisceoil, Seán, 'A personal memoir of the thirties', in H. Gustav Klaus (ed), *Strong Words, Brave Deeds: The Poetry, Life, and Times of Thomas O'Brien, Volunteer in the Spanish Civil War* (Dublin, 1994)
O'Leary, Don, *Vocationalism and Social Catholicism in Twentieth-Century Ireland: The Search for a Christian Social Order* (Dublin, 2000)
O'Malley, Kate, *Ireland, India and Empire: Indo-Irish Radical Connections 1919–64* (Manchester, 2008)
Ó Maolbhríde, Seán, 'The Curragh communists', in *Irish Times*, 16 June 1971
O'Riordan, Manus, 'Irish and Jewish volunteers in the Spanish Anti-Fascist war', lecture, Irish Jewish Museum, Dublin, 15 November 1987
——, 'The spy who grew up with the bold: the Irish republican education of Sir John Betjeman', in *Irish Political Review*, March–April 2010, pp 15–17, 12–14, 15–20
——, '1939 Greaves-Regan-O'Riordan conversations in Cork', in *Irish Political Review*, November, 2010, pp 14–18
O'Riordan, Michael, *Connolly Column: The Story of the Irishmen who fought in the Ranks of the International Brigades in the National-revolutionary War of the Spanish People 1936–1939* (Dublin, 1979)
O'Sullivan, Mark, 'Crossing Lines – John O'Reilly and Salaria Kee', in *Tipperary Historical Journal*, September 2020.
Payne, Stanley G., *The Spanish Civil War, the Soviet Union and Communism* (New Haven and London, 2004)
Paynter, Will, *My Generation* (London, 1972)
Permuy López, Rafael A., *Air War over Spain: Aviators, Aircraft and Air Units of the Nationalist and Republican Forces 1936–1939* (Hersham, 2009)
Petrou, Michael, *Renegades: Canadians in the Spanish Civil War* (Vancouver, 2008)
Ponting, Clive, *1940: Myth and Reality* (London, 1990)
Prendergast, Christopher, 'Diary', in *London Review of Books*, 27:6, 17 March 2005
Preston, Paul, *The Spanish Civil War, 1936–39* (London, 1986)
——, *Franco: A Biography* (London, 1993)
——, *The Spanish Civil War: Reaction, Revolution and Revenge* (London, 2006)
——, *We Saw Spain Die: Foreign Correspondents in the Spanish Civil War* (London, 2009)
——, *The Spanish Holocaust: Inquisition and Extermination in Twentieth-Century Spain* (London, 2012)
——, *The Last Days of the Spanish Republic* (London, 2016)
——, 'Britain and the Basque campaign of 1937: the government, the Royal Navy, the Labour Party and the press', in *European History Quarterly*, 48:3, 2018, pp 490–515
Prieß, Heinz, *Spaniens Himmel und keine Sterne: Ein deutsches Geschichtsbuch. Erinnerungen an ein Leben und an ein Jahrhundert* (Berlin, 1996)
Puirséil, Niamh, *The Irish Labour Party, 1922–73* (Dublin, 2007)
——, 'Catholic Stakhanovites? Religion and the Irish Labour Party, 1922–73', in Francis Devine, Fintan Lane, and Niamh Puirséil (eds), *Essays in Irish Labour History: A Festschrift for Elizabeth and John W. Boyle* (Dublin, 2008)

Quinn, John, *Irish Volunteers for Spain: A Short History of the Northern Irish Volunteers who fought in Defence of the Republican Government of Spain 1936 1939* (Belfast, 2011)

Quinn, Raymond J., *A Rebel Voice: A History of Belfast Republicanism, 1925–1972* (Belfast, 1999)

Radosh, Ronald, Mary R. Habeck, and Grigory Sevostianov (eds), *Spain Betrayed: The Soviet Union in the Spanish Civil War* (New Haven and London, 2001)

Regan, John M., *The Irish Counter-Revolution, 1921–1936* (Dublin, 1999)

Rhodes, Anthony, *The Vatican in the Age of Dictators, 1922–45* (London, 1973)

Richardson, R. Dan, *Comintern Army: The International Brigades and the Spanish Civil War* (Lexington, Ky, 1982)

Rilova Pérez, Isaac, *Guerra Civil y Violencia en Burgos (1936–1943)* (Burgos, 2016)

Rilova Pérez, Isaac (ed.), *75 años 1932–2007. Centro Penitenciario de Burgos. La Prisión en la Historia. Exposición Retrospectiva* (Burgos, 2007)

Robinson, J. K., 'Annual conference of the Northern Ireland Labour Party', *Inprecorr*, 49, 13 November 1937

Ruiz, Julius, "Work and don't lose hope': Republican forced labour camps during the Spanish Civil War', *Contemporary European History*, 18:4, 2009, pp 419–41

Rust, William, *Britons in Spain: The History of the British Battalion of the XVth International Brigade* (London, 1939)

Ryan, Meda, *Tom Barry: IRA Freedom Fighter* (Cork, 2003)

Rybalkin, Iurii, *Sovetskaia voennaia pomoshch'respublikanskoi Ispanii 1936–1939* (Moscow, 2000)

Schäfer, Max (ed.), *1936–1939, Spanien: Erinnerungen von Interbrigadisten aus der BRD* (Frankfurt am Main, 1976)

Schmidt, Ina, Stefan Breuer, Ernst Jünger, and Friedrich Hielscher (eds), *Briefe von Ernst Jünger 1917 1985* (Stuttgart, 2005)

Sheehy Skeffington, Andrée, *Skeff: The Life of Owen Sheehy Skeffington, 1909–1970* (Dublin, 1991)

Shelmerdine, L. B., 'Britons in An "unBritish" war: domestic newspapers and the participation of UK nationals in the Spanish Civil War', *North West Labour History*, 22, n.d., pp 20–47

Shaw, Liz, 'Joe Boyd – the last Brigader', in *Belfast Telegraph*, 18 June 2005

Shields, J., 'Struggle in Ireland entering a new stage', in *Inprecorr*, 54, 12 October 1934

Shovlin, Frank, *The Irish Literary Periodical, 1923–1958* (Oxford, 2003)

Skoutelsky, Rémi, *Novedad en el Frente: Las Brigadas Internacionales en la Guerra Civil* (Barcelona, 2006)

Slutsch, Sergej, 'Stalin und Hitler 1933 1941: Kalküle und Fehlkalkulationen des Kreml', in Jürgen Zarusky (ed.), *Stalin und die Deutschen: Neue Beiträge der Forschung* (Munich, 2006)

Staunton, Enda, 'Frank Ryan & Collaboration: a reassessment', *History Ireland*, 5:3, autumn 1997

Stephan, Enno, *Spies in Ireland* (London, 1965)

Stephens, D. P. (Pat), *A Memoir of the Spanish Civil War: An Armenian-Canadian in the Lincoln Battalion* (St John's, Nfl, 2000)

Stradling, Robert A., *The Irish in the Spanish Civil War, 1936–1939: Crusades in Conflict* (Manchester, 1999)

——, *Wales and the Spanish Civil War: The Dragon's Dearest Cause?* (Cardiff, 2004)

——, 'English-speaking Units of the International Brigades: war, politics and discipline', in *Journal of Contemporary History*, 45:4, 2010, pp 744–67

Swift, John P., *John Swift: An Irish Dissident* (Dublin, 1991)

——, 'John Swift, 1896–1990: a solitary voice that echoes still', in Francis Devine and Kieran Jack McGinley (eds), *Left Lives in Twentieth Century Ireland* (Dublin, 2017)

Thomas, Fred, *To Tilt at Windmills: A Memoir of the Spanish Civil War* (East Lansing, Mi, 1996)
Thomas, Hugh, *The Spanish Civil War* (London, 2012)
Thomas, Maria, *Faith and Fury: Popular Anti-Clerical Violence and Iconoclasm in Spain, 1931–1936* (Brighton, 2013)
Thorpe, Andrew, *The British Communist Party and Moscow, 1920–43* (Manchester, 2000)
Tisa, John, *Recalling the Good Fight: An Autobiography of the Spanish Civil War* (South Hadley, Ma, 1985)
Tremlett, Giles, 'Marxists are retards', in *The Guardian*, 1 November 2002
Turnbull, Patrick, and Jeffrey Burn, *The Spanish Civil War, 1936–39* (Oxford, 1978)
Ua Cearnaigh, Seán, 'From Tipperary to Jarama… The Story of Kit Conway, volunteer hero of the Spanish Republic', in *Ireland's Eye*, March 2006
Uhl, Michael, 'Die Internationalen Brigaden im Spiegel neuer Dokumente', in *Internationale Wissenschaftliche Korrespondenz* (IWK), Heft 4, 1999
*Ulster Year Book* (Belfast, 1938)
Vereinigung österreichischer Freiwilliger in der spanischer Republik 1936 bis 1939 (eds), *Österreicher im Spanischen Bürgerkrieg. Interbrigadisten berichten über ihre Erlebnisse* (Vienna, 1986)
Voros, Sandor, *American Commissar* (New York, 1961)
Walker, Graham, *The Politics of Frustration: Harry Midgley and the Failure of Labour in Northern Ireland* (Manchester, 1985)
Walshe, Eibhear, 'Lock up your daughters: From ante-room to interior castle', in Eibhear Walshe (ed), *Ordinary People Dancing: Essays on Kate O'Brien* (Cork, 1993)
Weber, Hermann, and Andreas Herbst (eds), *Deutsche Kommunisten: Biographisches Handbuch 1918 bis 1945* (Berlin, 2004)
Wharton, Barrie, and Des Ryan, 'The last crusade: Limerick's role in the Spanish Civil War', *Old Limerick Journal* (summer 2001), pp.13–17
Whelan, Barry, *Ireland's Revolutionary Diplomat: A Biography of Leopold Kerney* (Notre Dame, Indiana, 2019)
——, 'Ireland's Minister to Spain – L.H. Kerney's diplomatic efforts to secure the release of Frank Ryan', in *Saothar*, 37, 2012, pp 73–83
Wheeler, George, *To Make the People Smile Again: A Memoir of the Spanish Civil War* (Newcastle upon Tyne, 2003)
Williamson, Howard, *Toolmaking and Politics. The Life of Ted Smallbone: An Oral History* (Birmingham, 1987)
Wilson, David, *The Irish in Canada* (Ottawa, 1989)
Wintringham, Tom, *English Captain* (Harmondsworth, 1941)
Wolff, Milton, *Another Hill: An Autobiographical Novel* (Champaign, Il, 1994)

## Dissertations

Burton, William, 'The Spanish Civil War, Irish newspapers, journals, and periodicals: a thematic examination, 1936–39' (PhD, Ulster University, 2019)
Byers, Seán, 'Seán Murray, the Irish republican left and international communism, 1916–1962' (PhD, University of Ulster, 2012)
Convery, David, 'Cork and the Spanish Civil War' (PhD, UCC, 2006)

Cradden, Terence Gerard, 'Trade unionism and socialism in Northern Ireland, 1939–53' (PhD, Queen's University, Belfast, 1988)

Harbinson, John Fitzsimons, 'A history of the Northern Ireland Labour Party, 1891–1949' (PhD, Queen's University, Belfast, 1966)

Kendrick, Anna Kathryn, '"On guard with the Junipers": Ewart Milne and Irish literary dissent in the Spanish Civil War' (Senior thesis, Harvard, Ma, 2009)

McLoughlin, F.M., 'Irish neutrality during World War II, with special references to German sources' (MA, UCD, 1980)

Whelan, Barry, 'Ireland and Spain, 1939–55: Cultural, economic and political relations from neutrality in the Second World War to joint membership of the United Nations' (PhD, NUI Maynooth, 2012)

ONLINE

Census of Ireland, 1911

Dáil Debates, 1934

Diary of Major Robert Merriman, International Brigades, www.merrimandiary.com. Accessed 29 September 2014.

https://comeheretome.com/2018/08/21/gabriel-lee-1904-37-and-eoin-oduffys-irish-brigade/. Accessed 24 November 2019.

www.international-brigades.org.uk/memorials. Accessed 24 November 2019.

https://medium.com/@stewreddin/irish-citizens-of-basque-origin-the-story-of-ireland-s-basque-refugees-during-the-spanish-civil-war. Accessed 20 February 2019.

www.geocities.com/IrelandSCW/. Accessed 21 February 2019.

Kowalsky, Daniel, Stalin and the Spanish Civil War, http://gutenberg-e.org/kod01/frames/fkoding.html. Accessed 23 February 2004.

Ledesma Vera, José Luis, *La guerra civil y la comarca del Bajo-Aragon-Caspe (1936–1939)*, www.academia.edu/1765168/La_guerra_civil_y_la_comarca_del_Bajo_Arag%C3%B3n-Caspe_1936-1939_6. Accessed 10 December 2019.

*Oxford Dictionary of National Biography*, entries on H. C. Midgley and Monica Whately

Parr, Connal, 'The undefeated: radical Protestants from the Spanish Civil War to the 1960s', www.academia.edu/8238959/The_Undefeated. Accessed 27 December 2018.

Prieto, Julie, *Partisanship in Balance: The New York Times Coverage of the Spanish Civil War, 1936–1939*, pdf, pp 15–17, https://alba-valb.org/resource/partisanship-in-balance-the-new-york-times-coverage-of-the-spanish-civil-war-1936-1939/. Accessed 17 June 2020.

Rein, Raanan, 'A belated inclusion: Jewish volunteers in the Spanish Civil War and their place in the Israeli national narrative', *Project Muse*, muse.jhu.edu/article/460757. Accessed 17 June 2020.

# Index

Abraham Lincoln battalion 28, 109, 115,
    117, 121, 125–6, 140, 212
  advance on Belchite 209–10
  departure for Jarama 141
  fatalities 142, 156, 177, 261
  Friends of the Abraham Lincoln
    Brigade 361
  Machine-Gun Company 186
  Tumlison, Liam 156
  Veterans of the Abraham Lincoln
    Brigade 365, 374
Abyssinia 31, 73
  invasion of 3, 13, 22, 35
Albacete 91–3, 95, 99, 141, 193, 275, 313
  Cadres Department 158, 279, 286
  CPUSA representative in 218
  butcher of 120
  evacuation of 250
  formation of Washington battalion
    171
  fraternal party influence in 204
  Guardia Nacional barracks 273
  high command 152
  location 118
  march to railway station 119
  prison evacuation 276
All-Ireland Anti-War Crusade 42
Amalgamated Engineering Union 77–8
Amalgamated Transport and General
    Workers' Union (ATGWU) 15–16,
    71, 73, 77–8
American War of Independence 6
Amery, John 297
anarchists 7, 30, 40, 67, 89, 98, 187, 213, 307
  anti-clericalism 6
  Consejo (Council) de Aragón 205
  Farmers' Congress 40
  German 278
  Mas de la Matas (village) 285
  militiamen 162
  military leaders 211
  soldiers 169
  strongholds 306
  support for Frente Popular 1
  transport column 173
Ancient Order of Hibernians 64
Andalusia 118–19, 162–4
Anderson, Jane 297
Andrews, John M. 60, 365
Anglo-Irish Treaty 6
anticlericalism 6–7, 359
anti-Semitism 10
anti-socialism 60
Aragon 94, 99, 104, 202
  anarchist strongholds 306
  desertions 277–8
  end of the Spanish Republic 249
  failed offensive 202
  flight from 235
  landscape 228
  offensive 205
  second fascist offensive 232
  planned Republican attack 173
Arms for Spain Committee 70
Army of Africa 1
Army of the Centre 172, 277
Army of Manoeuvre 220
Association of Secondary Teachers 303
atheism 18–19, 349
Attlee, Clement, 69, 118, 219, 236
Australia 11, 102–3, 121, 250, 283, 311
Austria, 2, 14, 78, 90, 96, 120–1, 222

405

Barry, Tom 39, 52, 311, 320, 344
Basque Children's Committee 37
Basque Country 1, 7, 170
Beigbeder, Juan 332, 334, 337
Belchite 228–9, 243
  capture of 208–13
Belfast Anti-Fascist Committee 70
*Belfast News-Letter* 62
*Belfast Telegraph* 62–3, 67, 79
Belgium 33, 90, 342, 357
Belton, Patrick 12, 35
Bevin, Ernest 16, 78
Bilbao 34, 49, 79, 112, 170, 305, 332, 338
Blueshirts 6, 10–11, 14–15, 32, 296
Blum, Léon 4
Blythe, Ernest 39, 64
Bolshevik revolution 4
*The Book of the XV Brigade* 28, 145, 193, 206, 209, 217–20, 231, 253, 300
Briskey, Bill 144–5
Britain 72, 85, 90, 195, 235–6, 314
  diplomacy with Stalin 5
  field medical units 69
  Foreign Office 19
  IB volunteers 100–1, 103, 148, 217, 263
  IRA bombing campaign (1939–40) 338, 348
  massacres caused by 65
  news coverage 3
  possible war with Germany 249
  pro-Nazi organisations 79
  recognition of Franco 319–20
British Anti-War League 20, 23
British Army Field Regulations 208
British National Joint Committee for Spanish Relief 16
British Trades Union Congress Solidarity Fund 16
British Union of Fascists 3
*British Volunteers for Liberty* 125
*Britons in Spain* 109, 125
Brown, Jane 305–9
Brunete, Battle of 95, 99, 102
  background 169–72
  desertions 274–5, 281
  early days 173–92
  ruins 272
Bunreacht na hÉireann (Irish Constitution) 52
Burgos 149, 178, 236, 238, 241, 299, 303–4
  beginning of Frank Ryan trial 309, 314
  British POWs 323
  Irish Brigade chaplain 296, 299
  Kerney visits 335–40

Caballero, Largo, 32, 91–2, 111, 162, 169, 298
Cabanellas, Miguel 68, 306
Calaceite 149, 232–4, 301, 360
Callaghan, Brother Frank 78
Canada 142
  Canadian Pacific Railway 268
  IB volunteers 101–3, 115–6
  Royal Canadian Air Force 364
  Royal Canadian Mounted Police 116, 268
Carney, William 237–8, 242, 297, 302, 304
Carson, Edward 31
Castelldefels 276–7, 280–1
Catalonia 1, 34, 66–7, 255, 306
Catholic Church 1, 6, 11, 13–14, 370
  as a cause of Spanish decline 62, 74
  in England 37
  in Free State Ireland 60, 64
Catholic Young Men's Society 13, 16, 22
*Cemeteries of Liberty: Communist and Fascist Dictatorships* 15
Chamberlain, Neville 52, 241, 249, 330, 348
Chapayev battalion 143, 172, 179, 180–4, 191, 193
Chetwode, Sir Philip 318
China 78, 87, 95–6, 170, 172, 358
Christianity 31, 34, 53, 62, 71–72, 78, 111, 308
Churchill, Winston 33
Citizen Army 20, 22
Clarion clubs 65–6
Clissmann, Helmut 342–5
Cold War 30, 364, 370

Collins, Michael 65, 110
Commission on Vocational Organisation 9
communism 9, 14, 19, 33, 49, 71, 299, 308
   Irish 'red scares' 7, 370
   Spanish drift toward 2
   world party, as a 54
Communist International (Comintern) 4–5, 13, 21, 30, 89–97, 108, 363, 373
   agent in Dublin 17
   propaganda 19
Communist Party of Ireland (CPI) 15
   decline 53
Communist Party of Great Britain (CPGB) 17
Communist Party of the USA (CPUSA) 90
Confederación Nacional del Trabajo (CNT) 7
Connolly Column 28–9, 32–3, 36, 38, 43, 108–9, 117, 126, 356, 363, 370–1, 374
Connolly, James 28, 35, 44, 54, 126, 132, 157, 220, 341
Conradh na Gaeilge 22, 34, 303
Conway, Christopher (Kit) 144
Corona, Arturo 141
Cortes 1, 30, 91
   February 1936 elections 85
Cosgrave, W. T. 8, 39, 53, 302, 307, 311
Coyle, Eithne 34
Craigavon, Prime Minister (Northern Ireland) 30, 46, 75
Cripps, Stafford 38
Cumann na mBan 34, 362
Cumann na nGaedheal 8–9, 283, 296
Czechoslovakia 5, 37, 86, 250

Dáil Éireann 8
*Daily Mail* 3, 11, 47, 148
*Daily Worker* 11, 17–8, 94, 122, 126, 131, 196, 234
Dalton, Major Patrick 300
Daly, P. T. 320
*The Defence of Madrid* 69
de Maio, Tony 279, 281, 284
Denmark 37, 90, 344, 369

Department of External Affairs (Ireland) 238, 297, 307–8, 339, 347, 357–60
*Derry Standard* 63
desertion 193, 276
   Clarke, Fred 276
   Keenan, Patrick 275
   Magill, Joseph 276
   McGuinness, Charlie 275
   Mitchell, Charles (John Doyle) 276
   Tierney, John 276
Despard, Charlotte 60–1, 69
de Rivera, General Miguel Primo 2
de Valera, Éamon 9, 11, 22, 52, 53, 111, 237, 297, 301, 303, 305, 310–1, 321, 340
Dombrowski Brigade 140, 156
Donnelly, Charlie 44–6, 78, 111-12, 330, 378
Doran, Dave 212, 214, 218, 228, 230–1, 277, 359
Downing, Eugene (Eoghan Ó Duinnín) 46, 113, 122, 250, 252, 259–60, 266, 287, 290, 372–3
drunkenness 90, 96, 127, 141, 157, 274
Dublin Republican Congress 32
Dulanty, J. W. 323
Durruti, Buenaventura 306

*The Eagle Has Landed* 32
Ebro, Battle of 95, 178, 206–7, 213–4, 234, 249, 283, 287, 291
Economic War 10, 34, 52
Eden, Anthony 69
Edwards, Frank 20, 118–22, 162–3, 190, 321, 362, 373
Ejército Republicano Popular (ERP) 98
El Campesino 178
Emakume Abertzale Batza 34
Eucharistic Congress 1932 9, 20, 34, 80
Euskadi 37
European Conference for the Defence of the Spanish Republic 110
European Economic Community 10
Executive Committee of the Communist International (ECCI) 8, 16, 17, 34, 46, 50–1, 89, 91–3, 108
   *International Press Correspondence* 30

Fabian Society 67
fascism
    alleged Fine Gael sympathies 3
    and Ireland 10–11, 15, 50, 113, 298, 362, 371–2
    in central Europe 52
    in Nothern Ireland 46, 61
Fianna Fáil 30, 50–2, 363
    branches 331
    entry to government 9, 297
    impact on Free State politics 13–4
    position on Spain 11
Figueras 91, 102, 104, 268, 282, 284, 360
Fine Gael 30, 307
    alleged fascist sympathies 14
    formation 9
First World War 88, 93, 97, 103, 140, 143, 188, 274, 289, 342
Fischer, Dr Walter 154
Fleming, Lionel 10
Fox News 3
France 3–4, 37, 90, 249, 283–4, 291, 355
    diplomacy with Stalin 5, 86
    IB volunteers 100, 102
    Irish Minister to 357
    threats from Fascism 72
Franco, General Francisco 31, 50, 52, 297–301
    as a Christian soldier 11–2
    assault on Jarama 142
    emergence as an insurgent 2
    issues execution order 272
    pillars of Francoism in Ireland 9
Franco-Belgian battalion 121
Franco-Soviet Treaty of Mutual Assistance 5
*Franquismo* 2
Friends of Soviet Russia 17, 44, 60
Fuentes de Ebro 207, 213–6
Fry, Harold 144

Gaffney, Gertrude 37
Gaiety Theatre 35
Gal (János Gálicz) 143, 145–7, 150, 153, 157, 159, 171–2, 177–80, 182–3, 185–6, 191, 196, 207

Gandesa 230, 232–4, 250, 255, 257–61, 263, 300, 314
Garda Síochána 8, 20, 341
Garibaldi battalion 109, 123, 156, 169, 257
Germany 14
    anti-fascist defeats 2
    arms shipments from 88
    communist uprisings 172
    IB volunteers 10
    Intervention in Frank Ryan saga 340–2
    last free elections 94
    political exiles from 87
    re-armament 3–4
    resistance to Hitler 5
German Condor Legion 36, 144, 178, 183, 262, 317
Gilmore, George 23, 32–4, 111–12
globalisation 6
Gollancz, Victor 38, 43
Gonne, Maude 320
*Good-Bye, Twilight* 44–5, 46
Goodfellow, Charlie 182
Great Terror 87
Guadalajara, Battle of 239
Guardia Civil 98, 162, 181, 233, 306–7, 309
Guardia Nacional 194, 273
Guernica 36–7, 39, 63, 65, 297, 372
Gunning, Thomas 43, 119, 237, 263, 296–7, 300–3

Hedley, Jack 140–1
Hemingway, Ernest 157, 169, 218, 231, 297
Hempel, Eduard 340
Henry, Bill 150
Hitler, Adolf 3–5, 33, 47, 72, 81, 85, 339, 340, 344
Hodgson, Robert 241, 298, 299–300, 304, 311, 316–9
Hourihan, Martin 153
House of Commons 235, 322–3, 333
Hoven, Jupp 342–4

Indian Defence League 20
International Brigades (IB) 109, 148, 374
   and Comintern 89–97
   capital punishment 273
   control of 110
   dissolution 359
   fatality statistics 193, 260
   foundation 85, 108
   international volunteers to 100–1
   Irish contingent 29, 101–4
   punishment 278–81
   reorganisation 203–5
   Republican army 97–101
   War Commissariat of 355
International Brigade Association (IBA) 291, 330, 366
International Brigades Commemoration Committee 371
International Brigades Dependents' Aid Committee 70
International Federation of Trade Unions 15–16
International Lenin School 8, 119, 130
*Ireland To-day* 12, 31, 40–1, 45
Irish Army Volunteer Reserve 217
Irish brigadistas 101, 103, 364, 366, 372
Irish Christian Front 9, 12, 64
Irish Citizen Army 331
Irish Civil War 6, 103, 156, 203, 297, 303, 331
*Irish Democrat* 13, 28–9, 37–41, 51–2, 321, 372
Irish fatalities 147, 150, 156–7, 177, 188, 193, 211, 223–4, 259–60
Irish Film Society 42
Irish Foodship for Spain Committee 53, 71
Irish Free State Army 103, 116, 163, 284, 286
Irish Friends of the Spanish Republic 36–7, 42, 70, 361
Irish Iberian Trading Company 34–5, 312
*Irish Independent* 9, 12, 32, 35–7, 46, 50, 113, 300, 305, 308, 321
Irish National Teachers' Organisation 78, 303
Irish National Unemployed Movement 20
*Irish News* 64, 70–4
Irish Pacifist Movement 42

*Irish Press* 11–12, 35, 43, 112, 303, 363, 367
Irish Republican Army (IRA) 8, 18–20, 33, 39–41, 103, 275, 302, 311, 349, 363–4
   Belfast Brigade 65
   Dublin Brigade 32, 118, 131
   East Limerick Brigade 32, 303
Irish Society for the Study of International Affairs 42
*Irish Times* 10–11, 112,
Irish Trade Union Congress 15–16, 77, 331, 363
Irish Transport and General Workers' Union 15, 54, 71, 140, 373
Irish War of Independence 103, 357
*Irish Weekly* 1
Irish Workers' League 111, 366
*Irish Workers' Voice* 5
Italy 312, 355
   anti-fascist defeats 2
   diplomacy with Germany 3
   fascist power 85
   IB volunteers 100, 169
   military aid from 87–8
   nobility in 10
   parliamentary parties 14

Jarama 39, 95–6, 99, 104, 132, 138, 276, 301, 369
   American attack 149–51
   American battalion 140, 142–3
   Battleground 153–60
   British attack 143–9
Jews 44, 116, 128, 239, 374
Juan Marco battalion 186, 191

Kelly, Michael 141, 150, 170, 177
Kerney, Leopold H. 34, 237–9, 297–300, 303–4, 316–8, 320, 322–3, 332–40, 345–9

Laborda, Ramón 34–6, 70
Labour Defence League 20
Labour League Against Fascism and War 20, 22
Larkin, Jim 8, 29, 51, 54, 77, 363

Laski, Harold 38
Laverty, Maura 305
League Against Imperialism 20, 33, 44, 46, 342
League of Militant Atheists 18
League of Nations 53, 66, 99, 265, 267, 300, 342, 355
*Left News* 42,
Líster, Enrique 147, 175, 205
Locarno Pact 86
Lopera 119, 121, 126, 138, 188–9, 255

Macartney, Wilf 124, 131
Madrigueras 104, 121–4, 130, 139–40, 141, 160, 279, 364
MacKee, Seumus 50
Mackenzie-Papineau battalion 203, 214, 360
MacRory, Joseph 8, 13, 31, 33, 111
Madrid-Valencia highway 142, 147, 160
Maginot Line 4
Manilovski, Rodion (Colonel Malino) 175
Martin, Ambrose V. 12, 34
Marty, André 51, 89–97, 138, 142, 191–2, 203–4, 267–8, 279, 313, 355
McCullagh, Francis 50
McQuaid, John Charles 11, 14
Merriman, Robert 93–4, 139, 140–1, 150–3, 189, 203, 207–8, 212–14, 313
Mexico 5, 9
Mitchell, Máirín 28
Mola, General Emilio 1–2
Morata de Tajuña 142
Moroccan War 97
Mosquito Ridge 190–1, 193–4
Movietone 3, 148, 362
Mulcahy, Richard 39
*Mundo Obrero* 314
Munich Agreement 3, 61, 81, 267, 355, 361
Mussolini, Benito 3, 10, 72, 104, 169, 232, 317, 339

Nalty, Jack 102, 104, 160, 190, 250, 252, 250, 252, 266, 287 289, 291
National Centre Party *see* Fine Gael
National Corporate Party 10, 32

National Guard *see* Fine Gael
National Joint Committee for Spanish Relief 16, 70–1
National Sailors' and Firemen's Union 80
National Union of Distributive and Allied Workers 78
National Union of General and Municipal Workers 78
National Union of Journalists 303
National Union of Railwaymen 16, 366
  Belfast 66
Nazism
  Churchill kidnap plot 33
  Ireland 343
  Olympics 68
  radio propagandists 297
  Ryan, Frank 32
  Spanish struggle against 11
Negrín, Juan 169, 192, 249, 265
Negro Committee to Aid Spain 356
*A Negro Nurse in Republican Spain* 356
Nesterenko, Ivan 126
*New Northman* 70
New York Irish Workers' Clubs 20
*New York Times* 231, 237–8, 242–3, 297
Non-Intervention Agreement 4, 11, 78, 314
Non-Intervention Committee 4, 85, 97, 114, 252, 355
*Northern Whig* 62

Ó Briain, Art 275
O'Brien, Kate 49
O'Casey, Seán 28
Ó Ciamh, Pádraig 320
O'Connor, Peter 28, 103, 124–5, 128, 141, 155–6, 170, 186, 189, 195, 362, 366, 370, 373, 386
O'Daire, Paddy 162
O'Donnell, Blanca 337
O'Donnell, Peadar 12, 19–22, 31, 33, 47–9, 66, 69–70, 111–2, 114, 116, 321, 342, 372
O'Duffy, Eoin 8, 31, 65, 108, 112, 303, 331, 341, 369
O'Flanagan, Fr Michael 35, 53
O'Higgins, Kevin 110, 301, 310

Ontiveros, Juan García 321–3, 331, 334
O'Rahilly, Aodoghan 320
O'Riordan, Michael 109, 122, 126, 250, 252, 257, 260–1, 359–61, 363, 365–6, 370, 372–3
Orange Order 60, 76
Orwell, George 5, 19, 67, 170, 278
O'Sullivan Paddy 104, 217, 252, 259, 260
Otumba battalion 186, 191
Overton, Bert 144

Parti Communiste Francais (PCF) 87
Partido Comunista de España (PCE) 1
Partido Obrero de Unificación Marxista (POUM) 30
Partido Socialista Obrero Español (PSOE) 203
Partit Socialista Unificat de Catalunya (PSUC) 278
People's Anti-Imperialist Front 22, 30, 31
People's Army 95, 98, 228
Philby, Kim 237
*An Phoblacht* 19, 22, 36, 39, 302, 343
Pike, Dr William 154
Pingarrón 142, 149, 150, 156
Pollitt, Harry 21, 23, 30, 89, 94–6, 117–8, 125, 158, 219, 263, 355
Pope Benedict XV 7
Pope Leo XIII
    *Rerum Novarum* 6
Pope Pius XI 9
Popular Front/Frente Popular 1, 42, 85, 93, 98
Portugal 3–4, 31, 283, 286, 346, 355
Post Office Workers' Union 13
Power, John 103, 170, 182, 195, 217, 231, 257, 259–61, 264–5, 267, 291, 360, 362–3, 365
Pozorrubio 160, 189–90, 203,
Prieto, Indalecio 93, 185, 192, 203, 205, 211, 221
Progressive Publications Society 38, 70
Public Safety Bill (Ireland) 1931 8

*Quadragesimo Anno* 9
Quinto 207–8, 276

Rathmines Town Hall 20
Raylock, Max 23, 51
Red Cross 68, 95, 240, 242, 244, 318, 322, 335
Republican Congress 20–3, 29, 30–7, 46, 54, 111–18, 138, 141, 301, 310–1
Republican Labour Party (Kerry) 20
Revolutionary Workers' Groups (RWG) 5, 8
Robinson, Pascal 304
Rojo, Vicente 88, 170, 185, 187, 191–2, 211, 213, 220–1, 249
Rothermere, Lord 3
Royal Ulster Constabulary (RUC) 60
Russian Civil War 110
Russian Orthodox Church 8
Ryan, Frank
    accused of killing looters and protesters 238
    biography 32
    documentary on 32
    office 93
    release committee 53, 320–1
    trial and imprisonment 296
    views on Hitler-Stalin Pact 338
    writings 28, 147, 231
Ryan, Maurice Emmett 253–4, 258, 283–91

San Gregorio Military Academy 237
Sanjurjo, General José 1–2, 23
San Pedro de la Cardeña 149
Santa Clara
    abandoned convent 139
Saor Éire 8, 19, 39
Seanad Éireann 9
Second Rif War 7
Servicio Investigación Militar (SIM) 274 276, 278–9, 281–2, 284, 286
Sheehy Skeffington, Hanna 35, 37, 50, 112
Sheehy Skeffington, Owen 12, 34, 38, 40, 42, 45–6, 52
Shtern, Grigory 204, 272
Sierra Guadarrama 99, 170, 172
Sinn Féin 32–3, 128, 297, 321, 362, 371
Slav Dimitrov battalion 121, 149,
Smyllie, R. M. 'Bertie' 10–11

Soviet Union 143
  aid to Spain 5, 86–9
  foreign policy 5, 85–6
  intervention 85
  Politburo 86, 89, 91, 93, 131
Spanish Confederation of Right-Wing Autonomous Groups (CEDA) 1
Spanish Foreign Legion 97, 147, 320, 348
Spanish Medical Relief Committee 63, 69
Spanish Morocco 3, 4
Spanish Republican Air Force (FARE) 202
Stalin, Josef 4–5, 8, 12, 85–7, 89, 91–2, 97, 216, 338
St John of the Cross 6
Strachey, John 61
St Teresa of Avila 6, 50
Strauss, George 322–3
Student Vanguard 46
Suicide Hill 145–6, 189
Switzerland 37, 349, 368

Tarazona de La Mancha 194, 203, 214, 216–7, 230, 280–1
*TCD Miscellany* 31, 54
Teruel 99, 104, 172, 202, 277–8, 285
Togliatti, Palmiro 92, 97, 204
Torrado, General Asensio 92, 169
Treaty of Versailles 3, 342
Trinity College, Dublin 44, 297, 303, 320, 343
Trotskyism 92, 96, 278, 363

Uceley, Guillermo Escribano 315
Ulster Protestant League 60–1, 63, 74
Ulster Unionist Labour Association 60, 78
Unión Militar Española (UME) 98
Unión Militar Republicana Antifascista (UMRA) 98

United States 4, 102, 140, 349
University College Dublin 303
  Students' Representative Council 36
Vatican 7–8, 70, 300, 331, 338
venereal disease 157
Villafranca del Castillo 173
Villanueva de la Cañada 173, 175–6, 185–9, 212
Villanueva de la Jara 124, 130, 138–41
Villanueva del Pardillo 173, 177–8, 185–7, 191
*Voices from the Spanish Civil War* 287
*Volunteer for Liberty* 218
von Sperrle, General Hugo 178
Voroshilov, Klim 89, 97, 235
Vuillemin battalion 191

Wall, Rev. F. 13
Walshe, Joseph P. 297
Washington battalion 170–1, 179, 182–4, 193, 361
Waterford 15, 20, 39, 102, 116–17, 189, 239, 244, 321, 357, 362–5, 367, 383–4, 386–7
Wattis, Captain Clifford 150, 296
  trial 151–3
Wilson, Woodrow 2
Wintringham, Tom 119, 123–4, 132, 143, 145–7, 207
Workers' Union of Ireland 16, 363 366
World Congress of the Communist International (1935) 21, 30, 86
World-Wide Anti-God Campaign of Militant Atheism Exhibition 9

Young Communist League 102, 230
Youth Evangelistic Campaign 60
Yugoslav Communist Party 143

Zaisser, Wilhelm 99, 172, 185, 274